Knowledge Graphs

Knowledge Graphs

Fundamentals, Techniques, and Applications

Mayank Kejriwal, Craig A. Knoblock, and Pedro Szekely

The MIT Press
Cambridge, Massachusetts
London, England

This book was set in Times New Roman by the authors. Printed and bound in the United States of America.

Library of Congress Cataloging-in-Publication Data is available.

Names: Kejriwal, Mayank, author. | Knoblock, Craig A., 1962- author. | Szekely, Pedro, author.
Title: Knowledge graphs : fundamentals, techniques, and applications / Mayank Kejriwal, Craig Knoblock, and Pedro Szekely.
Description: Cambridge, Massachusetts : The MIT Press, [2021] | Series: Adaptive computation and machine learning series | Includes bibliographical references and index.
Identifiers: LCCN 2020028169 | ISBN 9780262045094 (hardcover)
Subjects: LCSH: Information visualization.
Classification: LCC QA76.9.I52 K45 2021 | DDC 001.4/226–dc23
LC record available at https://lccn.loc.gov/2020028169

10   9   8   7   6   5   4   3   2   1

Contents

List of Figures

List of Tables

Preface

Graphs have had a tremendous influence on both mathematics and artificial intelligence (AI), as evidenced by the large body of work on graph theory, as well as by the pervasiveness of graph models in subcommunities such as planning and knowledge representation. Knowledge graphs (KGs), a term that has become popular only in the last decade due to industrial-scale projects such as Google's Knowledge Graph and Amazon's Product Graph, may not seem particularly novel in this broader context. Certainly, *knowledge bases* (KBs), the predecessor to KGs in the Natural Language Processing (NLP) and other AI communities, have been around for a very long time, dating back several decades. Automatic construction and population of KBs, a prominent topic in this book, witnessed an explosion of research in the 1990s. Other techniques, such as instance matching (IM) and statistical relational learning (SRL), the focus of part IV of this book, have had an equally storied history. The first papers on what we designate as IM today were published more than a half-century ago, in the context of linking patient records.

The question might then arise: why is *now* the time to publish a textbook on KGs? Our answer to this (necessarily one of opinion rather than fact) is that the last decade has seen an astounding confluence of technologies and circumstances that have made KGs a relevant and popular branch of AI. Activities in both research and industry bear this observation out. Major conferences and journals regularly feature workshops, sessions, and special issues on KGs. The authors themselves have been involved heavily in many of these. Since the publication of encyclopedic KGs such as DBpedia, many KGs have been openly published on the web. Some already existed as KBs or general-purpose resources but are being repurposed or rebranded as KGs due to their relational properties. In fact, it is not uncommon to find KG "ecosystems," some in high-growth mode and others relatively mature. We dedicate an entire part of this book to describing these communities. Without a doubt, the emergence of data-driven decision science and the popularity currently enjoyed by AI, machine learning, and neural networks in the media, industry, and academia alike have both contributed to the flourishing of such ecosystems.

At the current time, the COVID-19 pandemic has further revealed how far KGs have come. Within a short time (just a couple of months), practitioners and researchers have taken publicly released data (such as an academic corpus) and set up public-facing KGs using toolkits that were well-established in the community for building domain-specific KGs. This not only illustrates that KGs offer a value proposition that is increasingly seeing mainstream adoption, but also demonstrates the maturity of the tools and algorithms themselves. Only a few short years ago, it would have required enormous personnel and resources to set up a KG from raw, heterogeneous web data.

Here, we attempt to provide a relatively comprehensive treatment of KGs. We recognize, however, that not every important piece of work can be covered (or covered in full) without making the book unwieldy. Our approach has been to pay careful attention to the fundamentals and techniques that have withstood the test of time thus far. We start from the very beginning and do not assume that the reader has a strong background in machine learning, NLP, or Semantic Web (the main areas that are allied with research in KGs). Nevertheless, having a basic background in these areas would make the reading of the text easier and more insightful. Hence, we believe that the book would be particularly suitable for courses taught at the upper undergraduate and graduate levels. We also hope that it will provide value to researchers who have some background in other areas of AI but are looking for an exposure to KGs as a way of enriching their own work.

We have attempted to make the chapters as independent and cohesive as possible, such that even a beginning researcher in the area could use individual chapters as short surveys or background on the subject matter. However, the book is best read in sequence, and in particular, chapters 1 and 2 are important for laying the foundation for the rest of the book. We also recommend reviewing chapter 2 prior to beginning part IV as many of the models in that chapter will be reconsidered and supplemented in chapters 11 and 12.

In teaching a course on the subject, we recommend a strong focus on the first two chapters, and depending on the course, selective focus on a mixture of the chapters in parts II, III, and IV. For example, if the instructor is particularly oriented toward the Semantic Web, less time may be allocated to the material in part II, and it may be more worthwhile to have multiple lectures on chapters 8, 12, and 14. A course more focused on text and natural language, on the other hand, would want to have multiple lectures on the chapters in part II (especially chapters 4 and 6), and chapters 11 and 13. A course focusing on advanced methods for NLP students may want to give significant attention to the chapters on nontraditional information extraction (IE) and KG embeddings (KGEs). Undergraduate classes may want to cover all the chapters in parts I–IV, not unlike introductory courses to machine learning and AI, where the goal is a broad exposure (with appropriate homework and assignments) rather than deep coverage. If the course is a seminar or at the graduate level, some of the key papers noted in the "Bibliographic Notes" section in each chapter should be assigned as required reading in addition to the chapter itself. Where possible, we recommend one classic and one recent paper. For many chapters, this approach is doable and provides valuable insight both into the research as it is relevant today and its origins as a problem statement.

Every chapter always concludes with a "Software and Resources" section, where we do our best to provide links and pointers to resources that (so far as we know) have been robustly adopted in their respective communities. We hope that these sections will be useful to practitioners and companies (especially companies not traditionally known for speedy technological adoptions) that are looking to *do* more with KGs. As a caveat, the very nature of such resources (almost always web-based) and the current fast pace of KG research indicate that we can never guarantee the persistence or relevance of the resource beyond the time that this book comes out. In attempting to mitigate the effects of such transience, we have given more weight to packages that already have a proven record of standing the test of time.[1] However, we recognize that it is inevitable that some resources that should have been included in the relevant chapter got omitted, despite our best efforts. The same goes for the "Bibliographic Notes" sections, where we have attempted to provide referential citations for almost all the material that we directly cover in the main body of the text. Because much of the material we cover has had a long history and is often the work of tens, if not hundreds, of researchers, we also extensively cite surveys on these topics that have inspired our own interpretation and rendition of the subject. This is also the main reason why we chose to opt for a relatively comprehensive "Bibliographic Notes" section at the end of each chapter, rather than crowd the main text with many citations, as would be the norm in proper academic research papers.

Additionally, the book has a set of exercises at the end of every chapter. In total, we have provided almost 130 exercises. We have tried to be consistent with our own pedagogical styles by having exercises at various levels of abstraction and difficulty. Toward the end of the book, as we delve deeper into part V, the exercises steadily become more project-oriented and thought-based, as would befit the chapters (on KG ecosystems) there. In earlier chapters, the exercises are more conceptual, challenging students and other readers to demonstrate a degree of mastery that would be expected after becoming acquainted with that material. Even in those chapters though, we have attempted to provide some abstract questions to provoke deeper thought from the (particularly attentive) reader.

Mayank Kejriwal, Craig A. Knoblock, and Pedro Szekely
April 2020

---

[1] The reader clicking on URL links directly in digital versions of the book should beware of "hanging" hyphens (i.e., at the ends of lines, when the URL runs long), because these may not be part of the true URL. If removing the offending hyphen or hyphens still does not yield a valid URL (or the desired resource), we recommend searching for that resource by its name using a search engine.

I KNOWLEDGE GRAPH FUNDAMENTALS

1 Introduction to Knowledge Graphs

Overview. Graph theory has long occupied an important place in computer science and mathematics, and the subject has become more relevant recently due to a resurgence of interest in the study of complex systems. In this decade, knowledge graphs (KGs) have emerged as the latest instance of using graphs for representing (and reasoning over) data that can be semistructured and web scale in origin and potentially marked by conflicts and inconsistencies. KGs as we understand them today became popular after the Google Knowledge Graph was introduced via an official blog post in 2011. In this chapter, we introduce KGs and provide some insight into why they have emerged as powerful and popular tools in multiple communities.

1.1 Graphs

Graph theory has long had a close connection with computer science, though its origins undoubtedly have been mathematical since Leonhard Euler first proposed a solution for the Königsberg Bridge Problem in 1735. As the story behind that problem goes, Königsberg, a quaint town in Prussia in the eighteenth century, was divided by the Pregel River into four divisions. Seven bridges span the river at various points, permitting crossing from one division into another (figure 1.1). According to folklore, the citizens of the city wondered whether it was possible to walk around the city while crossing each of the seven bridges *only once*. The starting point of such a route, if it existed, would not matter because the route would be a circuit. At the time, the citizens could not show such a route, but they also could not prove that such a route did not exist.

By modeling the problem as a graph, where divisions were nodes in the graph and the bridges were edges, Euler was able to prove the now-famous theorem such that a *Eulerian cycle* can exist in the graph if and only if every node has an even degree, with the degree of a node being the number of edges that were incident upon that node. In the graph representation of the problem shown at the right of figure 1.1, none of the nodes has an even degree; hence, the graph cannot possess an Eulerian cycle. The proof for the theorem is simple and elegant, expressing the power of using graphs to model and solve such problems.

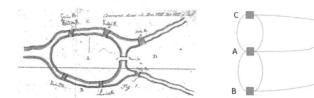

Figure 1.1: A version of the Königsberg Bridge Problem [as illustrated by Euler (1741) himself in his figure 1 from *Solutio problematis ad geometriam situs pertinentis*, Eneström 53]. On the right, the problem is modeled as a graph, with divisions as nodes, and bridges as edges. Figure obtained from MAA Euler Archive (copyright expired).

Graph theory, as the field came to be called (see the "Bibliographic Notes" section at the end of the chapter), became a popular area of study with the passage of time, as many scientists and mathematicians found that graphs could not only be used to model interesting phenomena in the real world (as Euler had shown), but that they were also sophisticated mathematical objects with complex properties. In modern computer science, graphs have taken on a life of their own starting several decades earlier, with algorithms like Edsger Dijkstra's shortest-path algorithm and computationally intractable problems like the traveling salesman problem now considered standard textbook material in any treatment of basic computer science theory, algorithms, and data structures. The connection of graphs to the field of artificial intelligence (AI) has been equally interesting, regardless of which lens we survey it through, including expert systems (and rule-based) research; sequential models like hidden Markov models (HMMs) and conditional random fields (CRFs); planning research (where state and action spaces are often drawn as graphs); constraint satisfaction (evidenced by the famous graph-coloring problem); databases (evidenced by the rise and study of graph databases, some of which we survey in chapter 12); networks, recommendations, and e-commerce; and the Semantic Web. It would be difficult to find an area in computer science or AI that has not been touched by graphs to at least some degree.

Considering this brief background on the influence of graphs, it is perhaps unsurprising that knowledge representation, reasoning, and inference would also come to be influenced by graphs. Yet, for a long time, it was not the norm to represent large data sets, such as we now see on the web, as graphs. Databases of various types, including object-oriented databases (inspired by object-oriented programming) and other relational models, were more popular, and in the machine learning community, there was far more interest in mathematical structures like matrices and tensors. Even in the Semantic Web (SW), a relatively recent offshoot of the broader web community, graphs had been predominantly used to model ontologies rather than enormous data sets until the advent of the Linked Data movement in the mid-2000s (chapter 14).

In industry, graphs as a means of representing Big Data had almost no discernible influence till the highly publicized announcement and exposure of the Google Knowledge Graph.[1] Arguably, KGs had existed for quite a while, and they were [and in communities like Natural Language Processing (NLP), still often are] referred to as *knowledge bases (KBs)*, as it was the norm to think of facts (knowledge) as entities, relations, and sets of triples rather than as a collection of nodes and edges. With the advent of the Google Knowledge Graph and its enormous influence on how we consume search results (as described in the next section), the rich relational information that ties together entities into a cohesive repository of knowledge has become much more apparent. At this time, the influence of KGs is being felt throughout society (as discussed in part V of this book), and KGs are being used in enterprise and government (chapter 15), in science (chapter 16), and even for addressing social problems like human trafficking and natural disaster response (chapter 17).

We introduce KGs formally in the next section by using a simple example to illustrate both the potential of and the challenges encountered when working with knowledge modeled as a graph. We then take a few examples of KGs in real-world domains.

1.2   Representing Knowledge as Graphs

Within computer science, as earlier indicated, graphs are commonplace and used to address a whole variety of problems. However, within AI, an interesting problem has always existed—namely, how should we "represent" knowledge within a machine so as to best facilitate "intelligent" agents and algorithms to reason over, and "work with," that knowledge? What *is* knowledge? These are deeply philosophical questions, with roots in the schools of epistemology, but they are also immensely practical because today, we are definitively living in an era characterized by Big Data, whether it be social media, open government data, sensor data, or e-commerce data such as used to power companies like Amazon, papers and academic research (such as found on PubMed or Semantic Scholar), and so on. To a machine, the collection of data is merely streams and sets of syntactic units such as strings. To a human being, data carries meaning (i.e., it can be said to have *semantics*). It is because of semantics that we are able to use the data to reason about novel situations, as well as to apply our knowledge in challenging scenarios. If a sufficiently rich *model* of semantics could be expressed to a machine, it could (with enough context) be used to derive sophisticated insights, such as allowing the machine to deal with uncertainty, answer questions, and even perform tasks of a causal nature, such as abduction and counterfactual reasoning.

---

[1] https://www.blog.google/products/search/introducing-knowledge-graph-things-not/.

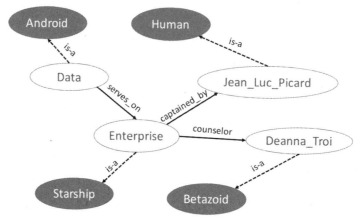

Figure 1.2: Representing knowledge as a graph: A simple KG fragment.

Although building such a "general AI" continues to be a far-reaching goal, an important milestone in achieving that goal is that a machine should be able to assign semantics, at a reasonable level, to "strings" of characters and numbers, if such semantics exist and can be perceived by humans in "natural" settings like plain English. Graphs provide one way to do this, as illustrated in figure 1.2. In the graph, we express our knowledge of personnel from a *Star Trek* show (namely, *The Next Generation*) by representing our *entities* of interest as nodes in the graph, and with relationships (also called *properties* or *relations*) between entities (including the *types* of those entities) expressed via directed, labeled edges. What we are looking at in figure 1.2 is the first example of a KG in this book. Because of the inherent structure present in the graph, we can pose well-defined queries to the system as (potentially sophisticated) *graph patterns* (e.g., the natural-language question "Who are all the personnel serving on the Enterprise?" can be expressed as a graph pattern "?x serves_on Enterprise," where "?x" represents a variable that needs to be bound). We will go into much more detail into such queries and the language used for graph patterns in future chapters, but the point that we hope to illustrate here is that, by making productive use of structure, we can avoid some of the ambiguity incurred through natural language.

The example question about *Enterprise* personnel is instructive because it also highlights a crucial thing missing in the KG fragment in figure 1.2. Here, our human knowledge tells us that Jean Luc Picard, Deanna Troi, and Data are all serving on the *Enterprise*, although only the roles of Jean Luc Picard and Deanna Troi are directly specified in the KG (as captain and counselor, respectively). However, if we were to execute the graph pattern query shown here *as is*, we would only get back "Data" as a result. Clearly, something beyond the explicit KG is required in order for all three answers to be returned. Specifically, the system needs to know that if a ship is captained by X, then X serves on the ship, and similarly for other "roles" such as counselor. We impart this kind of domain-specific (and

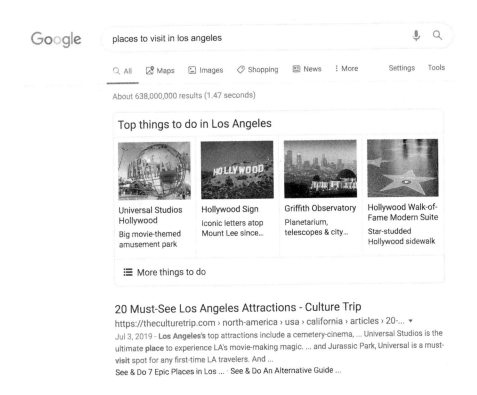

Figure 1.3: Results displayed by Google in response to queries such as "places to visit in Los Angeles," which include not just a ranked list of webpages, but actual entities corresponding to user intent.

in more universal situations,[2] "open-domain") knowledge by modeling the domain as an *ontology*. We already see the vestiges of an ontology, even in figure 1.2. For example, we see the *concepts* (also called *classes* or *types*) "Android," "Human," and so on. Entities in the KG are typed according to these concepts using the special relation *is-a*.

Actual ontologies are much more powerful, with hierarchies of classes (e.g., that *Capital* is a subclass of *City*), properties (e.g., the *serves_on* property is a superclass of another property, *captains*, not shown in figure 1.2), declarations that one property is related to another through a metarelation like *inverse* (e.g., *captains* is the inverse of *captained_by*), and other axiomatic declarations that help reasoners deduce additional knowledge that is not explicitly declared as facts in the KG.

---

[2] For example, if X is a *city*, then X is also a *location*.

The example in figure 1.2 may not seem to be "doing much," so to speak, but as a thought experiment, imagine that we are able to represent our domain knowledge in such a structured format, and also that we have a sufficiently rich ontology to model such knowledge. At web scale, the representation would allow us to pose increasingly complex queries and make sophisticated AI applications feasible. The most striking example of this is the web search, as evidenced by the Google Knowledge Graph mentioned earlier. Not very long ago, if a search were executed for a phrase such as "places to visit in Los Angeles," the Google search engine (and other generic search engines as well) would simply return a ranked list of webpages. It then would be up to the user to browse through these pages and put together answers to their original question. Worse, good answers may not even be retrieved if the system did not somehow know (e.g., through search logs) that when people refer to "Los Angeles," they are typically referring to Los Angeles *County* rather than the actual city of Los Angeles, which is only a small part of the greater metropolitan area.

By modeling entities and relations as shown in figure 1.2 and using that information with other powerful correlational tools like mining of web search logs and personalization, it became possible to interpret the query more deeply by using the KG to recognize that Los Angeles is a city and a county, and that the latter intent is more common when users search for tourist venues in Los Angeles. However, in more recent times, the Google KG has managed to go even further (figure 1.3) by directly providing a list of places to visit in LA (in response to the query), showing that it is able to grasp the semantics of the query better than string-matching approaches would have done. Searching has gotten more sophisticated and seamless as a result, and in many cases (as in this example), it may not even be necessary to click on a webpage link or go beyond the search engine for a response to the query. Tourist attractions are hardly the only examples of this; we see similar search results when searching for movies or concerts. When searching for a famous entity like a celebrity or geographical entity, Google also displays knowledge panels (figure 1.4), some of the content of which is derived from sources like Wikipedia. All of these search facilities are being powered, at least in part, by a large-scale proprietary KG.

Another important motivation for constructing and using KGs is that words and names can be deeply ambiguous and dependent on the *current* context of usage, which would include the user (and their past search history) initiating the search, but also their immediately preceding search. In the original blog post on the Google Knowledge Graph, "Taj Mahal" was used to illustrate this ambiguity because the name could be used to denote the famous monument in India, a local restaurant in any number of cities and areas, a casino in Atlantic City, New Jersey, and so on. If Google knew that the user happened to be in the Indian city of Agra at the moment when the search was executed, then the monument is the "relevant" (i.e., intended and desired) result. However, if the immediate search history involved restaurants in Los Angeles, then a nearby restaurant called Taj Mahal might be the relevant result. If no context is available, external information such as other people's

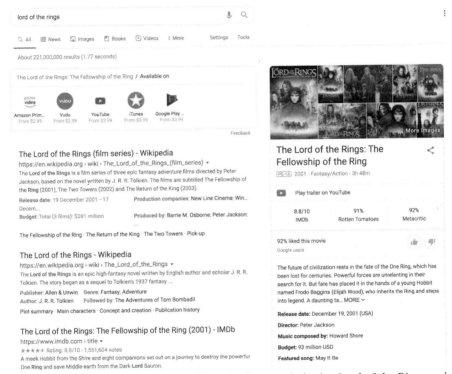

Figure 1.4: A knowledge panel describing the first movie in the *Lord of the Rings* series, in response to the keyword query "lord of the rings."

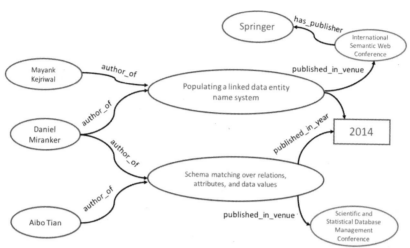

Figure 1.5: An illustration of an academic KG, showing two publications with overlapping authors. While oval nodes represent resources or entities, rectangles are used to represent literals, such as strings and numbers.

search histories could serve as an important prior. In practice, a combination of these factors, honed over time and at large scale using pragmatic and proprietary techniques, gives modern search engines a powerful edge in fulfilling everyday informational needs.

What these cases are intended to illustrate is that "Taj Mahal" and "Los Angeles" are ultimately *things, not strings*, and need to be *interpreted* as such by a machine to enable truly powerful applications. The primary application invoked here is called *semantic search*, but others exist, as described in part V, where KG ecosystems with significant footprints are detailed. In the next few sections, we provide a brief glimpse into KGs being used in some of these other influential domains.

1.3   Examples of Knowledge Graphs

This section provides a pragmatic view of how KGs are employed in the real world. Mostly, we rely on typical examples predominantly cited in the literature and used in industry, although some domains have achieved more mainstream success than others (e.g., e-commerce versus geopolitical events). We use these domains to illustrate the various aspects involved in constructing and applying KGs in the real world.

1.3.1   Example 1: Scientific Publications and Academics

As a first example of a domain-specific KG, let us consider an academic domain (figure 1.5). The two nodes in the center of the KG represent different publications. Some impor-

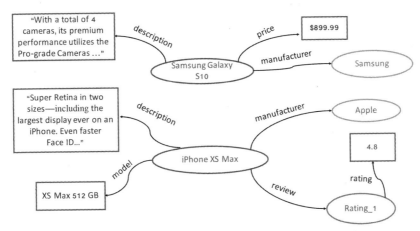

Figure 1.6: An illustration of a *Product* KG, showing two different products.

tant details concerning the publications are also shown, including their authors, dates of publication, and venues.

Despite its simplicity, the KG in figure 1.5 illustrates some of the expressiveness in *representation*, which is a much studied research area in communities such as the Semantic Web. The oval nodes in the KG represent *entities* or *resources* and are generally referred to (in the SW community) as internationalized resource identifiers (IRIs), a generalized form of uniform resource identifiers (URIs). We define these concepts more precisely in the next chapter, so we are limiting our current focus to the overall distinction between entities and literals (also known as *attributes*). Entities can have relationships with other entities (such as between authors and their publications) or attributes (such as the year of a publication). The distinction can be expressed by the fact that in a triple (h, r, t), t is either a literal (for the latter) or an entity (for the former). In SW representations of KGs, h is always an entity, and can never be a literal.

1.3.2   Example 2: E-Commerce, Products, and Companies

In the second example, inspired by the *products and e-commerce* domain, we expand upon the notions presented earlier for the academic domain. Once again, we see the distinction between literals and entities, but as illustrated in figure 1.6, there are numerous degrees of freedom, even when modeling the most basic structures in KGs. For example, the price of a product is modeled in a relatively simple way (as a relation incident upon a numeric literal object), but the rating is more complex. Potentially, the *Rating_1* resource shown in the KG could be used to define outgoing properties expressing not just the numeric *rating*, but also the review text, the person or website that provided the rating, and so on. We bring this up to illustrate that the choice of modeling can have implications for both upstream tasks

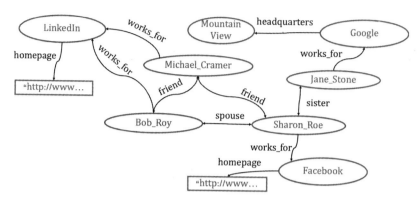

Figure 1.7: An illustration of a social network, illustrated as a KG.

(such as information extraction, used for constructing the KG in the first place, given such a model or *ontology*) and downstream tasks, such as instance matching (IM) and question answering, that become relevant after the initial KG has been extracted and made available for access. Availability of information can also vary, usually depending on the raw data sources from which the KG was extracted.

1.3.3   Example 3: Social Networks

Figure 1.7 shows yet another common domain (namely, social networks). Note that, in this example, "social network" does not mean a particular social network company or website like Facebook or Twitter (although an example could also be constructed for a website-specific KG), but an actual social network as it exists in the offline world between a group of fictional individuals. As the example shows, the social network illustrated therein can be used to express a range of complex relationships using the power of directed labeled edges, as well as shared relationships between entities of different types (people and organizations, but also organizations and locations such as <Google, headquarters, Mountain View>. This could be generalized even further to include fine-grained concepts, including schools, organizations, clubs, and alumni associations, as well as fine-grained relations such as membership, family relations, and professional hierarchical relations (e.g., supervised_of, project_lead). In fact, there is already a famous vocabulary called Friend of a Friend (FOAF) that contains many of these concepts and relations and can be used to express social domain KGs without inventing a new ontology.

1.3.4   Example 4: Geopolitical Events

Finally, we consider one of the more complex examples of a KG (specifically, in the geopolitical domain). Along with the artifices shown previously (such as the difference between entities and literals), the KG in figure 1.8 illustrates how "second-order" entities like events

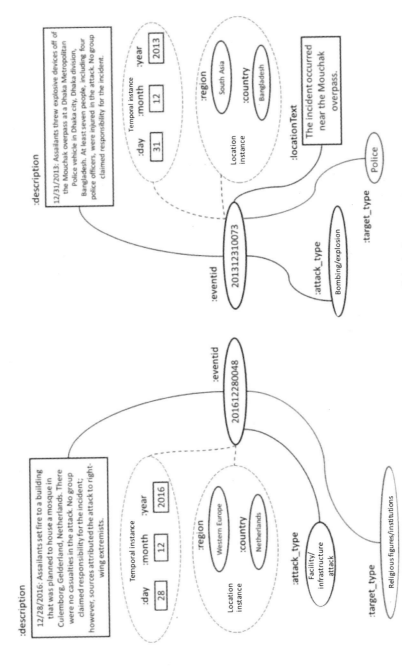

Figure 1.8: A fragment of an *Event* KG expressing distinct geopolitical phenomena.

can be modeled and represented. We refer to events as "second-order entities" because they have first-order entities like locations and times as their arguments. These first-order entities are themselves described further using attributes. Events may also be directly attributed and express relations between each other and to other entities. While precisely defining what separates an event from a (potentially *n*-ary, rather than a binary) relation in an ontology is a semantic rather than a syntactic issue, the practical differences are very real because extracting and resolving events with high quality (compared to extracting ordinary entities) constitute an active area of research. One of the best-known examples of a large-scale event KG that is also publicly available is the Global Database of Events, Language, and Tone (GDELT).

1.4   How to Read This Text

This text is broken into five parts following a "natural" order, but many of them can be read out of order depending on the reader's familiarity with KGs. Part I serves as an introduction to the core elements that make a graph a *knowledge* graph. Chapter 2, the only other chapter in this part, is heavier on technical details, including on models like Resource Description Framework (RDF), and is recommended reading to place the rest of the work in context, though not all the sections in that chapter are necessary.

Part II is self-contained and covers much of KG construction (KGC), including *domain discovery*, an important and relatively understudied area that covers how to *find* relevant data for *domain-specific* KGC to begin with.

Rarely is KGC adequate in terms of data quality and coverage. Often, there are missing links in the KG, and also many links are noisy. Part III covers *KG completion* (also called *identification* and *refinement*), which covers both well-studied techniques such as instance matching and more recent (often, neural network–based) KG-embedding (KGE) methods. Although part III is independent of part II, some of the concepts in part III will be understandable only in the context of the kinds of noise (and other problems) that are described in part II.

Part IV assumes that the KG has been constructed and completed, and it deals with the problem of querying and performing analytics on the KG. Some chapters, especially the more classically oriented (e.g., logic-based) ones, will have a higher quality than others, and they may require a review of the representational elements in chapter 2. Others will make fewer assumptions and tend to operate better in real-world systems and settings, but offer fewer theoretical guarantees. Personal preferences aside, each of these "schools" of querying comes with its own incumbent set of pros and cons, and which one to apply depends on the skills, design, and objectivity of the system architect.

Finally, part V, which is largely nontechnical and more descriptive than the rest of the book, describes the fruits of KG research—namely, *KG ecosystems*. This part is designed to be read by any reasonably knowledgeable practitioner or researcher with some familiarity with KGs (although chapter 2 is still recommended), but the technical depth of material covered in parts II–IV is certainly not required.

1.5   Concluding Notes

A KG is a practical and machine-readable way of representing information about the world, including entities, relationships, attributes, facts, beliefs, and even provenance, including justifications and uncertainty. In part, the proliferation and use of KGs has been predicated by the difficulty of getting machines to "directly" understand modalities such as natural language. Indeed, it is controversial how our brains process such input; it is certainly not outside the realm of possibility that we interpret the world in relatively structured ways, although the "natural" structure that we are comfortable with may differ significantly from the mathematical structure preferred by computer programs. By first "constructing" (and "completing"; see part III) KGs from raw data (part II), and then instituting systems that allow us to "use" the constructed KG, whether through structured querying or more natural question answering (part IV), the research community as a whole has been able to build powerful systems and applications with an underlying KG as the central representation (part V).

In practice, however, we must also deal with the uncomfortable notion that a KG is still not very well defined (which makes KG representation challenging because no one representation can be held to be the "correct" one), and also that it is rarely the case that the structure of a KG (the "ontology"), or the corpus over which the KG must be constructed, is either known or fixed. In addition to dealing with the dynamic nature of the world, we need to interpret the world not just as a collection of entities and relationships but also as a collection of entities, relationships, and complex, higher-order entities such as *events*. These are advanced topics of research, although some consensus is starting to emerge in topics like event extraction from text.

It is safe to say that KGs will continue to thrive as a research agenda in the foreseeable future. Entire KG ecosystems already exist, as described in part V, spanning the spectrum from academia to industry and e-commerce. As these ecosystems start to converge and collaborate, the potential for groundbreaking research continues to increase. This is an exciting era for KGS.

1.6   Software and Resources

Because this is an introductory chapter, we are not providing pointers to KG-specific resources just yet. However, one of the open-source packages that a layperson in graph theory or KGs may find useful is *NetworkX*. NetworkX, the full project page of which can be accessed at https://networkx.github.io/, is a Python package for the "creation, manipulation, and study of the structure, dynamics, and functions of complex networks." In the context of this book, a KG may be seen as a special kind of complex network because it is expressing knowledge in all its interconnectedness. Some of the advantages of working with NetworkX are that it is easy to set up in a Python environment, has been released under an open-source, 3-clause[3] Berkeley Software Distribution (BSD) license, and has been well tested with over 90 percent code coverage at this time. The package is also very flexible and versatile, allowing data structures for graphs, directed graphs, and multigraphs (and also *attributed graphs*, which are important for implementing KGs from a graph-theoretic perspective), many well-known graph algorithms (such as Dijkstra's shortest-path algorithm), and many measurements and diagnostics for analyzing network structure. It also includes generators for synthetic networks, random graphs, and classic graphs.

NetworkX is a good package, therefore, for becoming familiar with graph theory, and even building some toy KGs. However, it should be noted that it is not a standard package for building, or querying, real-world KGs; its primary use-case is in the network science realm. For example, it is not designed for querying, which is extremely important for getting useful information out of the KG, as we will cover in depth in part IV. Most real-world KGs are modeled using languages like RDF. Such models will be the subject of the next chapter.

1.7   Bibliographic Notes

We started this chapter by introducing the motivations behind graph theory, going all the way back to Euler and the Königsberg Bridge Problem. For a refresher on the problem, we encourage the interested reader to review Hopkins and Wilson (2004). Considering its long history, graph theory is a mature area of study in mathematics by now (although many interesting extensions have been proposed, and it continues to see research activity in mathematics under different guises), and several texts and handbooks are available for an interested and mathematically oriented reader. These include the introductory text by West (1996), the handbook by Gross and Yellen (2004), and going even further back, the work by Bondy et al. (1976) for a more application-oriented treatment.

The computer science and algorithms research community, as we noted in the introduction, has long had a close relationship with graphs. Now-classic work includes the search algorithms by Tarjan (1972) and Dijkstra (1959), to name just two. Because this is textbook material now, any preliminary treatment of graphs and algorithms such as shortest paths can be found in a good text in computer science, algorithms, computational complexity, or data structures. Some examples of such introductory works can be found in Frakes (1992) and Shaffer (1997). More recent analysis in computer science, though still fairly mature (going back to the 1990s and 2000s), has looked at interesting and fast ways of applying

---

[3] https://opensource.org/licenses/BSD-3-Clause.

some of these algorithms, especially Dijkstra's algorithm, including partitioning graphs, parallelization, and complexity analysis for such variants as graphs with weighted vertices. A good review of these may be found in the respective works by Möhring et al. (2007), Crauser et al. (1998), and Barbehenn (1998), among many others. For the reader who is looking for a good introduction to graph algorithms specifically, we recommend Even (2011).

Well before KGs, and quite disjoint from the algorithms community, researchers in physics and social sciences turned to graphs for modeling networks, which are useful in the study of complex systems, including protein-protein interactions, the growth of the web, and even ecological systems like the food chain in an ecological niche. *Network science*, as this field is called, is an actively researched, standard framework for studying complex systems that possess structure; see Barabási et al. (2016). Such systems, as evidenced in a range of works including Gavin et al. (2002), Hummon and Dereian (1989), and Borgatti et al. (2009), include the study of networks of protein-protein interactions, citation networks, and social networks, to name just a few. Recent research has led to many exciting advances in the construction and study of complex networks, especially from Big Data. For example, Chen and Redner (2010) study the community structure of the physical review citation network from the mid-1890s to 2007. Other domain-specific examples include the study by Li et al. (2007) of patent citation networks in nanotechnology and the study by Greenberg (2009) of the creation and influence of citation distortions.

Another highly active subarea of research in network science, and (arguably) one of the original motivations for employing network science as a scientific methodology for studying structure, is social networks. Work in this area can be traced back to at least the 1940s (and possibly beyond), when Moreno (1946) first proposed the "sociogram" as a way of studying such systems at a structural level. Since then, there have been tens of thousands of papers and articles on the subject; a standard, highly comprehensive treatment on social network analysis was provided by Wasserman and Faust (1994), along with a more recent book by Knoke and Yang (2008). More recently, pioneering work in this area includes a study of networks, crowds, and markets by Easley et al. (2010); social tie inference in heterogeneous networks by Tang et al. (2012); prediction of positive and negative links in social networks by Leskovec et al. (2010); and even ethics- and privacy-related challenges in mining social network data by Kleinberg (2007). Other important applications of network science includes bioinformatics, with research ranging from studies in systems pharmacology by Berger and Iyengar (2009) to tools designed for fast network motif detection as evidenced by Wernicke and Rasche (2006), and Schreiber and Schwöbbermeyer (2005), and tens (if not many hundreds) of other papers, many quite recent.

We cite all the previous works to make clear that there is considerable precedent, well before KGs were proposed, for using graphs for solving important problems and in studying myriad phenomena. Hence, it is not surprising that information retrieval and communities like Natural Language Processing would eventually be influenced by the promise of building, querying, and doing machine learning on large-scale graphs derived from sources like documents, tables, and webpages. Yet, perhaps because this spurt of research activity has emerged from different places and communities, there is no cohesive treatment of much of this research to explore KGs qua KGs. The original blog post touting the Google Knowledge Graph as treating queries as "things, not strings" is still available online and can be accessed at https://www.blog.google/products/search/introducing-knowledge-graph-things-not/ [at least as of late 2019; an official citation is Singhal (2012)]. Some other surveys and studies of KGs and their influence include a recent brief by Kejriwal (2019) that is an extended technical survey on a specific subarea (domain-specific KG construction), as well as Qi et al. (2020). In addition, a book on KG methodology, tools, and selected use-cases was published by Fensel et al. (2020).

There is no textbook specifically on KGs to the best of our knowledge, and in that sense, we hope that this book will serve as a standard for how to organize one. No doubt, as research on all the different areas we cover in this book continues at a breakneck pace, some of the material will have to be updated or supplemented with each independent attempt or edition. However, for those looking for perspectives on KGs, or a somewhat broad overview, we recommend Paulheim (2017) on KG refinement, as well as a more recent paper by Ehrlinger and Wöß (2016) that seeks to define a KG more precisely. A much more recent review on KGs was provided by Hogan et al. (2020), and another handy resource is Yan et al. (2018). While Nickel et al. (2015) delve much deeper into the relational machine learning side of KGs, it is also a good place to begin to get a gentle overview of KGs and their uses. For a survey and case study of enterprise KGs, we recommend Jetschni and Meister (2017). We cite more material on individual aspects of KG research in the upcoming chapters.

1.8 Exercises

1. To understand the general applicability of Euler's theorem (recall that the theorem states that a connected graph is Eulerian if and only if all vertices have even degrees), consider the three graphs on the next page. Do any of the graphs have Eulerian circuits? If so, label the edges and state the sequence of edges in the circuit starting and ending at node A.

2. What is the minimum number of "edges" you have to remove from the underlying graph representation of the Königsberg Bridge Problem such that an Eulerian circuit exists? Can you do it without violating connectedness? Draw the resulting graph.

3. You're trying to explain the Eulerian circuit problem to a friend. You show him the example of a connected graph where such a circuit does not exist (such as the Königsberg Bridge Problem) and tell him, "There is no way to start from node A and return to node A while traversing every edge in the graph exactly once." The friend responds that he

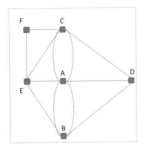 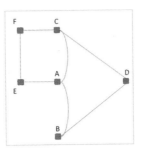 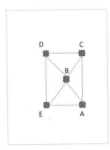

agrees with you, but that does not mean that such a "circuit" cannot exist for another node B. Write a simple proof by contradiction showing why the validity of your statement, in fact, does imply that such a circuit cannot exist for any other node in the graph.

4. Express as a KG the sentence "Michael's lawyer and friend, John Robbins, represented him on a felony charge in the District Court of Oz. Oz is the capital of Neverland. In attendance at the court were the Cowardly Lion and the Wicked Witch of the West." How many relations and entities are in your KG? Are there events in your KG?

5. Consider again the product KG that was introduced earlier in the chapter. How would you modify the graph (i.e., by adding, changing, or removing nodes or edges) in order to introduce competitor relationships between products (e.g., a Samsung phone and the iPhone). Also, is it true that Apple is the "manufacturer" of the iPhone? Is there any way in which you can make the relationship between Apple and iPhone more precise?

2 Modeling and Representing Knowledge Graphs

Overview. Before studying how to construct and use knowledge graphs (KGs), it is important to know how to *model* them. As indicated in the previous chapter, KGs have been heavily influenced by graph theory, and therefore it is unsurprising that many KG representations have an inherently graph-theoretic flavor. The diversity and subtleties of these different flavors is surprising and offer an interesting study in representational trade-offs. In this chapter, we study some KG representational models that have become dominant in KG-centric communities such as the Semantic Web. Chief among these models is the Resource Description Framework (RDF) model, as well as models that have been built on top of it, such as RDF Schema (RDFS). We also detail the Wikidata model and provide a brief primer on property-centric models such as the property graph and the property table. The chapter concludes with advanced research topics such as the Semantic Web Layer Cake, schema heterogeneity, and semantic labeling.

2.1 Introduction

Research in data-driven communities such as Relational Database Management Systems (RDBMSs) has a rich history in modeling the data that is being stored, processed, and queried. These models seem intuitive on the surface; to an unpracticed eye, an RDBMS "looks" like a set of tables, but there is much more subtlety in the formal machinery that goes into modeling such systems. Some of these may be familiar already to the reader who has dabbled in RDBMs, including decompositions, foreign keys, and functional dependencies. A critical feature is the separation between the "schema" of the system, which lays out a template for how the actual data can be modeled or represented, and the data itself.

KGs are less rigid than RDBMSs, but this makes a study of KG formalism all the more relevant. Without clear representational underpinnings, it is easy to think of any data item that has structure as a KG. What, for example, prevents us from calling an ordinary social network (such as an undirected friendship network) a KG? Why is Wikipedia not a KG? And most important, if we want to undertake the process of modeling and constructing KGs in our domain of interest, be it fighting fraud or designing a better e-commerce search engine, what formalism can we rely on to define and *constrain* the KG in appropriate ways?

In the previous chapter, we suggested (mainly through examples) an initial definition of a KG as a "labeled, multirelational, directed graph" (i.e., a graph where both nodes and edges have labels, and edges have directions). Even in this definition, a difference between formal and "normative" behavior quickly starts to emerge. In most typical KGs, the labels (or some significant fraction of them) tend to be human-readable or understandable (e.g., it is dubious whether a labeled graph where the labels are all random strings would be *perceived* as a KG). On the other hand, the definition is not always as rigid as it seems. In rare cases, KGs can be uni-relational—that is, in a simple product-customer KG, there may be a broad diversity in node labels, but only a single edge label ("purchase"). Some edges could even be undirected, though this is an easy formal fix (see the exercises at the end of this chapter). Our point here is that any definition or formalism involving KGs must be taken as a *guide*, rather than a strict, prescriptive statement resembling a mathematical definition (such as the definition of an irrational number). The KG community overwhelmingly relies on practice (rather than theory), as well as actual application of KGs in various domains, when deciding on such formal matters.

To drive this point home even further, let us take a second (arguably, even simpler) definition of a KG—namely, as a set of triples. A triple is like a "directed edge," where the first and third elements of the triple are the two nodes and the middle element is the labeled edge "going from" the first node to the third node. We will see in a subsequent section that this is an important definition on which models like Resource Description Framework (RDF) are grounded. It is also, however, the definition of a *knowledge base (KB)*, leading to the question of whether a KB is also a KG. Normatively, we argue that a KB cannot be a KG unless it has some kind of *structure*. In the extreme case, imagine that no two triples in the KB share any labels. Represented as a graph, such a set of triples starts looks highly disconnected, where the degree of every node is exactly 1. Put another way, a graph is clearly not the right data model for such a data set, any more than a table with lots of missing values is the right data set for an RDBMS. But when exactly does a KB morph into a KG? In borderline or ambiguous cases, the difference in terminology may be mere semantics. But more often than not, practice and application play a deciding role in whether a set of triples is just that, or can be visualized and described as something more (i.e., a KG). Furthermore, as we shall see when discussing the Wikidata data model, it is not always a good idea to describe every KG using the set of triples because it can lead to loss of representational power.

Graphs have always been an exciting area of research for algorithm research, but the rapid advent of KGs has brought graphs to the forefront of data-modeling research in this last decade. Graph algorithms still apply to KGs, and they play an important role when we discuss how to query KGs in part IV of this book. In this chapter, we describe some important languages that can be used to both model the KG, and define the schema or *ontology* for the KG. These languages have emerged as dominant forces in KG-centric communities

Figure 2.1: An example of a KG triple (:mayank_kejriwal, foaf:name, "Mayank Kejriwal") represented in RDF. The prefix *foaf:* is shorthand for http://xmlns.com/foaf/0.1/ (i.e., the subject in the triple is actually "http://xmlns.com/foaf/0.1/name," and similarly, the prefix *:* before mayank_kejriwal is meant to express that mayank_kejriwal lies in the *default* namespace). In this case, the "object" is a literal; by convention, literals are represented as rectangles, while URI nodes and blank nodes are elliptical.

like the Semantic Web (SW) and even Natural Language Processing (NLP), and most of them receive support from the likes of the World Wide Web Consortium (W3C). Research on them continues, but the primary aspects are well established by this time.

2.1.1 Resource Description Framework

Technically, RDF is a framework for representing information on the web, and not necessarily as a data model for representing KGs. However, because of the rise of KGs in the SW community, where the RDF model has been most developed and used, KGs in the SW have been represented either in RDF or in a "higher-level" representation based on RDF, such as RDFS. Because almost all models in the SW community ultimately derive from RDF, and some of these models, such as the Web Ontology Language (OWL), play a key role in part IV, when we describe reasoning and retrieval over KGs, we pay close attention to RDF and its design in this chapter.

At its core, RDF has an abstract syntax that reflects a simple, graph-based data model and has been motivated by several design factors, the most important of which is a way to represent information in a minimally constraining, flexible way. While an RDF can be used in isolated applications, where individually designed formats might be more direct and easily understood, the RDF's generality offers greater value from sharing. For this reason, it is a good fit for KGs that either derive from, or need to be published to, the web (whether publicly accessible or not). We note that many modern KGs (e.g., Wikidata) are connected to the web in some way, which may also explain why this model has emerged as a good fit.

The underlying structure of any expression in RDF is a collection of triples, each consisting of a subject, a predicate, and an object. A set of such triples is called an *RDF graph*. This can be illustrated by a node and directed-arc diagram, in which each triple is represented as a node-arc-node link. We illustrate such a triple in figure 2.1. The direction of the arc is clearly important because it always emerges from the subject and points to the object. Informally, the assertion of an RDF triple (s, p, o) says that the object o is related to subject s via a p relationship. The assertion of an RDF graph, a set of triples, equates assertion of all the triples in it; in other words, the *conjunction* of the statements corresponding to all the triples it contains.

The nodes in an RDF expose the relationship between between the RDF and the web. An RDF node may be one of the following:

1. Uniform resource identifier (URI) with an optional *fragment* identifier (URI reference, or *URIref*). For instance, "https://example.com/path/resource.txt #fragment" is a URIref.
2. Literal; for instance, "Mayank Kejriwal" but also numbers like 23 or dates.
3. Blank node, which is an abstract identifier that is locally unique and has no separate form of identification. Because they are not globally de-referenceable, blank nodes are not web artifacts but are used for establishing identities of resources (which may, for example, be unnamed[1]) within a local data set or *namespace*.

RDF properties are always URI references. A URI reference or literal used as a node identifies what that node represents. As mentioned previously, a URI reference used as a predicate identifies a relationship between the things represented by the incident nodes. Without additional constraints, a predicate URI reference may also be a node in the graph. This, along with other, similar observations, has motivated additional (subsequently described) models and vocabularies that "build upon" RDF by constraining it in the appropriate ways.

The most nonintuitive form that an RDF node can take is that of a blank node, which is neither a URI reference (in the proper sense) nor a literal. In the RDF abstract syntax, a blank node is just a unique node that can be used in one or more RDF statements but has no intrinsic name. There are many practical reasons for using such blank nodes. In many cases, it is because we want to use a local identifier for an unidentified resource in order to make assertions about it. The marriage example in the footnote here illustrates this use. However, note that the local identification semantics of the blank node has some important consequences when merging two or more RDF graphs because the blank nodes must be kept distinct if meaning is to be preserved; on occasion, this calls for reallocation of blank node identifiers. Formally, blank node identifiers are not part of the RDF abstract syntax, and the representation of triples containing blank nodes is entirely dependent on the particular concrete syntax used. In other words, the scheme for coming up with, and assigning, blank node identifiers is something that is entirely dependent on the person modeling and publishing the RDF data.

Concerning literals, datatypes in RDF allow the representation of values such as integers, floating point numbers, and even dates. There is a formal way to define datatypes in RDF, but many of the common types are already defined. A typed literal is a string combined

---

[1] As such an entity, consider the "second marriage of John Doe." The marriage has attributes that can be used to describe it, including the two participants in the marriage, the date of marriage, and the venue, but it may not make sense to give it a name and globally de-referenceable URI.

with a datatype URI (e.g., <xsd:boolean, "true">, where *xsd* is a shorthand prefix for XML Schema), while a plain literal is simply a string combined with an optional language tag.

2.1.1.1 Equivalences in RDF From the previous discussion, an RDF graph is a set of RDF triples, and the set of nodes in this graph is the set of subjects and objects of triples in the graph. What does it mean for two RDF graphs, G and G', to be equivalent? Formally, an equivalence holds if there is a bijection M between the sets of nodes of the two graphs, such that the following conditions are fulfilled:

1. M maps blank nodes in G to blank nodes in G'.
2. $M(lit) = lit$ for all RDF literals *lit*, which are nodes of G.
3. $M(uri) = uri$ for all RDF URI references *uri*, which are nodes of G.
4. The triple (s, p, o) is in G if and only if the triple $(M(s), p, M(o))$ is in G'.

We bring up the notion of equivalence to show that, unlike with ordinary graph theory, which primarily concerns unlabeled nodes and edges and where equivalences are usually established through graph isomorphisms, RDF (and by close extension, *knowledge*) graphs require a more stringent set of conditions. It is possible for G and G' to be isomorphic without being equivalent in the RDF universe; intuitively, this happens when two graphs are structurally identical but contain different *content*, which would lead to an incomplete or conflicting mapping between their respective nodes or properties. Note that two RDF URI references are equal if and only if they compare as equal, character by character, as Unicode strings. For literals, equality is slightly more complicated; the following conditions have to be met:

1. The strings of the two lexical forms compare as equal, character by character.
2. Either both or neither have language tags (and if the language tags exist, they must be equal).
3. Either both or neither have datatype URIs (and if the datatype URIs exist, they must be equal, character by character).

The last condition only applies to typed literals, while the first two conditions apply to both plain and typed literals. Sometimes, this means that adding more information to a literal can make the graph nonequivalent to another graph. For example, imagine the literal "Mont Blanc," which exists in two separate KGs. Now, however, the author of the second RDF KG decides to add language tags to all literals and appends the tag @fr to "Mont Blanc." The two literals, per the conditions given here, would now become unequal, and strictly speaking, the two graphs would become nonequivalent. Similarly, removing information can have the same effect (e.g., if both literals initially had the same language type @fr, but the author of one graph decides to remove the language tag).

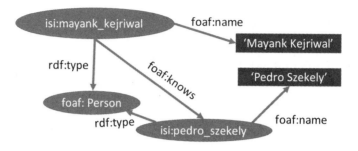

http://isi.edu/mayank_kejriwal http://www.w3.org/1999/02/22-rdf-syntax-ns#type   http://xmlns.com/foaf/0.1/Person
http://isi.edu/mayank_kejriwal http://xmlns.com/foaf/0.1/knows   http://isi.edu/pedro_szekely
http://isi.edu/mayank_kejriwal http://xmlns.com/foaf/0.1/name   "Mayank Kejriwal"
http://isi.edu/pedro_szekely http://xmlns.com/foaf/0.1/name   "Pedro Szekely"
http://isi.edu/pedro_szekely http://www.w3.org/1999/02/22-rdf-syntax-ns#type   http://xmlns.com/foaf/0.1/Person

Figure 2.2: A KG fragment in its conceptual graph representation (above), and N-triples representation (below). The *rdf* and *foaf* prefixes represent the namespaces indicated in the N-triples fragment. The authors' URIs are for indicative purposes only. Prefixes are not permitted in the N-triples representation.

2.1.2   RDF Serializations

The discussion so far illustrates that, conceptually, RDF can be represented just as a directed, labeled graph, or as shown in the case of the simplest KG representation possible, as a set of triples. RDF files that are meant to be downloaded as dumps are frequently formatted in just this way, and they are known as *N-triples* files. An N-triples file has a triple on each line, with each triple representing an edge in the RDF KG. Recall that subjects and properties in RDF graphs are necessarily URIs, and subjects can also be blank nodes, which are not globally de-referenceable in the way that ordinary URIs are. N-triples lines are "absolute" in that each line can be processed independently because full URIs have to be used in each line (prefixes and shorthands are not allowed). This also makes them amenable to a streaming setting where lines have to be read in (and parsed) from the file and then discarded.

However, it is not desirable to encode all RDF KGs this way. One reason is that N-triples files can grow to be very large because each URI tends to be a long string, including the namespace of the graph itself. For example, consider the simple KG fragment in figure 2.2. In N-triples format, the URI for a node would be repeated in as many lines as there are edges incident on that node.[2] This URI is long, and intuitively, it seems unnecessary to be repeating the URI so many times. Furthermore, because of their use of absolute URIs,

---

[2] For example, the URI for Mayank Kejriwal is repeated thrice as a subject in the N-triples representation provided below the KG fragment in figure 2.2.

```
@base <http://example.org/> .
@prefix rdf: <http://www.w3.org/1999/02/22-rdf-syntax-ns#> .
@prefix rdfs: <http://www.w3.org/2000/01/rdf-schema#> .
@prefix foaf: <http://xmlns.com/foaf/0.1/> .
@prefix rel: <http://www.perceive.net/schemas/relationship/> .

<#joker>
rel:enemyOf <#batman> ;
a foaf:Person ; # in the context of the DC universe
foaf:name "The Clown Prince of Crime" .

<#batman>
rel:enemyOf <#joker> ;
a foaf:Person ;
foaf:name "Dark Knight" .
```

Figure 2.3: A KG fragment expressed in Turtle as a predicate list.

N-triples files are not designed to be human-readable. The reason is that, while machines can ingest the file line by line and construct an RDF graph from it, humans typically find it inconvenient to parse all the long URIs. Thus, there are two needs here that have to be addressed.

First, is it possible to write out the RDF KG in a format that makes it readable by humans and machines alike, with humans being able to parse the KG and its contents rather intuitively?

Second, is it possible to shorten the URIs so that the RDF file is not quite as big as in its N-triples version? The two needs are interrelated in an intuitive sense: we can imagine that, if there were a way to avoid the frequent use of such long URIs, the RDF file would become more compact and take up less bandwidth and storage. The compactness would also make the file more readable.

The Terse RDF Triple Language, known as Turtle, is a concrete syntax for RDF that generalizes the N-triples format and makes it possible to not repeat full URIs throughout the document, among other syntactic facilities. As an example, let us consider the code snippet in figure 2.3, expressed in Turtle, of a hypothetical KG fragment describing Batman and the Joker in the DC comic book universe.

This snippet is written as a *predicate list*, which is convenient when the same subject is referenced by a number of predicates. Additionally, prefixes can be used to truncate URIs further. In this case, the subject <http://example.org/ #joker> has the *base* prefix http://example.org/, which once declared, does not need to be repeated. New prefixes can be defined using variables; for instance, *foaf* (Friend of a Friend) is a well-known namespace often used to model classes like *Person* and properties like *name* that are applicable to social entities like people, and has a full URI <http://xmlns.com/foaf/0.1/>. Just the use of prefixes alone makes the file a lot more compact and readable than the N-triples file, which may be considered to be a special case (known as Simple Triples) of Turtle. However, beyond prefixes, there are further savings and greater readability because the subject is not repeated.

An even more compact representation afforded by Turtle is the *object list*. For example, consider the triple *<http://example.org/#joker> <http://xmlns.com/foaf/ 0.1/name> "The Clown Prince of Crime," "The Ace of Knaves,"* which is actually expressing *two* triples, each with the same subject and predicate, but with different objects (in this case, both objects are literals). For large KGs, these compact representations can be attractive; however, one deficiency that should not be forgotten is that Turtle files, as expressed using object and predicate lists, cannot be parsed line by line, which make them more difficult to stream. A historical (though not current) limitation is that the W3C did not originally consider the Turtle language to be a standard (normative), although this changed in 2014, when the Turtle specification was published as a W3C recommendation. There are also multiple packages available for converting a valid RDF file in one serialization format to another.

2.2   RDF Schema

RDF Schema provides a data-modeling vocabulary for RDF data. It can be best understood as a *semantic extension* of RDF. As the name itself indicates, it is like a vocabulary (the language remains RDF; i.e., RDFS is an extension of, not a replacement for, RDF) for building schemas that provides semantics to RDF graphs. Nevertheless, one can refer to RDFS itself as a language due to its incorporated extensions. A common use-case is to specify a functional domain ontology using RDFS, with the actual KG being in RDF, but obeying the vocabulary and other constraints specified by the RDFS ontology. RDFS is a popular language for building such ontologies, though in the truest sense, it has limited functionality compared to more powerful Semantic Web languages like OWL, which permit broader reasoning capabilities as covered in part IV. This is one reason why RDFS is thought of as a *schema* rather than an *ontology* language.

2.2.1   RDFS Classes

The most important, and common, vocabulary unit in RDFS is *rdfs:Class*,[3] which is used to declare classes (equivalently called *concepts*). Fundamentally, a class is a *group* (e.g., Country) into which *resources* (e.g., United States, Germany) may be divided. The members of a class are known as *instances* of the class. In the RDF context, classes are not special entities, but are themselves resources because they are also identified by URIs (or more generally, as permitted by the RDF standards, by *internationalized* resource iden-

---

[3] The convention is to capitalize the word after the prefix for vocabulary units that are *nodes* in an RDF or RDFS graph, while *properties* (or edges) do not capitalize this word. We obey this convention in both this chapter and the remainder of this book.

tifiers, or IRIs) and may be described using RDF properties. The *rdf:type* property is typically used to state that a resource is an instance of a class. Notice how the prefix allows us to distinguish between whether a vocabulary element belongs to a core RDF (such as *rdf:type*) or RDFS (such as *rdfs:Class*).

An important aspect of classes to note here is that RDF distinguishes between a class and the set of instances that make up that class (also called the *class extension*). In other words, two classes may have the same set of instances but still be different classes (e.g., the "World Economies" and "Countries" would likely have the same set of instances, but are technically different classes). This distinction is important because it shows that a class is not exhaustively defined by the set of its instances. A name is not just a name; it clearly expresses semantics in this worldview. We can see that this often makes intuitive sense because "World Economies" and "Countries" arguably do not have the same semantics, even though as concepts, they apply to an identical set of instances. In logic, we would say that the *extensional equivalence* of two classes in RDFS does not imply their *equality*. Another reason why this is useful, beyond intuitive semantic differences, is that it allows different classes like "World Economies" and "Countries" to have exactly the same instances, and yet have different properties. A world economy may have a property like "GDP" defined for it, while the same property may not be defined for a country because it was not considered important or general enough for the class of countries. If we had chosen to identify classes with only their extension, this advantage would be lost, and modeling real-world KGs would have become near-impossible.

Technically, a class may be a member of its own class extension (in other words, an instance of itself). All RDF Schema classes are themselves grouped into a class called *rdfs:Class*. For example, if we had a class *:Dog*, then we would declare it as a class through the triple *(:Dog, rdf:type, rdfs:Class)*. The intuition is to declare the resource (an ordinary URI at the end of the day) as a class. For this reason, *rdfs:Class* should be thought of as a reserved resource in the RDFS world. Being declared an instance of *rdfs:Class* has specific semantics, as the example triple with *:Dog* illustrates. Other such reserved URIs include *rdfs:subClassOf* and *rdfs:Literal*. While their names make them relatively self-explanatory, it is important to understand all the semantic implications when using these terms. For example, if a class C is declared to be a subclass of a class C', then all instances of C must necessarily be instances[4] of C'. This affects the capability of reasoners, as we will see in part IV. For now, the important thing to remember is that these reserved terms are designed precisely to allow RDFS to incorporate standard semantics into some of its vocabulary elements.

---

[4] An alternative term that is sometimes used is *superclass*, which is the inverse of subclass. In other words, if a class C is a subclass of a class C', then C' is a superclass of class C. If a class C' is a superclass of a class C, then all instances of C are also instances of C'.

It is important to note that, in RDFS, instances and subclasses are different from one another. Specifically, recall that all things described by RDF are called resources, and are considered to be instances of the class *rdfs:Resource*. This is the putative "class of everything" (i.e., all other classes are subclasses of this class). Here, *rdfs:Resource* itself is an instance of *rdfs:Class*. Interestingly, *rdfs:Class* is also defined as an instance of itself, although this is not common among classes in general. Other important general classes that are critical for defining good schemas include (note again that some have the prefix *rdf:* and are technically defined in RDF, not RDFS):

1. **rdfs:Literal:** The class of literal values such as strings and integers. Property values such as textual strings are examples of RDF literals. Here, *rdfs:Literal* is an instance of *rdfs:Class*, and a subclass of *rdfs:Resource*.

2. **rdfs:Datatype:** The class of datatypes. All instances of *rdfs:Datatype* correspond to the RDF model of a datatype (we provided details on the different elements of this model earlier). Here, *rdfs:Datatype* is both an instance of and a subclass of *rdfs:Class*; each instance of *rdfs:Datatype* is a subclass of *rdfs:Literal*.

3. **rdf:LangString:** The class of language-tagged string values. Here, *rdf:LangString* is an instance of *rdfs:Datatype* and a subclass of *rdfs:Literal*.

4. **rdf:HTML:** The class of Hypertext Markup Language (HTML) literal values. Here, *rdf:HTML* is an instance of *rdfs:Datatype* and a subclass of *rdfs:Literal*.

5. **rdf:XMLLiteral:** The class of Extensible Markup Language (XML) literal values. Here, *rdf:XMLLiteral* is an instance of *rdfs:Datatype* and a subclass of *rdfs:Literal*.

6. **rdf:Property:** The class of RDF properties. Here, *rdf:Property* is an instance of *rdfs:Class*.

2.2.2   RDFS Properties

Recall that we earlier defined a property as a relation between subject resources and object resources. RDFS, however, goes further, introducing the concept of *subproperty*. The *rdfs:subPropertyOf* property may be used to state that one property is a subproperty of another. The semantics are as follows, and analogous to the subclass semantics. Specifically, if a property P is a subproperty of property P', then all pairs of resources that are related by P are also related by P'. The term *superproperty* is often used as the inverse of subproperty. Conversely, if a property P' is a superproperty of a property P, then all pairs of resources that are related by P are also related by P'. This specification does not define a top property that is the superproperty of all properties.

Another important element introduced by RDFS is the notion of a property's constraints on what it can take on as domain and range. The domain of a property is the set of values that can serve as its subject, while the range is the set of values that can serve as its object. RDFS introduces several role constraints by way of properties like *rdfs:range*, *rdfs:domain*, and *rdfs:subClassOf* (the last of which was described earlier). Here, *rdfs:domain* is an instance of *rdf:Property* that is used to state that any resource that has a given property is an instance of one or more classes. A triple *(P, rdfs:domain, C)* states that *P* is an instance of the class *rdf:Property*, that *C* is a instance of the class *rdfs:Class*, and that the resources denoted by the subjects of triples whose predicate is *P* are instances of the class *C*. Where a property *P* has more than one *rdfs:domain* property, then the resources denoted by subjects of triples with predicate *P* are instances of *all* the classes stated by the *rdfs:domain* properties (this is a subtle point that can lead to erroneous semantics and modeling by an inexperienced practitioner).

The *rdfs:domain* property may even be applied to itself. The *rdfs:domain* of *rdfs:domain* is a class *rdf:Property*, which states that any resource with an *rdfs:domain* property is an instance of *rdf:Property*. This seems intuitive enough, but without declaring it in the way we just described, it is not formalized.

In a similar vein, *rdfs:range* is an instance of *rdf:Property* that is used to state that the values of a property are instances of one or more classes. The triple *(P, rdfs:range, C)* states that *P* is an instance of the class *rdf:Property*, that *C* is an instance of the class *rdfs:Class*, and that the resources denoted by the objects of triples whose predicate is *P* are instances of the class *C*. Where *P* has more than one *rdfs:range* property, the resources denoted by the objects of triples with predicate *P* are instances of all the classes stated by the *rdfs:range* properties.

Just like *rdfs:domain*, the *rdfs:range* property can be applied to itself. The *rdfs:range* of *rdfs:range* is the class *rdfs:Class*. This states that any resource that is the value of an *rdfs:range* property is an instance of *rdfs:Class*. The *rdfs:range* property is applied to properties. This can be represented in RDF using the *rdfs:domain* property. The *rdfs:domain* of *rdfs:range* is the class *rdf:Property*. This states that any resource with an *rdfs:range* property is an instance of *rdf:Property*. Similarly, *rdfs:range* can also be applied to *rdfs:domain* with similar intuitions—namely the *rdfs:range* of *rdfs:domain* is the class *rdfs:Class*, which states that any resource that is the *value* of an *rdfs:domain* property is an instance of *rdfs:Class*.

2.3 Property-Centric Models

The RDF and RDFS models provide some sophisticated capabilities, but we saw (at the very beginning of this chapter) that simpler models, such as the set of triples, can often suffice for certain use-cases and communities. Such simple models have an advantage in that they are easy to express, use, and transfer between programs, but do not come with the sophisticated knowledge representation of RDF and other languages that build on it. Usually, the choice is not so extreme. In the next section, we present the Wikidata model, which offers a different trade-off between simplicity, expressivity, and formal or representational sophistication. In this section, we provide yet another perspective by describing a

Figure 2.4: A triple as it would be represented in a property graph model. Note how both the nodes and the edges are key-value data structures rather than URIs or literals.

simpler class of models that intuitively treat *properties* (or predicates) as first-class citizens.

The property graph is perhaps the simplest (and quite widely used) illustration of such a model. The Neo4j graph database, which is covered in some depth in chapter 12, uses this model as its primary representation of KGs. The most important difference between RDF and property graphs is that, while RDF uses Uniform Resource Locators (URLs) as identifiers (for relationships and entities), property graphs use purely local identifiers such as strings (recall that these were *literals* in the RDF context). At its core, a property graph is just a set of nodes and edges, where each node (and edge) may be thought of as a *data structure* of keys and values. An example is shown in figure 2.4. Because nodes and edges are both structures, complex information can be expressed quite succinctly, though without the same kinds of semantic and logical safeguards that RDF provides. In recent years, these models have become quite popular, and the Neo4j implementation also provides a querying language specifically designed for manipulating such graphs. The main reason why the property graph is thought of as a *property-centric* model (other than the similarity in their names) is precisely because of the support for key-value representations at both the node and edge levels. The philosophy is that it is natural for entities to have an associated bag of properties, and these properties are expressed using keys and values, exactly as shown in figure 2.4. In contrast, RDF is able to provide such support only by introducing new classes at a more abstract level or through reification (for example). For many ordinary practitioners, developers, and subject matter experts who have not necessarily been trained to understand such concepts, this concept can be difficult to convey. We provide more illustrations and formalism, including the querying language itself, in chapter 12. At present, it suffices to know that such models exist as pragmatic alternatives to RDF-like models. In actual practice, therefore, one must carefully consider the pros and cons of all these models (including the subsequently presented Wikidata model) before making a representational choice. We emphasize that, at the present time, there are enough good models, tool support, and representational choices available that inventing a new model and language for a task is usually considered wasteful.

Another kind of property-centric model is the *property table*. Property tables attempt to improve standard triplestore infrastructures, where each triple statement is stored in a three-

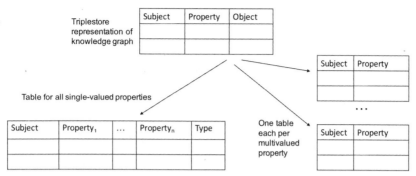

Figure 2.5: One approach to represent a set of triples or a triplestore as a property table. In a property-centric representation such as this, properties are elevated to the status of metadata as column headers (or even tables in themselves for multivalued properties) rather than values (the values in the cells of the second column in the original triplestore representation). In the derived tables, note that objects (or type) will always be the cell values, not including the first column, which is always the subject.

column table in a relational database (RDB) or other table-oriented infrastructure, by taking advantage of regularity in RDF data sets. Hence, unlike the property *graphs* described previously, the underlying model is usually still RDF, and the property table provides a more efficient mechanism for representing an RDF graph (given certain assumptions about the regularity). However, they are worth studying because one also could consider non-RDF variants of the concept.

The key idea (though variants also exist) is illustrated in figure 2.5. Let us assume that each subject in an RDF graph is associated with (at most) n single-valued properties. The multivalued properties (where, for a given subject s and multivalued property p, there are multiple triples of the form $< s, p, ?x >$, with $?x$ being a placeholder for an object) are treated separately; in essence, a separate two-column table with columns $subj$ and p_i is created for *each* multivalued property p_i. As is evident even from this brief description, the property table makes more sense when a table such as the one in figure 2.5 is relatively *nonsparse*. This tends to be the case for data that is more like an RDB than an irregular graph. Rather than choose between an RDB, with more efficient and intuitive structure for such data, and an RDF, which enables one to more naturally apply KG analytics, a practitioner could just use the property table. Semantic Web tools such as Apache Jena offer direct support for working with, and storing, such tables without sacrificing RDF as the conceptual mode of representation.

Figure 2.6: Info boxes for "The Joker" in the English and French Wikipedias, retrieved from *en.wikipedia.org/wiki/Joker_(character)* and *fr.wikipedia.org/wiki/Joker_(comics)*, respectively.

2.4 Wikidata Model

To understand Wikidata, we must first understand its relationship with the Wikipedia project, created with the vision of "a world in which every single human being can freely share in the sum of all knowledge." Wikipedia is a multilingual online encyclopedia created and maintained by volunteers who edit articles online using a simple markup language specifically designed for it. Wikipedia is available in over 300 languages, contains over 45 million pages, and has billions of visitors every month. While Wikipedia consists mostly of text documents, the pages in Wikipedia contain an enormous amount of structured data, including numbers, dates, coordinates, and relationships. Most structured data in Wikipedia is recorded in the *infoboxes* present in most pages. Figure 2.6 shows the info boxes for "The Joker" in the English and French Wikipedias. We see that the French Wikipedia has more data about the Joker, including aliases, gender, enemies, actors, and voices.

The goal of the Wikidata project is to build a central, multilingual KG to record the structured data for the subjects of Wikipedia articles, as well as to use Wikidata to populate the info boxes for all Wikipedia pages, in all languages. Doing so will remove the need for Wikipedia volunteers around the world to enter the same information manually in different languages. At this time, Wikidata contains data for more than 60 million items, and the migration of Wikipedia info boxes to Wikidata is well underway, with millions of Wikipedia pages already converted to query the data directly from Wikidata.

When we inspect the info boxes in figure 2.6, we see that most of the information can be represented in RDF. The subject is `:the_joker`, the property is derived from the attribute name, and the object is the attribute value. For example:

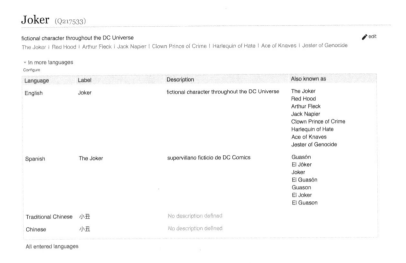

Figure 2.7: A KG fragment from Wikidata for "The Joker."

```
:the_joker :publisher :dc_comics .
```

In the French Wikipedia, we see the attribute "Interprété pa" to record the actors who played the Joker in a movie. For example, Cesar Romero played the Joker in the *Batman* movie of 1966, and Jack Nicholson in the *Batman* movie of 1989. The following is an incorrect attempt to record this information in triples:

```
:the_joker :performer :cesar_romero .
:the_joker :performer: jack_nicholson .
:the_joker :movie :batman_1966 .
:the_joker :movie :batman_1989 .
```

In this representation, we lost the information that Cesar Romero was in the 1966 movie and Jack Nicholson was in the 1989 movie. Triples allow us to represent the relationship between two items (character and actor), but in this example, the relationship is between three items (character, actor, and movie). Other examples include "spouse," where we need to record the person as well as the start and end dates of the relationship; and "population" for countries where we need to record the population and the year when the population was recorded. It also makes sense for other properties of countries to be recorded as *n*-ary, rather than as binary, relations (see the exercises).

Another important requirement follows from the nature of Wikipedia as a secondary source of information. Rather than publishing its own research, Wikipedia publishes findings recorded in primary sources, which include scholarly publications, news articles, and web sites, and records references to primary sources so that readers can judge the trustworthiness of the information. Wikidata is also a secondary source of information, so it also must record links to one or several primary sources. For every triple, we need the ability to represent links to primary sources where the information was published.

To faithfully represent the information in Wikipedia, we also need to represent uncertainty and units of measure. For example, the year when the famous *Mona Lisa* was painted is uncertain. Many art scholars believe that it was painted between 1503 and 1506, but recent research suggests that it was not started before 1513. In RDF, dates are represented as literals, but in this example, we need the ability to represent intervals. Units of measure are also important. For example, when we record the nominal gross domestic product (GDP) of the United States as 18,120,714,000,000, we must state whether this number is in US dollars, euros, or other currency.

In summary, the data representation requirements for Wikidata are:

- Representation of *classes, instances, properties, and literals*
- Representation of *n-ary relations* to record contextual or qualifying information about triples
- Representation of *references* to record links to the sources where the information was published
- Representation of the *units of measure* for quantities
- Representation of *uncertainty* for dates and quantities

The Wikidata KG, like all KGs, consists of nodes and edges. Wikidata uses two types of nodes, for *items* and for *properties*, and the edges are defined using *statements*. The main difference between Wikidata and KGs represented using RDF is that statements contain much more information than RDF triples; in addition to claims, which correspond to RDF triples, statements record references and qualifiers.

- **Item:** A thing being described in Wikidata. It can be a concrete thing, such as *Jack Nicholson*, the actor, a creation of the mind, such as *The Joker*, an event, such as the *Normandy landings* in World War II, or anything for which primary documentation exists.
- **Property:** Describes attributes that items can have, such as the *birth date* of a person, or relationships between two items, such as *place of birth*, which can be used to relate a person to a location.
- **DataValue:** Represents the value of an attribute of an item, such as dates, quantities, coordinates, and so on.
- **Statement:** Represents a specific piece of knowledge about an item, such as *Jack Nicholson's date of birth is April 22, 1937, according to the Integrated Authority File*, or *Jack Nicholson received the Academy Award for Best Actor in 1998 for his work in As Good as It Gets*. Statements include claims, references, and qualifiers.

- **Claim:** The part of a statement that records the factual knowledge in the statement, such as *Jack Nicholson's date of birth is April 22, 1937*, or *Jack Nicholson received the Academy Award for Best Actor*. A claim is specified using a property, such as *date of birth*; a value, such as *April 22, 1937*; or an item, such as *As Good as It Gets*.
- **Reference:** The part of a statement that records links to external resources or publications where the claim is documented, such as *. . . according to the Integrated Authority File*.
- **Qualifier:** A part of a claim that records contextual information about the claim, such as *. . . in 1998* or *. . . for his work in As Good as It Gets*. A qualifier, like a claim, is specified using a property and a value, but unlike claims, qualifiers may not have other qualifiers as parts.

2.4.1 Wikidata Items

Wikidata items are specified as tuples *(identifier, label, aliases, description, statements)*, where:

- **Identifier:** Every Wikidata item has a unique identifier, often referred to as a *q-node*, as they consist of the letter Q followed by an integer number. In the example in figure 2.7, we see the item corresponding to the Joker has identifier Q217533 in Wikidata.
- **Label:** Items have labels to denote the names of the concept that they represent. Wikidata encourages items to have labels in different languages, as it is intended to be a multilingual resource. An item can have at most one label in each language, and unlike identifiers, labels are not required to be unique, so multiple items may have the same label. Wikidata encourages capitalization to follow natural-language rules, where proper names are capitalized but other labels are in lowercase.
- **Aliases:** Because items can only have one label in each language, additional names for an item can be recorded as aliases. Wikidata encourages recording multiple aliases including colloquial and other commonly used names for items. Aliases are intended to improve recall of search engines.
- **Description:** Items have concise descriptions, one per language. Descriptions often provide information about the type of the item and are useful for distinguishing items that share labels.
- **Statements:** Items often have multiple statements to record attributes and relationships to other items. Each statement has a property, a value, zero or more references, and zero or more qualifiers. Items may have multiple statements for the same property. For example, in Wikidata's entry for the Joker, there are two statements using the property "member of," recording the fact that the Joker is a member of both the Injustice Gang and the Injustice League. When items have multiple statements using the same property, the user interface groups them in a statement group, but in the KG, each statement is a separate edge.

Wikidata statements are specified as tuples *(property, qualifiers, references, rank)*, with the following qualities:

- **Property:** A Wikidata property (defined next) that unambiguously specifies an attribute or relation for an item.
- **Qualifiers:** Each item/property/value triple may have multiple qualifiers that provide additional information about the triple. Qualifiers are defined using property/value pairs. While any property can be used in a qualifier, it is possible to define constraints to encourage or discourage use of properties as qualifiers (we describe constraints next). Qualifiers are often used to describe an interval of time when the triple is valid, but as the example illustrated, qualifiers can be used to record arbitrary details about a triple.
- **References:** Wikidata encourages recording of references for every item/property/value triple. References enable users of Wikidata knowledge to find the primary sources or other secondary sources for the information encoded in triples. References, like qualifiers, are described using property/value pairs. As figure 2.7 illustrates, not every statement in Wikidata has references.
- **Rank:** Wikidata records information about the world, and it is often the case that knowledge gets revised (e.g., Pluto is no longer categorized as a planet), primary sources provide conflicting information, or values differ depending on measurement methods or approaches. Wikidata does not attempt to represent the truth; instead, it wants to record different values and points of view, using qualifiers and references to enable users of the knowledge to select among opposing views. Wikidata defines three ranks, preferred, normal, and deprecated. When a statement has a single value, the rank should be set to normal. When a statement has multiple values, the preferred rank should be used for statements with references and qualifiers that provide further details in support of the validity of their values; for example, through the use of qualifiers with the properties point in time (P585), determination method (P459), and so on. The deprecated rank should be used for statements that contain errors (e.g., as a result of an incorrect measurement method, or that were believed to be correct, but have been disproven).

2.4.2 Wikidata Properties

Wikidata properties, like items, are also nodes in the KG. Property specifications include all the elements of items plus two additional elements, *datatype* and *constraints*. Properties are often referred to as *p-nodes*, as their identifiers consist of the letter P followed by an integer.

Datatype.   The datatype specifies the type of value that can be used in statements using the property. For example, the *educated at* property has type *Item*, requiring that the value be another item in Wikidata; the *start time* and *end time* properties have type *Time*, requiring that the values represent a point or time interval. The set of datatypes in Wikidata at the time or writing are:

- **Item:** Reference to an item in Wikidata.
- **Property:** Reference to a property in Wikidata.
- **Time:** A specification of a possibly uncertain time, specified as a tuple (time-point, timezone, before, after, precision, calendar), where:
    - Time-point denotes a point in time, represented as a timestamp resembling ISO 8601 (e.g., +2013-01-01T00:00:00Z; the year is always signed and padded to have between 4 and 16 digits; more extensive details about ISO 8601 may be found on the website: https://www.iso.org/iso-8601-date-and-time-format.html).
    - Timezone is a signed integer specifying an offset from UTC in minutes.
    - Before and after support specification of uncertain times as intervals [time-point − after, time-point + before]; before and after are nonnegative integers representing units of time given by precision.
    - Precision is an integer with meaning: 0—billion years, 1—hundred million years, 2—ten million years, 3—million years, 4—one hundred thousand years, 5—ten thousand years, 6—millennium, 7—century, 8—decade, 9—year, 10—month, 11—day, 12—hour, 13—minute, 14—second.
    - Calendarmodel is a reference to an item that represents a calendar model; for example, the Gregorian calendar (Q12138), Chinese calendar (Q134032).
- **Quantity:** A specification of a possibly uncertain quantity expressed with units of measure, specified as a tuple (amount, lower-bound, upper-bound, unit), where:
    - Amount represents the value of the quantity as a decimal number.
    - Lower-bound and upper-bound support the specification of uncertain quantities as intervals (amount − lower-bound, amount + upper-bound).
    - Unit is a reference to an item that represents a unit of measure; for example, centimeters (Q174728), euro (Q4916).
- **Monolingual text:** Specified as a tuple (string, language), where:
    - String is a Unicode string.
    - Language is a language code.[5]
- **String:** A Unicode string.
- **URL:** A generalized "URL" that identifies some kind of external resource, perhaps a link to an external site of some kind, or an identifier used for lookup in some kind of specialized resource.

---

[5] https://www.wikidata.org/wiki/Help:Wikimedia_language_codes/lists/all.

- **External identifier:** A string representing an identifier used in an external system.
- **Globe coordinate:** A specification of a geographical position specified as a tuple (latitude, longitude, precision, globe), where:
  - Latitude and longitude, specified as Geocentric Solar Magnetospheric System (GMS), or decimal degrees.
  - Precision specifies the resolution of the source of the coordinates, given as a decimal number.
  - Globe identifies a stellar body, such as Earth (Q2), the default, Mars (Q111).
- **Geographic shape:** A reference to a map data file on Wikimedia Commons.
- **Commons media:** A reference to a media file in Wikimedia Commons.
- **Tabular data:** A reference to tabular data file on Wikimedia Commons.
- **Musical notation:** A string describing music following the LilyPond (Q195946) syntax.
- **Mathematical expression:** A string expressed in a variant of LaTeX (Q5310).
- **Lexeme, form, and sense:** Datatypes to specify lexicographical data.[6]

Property Constraints.   Wikidata acknowledges that the world is full of exceptions, and consequently it does not enforce any constraints on the values of statements other than the datatype of properties described here. For example, if the datatype of a property is Item, any item can be used as a value. Property constraints are rules that specify how properties should be used, give guidance to human editors, and enable the construction of automated validators that flag statements with constraint violations, bringing them to the attention of human editors. It makes sense to define a constraint on the *head of government* (P6) property to state that the value should be a human (Q5), but exceptions are allowed. For example, the town of Talkeetna (Q668224) elected the cat Stubbs (Q7627362) as mayor, and Wikidata allowed this information to be recorded, tagging it with a constraint violation (Stubbs died at the age of 20 in 2017 and has since been replaced by a human mayor).

2.5   The Semantic Web Layer Cake

While RDF forms the basis of much of the Semantic Web, we have already seen that it is possible to extend its capabilities via modeling extensions like RDFS. Later in this book, in part IV, we will explore another set of extensions via OWL. However, even without knowing all the details of RDFS or OWL, we can see the broader trend here of a "modeling stack" or "layer cake" that consists of modeling facilities (often, but not always, languages and language extensions) for building and working with ever more sophisticated KG and ontological representations. A visualization of the famous Semantic Web Layer Cake is

---

[6] https://www.wikidata.org/wiki/Wikidata:Lexicographical_data.

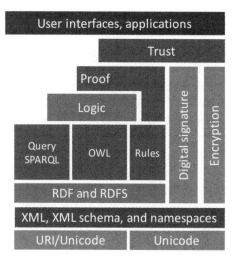

Figure 2.8: A simplified illustration of the Semantic Web Layer Cake.

illustrated in figure 2.8. We have already introduced many of the layers in this cake, starting from URIs and Unicode at the top all the way to RDF and RDFS at the bottom. At the very top are applications and user interfaces, which are necessary for actual users to be able to interact with KG representations. Proof and trust are important issues and remain areas of advanced research; the core idea is to be able to verify, in some way, the accuracy and provenance of the data that is being ingested and modeled in the system. As one can imagine, not all knowledge is equally trustworthy. We provide research pointers on these in the section entitled "Bibliographic Notes" at the end of this chapter for the interested reader. In the middle of the cake is a crucial layer (querying, OWL, and rules) that will form the subject of later chapters on reasoning.

One lesson to draw from a cake such as this is that representing and working with KGs is itself an interesting and important problem. Because of the visual ease of drawing KGs, it is easy to be misled into believing that representation itself is not a major issue. This is analogous to how we might be (naïvely) led to believe that an RDB is just a "set of tables." However, without proper models and representations, including powerful and consistent languages to express the knowledge in a KG in ways that machines would be able to efficiently query and ingest, a KG ecosystem would quickly fall apart. Instead, through the establishment of communitywide standards, whether of the SW, NLP, or the Wikidata communities, it has become feasible, even commonplace, to publish KGs on the web for the community to use and which are periodically updated. The original papers describing these KGs have garnered many thousands of citations and even won awards for their large-scale impact. Other KGs, such as the YAGO project, have been similarly successful.

2.6   Schema Heterogeneity and Semantic Labeling

As the Semantic Web and other related communities have expanded in scope, so have the schemas and ontologies that are currently in use. As we cover in detail in part V, there are entire KG ecosystems in place in areas as diverse as scientific inquiry, industry, and even artificial intelligence (AI) for social good. Even for generic domains such as encyclopedias and world knowledge (with the actual KG often derived from sources such as Wikipedia, Wikidata, and WordNet), there are multiple ontologies. It is not controversial to conclude that *schema heterogeneity*[7] is an important problem that needs to be addressed before different groups are able to work together on problems, and so that the potential of the web itself can be realized. While there are social aspects and solutions to this problem (an extreme being a mandate of sorts to use only one standard ontology per domain[8]), or one group using an ontology O for a domain could persuade another group to also use O rather than a different (possibly derived or hybrid) ontology O', the truth is that different groups and individuals have different use-cases, and ontologies and schemas are expected to serve those use-cases rather than the other way around. The problem then becomes: how do we address schema heterogeneity without having to pick one ontology over the other?

One important class of solutions that has been well developed both in the database and Semantic Web communities is to achieve (sometimes manually, but usually semiautomatically) a mapping between the two ontologies. In the database community, this has been referred to as *schema mapping* or *matching*. Rahm and Bernstein (2001) described the problem as finding a good fit for the "Match" operator, which takes two schemas as inputs and outputs a mapping between elements of both schemas that *correspond semantically* to each other. It is in the idea of semantic correspondence that the problem starts bearing a connection to AI because there is usually no clear mathematical formula for capturing the phenomenon of semantic correspondence. In contrast, for classic computational problems such as the traveling salesman problem, or even Euler's bridge problem (with which we began the previous chapter), the condition for success is usually well defined mathematically (though not necessarily easier to find computationally).

Even as early as two decades ago, when Rahm and Bernstein (2001) wrote on the matter, machine learning methods had started gaining in prominence. In fact, Rahm and Bernstein (2001) provide a full taxonomy of schema-matching approaches, some of which are based on constraints (using graph-matching techniques, for example) and others of which use linguistic cues, including word frequencies and information retrieval techniques, which

---

[7] One may wonder why we we do not refer to this empirical phenomenon as *ontological* heterogeneity, but the phrase simply has not caught on. It may be because schema heterogeneity was already a major problem in the broader database community that has exerted a prominent influence on research and application.

[8] Arguably, the Gene Ontology (covered in chapter 16) is one of the rare success stories to have achieved such a standing, though by decentralized and gradual community consensus rather than as a mandate.

are detailed in subsequent chapters. Our point here is that many approaches have been taken to the problem, and while good solutions have been developed and are in use, it is not a resolved matter, especially for difficult ontologies and new domains. A general machine learning approach to the problem is to designate one schema as a *source* schema, and the other as a *target* schema. The universe of elements (e.g., concepts) in the target schema then become akin to *labels* in the machine learning context, while elements in the source schema become the objects that need to be classified. Multiclass classification is applicable here, although other techniques can also be used.

Sometimes the matter is not as simple as automatically discovering a 1:1 correspondence, which the earlier machine learning–based approaches were more suitable for. There may be many-to-many correspondences, though correspondences usually tend to fall in the many-to-one (e.g., "phone number" and "extension code" in the source schema may correspond with a single, complete "phone number" field in the target) and one-to-many categories (e.g., a full "address" in the source schema maps to "zipcode" and "street address" in the target schema). Much subsequent research attempted to discover these correspondences with higher accuracy. Furthermore, even in the case of the 1:1 correspondence, simply discovering the match between concepts in the source and target schemas is not the end of the story, because the specific nature of the correspondence may also have to be discovered. Sometimes the mapping can be expressed as a syntactic transformation [e.g., if a phone is represented as xxx-xx-xxxx in the source and as (xxx) xx-xxxx in the target, a relatively simple program can be written, or given enough observations, *learned* by a pattern-mining or data transformation library, for mapping values between the two classes]. Sophisticated tools have been developed for learning such mappings and expressing such transformation programs in an adaptive fashion. The Karma semantic mapping and labeling system is a good example of an adaptive tool (see the section entitled "Software and Resources" for details) that also provides visual support to its users and supports multiple source and output formats (including spreadsheets and RDF).

Beyond direct schema and ontology matching, there are other use-cases of semantic mapping that we do not consider in this chapter, but provide pointers to in the section entitled "Bibliographic Notes." For example, SQL databases on the web or in industry may have to be transformed into Semantic Web standards such as OWL and RDF if the goal is to convert the underlying data to KGs and query them using graph pattern-matching languages such as SPARQL (chapter 12). Contrary to how they are first introduced, SQL databases are complex models in themselves (obeying, with some qualifications, relational algebra) and come with their own constraints such as foreign keys, column types, and primary keys. This mapping problem, therefore, is nontrivial. In fact, the R2RML mapping language was specifically adopted as a W3C recommendation[9] to formalize the mappings

---

[9] https://www.w3.org/TR/r2rml/.

from RDBs to RDF. Other research in the previous decade has given some valuable insight into the nature of this problem and potential solutions.

2.7 Concluding Notes

Unlike ordinary databases, KGs are particularly amenable to a visual graph-theoretic representation, which makes them easy for humans to understand and conceive. However, the modeling and representation of KGs are no less complex than for a sophisticated database. Representational decisions thus made can affect the entire application life cycle of the KG, including querying and other downstream applications that may need to access the KG. In this chapter, we started the topic of KG representation by briefly describing the simple triples model, still widely used in subareas of machine learning and NLP, followed by more sophisticated representational machinery like RDF and RDFS. We also described the Wikidata model, which, though not necessarily as rigorous as RDF, is extremely popular (and continuing to increase in influence) at this time, and sets itself apart due to the simplicity and ease of use without sacrificing core expressivity. We concluded the chapter with a discussion on how all of these models, with different degrees of expressivity and modeling capability, fit together within the context of a larger community. Understanding the various options available when modeling and representing KGs is an important skill to have when constructing or working with real-world KGs that are meant to support research and industrial applications for years to come.

2.8 Software and Resources

There are a number of resources available for working with, and validating, RDF. We do not focus here on the triplestores (packages that are useful for setting up RDF databases that can be queried and accessed), which will be the focus of chapter 12. One example of a simple command-line tool that can be used to convert different RDF serializations from one to the other is RDF2RDF, a Java tool that is wrapped into one single jar file for easy usage. It is licensed under GPL v2.0 and is publicly available at this link: http://www.l3s.de/~minack/rdf2rdf/. It can be run on the command line and is particularly convenient when the amount of memory available on the machine is proportionate to the RDF graph that needs to be converted.

A package that proves important for Python developers is RDFLib, which may be thought of as an RDF library for Python. The library contains parsers and serializers for RDF/XML, N3, NTriples, N-Quads, Turtle, TriX, RDFa, and Microdata. It also presents a *Graph* interface which can be backed by any of a number of *Store* implementations. The package is relatively complete in that a SPARQL 1.1 implementation is also included for supporting queries, and also update statements. RDFLib is available on PyPi and the open-source version is maintained using GitHub. Because of its plug-in–based architecture, several tools and projects have been built on top of RDFLib. Similar tools are also available in other languages, including Java. Several support the property-centric models that were discussed, including property tables and graphs. Neo4j, accessed at https://neo4j.com/download/, is an excellent example of the latter, and we describe it in detail in chapter 12. Apache Jena, mentioned as a software offering support for the former, maintains a homepage at https://jena.apache.org/.

The Wikidata project is completely available online at https://www.wikidata.org/wiki/ Wikidata:Main_Page. The main page contains links to a whole set of resources, including an introduction to Wikidata, tutorials on editing and contributing to Wikidata, and additional information on how to retrieve and use data from Wikidata. For the more advanced reader who has an interest in using Wikidata, this last set of resources is a useful place to begin.

Some of the vocabularies we mentioned in this chapter, including FOAF, also constitute an important set of resources for modeling RDF data. FOAF itself can be accessed at http://xmlns.com/foaf/0.1/, but other good examples include the Simple Knowledge Organization System (SKOS), which is accessed at http://www.w3.org/standards/techs/skos# w3c_all, and the Dublin Core (https://www.dublincore.org/). More advanced vocabularies, some of which may be considered languages for formally specifying detailed ontologies of concepts, properties, and constraints, will be discussed in part IV, when we cover the core of the OWL. The W3C has formal pages on RDF and RDFS, accessed at https://www.w3.org/RDF/ and https://www.w3.org/TR/rdf-schema/, respectively. More novel ways of expressing RDF and linked data, which are beyond the scope of this chapter, include JSON-LD, a full description of which can be found at https://json-ld.org/.

In the last section of the chapter, we mentioned schema heterogeneity and semantic labeling. A predominant tool for semantic labeling that comes with adaptive functionality and a fairly advanced user interface is Karma. It may be accessed at https://usc-isi-i2.github.io/karma/. It is described as an information integration tool that enables users to quickly and easily integrate data from a variety of data sources, including databases, spreadsheets, delimited text files, XML, JSON, KML, and web APIs. Users integrate information by modeling it according to an ontology of their choice using a graphical user interface that automates much of the process. Karma learns to recognize the mapping of data to ontology classes (hence, it is adaptive) and then uses the ontology to propose a model that ties together these classes. Users then interact with the system to adjust the automatically generated model. During this process, users can transform the data as needed to normalize data expressed in different formats and to restructure it. Once the model is complete, users can published the integrated data as RDF or store it in a database.

2.9   Bibliographic Notes

Knowledge representation (KR) has always been an important area in AI and computer
science. We cite Sowa (2014), Markman (2013), Brachman et al. (1983), Davis et al.
(1993), Gero (1990), Levesque (1986), Brachman and Levesque (1985), Sowa (2000), and
Zadeh (1996), though there are other works that are helpful. It suffices to say that, directly
or indirectly, many branches of AI depend on KR, and KG research is only one such area.
The references noted here are good places to begin, and have themselves cited, and been
cited by, other influential studies for readers who wish to deeply explore KR as an area in
itself.

The RDF model also has a long history (though not nearly as long as overall KR research), going back all the way to 1998, with the foundations of the model arising from
research conducted even earlier. An excellent resource going back to the early days is Lassila et al. (1998), as well as Decker et al. (1998), the latter especially helpful for querying
and doing inference on RDF data. Lassila et al. (1998) describe RDF as a "foundation
for processing metadata" by virtue of the model providing interoperability between applications that need to exchange *machine-understandable* information on the web. Unlike
other later publications that did not pay careful attention to defining metadata, the authors
describe it clearly as "data describing web resources," and even note the caveat that it is
now always clear what the distinction between data and metadata is, especially due to the
evolving and heterogeneous nature of information published on the web. Sometimes it is
inevitable that a particular resource will be interpreted in both ways simultaneously. The
broad goal of RDF, according to the authors, was to define a mechanism for describing
resources that made no assumptions about a particular application domain in that it did not
define (a priori) the semantics of any application domain. RDF in this sense was domain-
neutral; however, it was a sufficiently broad language that it could express information
about any domain using a systematic representation.

Inspiration for RDF was attributed to various communities and sources, including the
web standardization community [in the form of HTML metadata and the Platform for Internet Content Selection (PICS)], the library community, the structured document community
[in the form of Standard Generalized Markup Language (SGML), and more importantly
XML, which formed the basis for the first standard RDF serialization], and also the KR
community. The seminal article by Berners-Lee et al. (2001) in *Scientific American* is
particularly relevant here. Other relevant works are Lassila (1998), Manola (1998, 1999),
Connolly et al. (1997), and Berners-Lee et al. (1999). Akerkar (2009) may be a useful
guide for unifying the various strands mentioned in this chapter, including RDF, XML,
and ontologies. Other secondary areas that contributed to the RDF design include object-
oriented programming and modeling languages; see the relevant works by Cox (1986),
Calvanese et al. (1998), and Garcia-Molina et al. (2000) to gain an overview of some of
this work. The overall database community also had a strong influence on RDF.

It is important however to note the limits of some of these influences. For example, while RDF drew from the KR community, it does not specify a mechanism for reasoning. This mechanism would later be added (as evident in the Semantic Web Layer Cake). A good description of the layer cake, but also the foundations of the modern Semantic Web more generally, is provided in several works, including by Hendler (2009), Passin (2004), and Bénel et al. (2010). In summary, by characterizing RDF as a *simple frame* system, the idea was to build more sophisticated capabilities on top of it, including support for reasoning. This aim has largely been fulfilled in the last two decades with the development of OWL; see Antoniou and Van Harmelen (2004b) and McGuinness et al. (2004).

In Lassila et al. (1998), the phrase "knowledge graph" never appears because the term had gained neither the popularity nor standardized connotation that it has today. Yet the document makes it clear that what we know today as KGs were targets for RDF representation. The graph-theoretic interpretation of RDF was made clear in the document, with visual fragments of what we refer to as KGs rendered throughout the document.

Other representations covered in this chapter, including RDFS, can also trace their origins to work from the early 2000s; good references include McBride (2004), and Allemang and Hendler (2011). For actual standards descriptions, the best resource is the W3C's pages on these subjects. Beyond RDF, RDFS, and the Semantic Web, we also noted the rise of Wikidata and its data model as a simpler, though also less mature (in terms of reasoning and complex analyses), alternative to representing KGs. Some good readings on Wikidata, as well as its relationship to RDF and the Semantic Web, may be found in Vrandečić and Krötzsch (2014), Erxleben et al. (2014), and Hernández et al. (2015). Finally, good references on semantic labeling and the Karma system include Szekely et al. (2011, 2013), Knoblock et al. (2012), and Knoblock and Szekely (2015). We also mentioned that schema heterogeneity and mapping are problems that are not exclusive to KGs and the Semantic Web, but have also been prominent in the database community. A good survey of (now-classic) schema-matching approaches is Rahm and Bernstein (2001). There has also been work on mapping RDBs to RDF, and on ontological mapping. As a start, we recommend Choi et al. (2006), Sequeda et al. (2011), Sahoo et al. (2009), and Doan and Halevy (2005) for readers interested in these areas. For a broader overview of ontology matching, we recommend Euzenat et al. (2007).

2.10 Exercises

We will revisit the fragment from earlier in the chapter (see the image on the next page) for questions 1–3.

1. We want to give Batman a sidekick—namely, Robin. How or what would you add to the KG fragment to express this additional information (if you need to use relations

that are not expressed in the fragment given here, give them mnemonic names, and assume they are defined in the rel: vocabulary)?

```
@base <http://example.org/> .
@prefix rdf: <http://www.w3.org/1999/02/22-rdf-syntax-ns#> .
@prefix rdfs: <http://www.w3.org/2000/01/rdf-schema#> .
@prefix foaf: <http://xmlns.com/foaf/0.1/> .
@prefix rel: <http://www.perceive.net/schemas/relationship/> .

<#joker>
rel:enemyOf <#batman> ;
a foaf:Person ; # in the context of the DC universe
foaf:name "The Clown Prince of Crime" .

<#batman>
rel:enemyOf <#joker> ;
a foaf:Person ;
foaf:name "Dark Knight" .
```

2. The FOAF vocabulary can be accessed at the link that is provided in the prefix. Go to the link and study some of the classes and properties listed in FOAF Core. Can you use FOAF to add a single statement to the Turtle fragment that expresses the information that the Joker is 32 years old?

3. Write out the entire portion of the fragment from <#batman> downward in N-triples.

4. Let us try to compare the reduction in complexity that can be incurred by using Turtle instead of N-triples. Suppose we measure complexity in terms of both the number of terms as well as statements, for example, the fragment that you rewrote above in N-triples has four statements in Turtle, and seven terms (the single subject <#batman>, three predicates, and three objects, one of which is a literal). Suppose that you were told that your KG had only URIs and no literals. Furthermore, your KG has 1,000,000 nodes, each of which has four predicates (you may assume that these are all unique) linking it to four other nodes on average. You may also assume that everything has a single common prefix, so Turtle only involves a single additional statement declaring the prefix. Ignoring this prefix statement, how many statements and terms would be in your KG representation if expressed in Turtle? How about N-triples? What are the percentage reductions in statements and terms if Turtle is used over N-triples?

5. You are told that "John Green, Michael Brown, and Jerry Red are members of the Mensa organization," and that "Michael Brown is additionally a member of IEEE. Michael and John are friends, while Jerry's current project involves using AI for social good." Using FOAF and/or some of the vocabularies covered in the "Software and Resources" section, could you write out the "knowledge" expressed in that sentence in the Turtle format? For this question, you should not be using made-up terms (i.e.,

any terms that you use must be defined already in an established vocabulary). Values such as names and literals can be mnemonically proposed if necessary.

6. Returning to the motivation proposed behind the Wikidata data model, can you list properties of countries that must be recorded as *n*-ary ($n > 2$) relations?

7. State whether the statements below are True or False. If false, state the reason (simply) and correct the statement by adding, removing, or modifying elements.

    (a) RDF extends the linking structure of the web to use URIs to name the relationship between things and the two ends of the link (Subject and Object).

    (b) In Turtle (textual syntax for RDF) it is not allowed to use untyped (plain) literals.

    (c) RDF can be used to represent information only about things that can be directly retrieved on the web.

    (d) A resource can be represented by a blank node.

    (e) Copyright or licensing information of some resource cannot be represented with RDF.

    (f) The XML RDF syntax can describe some resources that cannot be described using the Turtle RDF syntax.

8. A friend remarks to you, "RDFS is a language intended to represent the structure of RDF resources." What does the word "structure" mean in this context?

9. Consider the academic KG example in chapter 1 (figure 1.5) and show what its representation would look like as (a) a property graph, and as (b) a property table. Make assumptions as appropriate. What is one good example of a multivalued property in figure 1.5, of which object values should belong in a separate table?

10. What is an example of a Wikidata entity that is an instance of *Item* and is linked to an instance of *Geographic Shape*? What property links the item to the geographic shape? *Note: You may have to look around on Wikidata to find such an entity.*

11. Look up the entry for COVID-19 on Wikidata[10] and answer the following questions:

    (a) What is COVID-19 an instance of?

    (b) What is the type of resource that COVID-19 is linked to via the property *number of deaths*?

    (c) What is the type of the resource linked via the property *significant event* (if there is more than one, pick the first one)? What is the Wikidata ID of this resource? Name the property that links this resource *back* to the COVID-19 resource you started from.

---

[10] https://www.wikidata.org/wiki/Q84263196.

II KNOWLEDGE GRAPH CONSTRUCTION

3 Domain Discovery

Overview. The problem of acquiring a relevant corpus of data from the web was recognized even in the early days, when the web had fewer than a billion documents. Since that time, the web has grown exponentially, leading to renewed interest in the problem. In the broadest sense, domain discovery is less about discovering the domain than about discovering relevant data describing the domain. However, in a real sense, discovering relevant data is akin to a *data-driven* discovery of the domain itself, because what is actually on the web will determine the content of the domain more than a normative definition. In this chapter, we cover the problem of domain discovery in detail. Our principal focus will be on intelligent and focused crawling, both of which continue to be the primary mechanisms through which a specific domain can be discovered; however, we will also pay some attention to a number of advanced topics that have been explored by the research community over the last decade.

3.1 Introduction

It has already become a proverbial cliché that we are awash in data, and the web has continued its relentless growth. While this growth is not disputed, it is always useful to put a number on the growth and statistics of the web, in order to provide some context and motivation for why raw data acquisition on a specific topic can be a problem. According to Internet Live Stats, a popular website on tracking the growth of the web and cited by the official World Wide Web's 25th anniversary site, the total number of *websites* (different from *webpages*, the count of which is much higher) on the web was almost 2 billion at the start of 2019, and there are more than 4 billion internet users. In contrast, in 1999, when motivations for focused data acquisition were already being touted by the academic community, there were only about 350 million *webpages*, with only 600 GB of text being changed every month. Today, those numbers are so enormous that even major search engines like Google may only be able to estimate them. What is abundantly clear, however, is that the web has truly become its own vast universe, and finding *relevant* data to answer a specific set of questions (or fulfill even a loosely bounded set of requirements) is like finding a needle in an ever-growing haystack.

Large data sets (Big Data) also exist in fields like genetics and space. However, those data sets tend to be well ordered and structured, and if available on the right infrastructure (whether a private cluster or the cloud), they can be indexed and searched with the right algorithms in place. The web is a different beast altogether. Even if it were possible to temporarily store large parts of the web on a massive cluster, which is currently only within the scope of major search engine providers, crawling the data has become problematic due to the rise of automated spiders and spam. Many websites now implement captchas, require logins or other credentials to access core data, or otherwise block computers and Internet Protocol (IP) addresses that make too many requests. In short, brute-force approaches are becoming harder to implement, requiring a healthy dose of automation and manual labor.

The web is also considerably heterogeneous compared to domain-specific data such as satellite images, or even social media. Here, heterogeneity can be thought of as variation along multiple dimensions, including syntactic structure of webpages, quality, textual and image content (which is how ordinary humans tend to think about heterogeneity), and method of access. For example, social media posts on Twitter can be crawled (within limits) by making calls to an application programming interface (API), but "normal" HTML pages have to be downloaded. Scraping useful content from such pages is even more challenging because there is so much on the pages that is not relevant (and also not visible to the human eye), but that is important for computer programs. For example, dynamic content on webpages is now mediated through embedded scripts, and because of modern web issues like search engine optimization (SEO), there may be hidden features on the webpages. To a computer program trying to "see" the page, all of these things are visible and must be handled gracefully. Because every website is different, and even webpages within a single website can be very different from one another, developing automated tools to construct KGs from such webpages is a difficult problem, and one that we pay attention to in the following chapters. The important thing to remember is that computers do not see the webpages in the same way that humans do, and this limits the expressiveness of any system that attempts to automatically characterize the relevance of a page to an input domain specification, usually using some form of machine learning.

By far, the predominant set of techniques that has been used in various guises to do good domain discovery is *focused crawling*. Intuitively, a crawler is a dynamic program that is supposed to go out on the web and acquire (via download, storage, and possibly indexing) a corpus that obeys certain criteria. Generic search engine crawlers are broad and not focused on a particular topic or user; they are the web-equivalent of a one-size-fits-all model. Focused crawling, as the name suggests, is either user- or domain-specific, though the latter is far more appropriate. User-focused search is akin to *personalized* information retrieval, for which a user model is required. Search engines like Google have invested significant effort in building such models, and can use them to provide relevant outputs to recurring users based on past search history and other artifacts, like the user's location and other information that becomes available when a user is signed into their accounts during search. In contrast, focused crawling is not about understanding user intent during search, but locating and downloading a "local universe" of documents that is relevant to some domain of interest. Specifying the domain is not always straightforward, however. In fact, we argue that there are four issues that need to be considered when designing (or choosing, customizing, and deploying) a focused crawler or other domain discovery tool.

First, how do we specify the domain to begin with? One easy, but naive, approach is to specify some keywords, but these could potentially be overloaded, ambiguous, or underspecified. It is also difficult to justify the difference between focused crawling and generic search (possibly with personalization) if inputs are always keywords, because the search engine learns over time how keywords map to user intent. Instead, in the vast majority of focused crawling literature, the crawler is given exemplar documents to begin with, but these could bias the system into discovering more of what is *already known*. This fundamentally defeats the purpose of domain discovery, especially because (in practice) many people are willing to commit to domain discovery to learn things about the domain that they might not have known, or even suspected. More recently, a functional view of domain discovery has also started to gain hold, especially for unusual domains like human trafficking and fraud. In such investigative domains, domain experts, such as law enforcement and workers in federal agencies like the Securities and Exchange Commission (SEC) and the Federal Bureau of Investigation (FBI), ideally want to construct a search system (whether based on KGs or other technology) to help them investigate leads about bad actors and make predictions about illicit activity before it actually happens and ends up causing damage. These kinds of investigative *queries* can also serve as inputs to the domain discovery process.

Second, how do we explore the *link structure* of the web to discover relevant webpages? Even when the web was "small," randomly following links from relevant root pages was found to yield suboptimal results compared to more intelligent approaches. Since those early findings, mostly emerging in the 1990s, many complex approaches have been proposed. A full exploration is not within the scope of this chapter; instead, we focus on important high-level discoveries that clearly illustrate how the link structure can be exploited to make good relevance determinations.

Third, how do we use the *content* of the webpage to determine relevance? In the simplest case, one could imagine an approach that is used by the search engines (namely, keyword matching and bag of words models like tf-idf). In other cases, we may want to extract other features to assist a machine learning classifier in making good relevance determinations.

Fourth, and related to the previous issue, is the question of what kinds of *user interactions* are permitted when doing domain discovery. A simple, relatively lightweight model would take the input domain specification from the user, attempt domain discovery over a (possibly self-determined) specified period of time, and not allow further inputs from the user. More practical systems, predicated on literature from both active learning and rein-forcement learning, may want to solicit occasional feedback from the user in the hope of achieving higher quality and coverage. Either approach has its pros and cons, but the latter is more favored in modern times, especially for complex domains.

There are also some practical and ethical issues related to domain discovery that we do not cover in this chapter (or indeed the entire book), mainly because they are tangential to the core concept of domain discovery itself, but also because they have not been resolved in a stable or established way. For example, how does a domain discovery system deal with captchas and login issues? While deep learning has shown some promise in dealing with automatic transcription of captchas, the problem is far from solved. There is also the question of infrastructure and best practices: how often should a webpage be recrawled, and what kind of infrastructure should be used to host the crawler? There is no real right answer to these questions, other than "It depends." For example, in our experience, when dealing with nefarious domains like human trafficking, some websites may have to be crawled more than four times a day to ensure data completeness. Furthermore, an old webpage should never be replaced by a recrawled version because the page could be useful for tracking activity and gathering evidence over time. However, if crawling news articles, it makes more sense to recrawl and replace, since the new news article may contain updated figures and redactions, rendering the previous version obsolete or even wrong.

Although we do not cover these issues in this chapter, we provide some guidance for the interested reader in the section entitled "Bibliographic Notes," at the end of this chapter. Our primary focus here will be focused crawling, though we take a broader view of domain discovery toward the end of this chapter.

3.2   Focused Crawling

Crawlers (equivalently known as *robots* or *spiders*) were designed for downloading and assembling web content locally. *Focused* crawlers were introduced for satisfying the need of domain experts or particular organizations for creating and maintaining subject-specific web document collections locally, usually for addressing complex needs that could not be satisfactorily handled by generic search engines. Focused crawling is especially important when results have to be high quality, relevant to the domain, and up-to-date, all without investing in wholesale resources (e.g., time, space, and network bandwidth) for acquiring a one-size-fits-all data set. In short, focused crawlers try to download as many relevant, domain-specific pages as they can, while keeping the number of irrelevant pages to a min-imum.

Recall that one of the issues alluded to in the introductory section was the level of user input. In early, and even recent, literature on focused crawling, the general assumption has been the crawler is given a *seed set* of webpages as input, with the immediate goal of extracting outgoing links in the seed pages and determining what links to visit next.

The primary difference between the various types and schools of focused crawling arise in assigning such *priorities* to links, though other differences are also relevant. Regardless of the criteria, webpages pointed to by these links are downloaded, and those deemed to be relevant (usually using some form of machine learning), are stored or indexed. Crawlers continue doing this until manually stopped or until a desired number of pages have been downloaded. Sometimes they stop by necessity because local resources get exhausted quickly as more pages are downloaded and stored. In yet other cases, crawling continues for a preset period of time. Decision criteria that depend on a crawler running until a resource (which could include time) runs out have an advantage in cloud infrastructure, because costs can be reasonably controlled or anticipated.

Crawlers used by generic search engines like Google retrieve massive web corpora regardless of topic or user-focused relevance. Focused crawlers accomplish the latter by combining both the content of the retrieved web pages and the link structure of the web. Based on how this is done, three classes of focused crawlers seem to have emerged in the literature, though some are much more popular than others. A classic focused crawler takes as input a user query that describes the topic, as well as a set of starting seed webpage Uniform Resource Locators (URLs) that can be used to guide the search toward other webpages of interest. The crawler incorporates criteria for assigning higher download priorities to links based on their likelihood to lead to relevant pages. Higher-priority pages are downloaded first, followed by recursively navigating to the links contained in the downloaded pages. Typically, download priorities are computed based on the similarity between the topic and the anchor text of a page link or between the topic and text of the page containing the link.

Text similarity is computed using an information similarity model, which in the modern era tends to almost always be a *vector space model* (VSM), although boolean models have been proposed in earlier eras. Put simply, a VSM attempts to represent a unit of data (in this context, a document) as a vector in some numeric space. Some VSMs that will recur throughout this book are the tf-idf VSM and embedding-based VSM, based on much more recent work in neural representation learning.[1] These VSMs have become extremely important in communities as varied as Natural Language Processing (NLP), information retrieval, and knowledge discovery. The reader without any knowledge of VSMs is encouraged to briefly review sections 10.1 and 10.2 in chapter 10.

3.2.1 Main Design Elements of a Focused Crawler

The principal goal of a focused crawler is to keep the overall number of downloaded web pages for processing to a minimum, while maximizing the percentage of relevant pages

---

[1] Another well-known VSM designed specifically for documents (and which we do not focus on as much in this book) is the topic model (formally known as Latent Dirichlet Allocation, or LDA).

retrieved. It was well recognized, starting from early work, that the performance of a focused crawler could be highly dependent on the selection of good seed inputs. One way
to infuse more robustness into this process is to accept a query from the user only as input
and to use a generic web search engine like Google to obtain the first set of seed pages
from this query. Regardless of how seed webpages are obtained, it is equally important to
understand what makes a seed page good. Generally, it has been found that such pages are
relevant to the topic (an obvious criterion), but less obviously, they can also be pages *from*
which relevant pages can be accessed within a *small* number of link traversals. For example, if the topic is e-commerce products, a good seed page may describe reviews of several
such products, along with links. Note that the review page itself is not all that relevant, but
it serves as a broker, and can be instrumental in a focused crawler, accessing many more
relevant pages than it would from a page describing a single e-commerce product.

The discussion here shows that there are many degrees of freedom in determining a
precise crawler design, from input to content processing. Yet the architecture itself (of a
focused crawler) is fairly standard, containing a uniform set of generic components. The
actual instantiation of the components depends on the crawler (e.g., Best-First Crawler versus Learning Crawler) and is amenable to varying degrees of innovation. Generic elements
that must always be taken into account when designing a crawler are discussed next.

Input Mechanisms. Crawlers take as input a number of starting (seed) URLs and (in
the case of focused crawlers) the topic description, which can be a list of keywords for
classic and semantics-focused crawlers or a training set for learning-based crawlers. More
recently, other innovative mechanisms for accepting the user's intent as input have also
been proposed.

Page Retrieval. The links in downloaded pages are extracted and placed in a queue.
A nonfocused crawler uses these links and proceeds with downloading new pages using
a first-in-first-out protocol. A focused crawler reorders queue entries by applying content
relevance or importance criteria, or it may decide to exclude a link from further expansion
(generic crawlers may also apply importance criteria to determine pages that are worth
crawling and indexing).

Content Processing and Representation. Downloaded pages are lexically analyzed
(e.g., using tokenization preprocessing modules) and transformed into a vector in some
VSMs. For example, in the tf-idf VSM, each term in a vector is represented by computing
a formula that trades off the term's frequency (in the document) and its inverse frequency
(in the full corpus), with the former contributing positively to the term's importance and the
latter contributing negatively. However, because computing inverse document frequency
(idf) weights during crawling can be problematic (there is no full corpus because the corpus
itself is being discovered and crawled), most Best-First Crawler implementations use only
term frequency (tf) weights. In general, using idf in a cold-start setting is problematic, but
because idf can be a useful feature, one other option is not to discard it completely, but

rather to rely on open knowledge bases (KBs; a background corpus), such as Wikipedia or the Google News Corpus.

Priority Assignment. Extracted URLs from downloaded pages are placed in a priority queue, with priorities determined based on the crawler type, as well as user preferences. These range from simple criteria, such as page importance or relevance to query topic (computed by matching the query with page or anchor text), to more involved criteria, such as that determined by a learning process.

Expansion. URLs are selected for further expansion, and all previous steps (page retrieval and download and priority assignment, among others) are repeated until some criterion is satisfied or system resources are exhausted. For example, the process may be stopped if the desired number of pages have been downloaded.

3.2.2 Best-First Crawlers

As the name suggests, Best-First Crawlers are the crawling equivalent of *best-first search*. Namely, every URL in the *crawl frontier* is assigned a "priority" score, which could be simple, using a tf-idf VSM, or a complicated combination of signals (as we describe later in this chapter with intelligent crawling). The URL with the highest priority score in the crawl frontier is selected for expansion. The links present on this downloaded page are then added to the frontier, and their priority scores are computed. Following this step, the next page to be crawled and downloaded is determined (based on the priority scores), and the entire process is repeated until the frontier is empty (i.e., there are no more pages to download).

Typically, Best-First Crawlers use only term frequency (tf) vectors for computing topic relevance. The use of inverse document frequency (idf) values (as suggested by the tf-idf VSM) is problematic because it not only requires recalculation of all term vectors at every crawling step but also, at the early stages of crawling, inverse document frequency values are highly inaccurate because the number of documents is too small. Generally, this is a problem with using inverse document frequencies when the document collection is compiled in a "cold-start" setting, whereby only a very small set of seed documents is initially available. Empirically, Best-First Crawlers have been shown to outperform several rival approaches (such as InfoSpiders and Shark-Search) as well as nonfocused Breadth-First crawling approaches. Historically, Best-First Crawling is considered to be the most successful approach to focused crawling due to its simplicity and efficiency.

Generalized versions of the Best-First Crawler also exist. For example, the *N-Best First Crawler* is a popular variant that, at each step, chooses *N* pages (instead of just one) with the highest priorities for expansion. In a similar vein, so-called intelligent crawling tries to combine various cues, including page content, URL string information, sibling pages, and statistics about relevant or irrelevant pages for assigning priorities to candidate pages. In some cases, this yields a more effective crawling algorithm that is able to learn to crawl without direct user supervision or training samples.

Variants of the classic Best-First Crawling strategy also exist, depending on how links in the same page are prioritized. We briefly describe some of these approaches below. Note that all variants draw on the formula for cosine similarity between the two vectors (represented in the same VSM space) $\vec{a}$ and $\vec{b}$:

$$cos\_sim(\vec{a}, \vec{b}) = \frac{\vec{a}.\vec{b}}{\|\vec{a}\|_2\|\vec{b}\|_2}. \tag{3.1}$$

Variant 1. All links on the page receive the same download priority by applying equation (3.1) on the topic and page content representations.

Variant 2. Priorities are assigned to pages by computing the similarity between the anchor text of the link pointing to the page and the query by applying equation (3.1). Unlike Variant 1, the links from the same page may be assigned different priority values.

Variant 3. This variant combines variants 1 and 2 by computing the priority of link l in page p as the average of the two similarities (query to page and query to anchor text). The rationale behind this approach is that a page relevant to the topic is more likely to point to a relevant page than to an irrelevant one. On the other hand, anchor text may also be regarded as a reasonably reliable summary of the content of the page that the link points to. However, anchor text is not always descriptive (or representative) of the content of the page that the link points to. By combining the two complementary signals, variant 3 is thus able to achieve a certain degree of robustness.

3.2.3 Semantic Crawlers

While classical Best-First Crawlers compute similarity via standard lexical term matching-based information retrieval (IR) (i.e., roughly, two documents are similar if they share common terms, and the more common terms they share, the more similar they are), it is too simplistic in certain settings where two documents are related even when they do not share many (or even any) common terms. Imagine, for example, a page describing "tourist must-visits" in Los Angeles, while another page describes "places to check out." The two pages share many lexical differences overall, but overlap heavily in terms of semantic content. Semantic crawlers address this problem by using term taxonomies or ontologies rather than relying solely on lexical matching or models like tf-idf. As we've seen earlier in this book when discussing KG ontologies and representational mechanisms, term taxonomies and ontologies conceptualize similar terms via typed links like *is-a*.

The basic approach of such crawlers is to first retrieve all terms conceptually similar to the topic terms from the ontology, and use these additional terms to supplement the topic description (e.g., by adding synonyms and other topically similar terms).

Where do general term taxonomies come from? One such famous resource is WordNet, a controlled vocabulary and thesaurus offering a taxonomic hierarchy of natural-language terms. It contains around 100,000 terms, organized into taxonomic hierarchies, and pro-

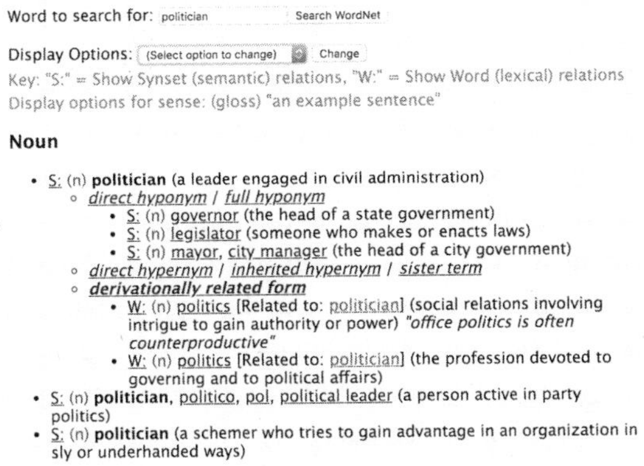

Figure 3.1: An illustration of the semantic information provided by the WordNet lexical resource for a common noun such as "politician."

vides broad coverage of the English vocabulary. Consequently, it can be used for focused crawling on almost every general-interest topic. Figure 3.1 illustrates an example for the word "politician." Intuitively, we can see that, if properly leveraged, WordNet can be used for expanding the lexical term "politician" to include terms such as "mayor" and "legislator." Pages containing these terms, compared to more random words (such as "garden" or "sky") would be assigned higher scores by a semantic crawler than by crawlers relying solely on term-matching VSMs.

Because the similarity between the topic and a candidate page is now computed as a function of semantic (conceptual) similarities between the terms they contain, how do we compute the similarity between related concepts that are not lexicographically similar? The definition of document similarity will clearly depend on the choice of semantic similarity function. A good choice (in the context of semantic crawlers) for computing the priority of page p is

$$priority_{semantic}(p) = \frac{\Sigma_i \Sigma_j sim(i,j) w_i w_j}{\Sigma_i \Sigma_j w_i w_j}. \tag{3.2}$$

Here, i and j are terms on the topic and candidate pages (or anchor text of the link), respectively, while w_i and w_j are their respective term weights. Further, $sim(i,j)$ is the semantic similarity between these two terms. Assuming a resource like WordNet, several semantic similarity measures are applicable, such as the following:

Synonym Set Similarity. Here, $sim(i,j)$ is 1 if i belongs to the synonym set of term j in the WordNet taxonomy, and 0 otherwise.

Synonym, Hypernym/Hyponym Similarity. Here, $sim(i,j)$ is 1 if i belongs to the synonym set of term j, 0.5 if i is a hypernym or hyponym of j, and 0 otherwise.

The download priority of a link can be defined as the average of the similarity of the topic description with the anchor text and the page content, both computed using equation (3.2).

3.2.4 Learning Crawlers

Learning crawlers learn user preferences on a topic from a set of example pages known as the *training set*. The method relies on a user providing a labeled set of pages, where the label expresses whether the page is relevant to the topic of interest. Training may also involve learning the link-path leading to relevant pages. Some methods only assume a positive training set (where we are given annotations expressing which pages are relevant, but no explicit annotations expressing which pages are irrelevant), while others require annotations expressing both relevance and irrelevance. The core idea, as with many supervised machine learning–based approaches, is to first train a classifier using a training set, and during crawling, use the classifier to classify each downloaded page as relevant or irrelevant (and also assign it a priority). Early approaches to learning crawlers used classifiers like Naive Bayes (trained on web taxonomies such as Yahoo!) for distinguishing between relevant and irrelevant pages, which was then expanded to more advanced classifiers such as decision trees, neural networks, and support vector machines (SVMs). For example, in one publication on learning crawlers, an SVM was applied to both page content and link context, with the combination shown to outperform methods using page content or link context alone.

The structure of paths leading to relevant pages can be an important factor in focused crawling, as first shown with *context graphs* by Diligenti et al. (2000). The idea is to work backward by following back links to relevant pages to recover pages leading to relevant pages. These pages, along with their path information, form the context graph. The original context graph method builds classifiers for sets of pages mainly at distance 1 or 2 from relevant pages in the context graph. The focused crawler uses these classifiers to establish priorities of visited pages. In a subsequent section on the *Context-Focused Crawler* (CFC) system, this methodology is detailed further.

An extension to the context graph method is the hidden Markov model (HMM) crawler, wherein the user browses the web looking for relevant pages and indicates if a downloaded page is relevant to the topic or not. The visited sequence is recorded and is used to train the crawler to identify paths leading to relevant pages. The significant aspect to note about these crawlers is that they were among the first to successfully model the crawling process as a *sequence-labeling* problem. As subsequent chapters of this book will illustrate, sequence labeling has emerged as an important subarea in machine learning and NLP, and today, problems like named entity recognition (a critical component in a KG construction pipeline) rely heavily on sequence labeling.

Yet another variant of a learning-based crawler uses two classifiers instead of one. This was best illustrated in an early paper that first used the open directory (Directory Mozilla, or DMOZ) web taxonomy to classify downloaded pages as relevant (or not), with a second classifier evaluating the probability that the given page will *lead* to a target page. While the two classification tasks should not be thought of as completely independent in the context of the modern web, we can nevertheless gauge that they are two separate classification tasks. Thus, using two classifiers has some benefits in this scenario.

We emphasize that learning crawlers are not necessarily exclusive from the crawlers described previously. Over the years, hybrid crawlers that combine ideas from learning and classic focused crawling have been proposed in the literature. We provide pointers to relevant reading in the "Bibliographic Notes" section at the end of this chapter.

3.2.5 Evaluation of Focused Crawling

Crawler performance is typically measured by the percentage of downloaded pages that are relevant to the topic (i.e., pages with similarity greater than a predefined threshold), a measure that is known in the literature as the *harvest rate*. Harvest rate can be adjusted (by using a higher threshold) to measure the ability of the crawler to download pages highly relevant to the topic.

How should we build a ground-truth for evaluating such measures? One suggested, and popular, approach is to issue each input topic as a query to Google and have the results be inspected by a user. Pages considered relevant by the user would constitute the ground-truth for the topic. Note that the size of a ground-truth set can be anywhere from a few tens to thousands of pages per topic. During evaluation, the results of a crawler per topic are compared with the ground-truth: for each page returned by the crawler, its document similarity (using VSM) with all pages in the ground-truth set is computed. If the maximum of these similarity values is greater than a user-defined threshold, the page is marked as a positive result (according to the method). The more positive the results of a crawler are, the more successful the crawler is (i.e., the higher the probability that the crawler retrieves results similar to the topic). The performance of a crawler is generally computed as the average number of positive results over all topics.

When evaluating multiple crawlers, it is also important to have the necessary controls in place. For example, all crawlers should be initialized using the same set of seed pages, and it is equally important for all experiments to be conducted between a similar time span and using a similar set of resources. A more nebulous problem that is hard to both diagnose and detect is *data set bias* (i.e., when the ground-truth itself is constructed in such a way or methodology as to bias the performance of one or more crawlers). The best way to account for such biases is to have the ground-truth be constructed by a team that is not involved in one or more system designs. By increasing the size of the ground-truth per topic, as well as increasing the number of topics, the probability of data set bias or overfitting is further reduced.

3.3 Influential Systems and Methodologies

As noted before, the design of a crawler is somewhat standard by now, although instantiations can widely vary. To gain a practical understanding of the trade-offs that are involved in engineering crawlers, in this section we consider some influential systems. Our goal is to be descriptive rather than prescriptive. The systems are described in the temporal order in which they have been developed within the community, in order to give a sense of how crawler design has advanced throughout the years.

3.3.1 Context-Focused Crawler

The CFC was one of the earliest crawlers to be predicated on the capability of preexisting search engines like Google. The basic intuition behind CFC is to take the seed documents, and to use a search engine to find and construct a representation of pages that occur within a certain link distance (defined as the minimum number of link traversals necessary to move from one page to another) of the documents. This representation is used to train a set of classifiers, which are optimized to detect and assign documents to different categories based on the expected link distance from the document to the target document. During the crawling stage, the classifiers are used to predict how many steps away from a target document the current retrieved document is likely to be. This information is then used to optimize the search.

Generally, there are two distinct stages to using the CFC when performing a focused crawl session, each of which is subsequently described in greater detail:

1. An initialization phase, when a set of context graphs and associated classifiers are constructed for each of the seed documents
2. A crawling phase, which uses the classifiers to guide the search and performs online updating of the context graph

3.3.1.1 Generating the Context Graphs The first stage of a crawling session aims to extract the context within which target pages are typically found, and then to encode this information in a *context graph*. A separate context graph is built for every seed element provided by the user. Every seed document forms the first node of its associated context graph. Using an engine such as Google, a number of pages linking to the target are first retrieved (known as the *parents* of the seed page). Each parent page is itself modeled in the graph as a node, with an edge declared between the target document node and the parent node. The new nodes compose "layer 1" of the context graph. The back-crawling procedure is repeated to search all the documents linking to documents of layer 1. These pages are incorporated as nodes in the graph and compose "layer 2." As figure 3.2 shows, we may intuitively think of these layers as ever-growing concentric circles. To simplify the link structure, visualization, and formalism, the convention is that if two documents in layer *i* can be accessed from a common parent, the parent document appears *twice* in the

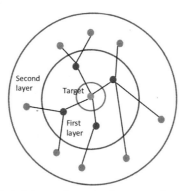

Figure 3.2: A context graph (with two layers) of a target document.

next layer (i.e., layer $i + 1$). This results in an "induced" graph, where each document in the layer $i + 1$ is linked to one (and only one) document in the layer i.

The back-linking process is iterated until a user-specified number of layers have been filled or some other convergence criterion is met (e.g., an upper bound on the total number of backlink traversals or the size of the context graph is breached). In practice, the number of elements in a given layer can increase suddenly when the number of layers grows beyond some limit. In these cases, one systematic approach is to statistically sample the parent nodes, up to some system-dependent limit.

The depth of a context graph is defined to be the number of layers in the graph excluding the level 0 (the node storing the seed document). When N levels are in the context graph, path strategies of up to N steps can be modeled. For example, a context graph of depth 2 is shown in figure 3.2.

By constructing a context graph, the crawler gains knowledge about topics that are directly or indirectly related to the target topic, as well as a very simple model of the paths that relate these pages to the target documents. As expected, in practice, we find that the arrangement of the nodes in the layers reflects any hierarchical content structure. Highly related content typically appears near the center of the graph, while the outer layers contain more general pages. For example, if we want pages on poker players and start with a seed webpage describing a particular player (e.g., Phil Hellmuth), the first layer may contain pages listing World Series of Poker champions, the next layer may contain pages describing a broader set of poker players, and the next layer after that may just describe the game of poker. Similarly, if we are given a professor's page as a seed page, the first layer would likely contain pages where the professor is mentioned (perhaps a class directory, as well as the group page of the professor's research group); the second layer would contain department-level pages; and the third layer may contain university-level pages. As a result, when the crawler discovers a page with content that occurs higher up in the hierarchy, it can use its knowledge of the graph structure to guide the search toward the target pages.

Once context graphs for all seed documents have been built, the corresponding layers from the various context graphs are combined, yielding a layered structure known in the original paper as a *Merged Context Graph* (MCG). This graph does not have to be connected, but on the other extreme, it is also rare to have a graph where at least two seed nodes do not share an undirected path.

3.3.1.2 Classifier Training   The next stage builds a set of classifiers for assigning any document retrieved from the web to one of the layers in the MCG, as well as for quantifying the (classifier's) belief in the assignment. The classifiers require a feature representation of the documents on which to operate. The original CFC implementation uses keyword indexing of each document using a (now not uncommon) modification of tf-idf called *reduced tf-idf*, which only uses the 40 highest scoring components in the tf-idf vector representation of the document. This process ensures numerical stability, reduces the amount of training data required, and can also make classification faster and low-dimensional. There is no reason why a modern VSM based on neural embeddings like word2vec or paragraph2vec cannot be used as a replacement.

Given the representation, the classifier is constructed to assign any web document to a particular layer of the MCG. However, if the document is a poor fit for a given layer, the document should be discarded and labeled as *Other*. A major difficulty in implementing such a strategy (using a single classifier mapping a document to a set of $N + 2$ classes corresponding to the layers $0, 1, \ldots, N$, as well as *Other*) is the absence of a good model or training set for *Other*. To solve this problem, the authors of the CFC work proposed a modification of the Naive Bayes classifier for each layer; further details can be found in Diligenti et al. (2000). Ultimately, the authors chose to use the classifier of layer 0 as the ultimate *arbiter* of topical relevance for a given document.

3.3.1.3 Crawling Phase   Once the classifiers are trained, the crawler can utilize them by first organizing pages into a sequence of $N + 2$ queues, N being the maximum depth of the context graphs. The *ith* class (layer) is associated to the *ith* queue, with i ranging over $0, 1, \ldots, N$. Note that queue $N + 1$ is not associated with any class, but rather reflects assignments to *Other*. Furthermore, the 0*th* queue will ultimately store all the retrieved topically relevant documents.

Initially, all the queues are empty except for the "dummy" queue $N + 1$, which is initialized with the starting URL of the crawl. The crawler retrieves the page pointed to by the URL, computes the reduced vector representation, and extracts all the hyperlinks. It then downloads all the children of the current page. All downloaded pages are classified individually and assigned to the queue corresponding to the winning layer (or the class *Other*). Each queue is maintained in a sorted state using the likelihood score associated with its documents. When the crawler needs the next document to move to, it pops from the first nonempty queue. The documents that are expected to rapidly lead to targets are therefore followed before documents that will (with high probability) require more steps to yield relevant pages. However, depending on the relative queue thresholds, frequently high-confidence pages from queues representing longer download paths are retrieved.

The setting of the classifier thresholds that determine whether a document gets assigned to the class denoted *Other* determines the retrieval strategy. In the original paper's default implementation, the likelihood function for each layer is applied to all the patterns in the training set for that layer. The confidence threshold is then set to be equal to the minimum likelihood obtained on the training set for the corresponding layer.

During the crawling phase, new context graphs can periodically be built for every topically relevant element found in queue 0. An alternative is to configure the focused crawler to ask for the immediate parents of every document as it appears in queue 0, and simply insert these into the appropriate queue *without* recomputing the MCG and classifiers. In this way, it is possible to continually exploit back-crawling at a reasonable computational cost.

3.3.2 Domain Discovery Tool

The simplicity of keyword queries is a strength and also a limitation. In theory, an analyst could improve the relevance of the results by issuing more specific queries. For example, if an e-commerce analyst were interested in collecting all reviews about a product over the web and the profiles of users using the product, she could potentially search all forums and user IDs associated with the sale of the product. To query for influencers, she could also search for whether a user is showing up in multiple forums and discussion boards. However, such queries cannot be expressed using ordinary search engines like Google. Even focused crawling tools like the CFC or Semantic Web (SW) search engines like Swoogle (see the section entitled "Software and Resources" at the end of the chapter), do not allow users to express such queries unless the data has already been gathered and parsed using an ontology.

To allow domain discovery over web resources, Krishnamurthy et al. (2016) recently proposed a Domain Discovery Tool (DDT) that serves as a visual analytics framework for interactive domain discovery. The framework augmented ordinary search engine functionality by directly supporting analysts in exploratory search. Specifically, DDT supports exploratory data analysis of webpages and translates analyst interactions with web data into a *computational model* of the domain of interest. One example of such a model that we saw in the context of systems like the enhanced HMM Crawler is a trained machine learning classifier. However, the model constructed by DDT is richer, leveraging more advanced machine learning. DDT is an open-source system and has been released on GitHub.

Just like the other focused crawling tools, DDT is a heavily engineered system that has several components working in tandem to achieve its goals. DDT is designed as a client-server model that has a web-based Javascript interface. This ensures that there is no clientside setup. Unlike most of the other systems, therefore, DDT has a strong ad-

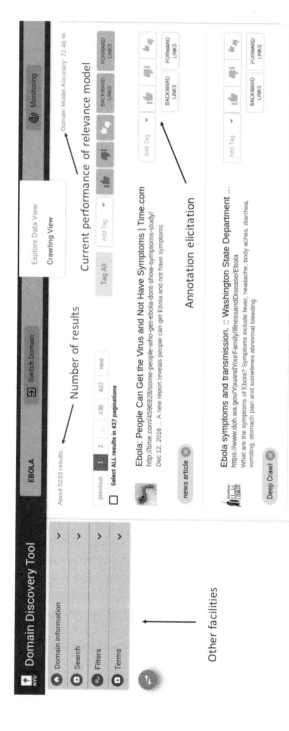

Figure 3.3: The interface of the NYU DDT, used for discovering relevant webpages over the web for an Ebola-related domain.

vantage: the analysts using the system could have a *nontechnical* background. Figure 3.3 illustrates the intuitiveness of the interface when someone is trying to crawl and discover relevant webpages around an "Ebola" domain that starts with just one or more keyword specifications. The other important components involved in DDT are described next.

3.3.2.1   Data Gathering and Persistence   Domain experts can use a variety of methods to gather pages of interest for analysis. First, DDT allows users to query the web using a search engine like Google. The users can leverage the large collections that already were crawled by these search engines to discover interesting pages across the web using simple queries. However, because search engines return only the URLs and associated snippets, DDT downloads the HTML content given by the URLs and stores it in the selected domain's index (using an Elasticsearch infrastructure). This content can be used later for analysis of the domain, and also as seeds for focused crawlers. Note also that because downloading a large number of pages (including raw HTML content) can be costly in terms of time, this operation is performed by DDT in the background.

Second, DDT also provides a mechanism for domain experts to directly incorporate their domain knowledge by allowing them to provide URLs either through the input box provided or by uploading a file containing a list of URLs. DDT then downloads the pages corresponding to these URLs and makes them available through its interface.

Finally, DDT automates the tedious and manual process that users often undertake when following links forward and backward from the pages they explore. Given a page, crawling backward retrieves the backlinks (the resources that contain a link to the selected page) of that page and then downloads the corresponding pages. Forward-crawling from a selected page retrieves all the pages whose links are contained on that page. Intuitively, these operations are effective and valuable because there is a significant probability that the backlink of a page, as well as the page itself, will contain links to other relevant pages. This same intuition was also relied upon earlier by the CFC.

3.3.2.2   Visual Summarization of Search Results   Similar to data gathering, DDT provides several mechanisms to give an analyst an overview of the pages they have explored. An important mechanism is Multidimensional Scaling (MDS); instead of displaying a list of snippets, DDT applies MDS to create a visualization of the retrieved pages (that maintains the relative similarity and dissimilarity of the pages). This allows the user to more easily select, study, and annotate a set of pages.

Because initially all pages are unlabeled, DDT needs an unsupervised learning algorithm to group pages by similarity. While a variety of clustering methods are applicable here, including K-Means and agglomerative clustering, the MDS implementation in DDT is currently achieved by principal component analysis (PCA) of the documents. Furthermore, to improve scalability, DDT uses Google's word2vec 300-dimensional pretrained vectors that were trained on part of a Google News data set comprising about 100 billion words, instead of using a vanilla tf-idf approach. A simple averaging-like formula is used to derive a document embedding (also with 300 dimensions) by combining the embeddings of all the words in the document. In turn, this yields a document matrix (over a corpus of n documents) of size[2] $n \times 300$, which is much smaller than the traditional *document $\times$ term* matrix. This smaller matrix is sent to the MDS algorithm as input.

Along with visualizations, DDT also dynamically updates and shows real-time page statistics, such as the total number of pages in the domain, number of pages marked as relevant, irrelevant, or "neutral" (pages that have yet to be annotated), and number of pages downloaded in the background since the last update. Other summarization facilities include dashboards for these page statistics, as well as other rich descriptive statistics, such as statistics over the entire content in the domain, such as the distribution summary of sites, the distributions and intersections of the search queries issued, summary of page tags and their intersections, and number of pages added to the domain over time. Similarly, the topic distribution dashboard visualizes the various topics contained in the domain, with the topics generated using the Topik toolkit. Using LDAviz, the DDT shows the topics, the overlap of topics, and the most frequent words contained in each topic.

3.3.2.3   User Annotations   DDT allows users to provide feedback for documents and extracted terms. Along with marking individual pages, users can select a group of documents for analysis and mark these documents as relevant or irrelevant. Users may also annotate pages with user-defined tags, which are especially useful for defining subdomains (e.g., *Information Extraction* could be a subdomain under the domain *Natural Language Processing*).

As with documents, keywords and phrases extracted by DDT can also be annotated by a user as relevant or irrelevant. Based on the relevant terms, the system reranks the untagged keywords and phrases by relatedness to the relevant terms (specifically, by using Bayesian sets). This allows capture of more related terms and phrases to help the user understand the domain further, as well as formulate new search queries. For more details on how the Bayesian set algorithm was adapted for this purpose, we refer the interested reader to the original paper. Users may also incorporate background knowledge by adding particular keywords and phrases customized for the domain. To guide users and provide them with a better understanding of the importance and discriminative power of extracted terms, DDT shows the percentage of relevant and irrelevant pages on which the term appears.

3.3.2.4   Domain Model and Focused Crawling   DDT uses the pages marked "relevant" and "irrelevant" (as positive and negative examples, respectively) to support the construction of a page classifier that serves as a model for the domain. This classifier, together with

---

[2] A matrix of size $u \times v$ has u rows and v columns.

a set of seeds (relevant pages), can be used to configure a focused crawler. DDT supports the ACHE Crawler, developed within the same group.

3.3.2.5 Summary   Despite the relatively simple mechanisms in it, early experiments and user feedback show that the DDT framework can considerably improve the quality and speed of domain discovery. DDT is a new exploratory data analysis framework that combines techniques from information retrieval, data mining, and interactive visualization to guide users in exploratory search. Many future avenues for research remain, not least of which is a comprehensive user study with a larger number of participants of diverse backgrounds. Krishnamurthy et al. (2016) are also planning to conduct evaluations of DDT's effectiveness on *nonweb* corpora.

3.4 Concluding Notes

Domain discovery is a fundamental step for any organization or individual that is looking to do end-to-end KG construction, querying, and analytics. The old saying "garbage in, garbage out" is relevant for domain discovery. A raw data set that does not contain useful information (i.e., that can help the user gain functional insights) to begin with will not become useful once it has been structured into a KG using the techniques that we will cover in subsequent chapters. The more difficult a domain is, the more important it is to do good domain discovery and find all relevant data on the web. Because the web is more difficult to crawl than ever, due to both size and the advent of captcha technology, a good domain discovery tool must have strong engineering and conceptual foundations. Focused crawling continues to be the favored approach to acquiring a domain-specific corpus, but the emergence of ecosystems like the Semantic Web, Linked Open Data, the Twitter stream, and Schema.org, as well as public resources like the Web Data Commons project and Wikipedia, indicate that it may not always be necessary to scrape raw webpages to acquire relevant data. While focused crawling design has remained relatively stable since the late 1990s, new techniques for capturing user interactions and allowing users to express their intent in finer-grained modalities mean that the book is not closed on this subject. Particularly exciting is the application of some of this work to illicit domains like securities fraud and human trafficking that have traditionally proved hard to tackle using mainstream artificial intelligence (AI) technology of any kind.

3.5 Software and Resources

Much of the classic work on focused crawling that was covered in this chapter does not have modern, open-source implementations that we are aware of; given how much the web has changed since even just 10 years ago, it is fruitful to reimplement those systems using recent versions of programming languages like Python and Java. However, some of the more recent systems are publicly available. A good example is the DDT tool covered in the section entitled "Domain Discovery Tool." At this time, it is available on GitHub,[3] and several demonstration videos[4] have been published on YouTube as well.

In some cases, however, we believe that implementing the classic systems in a modern setting has merit. Systems that the interested reader may want to look at include Ariadne (proposed in 2001 as a generic framework for focused crawling, and implemented in Java), CATYRPEL (one of the first proposed systems, also modular, that extended existing work in focused document crawling by not only using keywords for the crawl, but also leveraging high-level background knowledge with concepts and relations, which are compared with the text of the searched page), LSCrawler (a framework for a focused web crawler that is based on *link semantics*, and that has achieved better recall in practice than systems like Ariadne that do not incorporate any notion of link semantics or semantic similarity), and for the Semantic Web–focused user, Swoogle. Swoogle is not a focused crawling tool; instead, it was proposed as an SW search and metadata engine. We believe that it qualifies as a domain discovery tool because it is a crawler-based indexing and retrieval system for the Semantic Web [i.e., for web documents in the Resource Description Framework (RDF) or Web Ontology Language (OWL)]. It extracts metadata for each discovered document and computes relations between documents. When the original Swoogle paper was published, it was a prototype SW search engine that could facilitate several tasks, including finding appropriate ontologies, finding instances and characterizing or profiling the Semantic Web (e.g., by collecting metadata, especially interdocument relations that provided a wealth of knowledge on how different ontologies were referenced and how connected the Semantic Web was from an empirical viewpoint).

For those looking to do lightweight scraping or crawling, a number of convenient tools are available in languages like Python. An excellent example is Beautiful Soup, accessed at https://www.crummy.com/software/BeautifulSoup/bs4/doc/, which is popular enough that its documentation has been translated into multiple languages by its users. Beautiful Soup is a Python library for extracting data from HTML and XML files. It works with most web parsers and allows intuitive programmatic ways for navigating, searching, and modifying the parse tree. Numerous tutorials are available. Another good resource is Scrapy (Scrapy. org), which is described as an open-source and collaborative framework for extracting data from websites. Scrapy can be installed in a Python environment using pip, and it allows users to do a number of interesting things, including building and running their own web spiders. Documentation is fairly complete, and good tutorials are available throughout

---

[3] https://github.com/ViDA-NYU/domain_discovery_tool.

[4] https://youtu.be/XmZUnMwI10M, https://youtu.be/YKAI9HPg4FM, https://youtu.be/HPX8lR8QS4.

the web. Another good example is Import.io, accessed at https://import.io/, which is an interactive crawling platform.[5]

Although the examples given here are provided for Python, similar such packages are available in other languages as well, though they may not always be as easy to use as the abovementioned tools. We also note that there are command-line tools available in Unix-like systems for fetching webpages, an example being Scrape (https://github.com/huntrar/scrape), as well as some of the tools discussed on webpages such as https://linuxhint.com/top_20_webscraping_tools/. However, users should be cautious of deploying any of these tools at a truly large scale or for commercial purposes without first becoming familiar with their license or copyright status, as well as testing them in production scenarios. We also briefly note that, for companies or organizations that have a high stake in collecting, storing, or indexing web data (such as Google), the web crawling mechanisms are likely customized, internally developed, and refined.

3.6   Bibliographic Notes

What has been referred to (and described) as domain discovery in this chapter has a long and interesting history going back to the founding days of the web, and the concept was not necessarily always denoted as *domain discovery*. *Focused crawling* was a much more common term owing to the popularity of focused crawling techniques for building a domain-specific corpus from the web. More recently, as we described in the latter part of the chapter, the techniques have become significantly more diverse.

In the beginning of the chapter, we spent some space describing some statistics on the web, as well as why domain discovery on the web is both an important and difficult problem. Many of the statistics discussed can be found in several resources on the web; examples include Internet Live Stats (https://www.internetlivestats.com), Statista (https://www.statista.com/topics/1145/internet-usage-wo-rldwide/), and references such as Lyman and Varian (2003). A web search could reveal more recent statistics than were cited in this chapter.

Early papers on crawling were already surprisingly sophisticated, even in the 1990s. Some of the papers that we reference next, including those based on link analysis and machine learning paradigms like reinforcement learning, already existed well back in the early 2000s. Some good examples of early crawlers that used a variety of interesting techniques, algorithms, and methodologies include the collaborative web crawling approach described by Shang-Hua Teng et al. (1999) as the IBM Grand Central Station project, a "hidden web" crawler proposed by Raghavan and Garcia-Molina (2001), ontology-based web "agents"

---

[5] We provide a set of suggested exercises at the end of this chapter for the reader curious about Scrapy in the context of a real-world data set and task.

proposed by Luke et al. (1997) and Spector (1997), image search engines proposed by Sclaroff (1995), and even entire frameworks like SPHINX, proposed by Miller and Bharat (1998) to satisfy the need for a development environment that could enable practitioners to develop and test their own crawlers.

Much of the material in this chapter relied on the analysis by Batsakis et al. (2009), who describe the various kinds of crawlers (e.g., semantic, learning-based) in detail, and also mainly discuss ways to improve the performance of focused web crawlers. One of the primary approaches described in this chapter (focused crawling using context graphs) was originally described by Diligenti et al. (2000). Other relevant products include Ariadne, CATYRPEL, and LSCrawler, described by Ester et al. (2001), Ehrig and Maedche (2003), and Yuvarani et al. (2006), respectively. A good survey of focused crawling was provided by Novak (2004).

In addition, we mentioned several resources from the NLP community that have been increasingly used in some crawlers. Good references for some of these, including sequence models and WordNet, include Miller (1998), Rabiner and Juang (1986), and Sutton et al. (2012). An influential work on using WordNet to measure the relatedness of concepts is by Pedersen et al. (2004).

Chau and Chen (2003) provide a review of personalized and focused web spiders, defining a web spider as a software program that traverses the web "information space" by following hypertext links and retrieving documents using standard HTTP. This definition itself has a precedent in Cheong (1996). As Chau and Chen (2003) describe, web spider research directions have tended to fall along three dimensions (speed/efficiency, spidering policy, and IR, the last of which has attracted particularly prolific research).

Many crawlers and spiders have used link analysis (or more correctly, have been influenced by link analysis techniques). Relevant historical works that laid the groundwork for these techniques for many years to follow include Spertus (1997), Pirolli et al. (1996), Cho et al. (1998), Chakrabarti et al. (1999), and Weiss et al. (1996). Other creative crawlers used anchor text (clickable, emphasized text of an outgoing link in a webpage) or other cues, such as the text appearing near a hyperlink; see Amitay (1998), Armstrong et al. (1995), and Rennie et al. (1999). The last of these proposed reinforcement learning to efficiently crawl the web, which is worth noting considering the renaissance that reinforcement learning has been enjoying in game-playing. In other work, algorithms such as PageRank and HITS [Kleinberg (1999), Brin and Page (1998)], which give more weight to links from authoritative sources, have also led to revolutionary advances in modern web search. They are also relevant for domain discovery, especially with respect to the crawlers described in the "Focused Crawling" section in this chapter.

Since the early 2000s, the Semantic Web has also had an impact on crawling research. Earlier, we mentioned CATYRPEL, which is an ontology-focused crawler. Another example of an SW-inspired system is Swoogle, described by Ding et al. (2004), which was specifically designed to be a crawler-based indexing and IR system for the Semantic Web. Other examples include Multicrawler, BioCrawler [Harth et al. (2006); Batzios et al. (2008)] and other research such as by Hogan et al. (2011) and Rana and Tyagi (2012).

The DDT, an advanced system for domain discovery, was developed and described by Krishnamurthy et al. (2016). Other related studies by Felix (2019) and Moraes et al. (2017) would also be relevant for the interested reader.

The field of IR, detailed further in chapter 11, is intimately related to domain discovery, in that good search engines have to determine user intent and retrieve (and rank) a set of pages or documents that are *relevant*. Relevance was also a consideration for focused crawling and other domain discovery tools, and we noted the importance attached to it by both semantic and learning crawlers, which try to estimate it from various extracted features. Evaluation is also an important concern; an excellent reference is Fox et al. (2005).

More recently, crawling data (especially images) by third parties has been subject to ethical concerns. For the interested reader, we particularly recommend the work by Thelwall and Stuart (2006), Krotov and Silva (2018), and Sun et al. (2010).

Crawling has also become harder to do in an off-the-shelf fashion due to many websites now actively preventing "robots" from accessing some of their pages by imposing captchas and other "human-proving" tasks; see, for example, Von Ahn et al. (2003), Gossweiler et al. (2009), Egele et al. (2010), and Singh and Pal (2014). Whether such methods are truly effective remains to be seen, as computer vision, NLP, and other machine learning research (and tooling) continue to undergo rapid advancement and are being applied to "solve" captchas, as evidenced from Ye et al. (2018) and Csuka et al. (2018).

3.7 Exercises

1. In this and the next several questions, you will utilize web crawlers to collect webpages and extract data from the Internet Movie Database (IMDb) (https://www.imdb.com/). As we studied in this chapter, a web crawler is a program or *bot* that systematically browses the web, typically for the purpose of web indexing (web spidering). It starts with a list of seed URLs to visit, and as it visits each webpage, it finds the links in that web page and then visits those links and repeats the entire process. We recommend using Scrapy (https://scrapy.org), which is a crawler in the Python library, for these exercises. As a first step, download (and test) Scrapy and do a brief tutorial to ensure that you are familiar with the basics.

   Hint: To locate and extract the attributes, you may have to see the source HTML of some example pages. While there are some off-the-shelf tools (including regular expressions) that you can use for the extraction, if you are not confident about extracting data from HTML, you should return to this set of exercises after reading chapter 5.

2. Crawl at least 5,000 webpages of science fiction movies/shows in IMDb using Scrapy. Extract and generate, for each webpage, the attributes shown in the left panel of the image. Make sure to store your crawled data into a JSON-Lines (.jl) file. In this file format, each line is a valid JSON object (dictionary) that holds the attributes listed in the left panel for a single crawled webpage. More details on JSON can be found at https://www.json.org/json-en.html. While crawling and storing the webpages, did you encounter unexpected problems? If you did, how did you get around them? *Hint: While crawling, please make sure you obey the website's politeness rules (e.g., sleep time between requests) in order to avoid getting banned.*

3. Similar to the previous task, crawl at least 5,000 webpages of cast (i.e., actors and actresses) in IMDb using Scrapy. Extract and generate the attributes in the right panel for each cast webpage. Store the crawled data into a JSON-Lines file.

4. In the context of this task, answer the following questions using no more than two sentences for each question:

    (a) What is the seed URL(s) that you used for each task?

    (b) How did you manage to only collect movie/show or cast pages?

    (c) Did you need to discard irrelevant pages? If so, did you do it?

    (d) Did you collect the required number of pages? If you were not able to do so, please describe and explain your issues.

5. Ordinarily, focused crawlers (and many other types of crawlers as well) take as input traditional inputs such as some starting (or *seed*) URLs and, possibly, a topic description (e.g., a list of keywords). We suggested, however, that other innovative mechanisms can be used for representing a user's intent. Think of at least two such novel input types. What domains would they be particularly useful for?

4 Named Entity Recognition

Overview. Textual information has continued to proliferate rapidly in the digital realm, with many text repositories now available on the web. A significant part of this information, including online news, government material, legal documents (e.g., contracts and court rulings), corporate reports, medical notes, and even social media, tends to be transmitted as free-text documents that are difficult for machines to search or make sense of literally. This has led to the term *unstructured* being associated with free-text documents because the content is very different from "structured" data found in knowledge bases (KBs) and databases. To enable machines to do analytics over, or to build knowledge graphs (KGs) from, such data, there is a growing need to extract and interlink key pieces of information from the text. Typically, the first line of attack in building such information extraction (IE) systems is Named Entity Recognition (NER). In this chapter, we introduce IE and then delve deeper into NER. Compared to other IE techniques, NER has evolved over multiple decades of research, and has achieved impressive peak empirical performance in various domains across common entity types.

4.1 Introduction

IE is an unavoidable task in a broader KG construction (KGC) pipeline. Conceptually, IE can be defined simply as a class of algorithmic techniques to extract relevant information from raw data. As is so often the case in applied artificial intelligence (AI) and KG research, the devil is in the details. What do we mean by "relevant" and "information," for example? What is raw data? To understand the nuance behind this definition, we provide two applications of IE in figure 4.1. In the first application, the goal is to extract entities and relationships from web data. In chapter 3, for example, we covered the important problem of domain discovery and data acquisition, with the principal focus being on web data. Because almost every domain we can think of now has a significant web presence, the importance of minimally supervised web IE continues to grow. Fortunately, even though the problem is still not solved, in that no system is close to achieving human-level performance, the work is in a sufficiently mature stage that a range of options are available to the typical practitioner. We cover web IE in more detail in chapter 5.

In the second application, the raw data is free text, or *natural language*. Some authors have alluded to such data as being unstructured, but we discourage the use of this term because there is considerable structure (both syntactic and semantic) in natural-language data, and the study of such structure is an important goal of linguistics. However, it is also important to distinguish the various kinds of natural language, which can be quite diverse. The most obvious kind of variance arises from different languages (i.e., free text that is "natural" to a French speaker will not seem to natural to a native English speaker who has no knowledge of French). Beyond multilingual data, messages exchanged on social media platforms like Twitter have arguably yielded a whole other "dialect" that looks very different from the kinds of articles we read on Wikipedia or on newswire. Tabloids and more sensationalistic media fall somewhere in between, as do text messages, which have more regular spellings but are still short and can employ nonstandard characters like emojis.

Furthermore, as figure 4.1 suggests, the practical problem statement can have a strong dependence on the application. For example, is it relevant for an IE to be extracting e-commerce products from text when the downstream application is geopolitical forecasting? Generally, the scope of an IE task, like so many others in KG-centric pipelines, is defined through an ontology, which contains classes and properties of interest. If the IE is meant to be in support of the aforesaid geopolitical forecasting application, for example, then classes like *Country, Geopolitical Location, State Actor*, and *Politician* would obviously be of interest, while e-commerce classes like *Product, Color*, and *Price* would not. Properties tend to be defined by the classes in the ontology [e.g., *Geopolitical Location* would have (literal-valued) properties such as *latitude* and *longitude*, while in the e-commerce domain, *Product* and *Price* might be linked by properties such as *suggested_retail_price* and *factory_outlet_price*].

In short, without an ontology, IE tends to be an underdetermined term, both because it does not specify *what* needs to be extracted (e.g., are extractions limited to named entities like people and organizations, or should they be extended to events and relations like "President of"?), and also does not specify the *semantics* of such extractions (e.g., whether *Barack Obama* should have the semantics of a *Person* or the finer-grained *Politician* class). While ontology-guided IE is still the predominant form of IE, Open Information Extraction (Open IE), which does not rely on an ontology being provided, has also been studied. While Open IE has seen much improvement since it was first introduced, it remains considerably noisier and less feasible in practice than traditional IE. In this chapter, we focus primarily on extracting class instances, or *entities* (rather than property instances, or *relations*), from ordinary free text such as newswire, with Open IE and social media IE, left for a subsequent chapter. Relation extraction, as well as higher-order extraction problems such as event extraction, will be covered in chapter 6.

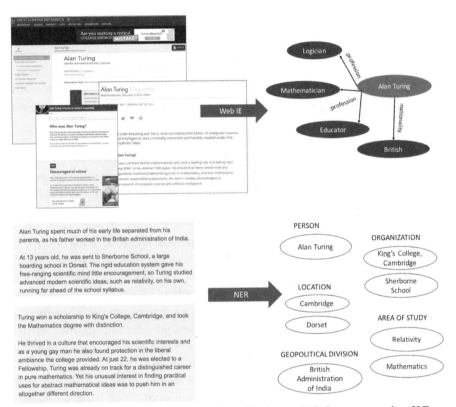

Figure 4.1: Two contrasting versions and applications of IE for constructing KGs over raw sources. Web IE operates over webpages, and attempts to extract a KG with entities, relations, or even events, while NER extracts instances of concepts such as PERSON or LOCATION. Concepts come from an ontology that can be domain-specific. To supplement the instances, and interconnect them with relations, relation extraction has to be executed as another step.

Specifically, we will focus on an extremely important (and best-studied) IE problem in the NLP community called NER. Note that entities in text can be named or unnamed. For example, in the sentence "Currently, it is unknown who killed Martha Jones, but the criminal is at large and a manhunt is underway," the person who killed Martha Jones is clearly an entity that exists in the real world (assuming someone *did* kill Martha Jones), but we do not have a name for that entity, even though we have the *type* (corresponding to a class like *Person* or *Criminal* in our ontology). In fact, we may never have a name for that entity, and we may (as a consequence) end up giving it an alternative name by way of reference (e.g., the Zodiac Killer). Extracting unnamed entities is also of interest, though we will focus mostly on extracting named entities in this chapter, which is now a mature research area with successful use-cases and implementation in several real-world applications.

We can define NER more precisely as the task of identifying the *instances* of a predefined set of concepts in a specific domain, ignoring other irrelevant information, where the input consists of a corpus of texts together with a clearly specified information need. As previously mentioned, concepts generally correspond to classes in an ontology, such as the simple model shown in figure 4.2. Identifying a concept's instances implies that an IE system must be able to locate specific *mentions* in the text, such that the mention *refers* to an instance of the concept. Furthermore, because different instances of the concept may actually be referring to the same underlying entity, these instances must be resolved. For example, consider the sentences "The United Nations sent food aid to Chad in 1980" and "The U.N. authorized a food aid mission to Chad in 1980." Correctly extracting the mentions "U.N." and "United Nations" as instances of the predefined concept "Country" is the task of an NER system. However, because both mentions refer to the same underlying entity, a further round of inference (known as *instance matching*) is required before the extractions can be queried, aggregated, or analyzed in complex ways.

We turn to instance matching in detail in chapter 8. In KG formalism, there is an easy separation between the two tasks of NER (and more generally, IE) and instance matching. One way to understand the separation is by thinking of NER as a KG *construction* problem (KGC), whereas instance matching is a KG *completion* problem. Solutions to both types of problems are necessary to achieve a high-quality KG.

4.2   Why Is Information Extraction Hard?

Even though this chapter is predominantly about NER, many of the techniques that we cover herein have directly inspired mainstream IE research for complex information types like relations and events. Thus, it is worthwhile taking a moment to understand what makes IE challenging to begin with. First, even in limited settings, IE is a nontrivial task due to the complexity and ambiguity of natural language. There are many ways of expressing the same fact, which can be distributed across multiple sentences, documents, or even

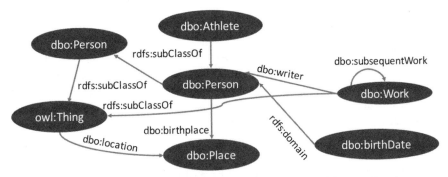

Figure 4.2: A simple concept ontology, named instances of which need to be extracted by an NER system. The ontology fragment is based on the real-world DBpedia ontology. RDFS and DBO, which stand for "Resource Description Framework Schema" and "DBpedia Ontology," respectively, indicate that the "vocabulary" terms (e.g., dbo:writer) lie in these namespaces.

knowledge repositories. Significant amounts of relevant information could be implicit and difficult to discern without a requisite (and enormous) amount of background knowledge that humans have managed to acquire despite a "poverty of the stimulus." In other words, we are able to use, learn, compose, and understand sentences in very creative ways, despite not having heard the vast majority of sentences we end up using and understanding. The general problem of natural-language understanding is far from being solved, though much progress has been made. Certainly, relation extraction and NER are important components in any computational system looking to understand language better. Furthermore, recent advances in NLP in developing robust, efficient, modular, high-coverage, and shallow text-processing techniques (predominantly based on statistical methods, especially deep neural networks), as opposed to deep linguistic analysis, have contributed to the customized deployment of IE techniques in real-world applications for processing large quantities of textual data.

Along with ambiguity, the other major challenge that IE tends to face is that models trained on concepts in a predefined ontology cannot be easily transferred when something significant changes, whether it is the genre of data (newswire versus social media) or the language. Not all text is equal, even for humans (e.g., even trained scientists have to expend considerable cognitive energy to understand a dense scientific report over reading and understanding a simple news article). The impact of the genre and the domain has generally been neglected in the NER literature, but some studies have shown that some leading NER systems, when tested on a corpus that comprised transcripts of phone conversations and technical emails (rather than a standard, widely used newswire collection called MUC-6), experienced degradation on standard metrics like precision and recall by as much as 20 to 40 percent. In recent years, some authors have made progress on this issue in difficult domains, but common-domain, newswire-oriented NER systems continue to experience the best performance. Another problem is when the ontology changes via the introduction of novel concepts and properties. Sometimes the ontology becomes finer-grained (e.g., an application may decide that a class like *Person* is too coarse-grained, and it may be better to subdivide that class into subclasses like *Politician, Actor,* and *Military Personnel*). Even simple changes like that can affect a trained IE model profoundly because the entity typing mechanism (which is responsible for assigning extractions to concepts in the ontology) may have to be retrained, and if the model jointly considers extraction and typing (as many modern systems do), the whole system may have to be retrained. The other problem is that the definition of relevance changes because not all persons are now relevant, which can lead to loss of precision. Some extractions may now also have multiple types (e.g., when an actor is also a politician, like Arnold Schwarzenegger), making both evaluation and extraction difficult.

Finally, Open IE and unsupervised NER, which require no ontology and/or training instances, still lag significantly in performance compared to supervised, ontologically mediated NER. This is not surprising, and it should also be noted that the performance of unsupervised NER has improved steadily over the past decade, especially with improvements in language models and self-supervised learning.

4.3   Approaches for Named Entity Recognition

Early approaches to NER tended to make heavy use of handcrafted rule-based algorithms, although this is an oversimplification because the actual techniques were quite diverse from one system to another. An early research paper in the 1990s was one of the first to formally recognize the problem as a *computational* task by proposing a system that aims to "extract and recognize names" (in this specific case, company names). This system relied on heuristics and rules. Research in the area expanded soon afterward, with the first major event aimed at properly defining and evaluating NER (among other NLP problems) being MUC-6. Since then, the popularity of NER as a field of study in both academic and industrial contexts has continued to rise. Other than Message Understanding Conferences (MUCs), other scientific avenues where the community came together to discuss techniques and evaluation standards for NER include HUB-4, MET-2, and HAREM. A more recent initiative is the Language Resources and Evaluation Conference (LREC), which has staged multiple workshops and conference tracks on IE since the early 2000s.

One bias that must be noted here is the almost singular focus of early research on English IE and NER. Some exceptions like German notwithstanding, multilingual NER only started becoming well studied since the early 2000s through conferences like the SIGNLL Conference on Computational Natural Language Learning (CoNLL). It was only in the mid-2000s that Arabic and less well studied languages like Bulgarian and Russian started

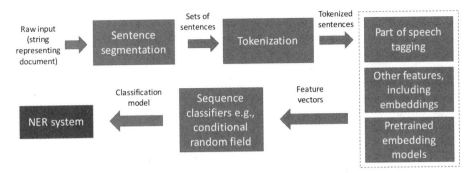

Figure 4.3: A practical architecture for NER can depend heavily on other elements of the pipeline, such as preprocessing and tokenization, as well as the availability of external resources such as lexicons and pretrained word embeddings (described in subsequent sections of this chapter). A complete description of these modules is beyond the scope of this book, but it may be found in any standard text or survey on Natural Language Processing.

becoming popular. Large-scale projects like Global Autonomous Language Exploitation (GALE) helped push for progress on multilingual NER. Much more recently, there has also been focus on low-resource languages like Uighyur. By "low-resource," we mean a language that has not been well addressed by the NLP community, but that is spoken by a large population. Government-funded programs like DARPA LORELEI have been instrumental in renewing the focus on multilingual and low-resource NER.

One last point that we note before diving headlong into the details of NER systems and approaches is that the performance of NER can strongly depend on other elements of a complete pipeline, including preprocessing and tokenization. *Tokenization* is the segmentation of the text data into "wordlike" units, which are called *tokens*. Often, their type also needs to be determined, which involves identification of capitalized words, hyphenated words, punctuation signs, and numbers, to name a few. In fact, a general architecture for NER can look like figure 4.3, with the NER step itself ensconced between other modules. Other NLP inference tasks have similar dependence on preprocessing; hence, the architecture can be built out even further with higher-level inference modules like relation and event extraction. Steps such as linguistic tagging (e.g., part-of-speech, or POS, tagging) and intermediate clusters can have a major impact on the overall performance of such modules. Linguistic tagging is one example of *syntactic analysis*, which includes computation of a dependency structure (most often, a parse tree) over a sentence. Other example tasks include phrase recognition (in particular, recognition of verb groups, noun phrases, and acronyms and abbreviations), sentence boundary detection, and morphological analysis. In short, to truly achieve impressive industry-scale performance on NER, much engineering effort is required, often extending well beyond training and tuning the NER model itself.

4.3.1 Supervised Approaches

The current popular paradigm for addressing NER is supervised learning, including such well-established statistical models as decision trees, maximum entropy models, hidden Markov models (HMMs), Support Vector Machines (SVMs), and conditional random fields (CRFs). Except for decision trees and SVMs, all of these are sequence-labeling techniques that do not make the famous independent and identically distributed (i.i.d.) assumption prevalent in many machine learning approaches and classifiers. To understand the difference, consider the sentence in figure 4.4. Suppose that, to keep the analysis simple, we were trying to classify each word in the sentence as a named entity "LOC" (for location) "PER," (for person) or "O" (for *others*, i.e., not a token or named entity of interest). Traditional classification would try to classify each word in the sentence *independently* (i.e., whether "the" gets a classifier as "O" has no impact on whether the next word is classified as "O," "LOC," or "PER"). Intuitively, this seems faulty. It seems more likely that "the" is going to be followed by a location like "United States" than not. Thus, we should not be classifying every token independently, but if possible, classifying the sequence as a whole. In the general case, the problem of taking all elements in a sequence and classifying them jointly is intractable for reasonable sequence sizes, but with some model assumptions, we can try to take some dependencies into account when classifying each token. Sequence labelers, including HMMs and CRFs, are examples of models that assign output states to input terms without making a strong independence assumption.

CRFs constitute an important enough class of models for NER (and other sequence-labeling problems) that we cover them separately in the next section. CRFs were first proposed and developed in the early 2000s, but they have continued to be an attractive solution even in the present day, though they are not state-of-the-art anymore due to the advent of deep learning methods like recurrent neural networks (RNNs). However, regardless of the technique, because supervised approaches involve a separation of labeled data into training and test sets, with the latter withheld until the model (and a suitable baseline) has been developed and tuned, proper evaluation is an important concern. One baseline that is considered almost as a "litmus" test consists of tagging words in the test corpus when they are annotated as entities in the training corpus. In other words, the performance of this system is a measure of the *vocabulary transfer* or the proportion of words, without repetitions, that appear in both the training and test corpus. In a study conducted over 20 years ago by Palmer and Day (1997), vocabulary transfer on the MUC-6 training data was found to have uneven vocabulary transfer across entity types (21 percent in the aggregate, but with 42 percent across locations and only 13 percent across person names). Actual recall of this simple baseline system is even higher because vocabulary transfer does not include repetitions, whereas many entities can be frequently repeated in the test corpus. A second study by Mikheev et al. (1999) that followed the original vocabulary transfer study on MUC-6 found, for example, that on MUC-7, this simple baseline tagger can achieve a recall of 76 percent for locations, and 26 percent for persons, with precision well over 70 percent. Other such consistent results were achieved thereafter by other authors (see the "Bibliographic Notes" section at the end of this chapter). The reason why we point this out here is to show that a high recall on some categories may not actually be as impressive as it would be in some other fields of AI (such as instance matching, covered in a later chapter) or in other categories. For example, if a system managed to achieve 78 percent recall on locations on MUC-7, this is not as impressive as achieving 78 percent recall on person names. Considering this litmus baseline tagger as a minimum viable NER is a good way of ensuring that performance numbers are not ratcheted above their true significance. It also helps to ensure that the test corpus is not too easy (or hard); while it's good to have some vocabulary transfer, the generalization of any method being evaluated becomes suspect if the test data set is too susceptible to achieve vocabulary transfer.

4.3.1.1 Conditional Random Fields   To set the stage for a CRF, let us formulate our input x as a *sequence* $(x_1, \ldots, x_m)$ of m tokens. Currently, it is best to think of the tokens as words, though in the most general case, they can be higher-order terms (such as phrases and clauses). The CRF is supposed to accept this sequence as input, and then output another sequence of *output states*, which we denote as $s = (s_1, \ldots, s_m)$. The output states are the named entity tags. Note that the number of output states equals the number of input states.

Formally, we can define a CRF on observations $\mathbb{X}$ and random variables $\mathbb{Y}$ by first defining a graph $G = (V, E)$ and letting $\mathbb{Y} = (\mathbb{Y}_v)_{v \in V}$, such that $\mathbb{Y}$ is indexed by the vertices of G. $(\mathbb{X}, \mathbb{Y})$ is a CRF when the random variables $\mathbb{Y}_v$, conditioned on $\mathbb{X}$, obey the *Markov property* with respect to the graph—that is, $p(\mathbb{Y}_v | \mathbb{X}, \mathbb{Y}_w, w \neq v) = p(\mathbb{Y}_v | \mathbb{X}, \mathbb{Y}_w, neigh(w, v))$, where $neigh(a, b)$ means that a and b are neighbors in G. Put even more simply, a CRF is an undirected graphical model with nodes that are partitioned into sets $\mathbb{X}$ and $\mathbb{Y}$, and with the conditional distribution $p(\mathbb{Y}|\mathbb{X})$ explicitly modeled.

CRFs attempt to output a good output sequence by expressively modeling the conditional probability $p(s_1, \ldots, s_m | x_1, \ldots, x_m)$. First, a *feature map* $\Phi(x_1, \ldots, x_m, s_1, \ldots, s_m) \in \mathbb{R}^d$ is defined that maps an entire input sequence x paired with an entire state sequence s to a d-dimensional feature vector. The probability can then be modeled as a log-linear model with the parameter vector $w \in \mathbb{R}^d$:

$$p(s|x; w) = \frac{e^{w.\Phi(x,s)}}{\sum_{s'} e^{w.\Phi(x,s')}}. \tag{4.1}$$

Here, s' ranges over all possible output sequences. For the estimation of w, the assumption is that there are a set of n labeled examples $\{(x_i, s_i)\}_{i=1}^n$. The regularized log-likelihood function L can now be defined as

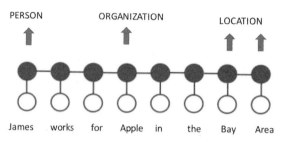

Figure 4.4: A CRF as applied to the task of NER. Unlike ordinary supervised classification, which would make an i.i.d. assumption and try to classify each term in the input sequence independently, CRFs (and other models like it) model dependencies to get better accuracy without necessarily becoming intractable. The dark nodes are output nodes that technically produce a probability over the full set of labels [which includes all concepts, and also a *Not Applicable* (NA)-type concept indicating that no named entity is present]. There are standard mechanisms for handling multiword extractions like "Bay Area."

$$L(w) = \sum_{i=1}^{n} log\, p(s^i | x^i; w) - \frac{\lambda_2}{2} \|w\|_2^2 - \lambda_1 \|w\|_1. \tag{4.2}$$

The nonlog terms in equation (4.2) force the parameter vector to be parsimonious in its respective norm, penalizing model complexity. This is the phenomenon of regularization witnessed in regular supervised models like SVMs. The parameters λ_1 and λ_2 allow the system designer to control the level of regularization. Finally, the parameter vector w^* is estimated as $w^* = argmax_{w \in \mathbb{R}^d} L(w)$. Once estimated, w^* can be used to tag a sentence by outputting state s^* using the equation $s^* = argmax_s p(s|x; w^*)$.

An important point to note in the mathematical treatment of a CRF given here is that it is dependent on the kinds of features included in the feature map. If the features are not discriminative, then there is little that a CRF can do. Generally, a standard set of features that have been found to work well in the NLP community for this problem includes testing the word for such aspects as: Is the word uppercase? Is the word a digit? Other features include the POS tag of the word. A key element of the feature map where the power of CRFs over nonsequential models like SVMs emerges is that features can be crafted over words that occur before or after the target word. For example, we may want to include the word that appeared three steps earlier as a feature in itself, or we may want the POS tag of the words that come after within a window of size 2. In more recent work, features that are not directly crafted, but rely instead on neural models, are word embeddings, described next. The key concept to bear in mind is that features should be diverse and discriminative, and they also should (in the CRF formulation) depend on at least some of the tokens before or after them.

Note that exact inference in CRFs is intractable except in some special cases (e.g., if the graph is a chain or tree, message passing does yield exact solutions, analogous to the Viterbi algorithm for the case of HMMs), or if the CRF contains only pairwise potentials with submodular energy. Generally, approximate solutions are employed, including loopy belief propagation and mean field inference. Learning the parameters themselves (the training phase) is usually done using maximum likelihood; a convenient property of CRFs is that, if all nodes have exponential family distributions and all nodes are observed, the optimization is convex and can be solved using ordinary gradient descent. However, approximations have to be used when some of the variables are unobserved.

4.3.2 Semisupervised and Unsupervised Approaches

Modern supervised approaches (and in particular, deep learning approaches that we describe in the next section) for solving NER can require a large amount of labeled training data in order to learn a system that achieves good performance. The approaches covered thus far assumed that labeled training data is available and can be provided. In fact, the more expressive the model is (and the more parameters it has), the more training data is usually required. However, acquiring such annotations at scale not only involves high degrees of manual labor, but is expensive, time-consuming, and (hence) impractical. In fact, training data is not only difficult to acquire, but it is not always clear that it can even be made available to system developers, especially if the data sets are sensitive or protected under law (such as with health data). Ironically, some of the earliest systems did not require much training data (e.g., in the late 1990s, Collins and Singer only used a few labeled seeds and seven features such as entity context and orthography for NER). More recently, there has been renewed interest in semisupervised information extraction from large corpora. A particularly influential approach has been *weak supervision*, which requires some amount of human supervision, usually in the very beginning when the system designer provides a starting set of seeds, which are then used to bootstrap the model so that it can proceed without further supervision (until some convergence condition is met). Another set of approaches, building on more classic machine learning theory, is based on active learning, which requires small but periodic interventions from human annotators. The idea behind active learning is that the annotator initially provides a small set of examples, based on which the learner actively decides which other examples to present to the human teacher next for maximal gain. Usually, these samples are just the ones on which the learner's prediction has the greatest uncertainty; by resolving these samples, the human annotator is giving the system the data that benefits it most. Another way to look at this is that it makes annotation more efficient by preempting the labeling of redundant samples that the system is able to automatically label with high certainty. Active learning is one example of "human-in-the-loop" learning that has recently witnessed resurgence, because it represents a hybrid situation where an appropriate balance of system design, data labeling, knowledge engineering, and human intervention together lead to effective performance.

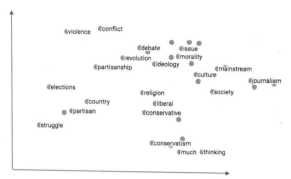

Figure 4.5: Representation learning ("embedding") over words, given a sufficiently large corpus of documents (sets of sequences of words). We show words in the neighborhood of "politics." For visualization purposes, the vectors have been projected to two dimensions. The mechanics behind representation learning are detailed in chapter 10, which describes how to embed KGs, including the actual neural network architectures that tend to be used for these embeddings.

However, by and large, the reliance on labeled training data has not disappeared (in the interest of having higher accuracy), but what has changed is the heavy reliance on manual feature engineering. Representation learning has emerged as a key trend in this direction. The basic problem of representation learning is to design an architecture (usually some kind of neural network) that takes as input raw data, such as a sequence of words (or even characters) and outputs a vector (representation) for the unit of interest (typically words, but also sentences and paragraphs). We illustrate classic representation learning over words (given a sufficiently large text corpus) in figure 4.5. As it turns out, representation learning is an important factor attributed to the success of deep neural networks because the layers in such networks learn increasingly sophisticated representations (with increasing depth) of the kinds of objects fed to them. For convolutional neural networks (CNNs), these input objects are usually images, while for RNNs, they are sequences, not unlike the inputs fed to CRFs. It would not be incorrect to think of RNNs as advancing the state-of-the-art over CRFs. Because sequence labeling is the main problem that needs to be solved here, we focus on RNNs in the next section. However, this will not be the only coverage of representation learning in this book. In chapter 10, we describe how the notion of representation learning as applied to words here can be extended to embed nodes, relations, and even complex structures in KGs.

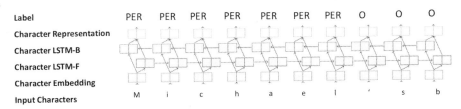

| Label | PER PER PER PER PER PER PER O O O |

Figure 4.6: A character-based RNN architecture as applied to NER for an input sentence such as "Michael's birthday is coming."

4.4 Deep Learning for Named Entity Recognition

Starting with seminar work in 2011 that relied on representation learning for solving several NLP problems like POS tagging and NER in a unified feature framework, neural NER systems with minimal feature engineering have gained in popularity. Such models are appealing because they do not normally require domain-specific resources like lexicons or ontologies and can scale more easily without significant manual tuning. Several neural architectures have been proposed, mostly based on some form of RNN over word, subword, and character embeddings.

The simplest possible definition of an RNN is that it is a network with loops in it, which allows information to persist. Because they have loops, RNNs can be unrolled (in time or over a sequence), meaning that the network can also be thought of as multiple copies of the same network, each passing a message to a successor. RNNs' chainlike structure has made them well suited to any problem that has involved sequences and lists, including speech recognition, language modeling, translation, image captioning, and NER. Just like CRFs, RNNs generally accept an input vector as input and then output another vector. However, here the output vector's contents are influenced not only by the current input, but the entire history of input fed into the network in the past.

In practice, a particular kind of RNN—namely, Long Short-Term Memory (LSTM)—is used widely in the NLP community owing to its more powerful update equation and some appealing backpropagation dynamics. Despite becoming popular only recently, LSTMs were actually proposed well back in the 1990s, initially as a solution to the vanishing gradient problem in neural networks. LSTMs help preserve the error that can be back-propagated through time and layers. By maintaining a more constant error, these RNNs can continue to learn during thousands of time steps, allowing potentially remote linkages between causes and effects to be modeled and discovered. LSTMs contain information outside the normal flow of the recurrent network in a gated cell. Information can be stored in, written to, or read from a cell, much like data in a computer's memory. The cell makes decisions about what to store and when to allow reads, writes, and erasures via gates that open and close. Unlike the digital storage on computers, however, these gates are analog, implemented with elementwise multiplication by sigmoids, which are all in the range of 0–1. Being analog, they are differentiable, which makes them amenable to backpropagation.

Returning to the application of LSTMs and RNNs to NER, the most recent models have significantly outperformed feature-engineered systems, despite the latter's access to domain-specific rules, knowledge, features, and lexicons. An example of an RNN-based model is a *character-based architecture* where a sentence is modeled as a sequence of characters, with the sequence passed through an RNN that predicts labels for each character (figure 4.6). These labels are then transformed into word labels via postprocessing mechanisms. The potential of character NER neural models was first established empirically in the mid-2010s (e.g., a system in 2016 used highway networks over CNNs on character sequences of words, followed by an LSTM layer and softmax for the final predictions). Character-level architectures may be thought of as a finer-grained generalization of word-level architectures, where the RNN is input a sequence of words, not dissimilar to the CRFs discussed earlier. LSTMs and CRFs have also been combined in this context (e.g., in 2015, a proposed system showed that by adding a CRF layer to a word LSTM model, performance could be improved by more than 84 percent F1-Score on the CoNLL 2003 data set). Similar improvements were illustrated in domain-specific NER systems such as DrugNER, as well as the medical NER system proposed by Xu et al. (2017). Even more recently, models have been proposed that have not only combined word and character architectures, but also have further supplemented them with one of the most successful features from feature-engineering approaches (namely, *affixes*). While affix features have been used in NER systems since the early 2000s, as well as biomedical NER, they had not been used in neural NER systems until quite recently. A number of experiments in 2018 and later showed that affix embeddings capture information complementary to that of RNNs over the characters of a word. In fact, embedding affixes was found to be better than simply expanding the other embeddings to reach a similar number of hyperparameters. Clearly, the affixes are adding more to the model than just plain expressiveness.

To summarize these threads of research, the general finding has been that word and character hybrid models tend to outperform individual word and character-based models (sometimes by more than 5 percent on the relevant metric). However, research in this area is significantly underway, and some findings show that progress is still to be made by incorporating key features of past feature-engineered models into modern Neural Network (NN) architectures. For example, a recent system managed to achieve a state-of-the-art result for Spanish, Dutch, and German NER (while performing within 1 percent of the best model for English NER) by incorporating affix features into an earlier system. In keeping with this trend, it is likely that (rather than a complete replacement of feature-engineered systems with representation learning) innovative hybrid models will continue to make further improvements beyond the state-of-the-art NER approaches.

4.5 Domain-Specific Named Entity Recognition

An excellent, and high-impact, example of domain-specific NER is in the patient and biomedical domain. There has been so much interest in this field that open-source packages implementing executable surveys of advances in the field (such as BANNER) have even been published. There is much motivation behind biomedical NER, owing mostly to molecular biology rapidly becoming an information-dense field. As such, building automated extraction tools to handle the large volumes of published literature has become a pressing focus. An accurate NER system can go a long way in making sense of these large quantities of text. Significant progress has been achieved over the last decade, as demonstrated in challenge evaluations such as BioCreative (where teams around the world implemented creative solutions to challenges such as the out-of-vocabulary[1] problem). As a result, several systems exist to address this (e.g., ABNER and LingPipe). We note that deep learning has also had a strong influence on biomedical NER (e.g., a system called DrugNER, which is based on a word and character neural network model, has outperformed the best feature-engineered system by almost 9 percent on MedLine test data and 3.5 percent on the overall data set).

In work that we cover in part V of this book, NER has also been applied to more unusual domains, such as illicit advertisements (e.g., containing solicitations for drugs or sexual services) crawled over the web. Extracting key pieces of information from these ads, including phone numbers, physical attributes, and locations, is an important problem because it can help law enforcement find victims of human trafficking or crack down on rings and perpetrators engaging in such activities, sometimes under a legitimate front (e.g., a massage parlor). NER is significantly more difficult in such domains due to different language models and obfuscation of identifying attributes, the heavy presence of long-tail entities (meaning that it is very difficult to get any representative training data), and the noisy nature of web data. Domain-specific techniques are required to achieve the level of accuracy necessary for useful predictive analytics.

Other kinds of special NER also exist. For instance, NER from social media usually involves a different (or at the very least, differently configured) set of techniques compared to newswire; similarly, NER in the absence of an ontology (Open IE) can be much more challenging than ordinary NER. Because these special kinds of NER have become all too frequent due to the advent of big, irregular data sets and growth of social media on the web, we return to them in chapter 7. It is quite likely that as more data sets continue to be released, and as more applications start to emerge, new kinds of NER will be proposed and investigated. At the same time, it is unlikely that the wheel will have to be completely reinvented; most flavors of NER are largely based on a common set of techniques and prin-

---

[1] This problem occurs when the test corpus contains words that were never encountered during training.

ciples, with a continued heavy dependence on advances in sequence-labeling architectures like RNNs.

4.6 Evaluating Information Extraction Quality

As the previous sections illustrate, there are many approaches for tackling IE. Evaluating these systems is an equally important problem. The most important metrics used for evaluating IE performance are *precision* and *recall*, which were adopted from the information retrieval (IR) research community and may be seen as measures of *correctness* and *completeness*, respectively. To define such metrics for IE, let #total denote the total number of slots that should be filled according to an annotated reference corpus (the ground-truth). Let us further denote #correct and #incorrect as the number of slots correctly and incorrectly filled by the system, respectively. Incorrect responses arise for two reasons. Either the slot does not align with a slot in the gold standard (spurious slot) or the slot does align but has been assigned an invalid value. With these notions in place, precision and recall may be defined as follows:

$$Precision = \frac{\#correct}{\#correct + \#incorrect}. \tag{4.3}$$

$$Recall = \frac{\#correct}{\#total}. \tag{4.4}$$

Another way to think about precision is that it is the ratio of true positives to the sum of true positives and false positives, where a positive (whether true or false) is defined as a slot that has been produced by the system. In contrast, *recall* is the ratio of true positives to the sum of true positives and false negatives (slots that exist in the ground-truth but were never output by the system).

There is a clear trade-off between precision and recall, in that improving one usually leads to a loss in the other (although it is not theoretically necessary). Generally, to obtain a finer-grained picture of IE performance, precision and recall may even be measured for each slot type separately. Nevertheless, to navigate the trade-off between the two, a single number is required. An alternative is a plot, but in practice, it is fairly common to report the F1-measure, which is used as a weighted harmonic mean of precision and recall, defined as follows:

$$F1 = \frac{2 \times Precision \times Recall}{Precision + Recall}. \tag{4.5}$$

A metric that is specific to IE is the *slot error rate* (SER), defined as follows:

$$SER = \frac{\#incorrect + \#missing}{\#total}. \tag{4.6}$$

Here, *#incorrect* was defined earlier, while *#missing* denotes the number of slots in the reference that do not align with any slots in the system's outputs. Put differently, it is the ratio between the total number of slot errors and the total number of slots in the ground-truth.

A final note with regard to evaluation is that many of the metrics given here can be further customized depending on what is required by the IE system. For example, we could modify *F1* to place higher weight on precision over recall (by toggling a parameter β that is set to 1.0 in the current definition of *F1* and equally emphasizes precision and recall), and similarly, we may modify some of the other metrics to put more weight on spurious slots. In NER systems that rely heavily on some form of machine learning, a *validation* set is often necessary to ensure that the system's hyperparameters are tuned such that its outputs are optimized for the metrics of interest.

4.7 Concluding Notes

NER is often the first line of attack when constructing a KG over raw sources, and in particular, free-text or natural-language documents. NER has been well studied since at least the 1990s, aided in great part by the MUCs. Today, there are a variety of data sets and systems available. More recently, deep learning approaches have led to breakthrough performance increases in several NER tasks. Yet the performance starts declining with lower quantities of training data, and when applied to irregular (or not as well studied) domains, languages, or styles of writing. In later chapters, we return to this issue, especially with respect to extracting entities from messages posted on social media platforms such as Twitter.

4.8 Software and Resources

At this time, there are several excellent openly available packages for NER. We enumerate some popular ones here, though this is not meant to be an exhaustive list:

1. The Stanford NER, accessible at https://nlp.stanford.edu/software/CRF-NER.html, is a Java-based NER published by Finkel et al. (2005), and is also known as CRFClassifier because it provides a general implementation of linear-chain CRF sequence models. It is available for download, licensed under the GNU General Public License. The source is also included. The general software for doing not just NER, but other NLP tasks as well is called Stanford CoreNLP (https://stanfordnlp.github.io/CoreNLP/), and it includes support for several languages, can be run as a simple web service, and has an integrated NLP toolkit with a broad range of grammatical analysis tools, among other facilities. We also recommend Manning et al. (2014) for more details.

2. The Natural Language Toolkit, or NLTK (https://www.nltk.org/), is a Python-based platform for NLP and provides easy-to-use interfaces to many standard corpora and

lexical resources, including WordNet. It also includes text-processing libraries for classification, tokenization, stemming, tagging, parsing, and semantic reasoning, as well as wrappers for industrial-strength NLP libraries. In addition, there is an active discussion forum.

3. SpaCy (https://spacy.io/) is another industrial-strength NLP toolkit that is designed for large-scale IE tasks. It uses memory-managed Cython, and independent research conducted a few years ago found it to be among the fastest extraction systems available, making it particularly amenable to web data. SpaCy can also be seamlessly operated with TensorFlow, PyTorch, and other neural network packages.

The more recent line of NER systems based on deep learning–based models can be implemented (or modified) using libraries such as TensorFlow, Keras, and PyTorch, accessible at https://www.tensorflow.org/, https://github.com/keras-team/keras, and https://pytorch.org/, respectively. Another excellent resource for knowledge extraction tools, including for multilingual data and more advanced kinds of IE covered in the next three chapters, is the project page maintained by the BLENDER group at the University of Illinois, Urbana-Champaign: https://blender.cs.illinois.edu/software/.

4.9   Bibliographic Notes

Much of the primary material on NER covered in this chapter has been inspired or derived from some classic surveys on the subject. A particularly useful survey was provided by Nadeau and Sekine (2007), but there at least a few others that have heavily influenced how we synthesized the material in this chapter, including Piskorski and Yangarber (2013), Appelt (1999), and Kaiser and Miksch (2005). In particular, Piskorski and Yangarber (2013) provide a broad overview of IE as a whole and break it down by task type, including NER, event extraction, and relation extraction. As expected, web IE is not given coverage because the NLP community has not overlapped much with the web community on the subject. [We state this as a historical note because it explains (in part) why we chose to write the chapter on web IE separate from this one.] Additionally, Jiang (2012) can be read as an accessible introduction to information extraction from text, but just like many of the mentioned surveys, it takes a broader overview of NER and relation extraction within a single chapter.

The study of NER itself dates back to the early 1990s in the version that we see today. Domain-specific NER started becoming more popular in the 2000s, although some of the earlier MUCs (discussed next) also had distinctly domain-specific flavors. Work that specifically covers domain-specific name recognition includes Collins and Singer (1999), Phillips and Riloff (2002), and Yangarber et al. (2002). For a reference to why IE is difficult and challenging, we recommend Huttunen et al. (2002).

The MUC series is largely responsible for directing the attention of the research community toward NER. Because these conferences hold a primary place in the history of modern NLP research, particularly for multisite evaluation of text understanding systems [see Chinchor and Sundheim (1995)], we briefly map out their evolution over time. The first five MUCs were held in the decade following 1987, but it was MUC-6 that truly led to systematic evaluation of NER. As noted by Grishman and Sundheim (1996), MUC-1 (held in 1987) was *exploratory* because each group designed its own format for recording the information in the document. There was no formal evaluation. By MUC-2 (held in 1989), the task had evolved to what is recognized today as template filling. MUC-2 worked out many of the details of primary evaluation measures, which were held to be precision and recall. By MUC-3, a domain-specific flavor was starting to emerge as the domain shifted to terrorist event reports from Central and South America, broadcast in articles by the Foreign Broadcast Information Service. The template became more complex, going from 10 slots in MUC-2 to 18 slots in MUC-3. MUC-4 remained largely the same, except that the number of slots increased to 24. MUC-5 represented a major shift compared to MUC-4, but it was since MUC-6 (held in 1995) that NER started to attract significant attention from NLP researchers. Several evaluation programs on this task, some of which will be covered later in the context of relation and event IE, include the Automatic Content Extraction (ACE) program, the shared task of the Conference on Natural Language Learning (CoNLL) in 2002 and 2003, and the BioCreative (Critical Assessment of Information Extraction Systems in Biology) challenge evaluation. Important references include Doddington et al. (2004), Hirschman et al. (2005), and Sang and De Meulder (2003).

While today, the phrase "named entity" is common, it was coined at MUC-6. The domain for IE was text (such as newspaper articles) describing company activities and defense-related activities, wherein it became clear that it is essential to recognize informational units such as names of people, organizations, and locations, as well as numeric expressions such as time, date, money, and percent. Identifying references to such entities in text was recognized as an extremely important subtask of the broader IE goal and was referred to as Named Entity Recognition and Classification (NERC).

IE as a sequence-labeling application goes back at least two decades, and possibly more. One of the earlier, more influential tools based on HMM was Nymble; see Bikel et al. (1998). CRFs became a standard method soon after; see Peng and McCallum (2006), Sutton et al. (2012), McCallum and Li (2003), and Sarawagi and Cohen (2005) for guidance. For more on the general application of supervised learning algorithms to NER and other similar NLP problems, excellent references are syntheses by Witten et al. (2016) and Manning and Schütze (1999), particularly the latter for NLP-focused work (although the content is now dated).

Semisupervised and unsupervised techniques have risen in popularity for at least a couple of decades. Early and heavily influential work include the multilevel bootstrapping approach by Riloff et al. (1999), but also Cucchiarelli and Velardi (2001), Pasca et al. (2006), and Lin (1998). Another interesting study, by Jones et al. (2003), was based on active learning for IE. Performance has steadily improved as well; in fact, Nadeau et al. (2006) reported that semisupervised NER was starting to rival supervised NER. Because some of the semisupervised approaches tended to rely on "seeds," Ji and Grishman (2006) explicitly drew attention to the problem of unlabeled data selection. Other important references include Alfonseca and Manandhar (2002), Evans and Street (2003), Shinyama and Sekine (2004), and Hearst (1992). Note that some of these cover, or intersect with, research on Open IE, which is the topic of chapter 7. The work by Hearst (1992) is important because it led to the adoption of so-called Hearst patterns for unsupervised labeling, and were in use more than a decade later, as evidenced by Cimiano and Völker (2005).

Finally, we note that many of the surveys cited here were prior to the advent of deep learning. A very recent survey on NER using deep learning models was provided by Yadav and Bethard (2019), and much of our analysis in this chapter on deep learning for NER relied on their work as a primary source. Rather than cite individual papers, we refer the interested reader to that paper for a comprehensive list of citations. Such a list, even in their case, would be incomplete, though, because new work continues to be proposed for improving NER performance even more using deep learning.

4.10 Exercises

Given the following set of words {*high, low, verb, semisupervised, automatic, noun*}, fill in the blanks for these statements. Note that some words in the set may be used more than once (and every word is used at least once):

1. Rule-based IE techniques are expected to have _____ precision and _____ recall.

2. Bootstrapping is an example of a(n) _____ technique for IE.

3. _____ extractors have _____ cost but usually lead to semantic drift.

4. Supervised extractors have _____ cost, but have _____ precision.

5. Semisupervised extractors require a _____ amount or training data.

6. One of the concrete subproblems in IE from natural-language text is defining the domain of interest. One simple approach to do it automatically is by setting any _____ phrase as a candidate entity and any _____ phrase as a candidate relation.

5 Web Information Extraction

Overview. Although information extraction (IE) has best been explored in the natural-language domains [particularly in the context of Named Entity Resolution (NER), as we described in chapter 4], the spectacular advent of the web from the early 1990s onward led to a large body of research output in extracting key information from web sources. Today, no other repository of public information is as vast or diverse as the corpus of searchable and indexable pages on the World Wide Web. This repository is now so vast that sophisticated methods are required simply to find and scrape domain-specific information (chapter 3) that could be of help in building a knowledge graph (KG) that has both high coverage and accuracy. Once we find these pages, we must develop IE modules, ultimately yielding a satisfactory KG that could be deployed in further downstream applications like question answering or querying. In this chapter, we cover influential web IE approaches and systems that were first proposed in the 1990s and have since been refined and combined with other methods.

5.1 Introduction

In chapter 4, we described IE methods for extracting key pieces of data from natural-language sources. Natural-language documents are often erroneously described as unstructured because each document is akin to a long sequence (whether it is interpreted as a sequence of characters, or words and punctuation) and has no syntactic structure beyond the language model itself. In contrast, a table has a very well defined structure, with columns that have headers and rows generally representing individual entities and their attributes. In proper RDBs, there are constraints on what kinds of values are allowed to be entered into the table, along with multitable constraints such as foreign key and functional dependencies.

Web sources, which arguably constitute the most voluminous category of information over which KGs (whether domain-specific or open-domain) can be constructed today, tend to fall somewhere in between the two extremes described here. The input to a web IE task tends to be either structured or semistructured rather than purely natural-language documents as in the previous chapter. In some respects, this makes the extraction problem easier, but in many other respects, it makes it much harder. An illustration of web IE for a real-world webpage is illustrated in figure 5.1. We use bounding boxes to illustrate the key pieces of information that should be extracted into a domain-specific KG (describing lawyers, their contact information, and their practices in California; see figure 5.2 for a sample KG fragment from this page).

In part, one of the difficulties illustrated in figure 5.1 is that structure can be as important as content (i.e., on some webpages, the only clue that a particular phrase on a webpage is a phone number is by virtue of its position on that page, as well as surrounding contextual elements). We provide details on some of the challenges later in this section, but one of them, which is mostly a product of how modern webpages are designed and rendered, is the presence of snippets of code and irrelevant content like advertisements (often dynamically rendered) on the page. Thus, an important task when doing web IE is *parsing the structure* of the webpage. Within a parsed substructure, such as a block of text, other IE techniques such as NER may have to be applied. For attributes like phone numbers and dates, regular expressions may be enough to normalize the value.

Unfortunately, a web source is rarely as structured as a pure RDB, though some webpages are highly uniform and templatized, making them more similar to structured tables than to natural-language documents. By and large, it is popular to refer to web IE inputs as *semistructured* precisely because their structure and content are so heterogeneous, both in terms of substance (the actual material on the webpage) and because of the way the material is laid out. There is also disagreement in the research community in how to formulate definitions of phrases like "semistructured" or "free-text." For example, some researchers treat postings (e.g., Airbnb rentals) on newsgroup websites or Facebook listings, medical records, and equipment and maintenance logs as semistructured, while HTML pages are treated as structured. Database researchers, as noted earlier, have a stronger view of what it means for data to be structured, and they largely treat only information stored in databases (with many limiting themselves to RDBs) as structured data. For such researchers, even XML documents are semistructured even with well-defined schemas, while HTML pages are unstructured.

Rather than argue about the merits or demerits of these terminological differences, we adopt a pragmatic viewpoint in this chapter. We consider HTML data as semistructured owing to the fair amount of regularity in how the content is presented on HTML pages. In several cases, the regularity is even programmatic, the best example being pages from the *Deep Web*, which is a term used often for dynamic webpages that are generated from structured databases with some templates or layouts. For example, the set of book pages from Amazon has the same layout for the author, title, price, comments, and other details, and a given such page is dynamically generated based on a query made by a user on the main Amazon search interface.[1] There are many other such situations where webpages

---

[1] Another way to think about dynamic webpages is that, caching and other such mechanisms aside, the HTML page *does not exist* (although the data for it does, in a database) until someone asks ("queries") for it.

Figure 5.1: A practical illustration of the web IE problem. We use bounding boxes to illustrate the elements that would need to be extracted. In some cases, the elements (like the "Contact us" link) may not be visible on the page itself, but they are obtained from the HTML via an < *a* href> tag or property. The KG fragment is illustrated in figure 5.2. The original webpage was taken from *lawyers.findlaw.com/lawyer/firm/auto-dealer-fraud/los-angeles/california*.

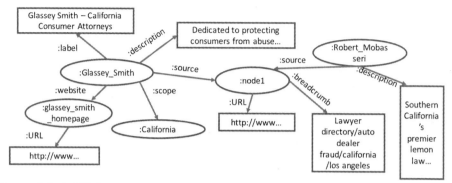

Figure 5.2: A KG fragment containing the extracted information from the webpage illustrated in figure 5.1.

are generated from the same database with the same template (program) and form a page class. Less extreme but still fairly regular, many page classes are not dynamic, but they still draw upon a common template. This is the case when we look at faculty pages (or course pages) on a given university's website. However, even in these situations, considerable heterogeneity exists. Even in the case of the Deep Web, page classes can be significantly different from one another and the original template-generating page may not be available to anyone outside the company or organization (and is also subject to change at any time). In the case of manually developed, nondynamic templates, differences can start emerging quickly even at the top domain level. For example, faculty pages from the engineering school and the business school may exhibit considerable difference in structure, even under the umbrella of a single university. Manually building web IEs for *every* page class is neither scalable nor sustainable in the long run. Building adaptive and robust web IEs that work for pages of the same class is a difficult enough task as is, and it is the primary focus of most web IEs proposed in the literature. However, some IE systems over the years have taken on the ambitious challenge of extracting key information from pages and page classes across various websites.

   Web IE is such an interesting problem that even its categorization attracts considerable diversity among researchers. One categorization that has become relatively popular is based on the *extraction target granularity* (e.g., are we building a system for record-level, page-level, and site-level IE tasks?). Record-level IE tasks involve the discovery of "record" (or *entity*) boundaries and their segmentation into separate attributes; page-level web IEs extract all data that are embedded in one webpage; site-level web IEs populate a database from pages of a web domain,[2] wherein the attributes of an extraction target are assumed to be spread across pages of a web domain. From the beginning of Web IE development, researchers have tended to devote more effort to developing record- and page-level data extraction, whereas industrial researchers have expressed more interest in building complete pipelines supporting site-level data extraction.

Web IE involves many challenges, some of which overlap with the challenges discussed in the previous chapter. For example, to achieve a high degree of automation, much human feedback and many manual annotations may be required, which limits both extraction generalization and adaptation. There is a clear trade-off that needs to be quantified before resources are allocated, because fewer annotations correspond to lower accuracy.

Volume is yet another challenge for web IE, especially in domains such as finance. Web IEs built over high-volume domains need to be scalable. In domains that are dynamic (i.e., the data gets stale quickly), streaming systems are obviously preferable. In the Big Data universe, this challenge is known as *velocity*. Streaming web IE can be highly challenging, especially considering that many machine learning techniques, including unsupervised algorithms, often need to see many documents (often over several epochs) before accurate inference is achieved or performance converges.

A more sociotechnical challenge that was not as relevant in the early days of the web, but is very relevant today, is that of privacy and ethics surrounding data collection and use. This challenge also applies to the problem of domain discovery earlier described. Some recent high-profile instances have shown that even scraping can be unethical, even though the data is public. In particular, Social Web domains require extra caution to be exercised because pages in these domains often contain personal information. Even if it is legal to do so, it may not be ethical. Beyond data collection, bias in training and testing are other concerns that must be dealt with in this context. The web may be diverse, but it also contains its fair share of racist, incorrect, or otherwise problematic information. If the extraction system is biased toward some kinds of attributes or text over others, this will inevitably lead to a scenario that does not work equally well for everyone.

A final challenge that we mention here is *maintenance*. A web IE that has been built and tuned, even for a specific website like Backpage.com, may end up breaking because the website undergoes changes in format or content. This problem is serious enough, and was recognized early enough in the development of web IE systems, that it has already spawned a considerable amount of research dedicated both to *detecting* when the extraction system has stopped working (i.e., producing meaningful results) and automatically repairing the system to get it functioning again.

---

[2] In this chapter, *web domain, top-level domain,* and *website* are all used interchangeably, with examples including craigslist.com and ebay.com. In contrast, a *webpage* is a specific HTML page. A web domain is also a webpage (called its *home page*).

5.2 Wrapper Generation

While traditional IE tools such as NER populate KGs from textual documents using sequence labels and other methods, web IE primarily involves the development and maintenance of wrapper generation systems, known for short as *wrappers*. Wrappers are designed to deal with webpages containing a diverse mix of information and structure, where the information contained in a web document is assumed to be defined by means of formatting markup tags. Wrapper generation systems can exploit these formatting instructions to define suitable wrappers for a set of similarly structured webpages.

However, wrappers based on very simple extraction rules are not able to effectively exploit these formatting instructions when dealing with pages with a complex structure. This has necessitated the development of different kinds of wrappers that are able to deal with specific kinds of pages. We enumerate three such page kinds here:

1. Pages that have a reasonable amount of text, and that require some amount of Natural Language Processing (NLP), most commonly, NER;
2. Pages that do not conform to a fixed schema, in that there is no separate description for the content categories on the page;
3. Pages with structural and syntactic constraints, which allows development of wrappers that are hybrid in nature (i.e., use both structural and natural-language features to extract information).

We note that modern wrappers exploit not only the structure within a web domain, but (just like domain discovery tools) can incorporate other contextual information such as hyperlinks, which are particularly relevant when the information needed to discover the attributes of an entity is nested under (or scattered across) many different webpages.

There has been a long tradition of work in wrapped generation, just like the NLP-based techniques covered in chapter 4. Because of this large body of work, it has become possible to synthesize many of the systems into one or more of several categories, including supervised, semisupervised, and unsupervised systems. Next, we describe work in each category in more detail.

5.2.1 Manually Constructed and Supervised Wrappers

In the wrapper generation literature, a manually constructed wrapper is generally taken to mean any wrapper building approach that requires the wrapper to be explicitly programmed using either high- or low-level tools. In other words, wrappers are not automatically constructed based on data and constraints. One of the earliest approaches for manual construction of web wrappers (called TSIMMIS) viewed the web IE task as one of programmatically building sets of pattern-matching expressions and assigning their outputs to variables. It did this by taking as input a specification file that declaratively stated (by a sequence of commands given by programmers) where the data of interest is located on the pages and how the data should be bundled into objects. Each command takes the form [variables, source, pattern], where *source* specifies the input text to be considered, *pattern* specifies how to find the text of interest within the source, and *variables* are a list of variables that hold the extracted results.

Other systems, such as Minerva, attempted to move beyond purely declarative approaches by combining their benefits with the flexibility of procedural programming in handling heterogeneity, irregularity, and exceptions. Minerva accomplished this combination by incorporating an explicit exception-handling mechanism inside a regular grammar. Exception-handling procedures are written in a special language called *Editor*. In the grammar used by Minerva, a set of productions is first defined with each production rule defining the structure of a nonterminal symbol (preceded by "$") of the grammar. For example, given a book review page, we may want to extract the book name, the reviewer name, the rating given by the reviewer to the book, and the text. The nonterminal productions $bName, $rName, $rate, and $text would be used to represent these attributes. Furthermore, suppose that the page were such that a book name was preceded by the HTML snippet "<b>Book Name</b>" and was followed by[3] "<b>." In the Minerva grammar, we could use a pattern such as "*(?<b>)," which matches everything before tag <b>, and place this pattern within a production rule such as <b>Book Name </b> $bName <b> to facilitate correct book name extraction (and similarly for the other attributes). A special, nonterminal $TP (Tuple Production) can also be used to insert a tuple in the database after each macro object (in this case, a "book," with all its attributes) has been parsed in terms of its attributes. For each production rule, it is possible to add an exception handler containing a piece of *Editor* code that can handles the irregularities found in the web data. Whenever the parsing of that production rule fails, an exception is raised and the corresponding exception handler is executed. This makes Minerva more robust than earlier systems like TSIMMIS; however, the rules and exceptions still have to be manually defined by a user.

Other influential examples of manually constructed wrappers include WebOQL (which is a functional language that relies on a data structure called a *hypertree* for querying and extracting information from the web and over semistructured data sets), W4F, which stands for WysiWyg Web Wrapper Factory, and is designed with WYSIWYG (what you see is what you get) support using smart wizards, and XWrap, which exploits formatting information in webpages to hypothesize about underlying semantic structures in the page. While all of these met with some success in their time, they were not able to scale and adapt with the explosive growth of the web.

As the brittleness of manually constructed web IEs became more apparent, and machine learning continued to evolve as a community, supervised WI started becoming more popu-

---

[3] This would happen if the very next line described another attribute of the book, such as "Reviewer," which would also be in bold (just like the attribute name "Book Name"); hence, the line itself would begin with <b>.

lar. Supervised wrappers take as input a set of webpages labeled with examples (of the data to be extracted) and output a wrapper. General users, rather than technical programmers, provide an initial set of labeled examples and the system (possibly via an interface) may suggest additional pages for the user to label, akin to the active learning paradigm in general machine learning. The user base of such systems can be broad, and they are cheaper to set up for a website, precisely because programming expertise is not required to the same extent as for manually constructed wrapper induction (WI) systems.

A good example is *Rapier*, which attempts field-level extraction using bottom- up, or *compression-based*, relational learning (i.e., it begins with the most specific rules and then replaces them with more general rules). Rapier learns single-slot extraction patterns that use syntactic and semantic information commonly employed in NLP, including a part-of-speech (POS) tagger and lexicons such as WordNet. Extraction rules consist of three distinct patterns: first is a prefiller pattern that matches text immediately preceding the filler, second is a pattern that matches the actual slot filler, and the last pattern is a postfiller pattern that matches the text immediately following the filler. Returning to the running example of books, an extraction rule for the book title might consist of a prefiller pattern that says that an extraction should be preceded by the the three "words" *Book*, *Name*, and **, a filler pattern that says that the name is a list of at most length 2, with the elements in the list labeled as "NN" or "NNS" by a POS tagger[4] and a postfiller pattern that is the word ** (see footnote 3 when describing Minerva). The precise syntax in which these rules are specified is not very important because it would depend on system implementation. The important point to note, though, is that the rules can employ complex cues, such as NLP outputs.

Another influential example is *Stalker*, which is a wrapper generation system that performs hierarchical data extraction by using an *embedded catalog (EC)* formalism to describe the structure of many types of "semistructured" documents. In the EC formalism, a page is described abstractly as a treelike structure with leaves as attributes to be extracted, and internal nodes are lists of tuples. For each node in the tree, the wrapper requires a rule for extracting the node from its parent. Additionally, for each list node, the wrapper needs a *list iteration* rule for breaking down the list into individual tuples. Stalker ultimately turns the complex problem of extracting data from an arbitrary document into several sequentially ordered (and easier) extraction tasks. The extractor is able to use multipass scans to handle missing attributes and multiple permutations. The actual extraction rules are generated via a *sequential covering* algorithm, which starts from *linear landmark automata* to cover the maximal number of positive examples, after which it attempts to generate new automata for the remaining examples. We illustrate an example of both a Stalker EC tree and rules in figure 5.3. The tree is simple to understand; it just says that a web document is

---

[4] In other words, the list contains one or two, singular or plural, common nouns.

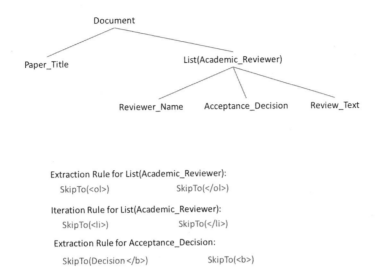

Figure 5.3: An EC model (above) of a hypothetical webpage describing reviews for academic papers, and some Stalker rules (below) for extracting reviewers and their accept/reject decisions.

a paper with a title, and a list of academic reviewers (who have reviewed that paper); each academic reviewer is described by their name, their acceptance decision (of the paper), and their review text. The Stalker rules, which mainly comprise tokens like *SkipTo*, are also intuitive to understand. For example, the list of academic reviewers is contained within the $< ol >$ and $< /ol >$ tags. The content within the tags can be further parsed to iterate over the attributes of an academic reviewer (the iteration rule in figure 5.3). The important aspect to remember about Stalker here is its EC representation of a webpage, as well as the simplicity of the rules, especially for dealing with fairly regular webpages containing nested and arraylike elements.

Supervised approaches have long been a popular way of tackling the wrapper generation problem. Besides Rapier and Stalker, other popular examples include SRV, WHISK, NoDoSE, WIEN, and DEByE. Similar to Rapier, SRV uses relational learning, but its algorithm is top-down rather than bottom-up. It frames web IE as a classification problem, wherein input documents are tokenized and all substrings of tokens (namely, fragments of text) are labeled as either positive (meaning it is an extraction target) or negative. SRV rules that are generated are logic-based and rely on token-based features and predicates that may be simple or relational. Simple features map a token into a discrete value (such as its length in terms of number of characters), while relational features map one token to another. Intuitively, the combination of relational and simple features, combined with a learning algorithm, can yield plausible rules. For example, SRV may be able to discover that the price of a product is a numeric word (possibly followed by a period and another numeric word), and occurs within an HTML tag. In contrast, WHISK uses a covering learning algorithm to generate multislot extraction rules. WHISK can be applied, not just to HTML documents, but also free-text and structured documents. WHISK rules are based on regular expression patterns that identify the context and exact delimiters of relevant phrases. To create the rules, it needs annotated training instances. WHISK learns rules top-down, starting from a general rule that covers all instances, and then extending the rule by adding one term at a time.

NoDoSE is even more interesting in that, rather than assuming that training examples can just be perfectly and completely obtained, it provides an interactive tool to its users to hierarchically decompose documents. It also differentiates between text and HTML code by having a separate, heuristic-based mining module for each. The goal of these modules is to infer a tree that describes the structure of the document. Given such a decomposition of a document, NoDoSE is able to automatically parse it to generate extraction rules.

Details of all these systems aside, we note that supervision in web IE arises in several forms, unlike with NER systems, where the primary source of supervision is annotation of named (and typed) entities within sentences and documents. NoDoSE, for example, uses supervision to infer an accurate treelike structure encoding the document, following which extraction rules are generated. On the other hand, Rapier is more traditional in the annotation-based supervision that it expects from users.

5.2.2 Semisupervised Approaches

Similar to the study of semisupervised NER approaches, semisupervised WI approaches use a variety of means to ensure that a wrapper can be learned without necessarily requiring large amounts of manual supervision. However, there are differences in how to reduce manual supervision. Some systems, like OLERA, accept incomplete, approximately correct examples from users for rule generation and are the equivalent of weakly supervised bootstrapping-based approaches in other areas of machine learning. Other systems, like IEPAD, require no labeled training pages at all, but do demand postprocessing effort from the user in order to select the correct target pattern and choose the data to be extracted. The majority of semisupervised approaches in web IE are built for record-level extraction tasks. Because extraction targets are unspecified for such systems, an interface is usually required for users to specify the extraction targets after the learning phase. The design of the graphical user interface (GUI) can play a role in the level of technical sophistication required from potential users. Brief descriptions of some of these systems are provided next, with citations of relevant papers in the section entitled "Bibliographic Notes," at the end of this chapter.

IEPAD was one of the earliest IE systems to generalize extraction patterns from unlabeled webpages by exploiting the fact that if a webpage contained multiple ("homogeneous") data records to be extracted, they are often rendered regularly using the same template (mainly for good visualization). Repetitive patterns can thus be discovered, assuming that the webpage is well encoded. By discovering the repetitive patterns, wrappers can be induced. To do so, IEPAD uses a data structure based on a binary suffix tree designed to discover repetitive patterns in a webpage. Because the original data structure only records the exact match for suffixes, IEPAD applies a center star algorithm to align multiple strings starting from each occurrence of a repeat and ending before the start of the next occurrence. A signature representation is used to denote the template to understand all data records.

In contrast, OLERA is a semisupervised IE system that acquires a *rough* example from the user for extraction rule generation. OLERA can learn extraction rules for pages containing single data records, which is not something that IEPAD can handle. OLERA executes three main operations. First, it encloses an information block of interest by leveraging approximate matching against a block that the user has marked in the rough example, and then generalizing an extraction pattern using a multiple string alignment technique. Second, it drills down or rolls up an information slot: *drilling down* allows the user to navigate from a text fragment to more detailed components, whereas *rolling up* combines several slots to form a meaningful information unit. Finally, just as in IEPAD, OLERA designates relevant information slots for schema specification.

Another approach that is similar to OLERA is Thresher, the GUI for which was designed to allow users to specify examples of content with semantic significance, by highlighting the content and describing their meaning via labeling. Thresher uses tree edit distance between the DOM subtrees of these specified examples to induce a wrapper, after which the user is allowed to associate RDF classes and predicates in an ontology with the nodes in the induced wrapper.

5.2.3 Unsupervised Approaches

Unsupervised IE systems do not use any labeled training examples and have no user interactions to generate a wrapper. Systems such as RoadRunner and EXALG are designed to solve page-level web IE, while others like DeLa and DEPTA (whose name stands for Data Extraction based on Partial Tree Alignment) are designed for record-level web IE. Compared to supervised systems, where extraction targets are specified by the users, the extraction target for unsupervised web IEs is defined as the data that is used to generate the page, or nontag textual content in data-rich regions of an input webpage. Because several schemas could potentially align with the training pages (due to the presence of nullable attributes), ambiguity is inevitable. Thus, rather than be completely unsupervised, practical unsupervised IEs often leave the choice of determining the right schema to users. Similarly, if not all data is needed, postprocessing may be required to select relevant data and assign it to the proper class in the ontology.

RoadRunner has been particularly influential as an unsupervised web IE; it frames the site generation process as an encoding of the original database content into strings of HTML code. Consequently, the extraction itself becomes akin to data *decoding*, with wrapper generation for a set of HTML pages corresponding to the inference of an HTML code grammar. RoadRunner uses the ACME matching technique to compare HTML pages of the same class. ACME, which stands for Align, Collapse, Match and Extract, was originally proposed by Crescenzi et al. (2001) as a technique to generate a wrapper by analyzing similarities and differences among some sample HTML pages of the class.

Using ACME, RoadRunner compares two webpages at a time by first aligning the matched tokens and collapsing the mismatched tokens. There are two kinds of mismatches: *string mismatches*, which are used to discover attributes (#PCDATA); and *tag mismatches*, which are used to discover iterators (+) and optionals (?). We illustrate these concepts using figure 5.4, which uses an example inspired by the original paper. The example showcases some of the more complex matching facilities that RoadRunner is capable of. For instance, in figure 5.4, the pages have a nested structure, with a list of books, and for each book, its editions are given. The algorithm starts by matching the sample (the second webpage) against the wrapper, which is initialized to equal webpage 1. The parsing first stops when a tag mismatch is encountered at the token <LI> (right before *Database Primer*). When trying to solve the mismatch looking for a possible iterator, RoadRunner does the following: first, based on the possible terminal tag (</LI> in the earlier line), the algorithm locates one candidate square occurrence on the wrapper right after (from <LI> all the way to the last occurrence of </LI>, as bounded by the dashed purple box); and second, it tries to match this candidate square against the upward portion of the wrapper. The square is matched backward, for example, by comparing the two occurrences of the terminal tag (the </LI> right at the end against the </LI> tag where the tag mismatch was first encountered), then moving to tokens $< /PI >$ and $< /PI >$ occurring before the occurrences of <LI>, and so on. This comparison is emphasized at the side of figure 5.4.

When trying to match the two fragments, *internal mismatches* can also be detected, such as involving the tokens $< /B >$ and $< P >$ in the graphic (bounded by a box). The internal mismatches can be dealt with in the same way that external mismatches are dealt with, meaning that the matching algorithm needs to be recursive. Every time there is a mismatch, a new matching procedure has to be started based on the ideas expressed here. The only difference is that this kind of recursive matching does not work by comparing one wrapper with one sample, but two different portions of the same object. In the example, the single external mismatch triggers two internal mismatches, one of which leads to discovery of the book editions, and the second of which leads to the identification of the optional pattern <I>Special!</I>. Without going into all the syntactic details of the final wrapper, we express it succinctly at the bottom of figure 5.4.

Because there can be several alignments, RoadRunner adopts union-free regular expression (UFRE) to reduce the complexity. The alignment result of the first two pages is then compared to the third page in the *page* class. The final wrapper is generated if RoadRunner succeeds in generalizing the wrapper each time a "mismatch" is found (i.e., when some

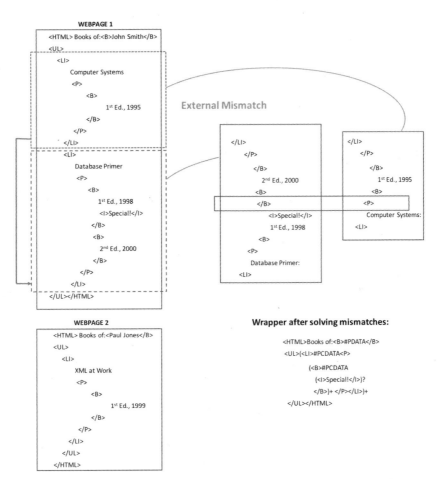

Figure 5.4: An overview of how RoadRunner performs unsupervised web IE.

token in the input sample does not comply with the grammar specified by the current wrapper). The final wrapper, therefore, is a common wrapper that has solved all mismatches encountered during parsing.

   Along with the module for template deduction, RoadRunner also provides modules for classification and labeling to facilitate wrapper construction. The first module, *Classifier*, analyzes pages and collects them into clusters with similar structural properties (the goal is to cluster together pages with the same template). The second module, *Labeler*, discovers *attribute names* for each page class. If RoadRunner is adapted to work with an ontology, the task of Labeler would be to assign concepts from the ontology to extractions from a set of pages belonging to the same class. Note that the RoadRunner system, as originally proposed, did not need any ontology or prior assumptions about the underlying schema or page contents; the schema was inferred along with the wrapper, and the system was fully capable of handling arbitrarily nested structures. Some preprocessing is required (e.g., an HTML page should be converted to an XHTML specification, which means that tags should be properly closed and nested), but these are not difficult to accomplish with mechanical tools. Experimentally, the algorithm was evaluated on some well-known websites at the time, including Buy.com and Amazon.com, and the authors showed that RoadRunner was able to successfully generate wrappers that matched many of the webpage samples and were consequently able to extract the requisite data on those pages.

   Besides RoadRunner, there are a number of other unsupervised web IE systems that have gained some influence. One such system is DEPTA, which is applicable to webpages that contain two or more data records in a data region. It relies on the insight that records of the same data region are reflected in the tag tree of a webpage under the same parent node. Hence, irrelevant substrings do not need to be compared as done in suffix-based approaches. The overall algorithm works in three steps: First, it builds the HTML tag tree for the webpage, and disregards text strings. Second, it compares substrings for all children under the same parent. This results in significant efficiencies. The final step handles situations when a data record is not rendered contiguously (an assumption made frequently in prior work). Recognition of data items or attributes in a record is accomplished using partial tree alignment, which is considered better than string alignment, as it takes structural cues into account. Because DEPTA was limited in handling nested records, a new algorithm called NET was later proposed, which used advanced techniques relying on visual cues to expand the scope of the system.

   Another unsupervised web IE system is DeLa, which is an extension of IEPAD and removes user interaction in extraction rule generalization while dealing with nested object extraction. It uses a novel WI algorithm called DSE (which stands for Data-rich Section Extraction), which extracts data-rich sections from webpages by comparing the DOM trees for two webpages from the same web domain. Data objects ultimately obtained by the system are transformed into a relational table, with multiple values of an attribute distributed across multiple table rows. Labels are assigned to the data table columns using heuristics (e.g., using maximal-prefix and maximal-suffix shared by all cells in the column). Potentially, this part of the system could be further enhanced using distant supervision techniques (e.g., Wikipedia or DBpedia concepts could be used to automatically label columns for "common" ontological types such as Country or Politician) if it were to be reimplemented in a more modern setting.

Finally, the EXALG system formulates the unsupervised WI problem in a novel way: by ingesting a set of pages assumed to be created from an unknown template T, as well as the values to be extracted. EXALG deduces the template T and uses it to extract the set of values from the encoded pages as an output. EXALG detects the unknown template by using techniques differentiating roles and equivalence classes. Per the former technique, occurrences with two varying paths of a particular token are understood to have different roles (e.g., it would assume that "Name" occurring in "Book Name" has a different role than when it occurs in "Reviewer Name"). The latter technique defines an equivalence class as a maximal set of tokens having the same occurrence frequencies over the training pages (called the occurrence-vector). The key insight here is that "template tokens" encompassing a data record have the same occurrence vector and form an equivalence class. To mitigate against the very real problem of false positives, the technique prevents data tokens from accidentally forming an equivalence class by filtering out equivalence classes with insufficient support (the number of pages containing the tokens) and size (the number of tokens in an equivalence class). Equivalence classes must also be mutually nested, and tokens within an equivalence class must be ordered, to comply with the hierarchical structure of the data schema. Equivalence classes that survive these checks can be used to construct the original template and thereby induce a wrapper.

5.2.4 Empirical Comparative Analyses

Given the wide variety of WI tools presented here, direct comparison of many of the tools can be a difficult proposition. Yet, without systematic comparison, it is difficult to ascertain progress, especially considering the nature of the problem. An influential survey has proposed that such a comparison be conducted along three dimensions: namely, the *task domain* or the difficulty of the Web IE task (i.e., why do certain Web IE systems fail to handle websites with some particular structure, while others succeed?), the techniques used in different systems, and finally, the user effort involved in the training process, as well as the system portability across different domains. From the user's point of view, the second dimension has been traditionally less important, but with the growth of GUIs and other efficient means of eliciting training data, it has become more important. Users may be willing to opt for a supervised system if acquiring labels and training data is easy but opt for a semisupervised or unsupervised system if it is laborious. If there are huge performance differences between using one technique or another, then the users may even be willing to put in some effort.

Many of the systems that we described in this chapter have indeed been compared across each of these three dimensions, mainly in terms of their capabilities and features used, rather than empirical performance on a common corpus (which unfortunately does not exist for web IE, unlike the data sets developed under MUC and other similar venues for NLP extraction tasks). Thus, we cannot claim that one system is better than another; however, some trends and limitations in the overall research area are revealed, as briefly documented here:

1. **Task domain dimension.** Analysis has shown that while manual and supervised web IE systems are primarily designed to extract information from cross-website pages, semisupervised and supervised web IE systems are mainly capable of extracting data from the template page, such as those found on the Deep Web. For better or for worse, there is a bias in the way unsupervised systems are designed: without the assumption of a common (or roughly common) template, they would not work well. This seems like a reasonable assumption, however, considering that they are not given labeled data. To take another example of analysis along this dimension, there is also considerable heterogeneity among wrappers in terms of their extraction levels (field-level, record-level, page-level, and site-level). While many wrappers are now able (or can be adapted) to extract at the record or even page level (e.g., RoadRunner and STALKER), almost no WI systems exist, to our knowledge, that can operate at the site level. Thus, this is clearly an open area of research. Other kinds of analyses along the task domain dimension are also possible, such as with respect to extraction target variation (e.g., is the IE robust to missing attributes and multivalued attributes?), template variation (e.g., can the IE support disjunctive rules and sequential patterns for rule generalization, to handle format variations in data instances?) and even non-HTML support.

2. **Technique-based dimension.** As observed in this chapter, many techniques have been proposed for WI over the decades. An analysis of these systems along the technique-based dimension could involve aspects such as the *number of passes* required over an input document to facilitate extraction (some wrappers, such as DEByE, require multiple passes, although most wrappers need only one); the *types of extraction rules* (e.g., is the wrapper relying on regular grammar or more powerful first-order logic?) induced by the wrapper; the *features* being supported by the wrapper (e.g., wrappers such as W4F use DOM tree paths, rather than just tag; literal or delimiter-bases content); the *tokenization schemes* supported by the wrappers (most of which support tag-level tokenization but some of which can support word-level tokenization, as well as tag-level encoding schemes to translate input training pages into tokens); and perhaps most important, the type of *learning algorithm* employed by the WI. Manual wrappers do not have any embedded learning algorithm, while wrappers such as DEPTA, DeLa, and IEPAD rely heavily on pattern mining. Even among supervised algorithms

that use some kind of linear programming or set covering, a distinction can be made between whether the learning occurs top-down (SRV, WHISK) or bottom-up (Rapier, WIEN, and Stalker).

3. **Automation-based dimension.** Analyses of web IE systems can be conducted with respect to such aspects as *user expertise* (e.g., many of the manual systems require users to have programming background in order to write good or even syntactically correct extraction rules); *fetching support* (e.g., does the WI system allow retrieval of pages dynamically using the URL?); *applicability* (how easily the approach can be extended to different domains due to architectural design decisions such as modularity); and even *output* or *application programming interface (API)* support, since some systems make it easy to retrieve the extracted data, but others can be accessed only programmatically or using specific data formats such as XML. Just as with previous dimensions, different wrappers offer different trade-offs among these various aspects. For example, concerning applicability, while manual and supervised systems often are modular and can be flexibly extended to other domains (assuming, of course, that a user is available to input the requisite amount of supervision), unsupervised systems are designed only for certain websites or domains. With respect to user expertise, while IEPAD (and OLERA) do not require labeling prior to pattern discovery, they do require postlabeling. Only DeLA seems to have successfully addressed the problem of assigning appropriate labels to extracted data in an unsupervised manner, though recently developed zero-shot learning techniques in NLP and computer vision communities may also be applicable (for the unsupervised schema and label assignment problem) in novel reimplementations of some of these systems, considering the broad availability of external concept data sets like DBPedia and WordNet.

5.3   Beyond Wrappers: Information Extraction over Structured Data

Thus far, we have mainly considered IE for webpages. Although webpages are not natural-language sources (despite the high prevalence of natural-language content on the webpage), the assumption still is that they are relatively free-form compared to tables or graphs. Yet tables and databases have become very common on the web, with some referring to the vast set of databases powering dynamic webpages as the Deep Web. We already discussed the Deep Web earlier in this chapter, in the context of wrapper generation. To recap, when we search for a product on an e-commerce website like Amazon, the webpage for the product is usually not a precreated (or even stored) HTML; rather, it is created on the fly using entries on that product in internal Amazon databases. This allows the webpage to contain up-to-date information, be highly standardized (since only the metastructure of the webpage and how it links to, and incorporates, database entries on the fly), and not be overly sensitive to a database that is always highly in flux due to the frequency of product

sales and introductions. According to most estimates, the Deep Web far trumps the normal
web in size (by factors as large as 90 to 100 times).

The reason for bringing this up here is to illustrate that, when it comes to web sources,
the information-generating sources may predominantly be structured rather than natural
language. While much of the Deep Web is inaccessible directly (one cannot obtain the
Amazon or Walmart e-commerce databases althrough Google queries, or even through
scraping, although parts of the database may be obtained through a carefully managed
crawl), there is a growing movement on the internet to publish structured data sets directly
and make them queryable through open APIs. One good example, which we detail in part
V, is government data [e.g., the US government has released a large number of raw data
sets through portals like data.gov; besides federal efforts, some states and counties (and
even cities) have been instrumental in making their data sets public]. Some agencies and
federal bureaus, such as the Bureau of Labor Statistics (BLS), have had a long history of
making their data (largely structured) public. These tabular, tablelike, or otherwise highly
structured data sets can serve as rich sets of information with which to populate KGs.

Why would extracting KG nodes, relations, and literal attributes from tables be so hard?
Intuitively, it would seem that a table is a simple data structure where the type of an entity,
such as a country, is a column header, and the rows contain and describe the actual entities
(e.g., US, Switzerland). But in reality, this is not the case with many tables. However,
empirical observation has shown that there is no one type of table on the web. There is
considerable heterogeneity, as expressed in the examples illustrated in figures 5.5 and 5.6.
Crestan and Pantel (2011) were among the earliest authors who attempted to provide a
classification of the different types of HTML tables actually observed on the web. Their
taxonomy includes two broad categories:

1. **Relational knowledge tables.** These are subclassified into *listings*,[5] *attribute/value*,
   matrix (possibly subclassified further as *matrix calendar*), *enumeration*, and *form*.
2. **Layout tables.** These are subclassified further into *navigational* and *formatting*.

Semiautomatically detecting the type of the table is itself a challenging problem with
imperfect accuracy. Once detected, IE modules designed to handle that table type could
be used, but these do not have perfect accuracy either. One may also encounter a long tail
of tables (that could only be defined as type "other" since they may not fit well, or only fit
loosely, in the taxonomy described previously); see figure 5.7 for an example. Hence, this
continues to be an active and important area of research; we provide important references
in the "Bibliographic Notes" section.

Even when fixing the table type, some tables can be complicated. Consider, for example, the table in figure 5.8. This table was taken from Wikipedia (https://en.wikipedia.

---

[5] This is itself subclassified further into *vertical* and *horizontal* listings.

Horizontal listing

iPhone	Released with	Release date	Final supported OS	Support ended
iPhone	iPhone OS 1.0	June 29, 2007	iPhone OS 3.1.3	June 20, 2010
iPhone 3G	iPhone OS 2.0	July 11, 2008	iOS 4.2.1	March 3, 2011
iPhone 3GS	iPhone OS 3.0	June 19, 2009	iOS 6.1.6	September 18, 2013
iPhone 4	iOS 4.0	June 21, 2010	iOS 7.1.2	September 17, 2014
iPhone 4S	iOS 5.0	October 14, 2011	iOS 9.3.5	September 12, 2016
iPhone 5	iOS 6.0	September 21, 2012	iOS 10.3.3	September 18, 2017
iPhone 5C	iOS 7.0	September 20, 2013	iOS 10.3.3	September 18, 2017
iPhone 5S	iOS 7.0	September 20, 2013	latest iOS	(current)
iPhone 6 (Plus)	iOS 8.0	September 19, 2014	latest iOS	(current)
iPhone 6S (Plus)	iOS 9.0	September 25, 2015	latest iOS	(current)
iPhone SE	iOS 9.3	March 31, 2016	latest iOS	(current)
iPhone 7 (Plus)	iOS 10.0	September 16, 2016	latest iOS	(current)
iPhone 8 (Plus)	iOS 11.0	September 22, 2017	latest iOS	(current)
iPhone X	iOS 11.0.1	November 3, 2017	latest iOS	(current)
iPhone XS (Max)	iOS 12	September 21, 2018	latest iOS	(current)
iPhone XR	iOS 12	October 26, 2018	latest iOS	(current)

Navigational

Amazon Music — Stream millions of songs
Amazon Drive — Cloud storage from Amazon
6pm — Score deals on fashion brands
AbeBooks — Books, art & collectibles
ACX — Audiobook Publishing Made Easy
Alexa — Actionable Analytics for the Web
Amazon Business — Everything For Your Business

Amazon Fresh — Groceries & More Right To Your Door
AmazonGlobal — Ship Orders Internationally
Home Services — Handpicked Pros Happiness Guarantee
Amazon Inspire — Digital Educational Resources
Amazon Rapids — Fun stories for kids on the go
Amazon Restaurants — Food delivery from local restaurants
Amazon Web Services — Scalable Cloud Computing Services

Audible — Download Audiobooks
Book Depository — Books With Free Delivery Worldwide
Box Office Mojo — Find Movie Box Office Data
ComiXology — Thousands of Digital Comics
CreateSpace — Indie Print Publishing Made Easy
DPReview — Digital Photography
East Dane — Designer Men's Fashion

Fabric — Sewing, Quilting & Knitting
Goodreads — Book reviews & recommendations
IMDb — Movies, TV & Celebrities
Shopbop — Designer Fashion Brands
MYHABIT — Private Fashion Designer Sales Need
Jungle.com — Shop Online in India
Kindle Direct Publishing — Indie Digital Publishing Made Easy
Prime Now — FREE Delivery on Everyday Items

Amazon Photos — Unlimited Photo Storage Free With Prime
Woot! — Deals and Shenanigans
Zappos — Shoes & Clothing
Souq.com — Shop Online in the Middle East
TenMarks.com — Math Activities for Kids & Schools
Amazon Warehouse — Great Deals on Quality Used Products
Whole Foods Market — America's Healthiest Grocery Store
Withoutabox — Submit to Film Festivals
Subscribe with Amazon — Discover & try subscription services

Attribute/value

Brand	Apple Inc.
Manufacturer	Foxconn[1] (on contract) Pegatron[1] (on contract)
Slogan	*Say hello to the future*
Generation	11th
Model	A1865 (with Qualcomm modem) A1901 (with Intel modem) A1902 (sold in Japan)[2]
Compatible networks	GSM, CDMA2000, EV-DO, HSPA+, LTE, LTE Advanced
First released	November 3, 2017
Availability by Region	November 3, 2017 [show] November 23, 2017 [show] November 24, 2017 [show] December 1, 2017 [show] December 7, 2017 [show] December 8, 2017 [show] December 22, 2017 [show]
Discontinued	September 12, 2018
Predecessor	iPhone 7 / iPhone 7 Plus
Successor	iPhone XS / iPhone XS Max iPhone XR
Type	Smartphone
Form factor	Slate
Dimensions	H: 143.6 mm (5.65 in) W: 70.9 mm (2.79 in) D: 7.7 mm (0.30 in)

Figure 5.5: Illustrative examples of the *horizontal listing*, *attribute/value*, and *navigational* web table types.

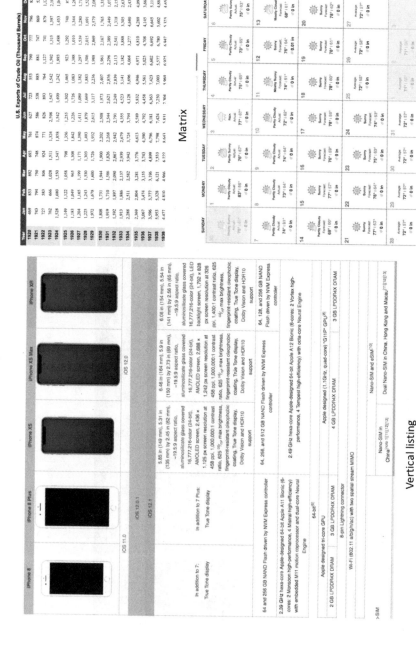

Figure 5.6: Illustrative examples of the *vertical listing*, *matrix*, and *matrix calendar* web table types.

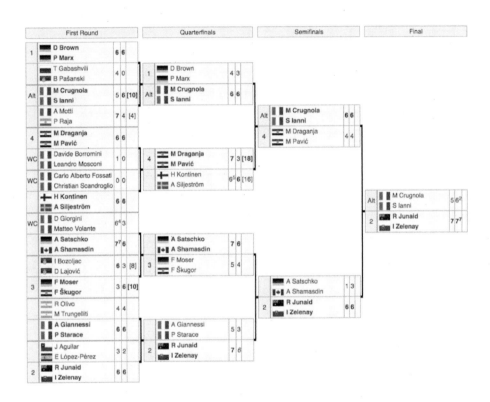

Figure 5.7: An "other" table type illustration that does not fit neatly into the taxonomy described in the text.

Pollster/Client	Date	Area	Sample size											
YouGov/The Times	13–14 Aug	GB	1,625	30%	21%	20%	4%	1%	1%	8%	0%	14%	2%	9%
BMG/The Independent	7–12 Aug	GB	1,515	31%	25%	19%	3%	1%	1%	6%	0%	12%	2%	6%
ComRes/The Daily Telegraph	9–11 Aug	GB	2,011	31%	27%	16%	3%	0%	1%	4%	0%	16%	2%	4%
Survation	6–11 Aug	UK	2,040	28%	24%	21%	4%	0%	0%	3%	–	15%	4%	4%
	10 Aug													
Richard Braine becomes leader of UKIP[7]														
Opinium/The Observer	8–9 Aug	GB	2,003	31%	28%	13%	4%	1%	1%	5%	0%	16%	0%	3%
YouGov/The Times	5–6 Aug	GB	1,628	31%	22%	21%	4%	0%	0%	7%	0%	14%	1%	9%
	1 Aug													
Brecon and Radnorshire by-election[8]														
YouGov/The Times	29–30 Jul	GB	2,066	32%	22%	19%	4%	1%	0%	8%	0%	13%	1%	10%
Ipsos MORI	26–30 Jul	GB	1,007	34%	24%	20%	4%	1%	1%	6%	0%	9%	1%	10%
ComRes/Britain Elects	26–28 Jul	GB	2,004	29%	30%	16%	3%	1%	1%	5%	0%	15%	2%	1%
Deltapoll/The Mail on Sunday	25–27 Jul	GB	2,001	30%	25%	18%	4%	1%	1%	4%	2%	14%	1%	5%
YouGov/The Sunday Times	25–26 Jul	GB	1,697	31%	21%	20%	5%	1%	0%	8%	0%	13%	1%	10%
Opinium/The Observer	24–26 Jul	GB	2,006	30%	28%	16%	5%	1%	1%	5%	0%	15%	1%	2%
ComRes/Sunday Express	24–25 Jul	GB	2,029	28%	27%	19%	3%	1%	1%	4%	0%	16%	0%	1%
YouGov/The Times	23–24 Jul	GB	1,715	25%	19%	23%	4%	1%	1%	9%	0%	17%	1%	2%
	23 Jul													
Boris Johnson becomes leader of the Conservative Party, and Prime Minister the next day														
	22 Jul													
Jo Swinson becomes leader of the Liberal Democrats[9]														
YouGov/The Times	16–17 Jul	GB	1,749	25%	21%	20%	4%	1%	0%	8%	0%	19%	1%	4%
ComRes/Britain Elects	15–16 Jul	GB	2,038	25%	28%	17%	4%	0%	1%	5%	1%	19%	1%	3%
ComRes/Sunday Express	10–11 Jul	GB	1,791	24%	28%	15%	3%	1%	1%	5%	1%	20%	2%	4%
Survation	10–11 Jul	GB	1,012	23%	29%	19%	4%	1%	1%	3%	–	20%	1%	6%

Figure 5.8: A tabular data source (containing information on polling from an instance of the UK general election, accessed on Wikipedia on October 18, 2019) for possible KG construction.

org/wiki/Opinion_polling_for_the_next_United_Kingdom_general_election) on October 18, 2019, and contains interesting data on opinion polling that, if extracted into a KG, could serve a useful purpose in forecasting and other such problem areas. However, extracting data from this table is no easy feat. While many of the columns contain numerical attributes, the numbers are not interpretable without both context and column headers. In this case, the column headers (not shown) are either abbreviations for UK political parties (such as Con or Lib Dem), which would be difficult to link to canonical entities without explicit domain knowledge, or for specific agendas such as Brexit. Other columns represent the area, which itself often contains an acronym value (e.g., GB stands for Great Britain), and in the case of the second column, a date range. Ontologizing such a data set is itself a challenging problem,[6] while extraction would be even more so, especially considering that the table would not normally come in a spreadsheet, but rather would be embedded within an HTML page.

Currently, state-of-the-art tools cannot easily handle such data sets without significant upfront modeling and annotation effort. However, the broader problem of table understanding has been picking up steam in the web IE research community, building on important work that has been published over the last decade. One compromise often made in many of these papers is to assume that the input, when it comes to the extraction system, takes the form of a well-formed spreadsheet. This may not be completely unreasonable because a web table understanding pipeline could be decomposed into two steps: extract a table from HTML and write it out as a CSV (or other similarly formatted) spreadsheet, and then use a more advanced IE system specifically designed to operate on spreadsheets. Some noise in the first process is inevitable, but it can be adequately addressed with state-of-the-art machine learning, especially with the availability of massive open corpora obtained and released by projects such as Web Data Commons.

An example of the second technique is the system published by Chen and Zipf (2017), which specifically addressed the problem of identifying spreadsheet properties that were hoped to lead to transformation programs that would eventually lead to automated conversion of spreadsheets into RDBs. Spreadsheet properties here are defined to be aggregation rows, aggregation columns, hierarchical data, and other elements. Identifying spreadsheet properties is akin to parsing the structure of the spreadsheet (but in a semantic sense), which is not dissimilar from WI on a set of webpages. In their work, they used *rule-assisted active learning*, wherein crude, easy-to-write rules provided by users are integrated into an active learning framework and are used to save labeling effort via the generation of additional high-quality, labeled data in the initial training phase. Experimentally, the approach

---

[6] One reason for this is that, while some cell values are clearly "values" or KG literals ("attributes"), others are instances ("entities"), and many are even concepts. Furthermore, subtables and rows are akin to *events* (opinion polls) due to a clear spatiotemporal dependence and the presence of actors, sources, and other event-centric arguments. Compiling all of these elements into a single ontology is not straightforward.

was able to perform impressively even with minimal training data and was robust to low quality in the initially provided rules. Whether the approach would be able to perform well on "wild" data, such as the formatted table in figure 5.8, is open to debate.

Another approach, proposed at roughly the same time, profiled the potential of web tables for augmenting cross-domain KGs like DBpedia and YAGO (detailed further in part V). The motivation for using tables is that the original cross-domain KGs have a low degree of completeness and are also far from correct (e.g., the population of the US changes every year, depending on data availability; however, the updated number may not appear in DBpedia for some time). In contrast, tables of the web, when properly extracted and analyzed, contain up-to-date information from many categories in web KGs that frequently become outdated. The cross-domain KG augmentation approach mentioned earlier compares several data fusion strategies for incorporating table knowledge into KGs, and determines that some strategies work better than others. The reason why this work, as an empirical study, is important is because it shows that even when we don't use web tables to construct KGs from scratch, we could still use them to improve existing KGs, or KGs that have been extracted over ordinary webpages and natural-language documents. In keeping with motivation, several other papers have been, and continue to be, proposed in extracting data from tables and mapping them to KGs (including deep learning approaches). We do not believe there is consensus yet on this problem, though progress is being made. We provide instructive pointers for the interested researcher in the "Bibliographic Notes" section.

5.4   Concluding Notes

The web is the richest and more voluminous source of data in existence today, and large swathes of it are accessible publicly. However, before we can do complex analytics or answer questions on such webpages, we have to find the relevant data (domain discovery, as covered in chapter 3) and then develop web IEs for constructing a KG over the data. This chapter covered web IE techniques and challenges, particularly wrapper generation. Wrappers were first proposed in the 1990s for parsing the structure and content in webpages to extract entities and attributes, and they have come a long way since then, with the development of numerous supervised, semisupervised, and unsupervised variants.

It is important to note that very frequently, web sources cannot be classed along neat lines as structured or unstructured, and neither can a real-world web IE system. Frequently, a combination of assumptions and heuristics yields the best performance; in a real sense, many web IE approaches (if not all IE approaches) are hybrid due to the restrictive quality requirements of downstream applications that must consume IE outputs and the constructed KG. An interesting use-case of a real-world, effective hybrid web IE system executed over semistructured data is the DBpedia project, which has been hugely influential in the Semantic Web community. We provide details on DBpedia in part V; in this chapter, we note that DBpedia is a KG that has been constructed over structured data (namely, infobox attributes) over Wikipedia webpages. Because Wikipedia webpages are not free-form webpages, but rather have a somewhat predictable metastructure, including the infoboxes, links to other Wikipedia pages, a chapterlike structure, and reasonably high quality due to crowdsourced vetting, IE techniques such as those used by DBpedia can account for such regularities in delivering a higher-quality KG that might be output by a program that makes no such assumptions or is not developed to explicitly look for, and extract from, Wikipedia infoboxes.

Finally, we concluded the chapter with a note on extracting KG entities and attributes from web tables. Contrary to perception, web tables can be as messy as web documents, and extracting KG entities from them is problematic, as the entity could be a row or a value in a cell. Columns may represent attribute values, but they also could contain identifiers for other entities. Doing representation learning and information extraction over tables continues to be a new and exciting area, therefore—one that is poised to become still more important as more raw data is released in the form of tables due to efforts such as open data and open government.

5.5 Software and Resources

Unlike NER and other kinds of IE on natural language, open-source and widely used tool-kits for web IE are rare. This may be because many of the classic algorithms mentioned in this chapter were developed and first published more than two decades ago (in most cases); even if implementations were released at the time, they are likely not relevant anymore and will have to be reimplemented for modern HTML pages and standards than were prevalent in the early days of the web. For many of the algorithms, we do recommend a reimplementation. For those looking for off-the-shelf tools that work reasonably well, we recommend w3ilb (https://github.com/scrapy/w3lib) and scrapely (https://github.com/scrapy/scrapely). The former is useful for working with various kinds of web data, including HTML, forms, and URLs. The latter is more closely related to the content of this chapter, and it is also useful for extracting structured data from HTML pages. Even if *Scrapely* is not directly used or preferred, it can still be used to preprocess the HTML page in a way that then makes it more amenable to the application of advanced algorithms, including recurrent neural networks and sequence-labeling architectures. Another useful package that is implemented in Python and that is invaluable for working with, and preprocessing, web data, is *Beautiful Soup* (https://www.crummy.com/software/BeautifulSoup/bs4/doc/).

In some cases, it is possible to locate a version of the source code (of the more advanced algorithms). For example, RoadRunner maintains a homepage at http://www.dia.uniroma3.it/db/roadRunner/, with resources for publications, experimental results, and downloads. It is also possible to find implementations of web extractors hosted on GitHub, but these should be treated with caution, as they may not have undergone rigorous testing or quality control.

However, there are some excellent commercial tools available for web IE and crawling. One example is Inferlink, which offers domain discovery and web IE services (http://www. inferlink.com/). Others include Web Scraper (https://webscraper.io/), Scrapinghub (https:// scrapinghub.com/data-services), PromptCloud (https://www.promptcloud.com/), and Web Data Extraction Services (https://webdataextractionservices.com/), to list only a few options. Some are much more specialized (e.g., for e-commerce crawling and product matching) than others. An advantage of having so many service providers in this space is that one could obtain a reasonable amount of crawled and extracted data (via a customized process) relatively inexpensively.

5.6 Bibliographic Notes

Many approaches to web IE and WI systems, including machine learning and pattern-mining techniques, have been proposed, with various degrees of automation. The survey by Chang et al. (2006) condenses and synthesizes the previously proposed taxonomies for IE tools developed by leading researchers in this area. This chapter is largely based on the core material in that survey, as it was written shortly after the main WI techniques had become established as mainstream.

As noted in the previous chapter, the Message Understanding Conferences (MUCs) inspired the early work in web IE. There are five main tasks defined for text IE: named entity recognition (NER), coreference resolution, template element construction, template relation construction, and scenario template production. The significance of the MUCs in the field of IE motivates some researchers to classify IE approaches into different classes, as pointed out as well by Chang et al. (2006): *MUC approaches*, evidenced by work from Riloff et al. (1993), Huffman (1996), Kim and Moldovan (1995), Krupka (1995), Soderland et al. (1995), among others published during that era; and *post-MUC approaches*, evidenced by work from Soderland (1999), Mooney (1999), Freitag (1998), Kushmerick et al. (1997), Hsu and Dung (1998), and Muslea et al. (1999), among others.

Note that even as early as the late 1990s, enough wrapper systems had emerged that authors such as Hsu and Dung (1998) had begun taxonomizing them into categories (e.g., handcrafted wrappers using general programming languages, heuristic-based wrappers, wrappers using specially designed programming languages or tools, and WI approaches). Chang et al. (2006) respected this taxonomy and compared WI systems from the user's point of view by distinguishing IE tools based on the degree of automation. Consequently, their findings showed that IE tools could be categorized into (1) systems that need programmers, (2) systems that need annotation examples, (3) annotation-free systems, and (4) semisupervised systems.

These are not the only categorizations that exist: similar kinds of groupings were also proposed over the years by Muslea et al. (1999), Kushmerick and Thomas (2003), Sarawagi (2002), Kuhlins and Tredwell (2002), and Laender, Ribeiro-Neto, Da Silva, et al. (2002).

There were differences between how these authors looked at the web IE problem; for instance, Muslea et al. (1999) chose to categorize based on input document type and the structure and constraints assumed for the extraction patterns, Kushmerick and Thomas (2003) chose to categorize IE based on only two distinct categories (finite-state and relational), and Laender, Ribeiro-Neto, Da Silva, et al. (2002) proposed a taxonomy based on the primary *technique* used by each tool to generate a wrapper. Sarawagi (2002) classified wrappers into three categories depending on the extraction task (i.e., is the wrapper a record-level wrapper, a page-level wrapper, or a site-level wrapper?). The classification by Kuhlins and Tredwell (2002) may be the most simple (but perhaps not as useful for researchers), based on commercial versus noncommercial availability.

This discussion shows the importance of web IE (and WI, in particular) to the AI and World Wide Web communities. We are now in the phase, in fact, where metasurveys can be written about web IE tools rather than just surveys. The approach that we took for this chapter has elements of both a survey and a metasurvey, though we use specific system examples to convey the concepts where applicable. In particular, details on manually constructed and supervised wrapper systems, such as TSIMMIS, Minerva, WebOQL, W4F, XWrap, Rapier, Stalker, SRV, WHISK, NoDoSE, WIEN, and DEByE may be found in Hammer et al. (1997), Crescenzi and Mecca (1998), Arocena and Mendelzon (1998), Sahuguet and Azavant (2001), Liu et al. (2000), Mooney (1999), Muslea et al. (1999), Freitag (1998), Soderland (1999), Adelberg (1998), Kushmerick et al. (1997), and Laender, Ribeiro-Neto, Da Silva, et al. (2002), respectively. Details on semisupervised approaches mentioned in the chapter, such as OLERA, IEPAD, and Thresher, may be found in Chang and Kuo (2004), Chang and Lui (2001), and Hogue and Karger (2005). Details on unsupervised approaches, such as RoadRunner, EXALG, DEPTA, and DeLA, may be found in the papers by Crescenzi et al. (2001), Arasu and Garcia-Molina (2003), Liu et al. (2003), and Wang and Lochovsky (2002).

Toward the end of the chapter, we covered more recent work, including web IE for tables and dynamic webpages, such as those found on the Deep Web. For the former topic, we recommend Cafarella et al. (2008), Etzioni et al. (2005), Cafarella et al. (2009), and Gatterbauer et al. (2007). A related reference, for learning more about web-scale table census and classification (including the table types introduced earlier), is Crestan and Pantel (2011). For the latter, a good reading list should include Chen and Zipf (2017), Liu, Meng, and Meng (2009), Lehmann et al. (2012), Furche et al. (2013), An et al. (2007), and Hong (2010).

5.7 Exercises

1. Suppose that you were crawling the full website lawyers.findlaw.com (we showed an example webpage in figure 5.1, along with the KG fragment that would be extracted by a good web IE system in figure 5.3). How might you use the techniques described

in this chapter to convert this website to a rich KG representation? Would a system like RoadRunner be useful to apply in such a use-case?

2. Again using figure 5.3 as an example, can you design an EC model and some Stalker rules for the webpage shown in figure 5.1?

3. Can you think of example domains where both web IE and NER techniques (from the previous chapter, for instance) would have to be considered in tandem to give you a KG such as in figure 5.2? Give a rudimentary schematic of what a webpage from the domain you have in mind might look like.

4. With reference to the previous discussion in the chapter on web tables and information extraction, write down the table types of the three tables shown here.

iPhone	Release date	Final supported OS
iPhone	June 29, 2007	iPhone OS 3.1.3
iPhone 3G	July 11, 2008	iOS 4.2.1
iPhone 3GS	June 19, 2009	iOS 6.1.6
iPhone 4	June 21, 2010	iOS 7.1.2
iPhone 4S	October 14, 2011	iOS 9.3.5
iPhone 5	September 21, 2012	iOS 10.3.3
iPhone 5C	September 20, 2013	iOS 10.3.3

Table type: _____

PlayStation 4

Developer	Sony Interactive Entertainment
Manufacturer	Sony, Foxconn[1]
Product family	PlayStation
Type	Home video game console
Generation	Eighth generation

Table type: _____

	U.S. Exports of Crude Oil (Thousand Barrels)											
Year	Jan	Feb	Mar	Apr	May	Jun	Jul	Aug	Sep	Oct	Nov	Dec
1920	469	853	892	693	761	627	723	553	790	777	796	823
1921	743	794	750	748	874	586	538	885	881	747	869	525
1922	727	583	806	924	771	826	893	764	1,127	741	879	1,122
1923	762	666	1,028	1,511	1,324	2,598	1,547	1,542	1,592	1,315	1,397	2,103

Table type: _____

5. Mark a single triple on the table image (circle the subject, predicate, and object, and mark them with "s," "p," and "o," respectively).

6 Relation Extraction

Overview. Thus far in this book, the focus has been on extracting entities, whether from text or semistructured documents like webpages. However, the edges in a knowledge graph (KG) are relationships that exist between pairs of entities. Also, higher-order entities, such as events, serve an important purpose in modern KGs that explore complex domains such as geopolitics. This chapter introduces and covers techniques on relation and event extraction to construct such KGs. Although research on relation and event information extraction (IE) has been ongoing for a while now, empirical performance is still low compared to other IE subareas like Named Entity Recognition (NER), and there is still a long way to go. Recent progress has been encouraging, and some systems have been deployed in the real world.

6.1 Introduction

When constructing KGs, NER can be used to get the nodes in the KG. However, a KG also contains *relations*, such as *spouse_of* and *capital_of*. To get these relations, a different brand of IE has to be executed on the corpus. This kind of IE, relation extraction (RE), is the problem of detecting and classifying *relationships* between entities extracted from the text and involves its own set of challenges, being a significantly more difficult problem than NER. We illustrate RE via the following examples:

1. **spouse_of:** [John] was married to [Mary] in 1929.
2. **employed_by:** [Hardy] has been working for [Calmet Corporation] since he was a teenager.
3. **member:** The [Pepper Jack club] recently convinced [Mary Poppins] to join.

In these examples, mentions of named entities are in brackets, and named entity types are omitted for clarity. The directionality of the relation should be evident from the context (although it is harder for machines to do so automatically); some relations, such as spouse_of, are symmetric and bidirectional. An interesting point that is conveyed even by the simple illustrations given here is that, unlike named entities, where it is possible to distinguish the "mentions" in the text and then type them with a concept in the ontology, the relation "instances" cannot be described as cleanly at the mention level. Instead, a pair of entity mentions itself serves as a proxy for a relation instance, and the primary task is to determine if a relation of that type indeed exists between the two entities. In practice, it does not make sense to actually distinguish between relation "instances" and "types." The problem is instead formulated as one of *existence*—that is, does the relation employed_by exist between a given pair of entity mentions *(Hardy, Calmet Corporation)*?

RE may be classified as being *global-* or *mention*-level. Global RE is expected to produce a list of entity pairs between which a semantic relation exists. It takes as input a large text corpus and produces a global list of semantically related entity pairs as output (along with the relation itself). In contrast, mention-level RE takes as input both an entity pair and the sentence containing it, and also has to identify whether a certain relation exists for that entity pair within the context of the sentence. Both global- and mention-level RE systems have been actively researched in the literature. To understand the difference, consider again the example sentence for employed_by. Mention-level RE can determine (for an ideal system) that there is an employed_by relationship between Hardy and Calmet Corporation, but it cannot determine the nature of employment. However, another sentence (or context) may indicate that Hardy is now the chief executive officer (CEO) of this company, which would allow global RE to produce the fact that a more specific relation CEO_of (which is a *subtype* of the inverse relation *employs*) exists between Hardy and Calmet Corporation.

As with NER, we note that the set of relationship types (and subtypes) that are within scope for the RE system is specified by a predefined ontology. In many cases, the ontology constrains the named entity types between which a relation can be defined. For example, for the employed_by relation, an acceptable domain would be instances of the concept PERSON, and an acceptable range would be instances of the concept ORGANIZATION.

Much of the work on RE is based on the task definition from the Automatic Content Extraction (ACE) program and ontology. ACE focuses on binary relations (i.e., relations between two entities), with the two entities involved referred to as arguments. For example, the employed_by relation in the previous example could be described by one of several relation subtypes in ACE, including EMPLOY-EXEC, EMPLOY-STAFF, or even EMPLOY-undetermined (the last being true in this case), depending on the type of employment relation described in the sentence. We describe ACE in more detail in the next section.

We note that although RE may seem independent from NER, the quality of the two can be intertwined. Complex entity types, as well as errors in either entity extraction or typing, lead to problems for RE, which in typical formulations is a downstream task relative to NER. RE and NER can also interact in the context of another important problem (namely, *event IE*). Giving a good definition of this task is hard to do because of the difficulty in defining an event. Intuitively however, we may think of an event as a *higher-order spatiotemporal entity* that may comprise a related set of entities (called *arguments*), and with some kind of temporal or spatial span (whether explicitly extracted or mentioned in the text or not). For example, in the sentence "The G20 summit in 2019 took place in Osaka," *G20 summit* may qualify as an "event" extraction, but by itself, the extraction does not do justice to the event. The event clearly has *arguments* that include both the location (*Osaka*) and the time (*2019*), which is the year in this case. These arguments could be finer-grained and may even include ranges (e.g., a war that occurred between a certain time span could also be an event extraction). If the participants had been mentioned, they may have been extracted as additional arguments of the event. Ultimately, the underlying ontology is used for deciding what constitutes a correct, or even well-defined, event extraction. In practice, identifying events in free text can often equate to identifying who did what to whom, the time and place of activity ("when" and "where"), for what reason ("why"), and through what methods or instruments ("how"). Effective event IE entails simultaneous extraction of several entities and the relationships between them. To formalize what is meant by an event, an ontological definition of event IE is assumed, just like with named entities, concepts, and relations. In the next section, we will cover some important ontologies and vocabularies that are used for defining applicable relation and event types.

The distinction between relation and event IE is not always clear; in some rare cases, even the distinction between NER and event extraction can become blurred. We could think of event IE, for example, as a "downstream" inference that takes into account the sets of extracted entities and relations, as well as their contexts. However, the methods that have achieved state-of-the-art performance in event IE take a more sophisticated view of the problem and attempt to *jointly* extract entities, relations, and events in the hopes of improving performance on all three. Toward the end of the chapter, we return to event IE and joint IE. The vast majority of this chapter, however, is scoped to RE because it is the next most important (and well-studied) kind of IE for free text after NER. Furthermore, despite the growing importance of events, most modern KGs still do not contain complex event definitions in their underlying ontologies (i.e., entities and relations continue to reign as first-class citizens in the vast majority of published KGs).

6.2 Ontologies and Programs

Before we delve into techniques for event extraction and RE, it is important to scope out the problem. At this time, there is a fair amount of consensus on what these tasks entail, even though the actual techniques continue to be actively researched. Unlike NER, the concept of an ontology becomes important when dealing with event extraction or RE (especially the former). The reason is that it is not always clear what an event really is; without some kind of constraint, the problem would quickly become ill defined. The choice of ontology is important enough that it usually ends up influencing the actual techniques used to extract events. We begin by exploring a popular event ontology called ACE, which has been used as the definitional backbone for many relational and event IE tasks. In fact, many of the techniques we cover later in this chapter were a direct (or inspired) output of some of the government-funded programs that used ACE (or some minor modification thereof) as the underlying ontology in support of the IE (from text) problem.

6.2.1 Automatic Content Extraction

The ACE standard was developed by the National Institute of Standards and Technology (NIST) in 1999 and has evolved over time to support different evaluation cycles, the last evaluation having occurred in 2008. The objective of the ACE program was to develop IE technology to support automatic processing of source language data (in the form of natural as well as derived text, such as from optical character recognition). Automatic processing, as defined at the time of program institution, included classification, filtering, and selection based on the language content and semantics of the source data. The ACE program required development and refinement of technologies to automatically detect and characterize such semantics. Research objectives included detection and characterization of entities, relations, and events.

The Linguistic Data Consortium (LDC) developed guidelines for annotation, corpora, as well as other linguistic resources to support the program. Annotation was an important component of the program; for instance, ACE annotators tagged broadcast transcripts and newswire and newspaper data in three languages (English, Chinese, and Arabic), producing both training and test data for evaluating systems with three research objectives: Entity Detection and Tracking (EDT), Relation Detection and Characterization (RDC), and Event Detection and Characterization (EDC). A fourth annotation task, Entity Linking (LNK), grouped all references to a single entity and all its properties together into a Composite Entity. In the KG community, a similar problem arises that we have alluded to earlier (instance matching) and that will be detailed in chapter 8.

The type inventory of ACE includes Person, Organization, Geo-Political Entity (GPE), Location, Vehicle, Facility, and Weapon. ACE also further classifies entity mentions by including subtypes for each determined type (e.g., Organization subtypes include Government, Commercial, Educational, Nonprofit, and Other); if the entity does not fit into any subtype, it is not annotated. Furthermore, each entity was tagged according to its class (specific, generic, attributive, negatively quantified, or underspecified).

To support the RDC task (or what we designate as RE in this chapter), ACE relations included physical relations, including Located, Near, and Part-Whole; social/personal relations including Business, Family, and Other; a range of employment or membership relations; relations between artifacts and agents (including ownership); affiliation-type relations like ethnicity; relationships between persons and GPEs like citizenship; and finally, discourse relations. For every relation, annotators identified two primary arguments (namely, the two ACE entities that are linked), as well as the relation's temporal attributes. Relations that were supported by explicit textual evidence were distinguished from those that depended on contextual inference on the part of the reader.

Table 6.1: Occurrence counts of relations and subrelations in the ACE 2004 data set.

Type	Subtype	Count
PHYS	Located	745
	Near	87
	Part-Whole	384
PER-SOC	Business	179
	Family	130
	Other	56
EMP-ORG	Employ-Exec	503
	Employ-Staff	554
	Employ-Undetermined	79
	Member-of-Group	192
	Subsidiary	209
	Partner	12
	Other	82
ART	User/Owner	200
	Inventor/Manufacturer	9
	Other	3
OTHER-AFF	Ethnic	39
	Ideology	49
	Other	54
GPE-AFF	Citizen/Resident	273
	Based-in	216
	Other	40
DISC	Disc	279

Finally, to support the EDC task, annotators identified five event types in which entities participate, with targeted types including Interaction, Movement, Transfer, Creation, and Destruction events. Provenance information tagged by annotators included not only the textual mention or anchor for each event (catgorized by type and subtype), but also event arguments (agent, object, source, and target) and attributes (temporal and locative, as well as others like instrument or purpose) according to a type-specific template. Later phases of ACE involved the addition of event types and relations between events.

In summary, ACE can now be thought of as both a standard for defining relations (and is an ontology in that traditional sense) but also for evaluations conducted by NIST for EDT and RDC. One of the most widely known data sets used to report RE systems' performance in the literature is the ACE 2004 data set, although more recent ones (such as ACE 2005 and 2007) have also been adopted in evaluations. Some statistics on occurrence counts of relations and subrelations in ACE 2004 are compiled in table 6.1.

A similar standard to ACE is Entities, Relations, Events (ERE), which was created under the DARPA DEFT program as a more streamlined version of ACE, with the goal of easing annotation and ensuring more consistency across annotators. ERE attempts to achieve these goals by consolidating some of the annotation type distinctions that were found to be problematic in ACE, along with removing some of the more complex annotation features.

There are many interesting aspects of ACE that are beyond the scope of this chapter, but are nevertheless worthwhile exploring for readers looking to develop RE or event IE systems for an application. We provide pointers both to ACE and some of the other ontologies covered subsequently in the section entitled "Bibliographic Notes," at the end of this chapter.

6.2.2   Other Ontologies: A Brief Primer

ACE is far from the only ontology available for relations and events. The Rich Event Ontology (REO) provides an independent conceptual backbone to unify existing semantic role labeling schemas and augment them with event-to-event causal and temporal relations. It does this by unifying various other influential ontologies and vocabularies, including FrameNet, VerbNet, ACE, and Rich ERE resources.

Besides ACE and REO, the Conflict and Mediation Event Observations Event and Actor Codebook (CAMEO) event coding ontology (funded under the US National Science Foundation) is another well-known instance of a vocabulary that was developed over a decades-long period and is licensed under Creative Commons. The origins of the project were not as ambitious as they have recently become, because it was intended initially to be finished in six months of part-time work. Instead, it developed into a next-generation coding scheme designed to correct some of the long-recognized conceptual and practical shortcomings in vocabularies like World Event/Interaction Survey (WEIS), as well as including elements that were important for geopolitical domains (e.g., it included support for detailed coding of substate actors). Eventually, CAMEO was used extensively in the Integrated Conflict Early Warning System (ICEWS) project, funded by the Defense Advanced Research Projects Agency (DARPA), where it was found to serve a robust set of needs.

The CAMEO formal codebook includes descriptions and extensive examples for each category and is available in both print and web-based formats. Despite CAMEO originally being intended specifically to code events dealing with international mediation, it has worked well as a general coding scheme for studying political conflict. For example, it includes four-digit tertiary subcategories that focus on very specific types of behavior, differentiating, for instance, between agreement to, or rejection of, cease-fire, peacekeeping, and conflict settlement.

A detailed support for actors is an important component of CAMEO. As the authors describe in the CAMEO specification, the concept of "actor" is now diffuse in the post–Cold War global political environment due to proliferation of substate, nonstate, multistate, and trans-state actors, some of whom exert greater force or influence than the official states themselves. Furthermore, because of the focus on detailed support for actors, as well as many of the event and relation types mentioned here, CAMEO has become a domain-specific ontology for event IE, with geopolitical KG construction and understanding being the obvious use-case. In principle, the ontology can support events beyond geopolitics, but ACE still tends to be the preferred choice for generic event extraction.

6.3 Techniques for Relation Extraction

Effective techniques for RE face many challenges. First, there are many possible relations, which vary between domains. Given a pair of entities, the chances of error are high when RE is posed as a classification problem due to so many label choices. Nonbinary RE, which can start resembling event extraction, is more challenging and relatively less well studied compared to binary RE. We note that RE can be difficult even for humans, as evidenced by high interannotator disagreement on some corpora. This can make both training and testing nontrivial. Extending English RE systems to non-RE is more challenging than one might expect from similar multilingual transfer in tasks like NER, because RE systems have heavier language dependence.

As with NER, various flavors of machine learning, including supervised and semisupervised techniques, have been used to attack RE. Next, we detail some important findings.

6.3.1 Supervised Relation Extraction

Supervised RE generally applies to mention-level (rather than global-level) RE. As evident from the name, supervised methods require labeled data where each pair of entity mentions is tagged with one of the predefined relation types (obtained from the ontology used for the task, the common ontologies having been described earlier). A special relation type *None* or *NA* is usually used to label the entity pairs where no predefined relation type holds. As the field has evolved, two distinct kinds of supervised RE have emerged into the mainstream: feature-based supervised RE and kernel-based supervised RE.

6.3.1.1 Feature-Based Supervised RE Feature-based methods define the RE problem as a classification problem that we briefly suggested earlier as a potential formulation. Namely, for each pair of entity mentions, a set of features is generated and a classifier, which is defined broadly, because it could just be a single model, but it could potentially also be an ensemble of models, working together in a simple (e.g., averaging-based) or complicated manner is trained on labeled instances (i.e., pairs of mentions tagged with a relation label). The features are extracted again at test time for entity mention pairs whose labels are unknown or withheld, and the classifier is used to predict the relation, often probabilistically. Once a pair of entity mentions is converted to a feature vector, we are in familiar supervised machine learning territory. However, converting pairs of entity mentions to feature vectors is a nontrivial process.

In the research literature, several kinds of features have been explored, including lexical, syntactic, and semantic features. Specific feature types could include word features (which could be the words representing the mentions, as well as all words between the mentions in the sentence), entity types of the mentions (e.g., Person, Location), mention types (e.g., name or pronoun), dependency features [e.g., Part-of-Speech (POS) and chunk labels of words on which the mentions are dependent in the dependency tree], and even parse tree features (e.g., path of nonterminals connecting the mentions in the parse tree). This is not an exhaustive list, but only some examples. Note that feature types do not have to be generic, but they could be domain-specific to yield higher performance in certain domains, such as the biomedical or geopolitical domain.

An interesting category of features is *semantic* features, which were historically based on the use of semantic resources such as WordNet. WordNet senses and semantic classes can be especially useful when dealing with finer-grained relation subtypes, such as different kinds of social or interpersonal relations. Because WordNet is a general resource, the exact way in which it is used by a system to extract features can vary. Another interesting class of features is based on the observation that all of the ACE 2004 relation types are based on one of several constrained structures that are syntactic-semantic in nature; for instance, *premodifier* structure, where an adjective or proper noun modifies another noun (*American diplomat*); *possessive*, where the first mention is in possessive case (*California's legislature*); *preposition*, where the two mention entities are related via a preposition (*mayor of Torrance*); and finally, *formulaic*, wherein the two mentions are written in some specific form (*Austin, Texas*). The reason why this observation is important is because we can use some rules and patterns to identify the specific structure in play, and this identification helps RE performance because models specialized for one or more of these structures can be used instead of a one-size-fits-all model.

Concerning the classification step, there are several ways to frame the problem because it is nonbinary (there is usually more than one relation in any nontrivial ontology). For example, because a model such as SVM is a binary classifier, one way to generalize it to do multiclass classification is by employing a strategy such as *one versus others* or (more rarely) one versus one.

Experimentally, feature-based methods have been superseded by both kernel-based methods and more recent methods based on representation learning (via deep neural nets). In practice, even when feature-based methods were very popular, much of the effort was spent in tuning and devising the right set of features for a domain and data set. While this kind of manual feature engineering has slowly but surely fallen out of favor, it is still often a first line of attack because it is easy to implement and quite intuitive. In domains where a reasonable amount of training data is available and some noise is tolerable, such methods may be sufficient owing to low implementation overhead (and low training and model selection complexity compared to deep nets).

6.3.1.2 Kernel-Based Supervised RE Feature-based RE is heavily dependent on the features extracted from the mention pairs and the sentence. Word embeddings could be used to add more global context, but without manual feature engineering, feature-based RE methods have not traditionally yielded maximal performance. The problem of feature engineering has been long recognized in the RE community, and kernel-based methods were proposed to avoid such explicit feature engineering. Inspired by SVMs, kernel methods compute similarities between representations of two *relation* instances, with the SVM used for the actual classification.

Before proceeding further, we provide a brief primer on kernels. Kernel methods are based on the idea of kernel functions, which operate in a high-dimensional *implicit* feature space, without needing to compute the coordinates in that space because they only need to compute the inner products between the images of all data pairs in that space. This computation, which is much less expensive than explicit computation of coordinates, is often referred to in the machine learning and SVM literature as the "kernel trick." In essence, to employ the trick, we only need a similarity function over data point pairs in the raw representation. The task of engineering and extracting features is now replaced with the task of specifying the kernel.

Different kernels have been defined and used over the years, with some of the common ones including the *sequence* kernel, the *syntactic* kernel, the *dependency tree* kernel, the *dependency graph path* kernel, and even *composite* kernels. The *sequence kernel*, for example, is motivated by the (now-famous) *string subsequence kernel* and computes the number of shared subsequences between any two sequences. Relation instances, therefore, must be represented as sequences for the proper functioning of this kernel. One way to do so is to consider the sequence of words from the first mention to the second mention in the sentence. Furthermore, even this method can be made more robust by not considering just the word (as a singleton in the sequence), but also features extracted from the word. In this representation, each word itself is turned into a feature vector [with the domain of the features being not just the set of all words (i.e., the vocabulary), but also the set of POS tags, generalized POS tags, entity types, and so on, all of which can be leveraged to extract a specific set of features for a single word] and the sequence is a list of feature vectors. Although not considered in classic work, even word embeddings could be used as word feature vectors, though the continuous nature of the embeddings may be inappropriate for the sequence kernel.

To extend the sequence kernel to work well on multidimensional lists of features, a generalized subsequence kernel was proposed early in the literature on kernel-based RE. This kernel is able to efficiently compute the similarity for two sequences s and t using a recursive formulation. More details on the recursive formulation and its implementation can be found in the original paper (see the "Bibiliographic Notes" section). Another kernel, called the *relation kernel*, is based on the generalized subsequence kernel and is a sum of four subkernels. The relation kernel can either be used in a multiclass SVM that is trained such that each relation type corresponds with its own class (with an extra class for the NA or NONE relation), or in a binary SVM that first decides whether *any* relation exists between the two entity mentions, followed by a multiclass SVM (if a relation is found to exist) to decide the appropriate relation type. This two-level approach was found experimentally to yield better results than the former approach.

A full description of the other kernels is beyond the scope of this chapter; however, the diversity of kernels mentioned earlier (based on graphs, trees, including dependency and syntactic trees, and sequences, as just described) illustrates the fruitful history of progress that kernel-based RE has enjoyed over the years, especially prior to the advent of deep learning. Syntactic tree kernels, for example, use the structural properties of a sentence (including its constituent parse tree) as primary features, but other works have augmented these features with information about entities and relations. Because the natural representation here is a tree, one issue that arises is the efficient computation of the kernel, because the number of possible subtrees is very large and it is not viable to explicitly construct each instance's image vector. In the kernel literature, this problem has been addressed by devising a polynomial-time function that is based on a recursive definition and counts the number of common subtrees rooted at two nodes v_1 and v_2.

Similar to the sequence kernel, a good representation for relation instances is necessary for the proper functioning of this kernel. Several possibilities exist, most of which construct a subtree from the complete syntactic tree characterizing a particular relation instance (pair of entities). These possibilities include, for example, a *path-enclosed tree* (the *smallest* subtree that includes both entities; i.e., the subtree enclosed by the shortest path connecting the two entities in the sentence's parse tree) and a *minimum complete tree* (the complete subtree formed by the lowest common ancestor of the two entities). Experimentally, the former has been found to work quite well, though it can perform even better when contextual information is also included in the tree. For example, a *context-sensitive path tree* is an extension of the path tree, where one word to the left (right) of the first (second) entity are also included. Yet other work has tried to augment the tree by annotating the tree nodes with discriminant features such as WordNet senses and properties of entity mentions, and by designing a special kernel called the Feature-Enriched Tree Kernel to compute the similarity between such "enriched" trees.

Composite kernels were designed to combine information captured by all of these different kernels (e.g., by combining syntactic tree and sequence kernels). Such combination is nontrivial because it has to be a valid kernel function for the kernel trick to apply. Functions that can be used to ensure valid composition between two kernels include sum, product, and linear combination. Several researchers have leveraged this property to design sophisticated composite kernels capturing multiple information sets to improve performance. For example, an influential approach designed individual kernels for three levels of NLP processing (tokenization, sentence parsing, and deep dependency analysis), and then combined them so that processing errors in one of the kernels can be compensated using the information in the other kernels. Later state-of-the-art work went even further by trying to apply composite kernels in a distant supervision framework, leveraging Wikipedia infoboxes, and reporting significantly improved performance.

6.3.2 Evaluating Supervised Relation Extraction

As mentioned earlier, some of the popular data sets on which different systems have reported RE performance include ACE 2003 and 2004, though a few papers also report performance on the occasional nonstandard data set. Because RE is essentially a multi-class classification problem, performance can be evaluated in terms of precision, recall, and F-measure for the non-NA classes.

Recent surveys have attempted to compare reported performance across the techniques of RE described previously. Kernel-based RE systems were generally found to outperform feature-based RE. In one study across seven major relation types in the ACE 2004 data set, for example, a syntactic tree kernel with dynamically determined tree span was found to achieve the highest F-score (of 77.1 percent), outperforming feature-based RE systems (that used lexical, syntactic, and dependency tree features, as well as a classifier based on the syntactic-semantic structures previously described) by more than 5.5 percent, and other competitive kernel-based REs by margins almost as high. The fact that a syntactic tree kernel was able to achieve the best performance demonstrates the importance of incorporating the structural features of a sentence into any pipeline.

6.3.3 Semisupervised Relation Extraction

Acquiring labeled data at scale is always a challenge for any task, and RE is no different, motivating development of semisupervised techniques. A second motivation, however, is to also leverage the large amounts of unlabeled data currently available on the web, which could be used to significantly boost performance of existing RE architectures without necessarily requiring labeling effort.

The most notable semisupervised (alternatively called *weakly supervised*) method for RE is *bootstrapping*, which starts from a small set of seed relation instances and iteratively learns more relation instances and extraction patterns. While bootstrapping has been widely explored (as discussed in the next section), another learning paradigm called *distant supervision* has become a popular alternative because it uses a large number of known relation instances in existing large knowledge bases (KBs) to create a proxy for actual training data. A commonality between bootstrapping and distant supervision is that, for both paradigms, *noisy* training data is *automatically* generated. To achieve good performance, careful feature selection and pattern filtering need to be carried out. Besides bootstrapping and distant supervision, more traditional machine learning paradigms such as *active learning*, as well as recent paradigms such as *label propagation* and *multitask transfer learning*, have been explored. The key idea behind the former method is that the learning algorithm is allowed to ask for true labels of some selected unlabeled instances. The criterion for choosing these instances varies, but all such criteria have the common goal of recovering the underlying hypothesis as quickly as possible (i.e., with few labeled instances).

In contrast, label propagation is a graph-based, semisupervised method where labeled and unlabeled instances[1] in the data are represented as vertices in a graph with edges reflecting similarities between vertices. Using an iterative algorithm, label information for a vertex is propagated in a systematic way to nearby unlabeled vertices through these weighted edges. This process continues (i.e., the labels are spread out over the graph over several time steps). Ultimately, the labels of (previously unlabeled) vertices are considered to have been inferred when the propagation process meets a particular convergence criterion. An important advantage of label propagation is that the labels of (previously unlabeled) vertices are not only determined by nearby instances, but also by nearby unlabeled instances.

Multitask transfer learning models the semisupervised learning problem yet another way, by attempting to start from a few seed instances of the relation type of interest, as well as a large number of labeled instances of other relation types. By using common structural properties (usually syntactic) that many different relation types seem to share, the framework uses a transfer learning method in addition to human inputs in the form of entity-type constraints. By using a shared weight vector, knowledge learned from other relation types can be transferred to the target relation type (hence, it is a "multitask" learning paradigm).

6.3.3.1 Bootstrapping   We mentioned earlier that bootstrapping requires a large, unlabeled corpus and a few seed instances of a relation type of interest. Given the seed examples, bootstrapping is expected to extract similar other entity pairs having the same relation type. An important early algorithm for bootstrapping was called Dual Iterative Pattern Relation Expansion (DIPRE) and relied on an idea called *Pattern Relation Duality*, which states that (1) given a good set of patterns, a good set of entity pairs (related according to a prespecified relation type) can be found; and (2) given a good set of such entity pairs, a good set of patterns can be learned. DIPRE puts this idea in practice through an iterative process. Patterns are represented as a tuple with five elements: *order, urlprefix, prefix, middle*, and *suffix*, where order is boolean, and the others are strings. The algorithm was designed mainly for web data, as evidenced by the urlprefix pattern element. Experimentally, it was shown that using just three seed examples of author and book pairs, and using a corpus of about 24 million webpages, DIPRE was able to generate a list of 15,000+ author-book pairs.

---

[1] Put more accurately, labeled instances are instances with known labels, while the labels of "unlabeled" instances have to be inferred.

The Snowball system improved over DIPRE by incorporating named entity tags in the patterns, meaning that patterns such as "ACTOR acted in MOVIE" and "ACTOR-featuring MOVIE" could be learned from text. With these patterns, the system can further search the corpus and find more such pairs with the target relation. These entity pairs are then added to the set of seed relation instances, and the entire process is repeated until a certain condition is satisfied.

An important point to note with these bootstrapping methods is that the quality of extraction patterns has to be evaluated such that not too many noisy patterns are included during the extraction process. Heuristic methods have been proposed to this effect, with two factors (coverage and precision) typically considered. While coverage is related to the percentage of true relation instances that can be discovered by the pattern, precision is related to the percentage of correct relation instances among all the relation instances discovered by the pattern. The metrics of coverage and precision are recurring themes in evaluations of many KG-centric subcomponents, including (as we shall see later) instance matching.

6.3.3.2 Distant Supervision Bootstrapping draws upon only a small set of seed entity pairs for its initialization. However, with the growth of the web and the publishing of large-scale repositories covering all manner of subject areas (a good example being Wikipedia), much human knowledge, contributed by crowds of users, has been captured and stored in KBs. With such openly available knowledge, it has become possible to use a large set of entity pairs known to have a target relation to *generate* training data. This idea has become known in the community as *distant supervision*. In the earliest approaches leveraging this philosophy, the assumption was that if two entities participate in a relation, any sentence that contains the two entities expresses that relation. Because this assumption does not always hold, some of the approaches use features extracted from different sentences containing the entity pair to create a richer feature vector that is supposed to be more reliable. Representation learning has made this process significantly more robust, and new research continues to be published that lies at the intersection of embeddings and distant supervision. Many of these approaches enrich the feature space by defining lexical, syntactic, and named entity tag features. Standard multiclass logistic regression is often used as the classification algorithm. By using distant supervision, even the early approaches were able to empirically show that they could achieve almost 70 percent of precision based on human judgment. By using several sources (e.g., in one approach, both YAGO and Wikipedia documents were used for distant supervision), more improvements could be achieved, including F-measures well into the mid-70s. Being a general technique, distant supervision is a recurring theme in KG construction (KGC), and it has also emerged as a viable IE technique with respect to information types other than relations and genres beyond free text.

6.3.4 Unsupervised Relation Extraction

Earlier, we discussed RE when the types of relations to be extracted are known in advance. There are also cases where we do not have any specific relation types in mind but would like to discover salient relation types in a given corpus. For example, given a set of articles reporting hurricane and typhoon events, it would be useful if we could automatically discover that one of the most important relations for this domain is the *originate* relation between a typhoon and the place where it originated.

When first studied, this important problem was referred to as *unrestricted relation discovery* but it is now referred to as "unsupervised" RE. An early approach tackled this problem by first collecting a large number of news articles from different news sources on the web, and then using simple clustering (based on lexical similarity) to pinpoint articles discussing the same event. In this way, the feature representation of an entity could be enriched by using its many occurrences in various articles. The next step was to perform syntactic parsing and extract named entities from the articles. Each named entity could then be represented by a set of syntactic patterns as its features. For example, a pattern may indicate that the entity is the subject of the verb *originate*. As a final step, pairs of entities cooccurring in the same article were clustered using their feature representations. The results were tables in which rows corresponded to different articles and columns corresponded to different roles in a relation. The discovered tables were found to have an impressive accuracy of 75 percent.

Later authors tried to generalize unsupervised relation discovery in their formulation of the problem, mainly by assuming that the input of the problem consists of entity pairs and their contexts. An unsupervised relation discovery algorithm would cluster these entity pairs into disjoint groups, with each group representing a single semantic relation. An "other" or garbage cluster was also used to capture unrelated entity pairs or unimportant relations. The contexts for each entity pair consist of both the context of each entity, as well as the the cooccurrence context. An entity pair can be represented by a set of features derived from the contexts, although in the early papers, only surface pattern features (e.g., "arg-1" spoke in support of "arg-2") were considered for modeling cooccurrence contexts. Clustering was fairly standard as well, drawing on established techniques like hierarchical agglomerative and K-Means clustering. Impressively, however, these methods were able to discover relations such as CityOfState and EmployedIn despite being given no a priori knowledge of these relations.

As the field of relation discovery has matured (though it is still far from human-level performance), there have been increasing efforts to generalize it even further, with the most complex version of the problem seeking to automatically induce an IE template, with a template containing multiple slots playing different semantic roles. A straightforward solution is to identify role filler candidates first, followed by clustering of these candidates. However, this simplified approach neglects the important observation that a single document tends to cover different slots. Some solutions have been proposed, but the problem is far from resolved.

More recent work has tried to go beyond a single static template to discover multiple templates from a corpus and automatically give meaningful labels to discovered slots by performing two-step clustering. The first clustering step groups lexical patterns that are likely to describe the same type of events, while the second step groups candidate role fillers into slots for each type of event. A slot can be labeled using the syntactic patterns of the corresponding slot fillers.

In conclusion, while there is a lot of exciting research being conducted in the area of unsupervised relation discovery and template induction, the difficulty of the problem has prevented general-purpose solutions that are able to achieve roughly the same kind of performance as NERs. However, performance has steadily improved since the early days, even as the scope of the original problem has expanded to become ever-more complex and real-world. In the next chapter, for example, we study Open Information Extraction (Open IE), which attempts to discover entities and relations without any kind of ontological input. Open IE is a natural generalization of the problem of unsupervised relation discovery that we briefly covered in this section. In the literature, Open IE and unsupervised RE are sometimes considered as akin; for instance, Unsupervised RE System (URES) was a direct successor to the KnowItAll Open IE system, which we describe at length in the next chapter.

6.4   Recent Research: Deep Learning for Relation Extraction

As with NER, RE has also been considerably influenced recently by deep learning research. As discussed earlier, supervised deep learning techniques for any task, including RE, require large quantities of training data for learning. Using manually annotated data sets for RE takes enormous time and effort to compile and is clearly not scalable. Hence, techniques like distant supervision, which produces training data by aligning KB facts with texts, have become popular. Data sets acquired in this way allows the learning of more complex models for RE, including architectures based on convolutional neural networks (CNNs).[2] The noise in such data sets generated through distant supervision, however, must be dealt with using special modeling techniques such as multi-instance learning. In this section, we provide some details on these efforts. Note that much research is still being conducted on this problem even at the present day. However, interesting trends have started to emerge.

---

[2] This section assumes some basic knowledge of CNNs. If readers are completely unfamiliar, they should skip this section at a first reading. For the interested reader, an accessible introduction to CNNs is recommended before perusing this section.

Early work on using deep learning for RE started by employing the same supervised data sets used by non–deep learning supervised machine learning models described earlier in this chapter. These data sets include the ACE 2005 data set, but also SemEval-2010 Task 8, which is a freely available data set that contains 10,700+ samples, with a roughly 80/20 percent split for training and testing. There are nine ordered relation types. Because the relations are ordered, their directionality effectively doubles the number of relations, as a pair of entities is believed to be correctly labeled with a relation only if the order is also correct. The final data set, augmented using this principle, contains 19 (rather than 9) relation classes as a result, with a single extra class for *Other*.

Distant supervision-based approaches started to be used for the task following an influential paper in 2009, wherein documents were aligned with known KBs, under the assumption that if an entity pair in the KB is associated via a relation, then any document containing the mentions of the two entities would also manifest that relation. This is obviously a strong assumption, and it can frequently be violated. There are many documents that contain both *Sergey Brin* and *Google*, for example, without explicitly expressing the *Founder* relationship between Brin and Google. In 2010, a solution to this problem was proposed, wherein the assumption was relaxed by modeling RE as a multi-instance learning problem. *Multi-instance learning* is a kind of supervised learning wherein a label is assigned to a "bag of instances" rather than a single instance. In the specific case of RE, an entity pair defines a bag, with the bag consisting of all the sentences containing the mention of the entity pair. Instead of assigning a relation label to each sentence, a label is instead assigned to each bag of the relation entity. In effect, the original strong distant supervision assumption is relaxed to a much weaker one—namely, given that a relation exists between an entity pair, at least one document in the bag for the entity pair must express that relation.

The data set for distant supervision was created by aligning the Freebase KG with the *New York Times* corpus, both of which are well known in the NLP community. In the 2010 work, entity mentions were located using the Stanford NER tagger and were matched to the names of Freebase entities. Further, 52 possible relation types, including a special class NA (indicating that there is no relation between the two entities), were defined in the relation ontology. The data set thus compiled is quite large, with more than half a million sentences, 18,000+ relational facts, and 280,000+ entity pairs in the training data. The testing portion contains 172,000+ sentences, 96,000+ entity pairs, and almost 2,000 relational facts. Evaluation is typically done by comparing extracted facts against Freebase entries. While this evaluation is good for comparing different RE systems, it is important not to interpret any results in an "absolute" sense, since Freebase (or any KG, including Wikidata and DBpedia) was not complete, and false negatives would undermine model performance as a result.

Beyond distant supervision, we noted in chapter 5 how representation learning has yielded great impetus to extraction problems in the NLP community. Word embeddings are the most common kind of representation learning (serving as inputs to higher-order deep learning models such as CNNs, as subsequently described), but in RE, *positional embeddings* were an innovation that helped drive higher RE performance as well. By positional embedding, we mean that the input to the model is not just the word embedding, but also the relative distance of each word from the entities in the sentence is encoded and sent into the higher-order model. This ensures that the deep network can keep track of how close each word is to an entity. Words closer to target entities are expected to contain more useful information involving the relation type. For example, in the sentence "Los Angeles is an economic mainstay in California," "economic" has relative distance 3 to the head entity "Los Angeles" and relative distance of −3 to the tail entity "California." These positions can be encoded in a vector of appropriate dimensionality (usually two positional vectors are used, for the head and tail entity, respectively). Together, these vectors, along with the word-embedding vector, would be concatenated and serve as the full-feature vector of the word to a higher-order deep learning model. A sentence would be similarly encoded as a bag of its constituent (full-feature) word vectors.

CNNs have become quite popular in the RE community, starting as early as 2011. Originally, CNNs were proposed primarily for computer vision problems for reasons that are beyond the scope of this chapter. The early deep learning approaches for RE (that did not use distant supervision) applied supervised learning with CNNs to the problem by modeling it as multiclass classification. The earliest work that used CNNs to automatically learn features instead of handcrafting features was published in 2013, and built an end-to-end network that encoded the input sentence using both word vectors and lexical features. This was followed by a convolutional kernel layer, a single-layer neural layer, and the usual softmax output layer, which yields a probability distribution over the relation classes. The architecture also relied on synonym vectors instead of word vectors, wherein a single vector is assigned to each synonym class rather than assigning every unique word its own vector. Unfortunately, this fails to leverage the representational power of word-embedding models. Furthermore, the embeddings (rather than being trained in an unsupervised way on the corpus) are randomly assigned to each synonym class. However, the model does try to incorporate a few lexical features using artifacts such as word, POS, and entity-type lists. Despite the criticisms of the model in hindsight (because some improvements are clearly possible), at the time, it led to an improvement by over 9 points (on the F-measure metric) in the ACE 2005 data set, illustrating the clear promise of this kind of CNN architecture for RE and laying the groundwork for a significant spurt in more deep learning RE research.

Other work using CNNs for RE soon followed, with a CNN model using max-pooling proposed in 2014, and CNN with multisized window kernels produced in 2015. The 2015 work proposed to be rid of exterior lexical features altogether, and instead allow the CNN to learn the features itself. Word and positional embeddings are used, followed by convolution and max-pooling (hence, it is similar in this regard to the work in 2014), but a novelty in this architecture was the use of convolutional kernels of varying window sizes to capture wider ranges of *n*-gram features. Experimentally, using kernels with 2-3-4-5 window lengths was found to deliver the best performance. Furthermore, the word embeddings were initialized using pretrained word embeddings from the word2vec model, which yields further improvements compared to random initializations of word vectors or static word2vec vectors.

Earlier, we mentioned multi-instance learning as a possible paradigm for using distant supervision. In 2015, Zeng et al. (2015) proposed piecewise CNNs (PCNNs) for using this paradigm to build a relation extractor. While the model was similar other models constructed a priori, it had the important additional contribution of piecewise max-pooling across the sentence. The method worked by max-pooling in different segments of the sentence instead of the entire sentence. Zeng et al. (2015) used three segments, based on the positions of the two entities in question. Experimentally, PCNNs were found to outperform previous CNN models on precision at higher levels of recall (25 percent or more). Later models improved this even further (see the "Bibliographic Notes" section). Ablation studies have demonstrated the advantages of preferring PCNNs over CNNs, as well as multi-instance learning over ordinary learning.

The discussion of the approaches described here (which have continued to be superseded by even more advanced models that employ mechanisms like selective attention and exploit information across multiple documents in a bag) and their demonstrable empirical impact shows that deep learning has ushered in an exciting period for RE. While much work still needs to be done, progress is being reported almost every year, and often the state-of-the-art technology is superseded within the year. Particularly beneficial has been the use of distant supervision and the adoption of the multi-instance paradigm, later augmented with training mechanisms like selective attention over documents and cross-document max-pooling. Other works have even incorporated structured information into the pipeline in an effort to improve feature representations even further (e.g., by exploiting relation paths and relation class ties). Intuitively, the approach leverages relations such as sister_of and parent_of to extract instances for wife_of.

An interesting avenue of future work in this area that is already underway is to use recurrent neural networks (RNNs) instead of CNNs for encoding the sentences, since it seems that RNNs and LSTM networks naturally fit NLP tasks more than CNNs. There hasn't been much conclusive evidence on the empirical benefits of using RNNs over CNNs in NLP tasks (e.g., while there is some evidence[3] that RNNs can perform well on sentiment classification at the document level, some other papers have showed that CNNs could potentially outperform LSTMs on language modeling). However, the state-of-the-art and consensus on this issue keeps shifting. In chapter 13, on *question answering*, we cover a

---

[3] A good reference for this claim is Tang et al. (2015a).

recent model called BERT, which is not based on CNNs and achieves state-of-the-art (or near state-of-the-art) on several language-modeling tasks.

6.5   Beyond Relation Extraction: Event Extraction and Joint Information Extraction

We provided a brief introduction to event extraction at the beginning of this chapter. Event extraction has also been studied mainly using ACE data, but domain-specific (in particular, biomedical) event IE has been studied as well (e.g., for BioNLP shared tasks). To reduce task complexity, early work employed a series of classifiers (called a "pipeline") that first extracts event triggers, followed by argument extraction. CNNs (including some of the models we briefly discussed in the previous section) have been applied successfully to event extraction as well. However, because pipeline approaches suffer from error propagation and cascading, joint extraction of event triggers and arguments has become very popular in the community.

The assumption guiding such joint IE models is that events and entities are closely related; entities are often actors or participants in events and events without entities are rare. Another motivation is that interpretation of events and entities can have high contextual interdependence. While early work in event IE modeled and extracted events separately from entities, performing inference at the sentence level and ignoring the rest of the document, joint IE explicitly models the dependencies among variables of events, entities, and their relations, the goal being to perform joint inference of these variables across a document.

In essence, joint IE decomposes the learning problem into three tractable subproblems: learning for within-event structures, learning for event-event relations (such as causality and inhibition), and learning for NER. The typical approach is to learn a probabilistic model for each of these subproblems, with a joint inference framework integrating the learned models into a single model that can jointly extract events and entities across the entire document. Depending on the paper, a variety of models have been put forth for realizing these intuitions, including Markov Logic (which we study in detail in the context of KG completion in part III of this book), structured perceptron and dependency parsing. Early work on joint inference largely relied on heuristic search to aggressively shrink the search space, because joint inference of the kind described here can lead to combinatorial explosion quickly if dealt with in a naive manner. Later work attempted more sophisticated techniques for reducing the search space (e.g., in 2011, dual decomposition was used to solve joint inference with runtime guarantees).

As intuited previously, improvements in event extraction would not have been possible without exploiting document-level context. For example, in the ACE domain, there is work on utilizing and propagating event type cooccurrence information to influence event classification decisions (e.g., in a domain-specific corpus describing guerrilla warfare in a country, an ATTACK event might cooccur often with a TRANSPORT event). By designing appropriate features, causal and temporal (among other) relations can be handled as well.

Experimentally, approaches that have jointly tried to extract entities and relations have reported considerable improvements over the pipeline approach. In fact, joint IE not only improves relation and event extraction, but also leads to improvements in entity extraction. One reason is that RE information can be leveraged for entity extraction in a joint IE model, unlike the pipeline approach, where NER precedes RE, which is not allowed to propagate backward. Unfortunately, comparing the models has proven to be difficult because they do not use a standard data set for their evaluations. It is also important to note that the "jointness" in joint modeling approaches occurs in one of two scenarios: either joint inference is conducted on local, independently trained classifiers for entities and relations, or actual joint learning is conducted wherein a single model is learned for extracting entities, relations, and events. Despite the improvements, there is considerable room for developing even more sophisticated approaches for handling the joint modeling problem, while still being efficient.

6.6   Concluding Notes

RE is an important type of IE that is essential for building KGs from raw data. Although all kinds of IE involve challenges, RE has proved to be significantly more challenging than NER. A range of techniques has been proposed over the years, refined and evaluated via programs like ACE. Supervised techniques include both feature-based and kernel-based methods, and they have historically been the best performing. However, semisupervised and unsupervised techniques have recently benefited a great deal due to paradigms like distant supervision and representation learning. Deep learning methods are continuing to be applied to RE to further advance the state-of-the-art. Finally, extending RE to event extraction, as well as building joint models that extract entities, relations, and extractions all at once in the hopes of doing better on each individual extraction problem, are all being explored in the community to expand the scope of the problem and build richer KGs. It is likely that we will continue to see new research in this area for the foreseeable future.

6.7   Software and Resources

We mentioned multiple ontologies in the beginning of the chapter and provided links and resources for them here:

1. Resources pertinent to the ACE program are available at https://www.ldc.upenn.edu/ collaborations/past-projects/ace. In particular, we encourage the interested reader to consider the annotation tasks and specifications (ACE 2008 is the latest version), as well as many of the other language resources available in the broader pages of the LDC.

2. REO was presented relatively recently by Brown et al. (2017), where they claim that it is "temporarily available by request" but is planned to be migrated to an "in-house

server in the near future, where it will be freely available." However, the authors have not been able to locate a download link online, and prospective users may have to contact the authors of the original paper directly.

3. CAMEO, which is also very popular for events, is described extensively in a manual available at http://data.gdeltproject.org/documentation/CAMEO.Manual.1.1b3.pdf. The GDELT (Global Database of Events, Language, and Tone) project, described at https://www.gdeltproject.org/, has many associated resources, including data, documentation and solutions. GDELT uses CAMEO, along with ICEWS (Integrated Conflict Early Warning System), a DARPA-funded initiative. More details on ICEWS may be found on Harvard Dataverse: https://dataverse.harvard.edu/dataverse/icews.

To *do* RE, one set of resources that can be used is the NLP packages mentioned in the previous chapter. Those packages provide excellent facilities for training a custom RE pipeline, but pretrained modules compatible with some of the packages are also available. Otherwise, RE still hasn't delivered the same level of performance as NER, and consequently it is not as widely used (at least compared to NER) in industry and other sectors, where accuracy requirements are higher. Other useful resources for the interested practitioner for RE and event extraction include FrameNet and VerbNet, respectively, available at https://framenet.icsi.berkeley.edu/fndrupal/ and https://verbs.colorado.edu/verbnet/, respectively. A VerbNet Java application programming interface (API) can be downloaded at http://verbs.colorado.edu/verb-index/vn/verbnet-3.2.tar.gz. In the last ten years, broader initiatives (such as data sets and competitions) have done their part in advancing the state-of-the-art and leading to more research. One example is SemEval 2010 Task 8 (http://semeval2.fbk.eu/semeval2.php?location=tasks), which is a multiway classification task that contains nine general relations, along with an "OTHER" relation. Other interesting repositories and links are tracked on the page http://nlpprogress.com/english/relationship_extraction.html.

More recently, deep learning systems have been used for relation and event extraction, as noted earlier. Frameworks such as TensorFlow and PyTorch are useful tools in this regard, but so are advanced-language models (based on transformer architectures) such as BERT, which will be covered in more depth in chapter 13. Due to the interest in NLP and tasks such as RE that are important for question answering, industry has also been playing an active role in advancing the state-of-the-art. For example, a recent method published by Wang et al. (2019) at IBM was able to achieve state-of-the-art (or near state-of-the-art) performance with RE (https://www.ibm.com/blogs/research/2019/07/relation-extraction-method/). In a separate line of work, the DeepDive system is another example of a supporting infrastructure for extracting structured information from unstructured data (http://deepdive.stanford.edu/relation_extraction).

6.8   Bibliographic Notes

RE had been an important problem in the IE community long before the advent of KGs, which have only made them more relevant. The problem has also long been considered to be more difficult, in terms of achieving satisfactory empirical performance, than tasks like NER. The structure of our coverage is largely inspired by the recent survey of Pawar et al. (2017). They describe a clear distinction between global- and mention-level RE and also provide a good overview of resources like ACE. As they note, they are hardly the first to study RE; in many papers on IE, RE has at least some coverage. For a fuller scope, the interested reader should consider work by Sarawagi et al. (2008), Bach and Badaskar (2007), and de Abreu et al. (2013), the last of which covers techniques used for Portuguese and can provide a good sense of some of the challenges posed by RE when dealing with non-English text.

Good references for some of the ontologies, vocabularies and resources (such as ACE, ERE, REO, CAMEO, and WEIS) we mentioned include Doddington et al. (2004), Gerner et al. (2002a,b), Song et al. (2015), Aguilar et al. (2014), and Brown et al. (2017).

Individual references for many of the RE techniques (supervised and unsupervised) covered in this chapter can be found in Pawar et al. (2017), but more recently, surveys have been published on entire subareas of RE. For example, a lot of work has also been done on using distant supervision of RE; Smirnova and Cudré-Mauroux (2018) provide a survey of methods and research on this very specific topic. Similarly, Jung et al. (2012) summarize a specific area of research (kernel-based RE) that saw an explosion of research in the last two decades. For a good overview of domain-specific RE, we recommend Zhou et al. (2014) and Cohen and Hersh (2005), which cover the biomedical domain. In a similar vein, causal IE was surveyed by Asghar (2016).

Toward the end of the chapter, our focus shifted to deep learning methods for RE. This is a relatively novel area of research, but several good references should be perused by the interested reader. Important references include Zeng et al. (2014), Nguyen and Grishman (2015), Riedel et al. (2010), Zeng et al. (2015), Mintz et al. (2009), Hoffmann et al. (2011), Surdeanu et al. (2012), Lin et al. (2016), Jiang et al. (2016), Ye et al. (2016), Dauphin et al. (2017), Phi et al. (2019), and Yin et al. (2017). Finally, Kumar (2017) provides a synthesis of these and other methods that have used deep learning for RE.

Excellent references for joint IE and event IE (including event coreference) include Liao and Grishman (2010), Ahn (2006), Ji and Grishman (2008), Madhyastha et al. (2003), Humphreys et al. (1997), Yubo et al. (2015), McClosky et al. (2011), and Li et al. (2013). We note also that RE research has been intersecting with other kinds of IE, including Open IE (which we cover in chapter 7); see Zhang et al. (2019) for a very recent example of how the two can be fused in a large-scale setting.

6.9 Exercises

1. Consider the following paragraph (sourced from Wikipedia, accessed at https://en.wikipedia.org/wiki/Albert_Camus):

"Soon after Camus moved to Paris, the outbreak of World War II began to affect France. Camus volunteered to join the army but was not accepted because he had suffered from tuberculosis. As the Germans were marching towards Paris, Camus fled. He was laid off from Paris-Soir and ended up in Lyon, where he married pianist and mathematician Francine Faure on 3 December 1940. Camus and Faure moved back to Algeria (Oran) where he taught in primary schools. Because of his tuberculosis, he was forced to move to the French Alps. There he began writing his second cycle of works, this time dealing with revolt – a novel La Peste (The Plague) and a play Le Malentendu (The Misunderstanding). By 1943 he was known because of his earlier work. He returned to Paris where he met and became friends with Jean-Paul Sartre. He also became part of a circle of intellectuals including Simone de Beauvoir, Andr'e Breton, and others."

As a first step, design a small ontology that would allow you to express the kinds of entities and relations in this paragraph. Use reasonable assumptions, but make the ontology as nontrivial as possible. Express the ontology using RDFS (chapter 2).

2. Annotate the surface forms of the entities and relations in the paragraph (corresponding to instances of concepts and properties in your ontology), and express the annotations as an RDF KG.

3. Is there any real difference between a relation "instance" and a relation in the ontology? *Hint: Using the provided paragraph, or one inspired by it, can you think of cases where the "surface" form of the RE is different from its label in the ontology?*

4. Are there multi-arity (taking more than two entities as arguments) relations in the paragraph? If yes, what? If not, could you add a sentence to the paragraph to introduce a multi-arity relation? Is this multi-arity relation *pairwise decomposable*; that is, if the relation takes four arguments, such as $R(n_1, n_2, n_3, n_4)$, where n_i are entities, then is it possible to express the relation equivalently as a set (with cardinality $^4C_2 = 6$) of relations: $\{R'(n_1, n_2), R'(n_1, n_3) \ldots, R'(n_3, n_4)\}$? Note that R' does not necessarily have to be the same relation as R.

5. Give at least three examples of real-world multi-arity relations that would not be pairwise decomposable. One useful way to think about decomposability in this context is to ask yourself whether you would be able to soundly and completely recompose the original n-ary relations given a KB containing only the pairwise equivalents.

6. Informally describe a domain or scenario where joint IE, as we described it in the later part of this chapter, could prove to be important in reducing noise and getting relevant extractions. Try to find a paragraph, similar to the example from Wikipedia or a news source, that would allow you to argue your case concretely.

7 Nontraditional Information Extraction

Overview. In previous chapters, we covered various task areas in information extraction (IE) including web IE, Named Entity Recognition (NER), and relation and event extraction. We hinted at other kinds of IE, however, that have recently gained traction, and with steadily improving performance. One such nontraditional IE is Open IE, which does not depend on the provision of an ontology, although it is not accurate to say that Open IE can extract just anything. Other kinds of nontraditional IE tasks that have continued to become popular include IE from short texts and messages like Short Message Service (SMS) and social media, domain-specific IE in areas like crisis response, and multilingual IE. We provide a flavor of all of these areas in this chapter.

7.1 Introduction

In chapter 4 on Named Entity Recognition (NER), we found that some categories, such as *Person*, *Location*, and *Organization* tend to be frequent enough that generic NER approaches, as well as open tools, are expected to be able to extract instances of these concepts from text. However, in some domains, what constitutes a named entity can be unusual, and best understood by studying the needs of that domain. Intuitive examples of domain-specific IE, some of which we have already covered, or alluded to, in previous chapters include bioinformatics and geopolitics. In the former domain, for example, systems have addressed the extraction of medications and disease names (e.g., *Alzheimer's*). In the latter domain, named *entities*, as understood, are simply not enough, and we have to build systems for extracting relations and higher-order entities such as events.

Many other examples have been proposed, including "film," "scientist," "project name," "email address" and so on, depending on the domain under study. In conferences such as the Conference on Natural Language Learning (CONLL), the type "miscellaneous" has often been used to include proper names that are not instances of the classic concepts. Sometimes the class has been augmented with types such as "product," and in the Message Understanding Conferences (MUCs), "timex" types such as "date" and "time," and "numex" types such as "money" and "percent," have become quite common. In fact, since

Saint Philip Neri School @SPN_Alameda · 1h
Bake sale to help #CaliforniaFires victims sponsored by the Stident
Leadership Council at SPN school - come on down!!!

CFACT @CFACT · Nov 12
Hey Gov. Newsom, the wildfires are mainly due to prohibiting controlled
burns and not clearing enough dead trees, not because of utilities!
#CaliforniaFires #TuesdayThoughts

Michigan Engineering ✓ @UMengineering · Nov 15
In 2018, 1.8 million acres burned in #CaliforniaFires—a record high. Now
it could be months before #Australia has more than *100 million acres* of
bushfire under control.

Figure 7.1: An illustration of domain-specific IE (*natural disaster* domain) over social media data. Instances that might be extracted in such domains are underlined and include the natural disaster itself (*#CaliforniaFires*), support events (*Bake sale*) that themselves have arguments (*Stident Leadership Council*), span of the disaster (*1.8 million acres*), and even causal information (*prohibiting controlled burns*).

2003, a special community named TIMEX2 specifically proposed a standard for the annotation and normalization of temporal expressions.

Given classic concepts like *Person* and *Location*, as well as the existence of a catchall concept such as *Miscellaneous*, we can frame domain-specific IE as a type of *fine-grained IE*. Fine-grained IE is typically dependent on a more detailed ontology than we would normally expect with ordinary NER. Not all fine-grained IE has to be domain-specific. For example, some of the earliest work in fine-grained IE addressed the challenge of extracting not just a location, but multiple location subtypes, including city, state, country, and ZIP code. Even when considering an innocuous attribute like *Person*, fine-grained IE can become important in domains such as politics (where we want to construct a KG that has instances typed according to fine-grained concepts such as *Politician*, *Candidate*, and *Donor*). The distinction between fine-grained IE and domain-specific IE can become blurred; the two can often cooccur. The problem is generally harder than ordinary IE because (for supervised systems), domain-specific annotations and/or more finely annotated corpora are necessary. Unsupervised systems are even harder to build and have to rely considerably on model assumptions. The hardest version of the problem, where any solution is far from achieving human performance, is when domain-specific IE is required for a genre of data (such as social media) that is already difficult for ordinary IE to work with. Figure 7.1 illustrates a representative instance of this problem.

When domain-specific corpora are developed, they can prove to be important assets to the community. For example, due to the recent interest in bioinformatics, the GENIA corpus was created and led to many studies involving concepts such as *Protein*, *DNA*, and *Cell Line*. Other researchers have used the corpus to identify drug and chemical names. There has also been considerable research on extending domain-specific IE to be open-domain (as discussed in the next section)—that is, building IE systems that are not limited to a set of possible types to extract, but instead discovers types by itself.

Many of the IE challenges and approaches discussed in this chapter are more advanced than those in the preceding chapters, and remain the subject of evolving research. By necessity, there will be less discussion on some of the approaches relative to others, because the jury is still out on some subfields of IE. Where possible, we focus on general or established trends, and point the interested reader to other promising avenues in the section entitled "Bibliographic Notes," at the end of this chapter.

7.2 Open Information Extraction

Unlike traditional IE methods, Open Information Extraction (Open IE) is not limited to a small set of target entity types or relations that are given in advance (via an ontology). Rather, it extracts all types of relations and entities found in a text corpus. In total contrast with domain-specific IE, Open IE facilitates *domain-independent* discovery of relations and entities extracted from text and is consequently able to scale to large, heterogeneous corpora such as the web. An Open IE system takes as input only a corpus, without any prior specification of the relations and entities of interest. The output is a set of all extracted relations and entities.

We note here that extracting relations is a more predominant concern in Open IE than extracting entities. One reason for this is that comprehensive named entity hierarchies already exist, which contain a relatively robust specification of domain-independent concepts for a system to extract. This goes back to the mid-2000s, when Sekine and Nobata (2004) first defined a named entity hierarchy with many fine-grained subconcepts, such as *museum* and *river*, and added a wide range of concepts (e.g., *product, event, substance, animal, color,* and even *religion*). In essence, their hierarchy covered the most frequent name types and rigid designators appearing in standard news data. The total number of categories was initially 200, but was being continuously refined (e.g., popular attributes for each concept were being defined even back then, to try and turn the hierarchy into an open-world ontology).

Today, several open-world ontologies (e.g., DBpedia, Wikipedia classes, and YAGO) exist that can be useful for extracting named entities (without an underlying domain ontology), and can even be used to bootstrap NER systems using techniques like distant and weak supervision. Consequently, Open IE research at the frontier has primarily focused on extracting relations between entities without knowing relation types in advance. There are many clear benefits of Open IE. First, relations of interest do not have to be specified a priori before posing a query to the system, unlike most structured (or graph-based) querying systems, which only allow valid queries to be posed in terms of concepts and relations from a predefined ontology. Thus, the query can contain terms that correspond to "open relations" and "concepts," a much more natural and powerful way of accessing data. Second, if Open IE can be satisfactorily solved, especially with open web data and documents, it would provide a big boost to specialized unsupervised and semisupervised systems, because they would be able to benefit from distant supervision. Ideally, an Open IE solution would execute in time $O(n)$, where n is the number of documents in the corpus. An important vision that was presented as a motivation for Open IE originally was that of building (with low supervision) factual web-based question-answering systems capable of handling complex relational queries. Other applications include intelligent indexing for search engines and much lower accuracy degradation for domain-specific IE due to the provision of additional training data acquired through executing Open IE algorithms on web data.

Given these ambitious goals, it is natural to suppose that Open IE is not going to be realized without an equally formidable set of challenges. Some challenges that were identified as early as 2007 (in the context of an Open IE system called *TextRunner*) are automation, heterogeneity, and efficiency. These challenges are not unique to Open IE, of course; they will be a recurring theme for other subproblems, such as instance matching (IM), in building, cleaning, and querying knowledge graphs (KGs). But despite the common label, for each subproblem (including Open IE) these challenges take on a specific form that is important to understand in the context of the task.

First, automation is a challenge for Open IE because such systems must generally rely on unsupervised extraction strategies (i.e., instead of specifying target relations in advance, possible relations of interest must be automatically detected, usually in a single pass over the corpus). Moreover, the manual labor of creating suitable training data or extraction patterns must be reduced to a minimum by requiring only a small set of hand-tagged seed instances or a few manually defined extraction patterns. Second, heterogeneity presents a problem because it can trip up deep linguistic analysis tools like syntactic or dependency parsers designed for a certain kind of data, genre, or domain. Thus, core reliance has to be on shallow parsing techniques like Part-of-Speech (POS) tagging, or the downstream methods have to be capable of dealing with high quantities of noise and degradation (if deep linguistic parsing tools are used on data that significantly departs from the training data in its characteristics). Finally, as we noted several times in this chapter, the true power of Open IE is realized only when it is considered at web scale. In turn, this mandates that Open IE should be efficient, which is challenging given the nature of the problem.

Because Open IE, as a research area, is so much more advanced and recent than standard IE subareas like NER, the kind of research convergence and development witnessed in

NER has yet to take place in Open IE. However, some grouping of systems is possible due to the popularity of the problem among IE researchers. A recent survey on Open IE identified four such groups:

1. **Learning-based.** Learning-based Open IE was one of the earliest kinds proposed, and much of the state-of-the-art continues to fall within this paradigm. An early such system was TextRunner, which is described in some more detail later in this chapter. The idea behind learning-based Open IE is to use three modules and largely rely on *self-supervised machine learning*. Self-supervision here is similar to both distant and weak supervision, in that a heuristic means (and typically an external data set) is employed to approximately label a sample with positive or negative labels, and then use that heuristically labeled sample as a training set. With this paradigm, the first module (called the *extractor*) tries to generate candidate extractions from the raw data using a range of features. The second module, which is a *classifier*, further refines the outputs of the extractor, resulting only in good or trustworthy extractions being retained. The third module, which is an *assessor*, is generally designed to assign confidences or probabilities to each extraction output by the classifier, using global features, an example of which might be the frequency of occurrence of the extracted information on the web.

A learning-based system proposed after TextRunner, which also learns an extractor without direct supervision, is Wikipedia-based Open IE (WOE). It primarily uses Wikipedia as a source of distant supervision. WOE anticipated projects like DBpedia (discussed in part V of this book) by using entries in Wikipedia infoboxes as a bootstrapping source. The data thus extracted is used to learn extraction patterns on both POS tags and dependency parses. The idea behind using the latter is to try and discover long-range dependencies. In experimental results, dependency features were found to improve both precision and recall over shallow linguistic features, though at the cost of speed and scalability.

A more recent and well-known Open IE system is Open Language Learning for Information Extraction (OLLIE), which bootstraps the learning of patterns based on dependency parse paths, just like WOE. However, rather than rely on Wikipedia-bootstrapping, OLLIE relies on more precise weak supervision by relying on the outputs of the rule-based RE-VERB extractor (described later in this chapter). Furthermore, rather than ignore the *context* of a tuple and, as a consequence, extract propositions that may only be hypothetical or conditionally true (as opposed to an asserted fact), OLLIE also includes a context-analysis step wherein contextual information from an input sentence around an extraction is analyzed. By doing so, the precision of extractions is significantly improved. OLLIE also expanded the scope of Open IE beyond previous approaches by identifying both verb-based relations, as well as relations mediated by nouns and adjectives. At comparable precision, its recall (often called "yield" in the Open IE literature) also significantly improved compared to baselines. This expansion of scope has been a longer-term impact of OLLIE on the

Open IE community at large. For example, some other entirely learning-based approaches proposed after OLLIE, such as ReNoun, focused on noun-mediated relations.

2. **Rule-based.** These systems make use of handcrafted extraction rules, a primary example being REVERB, which is a shallow extractor that introduced a syntactic constraint expressed using a simple POS-based regular expression. The extractor was able to cover 85 percent of verb-based relational phrases in English. Hence, REVERB significantly reduces the number of incoherent and uninformative extractions that most previous Open IE systems had produced, and which had always been cited as a practical challenge in truly deploying Open IE in the wild. REVERB also uses mechanisms to deal with other important challenges in practical Open IE, including avoiding the production of relations that are too overly specific to be useful in downstream higher-order problems like question answering.

Another rule-based system that is specifically able to deal with the extraction of relations that are not just binary, but may have arbitrary arity, is KRAKEN, proposed in 2012. KRAKEN captures complete facts from sentences by gathering the complete set of arguments for each relational phrase (within a sentence); hence producing arbitrary-arity tuples. Furthermore, identification of relational phrases, with corresponding arguments, is designed to rely on handwritten extraction rules over typed dependency parses. A similar system is EXEMPLAR, proposed in 2013, which is also able to extract *n*-ary relations using handcrafted patterns based on dependency parse trees and uses semantic role labeling to assign each extracted argument its corresponding role (such as *agent* or *patient*).

Other approaches, proposed later, were more abstract and semantics-oriented, attempting to mitigate the challenge posed by dependency parses (that the previous two approaches relied on) because it is hard to ascertain the complete structure of a sentence's propositions using just the dependency parse tree. PROPS introduced a sentence representation, which was specifically designed to represent the proposition structure of an input sentence, and was generated by transforming a dependency parse tree into a directed graph. Propositional extraction becomes much more straightforward in this representation. A rule-based converter is used for the actual conversion. Another example of this kind of approach (where a more semantic structure is proposed or extracted, rather than directly extracting a sentence's propositions from the dependency parse tree) is PredPatt, which has the added benefit of being one of only a few Open IE systems that are multilingual.

3. **Clause-based.** Clause-based systems are based on the idea that the performance of an Open IE system could improve significantly if, rather than execute the system on a complex sentence directly, we first restructure the sentence into a set of syntactically simplified, independent clauses that are easy to segment into Open IE tuples. ClausIE, first proposed in 2013, is one example of such a *paraphrase-based* system, and it exploits knowledge of English grammar to map dependency relations of the original sentence into clause constituents, yielding a set of coherent clauses that have a far simpler linguistic structure than

the original input. Following this step, the clause type can be determined by combining linguistic knowledge of properties of verbs (often helped by the availability of domain-independent lexicons) with knowledge about input clause structure. Based on the clause type, one or more propositions can be generated from each clause, each representing a different information set. For example, consider the sentence "The chauffeur showed Jim to his car." The clause type is determined to be SVOA (where S, V, O, and A stand for Subject, Verb, Direct Object, and Adverbial, respectively), and a pattern for it could be $SV'OA$, where V' is now a complex-transitive verb. The derived clause would be "<The chauffeur, showed, Jim, to his car>."

The Stanford Open IE takes this approach further by using a classifier for splitting a sentence into logically entailed shorter utterances. It does so by recursively traversing the dependency tree and predicting (at each step) whether an edge should yield an independent clause. To further increase the utility of extracted propositions, each clause (which is self-contained) can be maximally shortened by using natural logic inference techniques. Ultimately, a small set of 14 hand-crafted patterns is used to extract a predicate-argument tuple from each utterance.

While a few other clause-based Open IE besides the ones mentioned here exist, this approach to Open IE is not as popular as the learning-based or even the rule-based approaches. However, clause-based IE has had some influence on the development of inter-proposition relationship modeling, which is where many of the more recent systems are best classified.

4. **Interproposition relationship modeling.** Many of the previously defined Open IE systems lack expressiveness, in that they are not able to *interpret* the context in which complex assertions are often made. For example, they cannot determine if the assertion is stated factually, conditionally or even hypothetically. There is clear value in separating these categories. Earlier, we saw an exception, OLLIE, which first introduced a context-analysis step for precisely making these determinations. OLLIE did so by extracting an *attribution context* that denoted a proposition as being reported by some entity. For example, OLLIE could extract something along the lines of: (*<the universe, originated at, the Big Bang>*, AttributedTo *modern physicists*).

By expanding the default Open IE representation with an extra attribute in this way, OLLIE is able to also determine if clausal modifiers such as "if" are used. Modifiers that claim or are clausal are identified by matching patterns with the dependency parse of the sentence, although the specific technique used for each is different. Other systems have followed OLLIE in improving this aspect of Open IE further. For example, OpenIE4, which combines two Open IE systems, SRLIE and RELNOUN, is able to produce similar outputs while also being able to mark additional temporal and spatial arguments. Successors to OpenIE4 have since been released and similarly take a hybrid approach to the problem, leading to improved performance and expansion of problem scope. Yet another approach is

CSD-IE, which uses a technique called *contextual sentence decomposition* to further specify propositions with information on which they depend. In essence, it uses handcrafted rules over a parser's output to split a sentence into subsequences that are semantically similar. Each such subsequence constitutes a context, but while each context now contains a separate fact, it is often dependent on surrounding contexts. In OLLIE, this is represented by extracting additional contextual modifiers, but later systems took a more sophisticated approach by allowing tuples to contain references to other propositions via separate, linked propositions. In order to link propositions, each extraction is assigned a unique identifier, and this identifier is allowed to be used in the argument position of an extraction for a later substitution (with the corresponding fact that the identifier alludes to). This is reminiscent of event extraction except that the extractions are not events. Other approaches have since followed up on the idea of linked propositions.

Much more recently, several Open IE systems have been proposed (relying largely on interproposition relationship modeling) and have achieved, or come significantly close to, state-of-the-art performance. MinIE is one such approach and aims to decrease the production of overly specific extractions by employing four "minimization modes," each varying in their aggressiveness, and thereby allowing the user or system designer to toggle between different precision/recall trade-offs. MinIE also semantically annotates extractions with information about polarity, modality, attribution, and quantities instead of directly representing the information in the actual extractions. Another example is Graphene, which is an Open IE framework inspired by decades-old work in rhetorical structure theory, which is able to transform complex sentences into compact structures by first using a set of handcrafted simplification rules and then removing clauses and phrases that do not fundamentally contribute to the input. Graphene is also able to identify rhetorical relations that connect core sentences with their associated contexts, and is thereby able to output semantically typed and interconnected relational tuples.

An important point that should be noted in the context of the taxonomy given here is that such a categorization is only a rough (and largely academic) guide for understanding the various classes of Open IE architecture. In practice, many of the architectures that have continued to prevail, such as OLLIE, Graphene, and OpenIE4 (and its successors) are often hybrid and rely on techniques that arguably fall within several categories. For example, we found that even in its original state, OLLIE relied on the outputs of a rule-based system to improve the precision of weak supervision. The Open IE series of systems have largely relied on hybrid combinations of approaches. In general, hybrid systems tend to work well in complex machine learning problems where it is difficult to identify one kind of approach that definitively yields good performance across all domains where it is being tested.

While detailing any individual system referenced here is beyond the scope of this chapter, we are presenting here examples of two successful and early Open IE systems, the designs of which have had significant influence in the community. While these systems are no longer state-of-the-art, the philosophies underlying their design have continued to withstand the test of time, especially with respect to learning-based architectures.

7.2.1 KnowItAll

KnowItAll is a self-supervised, web Open IE system that has spawned multiple variants. It relies on a small set of domain-independent extraction patterns (e.g., <A> *is a* <B>) to automatically instantiate relation-specific extraction rules (training data) and thereby learn domain-specific extraction rules iteratively in a bootstrapping process. KnowItAll is solely dependent on POS tagging rather than NER or deep linguistic parsing, which helps it better tackle the problem of heterogeneity (e.g., to other languages) and scale (because NER and deep linguistic analysis tools are expensive).

KnowItAll can autonomously extract facts, concepts, and relationships from the web. By seeding the system with an an extensible ontology (e.g., the YAGO ontology) and a small number of generic rule templates, KnowItAll creates text extraction rules for each class and relation in its ontology. Because of this seeding, KnowItAll should not be thought of as a completely unsupervised, open-ended IE, though in practice, such seeding is not difficult to accomplish and leads to higher quality (in terms of relevance) than relying on approaches that do not require any kind of seeding. KnowItAll relies on a domain-independent and language-independent architecture for populating the ontology with specific facts and relations, and it is capable of supporting scalability and high throughput. Early research used threading and asynchronous message passing to facilitate communication between individual KnowItAll modules. The important modules, some of which include the modules common to other learning-based systems (such as the extractor and the assessor), are described here:

1. **Extractor:** The extractor's goal is to instantiate a set of extraction rules for each class and relation from a set of generic, domain-independent templates. Using an example from Etzioni et al. (2004), the generic template "NP1, such as NPList1" indicates that the head of each simple noun phrase (NP) in NPList1 is an instance of the class named in NP1. This template can be instantiated to find, for example, politicians from such sentences as "In the conference, she got to mingle with famous politicians, such as Hillary Clinton, Bill Clinton, and Nancy Pelosi." KnowItAll would be able to extract three instances of the class *Politician* from this sentence, using the template as defined here. Other such templates can be defined, and if KnowItAll is combined with more recent work on inferring such templates automatically from large text corpora, the template specification process itself could be automated.

2. **Search engine interface:** This module is designed to automatically formulate queries based on extraction rules. Each rule has an associated search query composed of the keywords in the rule. For example, the previous rule would lead KnowItAll to issue the query "politicians such as" to a search engine like Google or Bing, download each

of the pages named in the engine's results in parallel, and apply the extractor module
to the appropriate sentences on each downloaded page. In 2004, KnowItAll used up
to 12 search engines, including Google, Alta Vista, and Fast. Because many of these
are now defunct, a modern version would have to modify, implement, and deploy its
search engine interface accordingly.

3. **Assessor:** This module assesses the likelihood that the extractor's conjectures are
   correct by using statistics computed by querying search engines. The assessor uses
   Pointwise Mutual Information (PMI) between words and phrases estimated from web
   search engine hit counts to do so, similar to Peter Turney's PMI-IR algorithm. For
   example, suppose that the extractor has proposed "George Bush" as the name of a
   politician. If the PMI between "George Bush" and a phrase like "politician named
   George Bush" is high, this gives evidence that "George Bush" is indeed a valid instance of the class *Politician*. The assessor computes the PMI between each extracted
   instance and multiple phrases associated with politicians. These mutual information
   statistics are ultimately combined via a standard machine learning classifier (in the
   original KnowItAll system, a Naive Bayes classifier is used, although, in principle,
   more modern and powerful classifiers could also be used).

4. **Database:** The database stores its information (including metadata such as the rationale for, and the confidence in, individual assertions) in a commercial Relational
   Database Management System (RDBMS) such as MySQL or Postgres. Using such
   databases in the design has some clear advantages over ad-hoc schemes because such
   databases are persistent, scalable, and support rapid-fire queries and updates. Again,
   a more modern implementation of KnowItAll could potentially take advantage of
   databases hosted in the cloud, or even a key-value store like MongoDB or Elasticsearch that will be covered in more detail in part IV of this book.

However, KnowItAll has some important limitations as well. For example, the system
can require many search engine queries for assessing the reliability of the eligible relation-
specific extraction rules, and it also requires as input the name of the relation of interest
to the system. In the case of adding or updating a relation, a new learning cycle is further
needed. This makes the overall approach rigid and not easily amenable to the scalable
addition of new relations.

7.2.2 TextRunner

There has been considerable research (and corresponding progress) since KnowItAll was
first proposed to address some of the aforementioned problems. We provide many pointers
in the "Bibliographic Notes" section, but by way of example, we discuss one such influential system called *TextRunner*. TextRunner is an Open IE system that is *learning-based*
in the taxonomy of the previously described approaches. It addresses the challenges of

naming relations in advance and scalability. Specifically, TextRunner needs just one pass through the corpus without the need to name any relations of interest in advance.

In brief, TextRunner operates as follows. First, given sample sentences from the Penn Treebank,[1] its learner applies a dependency parser to heuristically identify and label promising extractions as positive and negative training examples. In this sense, it is very similar to weak supervision. One argument made by the system authors for using the Penn Treebank in this manner is that most relations in English can be characterized by a set of several lexico-syntactic patterns (e.g., *Entity-1 Verb Prep Entity-2*). The weak supervision data can thus be input into a classifier (such as Naive Bayes, though others can be used as well) that learns a model of reliable relations by leveraging unlexicalized POS and noun phrase chunk features. The self-supervised nature of TextRunner mitigates the requirement for providing training data, while the use of unlexicalized features helps the system scale to web-sized corpora.

Following learning, the TextRunner extractor generates candidate tuples by identifying pairs of noun phrase arguments and heuristically classifying each word between the arguments as being part of a relation phrase (or not). Candidate extractions are presented to a classifier, and only reliable extractions are retained. An important advantage of TextRunner in this step is its efficiency and scalability due to the approach being restricted to use only shallow features. In the final step, an assessor, which is redundancy-based, assigns a probability to each relation extraction (RE) or retained tuple based on the number of sentences from which each extraction was found. In doing so, it exploits the redundancy of information on the web, assigning higher confidence to extractions that occur multiple times.

For each sentence, TextRunner ultimately returns one or more triples, each representing a binary relation between two entities [e.g., (London, capital-of, United Kingdom)], along with the probability of the triple being extracted correctly. In evaluations, TextRunner was found to achieve (on average) 75 percent on the precision metric, but one criticism was that the output of the system was nonnormalized to a large extent (e.g., problems of matching names referring to the same real-world entity or identifying synonymous relations were not handled). When handling the relation synonymy problem, for example, system performance (in terms of the recall metric) was found to improve. One issue with avoiding relation-specificity in the RE task is that it does not scale well to the web.

7.2.3   Evaluating and Comparing Open Information Extraction Systems

Open IE systems can be compared using both intrinsic and extrinsic evaluation approaches. An intrinsic approach in this context is one in which an Open IE system is compared to

---

[1] The Penn Treebank project is a corpus, available to members of the Linguistic Data Consortium (LDC), used widely in the Natural Language Processing (NLP) community for its POS annotations.

another Open IE system as a baseline, typically KnowItAll and TextRunner in the earlier years, and more recent approaches like OLLIE in recent years. For example, MinIE was compared to OLLIE, ClausIE, and Stanford Open IE as baselines. KRAKEN was compared to REVERB as a baseline, while ClausIE was compared to several systems, including REVERB, KRAKEN, OLLIE, TextRunner, and a version of WOE. In contrast with intrinsic approaches, an extrinsic approach uses a external competition, such as the TAC KBP Slot-Filling Challenge and the MCTest comprehension task, to compare and contrast different systems on the same challenge. Although the challenge allows us to evaluate competing systems using a single test set, the challenge does not control for crucial factors, such as the training paradigm and resources available for training and development. The use of a single competition or data set itself raises issues of broader validity.

Regardless of which approach is used, evaluation of Open IE is not as clear-cut as that of more traditional IE systems due to the lack (even today) of a formal specification that clearly states what constitutes a valid relational tuple. Unfortunately, the lack of a specification does not just pose theoretical problems; it also holds back the potential of the community because it has long preempted the establishing of a common large-scale annotated corpus serving as a gold standard for reproducible, cross-system evaluations. Hence, many Open IE systems were forced to be evaluated on small-scale corpora, which is problematic because one of the essential motivations for developing Open IE in the first place was that it could be applied on the scale of the web.

More recently, some researchers have attempted to address the problem, mainly by introducing large-scale gold standard benchmarks. For example, in 2016, a corpus was published that contained three features underlying the principles of many existing Open IE solutions. These principles are *assertedness*, which states that extracted propositions should be asserted by the original sentence rather than inferring propositions out of implied sentences; *minimal propositions*, which states that Open IE systems should extract compact, self-contained propositions that do not combine several unrelated facts; and finally, *completeness and open lexicon*, which implies that all relations asserted in the input text should be extracted. The last of these makes Open IE a truly domain-independent task because all relations must be extracted from heterogeneous corpora, and no assumption about a set of classes of relations is made or specified a priori. Many Open IE systems have traditionally incorporated this principle by considering all possible verbs as potential relations; however, by limiting themselves to verbal predicates, these systems have ignored complex relations mediated by syntactic constructs such as nouns or adjectives. A handful of systems, as we noted earlier, have been trying to broaden the scope of Open IE, however, with increasing success.

How was the corpus constructed in the first place? In the case mentioned here, the annotations in an existing *Question Answering–driven Semantic Role Labeling* benchmark[2] were converted to an Open IE corpus, leading to 10,000+ extractions over 3,000+ sentences originally from Wikipedia and the *Wall Street Journal* (WSJ). However, this effort was not the only one. In 2017, in an attempt to improve reproducibility, a set of researchers proposed RelVis, which is an Open IE benchmark framework that allows comparative analyses of systems at scale, supporting quantitative evaluation using standard measures like precision, recall, and F-score. Impressively, they also define a way to manually analyze qualitative errors to support empirical studies (e.g., studying and detecting errors such as redundant or uninformative extractions is possible using their framework).

We conclude the discussion on Open IE by noting that many important research issues remain. Perhaps the most urgent issue is for the community to agree upon, and start adopting, the benchmarks noted here for evaluation, since (at this time) not many researchers have actually used the two benchmarks we have described here. Another issue is that many Open IE systems still tend to focus on the extraction of binary relations within the scope of sentence boundaries. On a related note, using Open IE for events that have time, location, and potentially involve extraction of more than one relation that go beyond sentence level constitutes a challenging task that must be given more attention in the future. Multilingual and social media Open IE involve yet other challenges, to which very robust solutions do not exist. We describe some of the challenges in working with social media, in particular, in the next section. Finally, integrating good reasoners with Open IE systems is another challenging problem that could upend important fields, including answering general and powerful questions over the web without limiting the ontology or domain of discourse.

7.3 Social Media Information Extraction

Thus far, the implicit assumption has been that the IE is being executed on text that is fairly "regular." This includes not just domain-specific corpora like bioinformatics papers, but more generally, newswire and newswire-like data such as Wikipedia pages. In contrast, social media data tends to follow its own jargon, or *language model*, especially on length-constrained message platforms like Twitter. While this is also true for domain-specific corpora to some extent, the subject matter on Twitter and social media is not constrained by domain. People just communicate differently on such platforms, even when relaying mundane information like the outcome of a sports game.

Of course, there is no denying the prevalence (and more arguably, utility) of micro-blogging and social media services like Twitter that allow users to write large numbers of

---

[2] These are downstream tasks that may rely on Open IE as one solution. Question answering will be covered in more depth in part IV.

short text messages, and communicate, comment, and chat about products and events in real time. Social media usage trends have been climbing steadily, boosted in no small part by low-cost, low-barrier, and cross-platform access to such media, as well as the global popularity of smartphones and mobile devices. In many cases, social media provides information that is more updated than conventional information sources, including breaking news. They also allow people to communicate without a mediator, avoiding the suppression of certain voices (which may be too controversial for the mainstream), and to an extent, preventing or mitigating against biased coverage in news media by providing an alternative information source. All these features can be important not just in everyday life, but also in the context of natural disasters (as real-time information and microneeds on the ground can be streamed on social media), or mass political movements like the uprisings during the Arab Spring or other protests (where news coverage may be curbed or controlled by powerful players).

There is a clear benefit from performing automated analysis of social media content, and any comprehensive analysis that attempts to understand what is being said has to involve information extraction (IE). While the discussion thus far has provided some context about what might make IE on social media more challenging than in regular domains, we enumerate a few concrete reasons here:

1. First, texts on social media platforms like Twitter tend to be very short (e.g., Facebook limits status updates to 255 characters, whereas Twitter limits tweets to 280 characters).

2. Second, texts are noisy, exhibit much more language variation, and are written in a highly informal setting, with incumbent features including misspellings, lack of punctuation and unorthodox capitalization, nontraditional word use, heavy use of grammatically incorrect phrases and spellings, and extreme presence of out-of-vocabulary tokens.

3. Third, meaning in such texts can be conveyed by nontext cues that require some background knowledge, including use of emoticons, nonstandard abbreviations, and hashtags (in Twitter, but with similar equivalents in other social media sources).

4. Fourth, there is a low amount of discourse information per each microblog document, and a threaded structure is fragmented across multiple documents, flowing in several (sometimes meandering) directions.

5. Fifth, it is highly uncertain if the information conveyed in the text messages is reliable (e.g., compared to the news media) and should be extracted and incorporated into a central knowledge repository like a KG that will eventually be used for querying and analytics.

These challenges suggest that a straightforward application of standard NLP tools on social media content typically results in significantly degraded performance. This has also been an opportunity for researchers to develop new, powerful tools for tackling IE, especially methods that can extract information from short, noisy text messages. In fact, to combat the problems noted here, research has focused on microblog-specific IE algorithms, with particular attention dedicated to the normalization of microblog text, because such normalization can help remove linguistic noise from the text before sending the text through to POS tagging and NER. Note that higher-level IE tasks such as event extraction from Twitter or Facebook are more difficult than NER because not all information on an event may be expressed within a single message. Most of the reported work in the area of event extraction from short messages in social media has tended to focus on event detection rather than outright event extraction in the fine-grained way discussed in chapter 6.

Even at the present time, research on IE from social media is still in its early stages, and largely limited to English. Next, we describe the anatomy of some influential systems, notably TWICAL and TwitIE, to illustrate the key principles behind a typical social media IE architecture. Future research will likely focus on further adaptation of classic IE techniques to extract information from short messages used in microblogging services, tackling non-English social media, and techniques for aggregating and fusing information extracted from conventional text documents, such as news articles, and short messages posted through social media, such as those for using Twitter to enhance event descriptions extracted from classic online news sources with updates that are both period- and situation-specific.

7.3.1 TWICAL

TWICAL, first presented in 2012, was motivated by the observation that, despite the continuing rise of Facebook and Twitter, previous work in event extraction had largely focused on news articles. As we have noted, there are considerable challenges to processing such messages; however, the particular challenge that was identified in Ritter et al. (2012) was that, while a corpus of social media messages tended to be disorganized and noisy, individual messages were short and self-contained and did not feature the kind of complex discourse structure typical of texts containing narratives. Other challenges are that, due to the diversity of tweets, it is unclear in advance which event types are relevant (because TWICAL focused primarily on open-domain event extraction), and the language model in tweets (which is very informal) makes it difficult to design or adapt traditional NLP tools.

Given a raw stream of tweets, TWICAL extracts named entities in association with event phrases and unambiguous dates involved in significant events. Specifically, it extracts a four-tuple representation of events that includes named entity, event phrase, calendar date, and event type. The authors chose this representation to closely match the way that important events are typically mentioned in Twitter.

The overall procedure can be succinctly described as follows. First, POS tags are obtained for tweets. Second, named entities and event phrases are extracted, temporal expressions are resolved, and the extracted events are categorized into types. Finally, TWICAL measures the strength of association between each named entity and date based on the number of tweets they cooccur in, to determine whether an event is significant. NLP tools, such as named entity segmentation systems and POS taggers that were designed to process edited texts (e.g., news articles), perform very poorly when applied to Twitter text due to noise. TWICAL, in contrast, utilizes a preexisting, openly available NER system and POS tagger trained on in-domain Twitter data that had been previously described in Ritter et al. (2011). Thus, it is a good example of an early system that, rather than borrow systems trained on news data, used Twitter data directly to do its own training.

Experimentally, TWICAL was evaluated on about 100 million tweets collected on November 3, 2011, using the Twitter streaming application programming interface (API) by tracking a broad set of temporal keywords, such as "today," "tomorrow," names of weekdays, and other such words. Along with temporal expressions and event phrases, named additions were also extracted from the text of each of the 100 million tweets. The authors then added the extracted triples to the data set used for inferring event types, and performed 50 iterations of Gibbs sampling for predicting event types on the new data, holding the hidden variables in the original data constant. A rigorous annotation procedure was followed, with events annotated according to four separate criteria described in Ritter et al. (2012).

A supervised baseline was used to evaluate the success of the approach by measuring precision at different recall levels by varying a threshold parameter. The authors found that because their approach could leverage large quantities of unlabeled data, it was able to outperform the supervised baseline by more than 14 percent. The authors also found that TWICAL's high-confidence calendar entries were of surprisingly high quality. For example, if the data were limited to the 100 highest-ranked calendar entries over a two-week date range in the future, the precision of extracted (entity, date) pairs was found to be over 90 percent, an 80 percent increase over the baseline. This result has high practical significance, especially in interactive or IR-style approaches, because users' attention tends to drop rapidly after perusing the first few entries in a ranked list. More broadly, it illustrated that the premises underlying the system were promising for developing good social media IE tools.

7.3.2 TwitIE

TwitIE is an open-source NLP pipeline first presented in 2013 at a premier NLP conference by researchers from the University of Sheffield. It is an end-to-end system that can be customized to microblog text at every phase. It also includes Twitter-specific data import and metadata handling. TwitIE is a significant modification of a previous system called GATE ANNIE,[3] which was designed for news text. Just like TWICAL, the premise behind

---

[3] GATE is an open-source NLP framework while ANNIE is a general-purpose IE pipeline. GATE comes prepackaged with ANNIE.

its development is that social media presents challenges over news text that cannot be handled by only using minor modifications to an existing system.

There are five critical modules in TwitIE, namely: *Normalization, Stanford POS Tagging, NER, Language Identification,* and *TwitIE Tokenization.* Because of the language identification module, TwitIE can be used for non-English data. TwitIE uses the *TextCat* algorithm for language identification, which relies on models based on *n*-gram frequencies to discriminate among various languages. The authors integrated an adaptation of TextCat to Twitter, making it work for five languages. Accuracy was measured to be at 97.4 percent, with minor variation in per-language accuracy (99.4 percent for English versus 95.2 percent for French). Considering that language identification is a fairly coarse-grained task compared to some others (such as NER and tokenization), the results show that language identification is hard on tweets, but it still achieves fairly good accuracy.

One of the assumptions made by the system is that each tweet is written in only one language, an assumption that is reasonable mainly because of the shortness of tweets, but also by empirical observation. Given a collection of tweets in a new language, it is possible to train TwitIE's TextCat to support that new language as well by using an *n*-gram-based fingerprint generator (from a corpus of documents in the new language) included as a plug-in in the TwitIE package.

Reliable tweet language identification is also important experimentally because it allows processing only of those tweets written in English, with the TwitIE English POS tagger and NER (as discussed next), by making execution of these modules incumbent on successful identification of the language of the tweet being in English. Although Bontcheva et al. (2013) (the original paper) does not demonstrate multilingual capabilities, the authors note that the GATE components that they adapt for TwitIE provide POS tagging and NER in French and German as well; in principle, therefore, much of what is noted next is applicable to these languages with some effort.

While the other modules mentioned earlier are also customized, the case of POS tagging is particularly instructive. Despite more than 97 percent accuracy of general-purpose English POS taggers, they are not suitable for microblogs, where their accuracy has been measured to decline to below 75 percent in studies. For this reason, TwitIE contains an adapted Stanford tagger, trained on tweets tagged with the Penn TreeBank tagset. Extra tag labels were added for retweets, Uniform Resource Locators (URLs), hashtags, and user mentions. This adapted tagger was trained using hand-annotated tweets, the NPS Chat corpus,[4] and news text from the Penn TreeBank. While these adaptations yielded a model that was found to achieve 83.14 percent token accuracy, its performance still lags performance achieved on news content by 10 percent (though it was still clearly higher than a naive application of an ordinary POS target on social media text).

---

[4] Described at http://faculty.nps.edu/cmartell/NPSChat.htm.

Experimentally, compared to the previous system (ANNIE) from which TwitIE was adapted, as well as the Stanford NER system (often used as the default pretrained NER when performing IE for novel data sets), TwitIE was found to achieve superior experimental results, particularly on the precision metric (which in turn, influenced the final F-measure), although recall was comparable to that of ANNIE (83 percent).

While continuing improvements in social media IE performance are promising, as evidenced by systems like TWICAL, TwitIE, and several others more recently proposed, it should be noted that there is still a significant gap in NER performance on microblogs, as compared to news content. As mentioned earlier, some of this gap could be attributed to insufficient linguistic context (compared to longer, more self-contained news articles) and the inherent difficulty of extracting information from tweets, for all the challenging reasons covered earlier in this section. Another limitation, which the authors of TwitIE acknowledge, is a severe lack of labeled training data, which hinders the adaptation of state-of-the-art NER algorithms, such as the Stanford conditional random field (CRF) tagger. As more training data sets and services are released for nontraditional sources, not only for social media platforms, but also for videos and multilingual corpora, more progress is expected on this issue.

7.4   Other Kinds of Nontraditional Information Extraction

Open IE and social media IE are not the only kinds of nontraditional IE possible. We saw at the very beginning of this chapter, albeit briefly, how fine-grained IE with a domain-specific flavor can itself require nontraditional, minimally supervised techniques, not to mention development of novel corpora and annotation schemes. Other kinds of IE are nontraditional for more historical reasons. For example, multilingual IE was introduced into the MUC series of conferences since MUC-5. This followed more than a decade of IE research that was purely focused on English. One of the impetuses for the shift was a growing amount of textual data available in other languages. Even so, much of the focus on non-English IE tended to be limited to the NER problem, with relatively little work reported on higher-level IE tasks, including RE and event extraction. In recent years, this has started to change, especially with the establishment of ambitious government-funded projects like DARPA LORELEI, DEFT, and AIDA, all of which have components designed to work with non-English data; in many cases, with languages that are "low-resource" and have almost no computational resources like English-parallel texts or training data to bootstrap them.

Perhaps because it has been studied for so long exclusively on English corpora, IE in languages other than English is typically harder, and the performance of non-English IE systems is usually worse. One reason is the lack of core NLP components and underlying linguistic resources for many languages, but most of all it is due to the various linguistic phenomena that are nonexistent in English, a subset of which includes:

1. Lack of white space, such as in Chinese, which can make the problem of word boundary disambiguation more difficult.

2. Complex declension of proper names, such as in Slavic languages (e.g., Polish), which can make it more difficult to normalize named entities. For example, entire papers have been dedicated to the topic of lemmatizing and matching people's names in such languages (e.g., Polish). In contrast, declension in English is so simple compared to other languages that the term is rarely even applied to English.

3. Free word order and rich morphology, which is common for Germanic, Slavic, and Romance languages and can complicate tasks like RE.

Note that this is not an exhaustive list (e.g., the problem of zero anaphora is common in Japanese and Slavic languages). A *zero anaphora* in natural-language conversations is the practice of omitting an overt reference term. To consider zero anaphora with the nonzero case, such as in English, consider the sentence "John says he is coming," where the word "he" is linked by anaphora to the preceding noun John. However, a similar construction in Spanish has no corresponding element: "Dice Juan que viene" (literary translation is "says John that comes"). This kind of zero anaphora can present significant problems for an IE system that has been tuned to English where this problem does not occur in everyday parlance.

Another kind of nontraditional IE that is beyond the scope of this work, but that is rapidly gaining in popularity, is the extraction of instances, attributes, and relations from media sources, especially images and video. When dealing with such sources, techniques from both NLP and the computer vision community are necessary. The most successful models tend to be "joint," not unlike the event-entity joint IE model considered in chapter 6. Furthermore, because of the success of deep learning in the computer vision community in particular, state-of-the-art systems that do IE on media sources are also predominantly based on deep learning and representation learning. Because of the success of these models, which improve with availability of more data and experimentation, the 'blurring' of boundaries between text and nontext modalities will continue, and it may not be long before KG construction over such kinds of media will become mainstream. However, we do note that it is (relatively) more expensive to run and train such neural networks, and using pretrained modules is not as straightforward for these modalities as for text. Hence, there remain infrastructure and computation challenges that still need to be addressed before such neural models truly become staples in a KG construction pipeline.

7.5 Concluding Notes

In the previous chapters, we introduced some "traditional" IE problems such as web IE, NER, and relation (and event) extraction. However, the heterogeneous nature of the web and subject matter experts, as well as the limitations posed by the traditional solutions, have led to a robust set of research results addressing IE problems such as Open IE and social media IE. We describe these IE problems as nontraditional in this chapter, but we maintain that this is only a simplification. Social media, and IE on social media, have now been around for well over a decade, as has Open IE. Thus, whether we should continue to think of them as nontraditional is a matter of subjective opinion. Regardless, it is undeniable that these kinds of IE involve a different set of challenges and questions than traditional IE, which is largely concerned today with improving performance and with closing the gap between supervised and unsupervised systems. Social media IE is especially challenging because social media itself is continuously morphing, and there is considerable heterogeneity between various social media platforms, not to mention disparities that arise due to geographies, topics, and cultural norms.

Despite the considerable difference of opinion in the community on how best to tackle many of these challenges, certain trends have been emerging, as we have attempted to describe in this chapter. Open IE systems, for example, can be taxonomized in four categories in the way they approach the problem, although many of the best systems are hybrids that combine rule- and learning-based techniques. Yet it is unlikely that any of these approaches will be superseded anytime in the near future, and it is our prediction that novel state-of-the-art systems will draw on their predecessors in improving upon some aspect of these techniques, while adapting the best of other techniques to maximize performance. We expect to find something similar in the evolution of social media IE research.

Nevertheless, many interesting and open areas of research remain in all the different kinds of IE covered in this chapter, with some more theoretical, while others firmly empirical. While the most obvious agenda is to improve the nontraditional IE systems (because their performance is understandably still lagging that of more traditional IE systems that have witnessed significantly more research and community resources), it is equally important to make these systems more robust, and more amenable to capturing the richness of human language.

We also discussed how, in the last two decades, IE has moved from monolingual, task-tailored, knowledge-based systems to multilingual, adaptive architectures that deploy minimally supervised machine learning in order to automate many elements in an IE pipeline. Some such pipelines, such as for Open IE, are minimal in the inputs they require to the extent that even an ontology is not required. However, it is not the case that these systems are completely unsupervised, because they do rely on other kinds of user inputs, as we specified when describing some of the representative approaches. In particular, because of the reliance of many Open IE systems on techniques such as distant supervision or weak supervision, it is not clear if these systems can be successfully extended to domain-specific corpora. Some work in this area, especially bioinformatics, has been promising, however, and we will likely see more examples in the years to come.

Finally, considering all of the different kinds of IE that we have encountered in this chapter, is it still fair to use the performance metrics and evaluation protocol? Intuitively, in evaluating Open IE as opposed to ontologically grounded IE (such as the NER and RE cases considered in previous chapters), we must account for subjectivity in the definition of whether an extraction contributes positively to recall or not. An extraction that seems erroneous or trivial to us may matter to another user looking at the corpus through a different lens. Similarly, when considering social media IE, one must ask whether the independent and identically distributed (i.i.d.) assumption is a good one to make. Many people are able to make sense of social media only when presented with the broader context (e.g., a certain tweet may not make sense for someone who is not well versed in US politics or Hollywood celebrity culture and scandal). Therefore, when extracting from a tweet, it may not be fair to have a truly random sample, but to instead have a background corpus that is more topically cohesive and uniform. Arguably, this cohesiveness would provide an IE (or accompanying tools such as word embeddings) with a better chance of success at understanding and extracting from tweets and other sparse social media. There is still much to be decided, therefore, when evaluating what we have referred to as nontraditional IE in this chapter.

7.6 Software and Resources

Open IE has been experiencing a renaissance of late, and several good options for software implementations exist. Because Open IE is still experimental compared to standard NER, the interested practitioner is advised to test these on samples of their own data sets before settling on any given particular option. In some cases, no existing implementation may suffice, and it may be necessary to reimplement or customize an existing algorithm, with the systems discussed in this chapter only serving as guidance. Here, we list some promising options for existing implementations:

1. The Stanford NLP group, also mentioned in earlier chapters, offers an Open IE facility as well, published by Angeli et al. (2015): https://nlp.stanford.edu/software/openie.html.

2. The Allen Institute offers another excellent resource: https://demo.allennlp.org/open-information-extraction. There is a demo of a reimplementation of a recent bidirectional long short-term memory (BiLSTM) model by Stanovsky et al. (2018).

3. The resource https://github.com/NPCai/Open-IE-Papers maintained on GitHub is an impressive repository and taxonomic classification on various papers, including recent ones using neural networks. There is also guidance on available training and testing data.

4. Another excellent aggregation resource of Open IE is available at the webpage: https://paperswithcode.com/task/open-information-extracti-on/latest. It provides a list,

relatively well maintained and recent, of Open IE papers with code. At this time, 18 options were listed.

When it comes to social media IE, one option is to gather together a training corpus of tweets or other social media (such as messages from Facebook or WhatsApp) and train one of the systems listed in the NER and RE chapters. Many of those systems are based on CRFs or neural networks optimized for sequence labeling, and with enough data, nothing prevents them from serving as a good IE system for such data. Because social media is domain-specific, and also culture-specific (as we pointed out in the section entitled "Concluding Notes"), we always recommend such retraining. Even the word embeddings should ideally be retrained on a background corpus that is more akin to the social media data that the user is looking to process. Most pretrained word embeddings are trained on "normal" text, such as that found in Wikipedia and news articles, and these do not closely resemble the informal (or even irreverent) nature of social media.

However, there are a few preimplemented packages available for those looking to specifically experiment with Twitter data. One option is the TwitIE system by Bontcheva et al. (2013), which maintains a homepage accessible at https://gate.ac.uk/wiki/twitie.html. The system described by Ritter et al. (2011, 2012) is also available at https://github.com/aritter/twitter_nlp.

The BLENDER group at UIUC also has some tools that could prove to be useful for multilingual, joint and other kinds of IE covered both in this chapter and previous chapters: https://blender.cs.illinois.edu/software/. Another group that maintains an excellent set of NLP resources is ARK, at the University of Washington: http://www.ark.cs.washington.edu/. Several resources available for download are designed for Twitter. Some resources will not directly yield IE output, but their output could serve as features to robustly bootstrap downstream IE training. For example, the source code available at https://github.com/brendano/ark-tweet-nlp/ could be used for robust POS tagging on tweets.

7.7   Bibliographic Notes

Open IE has been an active and important area of research for about 15 years. As currently defined, the term seems to have been popularized at around the mid-2000s, with a seminal reference being Etzioni et al. (2008), although ideas that shared a (somewhat) similar philosophy had been occasionally proposed. In their survey, Niklaus et al. (2018) draw on that work to identify three major challenges for Open IE systems, which we also alluded to earlier in the chapter (automation, corpus heterogeneity, and efficiency). The TextRunner system was the solution proposed by Etzioni et al. (2008) to these problems. As mentioned in the chapter, TextRunner used the KnowItAll system devised by Etzioni et al. (2004) as a baseline. Piskorski and Yangarber (2013) also provides an important perspective on Open IE and its relationship to other kinds of IE.

Since then, a large body of work has emerged on the subject, with a handful of influential references including Wu and Weld (2010), Fader et al. (2011), Yahya et al. (2014), Akbik and Löser (2012), Mesquita et al. (2013), Stanovsky et al. (2016), White et al. (2016), Christensen et al. (2010), Del Corro and Gemulla (2013), Schmidek and Barbosa (2014), and Gashteovski et al. (2017), many of which covered important systems like OLLIE, REVERB, and ClausIE that we briefly described in this chapter. Recent work in Open IE has also been quite prolific; for instance, Cetto et al. (2018) proposed the Graphene OpenIE framework.

Social Media IE, though a more novel research enterprise than Open IE, has become increasingly popular over time, especially as social media itself has grown in volume and popularity. Good starting references for the interested reader include Morgan and Van Keulen (2014), Hua et al. (2012), and Atefeh and Khreich (2015). Among specific systems covered in this chapter, TWICAL and TwitIE were proposed by Ritter et al. (2012) and Bontcheva et al. (2013), respectively. Other selected references for the social media context (though some are indirect) include Sankaranarayanan et al. (2009), Popescu et al. (2011), Li et al. (2012), and Zhou et al. (2015).

Toward the end of the chapter, we described cutting-edge research areas in nontraditional IE, including multilingual, cross-lingual, and multimodal IE. While much work remains to be done in these areas, we recommend Poibeau et al. (2012), Mei et al. (2018), Zhang, Duh, et al. (2017), Zhang, Whitehead, et al. (2017), Gong et al. (2017), and Mouzannar et al. (2018) as essential readings for the interested researcher to get started in these areas, with the understanding that in these new papers, the boundaries between different research areas are getting increasingly blurred. For example, Zhang, Whitehead, et al. (2017) not only covers the multimodal setting, but deals with the more complicated challenges posed by event extraction. Similarly, Mouzannar et al. (2018) describes a social media–related IE task and uses multimodal deep learning to accomplish the task.

7.8 Exercises

1. We will try to do extraction on tweets using standard NER packages such as NLTK and SpaCy. You could use either one or both (or even other well-known packages that come with pretrained versions), but we recommend being consistent in usage in this, and the next several, questions. We assume NLTK is being used in these exercises. An interactive demo version for trying out individual texts is available at https://text-processing.com/demo/, but to do all the exercises, you will need to set up a local version of NLTK.

As a first step, let us try to play with Twitter data and observe what happens. Go to twitter.com and copy-paste five tweets (one at a time) into the "Tag and Chunk Text" portal in the demo.[5] Try to be diverse in your selection.

2. For each of the tweets, how well does NLTK identify named entities? What are the issues you observe? As a control, try to paste in five sentences from Wikipedia. What are the estimated differences in precision and recall between the control setting and the tweets?

3. Think of how you could improve such a model. List five features that you could extract from tweets that would help you do better. Use your own examples (and the NLTK errors in them) to argue for the utility of your features.

4. For this exercise, we will use a publicly available Twitter data set. There are several such data sets available, including on competition websites like Kaggle. One example is https://www.kaggle.com/crowdflower/twitter-airline-sentiment. Download this data set, and prepare the data so that it can be run through the NLTK extraction module. You will know that you have succeeded when the module runs seamlessly on a sample of this data and outputs named entities (though in all likelihood, many will be incorrect).

5. Randomly sample 100 tweets, and build a "ground-truth" set of entities. Restrict your ontology to persons, organizations, and locations, and be liberal in your definitions. Feel free to add or remove things from your (initially random) sample until you get to a set of tweets that has enough ground-truth extractions from all three classes. Looking at your output from the previous question, what are the precision, recall, and F-measure of NLTK outputs on each of the three classes on your ground-truth?

6. To understand the value of preprocessing, run your data set through NLTK with two kinds of preprocessing, and also without preprocessing. Once again, use the ground-truth set that you carefully constructed in exercise 5 to evaluate your results. Based on your results, what kind of preprocessing seems to work well? Could you "add" more preprocessing steps to make it even better? What is the best performance you are able to get, and what preprocessing steps did you have to take to get to that performance?

7. * The Stanford CoreNLP package supports Open IE: https://stanfordnlp.github.io/CoreNLP/openie.html. Use the module on your Twitter data set. Do a careful, comparative analysis between the Open IE outputs and your previous NLTK outputs. Despite the noise, does the Open IE discover new or interesting things that you didn't catch earlier (and if so, what)?

---

[5] If the demo is offline or not available (or not working), then you should switch to your local version (with your favorite pretrained model) for this exercise.

III KNOWLEDGE GRAPH COMPLETION

8 Instance Matching

Overview. Once constructed, knowledge graphs (KGs) may contain sets of nodes that refer to the same underlying entity. Instance matching (IM) is the problem of semiautomatically clustering *instances* in the KG, such that each cluster resolves to a unique *entity*. Such entities are ordinarily named entities, although IM can apply even if the entity is unnamed. This chapter introduces the instance matching problem in detail and summarizes the main set of solutions that have been proposed over several decades. While the problem remains an active area of research, much progress has been made, and several techniques have become standard.

8.1 Introduction

We begin this chapter with an example of a real-world KG fragment describing four citations extracted from the web (figure 8.1). The KG has already been constructed by this time using techniques such as Named Entity Recognition (NER) or table extraction that were covered earlier in part II of this book. Each citation (which we can assume is an instance of the class *Citation* that exists in an ontology describing the KG and its extractions) has its own *syntactic identifier* (1, 2, 3, and 4) in the KG. In other words, from the machine's perspective, each citation is distinct.

This artifact can result in an erroneous answer to the following question: How many unique papers are in the KG? A reasonable human being would say that there are only two. Citations 1 and 4, as well as citations 2 and 3, form two clusters that each refer to the same underlying entity. The reason why these citations were not automatically resolved is that there are fuzzy differences between them. Citation 1, for example, contains additional information that citation 4 does not, such as the publisher (Springer) and the editor (Stinson). Instance matching, which (ironically) also goes by alternative monikers in the literature (with some terms favored much more heavily by some communities) such as instance matching, deduplication, and record linkage, is the algorithmic problem of resolving such instances or syntactic mentions (which may be extractions, coreferenced groups of extractions, or even entities from semistructured data sets like web tables, wrapper outputs, and XML files) into clusters, such that each cluster refers to the same underlying entity.

Interestingly, the human-provided answer would become more controversial if we re-place *papers* with *citations* in the question that we just asked. Some academics, particularly librarians, may insist that the machine is right—there are four unique citations. Others, like us, may (if only unconsciously) interpret the assumed intent of the modified question to be the same as that of the original question.

The purpose of elaborating upon this possible scenario is to illustrate that it is difficult, if not impossible, to make a formal claim by way of a logical statement or an analytical formula that can be parsed by a machine. If this were possible, then a machine would be able to use such a claim to unequivocally decide the semantic equivalence of two syntacti-cally distinct entities that a human being with reasonable contextual knowledge (or, in the case of domain-specific KGs, an expert with domain knowledge) would say are equivalent. Broadly speaking, this kind of ambiguity is ubiquitous in artificial intelligence (AI), and ordinary human or common-sense reasoning does not typically permit a robust analytical characterization. Hence, IM, despite seeming like a simple problem that most ordinary humans would be capable to solving effortlessly in nonspecialized domains (or by domain experts in specialized domains), is a tough problem for AI to crack.

While it may seem intuitively obvious that detecting, and consequently resolving, such semantically equivalent mentions is good for the KG, we offer several concrete motivations for IM. One reason was mentioned earlier: without IM, one cannot do simple things like counting. Looking again to figure 8.1, we note that IM is typically not limited to one *type* of instance. In the bibliographic KG, there are *Author* nodes that refer to the same authors. Without additional information, a machine would also give us an incorrect count of the number of unique authors in the KG. More specifically, without IM, we cannot rely on algorithms to accurately perform aggregation operations, which include not only counting, but also more complex summarizations that are important for analysis.

Another reason relates to the construction of the KG itself: in at least one case, namely the *year* of publication of citation 1 or 4, we derive an inconsistency, under the reason-able assumption that citation 1 or 4 is referring to the same publication. However, it need not always be the case that conflicting information sets of this nature necessarily indicate inconsistency. For example, one citation may have been for an arXiv publication while another was for exactly the same paper, but formally published in a peer-reviewed con-ference. However, this is clearly not the case for Citations 1 and 4 in figure 8.1. This example also illustrates why context, and in many cases domain-specific knowledge, can be important for making an informed judgment.

Finally, IM also plays a proactive role by helping us obtain a richer information set about a given entity. Returning to the example, one citation mention may include details such as the proceedings and venue, while a different mention of the same citation gives the year and publisher. Usually, the information sets are not disjoint; rather, they overlap, which may or may not lead to inconsistencies, as earlier described.

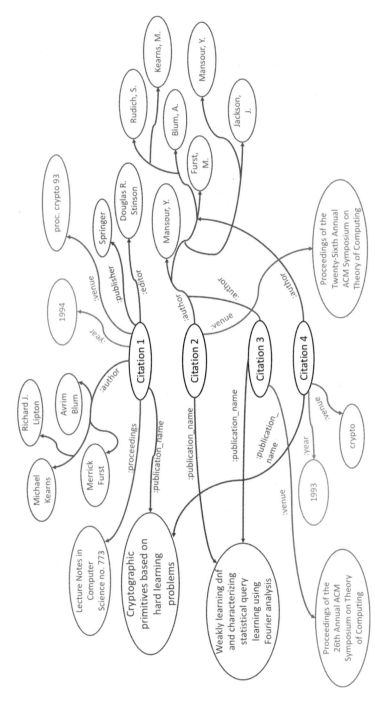

Figure 8.1: A fragment of a bibliographic KG illustrating the IM problem.

With these motivations in mind, we turn to the problem of how to solve IM. Like many difficult AI problems, at this time, the IM problem has not been completely solved, in that no adaptive IM system is able to achieve human-level performance across different domains, even with extensive systems tuning and training. However, much progress has been made on the problem over 50 years of research, and agreement has been reached on a number of issues.

8.2 Formalism

To lay out the formalism for IM, we assume the simplest graph-theoretic definition of a given KG $G = (M, R)$—namely, one that comprises a set M of mention nodes and a set R of directed, labeled edges. In the framework of KGs, the mention nodes are the instances we are trying to match. The term "instance," without qualification, is generally abstract because an instance could also be a record in a table, as is often the case in a database or data warehouse framework. Henceforth, except where occasionally indicated, we use the terms "instance," "entity," and "mention" equivalently. With this context in place, we can define a pairwise linking function $\mathcal{L}_p$ as follows.

Definition 8.2.1 (Pairwise Linking Function) *Given a set M of of mention nodes, a pairwise linking function $\mathcal{L}_p$ is a boolean function $\mathcal{L}_p : M \times M \rightarrow \{True, False\}$, which returns True for a pair of mention nodes iff they refer to the same underlying entity and returns False otherwise.*

Example 8.2.1 Considering figure 8.1 again, the putative pairwise linking function would return *True* for the (order-independent) pairs of mentions *Citation 1* and *Citation 4*, and also *Citation 2* and *Citation 3*, and *False* for any other pair (e.g., *Citation 1* and *Citation 3*).

Note that a mention node is always linked to itself by definition 8.2.1 (i.e., $\mathcal{L}_p$ obeys the property of reflexivity). In fact, it is almost always the case that of the three important properties of reflexivity, symmetry, and transitivity (RST), reflexivity and symmetry are generally obeyed by a real-world $\mathcal{L}_p$, and in many (but not all) cases, so is transitivity. In practice, the definition of $\mathcal{L}_p$ is applied to syntactically distinct mentions. By syntactically distinct nodes m_1 and m_2, we mean that $m_1 \neq m_2$ (i.e., the two nodes have distinct syntactic identifiers in the underlying KG G).

Furthermore, we refer to the function $\mathcal{L}_p$ as *fuzzy* (in lieu of boolean) when the range of the function is in [0,1] instead of $\{True, False\}$. It is easy to see that the boolean definition can be framed as a special case of the fuzzy definition. Many practical functions in the literature, which tend to rely on machine learning algorithms like neural networks and SVMs, are fuzzy; hence, by default, this term is usually omitted. We make this distinction, as it will prove important for the formalism. We also note that, although it is unsafe to assign strict probabilistic semantics to the output of $\mathcal{L}_p$, one can certainly assume probability-*like* semantics. In practice, the outputs are used in conjunction with a thresholding system and a manually annotated gold standard to plot either precision-recall or Receiver Operating Characteristic (ROC) curves.

One limitation of $\mathcal{L}_p$, as defined, does not easily extend to the case when more than two mentions refer to the same underlying entity. There are several ways, both theoretical and practical, that a pairwise linking function $\mathcal{L}_p$ can be extended to a clustering linking function $\mathcal{L}_c$. The semantics of such a function are similar to that of the pairwise linking function, in that all mentions in a cluster should refer to the same underlying entity, and clusters should be maximal in this respect.

Definition 8.2.2 (Clustering Linking Function) Given a set M of of mention nodes, a clustering linking function $\mathcal{L}_c$ is a function that partitions M into a set C of clusters, such that it is always the case that for each cluster $c \in C$, such that $|c| \geq 2$, all mention nodes in c refer to the same underlying entity e, and no other mention in G (i.e., $\in \bigcup C - c$) refers to e. If $|c| = 1$, the single mention in c exclusively refers to its own underlying entity.

Example 8.2.2 Given the four citation nodes in figure 8.1, the putative clustering linking function would return the partition {{Citation 1, Citation 4}, {Citation 3, Citation 2}}.

Unlike with the pairwise function $\mathcal{L}_p$, it is not completely obvious how definition 8.2.2 can be extended to make $\mathcal{L}_c$ fuzzy. In general, the pairwise function is much easier to formulate, and reason about, than the clustering function, and for that reason, it has been much better studied in the IM literature. In some cases, one can do without the clustering function altogether, while in other cases, the outputs of a pairwise function have to be somehow resolved into higher-level clusters. Reasonable clustering functions can be derived by combining the pairwise function with additional assumptions such as transitivity. Another popular technique is to materialize the outputs of an $\mathcal{L}_p$ function as a network-like graph (different from the original *knowledge* graph) and execute an off-the-shelf clustering algorithm on this graph. In the section entitled "Postsimilarity Steps," later in this chapter, we detail some of the possibilities.

8.3   Why Is Instance Matching Challenging?

Before proceeding to a description of standard IM solutions, it is useful to revisit the running example to achieve a better understanding of why the problem is so difficult for machines to begin with (but not the average human). We provided some intuitions in the introduction to this chapter, and to summarize those intuitions, IM is difficult to automate because (1) pairs of duplicate mentions are duplicates for a variety of reasons that are difficult to codify using a consistent and complete rule base, and (2) humans seem to draw on background (often intuitive) knowledge in several common IM domains that is hard to pin down in code. A third challenge that will become clear in the subsequent discussion is scale, because naive solutions to IM grow quadratically with the number of nodes in the

KG. In the rest of this chapter, we illustrate how current IM methods, which usually rely on machine learning techniques, can partially deal with these challenges. As noted before, human-level performance is yet to be achieved.

8.4 Two-Step Pipeline

As a thought experiment, it is useful to assume that we already know the *true pairwise linking function* $\mathcal{L}$. In the worst case, therefore, discovering all possible pairs of linked mentions in a KG is tantamount to solving a quadratic problem. Even for data sets with a few thousand nodes, the complexity quickly explodes. Data sets with more than 100,000 nodes, a not-unusual occurrence in the age of "Big Data," cannot be resolved with brute-force use of quadratic algorithms.

Recognizing this early on, the IM community has converged on a set of preprocessing techniques called blocking to mitigate this quadratic complexity. *Blocking* refers to the process of inexpensively clustering mentions that are approximately similar to (possibly overlapping) blocks. Only mentions that share a block are paired and evaluated by $\mathcal{L}$. A more formal interpretation of approximately similar is that, with high probability, a blocking algorithm should cluster mentions that are more likely to be duplicates (according to $\mathcal{L}$) than nonduplicates. Established blocking algorithms tend to be linear or superlinear but still subquadratic. In some cases, a blocking algorithm may theoretically still be quadratic, but it is still significantly faster in practice (sometimes terminating in less than 1 percent of the time that a full application of $\mathcal{L}$ would have taken).

Of course, the function $\mathcal{L}$ is usually not known in practice (some exceptions are described later), and must also be learned from data, or approximated using a heuristic. The output of blocking, usually a candidate set of mention pairs, is piped to the similarity step where the (known or learned) function $\mathcal{L}$ is applied. This leads to a *two-step* pipeline, as illustrated in figure 8.2. Here, $\mathcal{L}$ may be applied to each mention pair independently, which makes a strong independent and identically distributed (i.i.d.) assumption, or may leverage relational dependencies between mention pairs. Such collective methods have been proposed fairly recently, but they tend to be domain-specific and are continuing to be widely researched. While the majority of this chapter is focused on noncollective IM, which is established and relatively domain-independent, toward the end of the chapter, we briefly cover extensions to collective IM.

8.4.1 Blocking

Blocking is a preprocessing step that is used to mitigate the quadratic complexity of applying $\mathcal{L}$ to all (unordered) pairs of mention nodes from the set M. In the most general case, blocking methods use a many-many function called a *blocking scheme* to cluster approximately similar entities into overlapping blocks. We build up to the definition of a blocking scheme by first defining a simpler function called a *blocking key*.

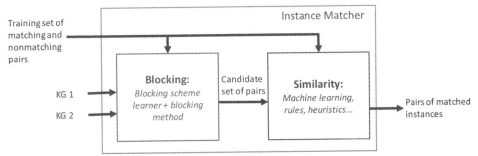

Figure 8.2: The two-step template that is often used for efficiently tackling real-world IM problems. The workflow can be customized in numerous ways, depending on both data modality and assumption about the underlying IM methods. For example, instead of linking entities between two KGs (say, Freebase and DBpedia), instances within a single KG may have to be resolved. For unsupervised methods, training sets may not be required (or the training set may be used only in blocking or similarity, not in both). If the KGs are modeled according to different ontologies and the IM or blocking is sensitive to this, then ontology matching may be necessary as a "step 0."

Definition 8.4.1 (Blocking Key) *Given a set M of mention nodes, a blocking key K is a many-many function that takes a mention $m \in M$ as input and returns a nonempty set of literals, referred to as the blocking key values (BKVs) of m.*

Let $K(m)$ denote the set of BKVs assigned to the mention $m \in M$ by the blocking key K. Furthermore, without loss of generality, the literals in definition 8.4.1 are all assumed to be strings.

Example 8.4.1 (Blocking Key) *A simple example of a blocking key is* Tokens(:label). *Given a mention node with a* :label *property (e.g., a* Person *instance with label "John Smith"), the blocking key would ostensibly yield the BKVs* {John, Smith}. *A more complex example is* Tokens(:label) ∪ Tri-Grams(:label), *which would yield a larger set of BKVs. Although we have used* :label *property in this example, any property could be used, but if an instance is not guaranteed to have a value for that property, then the blocking key has to be designed to deal with this behavior robustly (e.g., by returning the empty set).*

Given a blocking key K, a candidate set $C \subseteq M \times M$ of mention pairs can be generated by a blocking method using the BKVs of the mentions. Before describing some viable blocking methods, we introduce the notion of a blocking scheme that generalizes blocking keys to yield blocks instead of just literals-sets.

Definition 8.4.2 (Blocking Scheme) *Given a set M of mention nodes, a blocking scheme $\mathcal{K}$ is a boolean function that takes an unordered, distinct pair of mentions $(m_i, m_j) \in M \times M$*

(such that $m_i \neq m_j$) as input and returns True if (m_i, m_j) belong to a common block, and False otherwise.

It is important to note that it is *not* necessary for two instances that share a block to be paired together in the candidate set. In fact, it is often undesirable to do so, as example 8.4.2 illustrates. Furthermore, as shown in the example, while the definition of a blocking scheme makes no appeal to a blocking key, practical blocking schemes are built up by combining blocking keys using various set-theoretic operators. Such constraints are especially important when we consider that, theoretically, executing an arbitrary blocking scheme on a set of mentions (to obtain the set of blocks) is itself quadratic in the general setting and provides none of the benefits of blocking. Thus, a blocking scheme is purely conceptual, and actual blocking systems must apply efficient blocking methods (as subsequently described) that are approximately linear (or slightly superlinear) in the number of mentions, which almost always requires the provision of robust blocking keys.

Example 8.4.2 (Blocking Scheme) *An example of a blocking scheme, building on the previous example of blocking keys, is the function Tokens(:label)[m_i] $\cap$ Tokens(:label)[m_j] $\neq \{\}$ (we avoid subscripts by using square brackets for the argument). Even on instances of a simple type such as* Person, *a naive application of this blocking scheme as a candidate set generator would not work well in practice on a sufficiently large data set due to the presence of highly common names like "John" or "Tom," or surnames like "Smith." Considering that names in countries like the United States (and many other Western countries) follow a Zipf-like distribution, a candidate set generated using this blocking scheme, without any additional filters or refinements, would be roughly quadratic (in time and space complexity) in the number of mentions (problem 1). More generally, this problem is referred to as* data skew *and is a common problem in real data sets.*

In example 8.4.2, the naive application of the blocking scheme assumes a blocking method that was quite popular at one time (and that we will describe shortly), where two instances are paired and added to the candidate set if (and only if) they share a block. It is also easy to study the properties of this scheme—that is, it is reflexive and symmetric, but not guaranteed to be transitive (problem 1). By definition 8.4.2, this implies that blocks can be overlapping. None of these conditions are necessary for blocking schemes to be fulfilled. It is perfectly possible to devise blocking schemes where transitivity is guaranteed, and where blocking yields a partition (hence, if m_i and m_j belong to a common block, then it is guaranteed to be the only common block, which is sufficient, though not necessary, for transitivity).

We describe three influential blocking methods next [Traditional Blocking, Sorted Neighborhood (SN), and Canopies], all of which assume that a blocking key K is already specified by a user. Depending on the method, K must also obey some constraints. Subsequently, we also describe the automatic *learning* of a particularly robust class of blocking schemes that has been found to be extremely useful in practice for a variety of reasons.

8.4.1.1 Traditional Blocking We can generalize the way in which the blocking scheme in example 8.4.2 was generated from a blocking key. Specifically, given a blocking key K, an obvious solution is to generate the candidate set C as the set $\{(m_i, m_j)|m_i, m_j \in M \wedge m_i \neq m_j \wedge K(m_i) \cap K(m_j) \neq \{\}\}$. Note that the definition of C as a set further implies that m_i and m_j may share multiple BKVs. It is only necessary for two mentions to share *at least* one BKV for them to be paired and added to the candidate set. As previously described, C is not guaranteed to be transitive. This makes the method nonrobust, especially to the aforementioned problem of data skew.

Despite this problem, Traditional Blocking is often the first line of attack in practical systems. In recent years, researchers have modified Traditional Blocking to handle the large blocks that result from skew. A simple method that is easy to implement and difficult to outperform is *block purging*. The premise of the method is that, with a sufficiently expressive blocking key, blocks that are too large can be safely ignored. With this adjustment in place, the blocking scheme is still the same as before, but the blocking method is now nontrivial and requires the specification of a parameter (the size threshold, using whichever large blocks are discarded) that could, in principle, be learned from training data or experiments. Consequently, the candidate set complexity (in terms of both size and time taken to generate) is much more robust to the actual sizes of blocks generated by the original blocking scheme. The reason why the method performs so well experimentally is that blocks that are most likely indexed by BKVs that are equivalent to stop words like "the" or "an" tend to be large, and because stop words don't really contribute useful information about the instance, it is safe to discard such blocks without losing performance. The purging threshold could be specified in terms of pairs (i.e., discard all blocks that generate more pairs than this threshold) or in terms of block size (number of mentions in the block). While the threshold as an extra parameter may seem to involve extra effort, it has been found to be empirically robust to good default values (e.g., 100), so long as the default value is not too low. Because the method has time guarantees and runs quite fast, several iterations are possible to further tune the value. Another option, less used in the literature, is to start from a high threshold and set a timeout value based on a manually specified budget; namely, if the method has not concluded by the timeout value, then the threshold is reduced by a certain percentage and the blocking algorithm is reexecuted. Even more complex variants have been proposed, but there is no clear evidence that they provide much added value over simple block purging with a heuristically set threshold.

8.4.1.2 Sorted Neighborhood Another influential blocking method that was fundamentally designed to *guarantee* a bound on the size of the candidate set is the SN method, also known as *merge-purge*. The algorithm works as follows. First, a single BKV is gener-

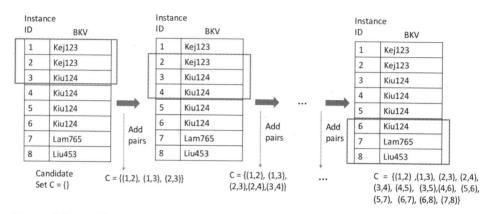

Figure 8.3: An illustration of SN blocking. On the left is a table with instance IDs and the instances' BKVs. The table is sorted according to the BKVs. A window of size 3 is slid over the table, and instances within the window are paired and added to the candidate set (initialized as empty). The final candidate set (sent on to the similarity step in the two-step IM workflow) is shown at the bottom right.

ated for each mention using a many-one blocking key. Next, the BKVs are used as sorting keys to impose an ordering on the mentions. Finally, a window of constant size w is slid over the sorted list. All mentions that share a window are paired and added to the candidate set. Figure 8.3 illustrates a workflow.

Example 8.4.3 (SN) *Figure 8.3 illustrates an example of SN from a US-based customer domain. We assume that the BKV is the concatenation of the first three letters of the last name of the individual, and three digits based on a hash of the social security number. Each instance (a customer) in the KG yields a single BKV and is represented using the customer ID in the sorted table shown. A window of size 3 is slid over the table, and the candidate set is generated. Because the table has eight instances, the total size of the candidate set is 13.*

The sliding window has two implications for candidate set generation. First, mentions that do not have the same BKV may still get paired. An example of such a pair in figure 8.3 is {2,3}. Second, some mentions with the same BKV may *not* get paired. For example, if the sliding window parameter w had been 2 instead of 3 in figure 8.3, the pair {3,5} would not have been added to the candidate set, despite the two instances having the same BKV.

In terms of the blocking scheme formalism, SN is interesting because the concept of a block is bypassed altogether. Instead, each window defines a block, which is of fixed size. The blocking scheme cannot now be defined analytically because it depends on the actual distribution of BKVs. Not only that, but there is a global dependence; that is, in order to determine whether two instances fall within a common block (in this case, window), we cannot *locally* compare their respective BKVs, for even as example 8.4.3 showed, having the same BKV is no guarantee that the two instances will be paired in the candidate set. In addition to the window size parameter, the pairing behavior of two instances depends on the BKVs of other instances (nonlocality). All things being equal, there is higher likelihood for two instances to get paired the more similar their blocking keys, and the fewer the instances that have the same BKV as the BKV of either instance (if distinct).

One source of nondeterminacy to bear in mind when using SN is that the order of instances that have the same BKV needs to be determined using some other information, or randomly. A variant of SN that has tried to deal with this problem instead slides a window over the sorted BKVs rather than the instances. This version loses size guarantees but tends to have higher recall and more predictable behavior because all instances with the same BKVs are always paired, by default, and the nondeterminacy problem noted here does not occur.

Assuming that the window size w is much smaller than the total number of mentions, SN has time and space complexity that is linear in the size of the data. For this reason, it has endured as a popular blocking technique in the IM community. Numerous variations now exist besides the ones alluded to here, including implementations in Big Data architectures like Hadoop and MapReduce. In general, the primary differences between the variants and the original version are input datatypes (e.g., XML Sorted Neighborhood versus Relational), specification of blocking keys, and various ways of tuning the sliding window parameter (e.g., adaptive versus constant) for maximal performance.

A key disadvantage of SN algorithms is that they rely on a single-valued blocking key. Hernández and Stolfo (1995) recognized this as a serious limitation and proposed *multipass SN*, whereby multiple blocking keys (each of which would still have to be single-valued) could be used to improve coverage. For a constant number of passes, the run time of the original method is not affected asymptotically. Practical scaling is achieved by limiting the number of passes to the number of cores in the processor.

However, because even in multipass SN, each blocking key remains single-valued, the use of expressive blocking keys (or even simple, token-based set-similarity measures that have high redundancy) is precluded. Extending SN to account for heterogeneous data sources is also nontrivial. For this reason, the application of SN to KGs and other heterogeneous, semistructured data sources has been limited. The use of a simple blocking method such as Traditional Blocking (combined with skew-compensating measures like block purging) has been more popular.

8.4.1.3 Canopies Clustering methods such as Canopies have also been successfully applied to blocking, especially in the context of relational databases (RDBs), although the application of Canopies to heterogeneous data like KGs is more straightforward than it is for SN. The basic Canopies algorithm takes a *distance function* and two threshold parameters *tight* ≥ 0 and *loose* $\geq$ *tight* and operates in the following way. First, a seed mention *m* is randomly chosen from *M*. All mentions that have a distance less than *loose* are assigned to the *canopy* represented by *m*. Among these mentions, the mentions with distance less than *tight* (from the seed mention) are removed from *M* and not considered further. Another seed mention is now chosen from all mentions still in *M*, and the process continues until all points have been assigned to at least one canopy. Unlike SN, and many other more traditional key-based blocking methods, Canopies does not rely on a blocking key; instead, it takes a distance function as input. For this reason, at least one work has referred to it as an instance-based blocking method and distinguished it from feature-based blocking methods such as SN and Traditional Blocking.

Similar to other popular blocking methods like Traditional Blocking and SN, several variants of Canopies have been proposed over the years, but the basic framework continues to be popular. For example, a nearest-neighbors method could be used for clustering mentions rather than a threshold-based method. In yet another variant, a blocking key can be used to *first* generate a set of BKVs for each mention, and Canopies can then be executed by performing distance computations on the *BKV sets* of mentions, rather than directly on the mentions themselves. Because this variant relies on a blocking key, it can no longer be considered an instance-based blocking method.

In the Canopies framework, each canopy represents a block. Concerning the choice of the distance function, the method has been found to work well with (the distance version of) a number of token-based set similarity measures, including Jaccard and cosine similarity (on tf-idf vectors). Such measures are quite robust to a number of issues (e.g., tf-idf based cosine similarity is insensitive to stop words and Jaccard is more sensitive to the number of unique tokens in a text fragment rather than the overall number of tokens, which allows it to discount frequently repeated words). However, token-based measures also have their blind spots, and not every information set or attribute associated with an entity can be decomposed into token sets to begin with. In practice, multiple distance functions and measures may make sense in order to correctly cluster entities with both high precision and recall. It is not completely clear whether one can extend Canopies in a way that seamlessly accommodates multiple functions. A systematic method might be multiview clustering, but at the risk of sacrificing the efficiency and simplicity of the original Canopies algorithm.

8.4.1.4 Learning Blocking Keys Thus far, we have assumed that a blocking key is specified a priori. This used to be a safe assumption when IM was principally applied to tables (wherein it is referred to as *record linkage* or *deduplication*) with relatively constrained schemas. In such a case, a domain expert or practitioner looking at the table would have a "feel" for what a good blocking key could be. With some trial and error, an initially posited blocking key could be refined until satisfactory performance was achieved. With KGs, the situation is somewhat different. First, KGs tend to be large and heterogeneous, even schema-free, in that many mentions may not have object values specified for all properties. For example, in figure 8.1, citation 2 does not have a specified publisher. Another problem that is common in KGs, but not RDBs, is that some properties have multiple object values specified. All the citations in figure 8.1 have multiple authors specified. If the same data were laid out in a table, there would be a single column for author name, and the authors would be separated using some agreed-upon delimiter (like a comma). The disadvantage of such compact representations is that one needs extra knowledge in order to parse the contents of the column.

Regardless of the trade-offs between tabular and graph-theoretic representations of data, the merits of automatically learning blocking keys should be evident. At the very least, an automatic, good blocking key learner or BKL would yield a key that is data-driven and relieve the domain expert of the effort of having to specify or discover one using costly trial and error. Beyond scale and convenience, such learners are important for systems that cannot expose their data for reasons of privacy.

The best-known procedure for learning blocking schemes from labeled training data was first published only a decade ago. The key idea is to model the blocking scheme as a Disjunctive Normal Form (DNF) rule. A DNF blocking key can be constructed by starting with a set of *indexing functions* that take a primitive datatype as input and return a set of primitives as output. Without loss of generality, *String* is assumed as the only available primitive datatype, although the formalism given in example 8.4.4 also applies with a mixture of primitive types.

Example 8.4.4 (Indexing Function) *An example of an indexing function introduced earlier in the context of blocking keys is* Tokens, *which relies on predetermined delimiters to tokenize a string (e.g., "John Smith") into a set of strings (e.g., {"John", "Smith"}).*

A *blocking predicate* $b_h(prop)$ on mentions is now defined by pairing an indexing function h with a property *prop*, and adopting the following semantics: Let two mentions in the KG be denoted by the symbols m_i and m_j. The logical predicate $b_h(prop)[m_i, m_j]$ is satisfied iff the intersection $h(prop)[m_i] \cap h(prop)[m_j]$ is nonempty, where $h(prop)[m]$ is defined as the set obtained by applying $h(prop)$ on the object value of m for property *prop*. Typically, the predicate mnemonically indicates the underlying indexing function. Similar to notation previously introduced, the property is included in parentheses and the argument in square brackets. Example 8.4.5 implements these ideas in practice.

Example 8.4.5 (Blocking Predicate) *An example of a blocking predicate is Common-Tokens(:label). CommonTokens indicates that Tokens is the underlying indexing function, while : label is the underlying property used by the predicate. If two mentions have so much as a common token in their labels, the blocking predicate would return True for the mention pair.*

What is the difference between the blocking key defined earlier and the indexing function? The most important difference is that the indexing function is a very general kind of function that takes the primitive datatype (rather than a KG instance) as input. On the other hand, a blocking key applies to instances of KGs, which means that it has to extract the relevant data (using properties like *:label*, for example) before applying an indexing function–like operation such as tokenization. The blocking predicate, being boolean, is like a simplified version of the blocking scheme introduced earlier, but it is much more specific in structure because it is not only always associated with an underlying indexing function, but it also applies intersection to the sets to determine the truth value. Recall that blocking schemes, in the general sense, were not bound by any such constraints; in fact, the underlying blocking scheme described by methods like SN (even given an analytic representation of the many-one blocking key itself) has no formulaic representation.

Before proceeding further, we must note the various ways in which predicates like CommonTokens can fail, most common of which is the data skew problem described earlier. To avoid such problems, one could envision ways to make the blocking predicate more complex (e.g., by considering an indexing function that is more sophisticated or discerning than tokenizing). However, it is unclear if even that would do the trick. What if the blocking key were too discerning? If a true positive pair does not make it through blocking, it has no chance of being flagged by the similarity step as being a matched pair of instances, which would hurt coverage metrics like recall. Clearly, we want a solution where a trade-off can be achieved between coverage and efficiency.

Intuitively, a combination of heuristics or predicates is usually required to achieve good performance on any linking task, including approximate tasks like blocking. The trick is to combine several blocking predicates into a single boolean expression, called a *DNF blocking scheme*, by using blocking predicates as atoms. For well-defined semantics, negated atoms are disallowed. Similar to the blocking predicates, a DNF blocking scheme takes a pair of mentions as input. The mnemonic considerations earlier stated also apply. Following example 8.4.6, we explain why such an expression is referred to as a scheme rather than a key, as well as the difference between the two.

Example 8.4.6 (DNF Blocking Scheme) *For a people's data set, consider the DNF blocking scheme CommonTokens(: label)∨HasExactMatch(: age)∧CommonSoundex(: label). Two new blocking predicates, named self-explanatorily, are introduced in the DNF expression: HasExactMatch uses the identity function as its underlying indexing function and returns True if two strings exactly match, while CommonSoundex uses a modified version of Tokens as its indexing function and returns True if two strings share at least one token that* sounds *the same (i.e., have the same* Soundex *encoding). The mention pair* (m_i, m_j) *is added to the candidate set C if it satisfies the scheme.*

It is fruitful to revisit the difference between a scheme and a key. Although the literature is not consistent on this issue (nor is it considered a touchy matter), we offer the following answer: A scheme takes a pair of mentions as input and returns either *True* or *False*; in other words, it is used to test for candidate set membership, but otherwise is not useful in practice because it is still pairwise. On the other hand, a DNF blocking key is a variation of the scheme that (1) operates on a single mention to extract a set of BKVs (based on the underlying indexing functions and properties), and (2) can be used to construct an inverted index of BKVs that can then be efficiently processed by a blocking method like the three described earlier.

Just as with arbitrary blocking schemes, it is possible for a pair (m_i, m_j) to be evaluated as *True* by a DNF blocking scheme, but not be included in the candidate set C. The reason, of course, is that the candidate set depends both on the BKVs and the blocking method used. Traditional Blocking can guarantee that a pair such as the one given here is always included in C, where a method like SN, as noted in an earlier caveat, would not. The converse is also true. Because of its sliding window methodology, a method like SN may include pairs in C that would be evaluated as *False* by the corresponding blocking scheme. For this reason, we recommend always thinking about blocking in terms of a blocking key and a blocking method rather than an idealized blocking scheme, although if available (especially in an analytical form) and paired with a reasonable or well-studied blocking method like Traditional Blocking, it can be instrumental for proving theoretical claims (such as membership or existence) about the candidate set.

As it turns out, one reason why DNF blocking schemes are attractive is that they can be learned using a training set of positive (matching) and negative (nonmatching) instance pairs. This is preferable not only because it means that adaptive methods can be used for automatically discovering the schemes, rather than constructing them using trial-and-error, intuition-based exploration, but because labeled pairs are usually available anyway for the state-of-the-art similarity steps based on machine learning. Thus, the labeled pairs can be used twice, maximizing the benefit of labeling them in the first place. DNF schemes are also not training hungry, so to speak; experiments have shown that with a few good training pairs, a robust scheme can be learned with good regularization mechanisms. Methods have been proposed to avoid labeling altogether by using heuristics like tf-idf to obtain an approximately correct training data set. Such methods are useful if the similarity step is unsupervised, which makes labeling unfeasible if the only goal is to use the labeled pairs for learning a blocking scheme.

What is interesting about DNF blocking scheme learners is that they do not rely on ordinary machine learning algorithms; instead, the problem is framed as an instance of *red-blue set covering*. This is a well-studied (and understood) problem that is known to be NP-complete, and greedy algorithms providing approximate solutions with guarantees have existed for at least a few decades. The basic version of the problem can be stated as follows. Given a finite set of red elements R, a finite set of blue elements B, and a family $S \subseteq 2^{R \cup B}$, the problem is to find a subfamily $\subseteq S$ that covers all blue elements, but which covers the minimum possible number of red elements. In the blocking context, the blue elements are the positive training pairs, and the red elements are the negative training pairs.

Note that, because blocking is only a precursor to similarity, false positives are expected, and the similarity step is expected to weed out those false positives in the second step. A candidate DNF scheme covers a pair if it returns *True* for that pair. The goal is to discover a candidate that covers all of the positive pairs, while minimizing coverage of the negative pairs. The actual algorithms used for discovering these schemes are not quite as simple, because the number of possible DNF schemes is at least exponential in the number of predicates. The usual mechanism for controlling the complexity is to set a parameter k (which is usually 2 or 3) and only consider k-DNF expressions as candidate schemes. A k-DNF scheme is a strict subset of all DNF schemes that allows conjuncts that have at most k blocking predicates. As we noted earlier, predicates are not allowed to be negated, which leads to an even smaller space. Even so, the full implementation of the learning algorithm can be tricky. For more details on semisupervised and unsupervised variants, including a variant proposed specifically for Resource Description Framework (RDF) KGs, we refer readers to resources listed in the section entitled "Bibliographic Notes," at the end of this chapter.

Work on red-blue set covering has continued in the algorithms community independent of blocking, instance matching, or KG. In principle, these developments can be used for speeding up learning, although we are not aware of any practical cases that have done so. Usually, the greedy algorithm suffices for learning a good DNF blocking scheme.

8.4.2   Similarity

Once blocking has been executed, the resultant candidate set C of pairs must undergo *similarity* computations to filter out (whether in a probabilistic or deterministic manner) the subset of C that comprises nonduplicate mention pairs. If the independence and identically distributed properties are assumed, each such pair is independently assigned a score, with higher scores indicating greater likelihood of the pair representing matching instances. Scores tend to be normalized to [0, 1], but this does not mean that they should be strictly interpreted as probabilities. The usual methodology is to either assume a threshold (all pairs with scores above this threshold are considered matching instance pairs) or to rank the pairs in descending order of score and consider only the top N. Either way, the threshold or N is an extra parameter that has to be determined using either a held-out validation set or some other kind of validation scheme, such as k-fold cross-validation.

The problem of choosing the pairs does not arise if the scores are deterministic (either 1.0 or 0.0), but this is rare in machine learning. In earlier research, when rules were used for determining if instances matched or not, this was much more common. However, to get good rules (or other heuristics), significant effort from domain engineers or experts had to be solicited and hence, in recent years, such methods have become increasingly obsolete. Furthermore, when using fuzzy scores, it turns out that there is a well-known theoretical model in early IM literature known as the *Fellegi-Sunter model*, named after Fellegi and Sunter (1969), who formulated it. The model makes the claim that *two* (not necessarily distinct) thresholds are actually necessary to achieve a desired optimal trade-off between minimizing false positives and minimizing false negatives, two goals that often conflict (and that influence *precision* and *recall*, respectively; see the section entitled "Evaluating the Two-Step Pipeline," later in this chapter, for more information). The goal behind using two thresholds is to partition the candidate set into three sets (matches, possible matches, and nonmatches). Possible matches are in the set that would benefit most from manual review. The ratio of conditional probabilities (the condition being based on whether the instance pair is assumed as matching or nonmatching) is used to compute the score that is compared to these thresholds to determine what set the pair should fall into. We provide original references for the Fellegi-Sunter model for interested readers in the "Bibliographic Notes" section.

This discussion assumes that we have a similarity function and have executed it on the candidate set to get scores or labels. But how do we learn such a similarity function to begin with? We principally assume a machine learning framework because machine learning models have emerged as state-of-the-art similarity functions. Notationally, let us denote the machine learning classifier as $\mathcal{L}^*$, or an approximation of the (unknown, true) pairwise linking function $\mathcal{L}_p$ defined earlier.

First, each mention pair in C is converted to a numeric (typically, but not necessarily, real-valued) *feature vector*. Figure 8.4 illustrates the procedure for two such mentions. Because instances in KGs do not have to contain values for every single property, some practical assumptions must be made if a given property does not exist for an instance or if (for whatever reason) the feature function returns an exception. A common practice is to use special (i.e., dummy) values in the event that (1) values for a given property are missing from both mentions, even though values for that property were observed for at least one other mention in the data set; and (2) the value for a given property is missing from one (but not both) mentions. By using not one but several dummy values, the missing information itself can be used to provide a (potentially useful) signal to the model. However, using too many "dummy" values for narrow classes of exceptions can impede generalization.

More specifically, given n properties, and m functions in a *feature library* (the set of feature functions), the feature vector would have at most mn elements. We say "at most" here because some features may be designed for specialized values (e.g., a feature that computes the number of milliseconds between two date values), and not be applicable to two arbitrary values or properties. In this case, the feature would be applicable only to those properties describing dates, and not *all n* properties. We also note that while more features are generally preferable, especially if they add value, care must be exercised because many feature functions may be correlated and could harm machine learning generalization, especially when the training set is small and highly heterogeneous, as is the case with real-world IM tasks. If it is not evident which feature functions should be retained and which should be discarded, a possible solution is to start by computing all possible (i.e.,

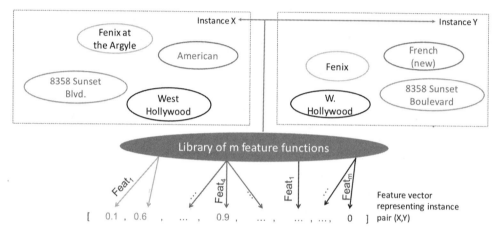

Figure 8.4: An illustration of feature extraction from a mention-pair of instances (X,Y) in the candidate set, given a library of *m* feature extraction functions. We have not drawn the property edges for clarity. Different concepts in the ontology are intuitively expressed by the text (e.g., the node "American" is of concept type "Cuisine" in the ontology). Not every feature function in the library may be applicable to every pair of attributes. Usually, a dummy value of −1 is used in the feature vector to express when one of the *m* functions is inapplicable to a concept. Given *k* attributes (in this case, *k* = 4) for each instance (of a given type), this ensures that each feature vector is of a dimensionality of exactly *km* unless a conscious decision is made to compare attributes across types. We use ... to indicate the presence of multiple unknown features and feature values.

Table 8.1: A non-comprehensive list of pairwise feature functions, classified by type, that are popular in IM and other related fields.

Type	Function	Type	Function
Character	Edit/Levenstein	Token	Monge-Elkan
	Affine Gap		TF-IDF
	Smith-Waterman		Soft TF-IDF
	Jaro		Q-gram TF-IDF
	Q-gram		Jaccard
Phonetic	Soundex	Numeric	Difference
	NYSIIS		Absolute Difference
	Metaphone		Magnitude/Factor
	ONCA		
	Double Metaphone		

NYSIIS stands for *New York State Immunization Information System* and ONCA stands for *Oxford Name Compression Algorithm.*

$\leq mn$) features and then apply a feature selection method like Lasso. A second, more traditional remedy is to invest domain engineering effort in assigning only a few features to each property. If no more than c feature functions are assigned to a property ($c << m$), the feature vector cardinality will end up being much smaller than mn, potentially yielding more robust performance during actual deployment.

Thus far, we have considered feature functions in the abstract, but what do *actual* feature functions look like? Luckily, there is an enormous body of work on several classes of useful feature functions—most notably, string similarity, but also phonetic similarity functions (although research on feature functions for numeric or date types is surprisingly sparse). We provide some guidance on available software packages in the section entitled "Software and Resources," at the end of this chapter. For the sake of completeness, we provide a list of functions that have been popularly used in table 8.1.

Another problem that also arises in the context of KGs when extracting features from pairs of instances is similar to the problem of exceptions noted here; namely, how should the features be extracted if there are multiple values for a property for an instance? In general, how do we deal with properties where the complete spectrum (no values, multiple values, or a single value) is observed over the KG? As one example, imagine a property called *:marriageDate*. Instances of people who were never married will have no value for this property, while those married more than once will have multiple dates. One way to deal with these cases is to use the dummy-assignment methodology if no values exist, and to use a *two-layer* similarity function if multiple values exist for the property for one or both instances in the pair. The first layer in such functions consists of an atomic similarity function (e.g., if the set consists of string values, this could be the normalized similarity version of Levenstein distance), and the second layer consists of an aggregation. For example, we could consider a symmetric aggregation function such as $max(editSim(s_i, s'_j))/(|S| + |S'|)$ where s_i and s'_j range over all strings in the two sets S and S'. The idea is that, for each string in S (and similarly for S'), we find the (not necessarily unique) string in the other set that has maximum normalized Levenstein similarity to that string. We collect all such similarities and then average them (the purpose of the denominator in the expression). This function is symmetric, but it may not be as robust to outliers. Other similar functions, not necessarily symmetric, could be devised as well. A more sophisticated variant of the second layer is not to use a function directly, but instead to model the problem as a weighted bipartite graph, and then calculate some kind of score (e.g., average weight over the edges in the shortest path spanning the maximum number of nodes) over this graph. The more sophisticated the aggregation, or the more expensive the atomic similarity in the first layer, the more expensive the feature extraction.

With feature extraction in place, each pair in C is converted to a feature vector. A machine learning classifier is trained on positively and negatively labeled training samples and used to assign scores to the vectors in the candidate set. Classifiers explored in the literature (see the "Bibliographic Notes" section) include classic models like random forest, multilayer perceptron, and support vector machine (SVM), all of which have been found to perform reasonably well. More recently, Siamese neural networks have been proposed for the IM task, although their effectiveness (specifically on IM) is still an open question, especially when training data is limited. A Siamese neural network uses (as the name suggests) the same weights while working simultaneously on two different input vectors to compute comparable output vectors. An intuitive analogy is fingerprint comparison or locality sensitive hashing (LSH), an advanced similarity technique that works well on large candidate sets when certain assumptions apply. In the "Bibliographic Notes" section, we provide some pointers to established work in these areas. One point to note is that, although these classifiers all tend to make the i.i.d. assumption, transitivity (which is a relational property that violates independence) plays a strong role in real-world IM determinations; if (m_e, m_j) and (m_e, m_k) are classified as matches with high probabilities, it is more likely than not that (m_j, m_k) also represent a matching pair, thus establishing a dependence between the similarity score of (m_j, m_k) and other pairs in which at least one of the two instances participated. While this observation is not typically employed at this stage, it motivates postprocessing steps such as clustering and soft transitive closure, as subsequently described.

8.5 Evaluating the Two-Step Pipeline

Because of the independence of blocking and similarity within the two-step formulation, the performance of each step can be controlled for the other when running experiments. This is convenient because of the increasing complexity of published blocking and similarity algorithms in recent years. Despite the potential disadvantages of this independence (in practice, there can be unintended interdependencies between blocking and similarity, because feature functions and biases could often be traded between the two, especially if training sets are shared), this methodology has resulted in the adoption of well-defined evaluation metrics for both blocking and similarity. In recent years, while the independence assumption has been challenged in a small number of applications and algorithms (as just one example, a blocking technique called *comparisons propagation* proposes using the outcomes in the similarity step to estimate the usefulness of a block in real time, the premise being that if a block has produced too many nonduplicates by the similarity algorithm, it is best to discard it rather than finish processing it), as we briefly detail in the "Bibliographic Notes" section, implementation and adoption of these algorithms have mostly been limited to serial architectures owing to the need for continuous data sharing between the similarity and block-generating components. Experimentally, the benefits of such techniques over independent techniques like SN or Traditional Blocking (with skew-eliminating measures such as block purging) have not been established extensively enough, or in enough domains, to warrant widespread adoption. The two-step workflow, with both steps relatively independent, continues to be predominant in the vast majority of IM research. With this small caveat, we describe these metrics next.

8.5.1 Evaluating Blocking

The primary goal of blocking is to scale the naive one-step IM that pairs all mentions (order-independently) with each other. A blocking system accomplishes this goal by generating a smaller candidate set. If complexity reduction were the *only* goal, the blocking system could simply generate the empty set and obtain optimal performance. Such a system would be useless because it would generate a candidate set with zero duplicates coverage.

Thus, duplicates coverage and candidate set reduction are the two goals that every blocking system seeks to optimize. To formalize these measures, let O be denoted as the *exhaustive set* of all $^{|M|}C_2$ pairs; in other words, the candidate set that would be obtained in the *absence* of blocking. Let O_D denote the subset of O that contains all (and only) matching mention pairs (i.e., semantic duplicates). O_D is designated as the ground-truth or gold standard set. As in previous sections, let C denote the candidate set generated by blocking. Using this notation, *reduction ratio (RR)* is defined by equation (8.1):

$$RR = 1 - \frac{|C|}{|O|}. \tag{8.1}$$

The higher the reduction ratio, the higher the complexity reduction achieved by blocking, relative to the exhaustive set. Less commonly, RR can also be evaluated relative to the candidate set C_b of a *baseline* blocking method by replacing O in equation (8.1) with C_b. Note that, because RR has quadratic dependence, even small differences in RR can have an enormous impact in terms of run time. For example, if O contains 200 million pairs (which would only take a mentions-set M with about 20,000 mentions—that is, a relatively common-sized data set that would not even remotely qualify as Big Data), and a hypothetical Blocking System 1 achieves an RR of 99.7 percent, while Blocking System 2 achieves 99.5 percent, their candidate sets would differ by 200,000 pairs. In short, small differences in the RR matter a lot, and the larger the mentions-set, the larger the impact of even a 0.1 percent improvement in RR.

We can also define a *coverage* metric called pairs completeness (PC):

$$PC = \frac{|C \cap O_D|}{|O_D|}. \tag{8.2}$$

One interpretation of PC is that it is nothing but a measure of recall (used for evaluating overall duplicates coverage in the similarity step, as described in the subsequent section) that *controls* for the errors in further learning or approximating $\mathcal{L}$, which is *not* known. In other words, PC gives an *upper bound* on the recall metric. More simply, it is the answer to the following question: If we know $\mathcal{L}$ and apply it to the candidate set C output by blocking, what would be the recall? For example, if PC is only 70 percent, meaning that 30 percent of the matching instance pairs did not get included in C, then coverage on the full IM task can *never* exceed 70 percent, and in most cases, will be below 70 percent (i.e., if the similarity step has nonzero false negatives). PC clearly represents an upper bound to overall IM recall.

There is usually a trade-off between achieving optimal PC and RR values in real-world blocking systems. The trade-off is achieved by tuning a relevant parameter. There are two ways to represent this trade-off. The first is a single-point estimate of the F-measure (FM), or harmonic mean, between a given PC and RR:

$$FM = \frac{2 \times PC \times RR}{PC + RR}. \tag{8.3}$$

A single-point estimate is useful only when it is not feasible to run the blocking algorithm for multiple parameter values. Otherwise, a more visual representation of the trade-off can be achieved by plotting a curve of PC versus RR for different values of the parameters.

Another trade-off metric, Pairs Quality (PQ), is less commonly used than the FM of PC and RR:

$$PQ = \frac{|C \cap O_D|}{|C|}. \tag{8.4}$$

Superficially, PQ seems to be a better measure of the trade-off between PC and RR than the FM estimate, which weighs RR and PC equally, despite the quadratic dependence of RR. PQ has often been described as a precision metric for blocking, intuitively because a high PQ indicates that the generated blocks (and by virtue, the candidate set) are dense in duplicate pairs. Unfortunately, in practice, PQ gives estimates that can be non-interpretable, if not outright misleading. For example, suppose there were 5,000 duplicates in the ground-truth, and *C* only contained 20 pairs, of which 12 are matching instance pairs. PQ, in this case, would be 12/20, or 60 percent. Assuming that *O* is large enough that RR is close to 100 percent, the FM (as defined here) would still be much less than 1 percent (as PC is only 12/5,000, or 0.24 percent). In other words, the negligible FM result would be correctly interpreted as an indication that, for practical purposes, the blocking process has failed. The result indicated by PQ alone, however, indicates otherwise, because 60 percent is not a bad performance to obtain on a difficult data set. An alternative, proposed by at least one author but (to the best of our knowledge) not used widely, is to compute and report the FM of PQ and PC.

8.5.2   Evaluating Similarity

Recall that the ultimate goal of the similarity step is to partition the provided candidate set *C* into sets C_D and C_{ND} of matching and nonmatching instance pairs respectively. Thus, two obvious (though not exclusive) metrics that apply to similarity are *precision* and *recall*:

$$Precision = \frac{|C_D \cap O_D|}{|C_D|}. \tag{8.5}$$

$$Recall = \frac{|C_D \cap O_D|}{|O_D|}. \tag{8.6}$$

In words, precision is the ratio of true positives to the sum of true positives and false positives, while recall is the ratio of true positives to all positives in the ground-truth. Similar to PC and RR defined earlier, there is a trade-off between achieving high values for precision and recall. An FM estimate can again be defined for a single-point estimate, but a better, more visual, interpretation is achieved by plotting a curve of precision versus recall for multiple parameter values.

Note that, because similarity is defined as a binary classification problem in the machine learning interpretation of instance matching, other measures such as accuracy can also be defined. One reason why they are not considered in the IM literature is because they also evaluate performance on the negative (i.e., nonduplicates) class, which is not of interest in IM. An alternative to a precision-recall curve is Receiver Operating Characteristic (ROC), which plots true positives against false positives. Historically, and currently, precision-recall curves dominate ROC curves in the IM community, but nowadays, important machine learning packages (e.g., sklearn in Python) allow a user to print out various metrics and curves without any programming. In real life, we recommend printing out both the precision-recall and ROC curves to evaluate both (1) how well the IM system is doing in an "absolute" sense; and (2) how well the IM system is doing above *random*.

8.6 Postsimilarity Steps

Although IM performance is strongly affected by various factors extrinsic to the actual classifier developed in the "Similarity" section, particularly the quality of the data being linked, much can be done to improve the IM process itself. Empirically, the performance of blocking affects the performance of overall IM, both by directly impacting the final recall score (and by extension, "trade-off" metrics like the FM), but also precision.

The features used in a classifier are also extremely important, although with the recent advent of KG embeddings (KGEs), feature crafting may soon belong to the past. However, there are limits to how much time one can spend refining features. Instead, a less labor-prone task may be to assume the scores as noisy inputs and use the dependencies between scores and mentions to obtain the final clusters of mentions (each cluster referring to the same entity), and to fuse the mentions in each cluster into a single composite entity. A problem that seems similar on the surface, but needs to be addressed at an earlier (i.e., similarity) stage, is that of modeling dependencies between mentions to obtain scores that reflect such dependencies. If domain knowledge is available, collective similarity methods, briefly described later, may be applicable, but if not, statistical methods like clustering and transitive closure can be used as a first line of attack. Another solution, which has been in vogue in the Semantic Web community, is to not "collapse" matching instances into clusters to begin with, but to instead embed them within an *Entity Name System (ENS)*. Next, we describe these two approaches.

8.6.1 Clustering and Transitive Closure

To recover clusters of mentions that refer to the same underlying entity, a naive method would be to first choose a duplicates threshold and then recover the connected components from the unweighted graph (figure 8.5). This method tends to have a high empirical failure rate, for the reason that a few noisy scores can lead to (1) disjoint clusters that, in fact, refer to the same underlying entity; and more commonly, (2) large, skewed clusters that got connected because of a few rogue links. Earlier, we saw that the data skew problem is quite common in the real world (due to nonnormal probability distributions often showing up in the context of common names and other such entities). While the first problem arises because low scores got assigned to matching (in the ground-truth) pairs, the second problem arises because high scores got assigned to nonmatching instance pairs. The latter problem tends to be more serious than the first precisely because of data skew. Namely, given a large connected component, how should we break it up into smaller components? We could ostensibly use network theory to try and identify the set of miscreant nodes and edges that caused the problem to begin with. But which network-theoretic measure should we use? Even for established concepts like centrality, several ways of defining and measuring it exist. Most nontechnical (and in many cases, technical) users grappling with

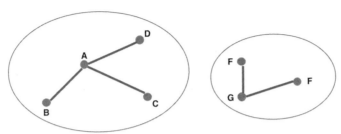

Figure 8.5: A naive hard-clustering method, based on connected components, for recovering instance clusters from thresholded, scored pairwise outputs obtained from a two-step IM pipeline. The nodes represent instances, the circles represent the clusters (in this case, equivalent to connected components), and an edge exists only between two instances if the similarity between them was above the threshold (and assuming also that they were compared in the first place—that is, were placed in the candidate set). A single edge between the two components (say, D and F) would "collapse" both components into one cluster. Soft clustering approaches take a more sophisticated approach. Other approaches do not apply thresholding but rather work directly with weighted edges in the graph.

the tuning and outputs of such algorithms do not have a deep enough knowledge of network theory to decide on the correct course of action.

Compared to algorithms that assume hard or unweighted edges, such as the connected components algorithm, we could go one step further and employ a class of *clustering* algorithms that generically accept a weighted graph as input, along with hyperparameters such as the number of clusters desired, and return the set of cluster assignments. Clustering is an important topic in the machine learning and data-mining literature, with applications well beyond IM. Examples of fairly established clustering algorithms include K-Means and spectral clustering. The important takeaway from this chapter is that, once we model the output of an IM similarity step as a weighted graph, any clustering algorithm can potentially be used, though some will achieve much higher performance than others. Unfortunately, it is not always clear which clustering algorithm is best for a given task or data set. Other considerations, such as the complexity of the algorithm, as well as its robustness to noisy scores, must also be taken into account. As mentioned earlier, in a typical IM pipeline, some high scores will inevitably get assigned to nonduplicate mentions and vice versa.

A potentially more serious problem is the specification of hyperparameters, which is by no means trivial in IM problems, even for simple algorithms like K-Means. The reason for this is that IM is (to use terminology proposed quite recently) a *microclustering* problem. In IM, the number of clusters grows much quicker with the size of the data than in traditional clustering algorithms. In many clustering evaluations applying the K-Means algorithm, k almost never exceeds 100, even when the data set to be clustered contains many instances.

In contrast, even simple IM benchmarks with a few thousand records can contain hundreds of duplicates.

What if we want to limit ourselves to the simple, but brittle, connected components scheme described here, but take the weights of the edges (the similarity score between instances paired in the blocking and evaluated in the similarity steps) into account to make the algorithm more robust? One way to think about this problem is as a *soft transitive closure*. A transitive closure occurs when we introduce a direct edge between A and B, if we observe a path between them. The idea is to recursively apply the transitive property: if A-B and B-C → A-C. As expressed here, the transitive property is a hard one (i.e., there is no fuzziness or uncertainty in the truth of the property). Instead, suppose that we assume that the property only holds with probability 0.8 in the general case. As another added layer of complexity, we also assume that the "edge" A-B itself has an associated strength, which is the score assigned to the pair by the similarity step. Per this representation, the resulting outputs of the similarity step constitute a body of rules embodying the transitive property (in practice, the rule base is represented simply as a set of weighted statements, with each statement encoding a scored pairwise match as output by the similarity step).

Given this rule base, there are a number of *soft transitive closure* procedures in the literature (just like normal clustering) that take this rule base as input and output truth values for all edges. A popular method is Probabilistic Soft Logic (PSL), which has other use-cases beyond IM and can, in fact, be applied to any similarly structured problem with dependencies and probabilities. In chapter 9, on statistical relational learning (SRL), we provide more details on the technical machinery that underlies such frameworks. Generally, however, true values are assigned only to edges that have already been assigned a nonzero score and all things equal, the higher the score, the higher the probability the true value will be assigned. Furthermore, all things being equal, the pair A-C will have a higher probability of being assigned a true value the shorter the weighted path between A and C. The specific way in which the algorithm takes the weights and links into account before making a true/false determination for a pair depends on the actual algorithm. Once the edges have been output, we could always rerun the connected component algorithm, this time with the hope that weaker links that lead to collapse of small components into large ones have been eliminated due to the probabilistic application of the transitive property (as opposed to the application of a single hard threshold, as in the naive case).

Another option that avoids the complexity of probabilistic frameworks while still maintaining a reasonable degree of robustness is to use either top-down or bottom-up (i.e., agglomerative) *hierarchical clustering*, which do not require the number of clusters to be specified. Hierarchical in this context means that the clustering algorithm creates the clusters by continually nesting data points. Initially, each data point is its own cluster (the "leaves" of the tree hierarchy), which in subsequent steps are combined into larger clusters. The final result, assuming the algorithm is allowed to fully terminate, is a treelike structure with a single large cluster (containing all data points or instances) as the root. A conceptually elegant way to think about this tree is as a set of levels, where each level represents a partition of the instance-set. For example, at the lowermost level, each instance is its own cluster (singleton), while at the topmost (root) level, there is only one set of instances. In the intermediary levels, we have different partitions of instance sets, although the sets get more coarse-grained as we move from the leaves to the root. In principle, some decision criterion (not dissimilar to a threshold) can now be used to determine the level of the tree that should be used to recover a single set of clusters forming a partition of the instances. More sophisticated variants delay making the choice, but rather wait until an actual query or application before returning results. For streaming data, dynamic clustering and other such methods can also be used. In fact, because this part of the IM pipeline intersects with clustering, any clustering algorithm can be used, although there is little evidence to suggest that relatively classic algorithms like spectral and hierarchical clustering (appropriately set up and tuned) can be outperformed by more learning-heavy algorithms after controlling for the quality of previous steps like blocking and similarity.

8.6.2 Entity Name System

Even if clusters of duplicate mentions have been identified, it still begs the question of what to do with them. For example, if there are five John Doe nodes in the KG, and we have managed to cluster them together, how do we collapse the five nodes into a single node, especially if there are inconsistencies between them? Different communities have converged on surprisingly different solutions to this problem. We list some of the important cases here. As it turns out, one of the solutions (ENS), proposed and adopted to varying extents in the Semantic Web (SW) community, has the interesting property that it can be implemented directly with pairs (the original output of the two-step pipeline), rather than clusters, though clustering and postprocessing can significantly improve the result.

In the Natural Language Processing (NLP) community, the issue of entity linking tends to arise with respect to an external knowledge base (KB) like Wikipedia or WordNet. We've already alluded to the importance of entity linking in some of the chapters on KG construction. For example, imagine an extraction called "Katmandu," which is a slightly unusual spelling of the Nepalese capital. If we're able to link this extraction to the canonical entity in Wikipedia, we not only preclude the issue of resolving mentions like "Katmandu" to other mentions in the text that refer to the same entity (e.g., "Kathmandu"), but we also reduce the error of typing the entity incorrectly (i.e., with successful entity linking, we would correctly deduce that this extraction has type "City" rather than "Person"). These KBs are already resolved, in that there is a single mention for each unique entity. Furthermore, once an entity extracted from text has been linked to an entity in the external KB, it can be represented canonically by using the representation or the label of the entity in the external KB. This option is also very popular in non-NLP communities when it is assumed that the external KB is complete, or stated more weakly, that it is not complete but contains all

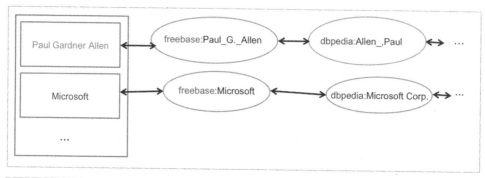

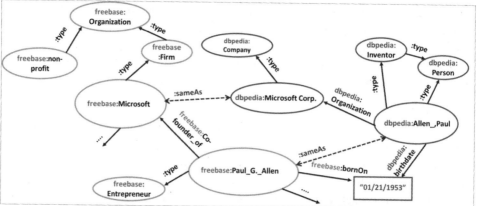

Figure 8.6: An ENS as a representation of IM outputs. The top image illustrates an ENS population given both a clustering scheme and entity linking, while the bottom image only assumes basic pairwise outputs from the similarity step. A population given either clustering or entity linking (but not both) is similarly feasible. Applications could directly query the ENS, sometimes in a pay-as-you-go fashion. Using additional RDF machinery, the *owl:sameAs* (or other ontologically equivalent) links could be further annotated with provenance, confidence, and other meta-attributes.

"entities of interest" (in other words, it is complete with respect to the domain). This also shows why this method of representation is not always appropriate (e.g., if there are many long-tail entities in the text or the input KG, we will obtain clusters of entities that do not resolve to an external KB node). Such clusters are known in the NLP community as NIL clusters. One way to resolve such NIL clusters is to choose a *preferred name* or a *canonical string* from the labels of the mentions in the cluster. Ideally, the label should have high information value. For example, "United Nations" would be preferred over "UN."

Even if we could somehow discover a good heuristic for selecting a preferred name, actual KGs have nodes that have richer information sets than just string labels. In the

SW community, the assumption is that structured data (including KGs) are published in a decentralized manner by parties that don't necessarily have equivalent interests or commitments to quality. At the same time, because of its flexible representational philosophy, the SW makes it easy to define the output of IM as a property (a labeled edge), just like any other relationship. One such property is *owl:sameAs*, and is near-universally employed by SW practitioners to represent the semantic equivalence of two RDF identifiers. Also, *owl:sameAs* is imbued with special semantics that are taken into account by SW reasoners that have to construct answers to aggregation queries and other complex SPARQL graph pattern queries. Given *owl:sameAs* links, we can construct a (usually distributed) ENS. The ENS is defined simply as a *thesaurus of mentions*, where each *owl:sameAs* link is treated as a declaration of synonymy. In practice, there are several ways to populate an ENS (figure 8.6). While the problem of reconciling inconsistencies does not go away simply by declaring *owl:sameAs* links or populating an ENS, it defers decisions to applications and querying infrastructure further down the pipeline. Provenance, reification, and other sophisticated facilities available in RDF and SW vocabularies and software can be used to resolve entities compactly without collapsing them into clusters and losing information. The reason that this works well is that applications have different needs and quality requirements, and it is not always clear what the optimal level of granularity is for entity clusters.

8.7   Formalizing Instance Matching: Swoosh

Swoosh[1] is a family of generic algorithms for solving IM. It assumes black-box functions for merging and pairwise comparison that are invoked by an IM engine. Given such black boxes, the idea behind Swoosh is to use an algorithm for *efficiently* performing the entire IM workflow itself (i.e., use strategies to minimize the number of invocations to the expensive black boxes). Although Swoosh sounds similar to blocking, its optimizations are based on answering a different question: given some specific properties obeyed by the black-box comparison and merge functions, what is an algorithm that optimally resolves a KB, where optimality is measured in terms of the number of instance comparisons?

While the algorithmic contributions of the proposed Swoosh variants (such as R-Swoosh, G-Swoosh, and F-Swoosh) are impressive in themselves, an important formal contribution is the formalization of the IM problem itself. Previously, the only other item that had presented significant formal work on IM was the Fellegi-Sunter model that we described earlier in the context of picking two thresholds. Swoosh presents a fundamental framework for generic IM by first defining the concepts of *merge* and *match* functions. Intuitively, as the name suggests, a merge function is a partial function from $M \times M$ (M being the set

---

[1] This section is advanced and may be skipped by a reader just looking to gain familiarity with the topic.

of mentions), and it captures the computation of merged instances (hence, the function is applicable only for pairs of matching instances); in contrast, the match function is like the pairwise linking function $\mathcal{L}_p$, defined over $\mathcal{M} \times \mathcal{M}$ and used to determine if the mention pair $(m_i, m_j) \in \mathcal{M} \times \mathcal{M}$ represents the same underlying entity. By way of terminology, if the match function returns true for (m_i, m_j), then we say that $m_i \approx m_j$; similarly, the instance obtained by merging by m_i and m_j is denoted by the symbol $< m_i, m_j >$.

Following these disclosures, a *merge closure* of a set of instances $\mathcal{M}$ is defined as the smallest set of instances S such that S is a superset of $\mathcal{M}$ and, for any two instances m_i and m_j, it is always the case that if $m_i \approx m_j$, then $< m_i, m_j >$ is in S.

Finally, the concept of *domination* is defined; intuitively, an instance m_i is dominated by m_j if m_j contains more information about the underlying instance than m_i. For example, imagine a simple instance represented only by a label "John White," and another instance with label "J. White" about the same individual. We could argue that the first instance dominates the second instance, because it contains information about the first name as well. For the sake of theory, let us assume that there is an oracle that returns true when presented with two instances, if the first instance dominates the second. We can now define a KG, G, to be dominated by another KG, G', if for every instance in G, there is at least one instance in G' that dominates that instance. Mathematically, KG domination is a *partial pre-order* (i.e., it is a reflexive and transitive relation). It is not a partial order because it is not antisymmetric (and neither is it symmetric): it is possible for G and G' to dominate each other. On the other hand, instance domination is antisymmetric: if m_i dominates m_j and m_j dominates m_i, then it is necessarily the case that $m_i = m_j$ (note the set-theoretic notion of *equivalence* has been used here, not the shorthand symbol for the match function).

The reason why these terms are important is that they can be used to provide a precise definition of IM: an IM is defined as the minimal set $\mathcal{M}'$ that meets two conditions: it is a subset of the merge closure $\mathcal{M}^*$ of the given mentions-set $\mathcal{M}$, and it dominates $\mathcal{M}^*$. By minimal, we mean that no strict subset of $\mathcal{M}^*$ satisfies both of these conditions. Although the definition does not impose any constraints upon $\mathcal{M}^*$, the authors of Swoosh prove the claim that it is, in fact, unique, given the definitions of merge closure and domination. In a slight abuse of terminology, we refer to $\mathcal{M}'$ as the IM of a given mentions-set, $\mathcal{M}$.

Without assigning additional properties to the match and merge functions, it is difficult to develop practical algorithms. The authors do propose an algorithm, G-Swoosh, as a baseline that does not require the match and merge functions to obey any specific properties. It improves over a brute-force algorithm that is iterative and pairwise (and therefore highly suboptimal in terms of the number of required comparisons) by intelligently ordering the match and merge calls. For the original pseudocode and proofs, we refer the reader to Benjelloun et al. (2009), also referenced in the "Bibliographic Notes" section. G-Swoosh also includes the guarantee that it will terminate and compute the IM for an instance-set if the IM is finite, and the authors present proofs that it is in fact optimal, in the sense that no algorithm that computes the IM of a mentions-set correctly will make fewer comparisons in the worst case.

To design algorithms beyond Swoosh, it becomes necessary to assign some properties to the match and merge functions. Interestingly, Swoosh defines four properties, labeled using the acronym ICAR, that are relevant for real-world IM scenarios:

1. Idempotence: An instance always matches itself, and merging an instance with itself yields the same instance.
2. Commutativity: For all pairs of instances, if and only if $m_i \approx m_j$, then $m_j \approx m_i$, and if $m_i \approx m_j$, then $< m_i, m_j > = < m_j, m_i >$ (again, note the equivalence and not the match symbol in this last equation).
3. Associativity: Associativity is defined on the merge operation; namely, if it is the case that $< m_i, < m_j, m_k >>$ and $<< m_i, m_j >, m_k >$ both exist, then the two are equivalent.
4. Representativity: If $m_k = < m_i, m_j >$, then for any m_l such that $m_i \approx m_l$, we have $m_k \approx m_l$.

Note that the last of the properties (representativity) is the least intuitive of the four. One way of thinking about it is that the instance m_k obtained from merging m_i and m_j represents the original instances, in the sense that any instance that would have matched m_i (or m_j by commutativity) will also match m_l (i.e., there is no negative evidence that can be created through the merge of m_i and m_j that would actually prevent m_k from matching any other instance that would have matched m_i or m_j). Another important point to note about these four properties is that they do not imply the transitivity of the match function.

Recall that the G-Swoosh algorithm did not assume the ICAR properties. In contrast, if we do assume the ICAR properties, it is possible to significantly improve on G-Swoosh (the authors term the new algorithm "R-Swoosh") in the worst case. Just like G-Swoosh, R-Swoosh maintains a certain optimality (i.e., it is possible to show that there exists at least one mentions-set where any algorithm has to perform at least as many comparisons as R-Swoosh to obtain the correct IM of the set). A third algorithm, F-Swoosh, further improves on R-Swoosh by eliminating redundant feature-based comparisons between values in the two mentions or instances being evaluated as a pair.

8.8 A Note on Research Frontiers

The differences between the three classic frameworks discussed earlier and the range of blocking, similarity, and postprocessing techniques that are described here have shown no signs of abating; in fact, we are just starting to see a renewed interest in the research community in addressing some long-standing challenges (and assumptions) in IM. Next, we very briefly describe some trends that seem to have taken root in various communities and are likely going to persist in the foreseeable future.

The first is the advent of collective methods for IM that we alluded to previously when describing soft transitive closure. Collective methods, including SRL, are not just limited to probabilistic application of the transitive property. In many domains in the real world, domain-specific relational dependencies are ubiquitous, if not always explicit. Here, we consider the classic example of resolving author names in the publication domain. The input is a large KG consisting of publications and their incumbent details (including authors), similar to the motivating example described in the introduction. One domain-specific relational dependency that is often found to be true in the publication domain is the tendency of coauthors to repeat being coauthors (i.e., if author A and author B have coauthored a publication P, it is quite likely that they have coauthored other publications as well). How can we use this for IM? Suppose that we were trying to resolve authors and publications in a domain-specific KG initially acquired through the methods described in part III of this book. Intuitively, we want the system to use the rule: if A and B have coauthored P, and if A' and B' have coauthored P', then the fact that $A = A'$ should positively influence the likelihood of $B = B'$. In other words, all things being equal, we are using coauthorship repetition (prior domain knowledge) to increase the score of the pair (B, B'), given evidence that $A = A'$ and coauthorship of $A - B$ and $A' - B'$. Note that this is very different from transitivity; we are not claiming that A and B are the same author. Collective methods like Markov Logic Networks (MLNs) and PSL allow domain experts to not only specify these rules (in many cases, probabilistically) using elegant formal frameworks, but also come with inference algorithms that can process these rules, along with actual IM outputs, to yield the underlying true KG with resolved instances. In chapter 9, we cover this class of techniques in much more detail.

Second, despite the advent of these sophisticated techniques, the fact remains that (with difficult domains especially), it is very hard to achieve reasonable IM performance, especially if labeled data is not available. Labeling is a nontrivial problem because, in IM, pairs have to be labeled rather than instances. Random sampling is precluded because of the quadratic growth in size of the set of pairs (recall the examples provided in the section "Evaluating Blocking," earlier in this chapter, in the context of the RR metric), as well as the fact that almost all pairs within this exhaustive set of all pairs are nonmatches. One way to select good samples for labeling, or in frameworks like active learning, is to employ efficient crowdsourcing, leveraging microworker platforms like Amazon Mechanical Turk, or more recently, services such as Amazon Sagemaker Ground-Truth. Several such frameworks for IM have been presented in the literature; we note a few papers in the "Bibliographic Notes" section.

Third is the advent of schema-free methods, which are especially apt when the KG has been constructed using Open IE (without the benefit of a domain ontology), or has an otherwise extremely broad domain, such as with DBpedia, or even the Gene Ontology. Schema-free methods are also relevant when two KGs have to be linked to one another and are individually typed using different ontologies (e.g., linking DBpedia instances to Freebase instances).

To understand the notion of schema-free, consider again the methods proposed earlier in this chapter when describing the similarity step. Therein, we constructed the feature vector (between two pairs of instances) of maximum cardinality mn, given m feature functions in the library and n attributes. The assumption, however, was that the two instances would share the same schema (i.e., have the same n attributes even though one or both of the instances might not have *values* defined for the attribute, in which case dummy values, or some other similar scheme, would have to be employed). This becomes problematic in several real-world scenarios. One scenario occurs when the set of attributes (roughly, the schema or ontology) is too diffuse, which happens when multiple approximately equivalent properties (e.g., *:birthdate* and *:bornOn*) are present in the ontology, likely due to historical reasons, as a consequence of which the two instances may define their values using these different properties. One instance may define the birth date value as the object of the *:birthdate* property, while another may use *:bornOn*. Short of cleaning up the ontology and the KG, which is almost never feasible in practice, or doing ontology matching (which is sometimes feasible but can lead to its own set of problems) by determining which concepts and attributes are equivalent to one another prior to executing an IM workflow, it is not clear how this problem can be resolved. A second scenario in which mismatched concepts or attributes present problems is when there are two differently ontologized or otherwise independently modeled KGs that need to be linked to one another, as noted previously with DBpedia, a KG that external data sets frequently have to link to in order to publish in the Linked Open Data ecosystem (chapter 14).

The earliest schema-free algorithms sought to address these problems by initially treating instances as bags of values, and then applying document-centric algorithms to obtain feature vectors (e.g., by using tf-idf or more recently, techniques like LSH). However, the limitations of this solution are fairly obvious. Consider, for example, date properties like *:bornOn* and *:diedOn*. Without the context of a property, it is difficult to distinguish between two instances where the birth date of one coincides with the death-date of another. With strings, the problem tends to be less severe, but with numbers, it can be even more severe than with dates. Another issue is that of blocking, as the state-of-the-art blocking scheme learners and blocking methods require a consistent and single set of attributes to be defined.

More recently, therefore, a new set of algorithms for these so-called highly heterogeneous information spaces has been proposed that is schema-free, but does not ignore the structure of the data by collapsing all values into bags of strings, numbers, and dates. Instead, the usual approach is to treat the instance as a set of key-value pairs, and by considering similarities not just between pairs of values, but also pairs of keys. Work on developing such schema-free algorithms has continued to flourish, particularly in the Semantic Web.

8.9 Data Cleaning beyond Instance Matching

In this chapter, our main focus has been on IM as one of the most fundamental KG completion problems that has to be solved in the real world, based on both empirical arguments that the problem is ubiquitous when entities, relations, and triples in the KG have been extracted from multiple data sources, and on historical arguments that IM has proved to be a difficult AI problem in the database (and NLP) communities. However, IM is by no means the only difficult data-cleaning problem that needs to be solved to achieve a truly robust and complete KG. In the world of databases, data cleaning has traditionally been defined as the general problem of detecting and removing errors and inconsistencies from data in order to improve data quality. Data quality problems are present in single data collections, such as files and databases (e.g., due to misspellings during data entry, missing information, or other invalid data), but also multiple data sources that need to be integrated (e.g., in data warehouses, federated database systems, or global web-based information systems).

Traditionally, data cleaning has tended to be associated more with structured than natural-language data. Arguably, natural-language tasks like coreference resolution can be interpreted as data cleaning, but the terminology hasn't caught on yet in the NLP community. One reason might be that in the database and structured data communities, the input is raw data in the form of tables and files. In NLP, the raw data is almost always text, and the mentions that have to be resolved are extracted to begin with. Any operations performed on the text, such as punctuation removal, tokenization, and lemmatization, are usually referred to as *data preprocessing*.

While such distinctions have worked well in the past, when all of these communities were relatively well separated, when it comes to KGs, the distinctions become blurred (or start overlapping completely), and we cannot pragmatically afford such distinctions if we want to build a good KG.

Historically, data warehouses have required and provided extensive support for data cleaning. Such warehouses load and continuously refresh large data sets from a variety of sources (e.g., a Walmart data warehouse may be pulling in data from many of its locations around the country on a periodic basis), and because of heterogeneity in the real world, not every source that is integrated is of equal quality. Data warehouses are used for decision-making, so good data quality is essential for avoiding wrong conclusions. Just like KG completion follows KG completion, data warehouses face the data-cleaning challenge during the so-called extraction, transformation, and loading (ETL) process, illustrated in figure 8.7, with the cleaning modules typically executed in a separate data-staging area before loading transformed data into the warehouse. A large number of tools of varying functionality are available to support these tasks, but a significant portion of cleaning often has to be done manually (or by low-level programs such as rule- or heuristics-based) that are accompanied by their own maintenance and robustness challenges.

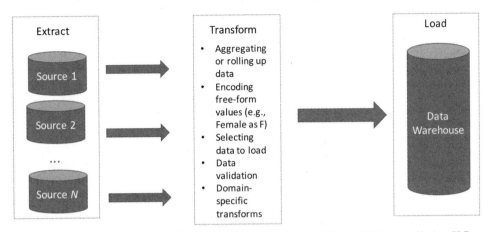

Figure 8.7: An illustration of ETL for database-centric workflows. When applied to KGs, the "extract" phase is equivalent to the methods described in part II of this book, while the "transform" phase would include steps like IM, SRL (described in chapter 9), and other approaches that lead to a single, clean KG. The "load" phase would upload the KG to an infrastructure where it can be queried, accessed, and used to facilitate analytics, a subject that will be covered in part IV.

Figure 8.8 provides a general taxonomy of data-cleaning problems seen through the lens of the database and data warehouse communities. In many cases, similar problems can arise with KGs (e.g., just like ordinary databases, KGs in particular domains can contain name and structural conflicts, as well as outdated spatiotemporal data). While in some of these cases, techniques can be framed or shared between the database and KG communities, in other cases, the problem has to be framed differently in a graph setting than in a tabular setting. For example, the missing value imputation problem, solutions for which are statistics-based methods, targets numerical columns (such as income or age) in databases, but it is better formulated as the link or relation prediction problem in KGs. In later chapters in this part of the book, we cover novel machine learning–based paradigms like KGEs and SRL for solving such problems in the KG setting more effectively than the numerical solutions traditionally presented for the missing value imputation problem.

Unsurprisingly, just as with IM, there is no one-size-fits-all solution for addressing data-cleaning. In fact, it is not even completely clear initially what data-cleaning steps need to be performed on a data set to begin with. Data profiling, therefore, is an important step prior to any composition or execution of data-cleaning workflows. Wikipedia defines data profiling as the "process of examining the data available in an existing data source" or as "collecting statistics and information about that data." In practice, data profiling is more shallow and mechanistic rather than adaptive (such as clustering or other descriptive

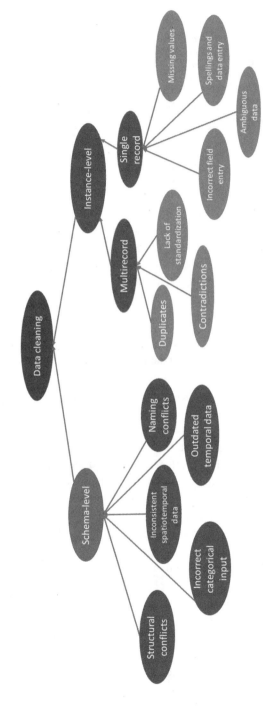

Figure 8.8: A taxonomy of data-cleaning problems, as originally conceived of in the database community.

data-mining procedures), but that does not preclude the value of good engineering. This is why, in good systems and applications, data profiling is systematic. Rather than issuing exploratory queries or randomly browsing the data rendered in a spreadsheet, the use of dedicated tools (of which the main ones are proprietary industrial solutions), such as Microsoft's SQL Server Integration Services and Informatica's suite of products, is common. Despite their differences, such tools have far more in common, in that they often use high-level inputs (often mediated via graphical interfaces) to issue requisite queries at the back end, and then using efficient (in many cases, highly specialized) aggregation algorithms to compute the profiles, statistics, and metadata desired by the user. The volume of the data dictates how long the process as a whole takes. For example, if an analysis of variance (ANOVA) is specified with large numbers of levels for some of the variables, the analysis could end up taking hours.

The actual output does not have to be highly formalized, though statisticians and experts may prefer it in sensitive or difficult cases. For ordinary practitioners, good tools employ a liberal use of tabs, charts, tables, dashboards, and a full suite of other visualization aids, many of which are interactive. The use-cases of such profiles are numerous, with data cleaning being an important one. A specific purpose of basic profiling is to reveal data errors, including inconsistent formatting within columns, missing values, and outliers. For example, in the database world, if a column is numerical and is missing values, it suggests the application of missing value imputation to that column. Outliers may be flagged for further study or removed altogether. In recent years, such interactive data cleaning has become very popular, with systems including early efforts, such as Potter's Wheel, which relies on a graphical user interface (GUI) to support a range of transforms along both the horizontal and vertical dimensions of a database; and more recent machine learning–based interactive systems such as ActiveClean, which relies on active learning to guide data cleaning toward instances where the analyst's attention is likely to result in high expected utility to the current model. Other systems, like Wrangler, try to find a balance between machine learning and programming-by-declaration techniques. Another interesting recent innovation is crowdpowered data cleaning, where the work starts intersecting more closely with KGs. Some of the crowdpowered techniques rely on external KGs like YAGO and DBpedia, but also special KGs like GeoNames, to develop well-curated data sets. Others use crowdsourcing, which helps alleviate the cost of using experts or large quantities of training data. These methods are promising, but outputs do not carry the same kinds of guarantees as declarative (but manual and expert-intensive) tools.

To the best of our knowledge, the development of such tools (especially at the scale and quality of some of the production-level industrial tools mentioned here) for KGs is a largely open issue and subject to disruption. Of course, there is always the option of trying to represent the KG as an RDB model and then profiling the transformed model. We cover some options for relational model of RDF KGs in part IV, when we discuss querying and infrastructure. However, while such modeling can work well for certain kinds of querying, where RDB infrastructure, query reformulation, and indexing mechanisms can be utilized to achieve speed at scale, it is more controversial whether the results of a profiler are even meaningful for a KG that is represented as an RDB. For example, a KG may be highly heterogeneous and not contain birth dates for many individuals (but in the cases that it does, the birth date may be precise and directly extracted from high-quality text). Applying missing value imputation or some other procedure to such a column is not wise, nor would it be appropriate to remove the column, despite its sparsity.

In general, such controversies arise due to KG models and RDB models relying on fundamentally different assumptions about the origins and quality of data. KG construction assumes that many instances will be incomplete in their attributes and relationships to other instances to begin with, because the algorithms are AI or NLP modules run over messy data. In contrast, data in RDBs tends to come from good, relatively higher-quality sources (if not outright manual inputs), rather than the interpreted outputs of AI algorithms. The schemas tend to be painstakingly designed, keeping in mind a narrower and better-defined set of business use-cases. Real-world KGs often have broad ontologies and are not strongly compliant with the ontologies. Hence, there is good reason to treat the data profiling and cleaning problem for KGs as being related to, but not the same as, data cleaning for RDBs and more structured data models.

8.10   Concluding Notes

In this chapter, we provided a definition and an overview of the IM problem. The IM problem arises frequently in several communities and domains and is an example of an AI problem that is much more effortless for humans than for machines. To make matters worse, naive solutions to IM are quadratic in the number of nodes in the KG. Techniques like blocking have to be used in practice to achieve acceptable reductions in the quadratic complexity, but at the potential cost of losing some recall in the final outputs.

IM has been researched for over 50 years, and a consensus has been reached on a wide range of issues. The problem has continued to attract new research ideas, some recent examples being the use of collective IM methods and novel frameworks like Swoosh, which, given some reasonable modeling assumptions, provide good theoretical guarantees. The microclustering nature of IM continues to be studied in the machine learning community, and more recently, the field has started to intersect with other research areas in computer science, including crowdsourcing and latent spaces. We provide some guidance for further reading on the former topic in the "Bibliographic Notes" section; the latter topic is covered more broadly in chapter 9.

8.11   Software and Resources

Because a practical IM solution is so dependent on input data formats (e.g., table versus graph), structure (the schema of the data), and domain (e-commerce versus biomedical IM), there are few standard implementations that could just be used without modification. A good example of such a system, proposed more than a decade ago, is Freely Extensible Biomedical Record Linkage (Febrl), a system introduced under an open-source license in 2008. Unlike Swoosh, which offers a theoretical framework, Febrl is an implemented system that was originally meant for a highly applied use-case (i.e., biomedical record linkage) and comes with no theoretical guarantees or formulation as such. It contains several reasonably advanced techniques for data cleaning and standardization, indexing and blocking, attribute value comparison, and record (in this case, instance) pair classification, all embodied within a GUI. Febrl can be seen as a training tool suitable for users to learn about and experiment with both traditional and new record linkage techniques, as well as for practitioners to conduct linkages with data sets containing up to several hundred thousand records.

The creation of Febrl was motivated by the fact that is important to have tools available that allow IM practitioners to experiment with traditional as well as advanced techniques, in order to understand their advantages and their limitations. Such tools should be flexible and contain many linkage methods, and also allow a multitude of configuration options for users to conduct a variety of experimental linkages. Additionally, as most IM users in the health sector do not have extensive experience in programming, an intuitive GUI should provide a well-structured and logical way on how to set up and run record linkage projects.

Presently, Febrl can be downloaded from the Source Forge portal (https://sourceforge. net/p/febrl/wiki/Home/). The homepage is at http://users.cecs.anu.edu.au/~Peter.Christen/ Febrl/febrl-0.3/febrldoc-0.3/manual.html, and contains extensive details on such aspects as indexing and field comparison functions. While the discussion given here may seem to suggest that Febrl is primarily geared toward the health sector, it can be used for other domains because it is customizable.

Another option, designed for Python users, is the Python Record Linkage Toolkit (https: //recordlinkage.readthedocs.io/en/latest/ref-datasets.html). It also allows the loading of Febrl data sets into the programmatic environment. A similar package is the Record Linkage Toolkit (RLTK), which can be applied in a Python environment using pip. The package is accessed at https://github.com/usc-isi-i2/rltk and is a general-purpose, open-source platform that allows users to build powerful Python programs for instance matching. One of the major innovations in RLTK compared to some of the other tools is its ability to handle large-scale data sets. RLTK supports multicore algorithms for blocking, profiling data, computing a wide variety of features, and training and applying machine learning classifiers based on Python's sklearn library. An end-to-end RLTK pipeline can be jump-started with only a few lines of code. RLTK continues to be under active maintenance and has been funded under multiple projects, including DARPA LORELEI (Low-Resource Languages for Emergent Incidents), Memex, and IARPA CAUSE.

There are some important packages for domain-specific instance matching. One example is DeepMatcher (https://github.com/anhaidgroup/deepmatcher), gaining popularity in e-commerce. It is designed mainly for the kind of product data scraped from web sources (and where details are embedded in Schema.org snippets). A good benchmark is available at http://webdatacommons.org/largescaleproductcorpus/. Just like biomedical and patient record linkage, e-commerce instance matching is such an important problem that it has drawn a small community around it (many of which are major industrial players). Recent state-of-the-art results in e-commerce IM, especially achieved by researchers working on the Product Graph at Amazon, have been impressive.

In the Semantic Web, some tools for instance matching, especially in the RDF and Linked Data settings, have been made available due to recent efforts. One early and very influential approach is the Silk framework (http://silkframework.org/), which is an open-source framework for integrating heterogeneous data sources, and thus is better suited to KGs than some of the other (more database-centric) tools mentioned thus far. In addition to generating links between related data items within different Linked Data sources, Silk helps data publishers to get RDF links from their data sources to other data sources on the web. It also offers facilities for applying data transformations to structured data sources. Silk offers a declarative link specification language, which has some attractive properties, including control and explainability of results. There is also an accompanying workbench GUI, in which link specifications can be intuitively declared.

Another resource in the SW ecosystem is LIMES (http://aksw.org/Projects/LIMES.html), a link discovery framework that implements time-efficient approaches for large-scale link discovery based on the characteristics of metric spaces (e.g., the triangle inequality). It can be configured using either a GUI or a configuration file. It is also offered as a Java library, and it is even available as a stand-alone tool.

There are also other resources for benchmarking instance matching, as collected in a tutorial accessed at https://www.ics.forth.gr/isl/BenchmarksTutorial/. One of the important resources mentioned in the tutorial is the Ontology Alignment Evaluation Initiative (OAEI), accessed at http://oaei.ontologymatching.org/, which offers IM benchmarking as a problem area, and even KG-centric matching tasks such as jointly matching instances and schemas. There is a workshop that includes several competitions organized each year, usually held in conjunction with the International Semantic Web Conference (ISWC) series. For those interested in benchmarking instance matching for traditional record linkage–like solutions, some solutions are available at https://dbs.uni-leipzig.de/en, with standard benchmark data sets for IM accessed at https://dbs.uni-leipzig.de/research/projects/object_matching/benchmark_datasets_for_entity_resolution. Another good resource is the Stanford Entity Resolution Framework (SERF), which is maintained by Benjelloun et al. (2009), who also authored the set of papers on Swoosh. It may be accessed at http://infolab. stanford.edu/serf/.

In many cases, the tools and packages mentioned here offer all the facilities that a user is likely to need to do feature engineering, train an IM classifier, and even evaluate the system on withheld test data. In some cases, however, it may be necessary to develop more advanced feature functions, including learnable string similarity metrics. As far back as the early 2000s, some systems relied on such learnable metrics, including Multiply Adaptive Record Linkage with INduction (MARLIN). MARLIN is a two-level learning approach that continues to be used and evaluated widely for its effectiveness on different classes of IM problems. First, string similarity measures are trained for every database field so that they can provide accurate estimates of string distance between values for that field. Next, a final predicate for detecting duplicate records is learned from similarity metrics applied to each of the individual fields. SVMs are employed for both tasks, and the authors show that they outperform decision trees, the favored classifier in prior work.

We are not aware of any obvious implementations for learnable string similarity, but using standard graphical models and dynamic programming, such similarity measures can be implemented by interested users in their favored programming languages and environments. Another approach, which is continuing to gain favor due to the rapid onslaught of neural networks and representation learning (including for KGs, as we cover in chapter 10), is avoiding feature engineering altogether and instead relying on vector space models and embeddings as the features. Even though such methods have many advantages, there are open questions that preclude getting rid of feature engineering altogether. For example, it is not completely clear how to embed or represent mixtures of text, numbers, and dates, as is often the case in KGs. Certainly, some modeling effort is required before an off-the-shelf embedding can be applied. Whether modeling is more preferable to feature engineering remains to be seen. More details on KG-embedding software and resources will be provided in chapter 10.

8.12   Bibliographic Notes

There has been extensive research on several variants of IM over the years. Ironically, this has led to the IM problem itself going by various names (mentions) in the academic literature, including deduplication, duplicate detection, entity resolution, merge-purge, record linkage (which is very common in the database community), entity reconciliation, instance matching, and coreference resolution (or equivalently, anaphora resolution). The last version of the problem is limited to the NLP community, while the data is still in the form of natural-language extractions and there is sufficient context for applying NLP techniques. The other terms are far more common when dealing with data in some kind of structured form, as we assumed in this chapter. An excellent, though by no means exhaustive, set of references that survey the problem in its various guises include Getoor and

Machanavajjhala (2012), Elmagarmid et al. (2006), Köpcke et al. (2010), Hernández and Stolfo (1995), and Elango (2005). Books and synthesis lectures by Christen (2012) and Christophides et al. (2015) offer thorough treatments, far beyond the scope of this lone chapter, including introductory and advanced material. Doan et al. (2012) offer a useful review of the broader area of data integration, within which research areas such as instance matching and schema matching have historically been embedded.

Much of the early (and a large portion of the later) research focused on the similarity step, as well as advanced methods for clustering entities directly. In the early days, rule-based approaches were popular, but as noted in the "Similarity" section earlier in this chapter, in the last decade, machine learning has emerged as the dominant paradigm for learning an approximate pairwise linking function from a training set of duplicates (positive class) and nonduplicates (negative class). An excellent review by Elmagarmid et al. (2006) provides more context for this evolution. Original references for Swoosh, Febrl, MARLIN, and the Fellegi-Sunter model include Benjelloun et al. (2009), Christen (2008), Bilenko and Mooney (2003), and Fellegi and Sunter (1969), respectively. (Although there are many original references for Swoosh, we only cite Benjelloun et al., 2009, because it offers much of the content underlying the relevant section in this chapter.) Note, however, that more recently, blocking has become a popular subject of study due to the focus on Big Data. An excellent overview was provided by Christen (2011), where many of the original papers on individual algorithms such as SN were provided. Good references on learning blocking keys or schemes include Michelson and Knoblock (2006), Bilenko et al. (2006), Cao et al. (2011), Kejriwal and Miranker (2013), Ramadan and Christen (2015), and Shao and Wang (2018). McCallum et al. (2000) proposed the Canopy Clustering algorithm, which has also been enormously influential in both research and practice.

A similar evolution is already taking place in the Linked Data community (discussed in detail in chapter 14), where rule-based approaches, such as the Silk system proposed by Bizer, Volz, et al. (2009), still enjoy support but are being gradually supplanted by adaptive algorithms that rely on machine learning techniques such as active learning. The systems themselves have frequently undergone updates to reflect such changes. For other examples of IM systems prevalent in the SW community, we recommend Nentwig et al. (2017), Klímek et al. (2019), and Ferrara et al. (2011). Kejriwal (2016, chapter 3) compares many existing systems on some Big Data dimensions, but we also recommend Getoor and Machanavajjhala (2013), which gives slightly different perspectives. Kejriwal (2016) shows that, despite significant advancements, many of the systems were designed for the relatively homogeneous record linkage problem, and not for the heterogeneous KGs often published on the web. Whether they can be successfully extended is more of an empirical than a theoretical issue. Recent SW IM systems, especially leaning more on semisupervised, unsupervised, or self-supervised machine learning, are described by Kejriwal and Miranker (2015a,b), Nikolov et al. (2012), and Araujo et al. (2012).

We also mentioned some novel research frontiers. In particular, collective and statistical relational approaches to instance matching (which we revisit in the next chapter) include Bhattacharya and Getoor (2007) and Singla and Domingos (2006). Examples of work that involve instance matching and crowdsourcing include Wang et al. (2012), but a more recent overview can be found in a survey of data cleaning by Chu et al. (2016). Whang et al. (2009), and Papadakis et al. (2011) provide guidance on IM systems that violate the independence between the blocking and similarity steps in the two-step workflow, and instead choose to interleave the two. Finally, deep learning approaches for instance matching are still in their relative infancy, although recent research by Mudgal et al. (2018), Ebraheem et al. (2017), and Kooli et al. (2018) are illustrative and relevant.

8.13 Exercises

1. Instead of resolving instances within a KG, suppose that we wanted to resolve instances between two KGs, G and G' with m and n instances, respectively. We will study the effects of blocking.

   (a) What is the cardinality of the exhaustive set O of instance pairs?

   (b) What would be the cardinality of O if both KGs were individually noisy (i.e., if we wanted to do instance matching both within and across the two KGs)?

   (c) Using the results of the previous parts of this exercise, prove (using arguments, without algebraically expanding the terms) that $\frac{(m+n)(m+n-1)}{2} = mn + \frac{m(m-1)}{2} + \frac{n(n-1)}{2}$.

2. ** This question concerns the terminology used for Swoosh. Given two instances m and n, such that m dominates n, construct the KGs G and G' in terms of these instances so they dominate one another.

3. This exercise concerns the KG fragment in figure 8.1.

   (a) What would be a good blocking key for this KG if the goal were to link citations?

   (b) Suppose that the blocking key was *CommonToken(:author)*. Assume that author names are perfectly tokenized by the blocking algorithm (i.e., "Rudich, S." is properly tokenized to yield the bag {"Rudich", "S."}). What would be the PC if this blocking key were to be executed? Does this make it a good blocking key? Why or why not?

   (c) Suppose that we decided that *CommonToken(:author)* is the matching function (i.e., if two citations have a common token in their author node, then they are matching). What would be the precision, recall, and FM of executing such a matching function on the exhaustive set of pairs?

4. In this exercise, we look at a slightly different version of entity resolution—namely, entity linking, which is the problem of linking a word or phrase (usually an extracted named entity) in natural-language text to no more than one entry in a preexisting KG

such as Wikidata. Although many methods for entity linking exist, we consider two intuitive ones here:

(a) **The popularity method:** Selects the entity that is the most popular among the list of candidates in the KG. Although different notions of popularity exist, consider the most intuitive definition that comes to mind. For example, given "Paris," Paris, France, would be more popular as an entity than Paris, Texas (which also exists).

(b) **The joint assignment method:** Selects the entity in the KG that is consistent (using some measure of consistency, such as coreference, or membership in the same semantic class) with the other mentions of entities. For example, if the extraction "Charlotte" were linked to a city, rather than the name of an individual, then a cooccurring extraction (e.g., in the same sentence) of "Paris" would be more likely to be linked to the city of Paris rather than the name of an individual (e.g., Paris Hilton).

For each of the following sentences, we only want to disambiguate the extraction "Arizona." We also italicize the *detected* entities. For each sentence, explain which of the two methods given here (or neither, or both) would be appropriate for getting to the right answer, and why. If neither method is appropriate, try to think of a better method and explain your intuitions in a few sentences. You may assume that there are only three candidates in your KG: (i) Arizona (state); (ii) Arizona (restaurant in New York City); (iii) Arizona (snake).

(a) *Arizona* is my all-time favorite *restaurant* in *New York City*.

(b) The best *BBQ* I've tasted is in *Arizona*.

(c) Very few *people* have been attacked by an *Arizona*.

5. Recall that earlier in the chapter, we presented string similarity features as one possible methodology for getting sets of features between pairs of entities that have been approved by blocking, and that are now being input into some similarity module. This exercise tests you on some common similarity measures (you should look up the details and formulas online because many sources describing the measures given here are available). For each string similarity measure, look up a definition online and provide the formula. Provide both a positive and negative use-case for the measure (i.e., what is one good use-case for each where you would, or would not, use this string similarity measure as a strong feature for entity resolution)?

(a) Needleman-Wunsch

(b) Soundex

(c) Monge-Elkan

(d) Levenstein

(e) Jaro-Winkler

6. Suppose that you could use only one string-matching function (appropriately thresholded) to determine whether entities in two KGs are linked. Would you want to use the Jaro-Winkler or Smith-Waterman similarity for linking the entities in the KGs shown in this table? Why?

Knowledge Graph A	Knowledge Graph B
Actor Jackie Chan	Tom Michael Mitchell, E. Fredkin University Professor
Professor Tom M. Mitchell	Jackie Chan Kong-san

7. In a similar vein, considering the two KGs in this table, would you use tf-idf or Levenstein distance?

Knowledge Graph A	Knowledge Graph B
Apple Corporation	Apple Corp
IBM Corporation	IBM Corp

8. Consider the data sets shown here, represented as tables, between which we want to match entities. The "Match" relation indicates the ground-truth, which would not be available to an entity resolution algorithm. We will use the following blocking key: the first letter of the last name concatenated with the last four digits of the phone number. Assume that Traditional Blocking is the blocking method. As a first step, list the blocking keys and the IDs of entities that fall into the blocks.

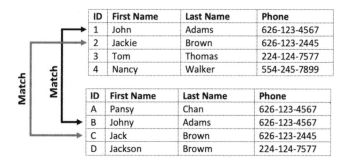

9. What are the RR and PC of the blocking?
10. Suppose that we decided to go one step further and declare that entities e_1 and e_2 (from the two data sets, respectively) match if they have the same blocking key. What would

be the precision and recall? *Hint: Do we even need to compute the recall if we have the answer to this question?*

11. Now, consider a blocking algorithm that is somewhat more advanced and robust than Traditional Blocking: namely, Canopies (also called Canopy Clustering). Although we provided a description in the chapter, it would be instructive to read the original paper (McCallum et al., 2000), because it has been very influential in the entity resolution and blocking literature. Consider both this question and the next three questions in the context of the image shown here. Assume that *d* (at the center) was the query entity that was used to generate the canopies. The inner, dotted circle represents the inner, tight canopy, while the outer, solid circle represents the outer, loose canopy. Suppose that these entities were restaurants (with attributes such as name, address, and structured representations of their menus). What would be good examples of similarity measures and thresholds to try in this context for getting reasonable blocking outputs?

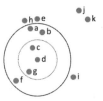

12. What is the valid set of entities from which we randomly pick our next query (i.e., for iteration 2)? *Hint: Would c be in this valid set? Why or why not? What about g?*

13. Assuming that the chosen element (iteration 2) is the first alphabetic element from the set you picked in exercise 12, what is the valid group of elements for iteration 3? Try to approximate the similarity functions and thresholds by drawing circles of similar radii as you see in the image.

14. Has the algorithm converged to a set of blocks? What is the minimum number of iterations that are still needed?

15. In general, can you think of cases (when applying Canopies) where, given *n* data points and two thresholded similarity functions, you need *n* iterations to converge? If you were told that the algorithm took *n* iterations before converging, what could you conclude about the PC and RR of the algorithm?

16. Can you think of ways to avoid the problem in exercise 15, short of replacing or redesigning the similarity measure?

9 Statistical Relational Learning

Overview. In addition to the explicitly modeled relationships, knowledge graphs (KGs) also contain many relational dependencies that violate the independence and identical distribution (i.i.d.) assumptions. Statistical relational learning (SRL) frameworks like Probabilistic Soft Logic (PSL) and Markov Logic Networks (MLNs) can help model (and infer over) such dependencies by combining powerful elements from both logic and probability theory. Although SRL is an entire field of research in its own right, some elements are particularly relevant to the study of KGs. We introduce SRL in this chapter, with a strong focus on frameworks that have been successfully applied to KGs and the KG identification problem.

9.1 Introduction

Working with KGs requires a systematic treatment of both uncertainty and relational information. Uncertainty can arise from several sources, some of which we have already explored in this book. For example, when extracting named entities, relationships, or events from raw data during the KG construction (KGC) phase, uncertainty arises due to the probabilistic nature of these algorithms. In general, most machine learning algorithms that we have seen, both during KGC and in steps like instance matching, output scores, or probabilities rather than hard labels. To convert these probabilities to hard labels, we have to use techniques like thresholding that either require clever guesswork (or experience), or if we are lucky, a validation set that helps us to systematically optimize the threshold to yield good results on an accuracy metric like the F-measure.

One of the intriguing questions that immediately arises in the context of this discussion is: what if we don't discard the uncertainty output by these algorithms, but somehow use it to build a more refined KG (i.e., as a *feature* or source of information in itself)? Key to the success of any approach that manages this difficult task is to use *collective* information being output by such algorithms. For example, an extraction algorithm might recognize an instance of a named entity with probability 0.6, but other instances of the same named entity (say, from other documents or sentences) may be output with higher probability. In the instance matching (IM) step, we might find that the controversial instance is being matched to other equivalent instances with similarly ambiguous probability. Looking at the two pieces of evidence together (ambiguity in extraction, and ambiguity in resolution), we may then conclude that the instance should not have been extracted in the first place or, at the very least, that it deserves more manual scrutiny than other instances. If we err on the side of precision, as many practitioners do, we would want to discard the instance rather than integrate it into the complete KG.

This example illustrates a relatively clear-cut case (namely, a sequence of ambiguous probabilities, which ultimately leads us to reject or manually label the wayward instance). Less interesting is the scenario where we have a sequence of low (or high) probabilities because these are clear rejects or accepts, respectively. However, the situation becomes much more interesting when we consider that some algorithms are more uncertain than another; furthermore, what one algorithm finds difficult may not yield uncertainty for another algorithm. This can happen within tasks [like Named Entity Recognition (NER)] or across tasks. The former problem is well studied in machine learning and is often a central focus of ensemble approaches. The latter problem is a more novel issue that has received attention relatively later in the history of machine learning, and that will be the main focus in this chapter. To generalize the problem further, imagine a range of algorithms that operate on a data set, with each algorithm outputting its own probabilities. Every entity and relation in our KG has an associated set of algorithmic traces and probabilities (with the origins of the trace going all the way back to the raw data, and possibly domain discovery itself). There is, thus, a lot of collective information that could potentially be used to "derive" a better KG than the original KG that has been handed down to us as a roughly sequential series of thresholded algorithmic outputs.

In the general case, we cannot do much about a mixed bag of probabilities about which we know nothing or can make no assumptions. But almost always, this is not the case. We know in what order the algorithms are run and what they are doing, in addition to a whole host of relevant details; for example, we know that information extraction (IE) precedes instance matching; we may even have a suspicion that the quality of instance matching is higher than the quality of our extractions. In fact, in many domains, we know a whole lot more, embodied by a body of useful knowledge that goes under the broad term of "domain expertise." The question then becomes: How do we use domain expertise and algorithmic uncertainties to yield a more complete and less noisy KG than would be yielded by executing a series of individual KG construction and instance matching algorithms? As a framework, SRL is one of the best-known paradigms that can help us formally conceive, and come up with viable solutions to, this problem. Modern state-of-the-art SRL frameworks like PSL allow modelers to robustly incorporate broad sets of domain rules, including domain-specific similarity functions (at the levels of individuals and sets), different types of relations (which is important for KGs), and differing levels of importance (using real numbers) for different domain rules. We provide some background on how these models are realized in the next section. In the second half of the chapter, after providing essential background on one of the earliest SRL frameworks (MLNs), we introduce PSL and its specific application to the KG completion problem.

9.2 Modeling Dependencies

One of the most important sources of domain expertise arises in modeling relational dependencies, and the strengths of such dependencies, in the selected domain. For example, let us consider the standard example of a social network, which typically has a simpler ontological structure than a full-fledged KG. Let us limit our ontology to the *Person* concept, and to a simple set of mnemonically specified relations such as *friendOf*, *spouseOf*, and *votesFor*. Note that only the first of these three relations is symmetric. Even in this domain, which is conceptually simple, a whole host of relational dependencies could be specified by largely building on knowledge acquired through social science research. For example, we may want to encode the rule, or *dependency*, that spouses largely vote for the same candidate. A weaker version of the rule is that friends often vote for the same candidate. Our research (or intuition) suggests that the spouse rule should have more importance than the friends rule, because the latter is true more often in the real world. However, in both cases, we do not want to treat the rules as deterministic; there is always *some* chance that the rule is violated.[1]

Informally, this information was easy to specify in plain English, but the beauty of SRLs is that they give us the mathematical machinery to formalize these notions. For most rules (and the only kind considered in this chapter), a simple form of first-order logic, namely with conjunctive bodies and single literal (nonnegative atoms) heads, is enough. For example, some rules for the social network domain described informally here are expressed next using this kind of conjunctive structure:

1. 0.8: *Spouse(A, B)* ∧ *VotesFor(A, P)* → *VotesFor(B, P)*
2. 0.1: *Neighbors(A, B)* ∧ *VotesFor(A, P)* → *VotesFor(B, P)*
3. 0.4: *Friends(A, B)* ∧ *VotesFor(A, P)* → *VotesFor(B, P)*

The uppercase arguments to the predicates (e.g., *A, B*) are logical variables that must be *grounded* by substituting them for concrete persons. The predicates can be constrained in practice in terms of which grounded objects they accept. For example, the *VotesFor* predicate can be constrained to only allow groundings (for *A*) from a set of persons, and groundings (for *P*) from a set of political parties. The weights indicate the importance of the rules, with higher weight indicating more importance. For example, the first rule, which has a weight of 0.8, is more important in this context than the third rule, which has

---

[1] As it happens, the deterministic case does not require special treatment and can be treated as a single instance of the formal machinery to follow.

a weight of 0.4. In other words, it is much more likely for spouses to align on political voting preferences than friends. There is an even lower likelihood (though still nonzero) for neighbors to align on these preferences.

Note that, although the mathematics may not always be easy to explain to a domain expert who is not versed in these frameworks, the rules themselves are fairly easy to elicit. There has even been work to extract such rules automatically (from data, documents, or even scientific literature) or to learn the structure of the rules from data, given a fixed set of predicates like *Friends* and *Neighbors*. Of course, we must always bear in mind that the situation quickly becomes more complicated as the numbers of concepts and relations increases, as is the case with real-world KGs.

9.3 Statistical Relational Learning Frameworks

As we saw earlier, modeling relational dependencies is an important aspect of many modern application domains. At the same time, such domains are also characterized by uncertainty (e.g., considering the example in the previous section, it is clear that we are not, or should not be, equally confident about every rule). Statistical learning is mainly focused on uncertainty and probability, while relational learning is focused on modeling relational dependencies. SRL is a powerful, relatively novel framework that attempts to combine the benefits of both lines of work. Key SRL tasks include collective classification, link prediction, and link-based clustering, all of which are described later in this chapter. Because of these applications, as well as increasing maturity in the individual research areas of relational learning and statistical learning, SRL has emerged as a feasible research agenda.

In early work on the subject, several critical features were identified that a unifying framework (where the unification is of statistical and relational models) must necessarily do all of the following:

1. Incorporate both first-order logic and probabilistic graphical models.
2. Permit simple representation of canonical SRL problems such as link prediction and collective classification.
3. Permit viable mechanisms for using and representing *domain knowledge* in the SRL spirit.
4. Allow extension and adaptation of techniques from statistical learning, probabilistic (and also logical) inference, and inductive logic programming.

Note that some of these requirements are functional, while others were deemed to be more pragmatic. For example, the third desideratum is necessary because the search space for SRL algorithms is very large even by artificial intelligence (AI) standards, and domain knowledge can be argued to be critical to success. Additionally, the ability to incorporate rich domain knowledge is an attractive feature of SRL, as we shall see when studying both MLNs and PSL.

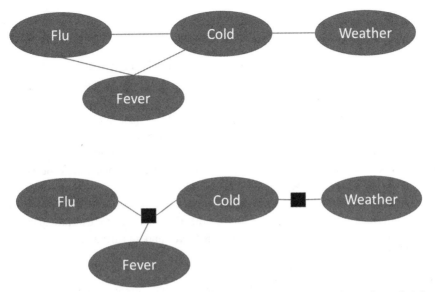

Figure 9.1: A visual representation of a Markov Network as an undirected graph (above) and a factor graph (below).

9.3.1 Markov Logic Networks

Markov Logic was proposed as a framework that was capable of meeting all desiderata mentioned in the previous section. However, before delving into Markov Logic, we start with a simpler concept (namely, a *Markov Network*, also called *Markov Random Field*). Markov Networks were proposed as a model for the joint distribution of a set of variables $X = (X_1, \ldots, X_n) \in \mathcal{X}$. Visually (see figure 9.1), we may think of this network as an undirected graph G and a set of potential functions ϕ_k. For each variable, there is a corresponding node in G, and for each *clique* in the graph, there is a potential function. A potential function is a nonnegative real-valued function that characterizes the state of its corresponding clique. Because the network is a model of a probability joint distribution, the joint distribution, as represented by a Markov Network, is encapsulated by the following equation:

$$P(X = x) = \frac{1}{Z} \Pi_k \phi_k(x_{\{k\}}). \tag{9.1}$$

Here, $x_{\{k\}}$ is the state of the kth clique (or equivalently, the state of the variables that are in the clique). Z is known as the *partition function*, and it is given by the expression $\Sigma_{x \in \mathcal{X}} \Pi_k \phi_k(x_{\{k\}})$. A Markov Network can also be conveniently be represented as a log-linear model, where each clique potential is replaced by an exponentiated weighted sum of features of the state:

$$P(X = x) = \frac{1}{Z}e^{\sum_j w_j f_j(x)}.$$ (9.2)

Here, a feature may be any real-valued function of the state. It is common to focus on binary features $f_j(x) \in \{0, 1\}$, with the most direct translation from the potential-form function being that there is one feature corresponding to each possible state $x_{\{k\}}$ of the clique, with the weight being $log\phi_k(x_{\{k\}})$. Unfortunately, this full representation is exponential in the size of the cliques; in practice, a much smaller number of features (e.g., logical functions of the state of the clique) can be used, allowing for more compact representations (particularly in the presence of large cliques in the graphical model) than the potential-function form. MLNs take advantage of this, as we describe later in this chapter.

How can inference be done in Markov Networks? Unfortunately, it has been shown that exact inference in such networks is #P Complete, and one has to resort to approximate inference, such as Markov Chain Monte Carlo (MCMC) and, in particular, Gibbs sampling, which samples each variable in turn, given its Markov blanket.[2]

To compute marginal probabilities, a Gibbs sampler is run with the conditioning variables clamped to their given values. A second popular method for inference in Markov Networks is belief propagation. Maximum Likelihood and also Maximum a Posteriori estimates of a Markov Network's weights cannot be computed in closed form, but the log-likelihood is a concave function of the weights and can be found efficiently using several established methods in the optimization community, including quasi-Newton optimization algorithms. Other alternatives include iterative scaling. If features are not specified, but data is available, features can be learned from the data by greedily constructing conjunctions of atomic features.

Syntactically, rules in a Markov Logic framework are indistinguishable from *first-order logic* formulas, except that each formula has a weight attached. Semantically, a set of Markov Logic formulas represents a probability distribution over possible worlds, where each world has a specific formal form, as described later in this chapter. First, however, we introduce some key elements of first-order logic that are important for putting the rest of this section in its proper context.

9.3.1.1 First-Order Logic

A *formula* in first-order logic is constructed using four types of *symbols* (namely, constants, variables, functions, and predicates). Constant symbols represent objects in the domain of interest (e.g., if the domain of interest is *cities*, constants could be *Los Angeles, Tokyo*, and *Shanghai*). Variable symbols range over the objects in the domain. Function symbols (e.g., *locatedInCountry*) represent mappings from tuples

---

[2] In a graphical model, the Markov blanket of a node is the minimal set of nodes that renders it independent of the remaining network. Conveniently, in a Markov Network, this is simply the node's neighbors in the graph.

of objects to objects. Predicate symbols represent relations among objects in the domain (e.g., *SisterCity*) or attributes of objects (e.g., *HighlyPolluted*).

An *interpretation* indicates which symbols represent what objects, functions, and relations in the domain. Note that variables and constants may be *typed*, in which case variables range only over objects of the corresponding type and constants can represent only objects of the corresponding type. For example, a typed variable x (with type *City*) is constrained to range only over cities.

A *term* is any expression representing an object in the domain, and it can be a constant, variable, or function applied to a tuple of terms (in this sense, the definition of a term is recursive). For example, *Tokyo*, y, and LeastCommonMultiple(x, y) are all terms. An atomic formula or atom is a predicate symbol applied to a tuple of terms, an example of which is *SisterCity(x, CapitalOf(Japan))*. Formulas are recursively constructed from atomic formulas using logical connectives and quantifiers. The familiar logical rules of composition apply. That is, if F and G are formulas, so are the following:

1. Negation: $\neg F$
2. Conjunction: $F \wedge G$
3. Disjunction: $F \wedge G$
4. Implication: $F \implies G$
5. Equivalence: $F \iff G$
6. Quantification (universal): $\forall x F_1$ (true if F_1 is true for every object x in the domain)
7. Quantification (existential): $\exists x F_1$ (true if at least one object x exists such that F_1 is true)

As with ordinary mathematical expressions, parentheses are typically used to signal precedence. A positive literal is defined as an atomic formula, while a negative literal is a negated atomic formula. Interestingly, we can define a KG (or any set of triples) as a single large formula that is a conjunction of several formulas (with a triple intuitively representing a single formula). This is also true for a *knowledge base*, or KB (a set of sentences or formulas in first-order logic), a more general model of data than a KG (which deliberately imposes a graph-theoretic interpretation on its triples-set). Bearing this generality in mind, we assume in the rest of this section that we are dealing with KGs rather than first-order KBs.

A final piece of machinery that is necessary is that of a *ground term*, which is a term containing no variables. A ground atom or ground predicate is an atomic formula whose arguments are all ground terms. A possible world (also called a *Herbrand interpretation*) assigns a truth value to each possible ground predicate. These possible worlds express the semantics (what it *means* to be true) of predicates in first-order logic, whereas the construction rules noted here (such as conjunction and implication) express the syntax. We say that a formula F is satisfiable if and only if there exists at least one world in which it is true.

We now have the machinery to define the problem of inference in first-order logic in the context of a KG—namely, the basic inference problem in first-order logic is to determine whether a KG *entails* a formula F: if F is true in *all* worlds where KG is true (represented symbolically by the expression $KG \models F$). Another way of putting it (called *refutation*) is that $KG \models F$ if and only if $KG \cup \neg F$ is unsatisfiable. Unfortunately, this makes a strict interpretation of the KG nonrobust because if a KG contains even a single contradiction, all formulas trivially follow from it. For automated inferential tasks, it is convenient to convert formulas to conjunctive normal form (CNF), or clausal form. As the name suggests, a CNF is nothing but a conjunction of clauses, where a clause is a disjunction of literals. A KG can be represented by a single CNF. Furthermore, every KG in first-order logic can be mechanically converted to clausal form. The advantage of clausal form is that it can be used in *resolution*, which is both a sound and refutation-complete inference procedure for first-order logic.

Theoretically, inference in first-order logic is semidecidable, and for this reason, KGs are constructed using restricted subsets of first-order logic that have desirable properties (such as decidability), the most commonly used of which are Horn clauses. A Horn clause is a clause that contains at most one positive literal. The famous Prolog programming language is, in fact, based on Horn clause logic; Prolog programs can be mined from data using inductive logic programming techniques, by searching for Horn clauses that (possibly approximately) hold in the data.

Already, the machinery described here starts to illustrate why we cannot limit ourselves to purely symbolic approaches when representing and working with (i.e., doing reasoning and inference on) KGs. The single biggest limitation is that many formulas in KGs are typically true in the real world, but it is rarely the case that they are *always* true. It is simply not feasible, in most domains, to come up with nontrivial formulas that are always true, and where it is feasible, such formulas capture a small portion of the relevant knowledge in that domain. While there are a number of solutions (many ad hoc) that have been proposed as practical extensions of first-order logic to deal with these challenges, a more systematic approach is Markov Logic, which we already introduced as fulfilling some of the desiderata that have been described. Armed with the tools and terminology of first-order logic, we take a deeper look at Markov Logic next.

9.3.1.2 Markov Logic The key motivation for Markov Logic was to address the limitation we noted previously; namely, that if we represent a KG using only first-order logic predicates and constraints, we would have a set of "hard" constraints on the set of possible worlds; hence, if even one world violates one formula, that world has zero probability. To counter this brittleness, Markov Logic was proposed to soften these constraints so that when a world does violate a formula in the KG, it only makes it *less probable*, not *impos-*

Table 9.1: Examples of MLN rules (in clausal form) with weights, encoding domain knowledge expressed as natural-language sentences.

Weight	MLN rule	Natural-language description
0.6	$\neg\text{Friends}(x,y) \vee$ $\neg\text{Spouse}(y,z)\vee\text{Friends}(x,z)$	If Mary and Bob are espoused, and Mary and Joan are friends, then Bob and Joan are friends.
2.0	$\text{Friends}(x,y)\vee\neg\text{Spouse}(x,y)$	If two people are not friends, then they are not spouses.
1.6	$\neg\text{Spouse}(x,y) \vee$ $\neg\text{Smokes}(y)\vee\text{Smokes}(z),$ $\neg\text{Spouse}(x,y)\vee\text{Smokes}(y) \vee$ $\neg\text{Smokes}(z)$	If Mary and Bob are espoused, then either both smoke or neither does.
1.2	$\neg\text{Stress}(x)\vee\text{BackPain}(x)$	Stress causes back pain.

sible. Extending this notion, the framework was designed so that the fewer the formulas that a world violates, the higher its probability. Just like in the motivating example at the beginning of this chapter, Markov Logic associates its formula with a weight reflecting the strength, or importance, of that constraint. The higher the weight, the greater the difference that formula's violation will make to the probability of the world (in log space).

With these ideas in place, a Markov Logic Network (MLN) is defined as a set L of pairs (F_i, w_i) such that F_i is a formula in first-order logic and w_i, its associated weight, is a real number. Additionally, a finite set of constraints $C = \{c_1, \ldots c_{|C|}\}$ is also associated with the MLN, denoted using the symbol $M_{L,C}$. As an example, we provide instances of MLN formulas, with weights, given a set of English sentences in table 9.1. As we noted before, the formula itself may be difficult to elicit from a domain expert without knowledge of first-order logic, but the English sentences are usually fairly easy to elicit from experts or from known scientific fact. Typically, some manual work is necessary in making the leap from the English sentences to the clausal forms noted in figure 9.1. Note that weights do not have to be between 0 and 1 and should not be interpreted as probabilities.

Beyond examples, it is best to think of an MLN as a *template* for constructing Markov Networks, because different sets of constraints will produce different networks. These networks may be of varying size, but they nevertheless share regularities in structure and parameters, specified by the MLN. At minimum, the formula weights are shared across the networks, meaning that all groundings of the same formula will share the same weight. In the literature, these networks are designated as *ground Markov Networks* to distinguish them from the (template) MLNs specified in first-order logic. From formulas previously introduced, the probability distribution over possible worlds x specified by the ground Markov Network $M_{L,C}$ is $P(X = x) = \frac{1}{Z}e^{\sum_i w_i n_i(x)}$, which in turn equates to $\frac{1}{Z}\Pi_i\phi_i(x_{\{i\}})^{n_i(x)}$, with $n_i(x)$ being the number of true groundings of F_i in x, and with $x_{\{i\}}$ being the state (or

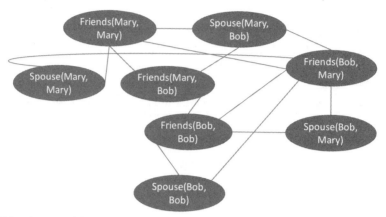

Figure 9.2: A ground Markov Network, assuming that the constants {Mary, Bob} are applied to the first two formulas in figure 9.1.

truth values) of the atoms appearing in F_i ($\phi_i(x_{\{i\}}) = e^{w_i}$. Other formulations of this are also possible (e.g., using products of potential functions rather than log-linear models), but this is the most convenient approach in domains where hard and soft constraints are both present.

Because the ground network can be difficult to work with as a pure mathematical structure, it is helpful to visualize it. Assuming constants {Mary, Bob}, we apply them to the first two formulas in figure 9.1 to obtain the graph shown in figure 9.2. The construction is fairly simple and mechanistic: each node in the graph is a ground atom, and an edge is declared between two nodes if their corresponding ground atoms appear together in some grounding of a formula. Using this network, there are well-defined inference procedures that can help us determine the probability of Friends(Bob, Mary), the probability of Friends(Bob, Mary) ∧ Spouse(Mary, Bob), and so on.

A full discussion of either the formalism of, or assumptions behind, MLNs is beyond the scope of this chapter (we provide pointers to primary material on the subject in the section entitled "Bibliographic Notes," at the end of this chapter). There are, however, some important propositions that have been proven about them. For example, it was shown that every probability distribution over discrete (or finite-precision numeric) variables can be represented as an MLN. These propositions are important because they show that MLNs are a rigorous mechanism for knowledge representation. More subjectively, their support for combining logic rules, weights, and probabilities makes them have many of the unifying features noted in the list in the previous section. Yet another important aspect that led to the uptake and popularity of the MLN framework when it was first proposed is that, as its authors showed in an influential work, SRL approaches like probabilistic relational models, knowledge-based model construction, and stochastic logic programs can all be mapped into an MLN framework.

9.3.2 Probabilistic Soft Logic

Similar to MLNs, PSL is a framework for collective, probabilistic reasoning in relational domains. However, there are some key differences, the most important of which is that, unlike MLN, PSL uses *soft*-truth values in the interval [0,1], rather than the binary values {0,1}. This one feature yields several convenient outcomes, including allowing the incorporation of similarity functions at the levels of individuals and sets. Another advantage to employing continuous-valued random variables rather than binary variables is that the most probable explanation (MPE) inference problem can be cast as a convex optimization problem that is significantly more efficient to solve than its combinatorial counterpoint in MLNs (polynomial versus exponential).

Simply put, a PSL model is composed of a set of weighted, first-order logic rules (just as with MLNs), where each rule defines a set of features of a Markov Network sharing the same weight. To recap, the formula $w : P(A, B) \land Q(B, C) \rightarrow R(A, B, C)$ is a valid PSL rule, with w being the weight of the rule, A, B, and C being universally quantified variables, and P, Q, and R being predicates. A grounding of a rule comes from substituting constants for the universally quantified variables in the rule's atoms. In this example, assigning the constant values a, b, and c to the respective variables in the example rule would produce the ground atoms P(a,b), Q(b,c), and R(a,b,c). Each ground atom takes a *soft-truth* value in the range [0,1], as opposed to MLNs, where the ground atom would have taken one of the two values in {0,1}.

PSL associates a *numeric distance to satisfaction* with each ground rule that determines the value of the corresponding feature in the Markov Network. The distance to satisfaction is defined by treating the ground rule as a formula over the ground atoms in the rule. PSL uses the Lukasiewicz t-norm and co-norm to provide a relaxation of the logical connectives, AND ($\cap$), OR ($\lor$), and NOT($\neg$), as follows (where relaxations are denoted using the symbol over the connective):

1. $p \tilde{\land} q = max(0, p + q - 1)$
2. $p \tilde{\lor} q = min(1, p + q)$
3. $\tilde{\neg} p = 1 - p$

As with many SRL frameworks, an important feature of PSL is that it restricts the syntax of first-order formulas. Instead of allowing arbitrary first-order formulas, PSL formulas must have conjunctive bodies. For example, the soft transitive rule:[3]

$0.8 : friend(Joe, Mark) \land friend(George, Mark) \rightarrow friend(Joe, George)$ is acceptable

---

[3] Stated intuitively, this rule says that a friend of a friend is (with high probability) a friend.

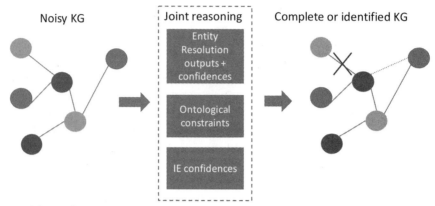

Figure 9.3: An illustration of KG identification.

in PSL, whereas a rule such as $0.95 : (friend(Joe, Mark) \land friend(George, Mark)) \lor roommate(Joe, George) \rightarrow friend(Joe, George)$ is not, but it could potentially be reformulated into several valid PSL rules (see the exercises at the end of the chapter).

9.4   Knowledge Graph Identification

We provided some intuition earlier in this chapter on the importance of modeling relational dependencies, especially in KG ecosystems that are rich in such complexities. In the next two sections, we provide concrete examples of SRL frameworks that have been used by researchers for the important application of *KG identification (KGI)*, alternatively known as *KG completion*. The core motivation behind KGI is based on the real-world observation that KGs constructed using Natural Language Processing or other techniques are inevitably noisy (i.e., have incorrect links) and sparse (i.e., have missing links). KGI refers to the problem of identifying the true KG from an input set of messy triples. Arguably, a good solution to the problem should incorporate domain knowledge, knowledge of the various kinds of noise and inconsistencies that could be present in the input, and knowledge of the confidences of systems that constructed the KG in the first place. Because these are different sources of information that rely on both relational dependencies and statistical regularities, SRL is an apt framework for modeling the KGI problem. We present one such model that has been recently published in the literature and that incorporates multiple algorithms and sources of information, especially IE and IM. The framework is presented abstractly in figure 9.3.

KGI assumes that, at its core, a KG contains three types of facts: about entities, entity labels, and relations. KGI represents entities with the logical predicate $ENT(E)$ and labels with the logical predicate $Lbl(E, L)$, where entity E has label L. Relations are represented with the logical predicate $Rel(E_1, E_2, R)$, where the relation R holds between the entities

E_1 and E_2 [e.g., $R(E_1, E_2)$]. Note that while this notation is a little different from what we have seen thus far, there is a straightforward mapping between such notations, all of which ultimately rely on the notion of a KG as a directed, labeled graph. The KGI problem is then defined as identifying a true set of atoms from a set of noisy extractions. To do so, one of the earliest approaches to KGI incorporated three components into an SRL framework: capturing uncertain extractions, performing entity resolution, and enforcing ontological constraints. By creating a PSL program that included these three components, KGI was able to relate the program to a distribution over *possible* KGs. Efficient inference was used to identify the most probable KG. Experimentally, this system was found to work well for KGI, even when the KG was built with extractions from web data, an important source for many real-world KGs (as discussed in chapter 5).

9.4.1 Representing Uncertain Extractions

Output from an IE system can be noisy and are related to the logical predicates [e.g., ENT(E)] via introduction of *candidate* predicates. Specifically, for each candidate entity, a corresponding predicate $CAND\_ENT(E)$ is introduced, and similarly for labels and relations generated by the IE system. Uncertainty in the extractions is expressed by assigning the candidate predicates a soft-truth value equal to the confidence value from the extractor. For example, an IE might generate an entity extraction *Charlotte* with confidence of 0.7, which the KGI system would represent as $CAND\_ENT(Charlotte)$ with a soft-truth value of 0.7.

Note that, in general, KGC systems tend to rely on several different IEs (see part II of this book, for example). The KGI system represented metadata about the specific technique or algorithm used to extract a candidate by using separate predicates for each such algorithm or technique. Notationally, if algorithm A was used to extract candidate entity E, the candidate predicate is denoted as $CAND\_ENT_A(E)$. Relations and labels are treated analogously. The predicates are related to true values of attributes and relations using weighted rules [e.g., $CAND\_REL_A(E_1, E_2, R) \stackrel{w_{CR-A}}{\Longrightarrow} REL(E_1, E_2, R)$ and $CAND\_LBL_A(E, L) \stackrel{w_{CL-A}}{\Longrightarrow} LBL(E, L)$]. The set of candidates generated from grounding these rules, using the IE outputs, is denoted using the symbol C.

9.4.2 Representing Instance Matching Outputs

The IM algorithms may output confidences along with their predicted matches, which also should be looked upon as candidates. In the KGI system, a predicate called $SAME\_ENT$ is used to capture the similarity of two instances [e.g., $SAME\_ENT(Delhi, NewDelhi)$]. To incorporate IM outputs in the PSL framework, three rules were proposed:

1. $SAME\_ENT(E_1, E_2) \tilde{\wedge} LBL(E_1, L) \stackrel{w_{EL}}{\Longrightarrow} LBL(E_2, L)$
2. $SAME\_ENT(E_1, E_2) \tilde{\wedge} REL(E_1, E, RL) \stackrel{w_{ER}}{\Longrightarrow} REL(E_2, E, R)$
3. $SAME\_ENT(E_1, E_2) \tilde{\wedge} REL(E, E_1, R) \stackrel{w_{ER}}{\Longrightarrow} REL(E, E_2, R)$

The intuition behind these rules should be fairly clear—namely, that when two instances are very similar, they will have high truth value for $SAME\_ENT$.

9.4.3 Enforcement of Ontological Constraints

The outputs of IE and instance matching are only one kind of knowledge that can assist in identifying a good KG. Another source of knowledge that brings out the power of SRL frameworks like PSL is the set of rules corresponding to an ontology. Each type of ontological relation can be represented as a predicate, with the predicates representing ontological knowledge of relationships between labels and relations. Predicates such as DOM and RNG can be used to limit the domains and ranges of certain relations (e.g., we can specify that the domain of a relation *Friend* is *Person*). Similarly, a predicate such as MUT can be used to specify that the labels corresponding to concepts such as *Country* and *Person* are mutually exclusive (i.e., an entity cannot simultaneously have both labels). Other predicates for enforcing the subsumption of labels (SUB), subsumption of relations (RSUB), and inversely related functions (INV) can be similarly devised. In Pujara et al. (2013), in fact, seven ontological constraints were specified (technically, these should be thought of as *types* of ontological constraints), reproduced here for the sake of completeness:

1. $DOM(R,L) \tilde{\wedge} REL(E_1, E_2, R) \overset{w_o}{\Longrightarrow} LBL(E_1, L)$
2. $RNG(R,L) \tilde{\wedge} REL(E_1, E_2, R) \overset{w_o}{\Longrightarrow} LBL(E_2, L)$
3. $INV(R,S) \tilde{\wedge} REL(E_1, E_2, R) \overset{w_o}{\Longrightarrow} REL(E_2, E_1, S)$
4. $SUB(L,P) \tilde{\wedge} LBL(E,L) \overset{w_o}{\Longrightarrow} LBL(E,P)$
5. $RSUB(R,S) \tilde{\wedge} REL(E_1, E_2, R) \overset{w_o}{\Longrightarrow} REL(E_1, E_2, S)$
6. $MUT(L_1, L_2) \tilde{\wedge} LBL(E, L_1) \overset{w_o}{\Longrightarrow} \tilde{\neg} LBL(E, L_2)$
7. $RMUT(R,S) \tilde{\wedge} REL(E_1, E_2, R) \overset{w_o}{\Longrightarrow} \tilde{\neg} REL(E_1, E_2, S)$

9.4.4 Putting It Together: Probabilistic Distributions over Uncertain Knowledge Graphs

All of the three classes of representations defined thus far can be combined into a single PSL program Π. A set of ground rules R can be instantiated using the inputs of the KGC and IM process, including the union of groundings from the set C of uncertain candidates, matching entities and ontological relations. The distribution over the set I of interpretations also corresponds to a distribution over the set G of KGs, and is given using equation (9.3), as follows:

$$P_\Pi(G) = f(I) = \frac{1}{Z} e^{\sum_{r \in R} w_r \phi_r(I)^p}. \qquad (9.3)$$

By conducting inference, the most likely interpretation can be identified, which (in the case of PSL) is an assignment of soft-truth values to entities, relations, and labels comprising the KG. In Pujara et al. (2013), the approach to converting these soft values into discrete elements that could be used and reasoned with was to choose a threshold and select the corresponding set of facts of appropriate quality to include into an "identified" KG.

9.4.5 A Note on Experimental Performance

Pujara et al. (2013) evaluated the method on both a synthetic KG derived from the Linked-Brainz project, which maps data from the MusicBrainz community using ontological information from the Music Ontology project, and also real data extracted using web IE and NLP techniques from the Never-Ending Language Learning (NELL) project. They compared KGI to simple baseline methods, as well as a simpler version of KGI that used the output of instance matching (or ontological constraints) only, rather than the complete KGI pipeline. In all cases, the complete KGI method was found to lead to the highest F1 score (over 91.9 percent) and an AUC metric of more than 90 percent. In fact, compared to previous work on the NELL data set, including MLNs, KGI was found to demonstrate substantial improvement.

9.5 Other Applications

Because of the generality of statistical relational frameworks like MLN and PSL, as well as their expressiveness in terms of representing and reasoning over relational models and dependencies, many applications have been proposed besides KGI, and many don't assume a KG at all, but are designed to operate on networks or even relational databases. We briefly describe some of these applications next. Further guidance is provided in the section entitled "Software and Resources," later in this chapter.

9.5.1 Collective Classification

While ordinary classification tries to predict the class of an object given its attributes, collective classification also takes into account the classes of related objects. Attributes can be represented either in Markov Logic or PSL as predicates of the form $A(x, v)$, with A being an attribute, x an object, and v, the value of A in x. The class, designated as an attribute C, is represented by the symbol $C(x, v)$, with v being the class of x. Classification is now modeled as the problem of inferring the truth value of $C(x, v)$ [for all x and v of interest, given all known $A(x, v)$]. An interesting aspect of this formulation is that it allows uniform modeling of ordinary and collective classification, because ordinary classification is merely the special case that guarantees independence of $C(x_i, v)$ and $C(x_j, v)$ for all x_i and x_j [and given the known $A(x, v)$]. However, collective classification includes other $C(x_j, v)$ in the Markov blanket of $C(x_i, v)$, even after conditioning on the known $A(x, v)$. Relations between objects are represented by predicates of the form $R(x_i, x_j)$. The framework exposes some generalizations as well; for instance, $C(x_i, v)$ and $C(x_j, v)$ could potentially be indirectly dependent via *unknown* predicates [and possibly even including $R(x_i, x_j)$].

9.5.2   Link Prediction

A link prediction system aims to determine whether a relation exists between two objects of interest (e.g., whether Craig is Jay's supervisor) given object properties (and possibly other known relations). In Markov Logic, link prediction can be formulated in a way that is near-identical to the MLN formulation of collective classification. The one key difference is that the goal now is to determine $R(x_i, x_j)$ for all object pairs of interest, rather than $C(x, v)$, as was the goal in collective classification.

9.5.3   Social Network Modeling

Social networks are like simpler versions of KGs, with nodes representing social actors (e.g., people) and edges representing relationships (e.g., friendship) between the actors on which they are incident. Social network analysis involves building models relating actors' properties and their links. For example, the probability of two actors forming a link may depend on the similarity of their attributes (a phenomenon called *homophily*); conversely, two linked actors may be more likely to have certain properties in common. These models can be expressed as Markov Networks, with succinct formulaic representations [e.g., *0.8: A(x,p) ∧ A(y,p) → R(x,y)*, where x and y are actors, $R(x, y)$ is a relationship between them, $A(x, p)$ represents an attribute of x (with p being the value taken by x for that attribute), and the weight of the formula captures the correlation strength between relation and the attribute similarity]. For example, we can design a model stating that friends tend to have similar movie preferences. In fact, not only can MLNs and PSL encode observations and rules in ordinary social networks, they also allow richer dependencies to be intuitively stated (e.g., by writing formulas combining and interleaving multiple types of relations and attributes, and their potentially complex interdependencies).

9.6   Advanced Research: Data Programming

While graphical models have generally led to noted advances in the machine learning community[4] and are certainly relevant to the problem of KG completion in a specific "flavor" (MLNs or PSL), a very recently published and relevant advance has been the so-called paradigm of data programming by Ratner et al. (2020). As defined by those authors, data programming consists of modeling multiple label sources without access to ground-truth, and generating probabilistic training labels[5] representing the lineage of the individual labels. The motivation is similar to that of weak supervision and active learning; namely, the dearth of a large quantity of labels that are necessary for modern machine learning

---

[4] For a complete overview of this topic, we recommend Koller and Friedman (2009).

[5] Note that this means that the labels cannot be guaranteed to be correct. In this sense, the labels are not unlike those acquired through other pseudolabeling techniques such as weak supervision.

architectures such as deep neural networks. Such labels are difficult to acquire due to the expense and manual labor required, especially for domain-specific cases like data analysis in the intelligence and defense communities, or medical image interpretation.

To illustrate the merits of data programming, Ratner et al. (2020) propose a system called *Snorkel* that enables users to write labeling functions instead of laboriously labeling data directly. Snorkel is an end-to-end system for combining weak supervision sources using this novel methodology. Because the labeling functions have different and unknown accuracies and correlations, Snorkel has to automatically model and combine their myriad outputs into a generative model. The resulting probabilistic labels output by the generative model can then be used to train a discriminative machine learning model.

We do not explore the full details of Snorkel in this chapter (we provide a link to the resource in the "Software and Resources" section), but we do use it as a means to illustrate the broad scope and use-cases of probabilistic graphical models. Systems like Snorkel show that graphical models can be used as a language for weak supervision. Other techniques covered in this chapter also show that it could be used as a metalanguage for combining outputs of IE, IM, and ontology constraints to yield a KG that is of higher quality, at least probabilistically. They are also a language for expressing the knowledge of domain experts in a tangible format. Most likely, other applications (or combinations and variants of existing lines of research and application) of graphical models and PSL will continue to emerge, especially as we start to witness more mainstream uptake of collective and joint reasoning solutions.

9.7 Concluding Notes

In this chapter, we described the importance of modeling relational dependencies and uncertainty in a joint framework that also makes it easy to elicit and represent domain knowledge. We described two unifying frameworks that meet many of the desiderata identified for SRL: MLNs and PSL. MLN, being an earlier framework, assumes that random variables are binary, while PSL, in modeling random variables as continuous, is able to turn the optimization problem into a convex form. We also described how PSL can be used for KGI by jointly representing and modeling IE, IM, and ontological constraints. Through inference, the most probable KG is thus identified. Finally, we briefly covered various other applications of SRL, including link prediction and collective classification. Although these are popular applications, they are by no means the only ones. Other sample applications that we did not describe, but that have also found SRL as a useful framework for formalizing the problem and devising robust solutions, include link-based clustering (i.e., cluster objects in a specific way—namely, that if they are more closely related via their links, they are more likely to belong to the same cluster), and instance matching.

9.8   Software and Resources

There are also numerous slides and classroom material that have been released by a number of instructors, owing to the popularity of SRL (or related SRL areas, such as probabilistic graphical models) in graduate curricula in computer science and AI. Because entire books have been written on this, an excellent resource is the book webpage of a relatively recent work on this subject by Getoor and Taskar (2007). The book webpage is accessible at cs.umd.edu/srl-book/. It lists courses at University of Maryland (cs.umd.edu/class/spring2005/cmsc828g), Purdue (cs.purdue.edu/home-s/neville/courses/CS590N.html), University of Washington (cs.washington.edu/education/courses/574/05sp), and University of Wisconsin (biostat.wisc.edu/~page/838.html).

The webpage also lists software, data, and links to workshops and meetings. We recommend thoroughly reviewing these. Webpages for specific groups that do research on this subject also list important resources and publications. We especially recommend the Lise's INQuisitive Students (LINQS) group (https://linqs.soe.ucsc.edu/home), as it provides fairly comprehensive information on data sets, publications, and resources. We also mentioned Snorkel as a software embodying the principles of data programming. Project details and tutorials on Snorkel are available at https://www.snorkel.org/.

9.9   Bibliographic Notes

SRL has a long history in recent AI literature, and it has found many applications beyond KGs. Like many areas of study in this book, providing a complete and exhaustive treatment of related work and bibliographic notes is infeasible, and we focus on key references and surveys instead, including the main papers that have guided the flow of material in this chapter. The application to KGs, and in particular, KGI, is a relatively recent phenomenon; we cite Pujara et al. (2013) as one of the important papers that took a detailed and systematic approach to KGI using PSL and showed that it could be successful with real-world data sets compared to rival approaches. However, a number of other important papers should be perused by interested readers, including Khosravi and Bina (2010), Getoor and Mihalkova (2011), Neville, Rattigan, et al. (2003), Rossi et al. (2012), and Kimmig et al. (2015). Some treatments are more domain-specific, but still extensive; for example, see Esposito et al. (2012) for a survey of SRL and social networks. Other applications for such probabilistic frameworks include trust analysis, drug-target prediction, and recommender systems, just to name a few [Kouki et al. (2015), Fakhraei et al. (2014), and Rettinger et al. (2011)].

Key references for learning about relational dependencies, and MLNs in particular, include Richardson and Domingos (2006), Wang and Domingos (2008), Kok and Domingos (2009), Domingos and Lowd (2009), Kok and Domingos (2005), and Singla and Domingos (2005). In one of the earliest papers by Singla and Domingos (2006) that applies Markov

Logic to a task (entity resolution) that is clearly relevant to KGs, we see some hint of techniques to come in the later part of the decade and the early 2010s. Some references go into much more detail than others. Koller and Friedman (2009), on probabilistic graphical models, is a key reference for learning about various kinds of probabilistic formalism that allow modeling joint distributions over interdependent unknowns using graph-based structures. For collective methods and their applications to link mining (closely related to some of the application areas covered toward the end of the chapter), we recommend Getoor and Diehl (2005) and the papers cited therein, in addition to some of the general resources covered in the "Software and Resources" section. For those looking for a more cursory treatment, a short and accessible introduction was also provided by Kimmig et al. (2012). Bach et al. (2017) provides a more complete and theoretical treatment of hinge-loss Markov Random Fields, which is a new type of probabilistic graphical model that generalizes different approaches to convex inference. PSL makes these fields easy to define and work with by using a syntax based on first-order logic.

The range and diversity of SRL approaches continue to grow, with some proposals including relational dependency networks, stochastic logic programs, and structural logistic regression, among many others. Important references include Wellman et al. (1992), Ngo and Haddawy (1997), Kersting and De Raedt (2001), Muggleton et al. (1996), Cussens and Pulman (1999), Sato and Kameya (1997), Dehaspe (1997), Friedman et al. (1999), Taskar et al. (2004), Neville et al. (2003b), Popescul and Ungar (2003), Cumby and Roth (2003), and Costa et al. (2003), to list only a few that were relatively early and influential. Toward the end of the chapter, we also mentioned data programming as an advanced area of research that draws on graphical models. The best reference for it to date is the open-access article by Ratner et al. (2020).

9.10 Exercises

1. Consider again the unacceptable PSL rule: 0.95 : *(friend(Joe, Mark) ∧ friend(George, Mark)) ∨ roommate(Joe, George) → friend(Joe, George)*. How would you break it up into a set of acceptable PSL rules?

2. Consider the rules and data shown here. Compute the penalty of the three ground PSL rules, where *X = Bob*. Show your steps.

Given the following ground PSL rules:
```
1.  HS(X)  -> GG(X)
2.  !HS(X) -> RC(X)
3.  HS(X) & GG(X) -> !RC(X)
```

HS:	HardWorkingStudent
GG:	HasGoodGrades
RC:	RetakesClasses

And observations:
- HS(Bob): 0.7
- GG(Bob): 0.5
- RC(Bob): 0.3

```
!Q = 1-Q
P -> Q = max(0, P-Q)
P &  Q = max(0, P+Q-1)
P |  Q = min(1, P+Q)
```

3. When would it be advantageous to use MLNs over PSL? When would it *not* be advantageous? Think of one good use-case for each.

4. You told a friend that "Michael is a stock market contrarian. When his friends, John and Bob, place a bet on a stock, he always bets against it." Your friend claims that statements like that cannot be expressed in PSL, and you are determined to prove him wrong. Making appropriate assumptions, and assuming that we have data on stocks, as well as "bets" that Michael, John, and Bob have placed on the stocks, provide PSL rules and observations (not unlike the short program and observations from exercise 2 for testing your hypothesis). What would be one way for you to know whether you're right or wrong about Michael?

5. You are trying to express your domain knowledge that A is more likely to follow the same celebrity on Twitter if (a) A's friend B follows that celebrity, and if (b) A has the same musical tastes as B. Express the two rules as PSL. Assume that you are equally sure about both rules.

6. Later, it occurs to you that you're not very sure about (b). Given a training data set of Twitter users, their musical tastes, celebrities, and their followers, what would be a way for you to test whether the second rule should be included? Do you have to make an include/not include decision? If not, what would be a methodology to maximize performance on a test data set without discarding the rule altogether?

10 Representation Learning for Knowledge Graphs

Overview. Neural networks have achieved powerful advances in recent years. An area of research that has been particularly affected is representation learning. In typical applications, representation learning involves embedding a data element, be it a span of text, an entity (or relation) in a knowledge graph (KG), or even an entire document, into a vector space. Usually, the vector space is real-valued and low-dimensional, which creates a robust representation. In the vector space, mathematical operations can be used in a variety of interesting ways (e.g., in the case of text, it has been found that one can derive relations such as King − Man + Woman ≈ Queen using completely unsupervised embedding techniques). In this chapter, we consider embedding KGs in vector spaces. Although KG embeddings (KGEs) constitute a relatively recent research area, the field has already witnessed a surge of research output, and relatively powerful techniques have emerged as a result. We describe some currently influential techniques that have been adopted and have yielded extremely competitive results.

10.1 Introduction

An old English saying that is often quoted is, "Birds of a feather flock together." J. R. Firth's hypothesis, also known as *Firth's axiom*, reinterprets this saying in the computational linguistics community as, "You shall know a word's meaning by its context." Though simple, the principle marks a dramatic shift in how semantics are realized, essentially spawning a successful *statistical* model of semantics that was far more robust and amenable to modern machine learning pipelines than ever before.

Even though the principle behind Firth's axiom is abstract, and open to multiple paths of realization, the dominant approach has been a vector space model (VSM). The idea is to convert (or somehow derive) a vector for the data unit under consideration. In the case of KGs, the data unit would be nodes and edges, but in the case of normal networks (such as a *friend-friend* undirected social network), the nodes constitute the data units, and in the case of natural language, the units are typically words. We saw in chapter 4, for example, how deep learning systems for Named Entity Recognition (NER) rely on good representation learning over words, and even characters. However, it is not enough to just obtain a vector for each unit, because we could randomly assign a vector to a word or node if this was

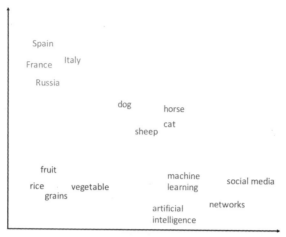

Figure 10.1: An illustration of Firth's hypothesis over a common corpus like Wikipedia pages. Words that are in the same semantic class (such as "cat" and "dog") tend to share similar contexts and are clustered close together in the vector space. Because the projection of the vectors (which are usually in the tens, if not hundreds, of real-valued dimensions) is in 2D, the "clusters" appear closer together.

all that was required. The vectors clearly have to fulfill some criteria, and one criterion is deciding the interpretation of context. In natural-language documents, the context of a word is interpreted to be the neighborhoods (surrounding set of words) that the word occurs in. Ignoring the issue of *word sense*, for example, a two-dimensional VSM model that is faithful to Firth's axiom in a reasonable corpus, as opposed to one that is not, is shown in figure 10.1. We immediately see that words that generally seem to belong to the same semantic class tend to occur closer together in the vector space, although there is also a nontrivial relationship between the semantic classes themselves (one would expect US government agencies like the National Science Foundation and National Institutes of Health to be closer to US politicians in the VSM than to Canadian politicians). In some sense, it is not incorrect to assume that, at least in natural language, word vector clusters that obey Firth's axiom tend to capture a continuous version of an ontology, or some latent space model of meaning that we have in our heads and capture through observable artifacts such as written documents.

VSMs existed long before neural networks: for example, the famous *term frequency-inverse document frequency* (or tf-idf) representation of documents was also a VSM, albeit with very different features than the representations that we are going to study in this chapter. The vectors obtained using tf-idf are usually very sparse (with only a few nonzero entries), high-dimensional (proportional to the vocabulary of the language), and not altogether apt for short texts. It is also not clear how we can use the model to get vectors for words. Another similar example, though lower-dimensional and more robust, is Latent Dirichlet Allocation (LDA), colloquially known as a *topic model*.

Firth's hypothesis has enjoyed a startlingly successful renaissance in the age of neural networks. While the best-known application of Firth's hypothesis is fittingly in Natural Language Processing (NLP), as embodied in now very well known algorithms like word2vec, fastText, and GloVe, many other applications, datatypes, and use-cases have been targeted by researchers in recent years, including KGs and networks. In the modern context, vectors derived in this way (whether using neural networks or another loss-minimizing optimization like matrix factorization) are generally referred to as *embeddings*. On the surface, it seems infeasible that such embeddings could be good. After all, natural language, and other real-world manifestations of naturalistic data (like social networks), have lots of irregularities and corner cases and can even contain outright contradictions and noise, as many symbolic and expert systems have discovered to their dismay. Is it not reasonable to assume a neural network might trip up in the same way? Other issues relate to logistics: How much data is required to train a good model? How should we set the dimensions of the learned vectors and optimize other hyperparameters? Some of these questions are better understood than others, but what is not disputed is that, given a reasonably sized corpus, the embeddings are relatively robust to noise and the occasional odd case. In part, this is because the embeddings are both lower-dimensional and continuous, allowing the learned model to be compact and robust. But the actual optimization, and the loss function that needs to be minimized, also greatly matter for the embedding to be useful.

Although Firth's axiom seems to call out words explicitly, there is no reason why it can't apply to other data units; we already cited document VSMs as an example and mentioned earlier how nodes and edges in a KG could potentially be embedded. But how do we define context in a KG? This is the question that will concern us through much of this chapter. We start with a description of the skip-gram and continuous bag of words (CBOW) models that have become classic studies in good, fast embeddings for not just natural language (their original purpose), but a whole host of inspired data formats, including networks and graphs. As such, understanding these models is important for a true appreciation of other embedding models proposed specifically for KGs. Next, we provide a general overview of KGEs and the schools of thought that are currently prevalent. Because a general theory of what constitutes a good KGE is not fully formed, it is informative to study specific, highly influential KGEs that continue to be used and repurposed in real-world KG applications.

10.2   Embedding Architectures: A Primer

Many types of models have been proposed for estimating continuous representations of words, including the well-known LDA and Latent Semantic Analysis (LSA) models. One motivation for using neural networks, however, is that they can outperform LSA by better preserving linear regularities among words; furthermore, topic models like LDA become more expensive on larger data sets due to their generative nature.

A basic probabilistic feedforward neural network language model (NNLM) consists of input, projection, hidden, and output layers. The assumption is that the NNLM is applied to a corpus, which may be assumed to be a set of word sequences (we do not distinguish between sequences that belong to the same document in a corpus, and those that do not). To visualize how the network works, imagine that a window of size N is slid over each sequence; it is these windows that serve as piecewise inputs to the neural network itself. Namely, at the input layer, N *previous* words are encoded using 1-of-V coding, where V is the size of the vocabulary. The input layer is then projected to a projection layer P that has dimensionality $N \times D$, using a shared projection matrix. As only N inputs are active at any given time, composition of the projection layer is a relatively cheap operation; however, the architecture becomes complex for computation between the projection and the hidden layer, as values in the projection layer are dense. Common choices are $N = 10$, with the projection layer having size 500–2,000 and the hidden layer, 500–1,000. Because the hidden layer is used to compute a probability distribution over all the words in the vocabulary, the output layer ends up with dimensionality V, leading to a per-training-example computational complexity of $(N \times D) + (N \times D \times H) + (H \times V)$. The last expression $(H \times V)$ clearly dominates, but several practical steps can be taken to avoid it, including using hierarchical versions of the softmax as discussed next, or avoiding normalization during training. With these steps in place,[1] most of the complexity is caused by the term $N \times D \times H$.

Hierarchical softmax is a popular method for addresses the complexity challenge of fully computing and materializing a probability distribution over all the words in the vocabulary by representing the vocabulary as a *Huffman binary tree*. Huffman trees assign short binary codes to frequent words, and this further reduces the number of output units that need to be evaluated. This is more efficient than a balanced binary tree, which requires $log_2(V)$ outputs to be evaluated. The Huffman tree, in essence, leverages the effect of data skew by requiring only about $log_2(UnigramPerplexity(V))$ outputs[2] to be evaluated, leading to non-trivial speedups (e.g., 2x) for realistic vocabulary sizes (more than 1 million words). Note that this step, by itself, cannot address the high complexity caused by the term $N \times D \times H$, but other architectures that have since become popular in the community (including skip-grams, as discussed in the next section) do address this problem. In those architectures,

---

[1] For the lay reader who is not very familiar with neural networks, some of this material specifying how the layers of the network work, or are structured, can be skimmed or skipped. A full discussion of neural networks is not within the scope of this work; there are various surveys and texts that can instead be perused by the interested reader or engineer looking to build or modify these networks.

[2] In NLP, perplexity is a way of evaluating language models, and is dependent on the probability distribution of the words.

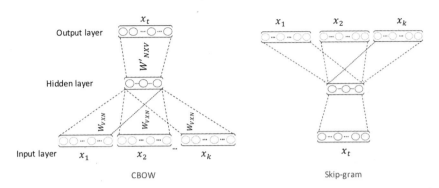

Figure 10.2: Comparative illustrations of the skip-gram and CBOW neural models, which have become extremely popular in the word representation learning ("embedding") due to their speed and good performance on word analogy tasks. Here, x_t is the target word, and $x_1, \ldots, x_k$ are the "context" words for some predetermined window size k. While CBOW takes the context words as input and predicts the target word, skip-gram operates in the opposite way.

efficiency of the softmax normalization becomes important, and the benefits of using a hierarchical softmax and a Huffman binary tree become more readily apparent. Clearly, the larger the vocabulary, the higher the benefit of using this methodology in the output layer.

10.2.1 Continuous Bag of Words Model

The CBOW model is similar to the feedforward NNLM, but the nonlinear hidden layer is removed and the projection layer is shared for all words, not just the projection matrix; hence, all words get projected into the same position because their vectors are averaged. The reason why this architecture is called a "bag of words" model is because the order of words in the history does not influence projection. By sliding a window of roughly size 8 over the corpus, the training criterion becomes to correctly classify the current (middle) word by leveraging words from both the history (four previous words) and the future. The training complexity becomes $(N \times D) + (D \times log_2(V))$, which is substantially less than the original complexity of (approximately) $N \times D \times H$.

Why is the model called the *continuous* bag of words model? The main reason is that unlike the classic bag of words model, the representation of the context is both continuous and distributed. Figure 10.2 expresses the CBOW architecture, along with the similar skip-gram architecture described next. The weight matrix between the input and projection layer is shared for all word positions, just like in the NNLM.

10.2.2   Skip-Gram Model

Skip-gram is similar to CBOW, but instead of predicting the current word based on the context, it tries to maximize classification of a word based on another word in the same sentence. Figure 10.2 expresses the intuition behind the difference between CBOW and skip-gram. Each current word is used as an input to a log-linear classifier with a continuous projection layer, and words are predicted within a certain range both before and after the current word. Mikolov et al. (2013) found that, while increasing this range could improve the quality of the resulting word vectors, it came at the cost of increasing the computational complexity. Because the more distant words are usually less related to the current word (compared to closer words), less weight is given to the distant words by sampling less from those words in the training examples. Consequently, the training complexity of the architecture is proportional to $C \times (D + (D \times log_2(D)))$, C being the maximum distance of the words. For example, if $C = 4$, then for each training word, a number R is randomly selected in the range $< 1, 4 >$, following which R words from both the history and the future of the current word are used as correct labels, requiring $R \times 2$ word classifications (with the current word as input, and each of the $R + R$ words as output). In the original paper on skip-grams, a value of $C = 10$ was suggested as appropriate.

10.3   Embeddings beyond Words

We suggested earlier that, generally, any data unit can be embedded in a vector space, so long as an appropriate context is available, and Firth's axiom is applicable. However, the devil is often in the details, as we saw even with word embeddings. What, for example, are we trying to optimize, and what should serve as a context? How do we model graphs, networks, or other structured data sets so that they are amenable to similar procedures?

Over the last decade, the machine learning community has vigorously taken up the challenge of embedding myriad datatypes and modalities, including KGs. As we describe in the section entitled "Bibliographic Notes" at the end of the chapter, this field is popular enough that it now goes under the general name of *representation learning*. In addition to being a staple at classic machine learning conferences, representation learning now even has its own conference series. Starting with the next section, we will be exclusively focusing on KGEs; however, before moving on to KGEs, we provide a brief primer on how the same intuitions behind models like skip-gram can be applied to network embeddings.

A network, such as a social or telecommunications network, is like a simpler version of a KG, in that (in the simplest and best-known cases) the nodes are of a homogeneous type, and there is only a single kind of edge. If an ontology were to be formalized for such a network, it would have only one concept (e.g., Person) and one relationship (e.g., friend). Even this simple network is very important, and many real-world social phenomena can be modeled this way (e.g., the Facebook friendship network, the Twitter hashtag cooccurrence network, and so on). There are important problems entailed by such networks, such as *link*

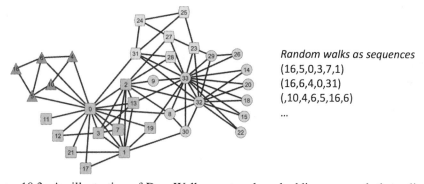

Figure 10.3: An illustration of DeepWalk, a network-embedding approach that relies on word embeddings as an underlying mechanism, on the Zachary Karate Club network. The concept is relatively simple: first, a "corpus" of random walks is constructed, with each random walk interpreted by the word-embedding algorithm (e.g., CBOW or skip-gram, but more modern embedding implementations could also be applied) as a sentence, and with nodes as words. The result is an embedding for each word (in this case, node). The algorithm can be extended in multiple ways (e.g., for directed graphs) and at this time, more sophisticated embeddings of this type have been proposed in the network community as well (LINE, node2vec, and several others). However, the algorithm continues to be reasonably popular, probably owing to its simplicity.

prediction, predicting when two people are friends or otherwise socially or professionally connected (in which case, a friend invitation can be recommended by a social network company like Facebook); but also *node classification* (e.g., if a particular person is wealthy and hence, amenable to targeted advertising of expensive watches). In the social sciences, it is well understood that the structure of the network alone can provide valuable clues to solving such problems. Concerning friendship prediction, for example, it is well known that a friend of a friend is more likely to be a friend than not; furthermore, the more friends A and B have in common, the more likely it is that they themselves are friends. Similarly, phenomena like the *rich club effect* suggest that wealthy people are connected to other wealthy people.

How do we extract good features using only the structure of the network? Classic (and even some modern) techniques relied on methods like matrix factorization (on an appropriate graph representation, like the adjacency matrix), but in the last few years, node embedding algorithms, based on neural networks, have become popular for featurizing nodes using structural context. An early such model was DeepWalk, which has a very intuitive algorithm behind it. The core philosophy is illustrated in figure 10.3. As a first step, the algorithm initiates *random walks* starting from each node. Each random walk can be thought of as a sentence, because it is just a sequence of nodes. The full set of random walks is exactly like a corpus, with nodes as words and can be embedded using a standard word-embedding algorithm such as word2vec. Although it sounds simple, DeepWalk achieved impressive results on a number of standard social network problems, and because of its reliance on word2vec, has fast execution times. Other node embedding algorithms have since superseded DeepWalk as state-of-the-art, including LINE and node2vec, but the basic philosophy behind these algorithms is similar to that of DeepWalk.

10.4   Knowledge Graph Embeddings

The previous section discussed some exciting possibilities for embedding ordinary networks using techniques inspired by word embeddings, as well as other representation learning methods first defined in related communities like NLP. There are limitations to some of these techniques, however, especially when applied to KGs. Take, for example, the random walk methodology adopted by DeepWalk for learning node representations. How can we extend it to learning about *edge* representations? One option is to incorporate the edge label in the random walk itself—that is, inserting the edge label between every two (consecutively traversed) nodes. It is debatable whether this will work, because the number of unique relationships (specified in an ontology) may be small compared to the number of unique nodes (instances in the KG). Furthermore, the directionality of edges can cause problems for algorithms inspired by word embeddings. Yet another problem is connectivity; there is no guarantee that KGs are connected graphs, and even when there is connectivity, it tends to be a result of hub nodes (e.g., "United States" may be a hub node

Table 10.1: Parameter descriptions of some well-known KGE architectures.

Algorithm	Entity Embedding	Relation Embedding
TransE	$\mathbf{h}, \mathbf{t} \in \mathbb{R}^d$	$\mathbf{r} \in \mathbb{R}^d$
TransH	$\mathbf{h}, \mathbf{t} \in \mathbb{R}^d$	$\mathbf{r}, \mathbf{w}_r \in \mathbb{R}^d$
TransR	$\mathbf{h}, \mathbf{t} \in \mathbb{R}^d$	$\mathbf{r} \in \mathbb{R}^k, \mathbf{M}_r \in \mathbb{R}^{k \times d}$
TransD	$\mathbf{h}, \mathbf{w}_h \in \mathbb{R}^d; \mathbf{t}, \mathbf{w}_t \in \mathbb{R}^d$	$\mathbf{r}, \mathbf{w}_r \in \mathbb{R}^k$
TransSparse	$\mathbf{h}, \mathbf{t} \in \mathbb{R}^d$	$\mathbf{r} \in \mathbb{R}^k, \mathbf{M}_r(\theta_r) \in \mathbb{R}^{k \times d}$; $\mathbf{M}_r^1(\theta_r^1), \mathbf{M}_r^2(\theta_r^2) \in \mathbb{R}^{k \times d}$
TransM	$\mathbf{h}, \mathbf{t} \in \mathbb{R}^d$	$\mathbf{r} \in \mathbb{R}^d$
TransF	$\mathbf{h}, \mathbf{t} \in \mathbb{R}^d$	$\mathbf{r} \in \mathbb{R}^d$
TransA	$\mathbf{h}, \mathbf{t} \in \mathbb{R}^d$	$\mathbf{r} \in \mathbb{R}^d, \mathbf{M}_r \in \mathbb{R}^{d \times d}$
TransG	$h \sim \mathcal{N}(\mu_h, \sigma_h^2 \mathbf{I}); t \sim \mathcal{N}(\mu_t, \sigma_t^2 \mathbf{I})$; $\mu_h, \mu_t \in \mathbb{R}^d$	$\mu_r^i \sim \mathcal{N}(\mu_t - \mu_h, (\sigma_h^2 + \sigma_t^2)\mathbf{I})$; $\mathbf{r} = \Sigma_i \pi_r^i \mu_r^i \in \mathbb{R}^d$
SE	$\mathbf{h}, \mathbf{t} \in \mathbb{R}^d$	$\mathbf{M}_r^1, \mathbf{M}_r^2 \in \mathbb{R}^{d \times d}$

Emb. stands for Embedding. $\mathcal{N}$ is the normal distribution with the usual mean μ and standard deviation σ parameters. d is the embedding dimensionality (set by the user, and generally in the range of tens to hundreds), n and m are the numbers of entities and relations, respectively, in the KG to be embedded, and SE means "structured embedding." Other symbols are algorithm- or system-specific, although some (such as k) can be specified by the user. For example, in TranSparse, θ is the average sparseness degree of projection matrices. For more formal definitions of parameters, we refer the reader to the individual papers or to a recent condensed survey (see the "Bibliographic Notes" section).

connecting many, though not all, nodes in a KG of pop artists, who may not share much in common but may mostly be based in the US or born in the US). Another reason for favoring special embeddings for KGs is that most KG nodes and edges have *meaningful* labels, and using only structural information is likely not going to yield the best performance, as some valuable text information is being thrown away in the process. Beyond these reasons, experimentally, we are not aware of any methods directly inspired by word embeddings that have yielded successful state-of-the-art results on KGs.

Instead, separate embedding algorithms have been designed, refined, and evaluated for KGs since they first started to become popular (in the early 2010s). In just this last decade, tens of algorithms have been proposed, some of which are variations on a common theme (but remain very valuable due to the improved experimental results on challenging benchmark data sets). In this section, we cover some of the important ones that have withstood the test of time thus far and inspired others like themselves. First, however, we provide a general overview of *energy functions*, which dictate how KGEs are optimized. In practice, the difference between KGE algorithms often boils down to a difference in their respective energy function formulations.

10.4.1   Energy Functions

Recall that, in an ordinary machine learning context, the primary goal of optimization is to infer model parameters that lead to a minimization of a loss function. For example, when training a linear regression model, the loss function most commonly squared is based on *least squares* (i.e., minimizing the sum of squares of errors, or residuals, where the error is defined as the difference between the predicted value (by the regression line) and the actual value).

In the context of KGEs, an *energy function* is a function (sometimes also called a *score function*) that is usually input into a margin-based objective function and that must be minimized (just like a loss function). A good example of a margin-based objective function, given an energy function $f(h, r, t)$, is

$$\mathcal{L} = \sum_{(h,r,t) \in \mathcal{G}, (h',r,t') \in \mathcal{G}'} [\gamma + f(h, r, t) - f(h'r, t')]. \tag{10.1}$$

Notice how the energy function is typically just a function of the *triple*, which is the most intuitive context for a relationship and entities (that constitute that triple). Recall that Firth's axiom was an abstract principle, and it is up to the designer of an embedding algorithm to determine the appropriate context for each data unit. A very simple energy function (used in one of the earliest KGE algorithms) is $\|v_h - v_t\|_{l_{1/2}}$ (i.e., the second norm of the difference between the vectors representing the head and tail entities). The energy should be high for *correct* triples, assumed to be in the graph $\mathcal{G}$ in equation (10.1) and low for *incorrect* triples (assumed to be in the graph $\mathcal{G}'$). Generally, $\mathcal{G}$ is assumed to be an initial KG (albeit incomplete) input into the algorithm, while $\mathcal{G}'$ is not explicitly provided, but is constructed from $\mathcal{G}$ using various sample-and-replace permutations. While there are sometimes differences in how this training data is constructed, the basic principle behind constructing the negative graph $\mathcal{G}'$ is that a random replacement of a head entity h or tail entity t with some other entity (denoted as h' or t' depending on whether the head or the tail entity is getting replaced) in the graph will almost always yield an incorrect triple. This principle is important precisely because the original graph is incomplete. Without this assumption (or even with it, frankly), we cannot always guarantee that a triple in $\mathcal{G}'$ is truly incorrect. When evaluating KGEs, it is common to check that triples in $\mathcal{G}'$ are truly incorrect by ensuring that the triple does not occur in either $\mathcal{G}$ or in the withheld test set of correct triples that the KGE does not access when learning the embedding. Notice also that the simple energy function we used does not depend on r. In more practical and realistic KGEs, however, vector (or matrix representations) of both entities and the relationship in the triple are involved in computing the score.

The energy function is directly related to the number of model parameters that the KGE algorithm is trying to infer. The more parameters there are, the more data is usually required to learn them well. Table 10.1 succinctly expresses the energy functions of many established KGE architectures, with table 10.2 expressing the time and space complexity of these architectures in terms of the relevant parameters. The classic TransE algorithm, which has been hugely influential in the KGE community, requires $2d$ parameters to be inferred *per entity*,[3] and d parameters *per relationship* (unique edge label). d, the embedding dimensionality, is usually some small fixed constant, such as 100. Even so, the number of parameters is certainly not trivial, even for this relatively early and pithy model (see the exercises at the end of this chapter). In general, both time and space complexity are affected, as table 10.2 demonstrates.

Unlike least-squares linear regression, which has some impressive theoretical properties (on the condition, of course, that the underlying assumptions are valid), modern deep learning and machine learning optimizations tend to be based more on the desiderata of the task, and can even be a matter of experimentation and trial-and-error. For example, it is still not completely clear, despite significant theoretical progress, how many layers should be included in a deep neural network, or what the effect of other model mechanisms (like dropout) will be on the final optimization outcome. The actual optimization procedure used in KGE implementations is fairly standard, with Stochastic Gradient Descent (SGD) being a common choice. Other alternatives include SGD+AdaGrad, SGD+AdaDelta, and L-BFGS.

Similarly, in the KGE community, it is not always clear whether (for example) relationship embeddings should be represented as vectors or matrices, or if enforcing sparsity has some value. The situation becomes even murkier when we deal with sparse KGs. Some recent influential work, for example, has shown that KGEs may not be appropriate if the underlying KG is too sparse and narrow, and that statistical relational algorithms do a better job (see the "Bibliographic Notes" section). Currently, there is a resurgence of interest in the broader artificial intelligence (AI) community to develop algorithms that are either inherently more explainable or methods that can extract some kind of interpretation from complex, black-box models (almost always based on optimizing a loss or energy function in a nonconvex space, usually using some kind of neural network or deep learning) trained on a good deal of data. It is likely that we will see some of this research play out in the context of KGEs as well.

10.5   Influential KGE Systems

In this section, we describe some important KGE systems that are now considered established baselines. However, it is important to note that the research on KGEs is continuing

---

[3] More precisely, this means d parameters for every entity that occurs at least once in a head position [in the triple (h, r, t), the entity h is said to occur in the head position, and t in the tail position], and d for every entity that occurs at least once in a tail position. Generally, an entity occurs in both positions; hence, $2d$ is an appropriate bound for the number of parameters learned per entity in the KG.

Table 10.2: Time and space complexities of the KGE architectures in table 10.1.

Algorithm	Space Complexity	Time Complexity
TransE	$O(nd + md)$	$O(d)$
TransH	$O(nd + md)$	$O(d)$
TransR	$O(nd + mdk)$	$O(dk)$
TransD	$O(nd + md)$	$O(max(d, k))$
TransSparse	$O(nd + (1 - \theta)mdk)$	$O(dk)$
TransM	$O(nd + md)$	$O(d)$
TransF	$O(nd + md)$	$O(d)$
TransA	$O(nd + md^2)$	$O(d^2)$
TransG	$O(nd + mdc)$	$O(dc)$
SE	$O(nd + md^2)$	$O(d^2)$

to evolve, and it is likely that several other good systems will have been published by the time this book has been published. Nevertheless, it is unlikely that any of these systems will mark a radical departure from the core concepts embodied in the systems described next.

10.5.1   Structured Embeddings

The technique of structured embeddings was among the first proposed for embedding KGs. The initial formalism, data sets, means of evaluation, and other aspects of the work have all continued to be influential on future lines of work. Hence, it is useful to introduce the model from the beginning starting with the core ideas.

First, as we've already seen, entities in KGs (just like words in documents) can be modeled in a d-dimensional continuous vector space, referred to as an *embedding space*. For the sake of notation,[4] assume that the *ith* entity (in a list of entities in the KG) is assigned a vector $E_i \in \mathbb{R}^d$.

Second, within the embedding space, there is a specific similarity measure that captures (not necessarily symmetric) relationships between entities. For the *kth* relation, let us assume a pair of $d \times d$ matrices (R_k^{lhs}, R_k^{rhs}); the similarity function S_k for two entities related through R_k is then defined as $S_k(E_i, E_j) = \|R_k^{lhs}E_i - R_k^{rhs}E_j\|_p$, using the p-norm (with $p = 1$ in the original paper).

The intuition is that the matrices and vectors should be learned so as to maximize, to the greatest extent possible, similarities between entities that are truly related through a relation, and to minimize similarities between entities not thus related. This intuition needs to be modeled as a neural network, which can be seen as a generalization of a Siamese

---

[4] We use the notation employed by Bordes et al. (2011) for this discussion.

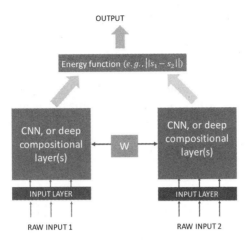

Figure 10.4: Illustration of the architecture of a Siamese neural network.

network that generally takes a pair of inputs and tries to learn a similarity measure (figure 10.4 illustrates the general principle behind a Siamese network). Specifically, the energy function (note the change in notation) $f(e_i^l, r_i, e_i^r) = \|R_{r_i}^{lhs} Ev(e_i^l) - R_{r_i}^{rhs} Ev(e_i^r)\|_1$ parameterizes a neural network and is trained to rank the training samples below all other triplets using 1-norm distance. Here R^{lhs} and R^{rhs} are $d \times d \times D_r$ tensors, where R_i^{lhs} is designed to select the *ith* component along the third dimension of R^{lhs}, yielding a $d \times d$ matrix slice. d is usually small for most KGs, with a recommended value of 50 in the original paper. E is a $d \times D_e$ matrix containing the embeddings of D_e entities, while the vectorization function $v(n) : \{1, \ldots, D_e\} \to \mathbb{R}^{D_e}$ maps the entity dictionary index (n) into a sparse vector of dimension D_e consisting of all zeros except for a one in the *nth* dimension (1-hot encoding).

The learning of the matrix E is an example of *multitasking* because a single embedding matrix is used for all relations, with the embedding of an entity containing factorized information contributed to by all relations in which the entity is involved. For each entity, the model learns how it interacts with other entities with respect all the relation types. A major advantage of this formulation is that it is memory inexpensive, and also scalable.

Training is done using SGD, and the negative training set is constructed in a way that is very similar to what we described in the previous section—namely, a positive training triple (i.e., a triple that exists in the initial graph) is randomly selected, and either its head or tail entity is randomly replaced, such that the new triple is not a positive training triple. Furthermore, during training, normalization is enforced (i.e., each column $\|E_i\|$ equals 1 for all values of i). Other details are provided in the original paper (see the "Bibliographic Notes" section).

An interesting aspect of SE is the method chosen to estimate the probability of an arbitrary triple being correct (after the model has been trained). The authors introduced a *kernel density estimation* (KDE) function that can estimate the density for any triple. This function can be used for ranking [e.g., given the relationship r and head entity h, candidate tail entities can be ranked by creating a triple (h, r, t) for every candidate tail entity t and computing the density for that triple using the KDE proposed in the paper]. The higher the density of the triple, the more probable that it is correct, and hence the better the rank of the candidate tail entity. In this way, a full ranking can be produced over all such candidates. A similar procedure can be adopted regardless of whether it is the tail entity, the head entity, or the relationship that is missing.

Empirically, Structured Embeddings, being one of the first embeddings proposed, was evaluated against a simple, nonembedding baseline, as well as variants of the proposed algorithm. Two tasks were considered: a ranking over missing tail entities in triples, and over missing head entities in triples. The authors reported the mean ranks (lower is better) and Hits@10 (between 0 and 1; higher is better) or the rate of correct predictions ranked in the top 10 elements per triple query. Two benchmark data sets, which were also adopted by other authors in the community, were used for the evaluations (namely, WordNet and Freebase). WordNet is a general resource valuable across NLP and information retrieval, and it has been brought up in several chapters of this book. For our current purposes, it suffices to think of it as a KG of words, with relationships expressing word semantics such as synonymy. Freebase, which was acquired by Google in 2010,[5] was originally a crowdsourced KG (not unlike Wikipedia, which is a crowdsourced encyclopedia) where users could contribute facts.[6] The version of Freebase used for the evaluations is still publicly available and has allowed many other researchers to replicate the results (and compare it to their own embeddings).

10.5.2 Neural Tensor Networks

Following on the heels of structured embeddings, neural tensor networks (NTNs) were proposed as an alternative way to achieve good KGEs.[7] The main difference was in the optimization function because the NTN replaced the standard linear neural network layer with a bilinear tensor layer that directly related two entity vectors across multiple dimensions. Specifically, the model computes a score of how likely it is that two entities are in a

---

[5] Source: https://www.cloudave.com/140/google-buys-freebase-this-is-huge/.

[6] Actually, Freebase was not purely crowdsourced, but rather composed in a hybrid way. Much of the information in it was crowdsourced, however, either directly or indirectly.

[7] This section is advanced and may be skipped by those unfamiliar with tensors.

certain relationship by the following function [using the notation[8] in Socher et al. (2013), where NTNs were first proposed], which is based on an NTN:

$$g(e_1, R, e_2) = u_R^T f\left(e_1^T W_R^{[1:k]} e_2 + V_R \begin{bmatrix} e_1 \\ e_2 \end{bmatrix} + b_R\right). \tag{10.2}$$

In equation (10.2), f is the *tanh* function, which is nonlinear and is applied element-wise, $W_R^{[1:k]} \in \mathbb{R}^{d \times d \times k}$ is a tensor and the bilinear tensor product $e_1^T W_R^{[1:k]} e_2$ yields a vector $h \in \mathbb{R}^k$ with each entry computed by one slide $i = 1, \ldots, k$ of the tensor ($h_i = e_1^T W_R^{[1:k]} e_2$). The other parameters for relation R are just like in a standard neural network ($V_R \in \mathbb{R}^{k \times 2d}$, $U \in \mathbb{R}^k$, $b_R \in \mathbb{R}^k$). A key advantage of the formulation of KGEs as a NTN is that the two inputs (entities) are related *multiplicatively* instead of (implicitly) through the nonlinearity that is standard in other neural network models where the entity vectors simply get con-catenated. Each slice of the tensor may be intuitively seen as being responsible for one type of entity pair or relationship instantiation. The model may, using this formulation, be able to learn that both a scientific paper and a piece of equipment have components [in the KG formulation, *(scientific_paper, has_component, x)*, where x might be abstract or exper-imental results from various parts of the word vector space]. Experimentally, the authors showed that this can lead to performance improvements.

The NTN is trained with contrastive max-margin objective functions, just like the struc-tured embeddings. Recall that the principal idea behind this optimization was that each triple in the training set should receive a higher score than triples where one of the entities is randomly replaced. In the NTN, each relation has its associated tensor net parameters. Letting Ω represent the set of all relationship parameters, the following objective should be minimized; g having been defined in equation (10.3) already:

$$L(\Omega) = \sum_{i=1}^{N} \sum_{c=1}^{C} max(0, 1 - g(T^{(i)}) + g(T_c^{(i)})) + \lambda \|\Omega\|_2^2 \tag{10.3}$$

As in other similar loss formulations, the hyperparameter λ serves as a regularization mechanism for ensuring that the parameters are sparse in their values to avoid overfit-ting. Another unique aspect of NTN was that, unlike KGEs, which randomly initialized entity vectors before optimization began, it decided to represent entities by their word vec-tors, and it initialized the word vectors with pretrained vectors. This allowed sharing of statistical strength between words describing each entity. Although this can cause some noise (e.g., "New York" and "York" would share some overlap in their initial vectors, even though York is no more similar to New York than, say, Paris), it can also have benefits (e.g., "Los Angeles" and "Los Angeles International Airport" would have similar initial vectors, as they should) and may potentially lead to faster convergence in some KGs. The authors

---

[8] A triple in this notation is represented as (e_1, R, e_2).

of NTN represent each entity vector by averaging its word vectors, and use unsupervised word vectors that are pretrained over common sources. The authors did experiment with Recurrent Neural Networks as a more sophisticated alternative to simple averaging, but without experimental benefits. Just like structured embeddings, NTN was evaluated over WordNet and Freebase. Compared to structured embeddings, it achieves an average improvement in accuracy of over 20 percent.

10.5.3   Translational Embedding Models

Translational embedding models exploit distance-based scoring functions by measuring the plausibility of a fact as the distance between the two entities, usually after a translation carried out by the relation. The intuition behind translation is shown in figure 10.5.

10.5.4   TransE

TransE is an energy-based model for learning low-dimensional embeddings of entities, such that relations are represented as translations in the embedding space: given a true triple or fact (h, r, t), the embedding of the tail entity t should be close to the embedding of the head entity h plus a vector that depends on the relationship r. TransE relies on a reduced set of parameters as it learns only one low-dimensional vector for each entity and each relationship.

The main motivation behind the translation-based parameterization is that hierarchical relationships are extremely common in KBs, and translations are the natural transformations for representing them. For example, consider tree representations wherein the siblings are close to each other and nodes at a given height are organized on the x-axis, with the parent-child relationship corresponding to a translation on the y-axis. In this context, a null translation vector corresponds to an equivalence relationship between entities, and the model can also represent the sibling relationship. This directly motivated the authors to use only one low-dimensional vector to represent the key relationships in KBs. A secondary motivation was guided by the analogical findings in the word-embedding and natural-language communities, where 1-to-1 relationships between various-type entities (like actors and movies) such as *starred-as* could be represented by the model as translations in the embedding space. Therefore, there may be empirical reason to suppose that such a thing might be achievable for entity embeddings derived from KGs rather than natural language.

More specifically, TransE represents both entities and relations as d-dimensional real-valued vectors in the same latent space (a subset of $\mathbb{R}^d$). Given a fact (h, r, t), the relation is interpreted as a translation vector $\vec{r}$ such that the embedded entities $\vec{h}$ and $\vec{t}$ can be connected by $\vec{r}$ with low error [i.e., $\vec{h} + \vec{r} = \vec{t}$ when (h, r, t) is a true fact]. The (relatively straightforward) intuition here arguably originates from the analog-style reasoning first presented and demonstrated convincingly in word-embedding papers from the NLP literature. In multirelational data, such an analogy is expected to hold by adopting generic approaches that

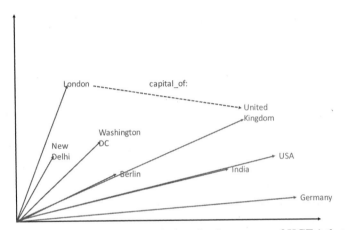

Figure 10.5: An illustration of basic translation (in the context of KGEs) that is exploited by all of the Trans* algorithms in increasingly sophisticated ways. In this example, an entity such as "London" can be translated into "United Kingdom" using the relation "capital_of:," which is a single vector that allows entities from one class (in this example) to be translated to entities from another class. In practice, translation tends to work well when entities can be (at least implicitly) clustered in such semantically meaningful ways, although more sophisticated variants are able to learn very general translations for relations that may not be between entities belonging to such well-defined classes.

can choose the appropriate patterns considering all heterogeneous relationships at the same time. The actual scoring function is given here (technically, either L_1 or L_2 norm could be used):

$$f_r(h, t) = -\|\vec{h} + \vec{r} - \vec{t}\|_{1/2}.$$ (10.4)

The score is expected to be large if (h, r, t) holds; the corollary is that large translational mismatch between the head and tail entities, where the relationship vector mediates the translation, will lead to a larger negative score.

For training the model, consider a training set T of triplets (h, r, t) known to be true. To learn good embeddings, TransE minimizes a margin-based ranking criterion over the training set:

$$\mathcal{L} = \sum_{(h,r,t)\in S'} \sum_{(h',r,t')\in S'_{(h,r,t)}} [\gamma + d(\vec{h} + \vec{r}, \vec{t}) - d(\vec{h'} + \vec{r}, \vec{t'})]_+.$$ (10.5)

where $[x]_+$ denotes the positive part of x, $\gamma > 0$ is a margin hyperparameter, and

$$S'_{(h,r,t)} = \{(h', r, t)|h' \in E\} \cup \{(h, r, t')|t' \in E\}.$$ (10.6)

The set of corrupted triplets, constructed according to equation (10.6), is composed of training triplets with either the head or tail (but not both at the same time) replaced by a random entity. The loss function favors lower values of the energy for training triplets than for corrupted triplets, and also is a natural implementation of the intended criterion. For a given entity, the embedding vector is the same regardless of whether the entity occurs in the head or tail position of the triplet. In this sense, TransE is different (sparser in its parameterization) than some other embedding algorithms that choose to learn more than one embedding for an entity, based on whether it occurs in the head position or the tail position.

Bordes et al. (2013) perform the optimization using SGD in minibatch mode over the possible head and tail entities, as well as relations. Embeddings for entities and relationships are first initialized following an established random procedure. The additional constraint in the optimization is that (when using L_2) the L_2 norm of the entity embeddings is 1 (no regularization or norm constraints are given to the relationship embeddings). This constraint is important compared to previous embedding-based methods because it prevents the training process from trivially minimizing L by artificially increasing entity embedding norms. At each main iteration of the algorithm, the embedding vectors of the entities are first normalized. The algorithm is stopped based on its performance on a validation set.

TransE is one of the simpler and more efficient embedding algorithms, but it has flaws in dealing with 1-to-N, N-to-1, and N-to-N relations. Taking 1-to-N relations as an example, given such a relation r [i.e., $\exists i = 1, ..., p$, such that (h, r, t_i) are all in the positive training

KG], TransE enforces $\vec{h} + \vec{r} \approx \vec{t_i}$ for all $i = 1, ..., p$, and then $\vec{t_1} \approx ... \approx \vec{t_p}$. The implication is that, given a 1-to-N relation (e.g., *AuthorOf*), TransE might learn very similar vector representations for *The Lord of the Rings*, *The Hobbit*, and *The Silmarillion*, which are all books written by *J. R. R. Tolkien*, even though they are different entities. The disadvantages for N-to-1 and N-to-N relations are potentially more severe.

10.5.5   Other Trans* Algorithms

To overcome the disadvantages of TransE in dealing with 1-to-N, N-to-1, and N-to-N relations, an effective strategy is to allow an entity to have distinct representations when involved in different relations. In this way, even if the embeddings of *Lord of the Rings*, *Hobbit*, and *Silmarrilion* turn out to be similar given the relation *AuthorOf*, they could still be far away, given *other* relations.

TransH implements this intuition using *relation-specific hyperplanes*. As shown in figure 10.5, TransH models entities again as vectors, but each relation r as a vector r on a hyperplane with $\vec{w_r}$ as the normal vector. Given a true triple (h, r, t), the entity representations h and t are first projected onto the hyperplane:

$$\vec{h_\perp} = \vec{h} - \vec{w_r^T} \vec{h} \vec{w_r},$$ (10.7)

and similarly,

$$\vec{t_\perp} = \vec{t} - \vec{w_r^T} \vec{t} \vec{w_r}.$$ (10.8)

The projections are then assumed to be connected by r on the hyperplane with low error if (h, r, t) holds (i.e., $\vec{h_\perp} + \vec{r} \approx \vec{t_\perp}$). The scoring function is accordingly defined as

$$f_r(h, t) = -\|\vec{h_\perp} + \vec{r} - \vec{t_\perp}\|_2^2,$$ (10.9)

similar to the one used in TransE. By introducing the mechanism of projecting to relation-specific hyperplanes, TransH enables different roles of an entity in different relations.

Training in TransH specifically proceeds as follows. First, the following loss function (similar to the margin-based function used by algorithms like TransE) is used to encourage discrimination between positive and negative (incorrect/corrupted) triples:

$$\mathcal{L} = \sum_{(h,r,t) \in P} \sum_{(h',r,t') \in N_{(h,r,t)}} [\gamma + f_r(h, t) - f_{r'}(h', t')]_+.$$ (10.10)

Notice the similarities between this loss equation and the one defined earlier for TransE. Once again, $[x]_+ = max(0, x)$, P is the set of positive triples, N is the set of negative triples constructed by corrupting (h, r, t), and γ is the margin separating positive from negative triples.

Concerning triples corruption, note that TransH takes a more sophisticated approach compared to previous methods like TransE. Recall that in TransE, negative triples were constructed by randomly replacing either h or t in a positive triple (but not both), according to a previously established procedure. However, as the authors of TransH note, real KGs are more complicated and incomplete, and there is always a chance that a true positive triple may accidentally get introduced this way (even though it is not in the training set). To mitigate this problem, the authors of TransH set different probabilities for replacing the head or tail entity when corrupting the triplet, which depends on the mapping property of the relation (i.e., one-to-many, many-to-one, or many-to-many). The authors give more chance to replacing the head entity if the relation is one-to-many and give more chance to replacing the tail entity if the relation is many-to-one. In this way, the chance of generating false negative labels is reduced. Specifically, among all the triplets of a relation r, the following two statistics are generated: the average number of tail entities per head entity (t_h), and the average number of head entities per tail entity(h_t). A Bernoulli distribution is then defined with sampling parameter $\frac{t_h}{t_h+h_t}$; namely, given a positive triple (h, r, t) of relation r, with probability $\frac{t_h}{t_h+h_t}$, the triple would be corrupted by replacing the head, while with probability $\frac{h_t}{t_h+h_t}$, the triple would be corrupted by replacing the tail.

Just like TransE, TransH also incorporates a number of constraints when minimizing the loss function. The first constraint is a *scale constraint*:

$$\forall e \in E, \|\vec{e}\|_2 \leq 1. \tag{10.11}$$

The second constraint is an *orthogonality constraint*:

$$\forall r \in R, \frac{|\vec{w}_r^T \vec{d}_r|}{\|\vec{d}_r\|_2} \leq \epsilon. \tag{10.12}$$

Finally, there is a *unit normality* constraint:

$$\forall r \in R, \|\vec{w}_r\|_2 = 1. \tag{10.13}$$

The unit normality and orthogonality constraints were clearly not applicable to TransE, as there was no concept of a hyperplane. The orthogonality constraint guarantees that the translation vector is actually in the hyperplane. Instead of directly optimizing the loss function with constraints, TransH instead uses the following *unconstrained loss*, with *soft constraints*:

$$\mathcal{L} = \sum_{(h,r,t) \in P} \sum_{(h',r,t') \in N_{(h,r,t)}} [\gamma + f_r(h,t) - f_r(h',t')]_+$$

$$+ C\{\sum_{e \in E}[\|\vec{e}\|_2^2 - 1]_+ + \sum_{r \in R}[\frac{(\vec{w}_r^T \vec{d}_r)^2}{\|\vec{d}_r\|_2^2} - \epsilon^2]_+\}.$$

Here, C is a hyperparameter weighing the importance of soft constraints. Similar to TransE, and other such algorithms, SGD is used to minimize the loss function. The positive triples-set is randomly traversed multiple times. When a positive triple is visited, a negative triple is randomly constructed as described previously. After a minibatch, the gradient is computed and the model parameters updated. Furthermore, note that the third constraint is missing from the unconstrained loss; instead, w_r is projected to a ball with unit radius before visiting each minibatch.

TransR shares the intuition of TransH, but it introduces *relation-specific spaces* rather than hyperplanes. As we saw earlier, both TransE and TransH assume embeddings of entities and relations being in the same space $\mathbb{R}^k$. However, an entity may have multiple aspects, and various relations focus on different aspects of entities. Hence, it is intuitive that some entities are similar, and thus close to each other in the entity space, but they are comparably different in some specific aspects, and thus far from each other in the corresponding relation spaces. One way to address this issue, adopted by TransR, is to model entities and relations in distinct spaces (i.e., entity space) and multiple relation spaces (i.e., relation-specific entity spaces), and performs translation in the corresponding relation space.

In TransR, entities are represented as vectors in an entity space $\mathbb{R}^d$, and each relation is associated with a specific space $\mathbb{R}^k$ and modeled as a translation vector in that space. Given a fact (h, r, t), TransR first projects the entity representations $\vec{h}$ and $\vec{t}$ into the space specific to relation r; that is,

$$\vec{h}_\perp = \mathbb{M}_r \vec{h}. \tag{10.14}$$

$$\vec{t}_\perp = \mathbb{M}_r \vec{t}. \tag{10.15}$$

Here $\mathbb{M}_r \in \mathbb{R}^{k \times d}$ is a projection matrix from the entity space to the relation space of r. Then, the scoring function is again defined as

$$f_r(h, t) = -\|\vec{h} + \vec{r} - \vec{t}\|_2^2. \tag{10.16}$$

Earlier, we provided a simple illustration of TransR in figure 10.5. Although powerful in modeling complex relations, TransR introduces a projection matrix for each relation, which requires $O(dk)$ parameters per relation. Thus, it loses some of the simplicity and efficiency that made TransE and TransH, which model relations as vectors and require only $O(d)$ parameters per relation so attractive. An even more complicated version of the same approach was later proposed, wherein each relation is associated with *two* matrices, one to project head entities and the other tail entities.

The training of TransR uses the same margin-based scoring function objective as some of the earlier methods; for reference, see equation (10.10). The difference, of course, emerges in the choice of the score function $f_r(h, t)$. Another more minor difference (between TransR and TransH) arises with respect to triples corruption for the generation of negative triples, because Lin et al. (2015) consider both the previous method used in TransE ("unif") and the Bernoulli-based method introduced first in the context of TransH ("bern").

A more complicated version of TransR, called cluster-based TransR or *CTransR*, was also proposed by Lin et al. (2015), and was motivated by the fact that models like TransE, TransH, and the original TransR all learn a *unique* vector for each relation, which may be underrepresentative for fitting *all* entity pairs under this relation, given that relations are often quite diverse. To better model these relations, the authors of TransR incorporate the idea of piecewise linear regression to extend the original model. The core idea is first, to segment input instances into several groups. Formally, for a specific relation r, all entity pairs (h, t) in the training data are clustered into multiple groups, and entity pairs in each group are expected to exhibit similar r relation. All such entity pairs are represented with their vector offsets $(\vec{h} - \vec{t})$ for clustering, with $\vec{h}$ and $\vec{t}$ obtained using TransE. Afterward, a separate relation vector r_c (and similarly, matrix $\mathbb{M}_r$) is learned for each relation r and cluster c. Projected vectors of entities are defined as $h_{r,c} = h\mathbb{M}_r$ and $t_{r,c} = t\mathbb{M}_r$, and the score function is defined as

$$f_r(h, t) = \|\vec{h}_{r,c} + \vec{r}_c - \vec{t}_{r,c}\|_2^2 + \alpha\|\vec{r}_c - \vec{r}\|_2^2. \tag{10.17}$$

Here, $\|\vec{r}_c - \vec{r}\|_2^2$ aims to ensure a cluster-specific relation vector r_c not too far from the original relation vector r, and α controls the effect of this constraint. Similar to TransR, CTransR enforces constraints on embedding norms of h, r, and t and mapping matrices. The learning process of both TransR and CTransR are carried out using SGD. To avoid overfitting, Lin et al. (2015) initialize entity and relation embeddings with the results of TransE rather than as random vectors. Relation matrices are initialized as identity matrices.

All of these examples (TransE, TransH, and TransR) show that translation is a powerful idea in the KGE literature that has taken hold. Many other algorithms have been proposed along these lines that are beyond the scope of this chapter. For example, TransD simplifies TransR by further decomposing the projection matrix into a product of two vectors; specifically, by introducing additional mapping vectors $\vec{w_h}, \vec{w_t} \in \mathbb{R}^d$, and $\vec{w_r} \in \mathbb{R}^k$, along with the entity/relation representations $\vec{h}, \vec{t} \in \mathbb{R}^d$ and $\vec{r} \in \mathbb{R}^k$. It is likely that this trend will continue, and translation will continue to be a part of more powerful KGE algorithms that continue will be proposed each year in academic venues.

10.6 Extrafactual Contexts

Many, if not all, of the algorithms described earlier fundamentally relied on observed facts in the KG for optimization. However, as described earlier in this book, especially in chapter 2, KGs in the real world contain much more than facts. In this section, we briefly discuss KGE techniques that further incorporate additional information besides facts. For example, there is now a growing volume of research that embed KGs by using entity types, relation paths, textual descriptions, and logical rules, in addition to the observed facts.

10.6.1 Entity Types

The first kind of additional information that could be considered in a KGE is *entity types*, which are concepts or semantic categories to which entities belong. More broadly, in our framework, this would be akin to considering the ontology and KG in tandem. One easy way to realize this intuition is to supplement the KG with *entity-type triples* by interpreting *:is_a* as an ordinary relation and the corresponding triples as ordinary KG facts.

A more sophisticated approach, called *semantically smooth embedding (SSE)*, requires entities of the same type to stay close to each other in the embedding space (e.g., the movie *Psycho* should be closer in the KGE space to another movie, *Avatar*, than to a song like "We are the World." To accomplish this goal, SSE employs two manifold learning algorithms (Laplacian eigenmaps and locally linear embedding) to model this smoothness assumption. For example, Laplacian eigenmaps require an entity to lie close to every other entity of the same type, giving a smoothness measure given by

$$\mathcal{R}_1 = \frac{1}{2} \sum_i \sum_j \|\vec{e}_i - \vec{e}_j\|_2^2 w_{ij}^1. \qquad (10.18)$$

Here, w_{ij}^1 is an indicator variable that is 1 if the entities represented by vectors $\vec{e}_i$ and $\vec{e}_j$ have the same concept type (and 0 otherwise). Both summations occur over all entities in the data set, indexed by i and j. A similar smoothness measure (say, $\mathcal{R}_\in$) can be devised for locally linear embedding. Together, these two terms are incorporated as regularization terms by SSE to constrain the KGE. Empirically, while SSE was found to perform better than straightforward methods, a major limitation is that the concepts are assumed to lie in a non-hierarchical ontology (essentially, as a set of tags) and an entity cannot have more than one concept type. In most KGs, including the ones that we have seen so far, as well as the KG ecosystems that we will be covering in part V, this assumption does not hold.

Other sophisticated approaches that have been proposed since SSE include *type-embodied knowledge representation learning* (TKRL), which handles hierarchical entity categories and multiple concept labels, which is especially useful for ontologies common in the Semantic Web (SW) community (albeit less common in computer vision, or even NLP). TKRL is a translational distance model with type-specific entity projections. Given a fact (h, r, t), it first projects h and t with type-specific projection matrices, and then models r as a translation between the two projected entities. The intuition behind such translations was presented earlier in this chapter, in the context of translational embedding models. Further details can be found in Xie et al. (2016a), also cited in the "Bibliographic Notes" section.

Beyond incorporating type information in the embedding itself, the ontology can be used during prediction (i.e., entity types can also be used as *constraints* of head and tail positions for different relations). To look at one example, head entities of relation *:movie_director_of* should have concept type *Person*, and tail entities should have a concept type that is a subclass of *CreativeWork*. Some systems attempt to impose such constraints in the training process, particularly during the generation of negative training examples. Negative examples that violate entity-type constraints are excluded from training, or generated with substantially low probabilities. Similar such constraints were implemented, for example, in RESCAL, a tensor factorization model, whose key idea was to discard invalid facts (with wrong entity types) and factorize only a subtensor composed of the remaining facts. Finally, note that the sample of techniques that we have briefly described here on incorporating concepts into the KGE process is not necessarily composed of mutually exclusive algorithms. There is nothing preventing us from using the ontology before the embedding (for generating nontrivial training samples as described here), during the embedding, and after the embedding (during prediction).

10.6.2   Textual Data

Using textual descriptions to augment KGEs is intuitive because in most KGs, there are concise descriptions for entities that contain rich semantic information about them. For example, in the DBpedia KG, description-like properties for the entity "The Terminator" include not only *rdfs:comment* and *dbo:abstract* (*The Terminator is a 1984 American science fiction film written and directed by James Cameron, produced by...*), but also *dbp:quote* (*Casting Arnold Schwarzenegger as our Terminator, on the other hand, shouldn't have worked. The guy is supposed to be...*) and even phraselike properties like *dbp:footer* (*Arnold Schwarzenegger, Linda Hamilton, and Michael Biehn played the film's leads.*). In the opening sections of this chapter, we described how representation learning really took off in the modern era because of algorithms like word2vec and GloVe that have been applied, with excellent results on tasks like word analogy, over large quantities of text. Furthermore, for common entities like movies and singers, textual information from external text sources like news releases and Wikipedia articles could also be leveraged to learn better embeddings.

Given these intuitions, it is not surprising that embedding KGs with textual information dates back to at least the NTN model, where textual information is simply used to *initialize* entity representations. We noted this earlier in our description of NTN, where we saw that entity vectors were initialized by considering simple averaging of pretrained word vectors (with the words as the constitutive words in the entity). Furthermore, the word vectors were acquired from a text-embedding model pretrained over an external news corpus. We also briefly noted the limitations of this method, particularly for phrasal entities where word composition does not apply. A later, more robust method attempted to initialize entities as average word vectors of their *descriptions* rather than just their names. A key limitation, however, of all of these methods is that they model textual information independent of KG facts, and hence fail to leverage interactions between them.

A first joint model that made better use of textual information during KGE optimization tried to align the given KG with an auxiliary text corpus, and then simultaneously conducted KGE and word embedding. Entities, relations, and words are represented in the same vector space, and operations such as inner product (similarity) between them are well defined and meaningful. Consequently, this joint model had three components or models: *knowledge, text,* and *alignment*. The knowledge model embedded entities and relations in the KG and was a variant of TransE. The text model embedded words in the text corpus and was a variant of skip-gram that was described at the beginning of this chapter. Finally, the alignment model guaranteed that the embeddings of entities, relations, and words shared the same space, using a variety of techniques, including (but not limited to) Wikipedia anchors and entity descriptions.

How does the joint model incorporate all of these possibly conflicting information sets, because they all have separate loss functions? One approach is to try to minimize the sum of the loss functions (as a single global loss function) but other approaches, including weighted averages, are also theoretically possible. The main feature of the joint embedding models, however, is to ensure that information is utilized at the same time from both structured KGs and unstructured text. KGE and word embedding are thus enhanced and supported by each other, especially due to the forced joint optimization of their respective loss functions. Moreover, by aligning these two types of information, joint embedding enables the prediction of *out-of-KG* entities, (i.e., phrases appearing in web text but not included in the KG yet). Of course, this is predicated on the fact that the textual source itself is rich enough to encompass the out-of-KG entities and vocabulary. More recent representation learning methods have even gotten around this problem, especially if the out-of-vocabulary (OOV) issue is arising due to misspellings and morphological variations, among other issues.[9] Recent conceptual approaches that have been proposed for enabling these kinds of joint embeddings include the description-embodied knowledge representation learning (DKRL), as well as the text-enhanced KGE (TEKE). In the "Bibliographic Notes" section, we refer interested readers to papers on these approaches.

10.6.3 Beyond Text and Concepts: Other Information Sets

While entity types (ontological or concept information), as well as external or supporting text corpora, have received maximum attention in the research community as ways of supplementing or improving the different kinds of KGE models, there are several other classes of interesting information sets that have also been found to be useful. Work on much of these is still in its relative infancy, but experimental results are very promising.

---

[9] We detail some popular packages in the section entitled "Software and Resources," later in this chapter, which are particularly adept at dealing with the OOV problem.

By way of example, one such class of information is *temporal information*. Some authors have observed that KG facts are usually time-sensitive (e.g., it may be that A and B were married in 1980, but not 1985). In communities such as the Semantic Web, such higher-order facts are expressed using a general technique called *reification*. However, if the higher-order information is temporal, we can utilize a *time-aware embedding model* to further improve the original KGE. The main idea is to impose *temporal order constraints* on time-sensitive relation pairs, classic examples being *:born_in* and *:died_in* (in contrast, the similarly named relations *:born_at* and *:died_at* are not time-sensitive). Given such a relation pair (r_i, r_j), the *prior* relation should intuitively lie closer to the *subsequent* relation after a temporal transition (i.e., $\mathbb{M}\vec{r_i} \approx \vec{r_j}$ where $\mathbb{M}$ is a transition matrix capturing the temporal order information between relations). At a high level, imposing such temporal order constraints is not very different from the entity-type constraints that we explored earlier in the context of several algorithms. Some researchers have been able to use these constraints to learn temporally consistent relation embeddings. Similarly, other researchers have tried to model the temporal evolution of KGs, by actions such as modeling changes in a KG via labeled quadruples, such as that (h, r, t, s) is *True* or (h, r, t, s) is *False*, with s being a time signature or stamp. These quadruples indicate that (h, r, t) appears or vanishes at time s, respectively. Such models perform especially well in dynamic domains, (e.g., KG representations of medical and sensor data). More details on this KG evolution model can be looked up in Esteban et al. (2016). Research in this area continues to flourish.

Besides temporal information, other information sets that are rapidly becoming popular for supplementing KGs and improving KGEs include relation paths (multihop, rather than single-hop, relationships between entities as a way of incorporating richer context), entity attributes, graph structural information, and even logical rules. The last is particularly exciting because it may represent a reconciliation between two paradigms (statistical versus symbolic) that had been considered incompatible (at least in practice) by many for a long time. Logical rules, which were once the staple of expert systems, and are still important in the design of precise ontologies in the Semantic Web, contain rich background information. As we saw in chapter 9, on statistical relational learning (SRL), they can also be used in probabilistic frameworks and generally yield more interpretable results than pure neural networks. There are a wide range of systems (e.g., WARMR and AMIE), furthermore, that can semiautomatically extract such rules from KGs. A central question that arises, however, is: can such rules be utilized to refine the embedding itself? A number of approaches have tried to affirm this utility. For example, in one work (called KALE), a joint model was proposed that embeds KG facts and logical rules simultaneously, not unlike the textual joint models seen earlier. There are some unique challenges that arise, unfortunately, when using logical rules, and research continues on addressing the issues. One particular problem that is common to many of the methods is that they have to instantiate universally quantified rules into ground rules before learning their models. The grounding is expensive, both in terms of time and space, especially with a large number of entities in the KG and a complex set of rules. Recent research has attempted to deal with this complexity issue, but the book on the subject is far from closed.

10.7   Applications

KGEs can benefit a range of downstream tasks such as KG completion, relation extraction (RE), and question answering. We describe these applications in this section (with the exception of question answering, to which an entire chapter is dedicated in part IV of this book). We also note that the evaluation of a particular KGE algorithm is intimately connected with the application that the KGE algorithm will be used for. In other words, embeddings do not necessarily have any intrinsic value, and it is far from clear that one embedding is universally superior to another; in theory, it is possible for an algorithm to yield embeddings that work well for one application (compared to another algorithm), but that do not work as well for a different task. Given that, we argue that one must always keep both the application and the data set (and its incumbent assumptions) in the forefront when making claims about one KGE algorithm outperforming another.

10.7.1   Link Prediction

Link prediction is typically referred to as the task of predicting an entity that has a specific relation with another given entity [i.e., predicting h given (r, t) or t given (h, r), with the former notationally denoted as $(?, r, t)$ and the latter as $(h, r, ?)$]. For example, a link prediction query $(?, DirectorOf, Basic\_Instinct)$ aims to predict the director of the film Basic Instinct, under the assumption that this triple is not explicitly declared in the original (training) KG, while $(Paul\_Verhoeven, DirectorOf, ?)$ tries to predict films directed by the specific person in the head entity position. For obvious reasons, this task is also sometimes called *entity prediction* or (less commonly) *entity ranking*. A similar idea can also be used to predict relations between two given entities, such as $(h, ?, t)$, a task referred to as *relation prediction*.

   With entity and relation embeddings learned beforehand, link prediction can be carried out using a ranking procedure. To predict the head entity in a query triple $(?, r, t)$, for example, we can take every entity h' in the KG as a candidate answer and calculate a score $f_r(h', t)$ for each (h', r, t). The structured embeddings method that preceded many of the Trans* algorithms provided a kernel density function for evaluating such function. However, if TransE is used, we can evaluate the function $f_r(h', t) = -\|\vec{h'} + \vec{r} - \vec{t}\|_{1/2}$ and rank the candidate head entities in descending order. Tail entity and relation prediction would work in the same way.

   How do we measure which algorithm is better? Because the problem has been framed as one of ranking, several evaluation metrics (mostly developed in the information retrieval community) are applicable, including *mean rank* (the average of predicted ranks), *mean reciprocal rank* (the average of reciprocal ranks), *Hits@n* (the proportion of ranks no larger than n; $n = 1, 5, 10$ are all common choices), and AUC-PR or the area under the precision-recall curve. We detail information retrieval metrics subsequently in a chapter dedicated to reasoning and retrieval.

10.7.2 Triple Classification

Triple classification is the task of determining whether an unseen (in the original KG) triple fact (h, r, t) is true or not [e.g., a good triple classification method would score the triple *(George_Lucas, DirectorOf, Star_Wars)* as *True* highly, while a triple like *(James_Cameron, ProducerOf, Star_Wars)* would get a low score.] Similar to link prediction, we can view this task as one of KG completion.

Once again, we can use either the kernel density function or a translational function (e.g., $-\|\vec{h} + \vec{r} - \vec{t}\|_{1/2}$ if using TransE) to score a triple (h, r, t), under the assumption that h, t, and r have all been observed in the training data set that was used to derive the KGEs, even though it is not necessary for them to have cooccurred in any triple in the training set. This is an important assumption, because in the general case, we cannot make claims about entities or relations that we have not seen at all in the training KG (in the context of other triples). Note, however, that some of the methods that used extrafactual contexts (e.g., joint embeddings that used both text corpora and KG), as well as straightforward extensions of the NTN algorithm (which used pretrained word embeddings for embedding initialization), may even be able to handle this eventuality. With these caveats in place, triple classification can be framed as binary classification by determining thresholding scores and predicting those triples to be true that have a score above the threshold. A slight modification of thresholding that works well in practice is to not have one threshold, but to introduce a threshold t_r for every relation r. The thresholds can be determined using a variety of well-established statistical methods. In the machine learning world, using a held-out validation set is a common mechanism.

To summarize, using relation thresholds, any unseen fact (h, r, t) containing relation r will be predicted as true if its score $f_r(h, t)$ is higher than t_r, and false otherwise. In this way, relation-specific triple classifiers are obtained. Such classifiers are amenable to metrics such as micro- and macro-averaged accuracy from the machine learning and NLP communities, which can be calculated and used to evaluate this application. Ranking metrics such as mean average precision can also be used.

10.7.3 Entity Classification

Entity classification, which is a specific instance of the more general "node classification" problem that shows up in graphs and networks, is defined as the problem of classifying entities into semantic categories (e.g., *Paul_Verhoeven* is a Person, and *Basic_Instinct* a CreativeWork. While it is not strictly necessary, entity classification is usually taken to mean (as the two previous examples show) the link prediction task $(h, IsA, ?)$ for an entity

x. Hence, similar prediction and evaluation procedures can be applied as for link prediction.

More complex versions of entity classification in the KG context have not been as well explored as node classification in the graph community. Considering the example given here, is it more appropriate to classify *Paul_Verhoeven* as a Person, Director, or Artist? In the general case, we want to try and predict the (possibly more than one) finest-grained semantic categories since the other categories can be inferred from those (i.e., Person can be predicted, given a reasonable ontology, from either Artist or Director). There are not a lot of methods that have aimed to solve multiclass entity classification, or to separately evaluate long- and short-tailed semantic categories. There is still much research to be done in this space.

10.7.4 Revisiting Instance Matching

As noted earlier in this book, instance matching (IM) is a complex problem, with over 50 years of research behind it. KGEs present yet another opportunity to improve performance on IM. Once again, just like entity classification, we can frame the problem as similar to those we have seen before. The ontology already contains a relation stating whether two entities are equivalent (denoted as sameAs), and an embedding has been learned for that relation. In this case, IM degenerates to a triple classification problem [i.e., the problem now is to judge whether the triple $(x, sameAs, y)$ holds (or how likely it is to hold)]. Triple scores output by an embedding model can be directly used for such prediction (see the "Triple Classification" section for details). This intuitive strategy, however, does not always work because not all KGs encode the sameAs relation. For this reason, some authors have proposed to perform IM solely on the basis of learned entity embeddings. For example, in Nickel et al. (2011), given two entities h_1 and h_2, and their vector representations $\vec{h_1}$ and $\vec{h_2}$, the similarity between h_1 and h_2 is computed as $k(h_1, h_2) = e^{-\|\vec{h_1} - \vec{h_2}\|_2^2 / \sigma}$, with the score used as the likelihood that h_1 and h_2 refer to the same entity. An advantage of strategies such as these is that they work even if the *sameAs* relation is not present in the input KG (this is exactly the unsupervised version of the IM problem). However, it is also important to remember that the utility of such methods is predicated on their modeling of the problem being correct. There is no evidence that the similarity function here, for example, would extend to arbitrary domains. In some domains, the function may not be the best guide to determining whether the argument entities match. Thus, it must be used with caution, and with a validation procedure in place, just like other unsupervised (e.g., clustering-based) algorithms.

Concerning evaluation, AUC-PR is the most widely adopted evaluation metric for this task, but standard precision, recall, and F-measure may also be used. The KGE community has not taken a close look at how to combine blocking-based methods with such embedding methods. Hence, several open research questions remain, and more developments in this area are likely forthcoming.

10.7.5 Other Applications

We have noted a subset of important applications in the previous sections of this chapter, but there are several more that we did not mention. For example, one exciting application is RE, detailed in chapter 6. As we argued there, RE is an important problem in NLP and KG construction (KGC). However, an alternative view is to see RE not as a means for KGC but as an application of KGs. For example, we could use preexisting KGs in a distant supervision framework to automatically generate labeled data and help improve an RE process. But such approaches are still text-based extractors, ignoring the capability of a KG to infer new facts by itself. Weston et al. (2013), for example, proposed to combine TransE with a text-based extractor to enhance RE performance. Yet other systems have drawn inspiration from recommender systems (which have themselves leveraged KGs to improve recommender performance) in using collaborative filtering techniques to improve performance on RE. These techniques factorize an input matrix to learn vector embeddings for entity pairs, textual mentions, and KG relations. The framework has been shown to be an improvement over traditional text-based extractors. Yet other authors have used matrix completion techniques instead of matrix factorization. In recent work, tensor-based variants have also been used. Suffice to say, there is still a lot of active research happening in this area, though advanced systems already exist.

One important point to note in the context of RE is that, as a KG application, it is different from the applications we considered previously in being out-of-KG. Out-of-KG applications are those that break through the boundary of the input KG and scale to broader domains. Many of the other applications we looked at, such as link prediction and entity resolution, are trying to improve the KG itself rather than scale to a broader domain. Another example of an out-of-KG application that was briefly mentioned earlier is a recommender system. Because these are out-of-KG applications, they rely on a number of areas in machine learning and NLP, and they are not exclusively married to KG technology or improvements.

10.8 Concluding Notes

As a research area, representation learning has come a long way, propelled by recent successes with neural networks. While word embeddings have been especially influenced by the advent of models like skip-gram and CBOW, a similar philosophy (Firth's axiom) has led to improved representation learning for other data units such as documents and (nodes and edges in) KGs. This chapter mainly concerned KGEs, for which many representation learning algorithms have been developed over the last decade. Among these algorithms, the translational algorithms have become especially popular, with numerous variants and extensions proposed in the research community following the initial success of TransE. KGEs have numerous applications, including link prediction, entity classification, relation prediction, and triple classification. More recently, KGEs have also been applied to out-of-KG applications such as recommender systems and RE.

While KGEs are continuing to proliferate into the mainstream research community, questions still remain on their effectiveness on graphs that exhibit both noise and sparsity. Recent work, for example, has shown that on real-world graphs, algorithms from the Trans* family may be significantly outperformed by SRL techniques like Probabilistic Soft Logic (PSL), described in chapter 9. That being said, these embeddings are continuing to get better each year in terms of significant performance improvements in standard KG application areas such as link prediction and triple classification. Because of their high utility, they have become a standard resource when addressing the basic issue of incomplete or noisy KGs.

10.9 Software and Resources

KGEs are a relatively novel and rapidly evolving area of research, and open-source software development has been scattered, sometimes provided only for the purposes of replicating experiments in support of a paper. Nevertheless, some valuable tools have emerged, especially in the last three or four years.

The OpenKE package includes some classic and effective models to support KGEs, including Trans{E,H,R,D}, RESCAL, DistMult, HolE, and ComplEx. They also provide other resources, such as pretrained embeddings on the website. The project page is accessible at http://139.129.163.161//index/toolkits#toolkits. A lesser-known project is https://github.com/BookmanHan/Embedding, which supports models such as TransA, TransG, and Semantic Space Projection (SSP).

Another excellent and widely used resource, released by Facebook Research, is StarSpace (https://github.com/facebookresearch/StarSpace). StarSpace is described as a "general-purpose neural model for efficient learning of entity embeddings for solving a wide variety of problems." These problems include KGEs, though the package can also be used for text classification, word embeddings, and information retrieval.

Recently, PyTorch-BigGraph (https://github.com/facebookresearch/PyTorch-BigGraph) was released to provide support for embedding larger-scale, graph-structured data. It also allows training of a number of models from the KGE literature, including TransE, RESCAL, DistMult, and ComplEx. Scalability is a key feature, which has been one of the concerns with OpenKE.

In earlier chapters, we provided resources on word embeddings. Resources for more advanced models such as BERT and RoBERTa will be provided in chapter 13, on question answering. An excellent general word-embedding package (but not the only one, by any means) that is robust to misspellings is fastText (https://github.com/facebookresearch/fastText), also released by Facebook Research. Finally, we mentioned network embeddings as an interesting line of related research that has a conceptual (if not algorithmic) connection to KGEs. Several good packages exist; for instance, we are mentioning DeepWalk (https://github.com/phanein/deepwalk), LINE (https://github.com/tangjianpku/LINE), and node2vec (github.com/aditya-grover/node2vec) as three of the most widely used ones.

10.10 Bibliographic Notes

KGEs are a very recent phenomenon, with the earliest study on the class of techniques covered in this chapter not appearing before the early 2010s, unlike many of the other areas we have covered thus far in this book, which have decades (and, in the case of entity resolution, more than a half-century) of research behind them, albeit not specifically attuned to KGs and their use-cases. As such, much of the material synthesized in this chapter was presented in their original form relatively recently, but in the last few years, some surveys and comprehensive overviews have also appeared. We highlight Wang et al. (2017) and Nguyen (2017) as influential in helping us organize the material in this chapter, as well as discussing the various KGEs using more uniform terminology and notation. Beyond KGEs specifically, a general survey on graph embeddings by Goyal and Ferrara (2018), as well as on KG refinement by Paulheim (2017), are also instructive, with the latter having more of an SW focus.

We mentioned both word and network embeddings as precursors to KGEs, in that they employ relatively similar techniques (a context-defining, objective function–based neural model). Among many others, good sources for the former include Mikolov et al. (2013), because it provides an early coverage of the skip-gram and CBOW models described in the earlier part of the chapter; and for the latter include Grover and Leskovec (2016), Perozzi et al. (2014), and Tang, Qu, et al. (2015). New representation learning algorithms are being proposed in these fields with great frequency, and we cite these earlier works as good avenues for researchers in these areas to begin exploring, as well as to acquire deeper context for the material in this chapter.

It is worthwhile for interested readers to study the original papers proposing many of the KGE techniques that we succinctly described in this chapter. The structured embeddings approach was first presented by Bordes et al. (2011). Many translational models have appeared over the years, with TransE and TransH remaining some of the more popularly used (perhaps owing to their available open-source availability, robustness, and ease and speed of use), and it is not possible to provide comprehensive references; good sources for TransE, TransH, TransR, TransD, TransSparse, TransM, TransF, TransA, and TransG are Bordes et al. (2013), Wang, Zhang, et al. (2014a), Lin et al. (2015), Ji et al. (2015, 2016), Fan et al. (2014), Feng et al. (2016), Xiao et al. (2015), and Xiao et al. (2016), respectively.

Beyond translational models, the NTN by Socher et al. (2013), the holographic embedding approach by Nickel et al. (2016), and the compositional vector space model by Neelakantan et al. (2015) are important and influential, and they have spawned variants with similar philosophies. Nontranslational models continue to be proposed, and many new models (as we discuss toward the later sections of the chapter) have tried to embed KGs while using additional information sets or context, including externally available text corpus or pretrained word embeddings, logic, temporal features, and other exotic artifacts that could potentially lead to better embeddings. While many good references have been cited in surveys, such as Wang et al. (2017), papers that we specially cite here include Zhong et al. (2015), Wang et al. (2014b, 2016), Xie, Liu, Jia, et al. (2016), Xie, Liu, and Sun (2016), Guo et al. (2015, 2016), Wei et al. (2015), and Trivedi et al. (2017).

10.11 Exercises

1. You have an ontology with 1,000 concepts and 2,000 relationships. You are trying to embed a KG (modeled on your ontology) with 100,000 unique instances. You may assume that an instance occurs both as a head and a tail entity (in separate triples). How many parameters must TransE infer? *Hint: Use table 10.1 for reference.*

2. For this question, we will consider the data in the table on the following page, which comprises 2D embeddings of entities. As a first step, plot this data on a graph. Do you see two obvious clusters? What does each cluster represent?

Bill Gates	$[0.1, 0.3]$
Sergei Brin	$[-0.5, 0.25]$
Larry Page	$[0.0, 0.0]$
Mark Zuckerberg	$[-0.25, 0.125]$
Jack Ma	$[0.0, 0.5]$
Facebook	$[1.5, 2.5]$
Google	$[1.5, 1.75]$
Microsoft	$[1.25, 1.25]$
Alibaba	$[0.0, 0.5]$

3. Recall the TransE objective (minimizing $\|\vec{h} + \vec{r} - \vec{t}\|_2$), and assume that the vectors in the table are fixed. Given that Gates, Zuckerberg, and Ma founded Microsoft, Facebook, and Alibaba, respectively, and that Brin and Page founded Google, what would be the optimal embedding for a founder relation (i.e., given training triples such as (*Google, founder, LarryPage*))?

4. Given the founder relation embedding in exercise 3, what would be the TransE loss (taken to be the sum of the expression given there, as applied to each triple in the KG.

5. Considering that there is only one pair of "cofounders" in this data set (Page and Brin), suppose you were asked to model a "cofounder" relationship based on this minimal amount of training data. Per the TransE objective, what would be the optimal value for this relation, assuming all other vectors in the table have to stay fixed? (Hint: *cofounder* is a symmetric relation.)

6. Suppose that we decided not to model cofounders separately, but to instead derive whether A and B are cofounders in the following way. Given that A founded a company X (but *without* the knowledge that B founded X), we determine a ranked list of A's possible cofounders by framing it as a tail-entity prediction problem [i.e., (X, *founder*, ?), with ? constrained via an ontology to only return *Person*-type instances]. We use translation to determine the scores of all entities (because we know that A is already founder X, we do not compute the score for A); namely, we compute the cosine similarity[10] between each Person-type instance vector and $\vec{X} + \vec{founder}$, and rank the instances in descending order of scores. What would the ranked list be if X is Google and A is Sergei Brin? What if A is Larry Page? In either case, do you get the true corresponding cofounder in the top one?

7. List one limitation of the TransE method compared to TransH and TransR. Give one example to demonstrate your point.

8. Considering the previous exercise, what would be one good reason to still use TransE? Could you think of KGs or use-cases where sticking with TransE, rather than advanced versions like TransH or TransR, might prove to be prudent?

9. This, as well as the next exercise, are both based on running an implementation of TransE. There are several such implementations available, as we highlight in the "Software and Resources" section. They usually come packaged with the Freebase and WordNet data sets (including train/test splits) that are often used as benchmarks in this space. We will only consider WordNet for these exercises.

   First, run a standard implementation of TransE on WordNet and compare some of the metrics to those reported by Bordes et al. (2013). Are there any differences that look significant? What might explain them?

10. Now, we will introduce noise and sparsity into the training set by randomly picking two triples and exchanging their relations. Given N-triples in the WordNet training data set, we consider the following two experiments:

    (a) **Noise injection:** For each triple t, we sample a constant number of p triples from the remainder set, where that set is the subset of the $N - 1$ triples that do not have the same head and tail entities as t. For each of the p triples, we create two new (noisy) triples by exchanging the relations between t and that triple, and then inject the two noisy triples into the training set. Note that the new training set thus created is a superset of the original training set, as we are not removing any of the original triples.

---

[10] This is not the only way to compute similarity scores for the purposes of ranking or prediction, but in this exercise, we assume that it suffices.

(b) **Deletion:** Randomly delete a fraction q of triples from the training set. If the deletion results in the complete elimination of a head/tail entity or relation from the training set, add one triple back to the training set (from the discarded set), such that every entity and relation in the test set is represented at least once in the training set.[11]

For different values of $p = \{1, 10, 50, 100\}$ and $q = \{0.01, 0.1, 0.4\}$ how does the performance of the algorithm on the test set change?[12] What general statements can you make about the robustness of TransE? What happens if we consider the most extreme change, where we first perform deletion with $q = 0.4$, and (on the remaining training set) noise injection with $p = 100$. Are the results even better than random?

11. If you used TransH rather than TransE, would your conclusions change? Is TransH necessarily better than TransE in dealing with noise?

---

[11] This is an important step, since otherwise, we will end up with entities and/or relations in the test set that we have never observed in the test set. In many implementations, this throws an error during test time.

[12] This would require a total of seven experiments, because you will be introducing only one change in each experiment compared to the original training set.

IV ACCESSING KNOWLEDGE GRAPHS

11 Reasoning and Retrieval

Overview. Thus far, the focus has been on the acquisition of data (domain discovery) to construct a knowledge graph (KG), and on KG construction (KGC) and KG completion. What happens once a KG is in place? At the bare minimum, such a KG needs to allow some set of users to "access" it. The notion of accessing a KG is complex because it potentially spans a broad continuum of possibilities, from simple keyword-based information retrieval (IR) to more complex reasoning tasks. Understanding the spectrum of possibilities is important because it influences the infrastructure required for supporting KG indexing and access. For example, reasoning is computationally demanding, but it can yield more insights and provide more guarantees than simple IR. Even without reasoning, querying a KG involves a diverse set of possibilities, from structured querying (not unlike SQL queries posed on relational databases) to answering questions posed in natural language. In this chapter, we cover reasoning and retrieval in some detail, especially in the context of constructed KGs. Although both of these areas are vast, and entire fields of research in their own right, we focus on the fundamentals in this chapter. In the next two chapters, we will specifically focus on querying and question answering.

11.1 Introduction

In the last few parts of this book, we have described how to construct and improve (complete) a KG. But once we have our KG, what should we do with it? How do we store and access it? These are issues that any real-world application has to deal with, and in many cases, it can make the difference between whether KGs are considered for that application or stakeholder to begin with. For example, if the schema of the data set is well defined and populated, and low latency on queries posed to the system is of utmost importance, it may make more sense to opt for a traditional Relational Database Management System (RDBMS) than a KG that, even today, can be slower than normal databases due to the inherently semistructured nature of the data. In contrast, if the goal is to do machine learning, analytics, or both in the absence of rigid structure or very high quality, using a KG obviously makes more sense but still involves important design decisions in the choice of infrastructure, especially for accessing the KG.

There are several criteria that can, and should, be taken into account when making these decisions, but one of the most important criteria involves the user who will be consuming the KG outputs. Will the user be doing a search on the KG in the same way as they query using Google? Do they expect a ranked list of outputs, some of which may not even contain the exact words they searched for, but are still semantically relevant (e.g., using Google, a user would not necessarily be upset, if upon searching for "top places to visit in Los Angeles," they would be shown a website somewhere at the top of the ranked list that lists "popular tourist attractions in LA" but does not otherwise contain phrases like "top places to visit"). The important thing to remember about such IR systems, including search engines such as on Google or Bing but also domain-specific or genre-specific portals like YouTube and Yelp, is that their primary goal is to satisfy user intent. Furthermore, although web search engines were initially designed for documents, like web HTML pages and text, the general definition of satisfying user intent (usually, but not always, expressed through keyword queries like the one described previously) can apply to any corpus, including video, social media, biological data, and semistructured KGs. The Google Knowledge Graph, which has been largely responsible for the recent popularity of this field, especially in industry, is the best example of a proprietary KG that expects to be accessed using this paradigm. When entities, or ranked lists of pages describing entities, are displayed to users in the Google search engine in response to a search, the goal is to satisfy user intent rather than look for strict or exact matches to the user's query.

However, we can imagine many use-cases where not only must the query be more sophisticated than a keyword query, but the user must require that the responses to the query (if more than one) to strictly meet the conditions specified in the query. This kind of scenario occurs most often in the context of ordinary databases and, with industrial behemoths like Walmart, data warehouses. For example, if a business analyst at Walmart wants to know the total revenue of all Walmart stores in California, they would not be pleased if the system displayed total net income, or included Arizona with California when making the calculations. In fact, it is perfectly reasonable (and desired) for the system to return no results at all if none of the conditions in the query are satisfied (e.g., maybe the system does not have data for California within a date range specified in the query), rather than return approximate results that are "close" to the final answer. In short, users desire accuracy when they pose such queries. Generally, though not always, such queries make sense when the data is of sufficient quality and when there is adequate structure in the data.

Although we have presented many flexible ways of constructing, completing, and even modeling KGs (chapter 2), the fact remains that a KG is a graph to begin with. Graphs have nodes and edges and are structural by definition. Most KGs are even more structured, because there is usually an underlying ontology in terms of which the KG was constructed to begin with. It is not infeasible to imagine that domain-specific, structural query languages such as those found in the database world (the primary example being SQL) could be devised to query graphs instead of relational tables.

Continuing with the notion of structure, we note that ontologies are actually far more than schemas because they tend to also be enriched with axioms and constraints. We saw this firsthand in chapter 2, when we discussed how RDFS extends the basic Resource Description Framework (RDF) model with additional well-defined (in other words, constrained) terms. We have also seen special properties like *owl:sameAs*, which are used to represent the result when two instances refer to the same underlying instance. Even in this simple example, wouldn't it be desirable (for some applications) to have a framework where, if the result of a query is node A and we know from the KG that node A and node B are matching instances via *owl:sameAs*, then node B should also be included in the answer set as a course of *reasoning*?

In the next few sections, we expand upon these intuitions of reasoning and retrieval. Although they seem very different at first sight and were researched and refined by completely disjoint research communities in the pre-KG era, they have always had similar practical underpinnings—namely, the need to access data and present them to users in response to some kind of query. In the KG era, these access modes have coincided because retrieval and reasoning both apply to KGs, in contrast to documents (where reasoning of the structured kind we have described here is hard to do), or to tables (where document-style IR can be less well defined or relevant). Which mode of access is more appropriate depends on the application and user, as well as on the quality of the KG itself. The choice can be important because it influences infrastructure, storage, and other practical and engineering requirements like latency. In the next chapter, we cover querying infrastructure in more detail; in this chapter, we provide background on both reasoning and retrieval and how they apply to ordinary KGs.

11.2   Reasoning

As the name suggests, a *reasoner* is a piece of software that can infer logical consequences from a set of asserted facts or axioms. The notion of a semantic reasoner generalizes that of an inference engine, by providing a richer set of mechanisms to work with. The inference rules are commonly specified by means of an ontology language, and often a *description logic* language. Many reasoners, in fact, use *first-order predicate logic* to perform reasoning; inference commonly proceeds by forward and backward chaining. Forward chaining is described logically as repeated application of modus ponens[1] and is a popular infer-

---

[1] We do not provide a formal description of modus ponens herein. Stated in plain English, it is a rule in logic where the hypothesis is a premise P, the statement $P \rightarrow Q$, and the conclusion is Q. For example, given the premise that today is Monday (P), and the truth of the statement "If today is Monday, then today is the first day of the week," modus ponens allows us to deduce that today is the first day of the week.

ence strategy for expert systems and production rule systems. Intuitively, forward chaining starts with the available data and uses rules to extract more data until a goal or conclusion is reached. In contrast, backward chaining, as the name suggests, works backward from the goal and is typically used in automated theorem provers and inference engines. Backward chaining tends to be more popular in artificial intelligence (AI) applications as well. Finally, while there are also examples of probabilistic reasoners, we do not cover them in this chapter (we point interested readers to relevant references in the section entitled "Bibliographic Notes," at the end of this chapter).

In the context of KGs, reasoning can be said to be the problem of *deriving facts that are not expressed in either the ontology or the KG explicitly*. Reasoning has been considered central to AI problems historically because it seems to come naturally to most human beings, including notions of implication, symmetry, transitivity, and equivalence (e.g., we are able to understand that the fact that a dog is an animal, and that Fido is a dog, together *imply* that Fido is an animal; also, we are able to understand that this is an *asymmetric* conclusion—that is, not every animal is Fido). However, machines do not have such capabilities built in a priori, which makes it necessary to formally specify axioms and constructs, as well as to design and construct an engine to process these axioms when given a KG. The output of reasoning, as the definition makes clear, is a set of new facts and conclusions. There are several practical reasons why such reasoning services are important when modeling and building KGs. In the design phase of an ontology, for example, we may want to do the following:

1. Receive warnings when making meaningless statements, such as testing satisfiability of defined concepts, because unsatisfiable, defined concepts are signs of faulty modeling.

2. See firsthand the consequences of statements made, such as testing defined concepts for subsumption, because unwanted, missing, or nonintuitive subsumptions may also be signs of imprecise or faulty modeling.

3. See redundancies, such as testing defined concepts for equivalence, because knowing about redundant classes helps avoid misconceptions.

Similarly, when modifying existing ontologies, we may want to avail ourselves of the services described here, in addition to automatically generating concept definitions from examples of instances or automatically generating concept definitions for too many siblings than we can possibly generate manually.

Although reasoning is a vast area of research, we focus on the Web Ontology Language (OWL) as a particular modeling language in the next section. However, before delving into OWL, it is useful to understand the basic primitives in a semantic reasoning engine. To begin with, a good modeling language allows a modeler to construct some fairly complex, but useful relationships among classes, which form the core elements of any ontology. Several such common building blocks are noted in table 11.1.

Table 11.1: Relationships between classes supported by most reasoners, especially based on languages like OWL.

Relationship	Informal Description	Example
intersectionOf	Every instance of the first class is also an instance of all classes in the specified list.	*:Brother :intersectionOf (:Man, :Sibling)*
unionOf	Every instance of the first class is an instance of at least one of the classes in the specified list.	*:Sibling :unionOf (:Brother, :Sister)*
complementOf	The first class is equivalent to everything *not* in the second class.	*:Sibling :complementOf :OnlyChild*
equivalentClass	The first class and the second class contain exactly the same instances.	*:Brother :equivalentClass :MaleSibling*
differentFrom	The first resource (usually meant to indicate an "instance" in the context of KGs) and the second resource do not refer to the same thing.	*:BobMarley :differentFrom :AlbertEinstein*
sameAs	The first resource and the second resource refer to the same thing.	*:Germany :sameAs :Deutschland*
disjointWith	The first class and second class have no instances in common.	*:Brother :disjointWith :Sister*

11.2.1 Description Logics: A Brief Primer

Description logics (DLs) are logics designed primarily to serve formal descriptions of concepts and roles (i.e., relations). These logics were created from previous attempts to formalize semantic networks and frame-based systems. Semantically, they are inspired by predicate logic, but their language is usually designed for more practical modeling purposes, and with the goal of providing good computational guarantees such as decidability. Research in DLs can be applied (e.g., how do the various DL constructs apply to real-world applications?), or theoretical and comparative (e.g., what is the impact or complexity of two DLs when evaluated against various reasoning frameworks?).

The knowledge representation system based on DLs consists of two components: the TBox and the ABox. We have already encountered them before, although we did not refer to them as such. The TBox describes *terminology* [i.e., the ontology in the form of concepts (or "classes") and roles (equivalently called relations, properties, and predicates in the KG context)], while the ABox contains assertions about individuals ("instances") using the terms from the ontology. Concepts describe sets of individuals, while roles describe relations between individuals.

KG and ontology descriptions using DLs employ constructs with semantics given by predicate logic. However, due to historical reasons, predicate logic and DL notations are different, because DL notation is closer to semantic networks and frame-based systems.

We do not cover these notations and formalism in this chapter, but only illustrate a very basic description logic (called *attribute language*, or AL) using a simple example.

Let us assume two concepts, *Human* and *Male*, generally referred to as *atomic* concepts. We can use the two concepts to refer to human men via the expression *Human ⊓ Male*; similarly, *Human ⊓ ¬Male* refers to humans who are "not male." Another twist on this expression is *¬Human ⊓ Male*, referring to males that are not humans (e.g., male lions).

A more complex example, using qualifiers like ∀ ("for all") and ∃ ("exists"), is an expression like *Human ⊓ ∃hasChild.⊤*, which describes all humans who have at least one child. The symbol ⊓ refers to an intersection or conjunction of concepts, while the expression *∃hasChild.⊤* says that all *successors* of the role *hasChild* are in ⊤ (i.e., in the set of everything). This is just a shorthand way of saying that there are no constraints on the successor so long as one exists. In the same vein, *Human ⊓ ∀hasChild.Male* describes all humans who only have male children. In this case, we have imposed a constraint on the successors of the *hasChild* role because the successors must be instances of the concept *Male*. Note the subtlety here between how machines and humans might interpret a formal statement like the last expression. If there is no restriction stating that humans can *only* have children that are *also* human, it is technically allowable for the KG to make assertions where a human has a child that is a male lion; such a human would still be described by this expression. Even in this simple example, one can see why reasoning, axiomatization, and conceptual modeling all require sophisticated thinking, making them double-edged swords. In prior decades, so-called expert systems had to contain many rules to avoid absurd conclusions like the one noted here, but this made them less robust to irregular occurrences. The problem has not been fully solved; most in-use reasoners can still be brittle. Probabilistic reasoning has helped, but the extent to which they have helped (or can help) is hotly debated.

11.2.2   Web Ontology Language

The W3C OWL is a Semantic Web (SW) language designed to represent rich and complex knowledge about things, groups of things, and relations between things. OWL is a computational logic–based language such that knowledge expressed in OWL can be exploited by computer programs (e.g., to verify the consistency of that knowledge or to make implicit knowledge explicit).

Why should we care about OWL as a modeling language compared to others? There are several advantages in using reasoners based on OWL:

1. OWL is *expressive*, making it particularly amenable to KGs. While legacy languages such as XML Schema Definition (XSD), Unified Modeling Language (UML) and SQL are adequate for listing a number of classes and properties and building up some simple hierarchical relationships (e.g., SQL allows us to build a new table for each class, a new column for each property, and so on), they have some severe limitations. SQL

does not allow easy representation of subclass relationships, while more expressive languages like UML can express static subclasses (e.g., *horse* is a subclass of *animal*) that are unchanging over time but cannot feasibly express dynamic relationships (e.g., all profits below $10,000 are tax-exempt in Country X). A distinguishing feature of OWL is that it can be used to express complicated and subtle ideas about data, which can be especially critical in domains like finance and medicine.

2. OWL is *flexible*, a valuable feature that is illustrated using the following example (inspired by relational databases). Suppose that we want to change a property in a database (in KGs, this would be the equivalent of modifying a property in the ontology). Perhaps it was because we had previously (erroneously) assumed that the property was single-valued, but real data shows that it is actually multivalued. For almost all modern relational databases, this change would require first deleting the entire column for that property and then creating an entirely new table that holds all of those property values (as well as a foreign key reference). The problem here, not taking into account the amount of work that would be required on the part of those maintaining the database, is that the change would induce *second-order effects* (e.g., it may end up invalidating any indices that deal with the original table, as well as related queries that users might have written). This is one reason (but not the only one) that legacy data models have rarely changed since being instituted, sometimes decades ago (usually, a new model is simply created if the change is unavoidable), due to the troublesome nature of such incremental modifications. In contrast, data-modeling statements in OWL are RDF triples and, by nature, incremental. Enhancing or modifying a data model after the fact can be easily accomplished by modifying the relevant triple. Most OWL-based tools take advantage of OWL's flexibility by supporting straightforward and incremental changes. Incremental changes are also important when dealing with KGs constructed over web or *streaming* data, especially over a period of time, because new requirements and unforeseen challenges tend to emerge in an organic fashion.

3. Last but not least, OWL is also fairly *efficient* compared to rival tools and languages in the KG/ontology reasoning space. OWL allows data models to support many kinds of reasoning tasks; in fact, various flavors of OWL have been proposed based on the expressive reasoning capabilities required by the application. More important, several software packages are now available for creating ontologies and performing reasoning with OWL. We cover some of these tools in the section entitled "Software and Resources," at the end of this chapter, the main one of which is the Protégé tool. Subsequently, we turn our attention to the various flavors of OWL.

11.2.2.1 Why Not Just RDFS? Recall that in chapter 2, we introduced the RDFS language for defining ontologies. While RDFS bears some similarities to OWL (in the SW stack OWL is built on top of RDFS, meaning that it has all the capabilities of RDFS plus some others), a principal difference is in vocabulary expressiveness. OWL includes

Table 11.2: A list of OWL class constructors, with corresponding DL syntax.

Class Constructor	DL Syntax
intersectionOf	$C_1 \sqcap \ldots \sqcap C_n$
unionOf	$C_1 \sqcup \ldots \sqcup C_n$
complementOf	$\neg C$
oneOf	$\{x_1\} \sqcup \ldots \sqcup \{x_n\}$
allValuesFrom	$\forall P.C$
someValuesFrom	$\exists P.C$
maxCardinality	$\leq nP$
minCardinality	$\geq nP$

the full vocabulary of RDFS, including *rdfs:type*, and *rdfs:domain*, but also includes other elements that are not included in RDFS. Table 11.2 provides an overview of the full range of class constructors in OWL, along with their corresponding DL syntax. The names of the constructors are fairly self-evident. An example of the constructor *unionOf* would be a statement like "Senators ⊔ Legislators." We introduced some of the more important and common constructs in the previous section, on reasoning primitives.

However, a more important difference is that, unlike RDFS, OWL not only tells us how we can use a certain vocabulary, but also how we *can't* use it. RDFS is much more constraint-free. For example, in RDFS, it is technically possible for anything to be an instance of *rdfs:class*. There is nothing stopping us from using a term both as a class and an instance. RDFS considers this to be legal because it does not constrain which statements can, or cannot, be inserted. However, in at least some flavors of OWL, such statements would not be legal (i.e., it would not be allowable to declare a term as being both a class and an instance). The full range of OWL axiom constructors are enumerated in table 11.3. In practice, which constructors can be used or are applicable depends on the flavor of OWL used, as subsequently detailed.

In summary, OWL imposes a much more rigid structure compared to the more free-for-all allowances made by RDFS. In turn, this permits more expressive and meaningful reasoning capabilities. Of course, some flavors of OWL choose to implement more constraints than others, primarily due to computational reasons because some kinds of inferences can be run really quickly, while others are intractable.

11.2.2.2 Flavors of OWL In the previous subsection, we referred several times to flavors of OWL. Technically, these are known as *sublanguages*. While many different sublanguages of OWL are theoretically possible, there are three sublanguages that are studied in practice because they are designed for use by specific communities of implementers and users:

Table 11.3: A list of OWL axiom constructors, with examples and corresponding DL syntax.

OWL Axiom	DL Syntax
subClassOf	$C_1 \sqsubseteq C_2$
equivalentClass	$C_1 \equiv C_2$
disjointWith	$C_1 \sqsubseteq \neg C_2$
sameIndividualAs	$\{x_1\} \equiv \{x_n\}$
differentFrom	$\{x_1\} \sqsubseteq \neg\{x_n\}$
subPropertyOf	$P_1 \sqsubseteq P_2$
equivalentProperty	$P_1 \equiv P_2$
inverseOf	$P_1 \equiv P_2^-$
transitiveProperty	$P^+ \sqsubseteq P$
functionalProperty	$\top \sqsubseteq\, \leq 1P$
inverseFunctionalProperty	$\top \sqsubseteq\, \leq 1P^-$

1. *OWL Lite* supports those users primarily needing a classification hierarchy and simple constraints. For example, while it supports cardinality constraints, it permits cardinality values of only 0 or 1. It should be simpler to provide tool support for OWL Lite than its more expressive relatives, and OWL Lite provides a quick migration path for thesauri and other taxonomies. OWL Lite also has a lower formal complexity than OWL DL (described next). Table 11.4 expresses the list of OWL Lite language constructs. Note that some of the constructs are derived directly from terms in RDF or RDFS (as evidenced by their prefix, such as *rdfs:label*). Many of the terms (such as *rdfs:domain, Class*, and *Individual*, which is an instance of a class) are self-explanatory, and we do not provide detailed descriptions of them here. Annotations within the ontology are generally supported by standard (and ubiquitous) properties like *rdfs:label* and *rdfs:comment*.

2. *OWL DL* supports those users who want maximum expressiveness while retaining computational completeness (i.e., all conclusions are guaranteed to be computable) and decidability (i.e., all computations will finish in a finite time). OWL DL includes all the OWL language constructs, but they can be used only under certain restrictions (for example, while a class may be a subclass of many classes, a class cannot be an instance of *another* class). OWL DL is so named due to its more direct correspondence with DLs compared to the other flavors. OWL DL contains all the constructs of OWL Lite, but it also contains constructs that OWL Lite does not contain. We provide some examples of these incremental additions in table 11.5.

3. Finally, *OWL Full* is meant for users who want maximum expressiveness and the syntactic freedom of RDF with no computational guarantees. For example, in OWL Full,

Table 11.4: A nonexhaustive list of OWL Lite language features.

OWL Lite Feature	Brief Description
Class	Defines a group of individuals that belong together because they share some properties, can also be organized in a specialization hierarchy using *subClassOf*. There is a built-in most general class named Thing that is the class of all individuals and is a superclass of all OWL classes. There is also a built-in most specific class named Nothing that is the class that has no instances and a subclass of all OWL classes.
rdfs:subClassOf	Class hierarchies may be created by making one or more statements that a class is a subclass of another class.
rdf:Property	Properties can be used to state relationships between individuals or from individuals to data values. Examples include *hasRelative* and *hasAge*. Both *owl:ObjectProperty* and *owl:DatatypeProperty* are subclasses of the RDF class *rdf:Property*.
rdfs:subPropertyOf	Property hierarchies may be created by making one or more statements that a property is a subproperty of one or more other properties (e.g., *hasBrother* may be stated to be a subproperty of *hasSibling*).
rdfs:domain	A domain of a property limits the individuals to which the property can be applied. If a property relates an individual to another individual, and the property has a class as one of its domains, then the individual must belong to the class.
rdfs:range	The range of a property limits the individuals that the property may have as its value. If a property relates an individual to another individual, and the property has a class as its range, then the other individual must belong to the range class.
Individual	Individuals are instances of classes, and properties may be used to relate one individual to another.
inverseOf	If the property $P1$ is stated to be the inverse of the property $P2$, then if X is related to Y by the $P2$ property, then Y is related to X by the $P1$ property.
FunctionalProperty	If a property is a *FunctionalProperty*, then it has no more than one value for each individual (it may have no values for an individual).
equivalentClass	Equivalent classes have the same instances, and can be used to create synonymous classes.

Table 11.5: Two examples of incremental language features supported by OWL DL, but not OWL Lite.

OWL DL Feature	Brief Description
oneOf	Classes can be described by *enumeration* of the individuals that make up the class, with members of the class being *exactly* the set of enumerated individuals (no more or less). A good example is the class *calendarMonths*, which would enumerate the 12 months. A reasoner could deduce the maximum cardinality of any property that has *calendarMonths* as its *allValuesFrom* restriction.
disjointWith	Classes may be stated to be disjoint from each other, which usually allows a reasoner to deduce an inconsistency (e.g., if an instance is declared to be an instance of two disjoint classes; also, a reasoner can deduce negative information such as, if X is an instance of A and A and B are disjoint, then X *must not* be an instance of B).

a class can be treated simultaneously as a collection of individuals and as an individual in its own right. OWL Full allows an ontology to augment the meaning of the predefined (RDF or OWL) vocabulary. It is unlikely that any reasoning software will be able to support complete reasoning for every feature of OWL Full. OWL Full also provides maximum flexibility for ontologists to define all manner of properties (e.g., for specialized kinds of complex annotations), or declarations of complex classes (e.g., that are boolean combinations of other preexisting classes).

There is an interesting relationship between these three sublanguages, as might be expected. Every *legal* OWL Lite ontology is a legal OWL DL ontology, and every legal OWL DL ontology is a legal OWL Full ontology. The inverses are not true, however. The same relation applies to conclusions (i.e., every *valid* OWL Lite conclusion is a valid OWL DL conclusion, and so on).

11.2.3 Sample Reasoning Framework: Protégé

An extremely important resource in the SW community for modeling ontologies using OWL is Protégé. Protégé was developed by the Stanford Center for Biomedical Informatics Research at the Stanford University School of Medicine. Protégé fully supports the latest OWL 2 and RDF specifications from the World Wide Web Consortium (W3C). It is highly extensible and is based on the Java programming language. In essence, it provides a plug-and-play environment that makes it a flexible base for rapid prototyping and application development.

Protégé's plug-in architecture can be adapted to build both simple and complex ontology-based applications. Developers can integrate the output of Protégé with rule systems or other problem solvers to construct a wide range of intelligent systems based on SW and

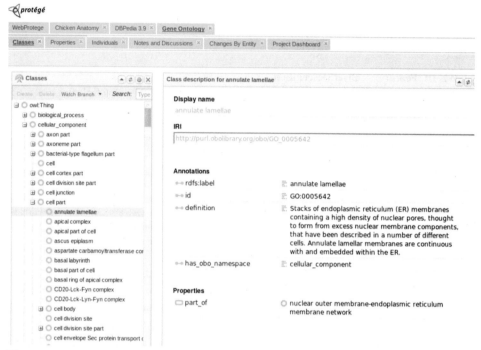

Figure 11.1: The Protégé interface in a biomedical domain (taken from the Wiki available at *protegewiki.stanford.edu/wiki/Main_Page*).

KG technologies. A visualization of the interface for the biomedical domain is shown in figure 11.1.

Protégé is not only a desktop-based tool; it also offers an ontology development environment for the web via WebProtégé. WebProtégé makes it easy to create, upload, modify, and share ontologies for collaborative viewing and editing. WebProtégé, just like the desktop version, fully supports OWL 2 and has a highly configurable user interface that can be used by both beginners and experts. Collaboration features include sharing and permissions, threaded notes and discussions, watches, and email notifications. A variety of formats are supported for ontology upload and download, including RDF/XML, Turtle, OWL/XML, and OBO. It is cross-compatible with the desktop version, and introduces the concept of web forms for domain-specific editing.

Perhaps the most important aspect of Protégé beyond all its technical capabilities is that it is actively supported by a strong community of users and developers that "field questions, write documentation, and contribute plug-ins." At this time, Protégé 5.5.0 was released and is the most recent version. It offers several new features compared to previous versions of Protégé, but like the other versions, is free to use.

11.3 Retrieval

As defined in a classic text on the subject, IR is defined as *finding material (usually documents) of an unstructured nature (usually text) that satisfies an information need from within large collections (usually stored on computers)*. As the definition indicates, IR has often been employed in the context of unstructured (a misnomer for natural-language) data, with the term and the field itself largely taking off because of the increased relevance of web search engines like Google and Bing. In fact, most IR systems tend to be distinguished by the scale at which they operate. Modern IR research in companies like Bing and Google has focused on web-scale systems where search capabilities have to be provided over billions of documents stored on entire clusters of computers. Good indexing techniques are vital, and even minor improvements can have a strong influence on the bottom line. Particular aspects of the web itself, including exploitation of hypertext, and robustness to site providers manipulating page content to boost search engine scores, have to be dealt with to satisfy the information needs of users.

Personal IR is at the other end of the spectrum and is not necessarily small-scale, though much smaller usually than most web search system. Personal IR is primarily relevant in operating systems (Apple's Mac OS Spotlight) and email search. Between personal IR and web IR lie *enterprise, institutional*, and *domain-specific* IR systems. Enterprise and institutional IR refer to the main customer bases or types they tend to serve. Domain-specific IR is an intriguing area of research, both in KGs and search, that has been rapidly exploding. An example of domain-specific IR is product search on Amazon or video search on YouTube. Beyond KGs, domain-specific IR involves building high-performance systems for (among others) searching legal documents like court filings, patents, medical documents, and research articles on topics ranging from sociology to chemistry.

Given that there is so much focus on documents, why discuss retrieval in the context of KGs? One reason is that KGs are rarely all symbolic, and often contain free-text fields like descriptions, phrases, and labels. For example, in encyclopedic KGs like DBpedia, which are derived from WIkipedia infoboxes, an entity like "Bob Marley" is described not only using an abstract and a label property, but has a birth date associated with him, and statistics like the number of awards won, links to some of his works (which in turn are subject nodes in the KG and have their corresponding links and literals), to only name a few. Symbolic reasoning may work with artifacts like dates, or even fields like awards, but would not work for description-like fields without either string matching (which does not work well for long strings like in the abstract field) or some kind of IR-inspired technique like tf-idf, which is described next. Furthermore, there are methods to represent KGs as *sets of key-value documents*, and systems like Elasticsearch support these representations seamlessly, as we describe in the next chapter. For example, for a single KG node, a document can be created, with the datatype properties of the node expressed as keys (and their corresponding object values, which are literals, expressed as values). More complex representations are also feasible, some of which are active areas of theoretical and practical research. Either way, by representing KGs as sets of key-value documents, IR toolkits and frameworks like Lucene become applicable, as do vector space methods.

11.3.1   Term Frequency and Weighting

By far, the dominant approach to ranking documents is the *vector space model* (VSM). The core intuition behind a VSM is to represent each document (and even free-text queries, which may be thought of as short documents) as a *vector*, not dissimilar to the word-embedding and KG-embedding (KGE) models we considered earlier. However, unlike those models, classic document VSMs yield document vectors where dimensions are interpretable, with each dimension usually encoding the *importance* of a word. For this reason, classic VSMs based on bag of words and its variants have the dimensionality of the language's common vocabulary (for English, a vocabulary of 50,000 is typically assumed, but it is not uncommon to consider the full dictionary as well), but are very sparse because most entries are zero (even in long documents, only a small portion of the language's vocabulary is usually observed).

The notion of importance is vital here, and the weighting scheme that has withstood the test of time and is still considered a highly competitive baseline or set of features in many settings is tf-idf. The tf-idf formula for term t in document d may simply be expressed by the following formula:

$$tf - idf_{t,d} = tf_{t,d} \times idf_t. \tag{11.1}$$

Here, the subexpression $tf_{t,d}$ is some measure of the frequency of term t in d, usually the number of occurrences of t in d. The idf_t term, which is dependent on the full corpus rather than any individual document, is the ratio N/df_t where N is the total number of documents in the corpus and df_t is the number of documents in which t occurs at least once. The reason why the model is said to be a bag of words model is because, as the formula illustrates, the order of the words is irrelevant to the vector representation. The sentences "The cow jumped over the moon" and "The moon jumped over the cow" would have the same vectors.

Variants of this formula also exist (e.g., using the logarithms of these expressions is quite common as a type of smoothing). Almost always, the logarithm of the *idf* is taken rather than the ratio N/df_t. In the case of *tf*, one could also consider relative frequency instead of absolute. Note that the length of the document is not as relevant as one might imagine after looking at the formula. The reason is that "matching" between vectors is usually done using a measure like *cosine similarity*, which measures the cosine of the angle between two vectors and is agnostic to their lengths. In essence, this equates to normalizing each vector (specifically, the 2-norm), and then applying dot product as the similarity measure between vectors. To take an example, if there were two documents d_1 and d_2, which contained only the term "knowledge" 10 and 20 times respectively, the vector representations for both documents would be identical after normalization (containing a 1 as the dimension value represented by "knowledge," and 0 in every other dimension). However, if even one other word were contained, the number of occurrences would start making a difference. Without a logarithmic adjustment, the effect of such "rare" words tend to be dampened, because the large frequencies end up dominating (both before and after normalization).

How could we use tf-idf for retrieving entities in KGs? One idea is to think of each entity as a "document" and to accept queries that are either free-text (a list of words), or more specific and semantic in origin (e.g., return a ranked list of entities matching the criteria "title: knowledge*, author: kejriwal*"). In fact, many form-based access mechanisms on the web (such as might be found on a university website) are based on such IR techniques. Of course, it is usually not the case that the underlying data over which libraries and other organizations retrieve is actually in the form of a KG. However, many modern tech-focused organizations like Amazon have far more structured data sets that resemble KGs. In any case, the point remains that IR techniques used for data sets that have descriptive text elements (with natural-language documents being an extreme case that only contains such elements) could be applied to KGs that have fields amenable to IR, such as "description," "label," and "comment," among others. We saw earlier that OWL and even RDFS allow for such annotation properties, and many well-established KGs like DBpedia make liberal use of these properties.

The corollary is that if such text(or *literal*) properties are not liberally used, or it is difficult to index the KG, then IR methods lose their advantage over reasoning methods. The next section details this tension further. Generally, the most difficult (and most real-world) KGs to access are both noisy, and have a high mix of structured and text information. Even cutting-edge, hybrid access techniques that combine retrieval and reasoning fail to achieve excellent performance, and there is much room for improvement in this domain. We cover such a use-case in the context of human trafficking in chapter 17, where we discuss the construction and use of domain-specific KGs for social impact projects.

11.4   Retrieval versus Reasoning

The situation becomes quickly more complicated with increasing sophistication in either the KG (which may adhere to a complex ontology, such as in scientific domains, or contains many nontext and even nonliteral structural information that is critical for retrieving good answers to queries) or to the query itself. In essence, an IR approach is inherently limited in its reasoning capabilities, relying mainly on surface semantic properties. Word and graph embeddings such as we have studied earlier can help resolve some of these issues, but not all. For example, KG embeddings and word embeddings, as we saw earlier, tend to embed each word or entity into a vector. A query, in contrast, is a subgraph, with some slots in the graph that are not known and have to be filled-in via query execution against the KG.

In recognition of the difficulty of so-called question-answering systems that are so crucial to the functioning of chatbots and intelligent agents like Alexa and Siri, the community has come up with a set of techniques specifically for question answering (see chapter 13). Some of the leading work in this space has been done in industry, and is not generally available to the public. Beyond natural-language question answering, a hybrid suite of approaches may be the best way to tackle querying in KGs.

One such approach is *fuzzy querying*. Work on fuzzy querying precedes the growth of KGs and was recognized mostly in the era of the early web, when noisy RDBMSs started becoming more common and data mining on such databases (which could sometimes be derived from web data, not unlike the web IE KG construction methods described in part II of this book) was desirable. Fuzzy querying meant retrieving answers to queries that corresponded more closely to imprecise natural language (e.g., "find all records such that almost all of the important fields are as specified," where by specification we mean a "constraint" or pattern in the query, such as *age* > 18). It was clear even back then that major extensions to languages like SQL would be necessary to accommodate such queries, including the extension of syntax, semantics, an elicitation and manipulation mechanism for specification of linguistic or fuzzy terms in the queries, and the embedding of fuzzy querying in native architectures (rather than designing completely new systems that would have likely had no impact on legacy architectures and primary users of database technology). Some of this work could potentially be extended to KGs.

More popular, however, is work on *query reformulation*. The idea there is to specify an ordinary query (rather than a fuzzy query that contains linguistic terms like "almost" or otherwise has an extended syntax) in a language like SQL or SPARQL, but not to assume strict semantics. Rather, the querying engine takes satisfying user intent to be the guiding semantic criterion for retrieval, and their evaluation is often done using IR metrics (a sample of which is described in the next section). As an example, suppose that we specify a SPARQL query that asks for the "population of the city of Los Angeles." If the query were to be executed with strict semantics, the population of the city of Los Angeles, if it existed in the KG or database, would be retrieved; otherwise, nothing would be retrieved by the query engine. However, many people actually mean the city of Los Angeles to be the greater Los Angeles metropolitan area, which includes other "cities" like Torrance and Santa Monica. A query reformulation system would try to satisfy user intent by using some kind of (statistical or expert-derived) heuristic to automatically reformulate the original query, in this case by expanding it to include these other cities in the greater LA metropolitan area. Furthermore, because the system itself may not know which cities to include in this expanded query, it would return, not a single answer, but a ranked list of answers that can be evaluated using various IR metrics. Note that query expansion is not the only form of query reformulation, which can also involve relaxations (in the extreme case, by deleting a specification, especially on a noisy, unreliable, or otherwise low-coverage predicate, to get higher recall), synonymy, soft string matching, and other operators to make the querying more robust. Whether fuzzy querying or query reformulation is appropriate depends on the preferred mode of user elicitation and expected output, as well as the actual quality of the KG. In more recent applications, like chatbots and question answering, both approaches may be apt.

In the introduction to this chapter, we stated that the reasoning and retrieval research communities had been fairly disjointed historically, with their own sets of researchers, data sets, and even publishing venues. KG research has brought both modes of data access into focus and placed it on common ground, primarily due to necessity. Most KGs have literals and free-text values, as we observed in the previous section, but they also have considerable structure that reasoning systems are better able to exploit. KGs not only span a range of genres, but also exist along a quality spectrum, with some KGs having high precision and others having good coverage of domain-specific instances, but also a lot of noise. KGs may be serving different sets of stakeholders, or they may be confined to one or more narrow use-cases. However, more often than not, trade-offs are involved, meaning that it is neither desirable nor wise to commit to a framework that is pure reasoning or retrieval. Approaches like fuzzy querying are useful for navigating such trade-offs. Because this is such an important problem, we expect research to flourish in this area for the foreseeable future.

11.4.1 Evaluation

In contrast with reasoning, IR practitioners always take a ranked list as the answer to be evaluated, given a corpus of documents and a free-text query. Several such corpora are available and have been constructed over many years in the community, including the Cranfield collection; the test bed evaluation series run in the Text Retrieval Conferences (TRECs) by the US National Institute of Standard and Technology (NIST); the NTCIR collection, which focuses mainly on East Asian language and cross-language IR; and CLEF (similarly focused on cross-language retrieval and European languages). For each ranked list, and a ground-truth of which entries are relevant (in its simplest and most popular form, relevance is just a binary measure—that is, with respect to a query, either a document is judged to be relevant and has a value of 1 in the corresponding ground-truth, or it has a value of 0 if it is considered irrelevant), an IR metric can be computed.

Several such candidate metrics have been, and continue to be, used in the literature and among practitioners, including Mean Reciprocal Rank (MRR), Normalized Discounted Cumulative Gain (NDCG), recall@k, precision@k, and Mean Average Precision (MAP).

Multiple systems can be evaluated fairly by having a large, broad corpus and many queries. For one or more of these metrics, a detailed set of performance data points can be obtained for each system. The usual tests of statistical significance (typically but not always *pairwise*, because all performance results are collected over a common set of queries) can be used to determine whether one system is statistically significantly better than another.

Mean Reciprocal Rank (MRR). Given a ranked list, the MRR for that list is the inverse of the rank of the single relevant document. MRR does not apply gracefully if there is more than one relevant document for a given query. As expected, the highest possible MRR is 1.0, and there is a rapid decline as the document moves down the list (e.g., the MRR is 0.5 if the relevant document is ranked second, 0.33 if ranked third, and so on).

recall@k. The recall at rank k (termed as *recall@k*) in a ranked list is the ratio of relevant documents in the top k to the ratio of the total number of relevant documents (for that query and corpus). For example, a recall@10 of 90 percent means that 90 percent of the relevant documents in the ground-truth for the query are in the top 10. Obviously, recall@m will be at least as much as recall@n if $m > n$. The lowest k at which recall reaches 100 percent tells us how many irrelevant documents we had to see before we saw *all* relevant documents for that query. To understand this better, let's take an example of a 10,000-document corpus. Note first that "document" should be understood here (and the rest of this discussion) in the looser sense of the word, because in the IR context, a document is any element that can be retrieved, and this could include a video or KG entity rather than a text document. Returning to the example, suppose that only 20 of the 10,000 documents are relevant for a given query. Furthermore, suppose that we observed that the lowest k at which recall@k of 100 percent is achieved is 50. One obvious thing that we should point out here is that recall@k can never be 100 percent for any k that is strictly smaller than the size of the ground-truth (in this case, 20). In this example, the number of irrelevant documents we saw is 30, because of the 50 documents that we saw before we saw all the relevant documents (20 in total), 30 had to be irrelevant. The k also gives us the rank of the last relevant document (see the exercises at the end of this chapter), and for all these reasons, it is an important number.

By itself, recall@k is rank-agnostic in that it does not tell us *where* in the top k the relevant documents are located. For example, if there are 10 relevant documents in the ground-truth and recall@5 is 10 percent, then this means that exactly one relevant document is in the top 5. However, the relevant document may have been at rank 4, 5, or 1; this would not affect recall@5. The measure is still fairly robust when it is plotted on a graph, with k on the x-axis and recall@k on the y-axis. When we plot recall in this way, we start to see the differences in ranking (e.g., in this example, if the relevant document was at rank 4, then recall@4 would also be 10 percent, while if the document was at rank 5, recall@4 would be 0). The graph of this would illustrate this difference.

For multiple queries, the different values of recall@k can be averaged for each value of k, yielding a single curve (with error bars, capturing the variance in recall values at each k). Note that, based on these observations, once recall@m has reached 100 percent, then recall@n where $n > m$ will also be 100 percent, yielding a flat line. So a full plot can be constructed for all values on the x-axis from $[1, \ldots, N]$, where N is the total number of documents in the corpus.

precision@k. The precision at rank k is analogous to recall@k, except that instead of computing the recall at rank k, it computes the precision [the number of relevant documents in the top k divided by $min(k, rel(q))$ where $rel(q)$, is the smallest rank at which recall@k reaches 100 percent; i.e., all relevant documents have been observed by that rank]. For example, suppose there are 10 relevant documents, and the last relevant document is achieved at rank 50. The precision@50 would then be $10 / 50 = 20$ percent, which stays flat at all values of k from 50 to N. Furthermore, unlike recall, the precision does not have to increase monotonically but can experience dips and increases. For example, if the very first document is relevant, then precision@1 is 100 percent, but if the second document is irrelevant and the third document is again relevant, then precision@2 drops to 50 percent, while precision@3 increases to 66.67 percent (since at rank 3, two out of three observed documents are relevant). By convention, to avoid dividing by 0, precision@k, where $k < k'$, k' being the lowest k at which the *first* relevant document is observed, is always 0. In the previous example, if the first document had not been relevant, then precision@1 and precision@2 would both have been 0 (while precision@3 would have been 33.33 percent).

When plotting the graphs, two kinds of conventions are common, based on the application. First, we can eliminate k altogether by plotting a graph of precision versus recall, precision being on the y-axis. k becomes like a hidden variable that is used to pair precision and recall values (at the same k) and allows one to see how precision changes with recall (see the exercises). This is a handy measurement because recall has to reach 100 percent at some k (in the most extreme case, recall@N is guaranteed to be 100 percent). In contrast, precision may never reach 100 percent for some queries (e.g., it is easy to show that if the first document is not relevant, then precision will never reach 100 percent) and unless all the relevant documents are always ranked at the top, precision@N will never be 100 percent. These extreme cases notwithstanding, in practice, there is almost always a trade-off between recall and precision, and a precision-recall curve helps us to evaluate this trade-off. Previously, in the chapter on reconciling KGs (chapter 8), we noticed similar trade-offs [e.g., both in the entity matching phase, where a precision-recall trade-off arose, as well as between Reduction Ratio (RR) and Pairs Completeness (PC) metrics in the context of evaluating blocking].

Interpolated Precision. The second convention is to use *interpolated precision* to remove "jiggles" in the precision-recall plot that do not allow us to see the general trends very easily. The interpolated precision at a given recall level r is simply defined as the highest precision found for any recall level $r' > r$. The reason for this adjustment is that, even though the recall stays constant between two ranks k_1 and $k_2 > k_1$ if all documents between those two ranks (exclusive) are irrelevant and documents at k_1 and k_2 are relevant (which means that recall@k_1 stays constant until recall@$k_2 - 1$ and then increases at recall@k_2), the precision will steadily decline between those levels, and then increase (i.e., precision@k_2 − 1 will be lower than precision@k_2) when a relevant document is encountered at k_2. These steady declines, followed by a steep and sudden rise at the rank when a relevant document is encountered leads to irregularity in the plot. By using interpolated precision instead of raw precision, the precision stays flat (and equal to precision@k_1) all the way from k_1 to k_2 − 1, leading to a smoother characterization of the trade-off between recall and precision at various levels of recall.

While precision@k and recall@k (and their harmonic mean, the F1-measure@k, which tries to quantify their trade-off at every value of k) are useful if considered graphically, and MRR is a useful metric if there is great emphasis on getting a single existent right answer at the very top (e.g., ads and e-commerce, because the user will often have a very short attention span), they have some limitations. In general, there has been controversy over which IR metric is the best one, because they are not always correlated. MRR, for example, is applicable only to ground-truths where each query has exactly one relevant document. Also, we saw how quickly the MRR declines as the relevant document slides further down the ranked list. For this reason, it has been criticized especially when it is analyzed in average over a set of queries. Imagine, for example, that there were two queries and a very large (roughly infinite) set of documents to rank. Suppose that system 1 got the right document in the top position for the first query, but ranked the right document last for the second query. Suppose also that system 2 got the right documents at the no. 2 and no. 3 positions for the two queries, respectively. Strangely, the average MRR for system 1 (0.5) would be higher than that for system 2 (0.42)!

Mean Average Precision (MAP). To address some of these issues, the TREC community in particular has preferred the MAP metric, defined using the formula below. Note that MAP assumes not only a given corpus D, but also a given set Q of queries. For each query $q \in Q$, the ground-truth $G_q \subseteq D$ is the set of relevant documents:

$$MAP = \frac{1}{|Q|} \sum_{q \in Q} \frac{1}{|G_q|} \sum_{g \in G_q} Precision(g). \tag{11.2}$$

There are some subtle aspects to equation (11.2), which is best explained from the inside out (namely, after fixing a query q and a relevant document g that belongs in the ground-truth G_q). For each query, we have a ranking over the documents over D. Precision(g) is calculated in the usual way: we note the rank k at which g occurs in the ranked list, and then divide k by the total number of relevant documents noted until k. The first inner sum and division then gives us the average precision in MAP for a single information need (i.e., query). For this query, the average precision is approximately equal to the area under the uninterpolated precision-recall curve (computed by using k as a hidden variable, as described here). When averaged over all queries, we get the single MAP score. Unlike MRR, MAP tends to be smoother and more robust in its distribution of scores. For most normal IR systems, MAP tends to vary between 0.1 and 0.7 according to a popular book on the subject. Indeed, it has been found that there can be more agreement between MAP scores of different systems for a single information need (query) than for MAP scores for different queries within the same system.

To summarize, the "average" in MAP is the average over precision values at different positions in the ranked list, while the "mean," just as with MRR, is the mean over all queries, because there is one average precision per query. Just like MRR, MAP also lies between 0.0 and 1.0, with 1.0 implying that for all queries, all relevant documents were always ranked at the very top. MAP has some distinct advantages over the previous metrics. First, unlike the precision and recall (@k) metrics, there are no fixed levels and interpolation is unnecessary.

Normalized Discounted Cumulative Gain (NDCG). Another metric that is highly important and that is most commonly used when relevance is not a binary measure but more nuanced (such as on a continuous scale from 0 to 1), is the NDCG (also written as nDCG). Intuitively, NDCG attempts to jointly quantify several aspects important to retrieval, namely (1) all else being equal, an item with higher relevance to the query should be ranked higher than an item with lower relevance; (2) the more relevant items there are for a query, the lower should be the contribution of any one relevant item to the evaluation of the ranking. In contrast, a metric like MRR is focused on optimizing the highest ranking of a single relevant item. Precision and recall are parameterized by k and form a continuum, rather than a single-point metric. The notion of binary relevance is another major limitation in all of the metrics considered thus far.

The NDCG is formally given by the following formula:

$$NDCG = \frac{1}{|Q|} \sum_{q \in Q} \mathcal{Z}_q \sum_{i=1}^{i=n} \frac{2^{R_q(i)} - 1}{log_2(1 + i)}. \tag{11.3}$$

We use three additional symbols in equation (11.3)—namely, $\mathcal{Z}_q$, n, and $R_q(i)$, of which n is a constant (i.e., query and corpus independent). Note that although NDCG does not necessarily require the (query-independent) parameter n, it is commonplace (in practice) to use it and set it to some reasonable number like 5 or 10. In essence, n means that, for any query, we only retrieve the top n results. n is generally assumed to be at least as large as the typical size of a ground-truth per query. Equation (11.3) also works if n is just set to D (the total size of the corpus). $R_q(i)$ is the *relevance* score (constrained to typically lie between $[0.0, 0.1]$) of the ith document in the ranked list retrieved in response to query q.

$\mathcal{Z}_q$ is a normalization factor that allows the NDCG to be constrained between $[0.0, 1.0]$ just like MAP and the other metrics. $\mathcal{Z}_q$ is dependent on the query q, and can be computed by setting the NDCG for that query (in practice, by letting $|Q| = 1$ in the equation (11.3), and getting rid of the outer summation since the averaging is over a single number) to 1 under the assumption of a perfect ranking. In other words, the inner sum, evaluated for a *perfect ranking* for that query is the reciprocal of $\mathcal{Z}_q$. Note that, unlike MAP and the other metrics seen thus far, the relevance score of a document (given a query) is directly taken into account in the NDCG. One reason why this is useful is interannotator disagreement over whether a document is relevant or not, given a query. For example, four out of five annotators may decide that d is relevant for query q. Rather than discard this disagreement, and round up or down, a more sophisticated approach is to designate the relevance of d given q as $4/5 = 0.8$. Furthermore, note that when a document is irrelevant and has relevance 0.0 for query q, the expression $2^{R_q(i)}$ evaluates to 1, which leads to the numerator taking on value 0.

Given all of these IR metrics and the way that we described how reasoning was evaluated earlier, how should one compare the performance of reasoning and retrieval? Generally, it is like comparing apples and oranges, and before the advent of KGs, the two had never been compared within the auspices of a single community or application. However, as we have argued at various points in this chapter, both reasoning and retrieval have a role to play in accessing the knowledge in the KGs. Reasoning is preferable when the KG is relatively clean and contains useful information that is only implicit in the KG itself, but can be derived by combining the KG and ontological axioms. Large KGs and ontologies can present problems of scale for reasoners, however.

A few government-funded research programs have yielded interesting and comparative insights on what happens when a reasoner is used to process queries (such as written in SPARQL, as discussed in chapter 12) without modifying the queries in any way, as opposed to a more IR-based system that is allowed to use the initial queries as a way to understand the actual user intent (which is to say, query reformulations and modifications are allowed, among other functionalities). Of course, scale starts becoming an issue even for well-designed IR systems once such complex operations are considered over large enough corpora.

11.4.2   Sample Information Retrieval Framework: Lucene

In the IR community, several tools are now considered mainstream for building fast and robust retrieval systems. A well-known system is Lucene, a full-text search library in Java that makes it easy to add search functionality to an application or website.

At a high level, Lucene operates by adding content to a full-text index, and then permitting query execution against this index, returning results ranked by either the relevance to the query or sorted by an arbitrary field such as a creation date. In Lucene, a *document* is the unit of search and index, with an index consisting of one or more documents. However (and this is a point that we alluded to earlier in this chapter, and shall repeat again in the next), a document either in the Lucene or IR context doesn't *necessarily* have to be a document, in the common English usage of the word. For example, a Lucene index can be created over a database table of products, in which case each product (i.e., row) would be represented in the index as a Lucene document.

In Lucene, a document consists of one or more *fields*. A field is simply a name-value pair (e.g., for a document describing this book, such a name-value pair might be "Title: Knowledge Graphs"). In this case, the field name is "Title" and the value is the title of that content item ("Knowledge Graphs"). Even though we've represented values as strings in these examples, they could potentially be other literals like numbers or dates.

In summary, indexing in Lucene involves creating documents comprised of one or more fields, followed by adding the documents to an *IndexWriter*. Similarly, searching involves retrieving documents from an index via a *IndexSearcher*. Many modern search and retrieval features are supported by (or can be implemented in) the basic Lucene framework, which has its own query syntax for doing searches. Lucene allows the user to specify which fields to search on and which fields to give more weight to (a process called *boosting*), and also it gives the user the ability to perform boolean queries, among other functionalities. In the next chapter, we will go deeper into boolean queries in the context of a key-value store called Elasticsearch, which has found value in some KG applications, and which has Lucene at its back end.

One reason why Lucene has survived the test of time is the flexibility and robustness of its query syntax, which anticipates the nature of IR being inherently difficult for machines (due to ambiguity in documents, length variance, different field reliability, etc.), and thus not amenable to a one-size-fits-all solution. The Lucene query syntax, in addition to supporting normal keyword matching against fields, also supports the following functions:

1. **Wildcard matching** (e.g., the query "Title: Knowledge*" will match any document that starts with "Knowledge" in its title)

2. **Proximity matching** (e.g., finding words that are within a specific distance from a word)

3. **Range searches** (e.g., match documents where the value in a "Date" field is between August 2001 and September 2004)

4. **Boosts** (e.g., customize which terms and classes are more important and should contribute high scores in terms of determining document relevance)

5. **Query parsing**, which makes it possible to do advanced tasks like programmatic query construction (allowing construction and deployment of dynamic and intelligent applications that can be programmed to construct their own queries via template or slot filling)

Another reason for Lucene's survival and popularity may very well be its open-source and community-driven status, as it is supported by the Apache Software Foundation. Bugfixes and releases are periodically released, and the project has a very active community around it. For example, at the present time, Lucene 7.7.2 was just released, containing nine bugfixes from the previous edition. The Apache Lucene project as a whole contains three subprojects:

1. **Lucene Core**, the flagship subproject, which provides Java-based indexing and search technology, spell-checking, hit highlighting, and advanced analysis/tokenization
2. **Solr**, a high-performance search server built using Lucene Core, with XML/HTTP and JSON/Python/Ruby application programming interfaces (API), hit highlighting, faceted search, caching, replication, and an admin interface
3. **PyLucene**, a Python port of Lucene Core motivated by the popularity of the Python programming language

11.5   Concluding Notes

Once a KG is constructed and completed, the data in it must be accessed and consumed by users and applications. Reasoning and retrieval are two dominant modes of accessing the KG. Reasoning is the more conservative, and formally well-defined, mode of access, but it expects a higher degree of quality and structure in the KG, and more conformance of KG data and assertions to the ontology. Many real-world KGs are not able to meet these strict requirements, and more often than not, with more extreme cases violating constraints in the ontology. As the KG grows in size, such violations become unavoidable, if not common. At the same time, there are domains where data from high-quality databases are being modeled as KGs. Reasoning and semantically well defined querying (where responses to the query strictly obey specifications in the query and do not interpret user intent liberally) work well in such cases, and are important in both scientific domains, as well as proprietary business analytics.

Contrasted with reasoning, IR is a more robust but approximate form of data access where, given a query from the user, the goal is to interpret the *user intent* and retrieve a set of results. The results are usually ranked, although there are exceptions (i.e., where results are sets rather than lists) that are beyond the scope of this chapter. Retrieval works well in the presence of free-text values and string literals, and when either the user query or corpus (or both) have noisy, missing, or implicit information. IR and reasoning have both been thoroughly researched in the AI and information sciences community, well before the advent of KGs. Whether reasoning or retrieval, or some combination or hybrid thereof, should be used for accessing and serving data in a KG depends both on the application and the KG itself. Applications with strict quality requirements, where the user is depended upon to produce queries that express their intent (usually through a domain-specific structured language like SPARQL or SQL) generally prefer reasoning, while retrieval is better suited for applications where the domain is too broad, the knowledge is too noisy or incomplete, or the user is not always aware of all the consequences of query specifications (but has some intent or goal in mind). In recent years, the choice has not been between "one or the other," but in how to best build systems where the benefits of both sets of approaches may be reaped. Fuzzy querying and query reformulation are two important, and reasonably well-established, classes of approaches in this promising direction.

11.6 Software and Resources

There are many good resources for both reasoning and retrieval, and two of the important ones, Protégé and Lucene, were given due attention in this chapter. These resources can be accessed at https://protege.stanford.edu/products.php and https://lucene.apache.org/, respectively. For those who do not want to install Protégé locally, an excellent alternative is WebProtégé, which is available at https://webprotege.stanford.edu/ and hosted by Stanford. We briefly described Lucene Core, Solr, and PyLucene toward the end of the chapter: these are available at https://lucene.apache.org/core/, lucene.apache.org/solr/, and https://lucene.apache.org/pylucene/, respectively. Many other packages use Lucene at their back end. Good packages for trying out structured IR-style querying are Elasticsearch and MongoDB, accessible at https://www.elastic.co/ and https://www.mongodb.com/, respectively.

There are several open-source software packages available that implement semantic reasoners. These resources include FaCT++ (available at http://owl.cs.manchester.ac.uk/tools/fact/), which is implemented in C++ and covers expressive DLs, Racer (https://github.com/ha-mo-we/Racer), Apache Jena (http://jena.apache.org/), and CEL (https://tu-dresden.de/ing/informatik/thi/lat/forschung/software/cel), among others. Some of these (e.g., FaCT++) are compatible with Protégé's DIG interface, which is a standard interface/protocol that was introduced to provide a common interface to DL reasoners.

Note that many programming languages today provide convenient packages for computing important IR metrics like NDCG and MAP. For example, the Scikit-learn package in Python provides functions for calculating NDCG, among many other metrics (https://scikit-learn.org/stable/modules/classes.html). More specialized metrics may require ad-hoc implementations.

11.7 Bibliographic Notes

IR holds an important place both in the history and the current practice of computer science. Even before massive success stories such as the Google search engine, IR has played an important role in academia, with SIGIR, the premier conference on IR, dating back all the way to 1971 (with the conference becoming an annual event starting from the second instance, in 1978). As Smeaton et al. (2002) report in an analysis of 25 years of SIGIR proceedings, even as early as 1971, databases and natural-language interfaces played an influential role, with the 1980s being dedicated more to the development of conceptual IR and KBs. Just as in other communities, therefore, research in the 1980s and early 1990s laid the groundwork for IR applied to the web, as well as the advent of large-scale KGs in the late 2000s.

By the early 2000s, there had been considerable interest in higher-level tasks like document summarization, cross-lingual IR, and distributed IR; selected overviews or influential papers include Nenkova and McKeown (2012), Callan (2002), Sharma and Mittal (2016), and Cahoon and McKinley (1996). Since that period, with the growth of companies like Netflix and Amazon, and due to public competitions like the Netflix challenge, as embodied in Feuerverger et al. (2012) and Ellenberg (2008), the IR community has started to see more work in recommender systems, which were already becoming popular due to the growth of the web; interested readers should consider Adomavicius and Tuzhilin (2005), Burke (2002), Bobadilla et al. (2013), and Yang et al. (2014) for a good start on exploring this vast body of literature. Machine learning has also become prominent in IR, just as in many other computing communities. Learning to rank was an important paradigm that led to a large body of output; see Liu et al. (2009), Chapelle and Chang (2011), and Cao et al. (2007). The LETOR benchmark is described in multiple papers; we recommend Qin et al. (2010) for interested readers. It was released by Microsoft Research Asia and is periodically updated, providing a huge boost to the research community in this area. Much more recently, neural networks and deep learning have become popular themes in IR, as in much of the AI literature; we cite selected, diverse papers by Li and Lu (2016), Severyn and Moschitti (2015), Zhang et al. (2016), and Pang et al. (2017) for interested readers to evaluate recent work in this area.

Several texts on IR have been published over the years, an excellent reference for studying classic textbook material is Manning et al. (2008). Additional references include Croft et al. (2010) and Tiwary and Siddiqui (2008), which does not include numerous task-specific overviews. For a primer on information organization, we recommend the short bulletin given by Glushko (2013).

Many of the metrics first proposed for evaluating IR systems have since percolated into other predictive applications and tasks, including NLP. Precision, recall, and F-measure are standard fare in that community, although certain metrics like NDCG and MRR remain specific to IR-centric tasks due to their special dependence on ranked outputs. Some good references for understanding and comparing these metrics include Radlinski and Craswell (2010), Sakai (2007), Sakai and Kando (2008), Hripcsak and Rothschild (2005), and Bellogín et al. (2017). The last considers statistical biases in IR metrics when they are applied to recommenders. These works, which form only a sample, show that while metrics like F-measure are standard in IR (and in IR-inspired communities that have to evaluate some measure of accuracy), they are interesting areas of study in their own right.

Much of the material on OWL and reasoning in this chapter has been derived from classic sources and official tutorials on the subject that we cite in chapter 12, when the matter is covered further in depth. We only cite some primers and introductory material herein for the sake of completeness, including Hitzler et al. (2009), Antoniou and Van Harmelen (2004a), and Krötzsch et al. (2012).

We briefly mentioned probabilistic reasoners, although a full description of these is beyond the scope of this introductory chapter. Good references for probabilistic reasoners include Schum (2001), and concerning the SW, Klinov (2008) and Da Costa et al. (2006). For a synthesis, especially as it pertains to the broader goals of building intelligent systems, Pearl (2014) is an invaluable guide, as is Neapolitan (2012).

Considering the issue of retrieval versus reasoning, we note that a growing body of work has chosen to not view these as being mutually exclusive, but has instead tried to combine the two areas to yield a more powerful and robust system for accessing KGs in an intelligent way. We mentioned query reformulation as an important research area where we see this amalgam occurring in practice, as evidenced by relatively recent work in the last two decades (especially in the SW community) from Calvanese et al. (2004), Straccia and Troncy (2006), Huang and Efthimiadis (2009), Buron et al. (2019), and Viswanathan et al. (2017).

11.8 Exercises

In the following questions, our primary focus will be on retrieval, as we cover reasoning and query execution in depth in the next chapter. Toward the end of the exercises, we consider questions of a comparative nature.

1. What is the rank of the last relevant document in the ground-truth, given the lowest k (call this k') such that recall@k' reaches 100 percent? Why? *Hint: Argue that the document at the $k-1$ position* must *be irrelevant.*

2. Show that, if the first document in a ranked list is not relevant, then there is no k for which precision@k reaches 100 percent.

3. Show that, for some $k > 1$, if precision@k is 100 percent, then it is necessarily the case that all top k documents are relevant. *Hint: What happens if only one of the documents is irrelevant?*

4. Is it ever possible for the precision@k versus recall@k curve to have slope 0 before recall@k reaches 100 percent?

5. We will be computing NDCG and MAP for two systems for a set Q of three queries q_1, q_2 and q_3. Assume a document set D with 10 documents $\{d_1, \ldots, d_{10}\}$. The (ultimate) goal is to determine which system is better, and by how much, on both metrics. We will proceed in steps. For the NDCG, assume binary relevance [i.e., $R(j,m)$ is either 1 or 0]. Consult the table here for specifics.

Query	System 1 (ranked list in order $[1, \ldots, 10]$)	System 2 (ranked list in order $[1, \ldots, 10]$)	Relevant items
q_1	$[d_1, d_2, d_3, d_4, d_5, d_6, d_7, d_8, d_9, d_{10}]$	$[d_{10}, d_9, d_8, d_7, d_6, d_5, d_4, d_3, d_2, d_1]$	d_2, d_5
q_2	$[d_1, d_3, d_5, d_6, d_7, d_2, d_4, d_9, d_8, d_{10}]$	$[d_{10}, d_9, d_8, d_7, d_6, d_5, d_4, d_3, d_2, d_1]$	d_3, d_6, d_7
q_3	$[d_8, d_7, d_2, d_3, d_1, d_5, d_4, d_{10}, d_9, d_6]$	$[d_{10}, d_9, d_8, d_7, d_6, d_5, d_4, d_3, d_2, d_1]$	d_1, d_2, d_3, d_4

(a) Suppose that we interpret the output of system 1 on q_3 as a set. What is the recall of system 1 on q_3?

(b) As a first step (toward computing and comparing ranked output metrics), for all three queries, compute the NDCG normalization factor (i.e., Z_{kj}, for $j = 1, 2, 3$).

(c) Compute the NDCG for both systems for each query. Which system is better on which query? What is the average NDCG for each of the systems?

(d) Compute the average precision (AP) for all three queries for both systems. Which system is better on which query?

(e) Compute the MAP for both systems.

(f) What is the correlation between the AP and NDCG per query? Are there any queries where one metric leads you to an inconsistent result on which system is better?

6. Rather than assigning relevance scores of 1 or 0 to the 10 documents in the table from exercise 5, we assign a relevance score of 1.0 to the relevant items (for each query) listed therein, and relevance scores of 0.5 to all other items. Is it still possible to compute the MAP? What about the NDCG? Has the average NDCG (across queries) gone up, down or is unchanged? By how much?

7. ** In the vein of the table, construct the output for two systems, and a single ground-truth (i.e., there is only one query and ground-truth but two systems have produced outputs) such that the MAP says one system is better than another, but the NDCG says otherwise. Assume a population of only five documents for simplicity.

8. Is it ever possible to derive such an inconsistency if the ground-truth has only one document? What if it has two documents?

9. Given inconsistencies, when would you justify the use of MAP versus NDCG?

10. Imagine a KG describing citations (we saw an example fragment of such a KG in chapter 8, on instance matching). The KG is vast and contains computer science papers. You have a user who issues queries (you may assume that the query is issued in a way that is unambiguously interpreted by the machine) such as "Find me papers that have been coauthored or authored by a scientist whose last name is 'Bloom' and the phrase 'Bloom Filter' occurs somewhere in the title." If you had access to both reasoning and retrieval facilities, how would you use them to construct a system that is able to answer queries such as these?[2] Would there be any advantage to your approach over using a pure retrieval- or reasoning-based system?

---

[2] The example using the Bloom filter (which actually exists) is only indicative, and meant to help you think about possibilities where keywords overlap. You should be thinking about the general case when answering this question.

12 Structured Querying

Overview. Once a knowledge graph (KG) is in place, it has to be queried in order to retrieve the desired information. Structured querying is one such mechanism, wherein a formal, database-like language (based on strong logical foundations, and with clearly defined semantics and syntax) is used to retrieve subgraphs or graph patterns from the KG. An alternative mechanism, which has continued to become more popular with improvements in both Natural Language Processing (NLP) and deep learning, is posing natural-language questions with the expectation that the underlying retrieval system would be able to understand the question and retrieve high-quality answers. In this chapter, we focus on structured querying, which continues to be the predominant method for accessing structured databases that are either tabular or graphlike. In the next chapter, we study question answering.

12.1 Introduction

In the data management community, querying has always been a fundamental component of research and practice. KGs are no different. With the advent of large data sets, including terabyte-sized or even petabyte-sized web corpora, large troves of structured data, including tables, relational databases, and spreadsheets, and other such Big Data, the final KG that is constructed is itself enormous.

With the assumption that the KG is generally semistructured (making a tabular serialization inherently unsuitable), and may contain many missing (or even non-conforming) values and semantics, two broad kinds of structured querying are applicable. The first, which is more traditional and has been inspired by the massive literature in the database community on SQL and SQL-like domain-specific languages (DSLs), is based on a graph pattern–matching language called SPARQL. SPARQL is heavily favored by the Semantic Web (SW) community, and is designed to work with Resource Description Framework (RDF), a modeling language for KGs that we covered back in chapter 2. A second kind of structured querying is based on key-value stores, which is inspired by NoSQL efforts in the relational database literature as well as the information retrieval community. These two kinds of structured querying offer their own sets of advantages and disadvantages. We return to this issue toward the end of this chapter, after describing both in detail.

12.2 SPARQL

The SPARQL query language is the official World Wide Web Consortium (W3C) standard for querying and extracting information from RDF graphs. It represents the counterpart to select-project-join queries in the relational model. It is based on a powerful graph-matching facility, allows the binding of variables to components in the input RDF graph, and supports conjunctions and disjunctions of triple patterns. In addition, operators akin to relational joins, unions, left outer joins, selections, and projections can be combined to build more expressive queries.

A basic SPARQL query is a *graph pattern*, which is defined as a set of triple patterns. Triple patterns are like ordinary triples, in that each pattern consists of subject, predicate, and object, but the twist is that each of these elements may now be a variable, an internationalized resource identifier (IRI), or a literal. In other words, the query specifies the known literals and leaves the unknowns as variables that can occur in multiple patterns to constitute join operations. A question mark is placed at the front of the token to indicate that it is a variable. For example, in the triple pattern *"?name foaf:name 'John'"* has the variable *"?name"* as the subject element; the pattern is essentially a query asking for the uniform resource identifier (URIs) that are linked to the literal *"John"* via the property *foaf:name* (specified in the predicate position using the IRI http://xmlns.com/foaf/0.1/name, for which it is a shorthand).

Given such a triple pattern, the query processor needs to find all possible *variable bindings* that satisfy the given patterns and return the bindings from the projection clause to the application. Join operations become necessary because, within the scope of a single graph pattern (recall that these are sets of triple patterns), triple patterns may share variables.

Generally, it can become unwieldy to specify SPARQL queries as sets of triple patterns; furthermore, triple patterns are not expressive enough by themselves to satisfy many real-world needs, including quantification, ordering, and grouping. In contrast, those familiar with SQL will recognize that these are core elements of the language and of extended relational algebra. SPARQL allows these facilities as well by providing a SQL-like way of specifying expressive queries to be executed against RDF data sets. A simple, yet powerful, query that illustrates this expressiveness is shown in figure 12.1.

We explain the various elements of this query here:

1. PREFIX: This is used to declare a shorthand (the "prefix") for a Uniform Resource Locator (URL) namespace. When the prefix is used, it is as if the full URL was used in its place.

```
PREFIX      foaf: http://xmlns.com/foaf/0.1/
SELECT      ?person, ?homepage
FROM        http://example.org/dataset.rdf
WHERE       ?person a foaf:Person ;
            foaf:homepage ?homepage .
ORDER BY ?homepage DESC
LIMIT 5
```

Figure 12.1: A simple SPARQL query, the elements of which are described in the text.

2. SELECT: This is similar to the SELECT often found in SQL queries (i.e., in the example given here, we can imagine the query execution returning a "table" with two columns, one for the *Person* and the other for the *Homepage* binding). The variable names are mnemonic; if we wanted, we could have declared the variable *"?person"* to be *"?p"* (assuming we also changed it in the other lines of the query).

3. FROM: Again, just like SQL, it is used to specify the data set over which the query will be executed.

4. WHERE: Like SQL, this is the place where the conditions are imposed. In this case, the conditions are graph patterns. In the example here, the condition says that anything that binds to *"?person"* must have type *foaf:Person* (where *foaf:* has the shorthand as expressed in PREFIX), and also possess a homepage.

5. ORDER BY: If we imagine that the results are retrieved as a two-column table, this says that the rows of the table must be ordered by descending order of homepage (where "descending" intuitively would be interpreted by the system in the usual way that comparators are defined for that datatype).

6. LIMIT: The number of rows in the answers-table is limited (to 5, in this case).

While all of the querying facilities expressed by this example query were supported by SPARQL 1.0, SPARQL 1.1, adopted as a W3C recommendation in March 2013, allowed for significantly more expressiveness. Specifically, it allowed aggregate functions inspired by the relational database community, such as COUNT, "grouping" functions (e.g., GROUP BY), and "having" functions (e.g., HAVING).

SPARQL 1.1 also contains support for subqueries (nesting queries within queries), negation and filtering, property paths, new variable introduction, basic federated querying, and support for graph patterns inside FILTERs. New built-in aggregate expressions include AVG, COUNT, GROUP_CONCAT, MAX, MIN, SAMPLE, and SUM with their usual meanings. All are allowed with or without DISTINCT. As noted earlier, the grouping of results can be optionally done as well, while HAVING executes a filter expression over an aggregation result.

Of the aggregation expressions mentioned, AVG, MAX, MIN and SUM are fairly self-explanatory and typically applied to numeric sets of results. By way of example, consider the query fragment in figure 12.2 (not all details may be specified to make this query

```
SELECT     min(?lowprice)
WHERE      {
                 ?dealer :last_name "Marshall" .
                 ?dealer :trades_in ?product .
                 ?product :estimated_price ?price .
                 ?price :low ?lowprice .
                 ?product :manufactured ?date .
                 FILTER (?date < "2019-01-01"^^xsd:date) .
           }
```

Figure 12.2: A partial SPARQL query illustrating an aggregation.

syntactically valid; see the exercises at the end of this chapter). What we are trying to discover is the lowest possible price (the minimum of low prices) offered by a certain dealer for products (that the dealer deals in, because we did not specify the product type in the query) that were manufactured after January 1, 2019. Similar queries can be composed with the other aggregation operators, such as MAX, AVG, and SUM. In a similar vein, COUNT only counts the number of elements, but COUNT(*) can be used to count all results. SAMPLE returns any element, which is useful if we have reason to believe that there is only one result, or we only want one result regardless (and we don't care which one it is). GROUP_CONCAT concatenates all elements and can be used in conjunction with separator expressions such as ", ".

12.2.1 Subqueries

Subqueries are the preferred way to embed SPARQL queries within other queries, which usually is done to achieve results that cannot otherwise be achieved, such as limiting the number of results from some subexpression within the query. Due to the bottom-up nature of SPARQL query evaluation, the subqueries are evaluated logically first, and then the results are projected to the outer query. Note, however, that only variables projected out of the subquery will be visible, or in scope, to the outer query. By way of example, consider the following (small) KG, expressed pithily (several triples are on one line):

@prefix : <http://people.example/> .

:martha :name "Martha", "Martha Marshall", "M. Marshall" .

:martha :knows :bob, :alice .

:bob :name "Bob", "Bob Brioni", "B. Brioni" .

:alice :name "Alice", "Alice Ace", "A. Ace" .

Now consider the query in figure 12.3, using the same prefix nomenclature as before. The overall query is evaluated by first evaluating the inner query, which yields a single minName for each y; i.e., we are essentially picking a canonical name for every person resource. We use MAX to pick the name with the most number of characters, as that would usually be the full name. The final result is a set of names (representing the people

```
SELECT    ?y ?minName
WHERE     {
                :martha :knows ?y .
                {
                        SELECT ?y (MAX(?name) AS ?maxName)
                        WHERE  {
                                        ?y :name ?name .
                                }
                        GROUP BY ?y
                }
          }
```

Figure 12.3: An example of a SPARQL query with a subquery.

Martha knows), but each name identifies a unique individual. Not doing the GROUP BY would have yielded a misleading result (see the exercises).

12.3   Relational Processing of Queries over Knowledge Graphs

Even though SPARQL looks very different from SQL, there has been a broad body of work on using decades-long query optimization work in the SQL and relational database communities to inform efficient query processing of SPARQL. Yet, as noted before, RDF and KGs cannot naturally be represented as "tables," and it is also not clear how one could easily convert SPARQL to SQL. However, relational database management systems (RDBMSs) have repeatedly shown that they are very efficient, scalable, and successful in hosting types of data that have formerly not been anticipated to be stored inside relational databases. In addition, RDBMSs have shown their ability to handle vast amounts of data very efficiently using powerful indexing mechanisms. Over the years, *relational RDF stores* have been proposed and developed in the community so that practitioners may have the best of both worlds to the greatest extent possible (i.e., have the representational benefits of KGs while being able to leverage findings from the RDBMS community to execute fast queries over these KGs, in addition to drawing upon other RDBMS benefits). These stores tend to fall broadly into three categories:

1. **Triple (vertical) table stores:** In these stores, each RDF triple is stored directly in a three-column table (subject, predicate, object).
2. **Property (*n*-ary) table stores:** In these stores, multiple RDF properties are modeled as *n*-ary table columns for the same subject.
3. **Horizontal table stores:** In these stores, RDF triples are modeled as one horizontal table or into a set of vertically partitioned binary tables (one table for each RDF property).

By way of example, alternative representations of the same RDF data set are shown in figure 12.4. We briefly describe each of the stores next.

Subject	Predicate	Object
:m_kejriwal	:homepage	:kejriwal_homepage
:kejriwal_homepage	:label	"http://usc-isi-i2.github.io/kejriwal/"
:m_kejriwal	:position	"research assistant professor"
:m_kejriwal	:organization	:USC
:USC	:label	"University of Southern California"
:c_knoblock	:organization	:USC

Triple (Vertical) Store

Subject	:homepage	:label	:organization
:m_kejriwal	:kejriwal_homepage		:USC
:kejriwal_homepage		"http://usc-isi-i2.github.io/kejriwal/"	
:USC		"University of Southern California"	
:c_knoblock			:USC

Property Table Store

Subject	:homepage
:m_kejriwal	:kejriwal_homepage

Subject	:label
:kejriwal_homepage	"http://usc-isi-i2.github.io/kejriwal/"
:USC	"University of Southern California"

Subject	:organization
:m_kejriwal	:USC
:c_knoblock	:USC

Horizontal Store

Figure 12.4: Relational RDF store representations (for all three categories described in the text) for the same RDF data set.

12.3.1 Triple (Vertical) Stores

The triplestore (also called a *triple table*) approach is the most straightforward way in which RDF can be mapped into an RDBMS. Each RDF triple is basically stored in one large table with a three-column schema (for the subject, predicate, and object). Indexes are added to each of the columns to make joins less expensive.

Unfortunately, because the triples are stored in a *single* RDF table, queries can be slow to execute in the general case. Scalability can be a major issue as well, with the RDF table exceeding the main memory size as the data (i.e., the number of triples) starts increasing. While simple, statement-based queries can be satisfactorily processed by such stores, they do not represent the most important mechanism of querying RDF data. Indeed, complex queries with multiple triple patterns (requiring many self-joins over this single large table) do not scale well.

A good example of a triplestore is 3store, which is based on a central triple table holding the hashes for the subject, predicate, object, and graph identifier (equal to zero if the triple resides in the anonymous background graph). A symbols table is used for enabling reverse lookups from the hash to the hashed value to return results. Furthermore, 3store allows SQL operations to be performed on precomputed values in the datatypes of the columns without the use of casts. For evaluating SPARQL queries, the triples table is joined once for each triple in the graph pattern where variables are bound to their values when the slot in which the variable appears is encountered. Subsequent occurrences of variables in the graph pattern are used to constrain any appropriate joins with their initial binding. To produce the intermediate results table, the hashes of any SPARQL variables required to be returned in the results set are projected, and the hashes from the intermediate results table are joined to the symbols table to provide the textual representation of the results.

Other examples of triplestores (or resembling triplestores) include RDF Triple eXpress (RDF-3X), and Hexastore. RDF-3X is designed as an RDF query engine that tries to avoid the expensive self-joins mentioned here by creating an exhaustive set of indexes and relying on the fast processing of merge joins. Triples in RDF-3X are stored (and sorted lexicographically) in a compressed clustered B+ tree. An impressive feature is that the physical design of RDF-3X is workload-independent (i.e., the design eliminates the need for tuning by building indexes over all six permutations of the three dimensions constituting an RDF triple). RDF-3X supports both individual updates and entire batch updates, making it a flexible choice for desiderata.

Similarly, Hexastore also focuses on scalability and generality in its data storage, processing, and representation, and it is based on the idea of indexing the RDF data in a multi-indexing scheme. Hexastore does not distinguish among the three elements in a triple and treats subjects, properties, and objects in an RDF triple equally, with each element type having its own special index structures built around it. By virtue of this design, it needs six distinct indexes for indexing the RDF data (hence the name), with the indexes materializing all possible orders of precedence of the three RDF elements. A clear disadvantage of this design principle, however, is a five-fold increase in storage compared to traditional triples stores.

12.3.2   Property Table Stores

Due to the proliferations of self-joins involved with the triplestore, the property table approach has been proposed as an alternative relational RDF store. Property tables improve triplestores by allowing multiple triple patterns that reference the *same* subject to be retrieved without an expensive join. In this model, RDF tables are physically stored in a representation closer to traditional relational schemas in order to speed up queries compared to triplestores. Intuitively, each named table includes a subject and several fixed properties (as columns). Improvements are also possible. For example, a variant of the property table, named property-class table, uses the *rdf:type* of subject resources to group similar sets of resources together in the same table.

An excellent, well-known example of a property table store is Jena, an open-source toolkit for SW programmers. The schema of the first version of Jena consisted of a statement table, a literals table, and a resources table. The statement table *(Subject, Predicate, ObjectURI, ObjectLiteral)* contained all statements and referenced the resources and literals tables for subjects, predicates, and objects. To distinguish literal objects from resource URIs, two columns were used. The literals table contained all literal values, while the resources table contained all resource URIs in the graph. Note, however, that this design requires each query operation to execute multiple joins between the statement table, the literals table, or the resources table (in the general case).

The *Jena2 schema* attempted to address this issue by trading off space for time and using a *denormalized schema*, in which resource URIs and simple literal values are stored directly in the statement table. To distinguish database references from literals and URIs, column values are encoded with a prefix that indicates the type of the value. A separate literals table is only used to store literal values of which the length exceeds a certain threshold (e.g., blobs). Other design considerations similarly applied and were implemented, with the increase in database space consumption addressed by using string compression schemes. Both versions of the Jena schema described here permit multiple graphs to be stored in a single database instance, with Jena2 additionally supporting multiple statement tables in a single database to accommodate applications that need to flexibly map graphs to different tables. In this way, graphs that are often accessed together may be stored together, while graphs that are never accessed together may be stored separately.

Other examples of property tables include RDFMATCH, Sesame, RDFSuite, and 4store. Technically, RDFMATCH is an Oracle-based SQL table *function* that can be used to query RDF data. An advantage of this approach is that its results can be further processed by SQL's querying capabilities and easily combined with other queries on traditional RDBMS. For efficient querying, the function uses B-tree indexes, in addition to creating materialized join views for specialized subject-property. A special module is also provided to analyze the table of RDF triples and estimate the size of various materialized views, based on which users are able to define a subset of materialized views.

12.3.3   Horizontal Stores

Horizontal stores (also called *vertical partitioning*) represent yet another mechanism for relational representation and storage of RDF data. In this approach, the triples table is rewritten into *n* two-column tables, with *n* being the number of unique properties in the RDF graph. In each of these tables, the first column contains the subjects that define that property, and the second column contains the object values for those subjects. The subjects that do not define a particular property are simply omitted from the table for that property. Each table is sorted by subject, so that particular subjects can be located quickly, and thereby enable fast merge joins for reconstructing information about multiple properties for subsets of subjects. For a multivalued attribute, each distinct value is listed in a successive row in the table for that property. An advantage of the horizontal store is that, while property tables need to be carefully constructed so that they are wide enough (but not too wide) to independently answer queries, the algorithm for creating tables in the vertically partitioned approach is straightforward and does not need to change over time. Another advantage, especially over the property-class schema approach (where queries that do not restrict on class tend to have many union clauses), is that because all data for a particular property is located in the same table, union clauses in queries are far less common.

A good implementation of the horizontal store defined here is SW-Store (the first time that vertical partitioning was proposed), which relies on a column-oriented DBMS, C-store, to store tables as collections of columns rather than as collections of rows (as in standard row-oriented databases such as Oracle, DB2, and Postgres, where entire tuples are stored consecutively). Column-oriented databases address a key problem encountered with row-oriented databases (namely, that if only a few attributes are accessed per query, entire rows need to be read into memory from disk before the projection can occur). By storing data in columns rather than rows, the projection occurs for free only where those columns that are relevant to a query need to be read. However, some authors have argued that storing a sparse data set, as is often the case with RDF, in multiple tables can cause problems, and have instead suggested storing a sparse data set in a single table and leaving the complexities of sparse data management to an RDBMS (usually with the addition of an interpreted storage format). However, this is by no means the only solution to the problem.

It is also important to note that, just as with many of the other advanced techniques in this chapter, the book is not closed on vertical partitioning, and indeed a number of papers have tried to extend it. For example, roStore proposes an ontology-guided approach to extend horizontal stores, and it outperforms SW-Store when it is necessary to reason over property hierarchies. The intuition is to use semantic query rewriting rules to improve performance by reasoning over the ontology schema of the RDF triples by having a single table for each property hierarchy. Such tables have three columns, one for each element of an RDF triple, with the remaining tables following the pattern design of ordinary horizontal stores. This design has the consequence of reducing the number of tables for ontologies containing several property hierarchies, a common occurrence in domains like biology and medicine. By reducing the number of property tables, there is a huge impact on query performance where the query requires joins over properties of the same property hierarchy due to the maintenance and generation of fewer relations compared to ordinary horizontal stores like SW-Store.

This brief discussion of roStore illustrates a subtle point—namely, that some systems explicitly choose to optimize for certain query classes. The success of those systems is both domain- and community-specific (i.e., those systems optimizing for a query class that is important and that occurs often enough in real workloads have a greater chance of being cited and used than a system that is designed for more obscure query classes and domains). To the best of our knowledge, there is no one system (in any of the three relational types of stores) that is guaranteed to trump every other system on *every* query class, metric, or eventuality. In querying, trade-offs are necessary.

12.4   NoSQL

One of the key limitations (though not necessarily a disadvantage) of using triplestores and the SPARQL query language is the need to represent data in RDF (or RDF-like) format. In many cases, especially where URIs are not involved or where the data is noisy and not always adhering to a well-defined, or stable, schema, RDF is not the desired format. One option is to use a normal relational database, but these are not apt or efficient when data is missing or noisy. We could even argue that a primary motivation for building KGs in the first place was to overcome relational databases' strong and conservative constraints on the kinds of data that an RDBMS can effectively operate over.

Over the last decade, the burgeoning NoSQL movement has become very popular. As the name suggests, NoSQL is best expressed as both infrastructure and querying that do not conform to the traditional RDBMs that use SQL as the primary querying interface. In fact, NoSQL as a term was originally coined (in 1998, by Carlo Strozzi) for an RDBMS that did not utilize SQL as the querying interface. Today, however, the term has been appropriated, especially by big companies offering cloud and data management services (such as Amazon and Google) to represent alternative data stores that store and process huge amounts of data as they appear in their applications. Although not evident in the terminology, NoSQL has come to be closely associated, just like KGs themselves, with web and Big Data.

Even in the very early days, there were various reasons why people searched for alternative solutions beyond RDBMSs for storing, accessing, and querying data. The rich feature set and the Atomicity, Consistency, Isolation, and Durability (ACID) properties implemented by RDBMSs might be necessary for some applications and use-cases, but do not scale as well *horizontally* (e.g., using commodity hardware). For many applications, a one-size-fits-all scenario is also not always appropriate, as it is simply more expedient to build systems based on the nature of the application and its workload. RDBMSs can also be expensive and generally follow a license-driven revenue model. Thus, costs do not fade in the future.

NoSQL has emerged as a *customizable* solution with shared-nothing horizontal scaling that is usually considered to be a prerequisite requirement that must be met by infrastructures claiming to be truly NoSQL. By "shared-nothing," we mean the ability to replicate and partition data over many servers. This allows the infrastructure to support large numbers of simple read/write operations in unit time and meet application needs with high (often irregular) throughput. Important features of typical NoSQL solutions are noted in table 12.1.

12.4.1   Key-Value Stores

Perhaps because of their simplicity, key-value stores continue to rise in popularity in the NoSQL world. Simply put, a *key-value store* (or key-value database) is a simple database

Table 12.1: Important features of typical NoSQL solutions.

	Use-case	Strengths	Limitations
Key-value	Objects need to be accessed via a key or an attribute.	Extremely scalable, easy to partition, and has fast random access if keys can be stored in memory.	Limited expressiveness, as objects can be queried only using the key; furthermore, without knowing the key, a user cannot easily query the object.
Document	Data is easily structured as documents, and the structure of the data is evolving.	The data motel is rich enough to store complex, even irregular data, including arrays, nested structures, and dictionaries. Secondary indices allow fast access.	Expressive languages where the structure provides the semantics cannot be used easily (if at all) with such models. There is also a lack of standard application programming interfaces (APIs) and query domain-specific languages for such models.
Graph	Excellent for data with relational characteristics.	Linked data sets can be queried easily, and it is also easy to map entity-relationship abstract models to this data model.	Efficiency and partitioning can be a problem, especially for big graphs, due to the high volume of internode message passing. Similar to document models, there is limited support for standard APIs and/or domain-specific query languages.
Wide-column	Parallel (and batch-oriented) processing of big, typically aggregated data (such as in data warehouses).	Suitable for storing large quantities of data, as it can be efficiently partitioned by both rows and columns.	Very difficult to use if the schema or ontology is evolving, and arbitrary querying is supported to a limited extent due to design constraints.

that uses an associative array (such as a map or dictionary) as the fundamental data model where each key is associated with one (and only one) value in a collection. This relationship is referred to as a *key-value pair*. In each key-value pair, the key is represented by an arbitrary string (or other primitive or hashable datatype, in theory) such as a file name, URI, or hash. The value can be any kind of data, such as an image, user preference file, or document. The value is stored as a blob, requiring no upfront data model or schema definition.

The storage of the value as a blob removes the need to index the data to improve performance. In a naive implementation, therefore, one cannot filter or control what is returned in response to a request *based* on the value, because it is opaque. In general, key-value stores have no query language. They provide a way to store, retrieve, and update data using simple GET, PUT, and DELETE commands. The path to retrieve data is a direct request to the object in memory or on disk. The simplicity of this model makes a key-value store fast, easy to use, scalable, portable, and flexible. However, the lack of expressive querying can be a disadvantage to some applications.

Scalability can also be a major advantage of key-value stores, because they tend to *scale out* by implementing partitioning (storing data on more than one node), replication, and auto recovery. It can be easier for key-value databases to *scale up* by maintaining the database in memory and minimizing the effects of ACID guarantees (a guarantee that committed transactions persist somewhere) by avoiding locks, latches, and low-overhead server calls. There are natural limitations to these strategies, but a full discussion is beyond the scope of this chapter. For extreme scalability, a different set of solutions, such as Apache Cassandra (which is essentially an ultrascalable key-value store) or HBase, both of which we describe subsequently, should be preferred. In practice, most KGs are amenable to key-value stores, especially with the advent of large memories on server-class machines and the support of horizontal scaling by major cloud providers like Amazon Web Services. Key-value stores are also good for servicing tasks such as session management at high scale, providing product recommendations, storing user preferences and profiles, ad servicing, and working effectively as a cache for heavily accessed, but rarely updated, data.

12.4.1.1 JSON Many key-value stores principally rely on the JavaScript Object Notation (JSON) format for passing and retrieving data. JSON is a lightweight data-interchange format that is meant for human readability, while still being easy for machines to parse and generate. It is built on two structures:

1. *A collection of name/value pairs:* In various programming languages like C++, Java, and Python, this is realized as an object, record, struct, dictionary, hash table, keyed list, or associative array. An example would be the data structure { "name": "A. Einstein", "age": 29}. An important thing to note is *what* datatypes are allowed as keys and values. The full specification (and formal definition) can be found on the

official website,[1] but the most common formats are integers and strings. However, datatypes such as fractions and hexadecimals are also permitted. Most important, the "value" (e.g., 42 in the snippet given here) can itself be a JSON, which makes this a *recursive* data-interchange format that can be used to express deep nested structures, if necessary.

2. *An ordered list of values:* In most languages, this is realized as an array, vector, list, or sequence. For example, ["A. J. Bose", "M. Kejriwal"] would be a valid JSON. Again, the elements of the list can themselves be JSONs.

A key advantage of JSON, even beyond the fact that it is preferred by key-value NoSQL systems, is that it is also highly amenable to storage on, and retrieval from, disk using programming languages like Python, which have become exceedingly popular in an era of machine learning applications. JSON objects on file can be read as Python dictionaries using only a single line of code.

Two excellent examples of key-value NoSQL databases are MongoDB and Elasticsearch. The former is arguably the most popular NoSQL database at the time of writing (for a justification of this claim, see the section entitled "Bibliographic Notes," at the end of this chapter). Conceptually, MongoDB is much more than a key-value store, because it can support any schema-free collected of documents. It relies on Apache Lucene, which is a fairly sophisticated, Java-based indexing and search functionality—exposing technology that is required for accessing many of the information retrieval (IR) facilities that is central to the hybrid querying (i.e., using a combination of text and nontext attributes) of these NoSQL databases. Similarly, Elasticsearch is a distributed, RESTful search and analytics engine capable of solving a growing number of use-cases. It is often compared with MongoDB; however, unlike MongoDB, it advertises itself more as a search engine than a NoSQL database system because of the strong focus on exposing robust search capabilities. There are also documented cases where Elasticsearch has been used to store and query KGs. However, for practitioners familiar with key-value stores, it is not a burdensome matter to transition from one to the other, and both their querying mechanisms rely on an IR technology like Lucene.

MongoDB and Elasticsearch can serve also as "semistructured" search engines, like other key-value NoSQL engines, due to their support for speedy querying (using Lucene indices). We say "semistructured" because the search is not purely text or keyword based, and hence, a purely IR-methodology like single inverted index does not apply. In fact, multiple indices are required, depending on the schema of the underlying key-value store. There is no one way to combine scores across multiple indices into one composite score, and it's more art than science.

---

[1] https://www.json.org/json-en.html.

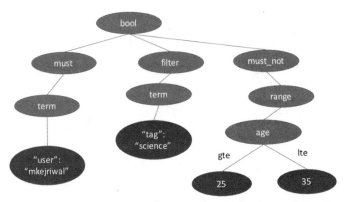

Figure 12.5: Illustrative (i.e., conceptual) example of Elasticsearch boolean tree query. Here, *gte* and *lte* stand for the symbols ≥ and ≤, respectively. The other leaf nodes are key-value pairs.

Because there has been much interest in the kind of semistructured or hybrid search that Elasticsearch exposes via its query DSL, we cover it in this section both as a model and an example (in use) of such kinds of search. An interesting functionality of the Elasticsearch query DSL is that it is used to expose the power of Lucene through a JSON interface, and it employs a combination of text and structured attributes. Intuitively, the Elasticsearch query DSL gets much of its power from using a recursive boolean-like representation that is both intuitive (can be drawn as a tree) and expressive. An illustrative example is provided in figure 12.5.

At the most basic level, the Elasticsearch query DSL uses JSON to define queries via two types of clauses. First, a leaf query clause looks for a particular value in a particular field by using query terms like *match, term,* and *range*. Second, compound query clauses wrap other leaf or compound queries and are used to combine multiple queries in a logical fashion (examples being the *bool* and *dis_max* queries) or to alter their behavior. Figure 12.5 illustrates such an example. Intuitively, the query first filters all documents such that there is a key called "tag" that has the value "science." This select set of documents is then evaluated in other ways (i.e., if the "user" key has value "mkejriwal" and the age of the user is between 25 and 35).

Queries in Elasticsearch can be executed in either a query context or a filter context. A query clause used in the query context is interpreted in an IR sense; namely, the query clause calculates a score (for each document) representing how well the document matches the query, relative to other documents. By sorting in decreasing order of nonzero scores, a ranked list of candidate documents is returned for each query. The results should be evaluated using IR metrics, some of which (e.g., MRR and NDCG) were detailed in chapter 11. In contrast, the filter context is much more coarse grained (yes/no) compared to the more nuanced query context. Formally, a filter context query returns an unranked set of documents, and it cannot be evaluated using metrics like NDCG. It is not uncommon to embed filters into query contexts to speed up processing and provide an obvious avenue for culling document candidates. Intuitively, a filter is like a constraint (e.g., imagine that we want to retrieve books that have "Information" in their title and "Metric" in their content, but we only want books that have been published after January 1, 2017). We could insert a filter clause in the query to that effect, similar to the "tag:science" filter in the query in figure 12.5.

The date constraint has been embedded in a filter context, because it is a hard constraint rather than a search criterion for influencing relevance scores, in contrast with the other two criteria. Note that it is important to interpret user intent correctly here in deciding what to place in a filter context. The filter context comes closest to behaving like a reasoner, even though it does not have the capabilities of Web Ontology Language (OWL) reasoners such as those available in Protégé and other such ontology management systems. The query context offers a mechanism for IR over semistructured key-value documents.

For interested readers, we provide a few pointers to Elasticsearch tools and tutorials in the section entitled "Software and Resources," at the end of this chapter. At this time, Elasticsearch has gained enormously in market share and has documented uses in a variety of companies and projects. For example, Wikipedia uses it to provide suggested text for full-text search, the *Guardian* uses it to give editors current feedback about public opinion on published media through social and visitor data, Stack Overflow uses it to complete full-text search, geolocation queries, and source-related questions and/or answers, and GitHub queries billions of lines of code using Elasticsearch. Similarly, MongoDB has its own large community of users, with some well-known organizations using it, including large companies such as Adobe, Cisco, eBay and AstraZeneca, as well as nontraditional technology users like the City of Chicago, which has built its real-time geospatial analytics platform on top of MongoDB.

12.4.2 Graph Databases

Since the emergence of database management systems, there has been an ongoing debate about what the database *model* for such systems should be. The discussions thus far make it clear that there is no single correct way of doing data modeling. A similar conclusion was reached in chapter 2, which presented multiple options for *representing* KGs and argued that there was no single correct way of achieving a representation that fulfills all desiderata.

The parameters influencing database model development are manifold, and among the most important influences are the characteristics or structure of the *domain* to be modeled, the capabilities of a user (both from the standpoint of querying and modeling), and their willingness to accept certain assumptions and constraints on software and infrastructure. In this context, *graph database models* can be loosely defined as models where data *structures* for the schema and instances are modeled as graphs (or generalizations thereof), and data *manipulation* is expressed by graph-oriented operations and type constructors. Graph database models used to be very popular in the 1980s and 1990s, along with models like object-oriented models, but were superseded at the time by other exotic models, such as geographical, spatial, and XML models.

With the advent of KGs, however, and other graphlike data sets on the web (including web and transportation, social, and biological networks), graph database models have enjoyed a resurgence while XML-like models have declined in popularity. However, we note that although KGs are a major application thrust, graph databases are not just KG-driven, but amenable to a wide range of graph-theoretic applications, such as large social networks. Just like the other NoSQL models and notions like key-value stores or hybrid search, little effort has been made to formally and explicitly define a graph database model. A rough definition was provided earlier in this discussion by deferring to the graphlike orientation of data structures and manipulation, both of which are core components of any database model and management system. Applications of graph database models tend to arise where data interconnectivity or topology is at least as important as the data itself. Clearly, KGs fulfill this desideratum.

Introducing graphs as a modeling tool offers some clear advantages for structured (but inherently nontabular) data. The single biggest advantage is that modeling is more natural because graphs have the advantage of being able to retain information about an entity in a single node and expose relational information via edges. However, a second advantage arises during querying, because (as we have seen with SPARQL), the body of research on graph-querying languages (as well as graph algorithms like shortest path) can be utilized compared to more ad-hoc data models. Put another way, by explicitly allowing such operations in querying, a suitable algebra (and querying DSL) designed for graph models allows users to express a query at a high level of abstraction, making querying natural as well. Last but not least, several influential implementations, such as Neo4j, have made graph databases more mainstream. Today, generic graph databases are more popular than SPARQL- or RDF-specific graph databases, such as the relational RDF stores described previously. However, there is also a lot of flux in database rankings (typically based on adoption) every year due to rapid advancements in both graph databases and the Semantic Web. We also note that these systems are not mutually exclusive; for instance, the Neo4j graph database can support the reading and writing of RDF data, and it is not very difficult (in practice) to translate SPARQL queries to the Cypher DSL supported within Neo4j.

The representation of entities and relations are identified as being fundamental to graph databases. We have covered many of these representational issues in chapter 2, but we review some of the critical elements here for the sake of completeness. Recall that an entity or object represents something that exists as a single and complete unit. A relation is a property or predicate that establishes a connection between two or more entities. As with KGs, relations in graph databases embody connectivity among entities.

Besides entities and relations, most modern graph databases support a variety of interesting artifacts that we summarize next.

12.4.2.1 Hypernodes and Hypergraphs Most modern graph databases support a kind of "nesting" through the use of *hypernodes* and *hypergraphs*. These metastructures are motivated by the fact that representing the database as a simple, flat graph (with many interconnected nodes) has the drawback of not being intuitively presentable to a user (or modeler). To address this challenge, a hypernode database is used, which consists of a set of nested graphs with intrinsic support for data abstraction and the ability to represent each real-world object as a separate database entity. Hypergraphs further extend this concept and are mathematically defined as a generalization of a graph, where an edge can join any number of vertices, rather than just two. This simple extension shows why such graphs can be powerful for modeling relational data, because each record or entity is, in many cases, more naturally thought of as a collection of properties (hyperedge), rather than a set of binary relations between the entity and each of its properties. In the RDF formalism, a hypergraph sometimes considered a conceptually more elegant way of representing n-ary data than mechanisms like reification.

12.4.2.2 Schema and Instance Graphs Unlike RDBMSs, the separation of schema and instance data is not as easy in graphs. An advantage of KGs is that, for most domains, this decomposition is easier than for generic graphs, because KGs tend to be extracted according to (and modeled on the basis of) a specified ontology. It is more difficult to maintain this distinction in domains like e-commerce and bioinformatics, as we describe in part V when we describe various KG ecosystems. A well-defined separation of schema and instance is a key advantage of RDBMs, where the schema is informally defined as a set of tables (and where each table itself is represented as a set of attributes with datatypes and other metadata). With the advent of object-oriented data models, more complexity is possible, but schemas are still distinct from instances. Just like with KGs, separation in graph databases can be maintained only if two types of graphs are defined: schema graphs and instance graphs. At minimum, a schema graph defines entity types represented as nodes labeled with a type name (alternatively referred to as "concept" or "class" throughout this book). However, similar to sophisticated domain ontologies, a schema graph may contain much more than just a flat set of concepts.

On the other hand, an instance graph contains concrete entities represented as nodes labeled by either an entity-type name or an object identifier; primitive values represented as nodes labeled with a value from the domain of a primitive entity; and relations represented as edges labeled with the corresponding relation-name according to the schema.

Just like with RDBMSs, this simple model has been expanded in multiple ways over the years, such as by including support for nodes for explicit representation of tuples and sets (*PaMaL, GDM*), n-ary relations (*GOAL,GDM*), hypernodes (*Hypernode model, Simatic-*

XT, and *GGL*), and hypergraphs (*GROOVY*)—extensions that provide support for nested structures, as discussed earlier. A novel use-case of hypergraphs in GROOVY is to use them for defining value-functional dependencies. Similarly, the hypernode model can use nested graphs at both the schema and instance level. A database consists of a set of hypernodes defining types and their respective instances. However, although hypernodes are used in several models, there are differences in usage. For example, while *Simatic-XT* and *GGL* use hypernodes as an abstraction mechanism consisting of packaging other graphs as an encapsulated vertex, the *Hypernode model* also uses hypernodes to represent other abstractions (e.g., complex objects and relations). In a similar vein, graph models based on simple and extended graph structures are also differentiated in their support for defining nontraditional datatypes. While *LDM, PaMaL, GOAL*, and *GDM* allow the representation of complex objects by defining special constructs (tuple, set, or association nodes), hypernodes and hypergraphs are arguably more powerful, because they are flexible data structures that support the representation of arbitrarily complex objects and present an inherent ability to encapsulate information.

Clearly, there is more research to be done in this area, though the proliferation of systems, tools, and capabilities noted here shows that graph databases are starting to converge in their approach to modeling and querying semistructured data. Next, we briefly note a few other features, followed by a popular graph database implementation (Neo4j) that has continued to gain in database adoption and market share and even has its own intuitive DSL for querying.

12.4.2.3 Integrity Constraints   Another important feature, borrowed from RDBMSs, is integrity constraints. Integrity constraints are general statements and rules defining the set of consistent database states or changes of state (or both). Previously, such constraints (in the context of KGs) were seen in the context of ontologies specified using languages like OWL. For example, one such important constraint was schema-instance consistency. For example, entity types and type checking constitute a powerful data-modeling and integrity checking tool, as they allow database schemas to be represented and enforced. However, checking consistency is also related to restructuring, queries, and updates of the database. In some cases, the problem can be undecidable (e.g., statistically checking consistency following an edge addition in an arbitrary graph object-oriented program). Another kind of integrity constraint is schema-instance separation (i.e., the degree to which schema and instance are different objects in the database). However, while in most models there is a separation between database *schema* and *instance*, many KGs may not necessarily have this separation. Another exception arises in some hypernode models, where the lack of typing constraints on hypernodes enables changes to the database to be dynamic (and makes the checking of this integrity constraint inapplicable). Yet another special kind of integrity constraint is data redundancy, but as we saw in chapter 8, on instance matching, this kind of constraint is much harder to enforce syntactically and requires advanced artificial intelligence (AI) solutions.

12.4.2.4 Example: Neo4j Neo4j is an open-source, NoSQL, native graph database that has been in development since 2003, but was only made publicly available starting in 2007. Just like other similar software in this space (motivated by for-profit enterprise needs, but without sacrificing the benefits of open-source, community-driven development), Neo4j has both a Community Edition and Enterprise Edition.

Neo4j relies primarily on the *property graph* model, where data is organized as nodes, relationships, and properties (data stored on the nodes or relationships). Nodes are the entities in the graph and can hold any number of attributes (key-value pairs) called *properties*. Nodes can be tagged with labels, representing their different roles in the domain. Node labels may also serve to attach metadata (including index or constraint information) to certain nodes. On the other hand, *relationships* provide directed, named, semantically relevant connections between two node entities. Relationships always have a direction and type; importantly, like nodes, relationships can have properties. This makes artifacts like reification much easier and more seamless in the property graph model and Neo4j than in traditional RDF settings. In practice, relationships tend to have quantitative properties, such as weights, costs, ratings, and time intervals. Due to the efficient way that relationships are stored, two nodes can share any number or type of relationship without sacrificing performance. Although they are stored in a specific direction, relationships can always be navigated efficiently in either direction.

Neo4j is referred to as a *native* graph database because it efficiently implements the property graph model down to the storage level. Other important features include *Cypher*, which is a declarative query language similar to SQL but optimized for graphs. The query language started out as being specific to Neo4j but has since been adapted by other databases like SAP HANA Graph and Redis (via the openCypher project); *drivers* for popular programming languages like Python and Java; and *ACID transaction compliance*, which makes it amenable for using in production scenarios. Next, we briefly describe the key features and syntax of the Cypher query language due to its importance and continuing adoption in industrial graph databases like the examples mentioned previously.

Cypher DSL. Although a machine language, Cypher was designed to also be human-readable, with constructs based on English prose. Nodes in Cypher take the form (x : *label*), where x is a variable and *label* is a node that typically represents the type of the variable. For example, if the variable was meant to denote a company, the label would be *Company*, which helps Neo4j determine how to group nodes together. Note, however, that labels do not necessarily have to be types; they can be another way of grouping nodes. It is highly recommended to declare labels for nodes, because Cypher uses such labels for filtering during query execution, similar to how SQL uses table names. Relationships in Cypher are represented by –> or <–, depending on the directionality. Additional properties

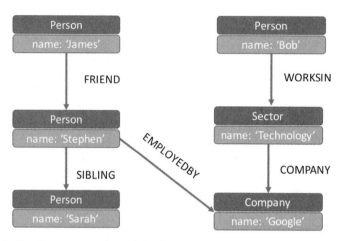

Figure 12.6: Graph representation of the Cypher snippet described in the text.

of the relationship, such as the relationship type, can be placed in square brackets inside the arrow. An example bringing these syntactic notions together, is illustrated here:

```
CREATE (bob:Person {name: "Bob"})
CREATE (james:Person {name: "James"})
CREATE (stephen:Person {name: "Stephen"})
CREATE (sarah:Person {name: "Sarah"})
CREATE (google:Company {name: "Google"})
CREATE (tech:Sector {name: "Technology"})
CREATE (bob)-[:WORKSIN]->(tech)-[:COMPANY]->(google)
CREATE (stephen)-[:EMPLOYEDBY]->(google)
CREATE (james)-[:FRIEND]->(stephen)-[:SIBLING]->(sarah)
```

A graph representation of the snippet here is illustrated in figure 12.6. Note that, because of edge or relationship directionality, a query such as "MATCH (p:Person)<-[:WORKSIN]-(tech:Sector)" will not yield results given the declarations here. However, a query that leaves the direction open can also be specified as "MATCH (p:Person)-[:WORKSIN]-(tech:Sector)," which would yield a positive match.

Just as we did with nodes, if we want to refer to a relationship later in a query, we can give it a variable like *[r]* or *[rel]*. We can also use longer, more expressive variable names like *[likes]* or *[knows]*. If we do not need to reference the relationship later, we can specify an anonymous relationship using two dashes −−, +−−>, or +<−−.[2] As an example, we could use either -[rel]-> or -[rel:LIKES]-> and call the *[rel]* variable later in a query to reference the relationship and its details. Note the difference between -[LIKES]-> and -[:LIKES]->; in the latter case, LIKES represents a variable and not a relationship type, which means that Cypher will end up searching all types of relationships when a query is issued.

Graphs declared using Cypher do not just support nodes, relationships, and labels. A last important feature to note here is *properties*. Note the important difference in nomenclature; while properties and relationships were considered synonymous in chapter 2 and other chapters of this book where we paid considerable attention to the RDF data model, they are different in Neo4j. In Neo4j, properties are name-value pairs that provide additional details to nodes and relationships. When applied to nodes, they are akin to datatype properties; however, when declaring properties for relationships in RDF, one has to rely on complex schemes like reification.

Properties in Cypher can be declared using curly braces. For example, a node property can be declared using a statement like $(p : Person\{name : "Mary"\})$, while a relationship property can be declared using a statement like $-[rel : WORKS\_FOR\{start\_date : 2017\}] \rightarrow$. Properties can have values with multiple datatypes; Cypher currently supports numbers (including integers and floats), strings, booleans, spatial types like *Point*, and temporal points like *Date* and *Time*.

While nodes and relationships make up the building blocks for graph patterns, these building blocks can be composed together to express simple or complex patterns. Patterns are the most powerful capability of Cypher graphs and can be written as a continuous path or separated into smaller patterns, tied together with commas.

An example pattern in Cypher is the statement "(:Mary)-[:LIKES]→(:Blockchain)." This pattern expresses the natural-language statement "Mary likes Blockchain." However, the statement, by itself, does not tell us whether we want to find this existing pattern in our current database or insert it in as a new pattern. To decide either way, we need to use qualifying keywords like MATCH and RETURN, similar to equivalent words in languages like SQL. MATCH searches for an existing node, relationship, label, property, or pattern in the database, and it is like SELECT in SQL. We saw some examples with MATCH earlier. In contrast, RETURN specifies what values or results we might want to return from a Cypher query (e.g., whether Cypher should return nodes, relationships, node and relationship properties, or patterns in the query results). Particularly, the node and relationship variables we discussed earlier become important when using RETURN. To bring back nodes, relationships, properties, or patterns, variables need to have been specified in a MATCH clause for the data we want retrieved.

---

[2] Of these, the first refers to an undirected relationship, while the last two are directed.

12.4.3 NoSQL Databases with Extreme Scalability

The NoSQL options covered so far in this chapter have demonstrable uses in KG applications, with Neo4j and Elasticsearch already employed in several such projects. In this section, we complete our treatment of NoSQL by covering two other systems, Cassandra and HBase, which are generally used across enterprises for their ability to handle extreme quantities of data. These databases are more a product of (and response to) the needs of Big Data rather than KGs per se. However, it is not unreasonable to suppose, as KGs become ever larger, especially in enterprise and medicine, that systems like these (or inspired thereof) will become more popular options for processing KGs. As such, any discussion on NoSQL would not be complete without a brief treatment of them. We also note that these two examples are, by no means, the only emblematic cases of Big Data NoSQL products, although they are among the two most popular products released under nonproprietary (in both cases, Apache) licenses. Brief notes on rival systems are provided in the "Bibliographic Notes" section.

12.4.3.1 Apache Cassandra   Apache Cassandra is a free (and open-source), distributed, wide-column store DBMS designed to handle large amounts of data across many commodity servers. Cassandra offers support for computing clusters spanning multiple data centers making it extremely scalable. Fundamentally, Cassandra was designed as a Big Data enterprise solution, with support for such features as *asynchronous masterless replication* (allowing low latency operations for all clients); *elasticity* (read and write throughput only increase linearly as new machines are added to the cluster, with no interruption or restart); and *fault tolerance* (with support for replication across data centers, and failed node replacement with no cluster downtime).

Fittingly, the origins of Cassandra were in enterprise as well (namely, Facebook), in response to a set of enterprise-specific needs (the Facebook inbox search feature). It was released as open-source on Google code in 2008, and in 2009 became an Apache Incubator. By 2010, it had graduated to a top-level project. Over time, multiple releases were engineered, with addition of more sophisticated features with each release. For example, the 2010 release added support for integrated caching and MapReduce, and a release in 2011 added the Cassandra Query Language (CQL).

An instance of Cassandra typically consists of only one table, which represents a distributed multidimensional map indexed by a key. The values in the table are addressed by a triplet *(row-key, column-key, time-stamp)*, where the *row-key* identifies rows by a string of arbitrary length, and a *column-key* identifies a column in a row and is further qualified (e.g., as part of a column family). A consistent hashing function, which preserves the order of row-keys, is used to partition and distribute data among the nodes. The order preservation property of the hash function is important to support range scans over the data of a table. Consistent hashing is also used by other similar Big Data NoSQL enterprise systems like

Amazon Dynamo; however, Cassandra handles it in a fundamentally different way from Dynamo.

The single biggest requirement that Cassandra fulfills, especially in enterprise applications, is that it is durable because the cluster as a whole keeps operating even in the face of multiple failures, including potentially catastrophic ones (such as when an entire data center loses power). Cassandra has no single points of failure and no network bottlenecks, as every node in a Cassandra cluster is identical. However, an arguably weaker feature of Cassandra is consistency.[3] Finally, Cassandra also offers support for Apache Pig and Hive, making it suitable for deployment in a Big Data ecosystem.

While we are not aware of documented cases in enterprise that use Cassandra for managing KG data, its wide-column properties, as well as support for timestamps and representation of tabular data as a multidimensional map indexed by a key, make it particularly amenable for KGs with subjects that have many properties and have associated timestamps or are otherwise streaming. For example, a KG capturing supply chain and logistics across a large company may need an architecture like Cassandra if availability and partition tolerance are important. As we start seeing KGs and Big Data intersect more in the future, such architectures are predicted to become more commonplace, and they may even inspire the birth of new architectures.

12.4.3.2 Apache HBase Apache HBase is a distributed, scalable, NoSQL, Big Data store that runs on a Hadoop cluster. At its core, HBase has the ability to host very large (web-scale) tables and provides real-time and random read/write access to Hadoop data by using a wide-column data store modeled after Google Bigtable, the database interface to the proprietary Google File System. In essence, HBase provides Bigtable-like capabilities on top of Hadoop-compatible file systems (e.g., MapR or HDFS) by borrowing Bigtable features like compression, in-memory operation, and bloom filters on a per-column basis.

As a NoSQL database, HBase is significantly differentiated from traditional RDBMs by being designed to scale across a cluster. Basically, HBase groups rows into regions that define how table data is split over multiple nodes in a cluster. If a region gets too large, it is automatically split to share the load across more servers. However, even though HBase is NOSQL, it still stores data in a tablelike format, with the ability to group columns into column families. Such groupings allow physical distribution of row values on various cluster nodes. Because of this design element, tables with billions of rows and millions of columns can be processed and stored by HBase. Furthermore, data stored in HBase does not need to fit into a rigid schema like with an RDBMS, making it ideal for storing unstructured or semistructured data.

---

[3] In fact, Cassandra is typically classified as an "availability and partition tolerance (AP)" system, because availability and partition tolerance are generally considered more important than consistency in Cassandra.

HBase is architected to have *strongly* consistent reads and writes, which makes it different from many other NoSQL databases, including Cassandra, that are only *eventually* consistent. Once a write has been performed, all read requests for that data will return the same value. HBase tables are also replicated for failover. These features make HBase amenable to a number of applications. For example, HBase is used in the medical field for storing genome sequences and running MapReduce on them. Other applications include e-commerce, sports, and web analytics. At the present time, Facebook is known to use HBase storage to store real-time messages, and Mozilla is using HBase to store all crash data. HBase has also been used by both Yahoo! and Twitter, the former for storing document fingerprints to detect near-duplications, and the latter for providing a distributed, read/write backup of transactional tables in its production backend. As another example, Infolinks uses HBases to process advertisement selection and user events, as well as to generate feedback for their production systems. It remains to be seen, however, whether any applications that strongly rely on KGs also use HBase. In general, the relational structure of KGs makes it more difficult to use a MapReduce-based system; however, as KGs in enterprise grow in size, and as quality and consistency requirements also become more demanding, HBase may be a preferred system for storing and processing such KGs, as it is one of the few popular NoSQL options offering strong consistency.

12.5   Concluding Notes

In this chapter, we provided a detailed overview of how to query KGs. The focus was on structured queries (i.e., sets of triple patterns) rather than natural-language questions that human beings are typically interested in asking, but that are far less precise or reliable for critical applications like business intelligence, bioinformatics, and logistics. Furthermore, KGs, being a combination of natural-language and structured data, are amenable to graph-theoretic querying architectures, and with some adjustments, such as query reformulation, such systems can access the KG in very robust and expressive ways. NoSQL has become a popular mode of access and storage in recent years, owing to deep support from enterprise, release under open-source Apache licenses (which has yielded a flourishing community), and the inability of ordinary RDBMSs to handle many of the challenges of so-called new age data like massive tables and heterogeneous graphs. Research in this area continues to expand, although winners and losers are already starting to emerge. We expect the future to see a deeper convergence between KG and graph-theoretic architectures, ordinary RDBMSs, and NoSQL systems that are predicated on being extremely scalable.

12.6   Software and Resources

We mentioned several systems in this chapter, many of which were inspired by, or are heavily used in, industry applications. Here, we provide a concise list of links to some of the main resources discussed in this chapter. On occasion, it may be that a link is either broken or has been superseded by a newer version; hence, it is wise to do a fresh search if using any of these in a production environment.

1. **SPARQL:** There are numerous tutorials on SPARQL on the web, but a good official resource for SPARQL is the W3C page: https://www.w3.org/TR/rdf-sparql-query/.

2. **Amazon Neptune:** We mentioned a number of RDF triplestores in the first part of the chapter. For a particular system, such as RDF-3X, a reimplementation may be necessary and readers should refer to the original source (see the "Bibliographic Notes" section for a summary of the material that we relied on when writing this chapter). However, Amazon Neptune offers services in the cloud for processing and querying RDF data. More details can be found at https://aws.amazon.com/blogs/aws/amazon-neptune-a-fully-managed-graph-database-service/.

3. **JSON:** The official website of JSON (https://www.json.org/json-en.html) provides both an introduction and a formal standard of the JSON format.

4. **Apache Cassandra:** The official website of Apache Cassandra (http://cassandra.apache.org/) provides many resources, including download links, a blog, supported features, and extensive documentation.

5. **Apache HBase:** Similar to the Cassandra website, the official HBase website (https://hbase.apache.org/) is also well documented and provides many resources, including download links, features, and news.

6. **Apache Hadoop:** Hadoop is one of the classic Big Data systems and has many resources devoted to it on the web. The official website is https://hadoop.apache.org/, but tutorials can be found in several other websites, including https://www.bmc.com/blogs/hadoop-introduction/ and https://www.edureka.co/blog/hadoop-tutorial/.

7. **MongoDB:** The official MongoDB website (https://www.mongodb.com/) provides many pointers, including documentation and download links, to setting up and using MongoDB.

8. **Elasticsearch:** The official website of Elasticsearch (https://www.elastic.co/) is similar to that for MongoDB, and contains all the resources and pointers that users are likely to need to download, and get started with, a free version. Elasticsearch events and conferences are also actively promoted on the website, some of which (e.g., ElasticON) are global affairs that attract heavy participation from the Elasticsearch developer community.

9. **Neo4j:** The official Neo4j website (https://neo4j.com/) provides much of the information that is needed to download the system and get started, including free Ebooks, download links, and a "Neo4j Sandbox" that enables interested users to use Neo4j without downloading it first.

Note that , while many of these services are available in the cloud, we only cited Amazon Neptune as an example of this. Furthermore, one is not restricted to Amazon for accessing these services on the cloud; other providers include Microsoft Azure (https: //azure.microsoft.com/en-us/) and Google Cloud (https://cloud.google.com/). For learning more about SPARQL queries and trying some exercises to gain more proficiency in SPARQL, we recommend the website https://www.w3.org/2009/Talks/0615-qbe/.

12.7   Bibliographic Notes

A large part of this chapter was devoted to SPARQL. There are many resources and references for SPARQL, an important one of which is the W3C recommendation (https: //www.w3.org/TR/rdf-sparql-query/), mentioned in the previous section. Because the document can be superseded by other recommendations, it is always a good idea, however, to do a fresh search, especially in the W3C technical reports index, available at http: //www.w3.org/TR/.

Academic references to SPARQL are numerous. A relational algebra for SPARQL was provided by Cyganiak (2005), and the semantics and complexity were studied by Pérez et al. (2006). Other important references, including benchmarks, include Barbieri et al. (2009), Bizer and Schultz (2009), Sirin and Parsia (2007), Quilitz and Leser (2008), Schmidt et al. (2009), and Huang et al. (2011). Some of the studies, such as Huang et al. (2011), are specifically focused on scalability. The material on relational processing of RDF stores, especially vertical and horizontal stores, in this chapter is largely based on the synthesis by Sakr and Al-Naymat (2010). It has been cited by many newer papers since; for instance, see Sun et al. (2015), Abdelaziz et al. (2017), and Schätzle et al. (2016). It is worthwhile to note that, while XML is not as popular as it once was, some recent papers have been published on XML querying as well. A relatively recent survey on structural XML query processing is Bača et al. (2017).

The NoSQL movement in non-SW communities has been gaining steam since it achieved mainstream adoption about a decade ago. Some good syntheses of NoSQL may be found by Hecht and Jablonski (2011), Strauch and Kriha (2011), Leavitt (2010), Cattell (2011), and Han et al. (2011). These surveys are dated, however; for a much more recent treatment, see Davoudian et al. (2018). Graph databases have been surveyed by Angles and Gutierrez (2008), and much of the established material on graph databases in this chapter was based on that. More recent work by Reutter et al. (2017) includes executing regular queries on graph databases; Heidari et al. (2018), on scalable graph processing frameworks; Angles et al. (2016), on foundations of modern graph query languages [an alternative citation is Angles et al. (2017)]; and modern work on graph querying and big graph data by Angles et al. (2018) and Junghanns et al. (2017), respectively. Good references on Cypher, which we used as an example in the chapter, and on Neo4j generally, are Francis et al. (2018) and Miller (2013).

Cassandra and HBase, described as NoSQL databases for extremely scalable situations, are further detailed by Cassandra (2014), Lakshman and Malik (2010), Vora (2011), George (2011), and Khetrapal and Ganesh (2006). A definitive guide on Cassandra was provided by Hewitt (2010). Some of these sources are more industry-oriented and applied than academic in discourse. To understand how RDF stores based on HBase and MapReduce could be realized, Sun and Jin (2010) is a good starting point.

We also commented in this chapter on the relative popularity of document-based NoSQL stores like MongoDB and Elasticsearch. Not many academic studies measuring popularity exist, but the latest rankings can be obtained from some reputable sources on the web that industry often looks to, including db-engines (https://db-engines.com/en/ranking) and scalegrid.io (scalegrid.io). According to the most recent data, MongoDB ranks highly, right after traditional SQL RDBMSs like Oracle and MySQL. There have been some papers comparing databases like MongoDB to both traditional database systems (like Oracle) and NoSQL databases like Cassandra. We refer interested readers to Győrödi et al. (2015), Abramova and Bernardino (2013), Parker et al. (2013), and Boicea et al. (2012) on the subject. Generally good sources to learn about MongoDB and Elasticsearch, other than the official web documentation and tutorials, are Chodorow (2013), Banker (2011), Gormley and Tong (2015), Paro (2015), and Kuc and Rogozinski (2013).

12.8   Exercises

1. (a) Consider again the query and small KG in the "Subqueries" section. What would the set of results be if instead the executed query was the one shown here?

```
SELECT    ?y ?minName
WHERE    {
                    :martha :knows ?y .
                    ?y :name ?name .
            }
```

   (b) What's misleading about the set of results that are obtained now?
2. Would the statement *:q rdfs:domain :d* AND *:x :q :y* imply *:x rdf:type :d*?
3. Complete the SPARQL query shown on the next page (by filling in the blanks). The query retrieves the URIs of actors who have starred in more than 10 movies, and the number of movies they have starred in. Your query should also retrieve the actor's name, if it exists in the graph.
4. Would the statement *:w rdfs:subPropertyOf :p* AND *:a :p :b* imply *:a :w :b*?

Here's the schema of the graph:

* In addition to the classes and properties shown above, you are allowed to use the property `rdf:type`.

```
PREFIX rdf: <http://www.w3.org/1999/02/22-rdf-syntax-ns#>
PREFIX rdfs: <http://www.w3.org/2000/01/rdf-schema#>
PREFIX movie: <http://data.linkedmdb.org/resource/movie/>

SELECT _____ ?name  (COUNT(?film) as ?n_film)

WHERE {

     ?actor _____ movie:actor ;

          movie:performance _____ .

     ?film rdf:type _____ ;

     _____ ?performance .

     OPTIONAL { ?actor _____ _____ }

}
GROUP BY _____

HAVING    (_____ > 10 )
```

5. Translate the two OWL axioms shown here to English.

∃occupation.Student ⊓ Woman:

_____

_____

BrokeStudent ≡ Student ⊓ ∃study.PrivateUniversity:

_____

_____

6. Is the query in figure 12.2 a valid SPARQL query? If not, make a small set of changes (using assumptions where appropriate) to make it a potentially valid query.

7. Consider the data shown next for both (a) and (b).

OWL axioms:

```
HardWorkingStudent ⊓ LazyStudent ⊑ ⊥
∃hasGoodGrades.T       ⊑ HardWorkingStudent
HardWorkingStudent ≡ Student ⊓ ∀friend.HardWorkingStudent
```

Assertions in a KB:

```
1. John:                    LazyStudent
2. <John,  INF-558>:        hasGoodGrades
3. <Peter, INF-552>:        hasGoodGrades
4. <Peter, John>:           friend
```

(a) Assuming that *John* is a *LazyStudent*, what is the *minimal* set of assertions you need to remove to make the knowledge base (KB) consistent?

(b) Assuming that *Peter* is a *HardWorkingStudent*, what is the *minimal* set of assertions you need to remove to make the KB consistent?

13 Question Answering

Overview. Querying and information retrieval (IR) are both excellent ways of accessing a knowledge graph (KG), but human beings often desire a more intuitive means of access, without necessarily sacrificing expressiveness (e.g., by limiting oneself to just keyword queries). Motivated by this need, question answering (QA), where the questions are posed in English or some other natural language, has emerged as a popular way of accessing the KG. However, as an application, QA has an importance beyond KGs, as it is necessary for the proper functioning of chatbots, personal assistants, and other artificial intelligence (AI) applications inspired by advances in Natural Language Processing (NLP). Historically, KGs have been instrumental in helping QA systems achieve state-of-the-art performance, although the dependence of the best QA systems on KGs have diminished in the last three years due to the advent of sophisticated language models. Nevertheless, KGs continue to be influential in designing good solutions for general-purpose (or even domain-specific QA). Thus, when discussing QA in the context of KGs, two agendas arise: using KGs to support good QA performance and using QA to support easy access to KGs. These two agendas are more complementary than initial appearances suggest, despite their very different goals. In this chapter, we provide an overview of QA first from the perspective of using (or not using) KGs to deliver good QA performance, and then by the use of QA to support intuitive KG access.

13.1 Introduction

QA is a specialized area in the field of IR, primarily concerned with providing relevant answers in response to questions proposed in *natural language*. Questions posed by users can be factoid questions, such as "Who is the current president of the United States?" but more recently, more complex types of questions that require aggregation or even more sophisticated and spontaneous inference have also become important.

QA can rightfully be considered as an evolution in the IR landscape, which historically has just been about document retrieval (namely, as discussed before, a search engine in this vein takes some keywords as input and returns the relevant ranked documents that contain these keywords, whether explicitly or in some semantic sense determined by using techniques like word embeddings). Certainly, these traditional IR systems do not return answers, and accordingly users are left to extract answers from the documents themselves.

However, an answer to a question is precisely what users are often looking for. Hence, the main objective of all QA systems is to retrieve answers to questions rather than full documents or best matching passages, as most IR systems currently do.

QA has been considered as an important research problem for at least two decades, as is evidenced by the Text Retrieval Conference[1] (TREC) initiating a QA track back in 1999, which tested systems' ability to retrieve short text snippets in response to factoid questions. Following TREC's success, the workshops of both Cross-Language Evaluation Forum (CLEF) and NII Test Collection for IR Systems (NTCIR) started multilingual and cross-lingual QA tracks focusing on European and Asian languages, respectively. Generally, QA systems are classified as open-domain or closed-domain. Open-domain QA is far more challenging, as it could consider questions across any category and can rely only on a universal ontology and public information on the web. Crowdsourced, encyclopedic knowledge sources like Wikipedia and DBpedia are thus central to the performance of such systems. On the other hand, closed-domain QA deals with questions from a specific domain (e.g., music, weather forecasting) Such a domain-specific QA system usually involves heavy use of NLP subsystems and also benefits from the modeling, construction, and use of a domain-specific ontology and knowledge base (KB).

In this chapter, we will be considering two agendas and set of perspectives around the problem of QA. The first agenda is not primarily concerned with QA itself, but with providing a more intuitive (for humans) means of accessing the KG, which may itself be supporting other applications such as structured analytics, business intelligence, or recommendation. As observed in previous chapters, expressive querying is not an easy skill for nontechnical subject matter experts to pick up (perhaps not the best use of their time). Key value–based systems, as well as NoSQL (or even just vanilla keyword-based IR), may help but lose expressiveness in the process. What actual users would like, in the most ideal situation, is to simply tell the system in *natural language* what they would like to know. Taken this way, QA is just another way of querying the KG.

The second agenda treats QA as the main application to be solved and is inspired by the web community and the historically challenging enterprise of open-domain QA, which has become much more applicable and relevant due to release of open data sets, the power of search engines, including semantic search capabilities such as the Google Knowledge Graph (GKG), and the rising influence of digital assistants such as Siri and Alexa. The second agenda is not concerned with *how* questions are answered, so long as they can be answered correctly. Technically, KGs are not necessary for the second agenda, although they were considered necessary for the best solutions until quite recently. With the advent of more sophisticated language models and representation learning, the need for KGs to yield good performance on QA tasks has become less apparent, although the matter is

---

[1] https://trec.nist.gov/.

not considered closed. In this chapter, we focus much more on the first agenda than the second, because the goal of this entire section is to describe ways to access the KG, which has many documented applications and use-cases beyond QA. However, because the two agendas share many common strands, especially in the way that they have evolved in the research literature, we spend some time in the next section describing how KGs have been used in some influential QA systems, as well as how they have been superseded more recently by neurally trained language models. With this background in place, we then turn our attention to QA as a means of accessing the KG itself (a problem more broadly known as *semantic question answering* or, SQA), on which much research has been conducted in the Semantic Web (SW) community in particular.

13.2 Question Answering as a Stand-Alone Application

We just noted that, in the context of KGs, the applicability of QA arises in two senses. The first is simply as a means of accessing the KG, while the second is concerned with QA as a *stand-alone application*, regardless of whether a KG is even used for it. This second agenda, which we briefly describe in this section through the lens of both an early (though still quite recent) and state-of-the-art system, was originally very important for KG research. The reason was that KGs were believed to be useful for achieving state-of-the-art results on open QA, and even for domain-specific QA. It was widely believed that the best performance could be achieved only if an appropriate KG of entities and relationships could first be constructed over the domain-specific corpus.

13.2.1 Learning from Conversational Dialogue: KnowBot

Because the primary use-case of QA systems has been in natural-language dialogue settings in which the system is interacting with users (often in a domain-specific scenario such as a chatbot encountered on a specific company's website), an interesting possibility is to build a QA system that can learn about its domain from conversational dialogue and leverage KGs to yield good performance. In 2015, a system called KnowBot was presented with precisely this goal in mind. KnowBot learned to relate concepts in science questions to propositions in a fact corpus, store new concepts and relations in a KG, and use the KG to solve questions. An impressive contribution of KnowBot was that it was the first system that acquired knowledge for QA from open, natural-language dialogue without a fixed ontology or domain model that predetermined what users could say.

   More specifically, KnowBot grows a KG of commonsense semantic relations in open, conversational dialogue, and uses task progress to drive natural-language understanding. It assumes that the user intends to provide one or more novel relations and uses constraints to disambiguate noisy relations. Because KnowBot is an open-domain dialogue system, it is different from relation extraction (RE) systems that rely on predetermined ontologies to determine valid relation types and arguments, such as Never-Ending Language Learning

(NELL). KnowBot is able to quickly bootstrap domain knowledge from users via dialogue-driven extraction, thereby producing effective relations without annotation or significant engineering effort. It also improves with each interaction, acquiring relations that are especially useful in the context of a particular task, and is able to embed these relations in a an enriched dialogue context.

For example, KnowBot was tested on a science data set (called SciText) that is a corpus of unlabeled, true-false, natural-language sentences derived from science textbooks, study guides, and even Wikipedia Science. The QA task itself consisted of 107 science questions from the fourth-grade New York Regents Exam. While each question has four possible answers, the authors converted each of the four QA pairs into a true-false QA statement using pattern-based rules. The degree to which a SciText sentence supports a QA pair is the sentence's *alignment score*.

While the alignment score depends on keyword overlap, SciText needs domain knowledge to answer the questions. KnowBot conducts dialogue about science questions and learns how concepts in each question relate to propositions in SciText. KnowBot presents users with a question, prompts them to choose and explain their answer, and extracts relations (and puts extracted relations in the KG) in order to increase its confidence in the user's answer.

Concepts are the nodes in KnowBot's KG, but KnowBot concepts are defined a little differently than the ontological concepts we saw earlier. In KnowBot, a *concept keyword* is any nonstopword of at least three characters, and a *concept* is a set of concept keywords with a common root (e.g., {presiding, presided, presides}). The Porter algorithm is used for stemming. If the concept is acquired from a QA statement, it is called a *question concept*, while *support concepts* are acquired from SciText support sentences. As with other KGs, relations connect pairs of concepts and represent semantic correspondence.

KnowBot builds KGs at three levels: per utterance, per dialogue, and globally (i.e., over all dialogue). An utterance-level KG (uKG) is a fully connected graph with nodes comprising all the concepts in an utterance. Because this likely contains much irrelevant correspondence, aggressive pruning is used to remove many edges, with remaining edges updating a dialogue-level KG (dKG). Pruning obeys two simple constraints: an edge can only relate a question concept to a support concept (alignment constraint), and edges cannot relate concepts whose keywords are adjacent in the utterance (adjacency constraint). Upon dialogue termination, the dKG updates the global KG (gKG), which stores relations acquired from all dialogue.

There are many technical details behind KnowBot that we do not cover here. However, the important points to remember is that each dialogue focuses on a single question, and after each user turn, the system, after each user turn (in the dialogue) updates the dKG and rescores each of the four candidate answers using an alignment score formula (based on overlapping concepts between the QA statement and the supporting SciText sentence, as well as the number of relations between the two sentences). The dialogue terminates once the user's answer has the highest alignment score, implying that the user has successfully provided the missing knowledge required for answering the question.

At the same time, the gKG, which includes relations learned from every KnowBot dialogue, results in redundancy that is used by KnowBot (based on the intuition that relations that recur across dialogue are more likely to be relevant to the original problem) to improve performance. For example, it ignores singleton relations yielded by a lone user utterance.

Hixon et al. (2015) did extensive evaluation of dialogue strategies (e.g., are users able to successfully complete the complex dialogue task in the absence of trained semantic parsers for natural-language understanding?) and used baselines such as interactive query expansion (IQE), which was the most reasonable competitive system when KnowBot was proposed. Metrics such as task completion (the proportion of dialogue that ends in agreement) were used, as well as dialogue length and acquisition rate (of the number of edges in the dKG at the end of each dialogue). With its best strategies, KnowBot was able to achieve more than 50 percent task completion, compared to less than 6 percent IQE. It marked an impressive shift for open-domain QA.

13.2.2 Bidirectional Encoder Representations from Transformers

Bidirectional Encoder Representations from Transformers (BERT) is a recently proposed language representation model proposed by researchers into Google's AI language model. BERT, as well as its successor, RoBERTa, have proved particularly successful at QA (although BERT can also be used for other tasks, such as language inference, without substantial, task-specific architecture modifications), although they do not have a strong KG dependence. Because it is considered as being on the frontiers of QA research, if not state-of-the-art (because its successor now does better on the benchmarks), we describe it in some detail next.

To motivate BERT, we already noted in previous chapters how learning representations of words has been an active area of research for decades. Many of the classic techniques were nonneural, but more recently, neural methods like GLoVE, skip-gram, and continuous bag of word (CBOW) models have proved dominant. Regardless of which representation is the best one, the fact remains that pretrained word embeddings are an integral part of modern NLP architectures, and often offer substantial improvements over embeddings created from scratch. Furthermore, neural representation learning has since been extended to address data units of coarser granularity, including sentences, paragraphs, and (as we saw in chapter 10) nodes and edges in KGs. At the same time, word representation learning itself has undergone significant improvements (work on this did not stop with word2vec or GloVE, despite the immense popularity of these approaches). ELMo, for example, was presented in 2018 by researchers from the Allen Institute for Artificial Intelligence and the University of Washington, and it was a new type of deep contextualized word representation that models complex characteristics of word use, as well as how these uses vary across linguistic contexts. When published, ELMo advanced the state-of-the-art for several NLP tasks including QA, but BERT was able to advance it even further.[2]

BERT primarily relies on two steps: pretraining and fine-tuning. Pretraining is important in BERT because it marked a shift from previous models, such as those that used left-to-right or right-to-left language models to pretrain their systems. BERT instead uses two unsupervised tasks for pretraining. First, it uses a task called *masked language model* (traditionally known as the *Cloze* task, dating to the 1950s), wherein some percentage (in the paper, 15 percent of WordPiece tokens) of the input tokens are selected at random and masked, followed by the training of a deep bidirectional representation by trying to predict the masked tokens. Specifically, the hidden vectors corresponding to the masked tokens are fed into the output softmax layer (over the vocabulary), as with traditional language models. More details on this task, including the steps taken to address noise or robustness issues, are described in the original BERT paper by Devlin et al. (2018), which is also described in the section entitled "Bibliographic Notes," at the end of this chapter. The second unsupervised task used for pretraining is *next sentence prediction* (NSP). NSP is important because it helps BERT perform extremely well on downstream applications such as QA and natural-language inference, both of which are based, not just on the goodness of a language model, but on understanding the relationship between two sentences (that not directly captured by a language model). Once again, to ensure that results are robust and the model can be trained to deliver meaningful results, the authors make some important design decisions. For example, when choosing the sentences A and B for each pretraining example, the authors label B as the next sentence 50 percent of the time, while a random sentence from the corpus is used the other 50 percent. Finally, note that the data that was used for the pretraining was the BooksCorpus, which contains 800 million words, and the English Wikipedia (ignoring lists, tables, and headers). Because of the second NSP pretraining task, a corpus such as the Billion Word Benchmark could not be used because it contains sentences in a shuffled order.

Fine-tuning (which is task specific and depends on who, or for what application, BERT is being used for) is the next important component, but it is relatively straightforward, as a self-attention mechanism in the transformer allows BERT to model most downstream tasks of choice, whether the task involves a single piece of text or text pairs. The idea is to send in the task-specific inputs and outputs into the architecture and fine-tune all the parameters of the model in an end-to-end fashion. Examples of inputs (assuming two sentences S_1 and S_2), are paraphrased sentence pairs, hypothesis-premise (entailment task), and question-passage (for QA). For token-level tasks (e.g., sequence tagging, QA), the token representations of the inputs are fed into the output layer, while for classification tasks such as entailment or sentiment analysis, the representation for the special (CLS) token

---

[2] At the time of its release, BERT advanced the state-of-the-art for 11 NLP tasks.

(i.e., a *classification* token that is always the first token of every sequence and is meant for precisely this purpose) is fed into the output layer. Fine-tuning is much less expensive than pretraining.

Concerning experimental success, on the Stanford Question Answering Dataset (SQuAD v1.1), which is a collection of 100,000 crowdsourced Q/A pairs, BERT was able to outperform the top leaderboard system by 1.5 points on the F1-score when used in an ensemble, and 1.3 points as a single system. With SQuAD 2.0, which extended the 1.1 version by allowing for the null possibility that no short answer exists in the provided paragraph, there was a 5.1 percent F1-score improvement over the next best system. It also brought BERT to within 6.4 percent of human-level performance on the task.

However, as we mentioned previously, the results were far more impressive than just outperforming the leaderboard winner (at the time) on this one task, as the authors of BERT showed that it could achieve state-of-the-art performance on 11 NLP tasks. Another example of this is when BERT was evaluated on the General Language Understanding Evaluation (GLUE), which comprises diverse natural-language understanding tasks. BERT was fine-tuned on GLUE, and the best BERT model was found to outperform the next best non-BERT system (OpenAI GPT[3]) on GLUE by more than 7 percent (on average, across all the diverse tasks included in GLUE). On the task that GLUE is best known for, Multi-Genre Natural Language Inference (MNLI), there is a 4.6 percent absolute accuracy improvement. On the official leaderboard (which does not make the test set available), there was more than 7 percent difference between the two systems at this time, further validating BERT's superior performance on this benchmark. On another sentence-pair completion benchmark called Situations with Adversarial Generations (SWAG; the task in SWAG is, given a sentence, to choose the most plausible *continuation* among four sentence choices provided to the system), BERT was able to outperform OpenAI GPT by 8.3 percent accuracy and even outperform an expert human (with human performance measured with 100 samples) by about 1.3 percent. This result, while impressive on the surface, exposes a worrisome factor about many of these evaluations that has also been raised with other such tests (including those that rely on some variant of the Turing test). That the evaluation would suggest that either the natural-language understanding problem has been solved by machines (which defies what we actually observe when these systems are deployed in real-world settings, or asked to answer questions that ordinary humans would find simple but that models like BERT can still be tricked by), or that the benchmark is missing some critical element (or is subject to some kind of bias) begs the question as to whether it is *truly* measuring open-domain QA in its full scope. Because of the recency of BERT, we have not seen too much evidence of these benchmark (or evaluation) limitations by way of rigorous and replicable research, but a smattering of papers studying such issues have been slowly

---

[3] Generative Pre-trained Transformer.

Table 13.1: Comparative overview of post-BERT models, including RoBERTa.

System	Performance	Data
BERT (bidirectional transformer with MLM and NSP)	Outperforms state-of-the-art in 2018	16 GB of BERT data (BooksCorpus + Wikipedia); 3.3 billion words
RoBERTa (BERT without NSP)	2–20% improvement over BERT	160 GB of (16 GB BERT data + 144 GB as well)
DistilBERT	3% degradation from BERT	16 GB of BERT data
XLNET	2–15% improvement over BERT	Base model used 16 GB of BERT data, while the large model used 113 GB (16 GB of BERT data + 97 GB as well); about 33 billion words

emerging. We anticipate that "diagnosing" such language models and benchmarks (and discussing the full scope of their strengths and weaknesses) will itself become a hotbed of research by the time this book is published.

13.2.2.1 Subsequent Advancements Although BERT is quite recent, and its integration into the Google search engine was only announced in 2019, successors purporting to improve its performance even further have already started percolating into the research community. RoBERTa is a good example of a recently proposed successor. In studying the original BERT system, Liu et al. (2019) found that it was significantly undertrained and could match or exceed the performance of every model published after it. They propose an improved recipe for training BERT models (called RoBERTa), which matches or exceeds the performance of all post-BERT published methods. The modifications were reported to be simple, including longer training times with bigger batches, and over more data, removing the next sentence prediction objective, training on longer sequences, and dynamically changing the masking pattern applied to training data. The authors also collected and presented a new (and larger) data set of comparable size to other privately used data sets in order to better control for the effects of training set size.

On both GLUE and SQuAD, the modifications lead to significant performance improvements, including a score of 88.5 on GLUE (matching the 88.4 reported by another recent work in 2019) and matching state-of-the-art results on SQuAD and RACE. The best models in all of these cases were post-BERT and were somewhat different in their architectural choices. The implication for a while was that BERT's design or foundational elements may not be the best after all in the race to achieve ever-increasing performance on QA tasks. RoBERTA's results, however, seem to reinforce that with simple modifications in the training procedure, the fundamentals of BERT still make it reign supreme over (or at least equal to) these other more complex, post-BERT models. It also highlights the importance of training and design choices that can get overlooked when designing or training a new architecture. For the sake of illustration, we provide an overview of RoBERTa and some other post-BERT models (in comparison to the original BERT-large model) in table 13.1 in terms of data and performance.

13.2.3 Necessity of Knowledge Graphs

While systems like KnowBot depended on building and growing a KG to support open-domain QA, BERT showed that it may be possible to acquire knowledge and answer questions without relying on either growing or using an explicit KG. More recently, there has been some evidence that language models could be used as a substitute for a KG, as the model itself seems to be capturing some of the knowledge that was traditionally thought to be the necessary domain of KGs. In one recent paper out of Facebook AI Research and University College London, for example, Lewis et al. (2019) showed that in addition to learning linguistic knowledge, language models like BERT (that have been trained using recent advanced neural methods and practices) can answer queries that rely on relational knowledge. The authors argue that language models have many advantages over structured KBs in that they require no schema engineering, allow practitioners to query about open classes of relations (recall that Open IE had been a difficult problem to solve; if valid, the use of language models may preclude practitioners having to build KGs using Open IE techniques for answering questions), and are easy to extend or retrain as more data becomes available because they are unsupervised, in that human labeling is not required. An impressive aspect of the authors' work is that they do a rigorous comparison, using a language model analysis probe, to answer interesting comparative questions such as: Do language models store relational knowledge, and if so, how much? Without any kind of fine-tuning, how does the performance of such language models compare to methods that automatically extract symbolic KGs from text corpora?

The authors of the work described here concluded that the largest BERT model (BERT-large) was able to capture accurate relational knowledge comparable to that of an off-the-shelf RE system, as well as an oracle-based entity linking system. Surprisingly, the models could recover factual knowledge quite well from pretrained models, but one caveat was that the performance on many-to-many relations was poor. On open-domain QA, BERT-large was able to achieve 57.1 percent precision@10 compared to 63.5 percent for a KG that was constructed using task-specific RE.

While this work has been among the more influential in studying the phenomenon noted here, several points should be borne in mind before being rid of KG construction altogether. First, the obvious caveat is that a large quantity of text data is required to train a language model with the kind of power that BERT-large possesses. While BERT-large and its successors may be enough for embedding general-text corpora like Wikipedia, it is not always the case (and may be rare, in fact) that such large quantities of text are available for domain-specific applications. Second, there is still a performance difference, even in the results noted here, between BERT-large's performance and the RE. We could argue that this is because the latter system was trained in a task-specific way, but even if we were willing to give BERT-large the same advantage, how should we incorporate training data (when available) into a language model? This is a harder question for which there is no good answer. Another caveat is that RE itself is also improving, so it is not remaining stagnant while BERT and other models like it continue to improve.

While these are some challenges that stand in the way of replacing KGs with language models altogether (even for the specific application of complex QA), the paper described here shows that the gap is closing and that, at the very least, any QA system that does rely on a KG should use such language models as baselines. There was a time, not very long ago, when simply entertaining the question of whether language models could rival KGs as a store of some *kinds* of relational information would not have been viewed as very promising (recall that the exercise conducted in this paper could not show convincing, or even good, results for many-many relations, which may suggest that it is not capable of answering questions that are complex or that require some kind of nontrivial reasoning and are far too subtle for a model like BERT to currently capture). But as the power of language models and their performance in NLP tasks continue to become more impressive, the question of whether KGs are necessary anymore for open-domain QA is looking more favorable for language models than for painstakingly constructed (and identified) KGs. More research on this matter is likely forthcoming.

13.3   Question Answering as Knowledge Graph Querying

QA for querying a KG (also known as SQA) was motivated with making KGs easier to access, as it would not require the mastery of a formal language (e.g., SPARQL) or knowledge of the ontologies that were used for KG construction (KGC) in the first place. Over the years, due to SQA being a popular research area, many systems have been developed and proposed, many of which have considerable overlap with themselves and with earlier research in this domain. Despite this influx of ideas, much work still remains to be done, and human-level performance is far from being achieved. Nevertheless, just like so much of the rest of this book, common trends and themes have become manifest, indicating the maturity of some of the core conceptual ideas. We present some of these key ideas in this section, with brief guidance on systems implementing these ideas. A broader overview of related work is provided in the "Bibliographic Notes" section for the interested reader.

Most SQA systems follow a two-stage approach: in the first stage, a query analyzer attempts to break the original question into a structured format that is more amenable for retrieval from KGs, while in the second stage, actual retrieval takes place. Considerable research has been produced for refining both stages. A cursory view of the problem may suggest that the second stage is less of a problem, as it amounts to query execution and could draw on some of the techniques and infrastructures described in chapter 12. At this time, there are a number of commercial (and even freely available) products that can execute queries efficiently over most KGs under a reasonable set of constraints. However, a deeper analysis of SQA, as well as the study of actual QA systems and the challenges they face, make even the retrieval step nontrivial. In some of the more advanced systems, the query analyzer and retrieval may even be interlinked or iterative (e.g., the analyzer may yield an initial query, but based on the outputs of retrieval, it may decide to refine the query even further or come up with a whole new set of queries). At some point, a set of answers is compiled and returned to the user, possibly after postprocessing steps such as aggregation, if necessary.

One other point to note is that, while the SW community favors SPARQL as the structured query language into which natural-language questions are reformulated, it is not a strictly necessary feature of SQA. Questions could be reformulated into an Elasticsearch boolean tree query, or even as a combination of keyword queries. The primary observation is that, regardless of the actual language or syntax employed, some kind of structure is necessary to answer the kinds of questions posed to SQA systems, and mere keyword-based retrieval is unlikely to be very useful.

13.3.1 Challenges and Solutions

There are many challenges associated with building robust and expressive SQA systems, some of which include the *lexical gap* (an NLP problem that arises from the fact that the same intent or meaning can be expressed in a variety of ways); *ambiguity* (another dominant NLP problem that arises because the same phrase, word, or even sentence could have different meanings based on syntax, semantics, or overall context); *multilingualism* (which arises only in more international contexts); the ability to answer *complex queries*; the ability to answer queries when the *requisite knowledge* needed for answering those queries is *distributed*; the ability to answer questions of a difficult nature (e.g., *procedural, temporal* or *spatial* questions); and the ability for certain classes of SQA solutions (such as template-based solutions) to generalize in a sufficiently robust way when the underlying data set, ontology, or even question type changes. Almost always, there is a trade-off between expressiveness and correctness; that is, systems that are able to handle very expressive or difficult queries will, on average, return incorrect results (or in the case of ranking-based approaches, ranked answers with fewer or lower-ranked relevant answers) than systems that are far less expressive but yield higher-quality answers for the questions that they have been designed to take as input.

Rather than provide a systems-level description of existing SQA solutions, we discuss here how the community has dealt with some of these challenges, using examples of representative systems where applicable.

13.3.1.1   Addressing the Lexical Gap   The lexical gap in SQA arises primarily because the labels in the KG that is being queried are different from the ones used in the question. For example, the question might ask "Who was JFK's dad?," for which the KG may contain the answer but using the more formal property *"fatherOf."* In other words, the KG and the question are referring to similar concepts but using different terminology. In a survey that was recently conducted studying how SQA systems handled the lexical gap, a variety of NLP techniques were found to have been employed by the systems, including incorporating similarity features like Levenstein (accounting for possible misspellings), applying preprocessing tasks like stemming and lemmatization, using WordNet or other resources for supplementing words with their synonyms, and even using pattern libraries (e.g., the pattern "X sampled Y from the buffet" could be used as an equivalency pattern for "X tasted Y").

Considering each of these in some more detail, recall that string normalization and other similarity features have already been encountered in a variety of KG settings, including instance matching (IM). Common examples are Jaro-Winkler, an edit distance that measures transpositions; phonetic similarities like Soundex (particularly useful for strings representing names); and even n-grams. It must be noted, however, that such similarity functions are not cheap and can prove to be prohibitively expensive, even for a single question executed over a sufficiently large KG. One option is to use *fuzzy* implementations or approximations. For example, Apache Lucene (which we studied earlier in this book, in chapter 11) offers a Levenstein automaton that is more efficient than exact Levenstein computation. Other approximations rely on mathematical properties like the triangle inequality to prune large sets of candidates so that fewer strings in the KG have to be compared (using the expensive matching function) to the label in the question.

Synonyms and other such features can be incorporated into an *automatic query expansion* (AQE) framework. AQE is much more common and useful in standard IR, but it is less commonly used in SQA because it tends to lead to noisy results. However, it can be used as a supplement, especially if the original query does not yield any results. At least one empirical work has shown that when different lexical (based on synonym, hypernym, and hyponym relationships) and semantic [based on the use of Resource Description Framework (RDF) and RDF Schema (RDFS) constraints such as subclass and superclass relationships] features are used in an AQE framework, with machine learning used to weight their influence appropriately, SQA performance on a benchmark improved compared to direct matching.

Speaking of standard IR, it is worthwhile asking if we can model the problem of querying a KG as that of querying a document corpus, while still retrieving entities and KG resources as answers. One approach, which has been considered by at least one set of authors, is to convert each RDF resource in the KG into a key-value document, with keys being text attributes constructed over useful information sets such as title, property values, and

RDF inlinks. Once converted, ordinary document retrieval algorithms can be applied, with classic approaches being tf-idf and BM25. While it may seem simplistic to model the problem in this way, it has proved to have a surprising degree of empirical success and be efficient. One reason for this empirical success could be the IR community's progress in improving its algorithms by incorporating ever more sophisticated features (such as word embeddings) and learning methodologies (such as learning to rank). However, one severe limitation often arises in the types of questions that such systems are limited to answering, as the questions are often treated as bags of words, just like the generated documents. If the KG does not contain many text attributes, it leads to challenges of its own.

Pattern libraries are useful primarily because the feature classes considered previously are useful mainly for individuals, not properties. Properties tend to suffer worse ambiguity than individuals, because (in addition to label ambiguity) a property could syntactically be expressed as a noun and verb phrase that may not even be a continuous substring. For example, "Martha sang the national anthem as a duet with Christine" expresses a musical-collaboration relationship between Martha and Christine, but the specific words expressing the property are not consecutive. Positioning of arguments is yet another problem, as it is not always necessary that the first entity is always the subject in the extracted triple with that property. In particular, subject-object positions in an extracted triple would get reversed depending on whether the property is expressed using an active or passive voice (e.g., "sang" versus "was sung by"). These problems are similar to the ones encountered in chapter 6 on RE.

Pattern libraries help alleviate some of these issues, assuming that the library can be built in the first place. The PATTY system, for example, detects entities in a corpus of sentences provided for mining such rules, determines the shortest path between the entities (in the accompanying KG), and expands the path with occurring modifiers to mine the pattern. Similarly, BOA generates linguistic patterns using a corpus and KG, while PARALEX automatically learns its templates from paraphrases obtained from the WikiAnswers site. Distant supervision and advanced RE techniques can be employed here as well. Once constructed, the pattern library could be used at the test time to improve the process of formulating queries (that have a higher likelihood of succeeding when executed against the KG) from input questions.

Entailments could also be used to shorten the lexical gap. They rely on a corpus of already-answered questions (or linguistic QA patterns) to infer answers for new questions posed at the test time. A phrase or word entails from another phrase or word if it follows from it. For example, "man" entails "person" but not the other way around. One way (reminiscent of case-based reasoning) to employ entailments in SQA is to pregenerate a large set of possible questions for an ontology or KG. When a question comes in at test time, a systematic approach (based, for example, on syntactic and similarity features) can be used to identify the most similar match (from the pregenerated questions) and produce the answer to that matched question. Thus, entailment is being inferred at the test time from the user's question to one of the pregenerated questions, using a range of well-defined, empirically high-performing features. In practice, this method, by itself, turns out to be both nonrobust and limited in the types of questions that it is able to handle owing to the computational observation that the number of possible questions tends to grow super-linearly with the size of an ontology. The approach may be better suited to domain-specific QA, where the ontology is too complex for ordinary QA or NLP tools to apply, and also where questions tend to be limited in structure and not very natural. Another approach that has been recently explored is to find several matches (or variants thereof) and combine these more basic questions into a complex question.

We note that many of the approaches described here are complementary, and some of the more sophisticated approaches are built on such compositions. For example, the BELA system implemented a four-layered approach to addressing the lexical gap challenge. The first layer involves mapping the question to the concepts of the ontology using index-lookup. Next, Levenstein distance is used to improve the mapping (e.g., if a word in the question and a property in the ontology exceed a threshold in terms of their Levenstein similarity). Third, WordNet is used to find synonyms for given words. In the last layer, BELA uses sophisticated semantic analysis. However, empirical evaluations showed that the earlier, simple layers had maximal impact on performance improvements, while later layers had marginal influence.

13.3.1.2 Addressing Ambiguity   Ambiguity principally arises when the same phrase has different meanings, which may arise for syntactic or structural reasons (e.g., "conduct" as a verb has different meaning compared to "conduct" as a noun), or lexical and semantic reasons (e.g., "line" could refer to a queue or to a line drawn on paper). In practice, ambiguity affects precision in SQA systems, while the lexical gap mainly affects recall. For this reason, perhaps, the solutions that were proposed for addressing the lexical gap can sometimes have a negative effect on ambiguity. The looser the matching criteria become, the more candidates are retrieved that are less likely to be correct. To address ambiguity, *disambiguation* solutions are required in order to select from multiple candidate concepts to resolve the meaning of a phrase with uncertain meaning. Two types of disambiguation are important in the context of SQA.

First, *corpus-based methods* can be used to resolve the meaning of a phrase by computing statistics such as counts of phrases in a text corpus and applying the distributional hypothesis. Recall that algorithms like word2vec rely on this hypothesis, which states that the context of a phrase determines its meaning. By using a variety of statistical approaches (which can also include word2vec and other embedding approaches), context features like word cooccurrences, left and right neighbors, synonyms, hyponyms, and even the parse tree structure could be used to resolve the meaning of the phrase. Even more sophisticated approaches take advantage of user context, including the user's past queries and their profile.

Second, *resource-based methods* rely on the fact that candidate concepts are KG resources (usually in RDF), not just arbitrary phrases in text. Hence, resources can be compared using various scoring schemes based on structural cues such as the resource's properties and the connections between different resources. An assumption is that a high score between all resources chosen in the mapping implies a greater likelihood of those resources being related. This, in turn, yields a greater likelihood of those resources being correctly chosen.

Several methods have been employed for making these collective determinations, some of which we have seen already in previous chapters. For example, Giannone et al. (2013) uses hidden Markov models (HMMs) to select correct ontological triples based on DBpedia's graph structure. Another approach uses Markov Logic Networks (MLNs), previously encountered in this book when discussing KG identification or completion. Yet another system, EasyESA, is based on the distributional hypothesis and represents an entity by a vector of target words. A system called gAnswer tackles ambiguity using RDF fragments, which are starlike RDF subgraphs. In essence, it uses the number of connections among the fragments of candidates to score and select them. Wikimantic uses Wikipedia article interlinks for a generative model and can be used to disambiguate short questions or sentences, so long as the language is reasonable. DEANNA formulates SQA as an integer linear programming (ILP) problem by employing semantic coherence (the cooccurrence of resources in the same context) as a measure. It constructs a disambiguation graph encoding candidate selection for resources and properties, and also uses an objective function to maximize the combined similarity while constraints guarantee the validity of the selections. While a full formulation of the problem in this way is NP-hard, existing ILP solvers can yield good approximations. More advanced versions of the system have used DBpedia and YAGO with a mapping of input queries to semantic relations based on text search. Empirically, on the QALD 2 benchmark, DEANNA outperformed almost every system on factoid questions, as well as on list questions. It is limited, however, in the types of graph patterns that can be used in the query (complex queries or graph patterns cannot be handled by the system).

The systems described here are only a small sample of several other approaches over the year that have specifically attempted to improve disambiguation in the SQA context to improve overall system performance. At this time, the problem is not completely solved and an active area of research both in the SW and NLP communities. However, the variety of techniques mentioned here (ranging from graphical models to use of external resources like DBpedia, Wikipedia, and YAGO) seems to suggest that a hybrid, well-engineered solution may be the current best hope.

13.3.1.3 Addressing Multilingualism and Complex Queries

Unfortunately, the majority of QA research is still predicated on the assumption that questions and answers will be in English. The web, as well as human society as a whole, is far more diverse. RDF offers the convenient facility of allowing a single resource to be described in more than one language by using language tags (such as @en and @fr). Ideally, users want to express their questions (and receive answers) in their native language, as that is the most natural and intuitive way for them to communicate their intent. However, there is no denying that the resources (including open KGs) available in English, as well as other Western languages like German, are more complete than in other languages. Hence, one line of approach allows users to pose a question in their native language, but then tries to answer it by mapping the question in some way to the KG (which may be encoded in a different language). Multilingual versions of WordNet (such as GermaNet, which is part of EuroWordNet) are especially appropriate for doing good mappings. Other authors have shown that a partial translation of the question may be enough to answer it, since the recognition of other entities can be accomplished using semantic similarity and other relatedness scores between resources connected to the resources initially mapped in the KG using the partial translation. An example of a system that does this, as well as making good use of open resources, is QAKiS, whose name stands for "Question Answering wiKiframework-based System." This system automatically extends preexisting mappings between various Wikipedia versions (in different languages) to DBpedia.

A more fundamental problem that arises regardless of language is the issue of complex questions, or (somewhat equivalently) questions that are formulated into complex queries. In normal discourse, it can be subjective what is meant by complex or simple. In QA, simple questions are ones that can be answered by locating and translating a set of simple triple patterns. Complex queries, on the other hand, may require the simultaneous retrieval and combination (in some well-defined way that is dictated by the semantics of the question) of several facts, or when the resulting query has to obey restrictions (or require postprocessing) as a result of ordered, aggregated, or filtered results.

An excellent example of a QA system that is well known in the popular public and can handle complex queries is IBM's Watson. Watson handles such questions by first determining a focus element, which represents the searched entity. Information about this element is used to predict the answer *type*, which in turn restricts the range of possible answers. Indirect questions and multiple sentences can be handled by imposing such restraints on the answers. The full Watson system is much more complex than this one feature, but the use of the feature allows it to handle complex questions and avoid nonsensical false positives (such as returning the name of a building when a celebrity's nickname is being asked for).

Other systems also exist for handling questions of a complex nature. One example is YAGO-QA, which allows nested queries when the subquery has already been answered. For example, if the question is, "What is the date of birth of the founder of SpaceX?" and it is posed after the question "Who is the founder of SpaceX?" YAGO-QA would be able to answer the former question, assuming that it was able to answer the latter question to begin with. Another assumption is that the requisite information is contained in an open-world KG like WordNet, Wikipedia categories and infoboxes, or GeoNames, as those are the sources from which YAGO-QA extracts facts. The system also contains various surface forms such as abbreviations and paraphrases for entities.

Another system is Intui2, which is an SQA system based on DBpedia. Intui2 relies on *synfragments*, which map to a subtree of the syntactic parse tree. A synfragment, therefore, is a minimal span of text that may be interpreted as an RDF triple or as a complex query. The interpretation of a parent synfragment is derived from the combined interpretations of its child synfragments, ordered by both semantic and syntactic properties. The underlying assumption behind Intui2 is that an RDF query could be interpreted correctly by recursively interpreting its synfragments. Intui3 was an evolution of Intui2 in that it replaced ad-hoc (or manually engineered) components with libraries such as the neural network–based toolkit SENNA (primarily useful for doing NLP), as well as the DBpedia Lookup service.

Examples of other systems include GETARUNS and PYTHIA. The former system creates a logical form out of a query consisting of a focus, predicate, and arguments. The focus element, which also arose in the context of IBM Watson, identifies the expected answer type (e.g., the focus of the SpaceX founder question would be the ontological concept *"Person"*). If no focus element is determined, GETARUNS assumes that it is a binary, yes/no-type question. In a second step, the logical form is converted to a SPARQL query by using label matching to map elements to resources in the KG. Among other ways to improve quality, filters are used by the system to handle additional restrictions that cannot be expressed in a SPARQL query. Such restrictions can arise when dealing with data naturally expressed as a list (e.g., "Who was the sixth employee of Facebook?"). In contrast to GETARUNS, PYTHIA is an ontology-based SQA system that can potentially handle queries that are more linguistically complex, such as those involving quantifiers and numerals, but it has its own set of limitations and assumptions.

13.3.1.4 Other Challenges The challenges noted earlier are some of the main challenges encountered by SQA systems in the modern setting. However, these are not the only set of problems that must be solved for SQA to be truly successful. One challenge that we did not discuss in detail, for example, occurs when dealing with large KGs or even multiple KGs sitting in distributed infrastructure. For example, we may want to answer a question not only using DBpedia or some other KG, but a set of KGs whose resources are loosely (and, potentially, noisily) interlinked using *sameAs, equivalentClass*, and *equivalentProperty* links. If it is known in advance that several KGs need to be used, then such interlinking could be done in advance (or the KGs could be completed offline using instance matching and other techniques covered in part III), with links such as *sameAs* stored in a separate infrastructure like an Entity Name System (ENS) or a registrylike index). It is much more challenging to create these links in an online fashion when the query itself is posed, and there is still an open question on how best to do so without incurring a high time complexity.

Common approaches to this problem assume that such links already exist between a set of KGs, and the SQA system needs to use these links to answer a question that cannot be answered using only one KG. As just one example, the ALOQUS system uses the PROTON upper-level ontology to phrase the queries, and then aligns the ontology to other KG ontologies using the BLOOMS systems. Using the alignments, the original query can be executed on the target systems. A filtering system, using a threshold on the confidence measure, is used to improve both the speed and quality of the final results.

13.3.1.5 Special Question Types   In recent years, there has also been a lot of interest in SQA where the questions may be of a special nature or involve information modalities such as procedures, time, or space. Note that SQA involving these question types does not have to be domain-specific (but it could be). In practice, such question types are better suited for some domains than others. For example, if the KG has lots of geopolitical information or events (such as the GDELT KG), spatiotemporal questions are relevant for accessing that information. We provide core details on how SQA research currently handles some of these special question types.

Procedural questions tend to ask questions about the "how" of a phenomenon, rather than mere facts. Similarly, *causal* questions, which are an advanced area of research and beyond the scope of this book, ask about the "why." Current SQA systems cannot handle procedural QAs very well, mainly because there are currently no KGs (that are openly available and constructed at scale) that contain such knowledge. One option to addressing this problem is to assume that the procedural knowledge is somewhere on the web, and if the original problem can be satisfactorily solved by following the procedure on the webpage, it may be enough to find the webpage in response to a procedural question. The KOMODO system follows precisely this approach; it is able to return webpages with step-by-step directions on how to reach a user-specified goal. KOMODO operates by submitting the question to an ordinary search engine and then cleaning the highest-ranked returned pages to identify and extract procedural text using statistical distributions of Part-of-Speech (POS) tags.

Spatial and *temporal* questions have both been the focus of more SQA research, as there is more data available (in several KGs) on the spatiotemporal properties of incidents and events. In RDF, locations can be expressed as two-dimensional (2D) geocoordinates (latitude and longitude); however, support for three-dimensional (3D) location representations is considerably lower. Another alternative is to model spatial *relationships*, which is often more relevant to users because many users are not interested in geocoordinate-based retrieval.

Spatiotemporal QA can also be domain-specific. For example, the Clinical Narrative Temporal Relation Ontology (CNTRO), which is based on an Interval-based Temporal

Logic, was introduced and used by a set of authors to answer temporal questions on clinical narratives. The logic is convenient, in that it allows the usage of both temporal instances and intervals. Hence, temporal relations of events can be inferred from those of others, such as by using the transitivity relationship between temporal qualifiers like *before* or *after*.[4] In addition to other domain-specific features, CNTRO includes a Semantic Web Rule Language (SWRL)-based reasoner that can deduce extra time information (based on given information or facts), and even other temporal artifacts such as possible causalities (e.g., the relationship between a therapy for a disease and its application to cure a patient of that disease).

Several systems are capable of combining spatial and temporal reasoning. For example, QALL-ME is a multilingual SQA that is based on description logic (DL) and uses the spatiotemporal context of a question (if the context is not directly present, the location and time of the user asking the question are added to the query) to determine the language that should be used for the answer (which may differ from the question language). In a similar vein, the implicit temporal and spatial context of the user could also be used by a dialogue-based system to resolve the ambiguity challenge.

13.3.2 Template-Based Solutions

It should be evident from much of the earlier discussion that reformulating a question into a query in SPARQL, or even in a logical form, is a difficult problem. For complex questions in particular, the resulting SPARQL query contains more than one basic graph pattern, and the reformulation process is susceptible to (sometimes subtle) noise.

One of the more dominant class of techniques for yielding queries that are either correct reformulations or of sufficiently high quality is *template-based solutions*. These approaches map input questions to either manually or automatically created SPARQL query templates. While there has also been research in building SPARQL queries in a completely template-free manner (e.g., using only the given syntactic structure of the input question), we focus on template-based solutions in this section owing to their practical importance, as well as significant research output produced over the years. Note that the two approaches are not necessarily mutually exclusive. It may be possible, for example, to use a template-based solution to *bootstrap* the training of a question-understanding system, which may eventually learn to bypass templates (and even query reformulation) altogether, as recent language models like BERT have sought to do.

Importantly, many templates can be generated automatically. For example, the Casia system generates graph pattern templates by using the question type, POS tags, and even named entities. Generated patterns are mapped to resources using similarity measures and resources such as WordNet and PATTY. The possible combinations of graph patterns

---

[4] Transitivity arises from the fact that if A occurs *after* B, and B occurs *after* C, then A occurs *after* C.

are used to build SPARQL queries, with the system focusing on queries that do not need filters, aggregations, or superlatives. Other systems take a slightly different approach. The Xser system first assigns *semantic labels* (variables, entities, relations, and concepts) to phrases by formulating the problem as sequence labeling and solving it using a structured perceptron (trained on several NLP features, including n-grams of POS tags, named entity tags, and words). A major advantage of Xser over Casia is that it can handle complex graph patterns. Other examples of systems include TBSL and SINA.

Some such systems have also been domain-specific. For example, manually created (and also machine learning–created) templates have been created for the narrow medical patients–treatment domain. This domain is a natural use-case for templates, because the precision and quality of results are so important.

Template-based solutions are not just restricted to SPARQL. As a case in point, the TPSM system maps natural-language questions to Web Ontology Language (OWL) queries by formulating the problem as a fuzzy constraint satisfaction problem (CSP). Constraints include both surface-text matching, similarity of surface forms, and preference of POS tags. Correct mapping elements acquired by solving the fuzzy CSP are combined into a model using predefined templates. As NoSQL systems become more popular, more such non-SPARQL approaches (that attempt to automatically frame questions in such forms as Elasticsearch boolean tree queries) may correspondingly become more popular as well.

13.3.3   Evaluation of SQA

When discussing language model–based QA such as BERT, we noted their evaluations on community-developed QA benchmarks. Systematic evaluation of SQA has similarly met with vigorous support. One such evaluation is Question Answering on Linked Data (QALD), which is the best-known all-purpose evaluation of open-world SQA on DBpedia facts. DBpedia is a staple of the Linked Data ecosystem, as we cover in chapter 14. The QALD benchmark was instituted in 2011 and made progressively more difficult each year. The general task has been supplemented with additional challenges, including multilingual QA and hybrid QA that use text and Linked Data jointly. Another addition is SQA on statistical data by way of RDF Data Cubes.

Another benchmark is BioASQ, which is domain-specific and only actively ran until 2015. The task consists of both semantic indexing and SQA on biomedical data. Systems were expected to be hybrid, returning answers that comprised of matching triples and text snippets; partial evaluation using either modality was also permitted. An introductory version first separated the tasks of Named Entity Recognition (NER) and named entity disambiguation (on the question), as well as the answering of the question itself. The more advanced evaluation combined all these steps to evaluate a full system.

TREC LiveQA, which started in 2015, poses Yahoo Answers questions to the systems.[5] These questions are unanswered and were originally intended for other humans. The idea was to pose realistic questions formulated in the wild (so to speak) rather than cleverly contrived. It also went beyond just factual questions, such as the ones posed in QALD, BioASQ, and the old QA track of TREC.

Despite such efforts, however, it became increasingly clear that it was becoming difficult to compare systems in a uniform setting and to maintain a shared infrastructure for benchmarks. In the last few years, the HOBBIT project was funded in the European Union to achieve this goal, among others. HOBBIT seeks to provide an integrated platform with standardized interfaces that allows practitioners to benchmark their algorithms without complex installations. It is also able to generate benchmark data from real-world sources and runs yearly evaluation campaigns. As such, it has provided valuable impetus for the measuring and reporting performance of SQA systems more uniformly than was possible earlier. We provide more details on HOBBIT and some of the open challenges and benchmarks that it supports in the section entitled "Software and Resources," at the end of this chapter.

Herein, we note that, in one of the more recent challenges that took place around the present time, *Scalable Question Answering* was successfully executed on HOBBIT at the Extended Semantic Web Conference (ESWC) in 2018. The effort was established with the goal of providing a timely benchmark for assessing and comparing recent systems that mediate between many users who are expressing their information needs in natural language, and RDF KG. Successful approaches to this challenge were able to scale up to Big Data volumes, handling many questions and accelerating the QA process, with the highest possible number of questions answered with the greatest accuracy in the shortest possible time.

The data set was derived from the LC-QuAD data set, comprising 5,000 questions of variable complexity and their corresponding SPARQL queries over DBpedia. In contrast to the analogous challenge task run at ESWC in 2017, the adoption of this new data set ensured an increase in the complexity of the questions and the introduction of "noise" via spelling mistakes and anomalies as a way to simulate real-world scenarios in which questions may be served to the system imperfectly (due to speech recognition failures or typing errors).

The benchmark works by sending to the QA system one question at the start, two more questions after 1 minute, and a stream of $k + 1$ new questions after k minutes. Further, 1 minute after the last set of questions is dispatched, the benchmark closes and the evaluation begins. Precision, recall, and F-measure metrics are all reported, but an additional mea-

---

[5] Recall that the original TREC evaluations were designed for pure IR approaches, with document-level relevance annotations.

sure (called the *Response Power*) was introduced as the main ranking criterion. Response Power was defined as the harmonic mean of three measures (precision, recall, and the ratio between processed questions, wherein an empty answer is considered as processed and a missing answer is considered as unprocessed, and the total number of questions sent to the system).

While more than 20 teams expressed an interest in the challenge, teams from three countries (Canada, Finland, and France) were able to submit and present their systems at the conference (which is a requirement). The best system managed to achieve a Response Power of 0.472, showing that much work still remains to be done, although considerable progress has been made.

13.4 Concluding Notes

In this chapter, we described QA, both as a problem in itself (where users want answers to natural-language questions posed to search engines like Google or digital voice assistants like Siri or Alexa), as well as a solution for allowing users not versed in languages like SPARQL to access the rich trove of information in KGs, particularly large or complex ones.

Many open research questions remain in the field of QA, and we are likely to see more published research and commercially available tools owing to the popularity of the area. There is plenty of scope to combine the advantages or lessons of SQA and language model–based QA. Currently, the latter technique is used more for general QA because it has been trained on a large text corpus of a generic nature, while the former is more useful if a KG exists and needs to be queried using more natural and intuitive mechanisms, such as questions posed in English or other natural languages. Given the success of BERT and language model–based QA, it is reasonable to ask if there is some way to transfer their success to structured KGs. Researchers are only starting to investigate such questions.

13.5 Software and Resources

The main motivation behind the HOBBIT infrastructure and platform was that many of the SQA systems presented in the SW literature have not been very usable or available as packages that can be evaluated on standard benchmarks (the absence of such a benchmark was yet another problem in the community for at least a while, and to some extent even today). Hence, we describe the HOBBIT project and its resources in some detail, although papers on individual systems mentioned in the chapter, as well as in the "Bibliographic Notes" section, could be used to verify if any software links are given and still available. In many cases, if a specific system is required to be implemented, the user may have no option but to reimplement the system based on the paper guidelines. This is an unfortunate consequence of nonstandardization in the early days of SQA research.

We also describe resources for BERT and some of the other impressive language models discussed in the first part of this chapter. Note that BERT has also found usage in other modular architectures, attesting to its usability (e.g., BERTserini was proposed as an end-to-end QA system that integrates BERT with the open-source Anserini IR toolkit). BERTserini was shown to be capable of identifying answers from a corpus of Wikipedia articles, and only required fine-tuning the pretrained BERT (on SQuAD). It was deployed as a chatbot that users could interact with. Other such applications may also exist, some of which are likely proprietary and unpublished.

13.5.1 BERT and Language Model–Based Question Answering

The code and pretrained models for BERT are available om a GitHub project page: https:// github.com/google-research/bert. In general, the language model and language-embedding subcommunities in NLP have a strong and laudable history of releasing their models, both for training on domain-specific or arbitrary corpora, but also pretrained models that can just be downloaded, used, and evaluated in an off-the-shelf fashion. For general domain-independent QA, therefore, these pretrained models can be accessed and executed with relative ease. Resources for some previous word-embedding models (e.g., links to word2vec, GloVE, and fastText) have been noted in previous chapters. In chapter 10, other kinds of links for training embeddings were also provided. However, if QA is the specific goal, using tools like BERT and RoBERTa gives the best chance of achieving high performance. RoBERTa is accessible at https://github.com/pytorch/fairseq. Among other models, OpenAI and GPT-2 source code is available at https://github.com/openai/gpt-2. Pretrained PyTorch models for many of these models are available at https://github.com/huggingface/pytorch-pretrained-BERT.

13.5.2 HOBBIT

Earlier, we noted that HOBBIT as an important resource in the quest to standardize and evaluate QA systems in the context of KGs. The platform itself is a distributed Findable, Accessible, Interoperable, and Reusable (FAIR) benchmarking platform that is meant to be involved in the entire Linked Data life cycle, not just QA. As we are primarily interested in QA, however, we focus on that aspect of HOBBIT herein. We mentioned the Scalable Question Answering benchmark earlier, which came to a conclusion at ESWC 2018. It remains a valid resource to use for evaluating and benchmarking QA efforts, and due to its recency, the risk of benchmark bias is minimal. The main project page of HOBBIT is accessed at https://project-hobbit.eu/, and the scalable QA challenge details can be accessed at https://project-hobbit.eu/open-challenges/sqa-open-challenge/. As per the website, the online instance of the HOBBIT benchmarking platform is available at https://master.project-hobbit.eu, which also includes usage details and the platform wiki. The code of the platform and the benchmarks are accessible at https://github.com/hobbit-project, and the benchmarks are also available in CKAN (https://hobbit.ilabt.imec.be/), along with related publications and source code. The project also maintains a YouTube channel (https://www.youtube.com/channel/UC3eWNVAKXLqAdOhuQ5kd57g/featured) where tutorial videos can be found.

13.6   Bibliographic Notes

There has been enormous research in both QA and language models in the last decade, and the papers studying or extending models like BERT now number in the tens (if not hundreds). By necessity, our coverage here of related work was not comprehensive; it has focused on original, rather than secondary (or follow-up) papers. Furthermore, because the main focus in this chapter is on QA rather than on language models, we have focused more on QA. We also paid attention to the first agenda presented in the introduction (QA as a means of intuitively accessing the KG), in contrast to surveys and theses on QA that place more emphasis on the second agenda (QA, especially of the commonsense or open-domain variety, as the main application to be solved in and of itself, with or without a KG).

In the initial part of the chapter, we discussed the KnowBot system, which learns from conversational dialogue. Good references for this kind of learning include Hixon et al. (2015), Bordes et al. (2016), Weston (2016), and Wen et al. (2017). The first of these describes KnowBot directly; the other papers address the issue of learning from conversational dialogue.

Next, our focus in the chapter shifted to language models and BERT. There is a broad set of references that the interested reader should pursue for more information on this topic (including the use of language models for conversational QA). We recommend Devlin et al. (2018), Liu et al. (2019), Yang, Xie, et al. (2019), Reddy et al. (2019), Yang, Dai, et al. (2019), Sanh et al. (2019), Rajpurkar et al. (2016), Peters et al. (2018), Radford et al. (2018, 2019), Wang and Cho (2019), Wolf et al. (2019), and Rogers et al. (2020) as initial sources. The first of these covers BERT itself, but the other papers are also very instructive, and some cover language models that have become (or are becoming) at least as influential.

Before moving into the primary agenda described here (QA as a means of intuitively accessing the KG), we also asked the question as to whether the advent of these language models (and their excellent performance thus far) demonstrates that KGs may not really be necessary for open-domain QA. For those looking for more insight into this connection between KGs and (relatively) open-domain and open-world QA, we recommend Petroni et al. (2019), which was mentioned in this chapter as a recent example of language models being able to answer queries that rely on relational knowledge. Other important studies include Bosselut and Choi (2019), Roberts et al. (2020), and Bouraoui et al. (2019). All of these are extremely recent papers, and most likely will be followed by others exploring similar questions.

Moving beyond language models, the vast majority of the chapter focused on QA as one means of KG querying. This mode of QA, called Semantic Question Answering in the SW literature, has resulted in multiple papers over the years. The synthesis lectures on NLP for the Semantic Web by Maynard et al. (2016) may serve as a useful general reference. Another excellent survey, on which we relied on for our own synthesis in this chapter, was provided by Höffner et al. (2017). In this paper, the authors defined Semantic Question Answering as having three important features: first, users asked questions in natural language; second, they used their own terminology, rather than being constrained by a specific ontology or schema; and third, they obtained the answers by posing the queries to a KG (what the authors referred to as an "RDF knowledge base"). To study Semantic Question Answering, the authors identified about 72 publications covering 62 distinct SQA systems.

The challenges that we identified in this chapter were largely inspired by the analysis of those 72 publications. Good papers on addressing (and characterizing) the lexical gap include Ngomo (2012), Schulz and Mihov (2002), Usbeck et al. (2015), Zhang et al. (2013), and Biemann et al. (2015). Addressing ambiguity was at the forefront of the work by Giannone et al. (2013), Shizhu et al. (2014), Unger and Cimiano (2011b), Cimiano (2009), Freitas, Oliveira, O'Riain, et al. (2011), Freitas, Oliveira, Curry, et al. (2011), Carvalho et al. (2014), Boston et al. (2012), Zou et al. (2014), Shekarpour et al. (2012), and Yahya et al. (2012). Multilingualism and complex query handling have been the subjects of much more recent research; good references include Aggarwal et al. (2013), Buitelaar et al. (2009), Cojan et al. (2013), Deines and Krechel (2012), Gliozzo and Kalyanpur (2012), Unger and Cimiano (2011a), and Delmonte (2008). One of these, namely IBM's Watson, the DeepQA architecture of which is described by Gliozzo and Kalyanpur (2012), has garnered significant attention in the popular press, especially after beating human champions at the game show *Jeopardy!*.[6] More recently, Chakraborty et al. (2019) presented an introduction to neural approaches for QA over KGs.

These are not the only challenges being addressed, however; we also recommend papers by Joshi et al. (2012) and Damova et al. (2010) to gain a sense of challenges and approaches that we could not detail much in this chapter, including (for example), the challenge of querying large (or even multiple) KGs that are sitting in distributed infrastructure: Herzig et al. (2013) and Kejriwal (2014) are particularly relevant in this context. Special question types, especially of the spatiotemporal variety, have also become important recently; see Horrocks et al. (2004), Melo et al. (2011), and Younis et al. (2012).

In part, the ability of a system to do good SQA is limited by the state of NLP technology, which is not a dominant line of research in the Semantic Web. Template-based solutions have been conventionally presented in the context of answering complex questions by *reformulating* them as SPARQL queries in a semiautomatic fashion. Good references for template-based solutions in the SQA literature include Xu et al. (2014), Unger et al. (2012), Shekarpour et al. (2013), Zou et al. (2014), and Ben Abacha and Zweigenbaum (2012). As

---

[6] https://www.nytimes.com/2011/02/17/science/17jeopardy-watson.html.

we suggested in the chapter, it may even be possible to use template-based solutions to bootstrap the training of a question-understanding system, which may eventually learn to bypass templates (and even query reformulation) altogether, as recent language models like BERT have sought to do. Furthermore, with the advent of language models, the jury is still out on whether the natural-language understanding component of an SQA is truly the bottleneck, or if the challenge has now shifted elsewhere (e.g., in dealing with information sources of differing veracity or completeness, or reconciliation of answers that are semantically correct responses to a query but contain vague or contradictory components due to the quality of the KGs).

With so many systems, evaluation of SQA has been an important agenda in the community, and in the "Software and Resources" section, we introduced frameworks like HOBBIT that seek to provide standardized interfaces for practitioners to benchmark their algorithms. Other good references and resources for SQA evaluation (including for domain-specific tasks like biomedical SQA) that the interested reader can look to include papers by Bizer et al. (2009a), Höffner and Lehmann (2014), Tsatsaronis et al. (2015), Agichtein et al. (2015), Balikas et al. (2015), Tsatsaronis et al. (2012), and Dang et al. (2007).

13.7 Exercises

1. Making appropriate assumptions, draw an ontology fragment capturing the structure of the KG described in the paragraph below:

"MusicDB is a KG describing musical artists from the United States, including artists that are not officially represented by talent agencies or recording labels. It also contains information on concerts and performances, both past and upcoming, by those artists. For more famous artists, information on side projects such as acting roles and movie soundtracks is also maintained in the KG. Even when the artist has not officially published an album or single, the artist's work on alternative platforms like YouTube is stored in the KG. There is a state-of-the-art IM system that is able to discover (and store in the KG) *:sameAs* links automatically discovered between various modalities of the artist's work (e.g., the song on an album may have been performed in a concert, used as a soundtrack on a movie, and have a video officially posted on YouTube). The KG also has a special relation called *:cover*, which exists between two works A and B, when B is a 'cover' of A (i.e., B is the same 'work' as A but was performed by a different artist)."

2. Assuming that the KG corresponding to your ontology fragment exists and is of sufficiently high quality, what would be (using your own ontological classes and properties) the SPARQL translation of the following query in natural language to access the information requested from the KG: "Who are all of the musical artists that have performed in concerts in Germany, but not France, in the year 2017?"

3. Suppose that you ran the correct SPARQL query corresponding to exercise 2 but got back a sparse set of results, presumably because American artists who performed in Ger-

many also performed quite often in France. Hence, your boss asks you to instead return a list of artists who performed in Germany *relatively more often* than in France. As a first step, try to reframe this question in more precise terms, given your understanding of what is meant by the phrase "relatively more often." Next, pose your reframed question as a SPARQL query.

4. Given a model like RoBERTa, which has essentially been trained on extremely large natural-language corpora containing all manner of information, are KGs even necessary? Assuming the language model is near-perfect, what arguments could you think of to make the case that KGs are required in certain domains? Put more generally, what properties about a domain make it more amenable to a KG-centric approach as opposed to a purely NLP approach?

5. Design a semisupervised machine learning architecture that uses a language model (pre-trained on a large corpus) and a small set of training examples to automatically translate a natural-language question to a SPARQL query, *given* a KG. What would the training examples look like, and how might you constrain them? How might the language model help in reducing the need for too much training data? For purposes of illustration, you may use the same KG and ontology as exercise 1.

V KNOWLEDGE GRAPH ECOSYSTEMS

14 Linked Data

Overview. At this time, knowledge graphs (KGs) have been adopted in several communities and ecosystems. In many of these communities, adoption continues to grow; in some cases, it occurred superlinearly. A particular community that was an early adopter of publishing KGs on the web using a core set of principles is the Semantic Web (SW) community. The four principles, termed the *Linked Data principles*, have together yielded a web-based ecosystem that contains many interconnected KGs and currently spans many billions of triples. Many data sets in this ecosystem are open, which has led to the moniker *Linked Open Data* (LOD). In this chapter, we describe the principles and their collective impact. We also review important facts about the most central and influential KGs in the LOD ecosystem.

14.1 Introduction

At the core of the web's success is the ability for anyone, anywhere, to publish, link, and consume information using simple protocols like HTTP that can be "layered" over underlying Internet protocols like TCP and IP. Yet it is important to remember that much of this information is designed to be consumed by *humans*. Most webpages that you have likely browsed to date have consisted mostly of text and images, which, for context, are linked to other similar webpages with text and images. One of the motivations that we offered for KGs in the introduction is that they have a structure that machines can consume and reason over more easily, accurately, and scalably than they can consume text and images (at least at the present time). In this respect, KGs were offered as a convenient interface that can be produced, either directly or indirectly [i.e., via information extraction (IE)] by humans or from human content, and are more meaningful to machines than natural text representations. Unfortunately, and largely due to reasons both historical and rooted in convenience, the HTML pages that we often access and consume in our browsers do not have such machine-amenable structure.

Equally important is the growing need for making data, not just documents, the first-class citizen of the web in support of an emerging data economy. What this really means is that a *systematic* framework is desired for publishing, representing, and providing *direct* access to raw data that currently needs to be wrapped in an HTML document before being publicly exposed on the web. Yet, as noted at the start of this chapter, the web is designed to render documents on a browser for human consumption. How can we publish raw data using such a systematic framework without redesigning the web itself?

The Linked Data movement, a direct product of a grassroots effort called the World Wide Web Consortium (W3C) Linked Open Data (LOD) project[1] that was founded in January 2007, emerged as a potential (albeit, not unique) solution to this problem. In the years since, the movement has grown, and many data sets have been published using the Linked Data principles (described in the subsection entitled "Overall Impact"). Wikipedia is an important source of raw data that has often been used to populate several linked data sets. Figure 14.1 illustrates how Wikipedia infoboxes (described on the next page) can be a valuable source of structured data for populating knowledge bases (KBs) such as DBpedia. However, even before (and along with) the Linked Data movement, a number of need-driven efforts have attempted to induce some degree of structure to the web that makes its content more machine-readable. Important efforts are briefly described next.

1. **Microformats and Microdata:** Microformats and microdata are snippets of data embedded in HTML pages like regular markup. They are meant to describe structured data, usually are restricted to specific entity categories, and are constrained by choice of vocabulary. Although this limits their applicability, an advantage is that they can be seamlessly integrated into HTML and can be identified and extracted programmatically using syntax alone (figure 14.2). A major disadvantage, however, is that it is often impossible to use either microformats or microdata to express complex relationships between entities. While we do not go into the differences here, microformats are typically limited to the vocabulary officially maintained on the Microformats.org page, while microdata can use arbitrary vocabularies. In practice, however, the Schema.org vocabulary has rapidly emerged as the de facto microdata vocabulary due to widespread support and consumption by search engines like Google and Bing. At this time, the adoption of Schema.org has reached web scale, especially for popular domains like movies, tourist attractions, and products.

2. **Web APIs and Mashups:** Companies such as Amazon expose their product data via web application programming interfaces (APIs) that are consumed by third parties (many of which are small, specialized businesses) that attempt to generate or boost product sales by using Amazon as the centralized marketplace for conducting transactions. However, web APIs have a significant presence even beyond online marketplaces. Many key players in the emerging data economy mentioned in this discussion are data providers (e.g., Knoema.com) that provide programmatic access

---

[1] On occasion, also called the *Linking Open Data* project.

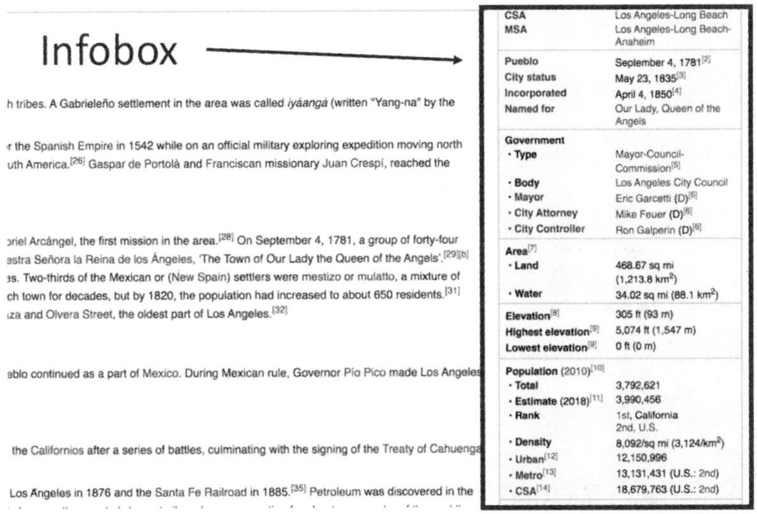
Infobox
h tribes. A Gabrieleño settlement in the area was called *iyáangá* (written "Yang-na" by the
r the Spanish Empire in 1542 while on an official military exploring expedition moving north
uth America.[26] Gaspar de Portolà and Franciscan missionary Juan Crespí, reached the
oriel Arcángel, the first mission in the area.[28] On September 4, 1781, a group of forty-four
estra Señora la Reina de los Ángeles, 'The Town of Our Lady the Queen of the Angels'.[29][b]
es. Two-thirds of the Mexican or (New Spain) settlers were mestizo or mulatto, a mixture of
ch town for decades, but by 1820, the population had increased to about 650 residents.[31]
iza and Olvera Street, the oldest part of Los Angeles.[32]
eblo continued as a part of Mexico. During Mexican rule, Governor Pío Pico made Los Angeles
the Californios after a series of battles, culminating with the signing of the Treaty of Cahuenga
Los Angeles in 1876 and the Santa Fe Railroad in 1885.[35] Petroleum was discovered in the
CSA Los Angeles-Long Beach
MSA Los Angeles-Long Beach-Anaheim
Pueblo September 4, 1781[2]
City status May 23, 1835[3]
Incorporated April 4, 1850[4]
Named for Our Lady, Queen of the Angels
Government
• Type Mayor-Council-Commission[5]
• Body Los Angeles City Council
• Mayor Eric Garcetti (D)[6]
• City Attorney Mike Feuer (D)[6]
• City Controller Ron Galperin (D)[6]
Area[7]
• Land 468.67 sq mi (1,213.8 km²)
• Water 34.02 sq mi (88.1 km²)
Elevation[8] 305 ft (93 m)
Highest elevation[9] 5,074 ft (1,547 m)
Lowest elevation[9] 0 ft (0 m)
Population (2010)[10]
• Total 3,792,621
• Estimate (2018)[11] 3,990,456
• Rank 1st, California 2nd, U.S.
• Density 8,092/sq mi (3,124/km²)
• Urban[12] 12,150,996
• Metro[13] 13,131,431 (U.S.: 2nd)
• CSA[14] 18,679,763 (U.S.: 2nd)

Figure 14.1: Wikipedia infoboxes have been used to automatically populate KBs such as DBpedia on a large scale.

through natively developed APIs. Social media platforms like Facebook and Twitter are also major adopters of APIs. Due to the proliferation of APIs, websites like ProgrammableWeb now maintain directories listing web APIs. One can creatively combine and use these APIs in tandem to create novel applications, called *mashups*.

3. **Templated HTML:** Many websites, such as Amazon and IMDB, are populated from a set of underlying databases (whether NoSQL or relational). Although the database itself tends to be proprietary, the pages can be crawled and, if there is sufficient regularity in the schema, the information can be extracted using wrappers and other IE tools. Unlike the other options, however, this one involves considerable noise and is only a partial solution to the original problem of exposing data wrapped in HTML documents. Even if it were possible to build perfect wrappers, a wrapper would have to be customized for each schema type in each website. This is clearly not a scalable solution to the problem of seamlessly accessing and using data published on the web.
4. **Infoboxes:** Infoboxes are structured pieces of information (usually key-value pairs) commonly employed by websites like Wikipedia to summarize and convey important information about an entity (figure 14.1). Despite their simplicity, their importance should not be underestimated, as it is far easier to extract infoboxes automatically than to wrap arbitrary website templates.

Interestingly, the efforts themselves illustrate a smoother spectrum (in realizing a machine-amenable web, while still keeping the web friendly for human and browser consumption) than one might have anticipated. For example, infoboxes on websites like Wikipedia were

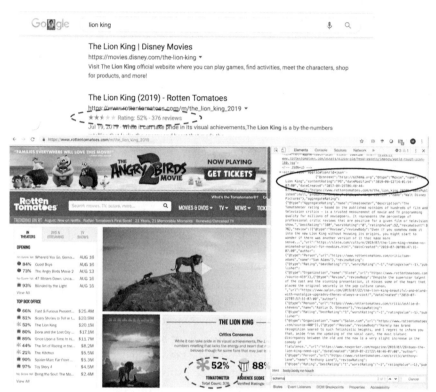

Figure 14.2: An illustration of microdata (Schema.org) for a movie website (the *Rotten Tomatoes* page for the 2019 *Lion King* remake). Elements such as the rating are embedded in the source HTML as Schema.org (shown using the dark, solid oval) and could be extracted into a KG based on syntax. Search engines find it easier to work with such semantically rich data for precisely this reason, leading to more informed search results for a querying user. The manifestations of Schema.org snippets (including the ratings both on the *Rotten Tomatoes* page and in a Google search) are shown using the two dashed ovals.

arguably designed to summarize the data for a human being, but are now used by search engines like Google and are also crucial to some specific Linked Data KGs like DBpedia (discussed in the subsection entitled "DBpedia"). On the other hand, APIs were almost exclusively designed to provide *programmatic access* to resources. It is still rather unusual to encounter non–computer scientists who use APIs directly in their work, as it is too low-level and primarily preferred by application designers.

Furthermore, although the options given here are powerful in their own right, they are also *piecemeal*, each option being designed organically to serve a particular niche or purpose. For example, it is difficult to define, extend, and consume web APIs in the same way as one would infoboxes. For any given option, there are severe disadvantages in adopting it for publishing arbitrary data over the web. Web APIs are customized to each data set and provider, and microformats express only a narrow range of entities and attributes (in addition to the interentity relationship specification problem mentioned earlier).

More fundamentally, the leading figures in the development of the web (including the inventor of the web, Tim Berners-Lee) have increasingly come to recognize that the next step in the web's evolution will be to move from an interlinked repository of documents, which is still how much of it is structured today, to an interlinked repository of *things*. Recall the advanced querying strategies covered in part IV of this book, and imagine that we could apply such techniques, or pose such queries, against the *entire web*, not just a stand-alone triplestore or a NoSQL server. This is the broader vision that Linked Data, as well as the larger SW ecosystem in which it is embedded, seek to fulfill. The vision seeks to make things (usually named *entities*) rather than documents first-class citizens of the web, but there must be a way to express rich (i.e., typed) relationships between things. In contrast, current hyperlinks on the web are untyped, and their semantics are unspecified. In other words, not only do we not know *why* a page is linking to another page, but we do not know what the link even means. For any application that needs to rely on a rich set of semantics, such as fine-grained search, untyped links are inadequate.

Although it is easy to confuse so-called Linked Data with the actual data being published (a tendency not helped either by the name or the occasional misuse of the term in the literature), Linked Data refers to a set of four principles that specify how data (especially structured data in the form of entities, attributes, and relationships) should be published on the web. The principles have a direct analogy to simple standards that have made the document web so popular (table 14.1). Furthermore, many Linked Data data sets have been published under an open license and are collectively referred to as *Linked Open Data* (LOD). More broadly, the *Web of Linked Data* comprises both open and nonopen data sets (and in some cases, even hybrid models like the Linking Open Drug Data initiative, wherein commercial entities share some of their data publicly) published using Linked Data principles.

Table 14.1: The Linked Data principles, enumerated.

Principle 1: Use URIs as names for things.
Principle 2: Use HTTP URIs so that people can look up those names.
Principle 3: When someone looks up a URI, provide useful information, using the standards (RDF*, SPARQL).
Principle 4: Include links to other URIs. so that they can discover more things.

14.1.1   Principle 1: Use Uniform Resource Identifiers for Naming Things

The W3C,[2] which is the main international standards organization for the World Wide Web [and by extension, the Semantic Web (SW)] has informally described[3] Uniform Resource Identifiers (URIs) as "short strings that identify resources in the web: documents, images, downloadable files, services, electronic mailboxes, and other resources." Uniform Resource Locators (URLs) are a special case of URIs, which are themselves special cases of Internationalized Resource Identifiers (IRIs). We do not delve deeply into all the differences between these terms; instead, the important thing to remember is that URIs codify a *naming standard* (i.e., not every short string is a URI).

What things can have a URI? The rule of thumb: is anything that can be given a name, which covers a surprisingly broader range than the document web, such as (1) "real," including flesh-and-blood, entities, such as celebrities and food items; (2) geographical entities, such as countries and cities; (3) mathematical and abstract entities like the Pythagorean theorem; (4) documents, such as the ones dereferenced on the document web; and (5) digital content, such as videos and web APIs. Referring again to table 14.1, because Linked Data builds atop the existing web architecture, the formal term "resource" is used to refer to all of these objects, and as per the first principle, a resource must be named and identified using a URI.

We also note that blank node URIs are generally not permitted [contrast this with the definition of Resource Description Framework (RDF) in earlier chapters, which allowed subjects and objects in triples to be blank nodes]. One reason for this is that blank node identifiers tend to be local to the data set and violate the second Linked Data principle, which calls for URIs to be dereferencable. If we want to publish a blank node using Linked Data principles, we would have to give a dereferencable name to the blank node. For example, if a particular blank node is describing all the marriages of celebrity X, then the node would have to be given a name like "Celebrity-X-Marriages" and specified using a *globally unique* URI.

---

[2] https://www.w3.org/.

[3] Source: https://www.w3.org/Addressing/.

Table 14.2: Examples of DBpedia entities with URIs.

Entity	URI
John Lennon	http://dbpedia.org/resource/John_Lennon
The Beatles	http://dbpedia.org/resource/The_Beatles
Billy Preston	http://dbpedia.org/resource/Billy_Preston
Pythagorean theorem	http://dbpedia.org/resource/Pythagorean_theorem
Judy Garland	http://dbpedia.org/resource/Judy_Garland

Table 14.2 lists examples of entities, along with real-world URIs in LOD data sets like DBpedia and YAGO. Note that it is no coincidence that the URIs strikingly resemble URLs (principle 2) that can be accessed using protocols like the HTTP. While it may seem obvious when stated explicitly, it is important to keep in mind that URIs are not the only established (or standardized) naming mechanism on the web. In particular, the first Linked Data principle does not allow naming standards like digital object identifiers (DOIs) that are predominant in the academic publishing community.

14.1.2 Principle 2: Use HTTP Uniform Resource Identifiers

Principle 2 states that it should be possible to look up URIs using the widely established HTTP. On the surface, there is not much to say about this rule, but its importance should not be neglected. Principle 2 is what brings Linked Data data sets into the web ecosystem, because a web protocol (and a browser) can be used for looking up things. Note that this is *not* true for naming schemes like Uniform Resource Names (URNs) and DOIs, which are not designed to be dereferenced using standard web protocols. Similar to DOIs, the protocol also establishes a uniqueness constraint on web access and visibility because two different resources cannot have the same URI and still be HTTP-accessible over the web. However, this does *not* mean that (1) the same resource cannot be referred to by different URIs, a rampant problem that can only be solved automatically, by instance matching (IM); or (2) every URI is HTTP-dereferencable. Technically, this also explains why principle 2 is necessary to begin with, as a URI can also be a URN (a globally unique name, but without an access mechanism). Because of principle 2, URN-URIs are ruled out, and even URLs are constrained, because the access mechanism must be HTTP and not some other protocol like the File Transfer Protocol (FTP).

14.1.2.1 The Problem of Dereferencing
There is yet another subtlety that comes into play when we consider what makes the URI representing a resource dereferencable. Taken literally, "dereferencable" means that the resource must be fetched over the wire. In programming environments, as well as the document web, the resource is a data item (such as the element of an array) or a document, and dereferencing the item does not involve

any controversy. However, recall that, as per the first Linked Data principle, resources can be used to name *actual* things, not just the documents describing that thing. Ludicrously, dereferencing the "thing URI" would mean sending the actual thing over the web.

By consensus, two workarounds have been devised to address this issue, without abandoning the conceptual elegance of principle 1. Both strategies are designed to ensure that there is no confusion between the objects themselves and the documents that describe them, and that both humans and machines can retrieve the representations best suited for them. The two solutions are called *303 URIs* and *hash URIs*. In the first strategy, the server responds to the client (when dereferencing the URI of an actual object) with a *303 redirect* by sending the HTTP response code *303 See Other*, along with the URI of a web document that describes the real-world object. Although it sounds simple, the 303 URI strategy involves four steps. First, the client has to perform an HTTP GET request. Next, the server receives the request and has to recognize that the URI identifies a real-world object or abstract concept. The server responds using the 303 direct, as described previously. Third, the client performs another HTTP GET request using the new URI provided by the server. Finally, the server now replied with an HTTP response code, *200 OK*, and sends the client the requested document.

The *hash URI* strategy was designed to address one of the main criticisms of the 303 URI strategy—namely, that it requires two HTTP requests to retrieve the description of the real-world object. The hash URI strategy avoids this by exploiting the property that a URI may contain a special part (the *fragment identifier*) separated from the base part by a hash symbol. For example, consider the URIs http://companyY.com/schema/division# Marketing and http://companyY.com/schema/division#Op-erations. When a client wants to retrieve such URIs, the HTTP protocol mandates the fragment part to be stripped off before making the request to the server. This implies that any URI that contains a hash cannot be *directly* retrieved, and thus does not identify a web document. Therefore, such URIs can be used to identify real-world objects and abstract concepts unambiguously.

How would the hash strategy work in practice? First, the client would truncate the URI, removing the fragment, and then connect to the server using a GET request (for either sample URI, it would be http://companyY.com/schema/division after stripping the fragment). The server answers by sending the requested document (typically RDF/XML). At this point, the client would need to be Linked Data aware, as it will inspect the response and find triples that tell it more about the resource that was originally requested (with the fragment). For example, if http://companyY.com/schema/division#Marketing was originally requested, the client would likely discard all triples that do not describe the marketing division, even though a single file (retrieved using GET on http://companyY.com/schema/division) describes all divisions.

Note that both the 303 URI and hash URI strategies have their pros and cons. The 303 URIs tend to serve resource descriptions that are part of large data sets, such as descriptions of individual concepts from open-world KGs like DBpedia. Meanwhile, hash URIs tend to be used for identifying terms within RDF vocabularies, and because the Linked Data–aware client usually has to do additional work on the fetched file, the file tends to be smaller. Hash URIs are also useful when RDF is embedded into HTML pages using RDF in attributes[4] (RDFa). However, we note that the two strategies are not mutually exhaustive, and in fact, it is possible to combine their benefits. We could use the hash (following it with an indicative word like "this") to distinguish between the URI for the actual object and the document (the stripped URI). No additional processing is required by the client because the retrieved file is the document describing that resource. Only one GET request is needed because the protocol itself mandates the stripping of the fragment identifier, so a 303 redirect is not required to begin with (because after stripping the fragment, the object URI turns into the document URI).

14.1.3 Principle 3: Provide Useful Information on Lookup Using Standards

Although principle 2 stipulates the lookup mechanism, it does not say anything about the content that should be retrieved upon lookup, or the representation of that content. Principle 3 bridges this gap. It states that when a resource is looked up using HTTP, useful information should be retrieved using standards like RDF and SPARQL. Generally, the latter implies that the information should be exposed using a SPARQL end point, while the former places restrictions on serialization and representation. However, it is not merely enough for the data to be accessible using SPARQL, or to be serialized in an official RDF format. The data must also be sufficiently useful, whether to a human or computer program, dereferencing the URI associated with the resource.

For this reason, unlike the first two principles, principle 3 is more subjective. It is easy to verify when a resource is fulfilling the first two principles, as there is nothing subjective or uncertain about mechanisms like HTTP or standards like URI. However, it is quite possible for a resource to display information that (arguably) is not useful, even if it obeys standards like SPARQL and RDF. Most people, however, have an intuitive sense of what makes a useful lookup (e.g., upon lookup, a basic description of the resource should be provided). An important aspect of usefulness is *vocabulary reuse*. For example, if we are trying to publish Linked Data about someone's dog, common properties (such as the name of the dog) can be borrowed from vocabularies like Friend of a Friend (FOAF; for more details, see the subsection entitled "Friend of a Friend"); a new property should not be invented for this purpose. This also illustrates the subjectivity of the rule, as we could potentially end up creating a property if an equivalent property from an established vocabulary cannot be found, or if the semantics of the property are different from what may have been intended. To follow this rule, therefore, some judgment (and good faith)

---

[4] https://www.w3.org/TR/rdfa-primer/.

is inevitably required, along with knowledge that is common to the Linked Data and SW communities, but not necessarily other communities.

14.1.4   Principle 4: Link New Data to Existing Data

The first three principles provide guidance on how to publish, represent, and access data, but they say nothing about how different data items should link to each other in the same way that documents on the regular web contain hyperlinks to one another. Connectivity among constituent elements is an important, if not the central, factor in what makes the web special and powerful. Because Linked Data is designed to ultimately serve the web, the fourth Linked Data principle states that new data should not be published in silos, but rather should be connected to existing data sets. Just as hyperlinks are crucial for connecting pages from different servers into a single global information space, principle 4 is crucial for maintaining the web's follow-your-nose architecture by mandating the publishing of typed links among URIs ("things") in different data sets. Several types of connecting links are possible, in addition to internal or local links that connect two or more URIs within the data set itself.

Note that, in addition to its other benefits, principle 3 facilitates easy syntactic adoption of principle 4 because RDF does not have to be limited to a single namespace. So long as the nonliteral elements in an RDF triple obey the definition of URIs, the namespace of the URI makes no difference to syntactic validity. Thus, the entire "data set," which is not just the data set itself but also its links to external data sets, can be released as a single RDF dump, or it may be queryable from a single SPARQL end point, if desired. In practice, it is not uncommon for LOD providers (such as DBpedia, discussed in the subsection "DBpedia") to publish external and internal links in separate files when exposing the data sets as N-triples dumps.

Suppose that the data set we want to publish using Linked Data principles declares its URIs in a single namespace. Assuming that the RDF triple is an object triple (i.e., the object is a URI, not a literal, typed or primitive), we say that the relationship represented by the triple is *external* if the namespaces of the subject and object are different, and *internal* otherwise. For example, the relationship in the triple (*dbr:Judy_Garland, owl:sameAs, yago:Judy_Garland*) is an external relation, where *dbr:* and *yago:* are shorthand prefixes for http://dbpedia.org/resource/ and http://yago-knowledge.org/re-source/, respectively. Conversely, in the triple (*dbr:Judy_Garland, dbo:spouse, dbr:Mickey_Deans*), the relationship is internal because the namespaces of the object and subject are identical.

Principle 4 encourages (or, stated more strongly, *requires*) the publication of external-relationship triples connecting entities among different RDF data sets (or sets of RDF triples that have different namespaces), and the properties that are most favored for doing so are *owl:sameAs* and *skos:related*. We've briefly alluded to *owl:sameAs* in chapter 2, but also when describing querying in part IV. The most important aspect to remember about such properties is that they are predefined with established semantics—that is, all practitioners are supposed to use these properties with roughly the same semantic intent (in the case of *owl:sameAs*). Here, *skos:related* is more controversial; it clearly depends on the subjective frame of reference of the data set publisher. Some publishers may be too aggressive in declaring two entities to be related, while others may see a weak or nonexistent relationship. We see such issues arise in the broader web as well. Many see this diversity as an advantage and a core feature of the web (and by extension, Linked Data), but on occasion, depending on the task at hand, it can lead to noise and quality problems, and it often requires a degree of technical sophistication on the part of the application consuming the data.

14.2   Impact and Adoption of Linked Data Principles

Because of the increasing adoption of Linked Data, there has been a concerted effort both to quantify the quality of Linked Data data sets and to assess the importance and rates of adoption of various principles. In the "Bibliographic Notes" section, we note some specific research papers that did thorough assessments of the quality and growth of LOD. These assessments started becoming commonplace once the size and number of LOD data sets reached a certain threshold [e.g., the State of the LOD Cloud report by Bizer et al. (2011) analyzed the adoption of linked data best practices by LOD data sets within various topical domains]. Some of the more recent key findings of the overall ecosystem are noted briefly next, followed (in the next section) by more details on impact and applications of specific highly influential LOD data sets.

Before describing these findings, we provide a methodological note on how these assessments are done to begin with. One method, which has become standard, is to crawl a snapshot of the Linked Data web, typically by using a specialized crawler (e.g., the LDSpider framework). For example, in Schmachtenberg et al. (2014), a group of SW researchers seeded LDSpider with 560,000 seed URIs originating from three sources:

1. All URIs of the example resources from data sets contained in the *lod-cloud* group in the datahub.io data set catalog, as well as example URIs from other data sets in the catalog marked with Linked Data related tags.
2. A sample of the URIs contained in the Billion Triple Challenge 2012 data set.
3. URIs from data sets advertised on the public-lod@w3.org mailing list since 2011.

Next, the researchers used the seeds to perform crawls during a specific month (in their case, April 2014) to retrieve entities from every data set using a breadth-first crawling strategy. All together, they crawled 900,129 documents describing 8,038,396 resources and made them available to the public for future replication. The crawled data belonged to 1,014 data sets, providing a representative sample for studying how well the Linked Data principles are being adopted across the spectrum of actual LOD data sets. Some of the main findings were as follows:

1. In total, 56 percent of all data sets in the crawl had links pointing to at least one other data set (external links). The remaining 44 percent were either only the target of RDF links from other data sets or were isolated. Thus, there is still a lot of work to be done in fulfilling the fourth Linked Data principle. One reason why this has not been straightforward is the challenge of implementing an efficient, high-quality IM system for a topical domain.

2. In further support of the first point, the in- and out-degrees varied widely, with a small number of data sets in each category being highly linked, while most data sets were sparsely linked. Overall, social networking data sets showed the highest degree values, while data sets with geographic and user-generated content showed an imbalance between in- and out-degrees (e.g., geographic data sets had much larger in- than out-degrees, measured by area under the respective degree distribution curves)

3. An analysis of the overall graph structure of the full crawl mostly yielded one large, weakly connected component consisting of almost 72 percent of all data sets in the crawl. There were three small components, one consisting of three data sets, and two consisting of two. Furthermore, within the large weakly connected component, there was one large strongly connected component consisting of approximately 36 percent of all data sets. What this shows is the unevenness of connectivity in LOD, as strong connectivity implies the entities within the strongly connected component are easily navigable to one another via one (or a few) short links. How this compares to the document web is not well understood at present; however, the fact that almost 30 percent of data sets can't be accessed from the other 70 percent is a cause for concern considering the motivations for proposing the Linked Data principles to begin with.

4. An analysis of *vocabulary usage* on LOD showed that the top vocabularies besides RDF, RDFS, and OWL are FOAF and DCTerms, with Simple Knowledge Organization System (SKOS) also in the top 10. Some vocabularies found much more growth on LOD than others (e.g., while FOAF was used by about 27 percent of all data sets in 2011, it was used by more than 69 percent of data sets in the crawl in 2014). In contrast, the Dublin Core vocabulary had less growth (though still a significant amount), going from about 31 percent of data sets in 2011 to 56 percent in 2014.

5. A negative finding by the report was the provision of alternative access methods for the data sets, such as SPARQL and dumps. In 2011, the numbers were encouraging, as more than 68 percent at the time provided end points, with almost 40 percent providing dumps. In 2014, these numbers were found to be much lower, but this was not necessarily due to lack of provision. Instead, one possibility indicated by the evidence was that the dumps and end points, if provided, were not easy to find using automated

methods such as the Vocabulary of Interlinked Datasets (VoID) descriptions[5] linked from the data sets. In reality, the number of end points and dumps may very well have increased over time. This illustrates the importance, not just of ensuring that the data set itself obeys Linked Data principles, but (to deal with the growth of the ecosystem) also providing adequate information about the data set–level metadata to make it easier for automated agents and applications to find and consume these data sets.

14.2.1 Overall Impact

The growth in the number of LOD data sets since its founding in 2007 is emblematic of the impact that the Linked Data principles have had on publishing and exposing structured data. In May 2007, LOD comprised only 12 data sets, including some of the ones that we cover next, such as FOAF and DBpedia. The growth was exponential for several years, though in current years, the growth has slowed. Topical domains represented in the LOD ecosystem include publications and bibliographics, bioinformatics and domain sciences, Open Government, social media, and most important, cross-domain data sets that are encyclopedic and open-world and play an important role in enabling the fulfillment of principle 4.

In enterprise and governmental organizations, we find that there is a healthy adoption of Linked Data by various organizations, especially those for which providing *background context* (e.g., by linking to DBpedia, as is commonly done) and *data integration* are both important. In addition to adoption, many important KGs in LOD are now used widely for a range of tasks and applications, from geospatial data integration to Natural Language Processing (NLP). Thus, when quantifying the impact of Linked Data, it is important to separate the impact of the *principles* themselves from the impact of the *data sets* that have been published using Linked Data principles (a task that may not be feasible or clear-cut in some cases). One could very well argue, in the case of DBpedia, that while Linked Data did not result in the publishing of new knowledge because much of the the raw information is already contained in Wikipedia, it unlocked new applications by republishing structured Wikipedia knowledge as RDF.

14.3 Important Knowledge Graphs in Linked Open Data

Here, we provide details on some significant KGs in the LOD ecosystem. These KGs are either heavily influential or widely used, and many have been part of LOD since the early days, continuing to grow with it.

---

[5] The VoID vocabulary is used for providing data set-level metadata, published as triples either in the data set itself, or back-linked in a separate VoID file.

14.3.1 DBpedia

DBpedia is as a crowdsourced community effort to extract structured information from Wikipedia and make this information available on the web. DBpedia makes this information accessible on the web under the terms of the Creative Commons Attribution-ShareAlike 3.0 license and the GNU Free Documentation license. These are liberal licenses that make it significantly easy to use, extend, and share the KB.

Although DBpedia is multilingual, like Wikipedia, the English-language version continues to be the largest, best-known, and most well maintained. According to the most recent posting on the DBpedia website, this version currently describes 4.58 million things, out of which 4.22 million are classified in a consistent (i.e., DBpedia) ontology, including 1,445,000 persons; 735,000 places (including 478,000 populated places); 411,000 creative works (including 123,000 music albums, 87,000 films, and 19,000 video games); 241,000 organizations (including 58,000 companies and 49,000 educational institutions); 251,000 species; and 6,000 diseases. Localized versions of DBpedia are available in 125 languages, which, in total, describe over 38 million things. Although there is significant overlap (almost 24 million of the 38 million) between the objects represented in the localized versions and in the English version, there are also almost 14 million entities that are specific to the locale.

In all, the full DBpedia data set contains over 38 million labels and abstracts, at least 25.2 million links to images, almost 30 million links to external web pages, almost 81 million links to Wikipedia categories, and numerous links to other linked data sets (an estimated 50 million). In practice, DBpedia has truly emerged as a Linked Data hub and is a primary source of linking for new data sets that want to be published using the Linked Data principles, especially principle 4, which that mandates interlinking.

Concerning infrastructure and architecture, the DBpedia RDF data set is hosted and published using OpenLink Virtuoso. The Virtuoso infrastructure provides access to DBpedia's RDF data via a SPARQL end point, alongside HTTP support for any web client's standard GETs for HTML or RDF representations of DBpedia resources.

14.3.2 GeoNames

GeoNames is a geographical KB that covers all countries and contains over 11 million names of places. It is available for download free of charge under a Creative Commons attribution license. It contains over 9 million unique features, including 2.8 million populated places and 5.5 million alternative names. GeoNames is also linked to DBpedia, which allows contextual knowledge to be shared across the two sources, an important goal of the Linked Data principles. The most important data sources used by GeoNames in the *Geo-Names Gazetteer* are the National Geospatial-Intelligence Agency (NGA) and the US Board on Geographic Names, the US Geological Survey Geographic Names information system (for names in the US), Ordnance Survey OpenData, and GeoBase for Canadian ge-

Table 14.3: A small subset of sources used for compiling the GeoNames KG.

Country	Name	Description	Website
Argentina	indec	National Institute of Statistics and Census of Argentina	http://www.indec.gov.ar/
Spain	cartociudad	National Address Database	http://www.cartociudad.es/portal/
Faroe Islands	um_stovnin _fo	Environment Agency	http://www.us.fo/
Ireland	osi	Ordnance Survey Ireland (OSi)—Open Data	https://www.osi.ie

A more complete list is available at geonames.org/datasources/.

ographical names, among others. Some other data sources, particularly for smaller countries, are listed in table 14.3. In the section entitled "Software and Resources," later in this chapter, we provide links to the full set of sources. An important point illustrated even by the small subset of sources in table 14.3 is that *without* GeoNames, a practitioner or user in this space would have to download, integrate (in terms of schemas), and otherwise invest considerable effort when working with multiple countries, or even one country when more than one data source is available for that country.

There is also a range of impressive features available for online users, including the ability to (1) search for names with full-text search (which itself could output results as a table or display outputs on a map); (2) browse capitals, the highest mountains, and the largest cities on a map; (3) browse names on map and show (or hide) feature classes and codes; (4) export names in a variety of formats, including as a comma-separated values (CSV) file or as a Portable Network Graphics (PNG) image; (5) geotag names (for registered users); (6) edit names in a wiki-style collaboration; and (7) send maps via email, among others. A number of companies and organizations are known to use GeoNames, including Apple Snow Leopard, Ubuntu, Bing Maps, DigitalGlobe, the *New York Times* (NYT), US Geological Survey, and Nokia, attesting to the usefulness, quality, and ease of use of this resource. In the academic community, especially Semantic Web and NLP (for such tasks as toponym resolution and location extraction or linking), the resource also has a loyal following.

14.3.3   YAGO

YAGO (whose name stands for "Yet Another Great Ontology") is a semantic KB derived using automatic extraction methods from three sources: Wikipedia (e.g., categories and infoboxes), WordNet (e.g., synsets and hyponymy), and GeoNames. YAGO is a joint project of the Max Planck Institute for Informatics and the Telecom ParisTech University. Currently, YAGO has knowledge of more than 10 million entities (like persons, organizations, and cities) and contains more than 120 million facts about these entities. The accuracy of YAGO was manually evaluated to be above 95 percent on a sample of facts. In keeping with the fourth Linked Data principle, YAGO has been linked to the DBpedia ontology and to SUMO (Suggested Upper Merged Ontology).

YAGO has continued to be maintained and updated over the years since its initial release in 2008, with YAGO3 being the latest version. The YAGO code recently went open source; the source code is now available on GitHub for anyone to work with. YAGO3 is provided in Turtle and tab-separated values (TSV) formats. To facilitate efficiency and exploration, thematic and specialized dumps have also been made freely available, along with dumps of the whole database. The KB can also be queried through online browsers and a SPARQL end point hosted by OpenLink Software.[6] A major application of YAGO is the Watson system, which is a question-answering AI developed by IBM that won the first prize in a 2011 competition of the *Jeopardy!* quiz show (beating two top human champions). Another important feature of YAGO is that it is anchored in time and space, with a temporal and spatial dimension attached to many of its facts and entities.

14.3.4   Wikidata

Wikidata describes itself[7] as a "free, collaborative, multilingual, secondary data-base, collecting structured data to provide support for Wikipedia, Wikimedia Commons, the other wikis of the Wikimedia movement, and to anyone in the world." Wikimedia launched Wikidata in October 2012; initially, it had limited features because editors were only able to create items and connect them to Wikipedia articles. In January of the next year, three Wikipedias (the Hungarian edition, followed by Hebrew and Italian) began to connect to Wikidata. In the meantime, the Wikidata community created more than three million items independently. The English Wikipedia followed in February 2013; all the Wikipedia editions subsequently connected to Wikidata in March.

The representation model in Wikidata is somewhat different from RDF, with the main principles behind the representation described earlier in chapter 2. However, note that an RDF version of Wikidata is currently available. In its native form, Wikidata uses a simpler data model to store structured data, much more like the key-value models used by NoSQL databases like Elasticsearch. In essence, data is described through property-value pairs: properties are objects and have their *own* Wikidata pages with labels, aliases, and descriptions. Unlike items, these pages are not linked to Wikipedia articles.

However, property pages always specify a datatype that defines the type of values the property can have. For example, "GDP" has datatype *Quantity*, "has mother" has datatype

---

[6] https://www.openlinksw.com/.

[7] Source: https://www.wikidata.org/wiki/Wikidata:Introduction.

Item because it relates to *mother*, and "postal code" has datatype *String* (by default, as the datatype is not explicitly mentioned or declared on the property page for "postal code"). This information is important for providing adequate user interfaces and ensuring the validity of inputs. There are only a small number of datatypes (mainly quantity, item, string, date and time, geographic coordinates, and URL). Data is international, although its display may be language-dependent (e.g., the number 1,007.8 is written as "1.007,8" in German but as "1 007.8" in French).

What about more complex data that property-value pairs cannot adequately represent? Although we do not revisit the Wikidata data model here (interested readers may want to review chapter 2), we do note that Wikidata provides intuitive support for citation-based provenance, which can prove to be a useful feature because there are so many contributors, and not all are equally careful or discriminatory in adding or verifying knowledge that gets added to the KB:

1. *Qualifiers* are used to state contextual information such as the validity time for an assertion, and they can also be used to encode ternary relations that fall outside the normal scope of the property-value model. As one example, we can use qualifiers to say that Audrey Hepburn played Holly Golightly in the movie *Breakfast at Tiffany's* by adding to the item of the movie a property *"cast member"* with value "Audrey Hepburn" and an additional qualifier *"role = Holly Golightly."* Qualifiers are extensible, not being "ontologized" in the sense that the set of qualifiers is fixed in advance. While qualifiers closely resemble the data found in Wikipedia infoboxes, they should not be misunderstood (though they often are) as a workaround to represent higher-arity relations in data models like RDF.

2. *Special statements* in Wikipedia allow a publisher to specify that (1) a property value is unknown, permitting conceptual assertion of nonknowledge; and (2) a property has no value. In chapter 8, on instance matching, we saw these issues arise when extracting features from pairs of instances in the similarity step, and therein proposed dummy values to provide signals to a machine learning classifier about missing property values and other such negative information. Special statements in Wikidata serve the same role as these predefined "dummy" values.

14.3.5 Upper Mapping and Binding Exchange Layer

Upper Mapping and Binding Exchange Layer (UMBEL) is a logically organized KG of 34,000 concepts and entity types that can be used in information science for relating information from disparate sources to one another. UMBEL[8] is an open-source extraction

---

[8] Note, however, that UMBEL is no longer supported by its editors (as of January 1, 2019) and support has instead migrated to a separate effort called KGpedia. Besides this change of terminology, many aspects still remain the same, insofar as we can determine; hence, we describe UMBEL as it was premigration.

of the OpenCyc KB and is able to take advantage of Cyc's reasoning capabilities. This is an important capability, as Cyc itself was created over many years and contains important knowledge about the world and common objects not necessarily contained in encyclopedic KGs like DBpedia. In recent years, this type of knowledge has gained increased prominence for moonshot problem areas in AI like common-sense reasoning.

UMBEL promotes semantic interoperability of information via two means. First, it uses an ontology of about 35,000 reference concepts, designed to provide common mapping points for relating ontologies or schema to one another; second, it uses a vocabulary for aiding that ontology mapping, including expressions of likelihood relationships distinct from exact identity or equivalence (we saw a similar case earlier with *skos:related* when describing the fourth Linked Data principle). Because the vocabulary is designed for interoperable domain ontologies, it is useful for fulfilling principle 3.

UMBEL is written in the SW languages of SKOS and OWL 2. It is a class structure used in Linked Data, along with OpenCyc, YAGO, and the DBpedia ontology. Besides data integration, use-cases of UMBEL include concept search, concept definitions, and ontology consistency checking. It has also been used to build large ontologies and for online question-answering systems, among other applications.

Including OpenCyc, UMBEL has about 65,000 formal mappings to DBpedia, PROTON, GeoNames, and Schema.org, and provides linkages to at least two million English Wikipedia pages. Reference concepts and mappings are organized under a hierarchy of 31 different (and mostly disjoint) *supertypes*. Each of these supertypes has its own typology of entity classes to provide flexible tie-ins for external content. A total of 90 percent of UMBEL is contained in these entity classes. It was first released in July 2008 and was updated periodically since.

14.3.6   Friend of a Friend

According to the published vocabulary specification, FOAF is devoted to linking people and information using the web. Regardless of whether information is in people's heads, in physical or digital documents, or in the form of factual data, it can be linked. Although it sounds like an ontology for publishing social network-like information (such as user profiles) FOAF is much broader and actually integrates three kinds of networks (namely, *social networks* of human collaboration, friendship, and association; *representational networks*, describing a condensed view of a toy universe (i.e., a deliberately simplified, hypothetical example) in factual terms; and *information networks*, using web-based linking to share independently published descriptions of this interconnected world). FOAF does not compete with socially oriented websites; rather, it provides an approach in which different sites can tell different parts of the larger story, and by which users can retain some control over their information in a nonproprietary format. Technically, the ontology is quite compact (19 classes, 44 object properties, and 27 datatype properties), and it is compatible with OWL 2

Table 14.4: Other Linked Data data sets.

Project	Webpage
Bio2RDF	https://bio2rdf.org/
BGS OpenGeoscience	http://data.bgs.ac.uk/
MusicBrainz	https://musicbrainz.org/
Science Commons	https://creativecommons.org/about/program-areas/open-science
Linked Sensor Data	http://wiki.knoesis.org/index.php/LinkedSensorData

A more complete list is available at w3.org/wiki/DataSetRDFDumps.

RL (meaning that it is convenient to materialize derived FOAF knowledge by performing reasoning using the ontology, in a triplestore).

Historically, FOAF is an important effort that was conceived many years before the Linked Data principles were codified or developed, and in fact even before the era of social media websites like Facebook or Twitter. Although the project is still maintained, it has not witnessed the rapid adoption that social media has. Nonetheless, its vocabulary continues to be reused for publishing many Linked Data data sets, as well as for fulfilling core tenets such as the third Linked Data principle. In particular, many computer scientists, especially in the SW community, have published their profiles using FOAF yielding a large, decentralized open social graph on the internet.

14.3.7   Other Examples

A number of other organizations have adopted the principles of the Linked Data movement and have even exposed SPARQL end points. We list some of these data sets in table 14.4, along with a brief description and the format in which the data can be accessed. Some of these data sets are discussed more fully in the next few chapters, depending on whether the application is enterprise specific (e.g., the BBC) or involves a specific community (e.g., biomedicine).

In some cases, we note that, even when organizations have chosen not to publish their entire data sets (what has been described as the KG in this book) as Linked Data, they have released their metadata, taxonomies, or even entire ontologies in that way. It is sometimes not completely clear in this context whether the data being published is part of the KG or the ontology. With this caveat in mind, we cite NYT as a well-known example. In early 2010, NYT added almost 5,000 new subject headings (or tags) to a set of 5,000 person-name subject headings that had been released in October 2009. The subjects include organizations, publicly traded companies, and geographic identifiers, ranging from Apple to Kansas to Williams College. We note that these tags are manually mapped to DBpedia, Freebase (which has since been acquired by Google, and of which the public equivalent is Wikidata), and in the case of geographic entities, GeoNames. This is obviously in fulfillment of the fourth Linked Data principle described earlier. Additionally, NYT incorporated DBpedia identifiers into their Article Search API for even more seamless integration.

Because the data was released to data.nytimes.com, it can be used for building complex, data-driven applications (e.g., designing and building a web app for finding alumni in the news, a feature now offered prominently on social media websites like LinkedIn as well). The important thing to remember is that, by publishing such data as LOD, the development of such applications is democratized and made significantly easier. If the data were not accessible in a structured, interlinked format, customized code would have to be written and developed for each application. Although significant coding is still involved (an issue we take up at length in chapter 17), data curation has now been largely automated.

14.4   Concluding Notes

In this chapter, we provided a first, well-established example of a *KG ecosystem* (namely, linked data). At its core, linked data is not data; rather, it is a set of principles for publishing data on the web. Unlike regular documents published as HTML, and primarily meant for human perusal and consumption, data sets published using the Linked Data principles are structured, almost always adhering to the RDF data model that we introduced in depth in chapter 2 and have alluded to frequently during the course of this book. The success and impact of these principles are best illustrated through the large and growing collection of data sets on LOD, which are open to the public and freely available to use, and also span domains that range from narrow (such as geographical and geopolitical entities in GeoNames) to open-world and encyclopedic (such as the Wikipedia-derived DBpedia KG). Enthusiastic adopters of these principles include the medical and scientific communities, as well as enterprise and government. In the next two chapters, we cover the adoption of KGs by these individual communities in more detail.

14.5   Software and Resources

Many of the data sets and LOD examples mentioned in this chapter can be found easily on the web. A full description of the Linked Data movement itself, including principles and the diagram showcasing the breadth of LOD, may be accessed at http://linkeddata. org/. Data sets that are available as RDF dumps are listed on https://www.w3.org/wiki/ DataSetRDFDumps. The website also contains links to other resources, including tools. Not all of the links may be active, however. For the sake of completeness, we provide links to the important Linked Data resources here:

1. The GeoNames resource is available at https://www.geonames.org/, while a full list of
    GeoNames data sources is available at urlhttps://www.geonames.org/datasources/.

2. The UMBEL resource was previously accessible at http://umbel.org/, but as mentioned earlier, support has migrated since early 2019 to KGpedia. However, a website for KGpedia is currently not available. Interested users still have the option of going to the UMBEL site and contacting the editors for a historical version of the resource.

3. DBpedia's main page can be accessed at https://wiki.dbpedia.org/. Previous versions are also available, and other resources are available for the interested practitioner, including a support forum, news on events and hackathons, and links to the latest research.

4. The YAGO resource is available at https://www.mpi-inf.mpg.de/departments/databases-and-information-systems/research/yago-naga/yago/.

5. FOAF, and several other important vocabularies like it that are important both for the Linked Data movement and for the Semantic Web more broadly, were previously described with links in chapter 2. FOAF itself may be accessed at http://xmlns.com/foaf/spec/.

6. Wikidata is accessible at https://www.wikidata.org/wiki/Wikidata:Main_Page. The default representation is not RDF or Linked Data (recall that we covered Wikidata as a separate model for KGs in chapter 2), but Linked Data versions are available (https://www.wikidata.org/wiki/Wikidata:RDF). The Wikidata query service offers a SPARQL end point as well (accessed at the URL https://query.wikidata.org/). A similar facility is available for some of the other major KGs like DBpedia as well.

14.6 Bibliographic Notes

The start of the SW movement can be traced back to a seminal article by Berners-Lee et al. (2001a), which describes the Semantic Web as the web of tomorrow that "will bring structure to the meaningful content of web pages, creating an environment where software agents roaming from page to page can readily carry out sophisticated tasks for users." It is a follow-up on a previous Semantic Web road map that had also been published by Berners-Lee et al. (1998). Other work that was influential right around that time include an article describing SW services by McIlraith et al. (2001); Hendler (2001), on agents and the SW; and an article on ontology learning by Maedche and Staab (2001), among many others in the spurt of research that followed soon after. However, the focus at the time was largely on the vision of the Semantic Web, as well as the sorts of reasoning and architectural capabilities that would be necessary for the agents in Berners-Lee's article to become commonplace.

The Linked Data movement and principles were still a few years ago, but some of the work that continued to be published in the mid-2000s bore hints of the movement to come. Among studies that we cite from this period include Antoniou and Van Harmelen (2004a) and Shadbolt et al. (2006). One of the earlier, highly cited articles on Linked Data (where it was referred to as an "emerging web") was Bizer (2009), although it itself cites an earlier document on design issues pertaining to Linked Data by Berners-Lee.[9] Other relevant work includes Berners-Lee (2011). Influential articles, including on DBpedia, that were used as much of the primary material for sections of this chapter include Bizer et al. (2007, 2008), Auer et al. (2007), and Kobilarov et al. (2009), the last of which discusses how the BBC used DBpedia and Linked Data to make connections.

For readers looking to go into much more depth into Linked Data than we were able to provide in this chapter, we recommend the synthesis lectures by Heath and Bizer (2011). For practitioners, especially web developers, Wood et al. (2014) is also recommended because it has step-by-step examples of increasing complexity, as well as practical techniques using popular tools like Python and JavaScript. Interesting (though by now, dated) perspectives are also found in Jain et al. (2010) and Bizer et al. (2011). More recent work related to this subject include Kendall and McGuinness (2019), Sakr et al. (2019), and Pan et al. (2017). Other books, which focus on more specific aspects of linked data (such as for libraries and museums), include Hart and Dolbear (2016) and Van Hooland and Verborgh (2014). A good comparison of some influential linked data KGs, including DBpedia and YAGO, is provided by Färber et al. (2015). A different line of study examines the quality of linked data, including adoption of best practices. We cite Schmachtenberg et al. (2014) as a particularly thorough example. A more recent example is Zaveri et al. (2016).

We mentioned earlier in the chapter that URIs codify a naming standard, which was defined and is controlled by the W3C. A good overview of definitions and syntax can be accessed in the W3C's RFC 3986 document (with more details provided in the updated RFCs 6874 and 7320). These RFCs may be accessed from the W3C's website.[10]

14.7 Exercises

1. Considering the data shown here, is either the first or second Linked Data principle violated? If either (or both) is violated, mention the line number where each violation occurs, and explain why it is considered a violation.

```
1  <http://szekelys.com/diego>
2      rdf:type                          "Dog" ;
3      <http://szekelys.com/name>        "Diego" ;
4      dbpedia-owl:species               "Labrador Retriever" ;
5      dbprop:country                    "Canada" ;
6      dbprop:color                      <ftp://pedro@ftp.szekelys.com/yellow> .
```

2. What about the third and fourth Linked Data principles?

---

[9] https://www.w3.org/DesignIssues/LinkedData.html.

[10] https://www.w3.org/TR/#Specifications.

3. For this exercise, go to the current DBpedia Downloads page: https://wiki.dbpedia.org/Downloads2015-04. Although this is not the latest version, the exact version does not matter for this and the next exercise, so long as it's a relatively recent version (i.e., 2015 or later).

   Is there evidence on the page that lends credence to the hypothesis that the fourth Linked Data principle is being honored? Why or why not?

4. When navigating to http://dbpedia.org/resource/Trojan, we noticed that the address on the browser has changed to http://dbpedia.org/page/Trojan. Explain why this happened, citing the relevant Linked Data principles.

5. Try to find examples of at least three LOD data sets that we have not mentioned in this chapter and that are online and accessible. Draw a table and list their names, URLs where we can access a SPARQL end point or dump, a subject domain, and one use-case where the data set could prove useful.

15 Enterprise and Government

Overview. Enterprises, nonprofits, and governments are important drivers of the modern economy. Although graphs have been prevalent in artificial intelligence (AI) for a long time, one could largely attribute the modern renaissance of the term *knowledge graphs* (KGs) to the Google Knowledge Graph, which was first advertised through a blog post in the early 2010s and has since become a paradigmatic application of web-scale KG construction and use. Since then, KGs have been taken up by all manner of companies and organizations, including start-ups and nontech organizations that have been traditionally conservative about using such technology. Governments have also started publishing much of their data, a lot of which is structured, as open data. Although these data sets do not typically constitute, in their raw form, a KG, they are rife with entities, relations, and events, and with the tools described in part II of this book, can be used to construct domain-specific KGs for applications like city planning, public transportation, and health informatics. In this chapter, we provide a brief overview of KG adoption in both enterprise and government.

15.1   Introduction

Because of the Big Data movement that started almost a decade ago, as well as the rapid rise of useful information on the web, KGs have had a big impact on industry. Recent pioneering work on KGs could arguably be traced to a blog post by a Google vice president at the start of the 2010s, which introduced the Google Knowledge Graph as revamping the search experience with "things" rather than "strings" as first-class citizens. Since that post, KGs have become increasingly popular in enterprise, and this has always served as a strong motivation for the academic KG research community. Informally, it is well known that many of the major companies have been building their own KGs, which are often domain-specific. Smaller companies, which do not have access to either the same kind of data or expertise as the bigger companies, have also made strides in applying KGs, sometimes by judiciously leveraging open-source packages and open-world KGs like DBpedia and Wikidata. Another manifestation of KGs in enterprise is the rapid onset of Schema.org publishing, especially when the entity (such as a movie or museum) needs to be prominently and accurately displayed in search engine results. As we described briefly in the previous chapter, Schema.org (or microdata) is an embedded knowledge fragment within a webpage; however, these fragments describe entities and their properties using established ontologies. The full set of published microdata on the web resembles a giant KG distributed across websites and companies with many common entities (such as the listing of the same movie by two different theater companies) that have to be indirectly resolved by search engines or aggregators using techniques like instance matching (IM) in response to a search ("query"). For this reason, it is fruitful to think about Schema.org as a massive, decentralized application of KG technology and concepts by a multitude of companies and service providers. Another example of KGs in enterprise is attribute-rich social networks, such as used by LinkedIn and Facebook, which tend to be hybrids between classic networks (where there is no ontology and relationships are untyped) and rich KGs with hundreds, even thousands, of relations and concepts. Yet another example, with increasing relevance, is the product graph used by e-commerce giants like Amazon. The fact that KGs are especially amenable to novel machine learning algorithms like tensor networks and representation learning compared to standard two-dimensional (2D) tables makes them even more attractive to companies looking to use and integrate advanced AI into their workflows.

Governments are one step removed from KGs, because they do not usually have the resources to construct full-fledged KGs, nor is there an urgent case for doing so. However, Open Government Data (OGD) has become much more commonplace, as is a focus on using more data-driven methodologies for driving efficiency and service quality improvements. Much of this data is open source, and some government data sets resemble KGs in form and content, if not in name or representation. In the hands of a moderately experienced practitioner, important subsets of OGD can be queried and analyzed just like the KGs we studied in chapter 14. In any case, we can always draw on the KG construction techniques described in part II to extract a KG from tables, documents, and government sources (like city webpages), ontologized according to our needs and preferences. For these reasons, we describe OGD and its possibilities in some detail in the second half of this chapter, even though it is not a true KG ecosystem.

15.2   Enterprise

Graphs and KBs have both historically been associated with academia, as the bulk of early AI research in these areas was mostly academic. However, the rise of tech giants like Google, Microsoft, and Amazon, as well as the importance of unstructured and semistructured data, much of it on the web (but also proprietary data, such as user search logs), has led to considerable industrial innovation and adoption around KGs. While all the details are not known, enough public information is available that we now know that many of these big companies are investing considerable effort into building proprietary KGs. Some of this effort is scientific, but much of it relies on careful engineering and infrastructure set up to ensure high efficiency and bottom-line impact. KGs have become popular enough in enterprise that even small and medium-sized companies are following suit, and there is a range of companies focused on providing KG services and application programming interfaces (APIs). More commonly, however, the KG is used in a supportive role. Sometimes this support is for a customer-facing service (the best example being rich semantic search, as we describe later in the chapter), but it can also be for the business side of the company (for running queries and aggregations over heterogeneous data that cannot be encapsulated properly or efficiently in a data warehouse), or for other divisions like sales, marketing, and data analytics. In most enterprise settings, with search being an exception, KGs tend to be domain-specific, though the domain could be very broad. For example, the product graph built and used within Amazon is technically a domain-specific KG (from the e-commerce domain), but it contains many entities that cannot be found, even in encyclopedic KGs like DBpedia. Interestingly, these KGs also have unique properties not well studied in academia; for example, many entities in the Amazon product graph are not even named entities, but are instead best described as sets of key-value pairs that provide the features (prices, ingredients, and so on) of the products.

Google is one of the first modern adopters of large-scale KGs, especially KGs constructed over web sources. The Google Knowledge Graph, which is an internal project at Google, seeks to incorporate semantics into regular keyword-based retrieval. One way for incorporating semantics, illustrated in figure 15.1, is through the *knowledge panel*, best illustrated for historic entities like Leonardo da Vinci. Before such a KG had been conceived, keyword search would usually just yield a list of webpages, and it was the user's task to click around these pages to satisfy their intent. Today, clicks may not even be required for many queries. For example, a search like "Los Angeles places to visit" would yield a list of candidate places to visit in Los Angeles on the Google search page itself, satisfying the intent of most users without requiring additional clicks or navigation. As another example of search extending beyond just webpage listing, a query such as "UK pound to USD" directly yields a calculator on Google, which is updated with the latest currency interchange rate and can be used to satisfy user intent for arbitrary pound and dollar values. While it is not clear that a KG underlies *all* of these facilities, the Google Knowledge Graph does play an important role in providing such rich semantics for many classes of Google searches.

15.2.1 Knowledge Vault

The mechanics of the Google Knowledge Graph are largely proprietary or unknown, but an important contributing technology is the Knowledge Vault (KV) devised by Dong et al. (2014), which is best described as a web-scale probabilistic knowledge base (KB) that combined extractions from web content (obtained via analysis of text, tabular data, page structure, and human annotations) with prior knowledge derived from existing knowledge repositories.

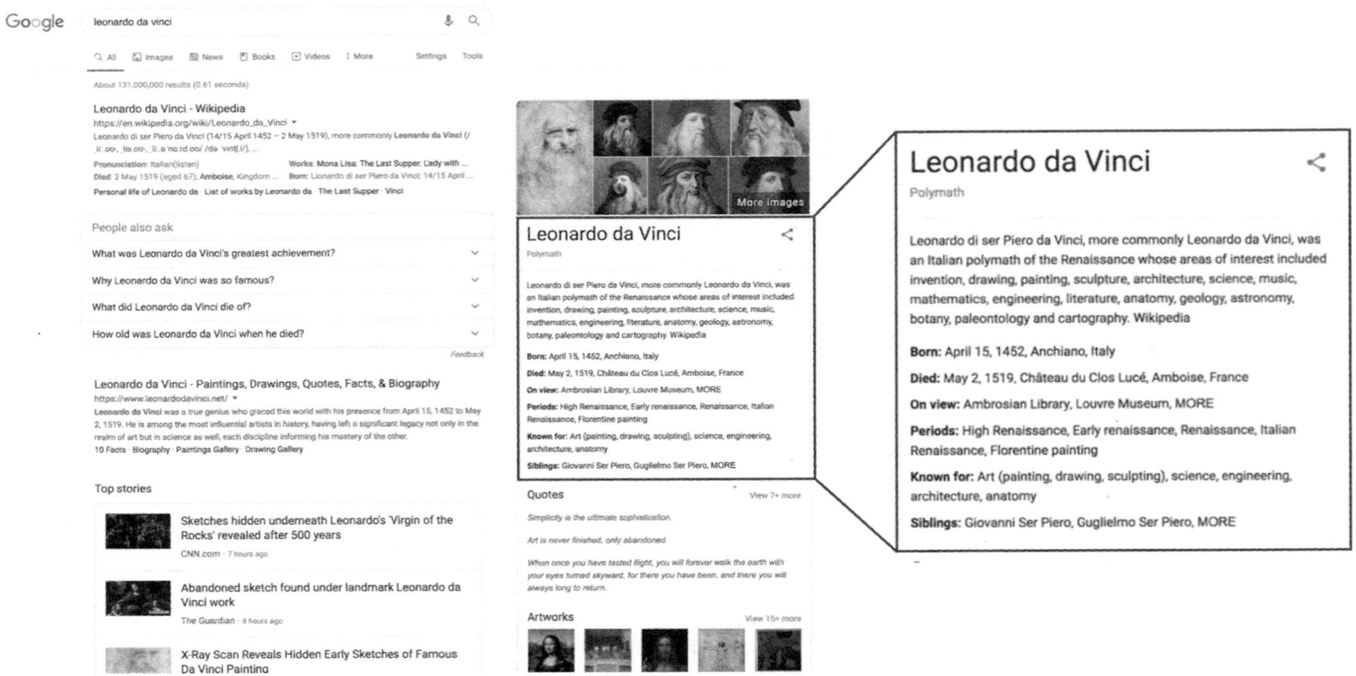

Figure 15.1: An example of semantics being incorporated into modern search engines like Google to satisfy user intent without requiring even a click. In this case, a search for an entity like "Leonardo da Vinci" yields a knowledge panel powered by the Google Knowledge Graph, and it provides some of the core information about the entity most likely to be useful to a typical user conducting the search. We also illustrate a magnified version of the panel (right).

KV used supervised machine learning models for fusing these information modalities. In the rest of this section, we describe the KV in more detail, in keeping with the goal of illustrating how KGs are deployed in industrial settings. Later in the chapter, we describe more recent refinements to the KV, although the extent to which these improvements have made it into actual enterprise KGs is not known. However, there is reason to believe that there is significant synergy between the publication and actual industrial systems, as the main authors of these papers tend to be from industry, usually large tech giants like Google or Amazon.

A primary motivation behind the KV stemmed from the fact that, although several large-scale KGs existed at present, such as Never-Ending Language Learning (NELL), YAGO, and DBpedia, and have been described in the previous chapter, they were highly incomplete. Dong et al. (2014) pointed out, for example, that in Freebase, which then was the largest open-source KG, 71 percent of people entities had no known place of birth, and almost 75 percent had no known nationality. Coverage also tended to be lower for relations that were not common, which meant that there was selection bias when it came to what knowledge was actually included in these KGs. Selection bias of this kind was emerging as a serious (and still not fully understood or quantified) problem in KBs that relied on crowdsourced content, the best example being Wikipedia. This may be a contributing factor in the growth of Wikipedia essentially plateauing over the last few years.

The KV was designed to be a fused knowledge repository that had greater coverage than any individual KG, while still being fairly precise. The KV was defined as a weighted labeled graph, with the weight $(G(s, p, o))$ for a triple (s, p, o) being 1 if that triple corresponds to a fact in the real world (and 0 otherwise). Because the binary problem is difficult to solve while still achieving both high coverage and correctness, the authors framed the problem as computing $Pr(G(s, p, o) = 1)$ for a *candidate* triple (s, p, o), where the probability is conditional on different sources of specified information.

15.2.1.1 Main Technologies KV relies on three broad sets of techniques to achieve the probabilistic knowledge fusion goals stated previously. Namely, it relies on the following:

- **Extractors**, similar to some of the modules covered in part II, especially web information extraction (IE) and relation extraction (RE), were designed to extract triples from a large number of web sources. Each extractor assigns a confidence score to an extracted triple, meant to represent uncertainty about the identity of the relation and its corresponding arguments. Examples of extractors used in Dong et al. (2014) are listed in table 15.1. The KV extractors were designed specifically for fact extraction from the web, including extraction from text documents, HTML trees and HTML tables. An important problem that arises when using these four fact extraction methods is *data fusion*. In the KV, this fusion is achieved by constructing a feature vector for each extracted triple and then applying a binary classifier to compute the probability of the triple being true, given the feature vector. To be fast and scalable, a separate classifier is used for each predicate.

Table 15.1: Examples of extractors used in the KV.

Input Modality	Extractor Techniques Used
Text documents	Relatively standard methods for RE from text, but adapted to be scalable. Training is done using distant supervision (first covered in the context of semisupervised information extraction in part II).
HTML trees	As with text documents, classifiers are trained, but the features input to the classifier are derived by connecting two entities from the Document Object Model (DOM) trees representing the HTML, instead of from the text. Specifically, the lexicalized path along the tree (between the two entities) is used as the feature vector.
HTML tables	Heuristic techniques are employed, because traditional extraction techniques (like for HTML trees and text) do not work well for tables. One such heuristic is to match the entities in the column to Freebase, and then using the matching results to reason about which predicate each column corresponds to.
Human annotated pages	Human annotations in this context refer to the microformat and microdata annotations described in the previous chapter. In the KV, only Schema.org annotations in the webpages are used (limited to a small subset of 14 predicates mostly related to people) by defining a mapping manually between these 14 Schema.org predicates and the Freebase schema.

How is the actual feature vector composed? The approach adopted by KV is to use two numbers for each extractor: the square root of the number of sources the extractor extracts the triple from, and the mean score of extractions from the extractor, averaging over sources. The classifier determines a different weight for each of these two components, and it can learn from the relative reliabilities of each extraction system. Because a separate classifier is fit per predicate, each predicate's individual reliability can be separately modeled.

For training this fusion system, the labels are acquired by applying a triple labeling heuristic called the *local closed world assumption* to the training set, and boosted decision stumps were used as the actual classifiers (because they were found to significantly improve over a baseline logistic regression model). This heuristic is described in all its detail in the original KV paper by Dong et al. (2014), but in essence, it expands upon the original notion that only the triples in the initial KG (used for training) are correct (and triples not in the initial KG are incorrect) in several ways. As per this heuristic, some triples are considered indeterminate, for example, and are not labeled as either correct or incorrect (and are hence discarded from the training and test sets); in principle, this set is like the possible matches set recovered from models like Fellegi-Sunter, proposed for the IM problem (as described in chapter 8).

• **Graph-based priors** encode the prior probability of each possible triple, with the values of the priors derived from triples stored in an existing KG. Prior knowledge is important because it allows the filtering of extracted facts that are too unreliable. It also allows link prediction, even when there is little or no evidence for the predicted fact that has been extracted from the web. Two algorithms were used: the path ranking algorithm (PRA) and neural network model (MLP, or multilayer perceptron). PRA is similar to distant supervision, in that the algorithm starts with a set of entity pairs connected by a predicate p. The algorithm performs a random walk on the graph, starting at all subject nodes, with paths reaching the object nodes being considered successful. The quality of the paths are measured in terms of support and precision metrics, similar to association rule mining. For example, PRA can learn that two entities connected via a marriedTo predicate often (but not always) have a path via another entity that is their child (the edges in the path being parentOf predicates).

Intuitively, these paths can be interpreted as rules. The rule equivalent of the path mentioned previously is that if two people are married, they are *likely* to have a common child. Because multiple rules or paths can apply for a given entity pair, the rules are combined by fitting a binary classifier (in this case, logistic regression) with the features being the probabilities of reaching an object node o from a source node s following different types of paths, and with labels again derived by applying the local closed world assumption on a preexisting, or initial, KG like Freebase. A classifier is again fit for each predicate independently in parallel.

The neural network model is different from the PRA and is more akin to the KG representation learning methods described in chapter 10, though the actual loss function and optimization is different from the Trans* and other algorithms described therein. KV favors tensor decomposition instead, in order to learn embeddings for entities and predicates (which in principle is not dissimilar from the neural tensor network model presented in that chapter). Although more advanced than the PRA, the authors of KV found that, when evaluated on a real test set, the performance of the neural method was roughly equal to that of PRA, with the Area under the ROC Curve (AUC) for the neural and PRA models being 0.882 and 0.884, respectively. This result illustrates an important (and ubiquitous) finding in industry: namely, that on real, industry data sets, more classic and conventional methods can sometimes perform as well as the state-of-the-art in the research community. Reasons for this phenomenon abound, with some of the popular ones being data set bias (and benchmark overfitting) and the limitations of research test sets.

The priors output by both of these algorithms are fused using a similar fusion method as the one described earlier for extractors. The main difference is in the features, as this component does not yield extractions. Instead, KV uses the confidence values from each prior system, as well as indicator values specifying if the prior was able to predict or not (similar to a dummy value distinguishing a missing prediction from a 0.0 prediction score). A boosted classifier is again used. The fused system achieved an AUC of more than 0.91, significantly improving over the individual AUCs.

· **Knowledge fusion** computes the probability of a triple being true, based on agreement between different extractors and priors. Once again, the same fusion method described previously (using boosted classifiers on feature vectors derived from component outputs and confidences) was used, and empirically (just as done earlier), the fusion was found to yield significantly improved quantitative performance. Furthermore, an interesting finding was that when priors and extractor outputs were fused, the number of triples about which KV was uncertain (for which the predicted probability was between 30 percent and 70 percent) declined. The moral of the story is that leveraging multiple sources and systems in large-scale, real-world systems, especially in industry, can be critical to obtain the best performance. Such fusion could, in practice, make all the difference between an architecture being viable in an actual deployment, and being relegated to the sidelines as a failed company research project.

15.2.1.2 Refinements Since the original publication, the KV has undergone several refinements, not all of which have been made public. One recently published and heavily improved version by Lockard et al. (2019) is *OpenCeres*. We have already covered aspects of this system in some of the chapters in part II, particularly RE and Open IE. OpenCeres builds on Ceres, which significantly improved its performance compared to KV by being able to automatically extract from semistructured sites with a precision over 90 percent using techniques like distant supervision. Semistructured sites are important because they contributed approximately 75 percent of total extracted facts and about 94 percent of high-confidence extractions. OpenCeres extends Ceres by providing feasible solutions for Open IE on semistructured websites. Because it is based on Open IE, OpenCeres is able to identify predicate strings on a website that represent the relations, as well as to identify unseen predicates by applying semisupervised label propagation. Unlike the web IE techniques we covered in chapter 5, OpenCeres is also highly novel, in that it is able to use visual aspects of the webpage for distant supervision and label propagation. Returning to the issue of data set bias and limitations of research benchmarks mentioned earlier, OpenCeres was evaluated on a new benchmark data set and online websites. It obtained an F-measure of 68 percent, higher than baseline systems, while extracting seven times as many predicates as present in the original ontology. On a set of 31 movie websites, OpenCeres yielded 1.17 million extractions with almost 70 percent precision. Work on OpenCeres continues in industry[1] at this time.

---

[1] The authors of Lockard et al. (2019) describing OpenCeres are currently employed at Amazon.

15.2.2 Social Media and Open Graph Protocol

Social network and social media companies like LinkedIn and Facebook have also become proponents of KGs. A major initiative in this direction is the Open Graph Protocol (OGP), which enables any webpage to become a rich object in a social graph. As one example, Facebook uses the OGP to allow any webpage to have the same functionality as any other object on Facebook.

The core idea behind the protocol is to add metadata to the webpage, with the four required properties being *og:title, og:type, og:image,* and *og:url.* The initial version of the protocol is based on Resource Description Framework in Attributes (RDFa). RDFa is itself an extension of HTML5, which was designed for helping web developers mark up entities like people and places on websites to generate better search listings and visibility on the web.

Good examples of OGP usage can be found on IMDB. For example, a partial OGP snippet on the IMDB page for the movie *The Lion King* (2019) is illustrated in figure 15.2. The snippet is relatively easy and modular to insert into the webpage, and with some scripting, it can even be generated from an existing database of information. Other than the compulsory properties, recommended properties include *og:description, og:site_name,* and *og:video,* among others. Interestingly, some properties can even have extra metadata attached to them, specified in the same way as other metadata in terms of property and content, but with the property having an extra *":".* For example, the *og:image* property has optional structured properties like *og:image:type* (a MIME[2] type for the image), and *og:image:width* (the number of pixels wide). While the OG is not quite as rich as an ontology, it serves that purpose when marking up a webpage with snippets.

While many different technologies and schemas exist and could be combined together, there does not exist a single technology that provides enough information to richly represent any webpage within the social graph (a richer version of the classical social network). The OGP builds on these existing technologies and gives developers a single path for implementation. In that sense, it is simple and unified, and has a significant web presence. At this time, it is being published by IMDB, Microsoft, Rotten Tomatoes, *TIME,* and several others. Additionally, it is consumed by both Facebook and Google. Adoption is also helped by lightweight plug-ins (e.g., on WordPress) that can be used to easily add Open Graph metadata to WordPress-powered sites.

15.2.3 Schema.org

In chapter 14 on Linked Data, we mentioned microdata as another means of adding more machine-amenable structure to the web. Schema.org is the best example of this effort, and it has witnessed massive uptake in the last decade, in part (if not mostly) due to the

---

[2] Multipurpose Internet Mail Extensions.

```
<link rel='image_src' href="https://m.media-
amazon.com/images/M/MV5BMjIwMjE1Nzc4NV5BM15BanBnXkFtZTgwNDg4OTA1NzM@._V1_UY1200_CR90,0,630,120
0_AL_.jpg">
    <meta property='og:image' content="https://m.media-
amazon.com/images/M/MV5BMjIwMjE1Nzc4NV5BM15BanBnXkFtZTgwNDg4OTA1NzM@._V1_UY1200_CR90,0,630,120
0_AL_.jpg" />

    <meta property='og:type' content="video.movie" />
    <meta property='fb:app_id' content='115109575169727' />

    <meta property='og:title' content="The Lion King (2019) - IMDb" />
    <meta property='og:site_name' content='IMDb' />
    <meta name="title" content="The Lion King (2019) - IMDb" />
    <meta name="description" content="Directed by Jon Favreau. With Donald Glover,
Beyoncé, Seth Rogen, Chiwetel Ejiofor. After the murder of his father, a young lion prince
flees his kingdom only to learn the true meaning of responsibility and bravery." />
    <meta property="og:description" content="Directed by Jon Favreau. With Donald Glover,
Beyoncé, Seth Rogen, Chiwetel Ejiofor. After the murder of his father, a young lion prince
flees his kingdom only to learn the true meaning of responsibility and bravery." />
    <meta name="keywords" content="Reviews, Showtimes, DVDs, Photos, Message Boards, User
Ratings, Synopsis, Trailers, Credits" />
    <meta name="request_id" content="5NMV6D2TWAASYERP9629" />

<script type="application/ld+json">{
"@context": "http://schema.org",
"@type": "Movie",
"url": "/title/tt6105098/".
```

Figure 15.2: An example of an OGP snippet embedded in the HTML source of the IMDB page associated with the *Lion King* (2019). By embedding these snippets, developers can turn their web objects into graph objects. The protocol has been extremely popular with developers catering to social media companies like Facebook. Accessed on Nov. 17 at *www.imdb.com/title/tt6105098/*.

official support and use of Schema.org markup by the major search engines in indexing and rendering search results.

On its homepage,[3] Schema.org is described as a "collaborative, community activity with a mission to create, maintain, and promote schemas for structured data on the Internet, on web pages, in email messages, and beyond." The vocabulary and initiative were founded by Google, Microsoft, Yahoo!, and Yandex (another search engine), with the vocabularies maintained and developed by an open community process. The vocabulary itself can be used with several encodings, including microdata and RDFa. Currently, at least 10 million websites are known (although the actual number is believed to be much higher) to mark up their pages and email messages with Schema.org snippets, and applications from Google, Microsoft, and Yandex, among others, use the Schema.org vocabularies as well.

However, while it is not possible for most people to obtain all the Schema.org fragments at true web scale, a large corpus of Schema.org data has been made directly available to the public as a result of the web Data Commons (WDC) project (see the section entitled "Software and Resources" at the end of this chapter), which extracts embedded structured data (including RDFa, microdata, and microformats) from several billion webpages. The project provides this extracted data for download and even publishes statistics about the deployment of the various formats.

As Schema.org has grown, mechanisms have been adopted to extend the Schema.org core to support more detailed and specialized vocabularies. Two categories of extension are (1) *hosted* extensions, managed and published as part of the Schema.org project, with the design led by dedicated community groups; and (2) *external* extensions, managed by other organizations with their own processes and collaboration mechanisms. As the name suggests, external extensions are more organic and driven by external needs, and external sources on the web must be referred to for documentation and development information. It is important to note that the steering group does not officially endorse these kinds of extensions. Hosted extensions, which are officially endorsed, include extensions on such diverse subjects as health and life sciences (Health-lifesci.schema.org), Internet of Things (Iot.schema.org), and bibliographies (Bib.schema.org).

The Schema.org movement continues to grow, and it is quite possible (although we are not aware of an official census) that the total number of Schema.org markups (expressed as RDF triples) has already exceeded the number of RDF triples published using Linked Data principles. However, it is important to note that Schema.org markups are complementary to Linked Data. The vast majority of Schema.org entities seem to be comprised of products, services, and local businesses and organizations that are vital to the proper functioning of search engines, especially when searching for localized and longtail entities (such as a restaurant in your city that does not have a Wikipedia page). In contrast, Linked

[3] https://schema.org/.

Data has seen uptake either from the scientific community (detailed further in chapter 16, on KGs for domain sciences), or relying heavily on primary data sources like Wikipedia and GeoNames. Efforts to bridge the two movements (i.e., crawl, study, and republish) as Linked Data Schema.org annotations are currently under way as a major research frontier in the SW. However, the fourth Linked Data principle is difficult to honor, as many long-tail entities likely cannot link to anything currently existing as Linked Open Data, and as we covered in part II, crawling and domain discovery are not easy problems to address, especially at scale.

15.3   Governments and Nonprofits

Governments and nonprofit organizations have also become significant adopters and con-tributors of structured knowledge. In many cases, this knowledge is ontologized and could be serialized as a KG, which can be queried using many of the techniques covered ear-lier. While Schema.org is as an excellent example of an ecosystem that organizations (both profits and nonprofits) have striven to be a part of, owing to its continued influence on search results, it is certainly not the only example of structured knowledge being published by governments and nonprofits. Next, we briefly cover some other influential examples.

15.3.1   Open Government Data

According to the Organisation for Economic Co-operation and Development (OECD), OGD[4] is a "philosophy, and increasingly a set of policies, that promotes transparency, accountability and value creation by making government data available to all." In mod-ern economies, both Western and emerging, public bodies produce and commission large quantities of data, usually with the goal of becoming more transparent and accountable to citizens. By encouraging the use, reuse, and free distribution of data sets, governments also attempt to promote business creation and innovative, citizen-centric services. The eight principles of OGD, according to 30 open government advocates who gathered in California to develop a more robust understanding of why OGD is essential to democracy, are briefly enumerated in table 15.2.

OGD can pose some tricky questions for governments, such as: Who will pay for the col-lection and processing of public data if it is made freely available? What are the incentives for government bodies to maintain and update their data? What data sets should be pri-oritized for release to maximize public value? These questions involve various trade-offs, and it is important to take steps to developing a framework for such cost-benefit analyses, including data collection and curation, as well as preparation of case studies to demonstrate the concrete benefits (economic, social, and policy) of OGD.

---

[4] http://www.oecd.org/gov/digital-government/open-government-data.htm.

Table 15.2: An enumeration of the eight OGD principles.

OGD Principle	Description of Principle
Complete	All public data is made available. Public data is data that is not subject to valid privacy, security, or privilege limitations.
Primary	Data is given as it is collected at the source, with the highest possible level of granularity, not in aggregate or modified forms.
Timely	Data is made available as quickly as needed to preserve its value.
Accessible	Data is available to the widest range of users, for the widest range of purposes.
Machine-processable	Data is reasonably structured to allow automated processing.
Nondiscriminatory	Data is available to anyone, with no registration required.
Nonproprietary	Data is available in a format over which no entity has exclusive control.
License-free	Data is not subject to any copyright, patent, trademark, or trade secret regulation. Reasonable privacy, security, and privilege restrictions may be allowed.

We credit the succinct descriptions provided at https://public.resource.org/8_principles.html.

The OECD OGD project aims to promote international efforts on OGD impact assessment. The mapping of practices across countries helps establish a knowledge repository on OGD policies, strategies, and initiatives and support the development of a methodology to assess the impact and creation of governance value, especially along socioeconomic dimensions, through OGD initiatives.

We iterate that this is not just an initiative that is being enthusiastically adopted in the rich economies. In the last decade, in particular, there have been many conferences and initiatives for (1) building OGD cultures, especially in the Middle East and North Africa regions to combat endemic corruption; (2) developing useful indices that can allow one to compare OGD success and adoption rates in a quantitative way across countries; and (3) promoting the movement, through reviews, blogs, and meetings.

A concrete application of OGD is *Smart Cities*. The Smart Cities Council describes[5] a smart city as one that "uses information and communications technology (ICT) to enhance its livability, workability, and sustainability." Smart Cities have become an increasingly important concept in the face of global pressures like climate change and village-city emigration in developing countries, leading to the rise of giant metropolises. Pollution, poverty, income inequality, food shortages, and imbalances are other severe problems, leading to a surge in antiestablishment populism in recent years. Smart Cities, through efficient re-

[5] https://smartcitiescouncil.com/article/hill-smart-cities-week-tackling-opportunities-and-challenges.

source mobilization and better governance and accountability, attempt to mitigate some of these issues to make cities more livable and sustainable.

The Smart Cities movement was not originally (and still is not) centered around KGs as the primary technology. However, due to their flexibility, KGs have been recognized as being important to the Smart City movement. Recently, for example, Santos et al. (2017) used KGs for supporting automatic generation of dashboards, metadata analysis, and data visualization. It is likely that this trend will continue, especially as cities release their data sets in highly heterogeneous formats, for which KGs are particularly apt as data representations.

15.3.1.1 US Government Data (Data.gov) A good example of an OGD ecosystem is Data.gov in the United States. Data.gov is managed and hosted by the US General Services Administration, Technology Transformation Service, is developed publicly on GitHub, and is powered by two open-source applications, CKAN and WordPress. Data.gov follows the Project Open Data (POD) schema, a set of required fields for every data set displayed on Data.gov. The POD schema addresses the challenge of defining and naming standard metadata fields so that a data consumer has sufficient information to process and understand the described data. This is especially important considering the vast number of data sets that have become available on Data.gov portals. Metadata can range from basic to advanced, from allowing discovery of the mere fact that a certain data set or artifact exists on a certain subject all the way to providing detailed information documenting the structure, quality, and other properties of a data set. Clearly, making metadata machine-readable increases its utility, but it also requires effective and consensus-driven standardization. By following the POD schema, Data.gov takes a step in this important direction.

Although the total number of data sets, which is available on the Data.gov Metrics page, can fluctuate, the range and growth has been impressive in recent years. According to official statistics, as of June 2017, there were approximately 200,000 data sets reported as the total on Data.gov, representing about 10 million data resources.

Importantly, we note that releasing data in many cases is now no longer voluntary. Under the terms of the 2013 Federal Open Data Policy, newly generated government data is required to be made available in open, machine-readable formats, while continuing to ensure privacy and security. For instance, federal Chief Financial Officers Act agencies are required to create a single data inventory, publish public data listings, and develop new public feedback mechanisms. Agencies are also required to identify public points of contacts for agency data sets.

As a distributed collection of JSON and semistructured files, it is not immediately apparent that Data.gov is a "knowledge graph." Certainly, integrating so many of the data sets (especially at the level of records, as discussed in chapter 8, on instance matching) is a challenging problem that is only partially helped by the use of a uniform schema. However, the use of the schema also motivates thinking of the collection as a KG. Research initiatives are currently underway to realize this vision, especially using free, open-source tools and NoSQL environments like Elasticsearch. Relevant research is noted in the section entitled "Bibliographic Notes," at the end of this chapter.

15.3.2 BBC

The BBC is a British public service broadcaster that is the world's oldest national broadcasting organization (and the largest broadcaster in the world measured by the number of employees). In fact, the BBC was also one of the first organizations to use linked data, with a highly successful public use-case being its Olympics coverage. However, even before that, BBC was obtaining existing uniform resource identifiers (URIs) for musical artists from MusicBrainz, a freely available linked data set that currently contains tens of millions of artists, albums, and songs. As noted in the previous chapter, most linked data sets on Linked Open Data (LOD) also connect to DBpedia as a hub source for fulfilling the fourth Linked Data principle, which is also true for MusicBrainz. This gave the BBC a large body of externally developed (and freely available) knowledge about the music industry. However, the path forward was not seamless, since (as also described earlier) Linked Open Data can suffer from quality problems. When an organization using these data sets discovers errors, they have a choice in whether to report it. The BBC made the strategic decision to help improve the MusicBrainz database when it found errors, in keeping with its charter to provide benefit to the public.

We used this example not only to illustrate an early example of a nonacademic organization using LOD (and by virtue, KGs), but also as an example of open data innovation. At the time, the open data movement was not as popular, but today, more companies and start-ups are starting to publish (and use) open data to create real business and social value. This movement started picking up steam in the late 2000s; for instance, Barack Obama issued a *Memorandum on Transparency and Open Government* on January 21, 2009, the very next day after he was sworn in as US president, endorsing the opening of government data and committing to accountability. Companies were slower to adapt to this trend, but today, it is not unusual for companies to give back to the community via open-source code and limited data set releases. In the media landscape, the BBC's adoption of linked data and KGs likely played an important role in other organizations (like the *New York Times*) taking up the challenge and discovering applied uses of KG technologies and data for solving some of their own problems.

15.3.3 OpenStreetMap

OpenStreetMap (OSM) is a *collaborative mapping* project with the overarching goal to create a free and editable map of the world. It is an instructive example of massive-scale, crowdsourced geographic information, with a direct analog to crowdsourced encyclopedic information sources like Wikipedia. OSM was created by Steve Coast in the United Kingdom in 2004, and it was inspired by both the success of crowdsourced efforts like

Wikipedia and the proprietary nature of existing map data in the UK. OSM currently has more than two million registered users, each of whom can contribute to the project by collecting data that uses techniques such as manual surveys, aerial photography, and Global Positioning System (GPS).

The data generated by OSM is used by websites such as Craigslist, OsmAnd, Geocaching, and Foursquare (to name just a few), and is an alternative to services like Google Maps. Map data collection is both a grassroots and crowdsourced effort, with data being collected from scratch by volunteers performing systematic ground surveys (using tools such as a handheld GPS unit, a notebook, or even a voice recorder). The data is then entered into the OSM database. Mapathon competition events are also held by the OSM team and nonprofit organizations and local governments to map a particular area.

Some government agencies have released official data under appropriate licenses. This includes the US, where works of the federal government are placed in the public domain. In the US, OSM uses Landsat 7 satellite imagery, Prototype Global Shorelines from the National Oceanic and Atmospheric Administration (NOAA), and TIGER data from the Census Bureau. In the UK, some Ordnance Survey OpenData is imported, while Natural Resources Canada's CanVec vector data and GeoBase provide land cover and streets. An important source of information that does not lead to copyright or licensing problems is out-of-copyright maps that serve as good sources of information about features that do not change frequently. Copyright periods vary, but in the UK Crown copyright expires after 50 years; hence Ordnance Survey maps until the 1960s can legally be used. A complete set of UK 1 inch/mile maps from the late 1940s and early 1950s has been collected, scanned, and is available online as a resource for contributors.

In February 2015, OSM added route planning functionality to the map on its official website. The routing uses external services (namely, OSRM, GraphHopper, and MapQuest). Three examples of software available for working with OSM include OpenStreetBrowser, which displays finer map and category options; OsmAnd, which is a free software for Android and iOS mobile devices that can use offline (vector) data from OSM, and which supports layering OSM vector data with prerendered raster map tiles from OSM; and Maps.me, which is another free software for mobile devices that provides offline maps based on OSM data.

A notable application of OSM has been in the area of humanitarian aid. For example, during the 2010 Haiti earthquake, OSM and Crisis Commons volunteers used available satellite imagery to map the roads, buildings, and refugee camps of Port-au-Prince in just two days, building one of the most complete digital map of Haiti's roads ever to exist. Other organizations that have used these data and maps include the World Bank, the European Commission Joint Research Center, and even the Office for the Coordination of Humanitarian Affairs. Other natural disasters in which OSM data played an important role include the northern Mali conflict, Typhoon Haiyan in the Philippines in 2013, and the Ebola epidemic in West Africa in 2014.

15.4   Where Is the Future Headed?

KGs in governments, nonprofits, and for-profit organizations have continued to grow, a trend that will most likely continue in the foreseeable future. In addition to growth in existing ecosystems, new initiatives are in the works, some with potentially transformative impact. Because any discussion of where the future will go is necessarily speculative and beyond the scope of this book, we focus on two well-realized trends. Interestingly, both are grassroots efforts, although one is primarily industrial and the other is primarily academic.

First, an encouraging sign of progress in the adoption of KGs in enterprise is the growing number of start-ups and nontech companies that have been using, building, or otherwise working with KGs recently. This trend has not gone unnoticed in business and consulting. For example, Gartner placed Graph Analytics on its "Top 10 Data and Analytics Technology Trend for 2019" report in the area of solving critical business priorities. While graphs are considered a general data model (or structure) in the academic computer science and math communities, it is fairly evident in the actual report that KGs and graph databases constituted the primary technologies in Garner's scope, as the following quote evinces:[6] "The application of graph processing and graph DBMSs will grow at 100 percent annually through 2022 to continuously accelerate data preparation and enable more complex and adaptive data science." Examples of start-ups that are offering KGs (whether by way of supporting technology, data, or both) as primary business offerings include Stardog, which has partnered with industry leaders like Morgan Stanley and the National Aeronautics and Space Administration (NASA), and Diffbot, which is attempting to assemble a web-scale KG of billions of facts and offers a subscription-like model with starter rates as low as a cable TV bill. Other examples also exist, some more specific to communities like SW than others. While most start-ups have focused on English-language data and cater to customers in Western economies, the rise of spending power, modernization, and economic importance of countries like India and China has led to a renewal of interest in building KGs from multilingual data sets covering more diverse domains and data genres such as Short Message Service (SMS).

Second, a very recent initiative that is motivated by the concern that enterprises like Google, Amazon, and Microsoft each have their own, currently proprietary KG ecosystem is the Open Knowledge Network (OKN). Proprietary KG ecosystems have two consequences: (1) repetition and redundancy, with similar technical problems being solved

---

[6] https://www.gartner.com/en/newsroom/press-releases/2019-02-18-gartner-identifies-top-10-data-and-analytics-technolo.

across similar talent pools (and for virtually identical markets); (2) the lack of openness, uniform standards, or public availability. It is notable that the challenges in the second point were addressed by movements such as Linked Data, and even Schema.org, but these initiatives do not have the centralized resources or personnel of the major technological firms. Alarmingly, it seems that large, interlinked KGs on the web (which would not include Schema.org, as the entities are not naturally linked in the way that Wikipedia, DBpedia, and other data sets on LOD are) fall within two camps: high-quality, closely guarded KGs being developed in industry, of which even basic details can sometimes be hard to publicly acquire (Microsoft Satori is one example), and open, crowdsourced KGs that have to be developed, hosted, and maintained in increasingly resource-light settings, or through small individual efforts by a massive collective (crowdsourcing).

OKN offers itself as an alternative by pushing for a small set of core protocols and vocabulary, as well as a web-style architecture, that encourage diversity (i.e., publishers and consumers of all sizers and stripes) and easy proliferation and publishing of services (e.g., search) that would lead to rapid application offerings. Invoking the analogy to the pre-web era, OKN would play the same role in the development, publishing, storage, and access of web-scale knowledge graphs that the HTTP protocol played, and continues to play, in the publishing and consumption of websites. It is controversial to what extent the initiative is different from either the SW or the Linked Data movement (which is broadly supported by the SW community, as noted in chapter 14). Interestingly, while the Linked Data movement is global in scope, with contributions from both US and European institutions, the scope of OKN has been limited to US agencies, institutions, and individuals thus far.

At this time, the initiative involves a number of important figures from academia and industry, with regular workshops organized and held by the US National Science Foundation. Important domains that key stakeholders believe will be affected by the effort include finance, geosciences, commercial applications like personal assistants, and biomedicine. Like any ambitious effort, the success of the movement is not guaranteed, but it is a principled step toward achieving an open, and truly web-scale, KG ecosystem that offers benefits to public, private, and individual players alike.

15.5   Concluding Notes

In this chapter, we covered the adoption of KGs in enterprise and government. Although the term "knowledge graph" became popular in modern times because of the Google Knowledge Graph, which is truly web scale in its scope and largely proprietary, it has since been widely adopted (as a technology) or constructed (as valuable data) by all manner of organizations. Most encouragingly, start-ups and nontech companies have taken up the mantle in discovering novel use-cases of KGs and employing them as a service. Governments are not far behind, although data sets on portals like Data.gov are still too raw compared to industry standards. Also important is the successful application of scientific principles like Linked Data by organizations like the BBC. More recently, initiatives like the OKN are seeking to democratize large-scale, all-encompassing KGs by incentivizing easy proliferation and publishing of KGs and KG-centric services like search. In a narrower domain, OSM has successfully democratized the publishing and use of map and geospatial data.

15.6 Software and Resources

The Schema.org resources are available at https://schema.org/, with the schemas available at https://schema.org/docs/schemas.html. For developers, there is a separate set of resources available at https://schema.org/docs/developers.html. The Knowledge Vault (KV), which was mentioned in the early part of the chapter, received a lot of press[7] (and was written about in several publications, as cited in the next section), but does not seem to have been made openly available. An adequate substitute for research purposes might be Wikidata, which is available at https://www.wikidata.org/wiki/Wikidata:Main_Page. However, more recently, researchers who previously worked on the KV research released a publication on OpenCeres (accessible at http://lunadong.com/publication/openCeres_naacl.pdf), which contains details that are replicable on large, openly available corpora. The Common-Crawl is an important resource in this regard, accessible at http://commoncrawl.org/. We recommend that interested readers also take a closer look at the WDC, which extracts structured data from the CommonCrawl and provides extracted data for public download to support academia and industry alike. WDC has its homepage at http://webdatacommons.org/.

Concerning social media efforts, the primary webpage for learning about the OGP is https://ogp.me/. Toward the end of that webpage, several implementations are mentioned, including libraries written in Python, Ruby, and Java, accessible at http://pypi.python.org/pypi/PyOpenG-raph, http://github.com/intridea/opengraph, and http://github.com/callumj/opengraph-java, respectively.

We have mentioned that OGD is becoming more common throughout the world. In the US, a good resource is https://www.data.gov/open-gov/. Another good resource is the OECD website on the subject: https://www.oecd.org/gov/digital-government/open-government-data.htm. Among other important resources, it publishes the OURdata Index, which assesses governments' efforts to implement open data in the three critical areas—the openness, usefulness, and reusability of government data. The most recent index showed that South Korea has the highest index, while the US ranked out of the top 10, but was slightly above the OECD average. Some sample websites of countries that have instituted open government efforts or portals include Singapore (https://data.gov.sg/), the

---

[7] Examples of such coverage include https://www.engadget.com/2014-08-21-google-knowledge-vault.html, https://zebratechies.com/google-knowledge-graph-knowledge-vault-and-how-its-impact-on-serp, and https://www.searchenginenews.com/sample/update/entry/understanding-googles-knowledge-vault.

United Kingdom (https://data.gov.uk/), and India (https://data.gov.in/). Most democratic nations today offer such platforms, although the ease of use and completeness of data vary significantly.

We mentioned the BBC as an important and early adopter of KG and SW technologies. A good webpage for accessing the ontologies and other resources is www.bbc.co.uk/ontologies.

The OSM resource is accessible at openstreetmap.org/#map=5/38.007/-95.844. It is free to use under an open license. For users interested in exploring download options, we recommend https://www.openstreetmap.org/export#map=5/38.007/-95.844, which provides export options licensed under the Open Data Commons Open Database License.

At this time, projects exploring the OKN have already received funding from the National Science Foundation. A "Dear Colleague" letter is accessible at https://www.nsf.gov/pubs/2019/nsf19050/nsf19050.jsp. An OKN report by the Networking and Information Technology Research and Development (NITRD) program is directly downloadable from https://www.nitrd.gov/news/Open-Knowledge-Network-Workshop-Report-2018.aspx.

15.7   Bibliographic Notes

We started this chapter by describing the effects of the Big Data movement on industry and government. While listing a full bibliography of Big Data would be a near-impossible task, we note some influential papers that have especially looked at industry, including Chen et al. (2012), Labrinidis and Jagadish (2012), Khan et al. (2017), Yin and Kaynak (2015), Xu and Duan (2019), Lee et al. (2014), and Bilal et al. (2016). There are fewer papers describing the influence of Big Data on government, but the output is still extensive, important examples including Kim et al. (2014), Bertot et al. (2014), Janssen and van den Hoven (2015), and Archenaa and Anita (2015). Janssen and van den Hoven (2015), in particular, describe an intersection of open Big Data with Linked Data, which has been discussed in previous chapters, but note that such a combination could potentially present challenges to transparency and privacy. When applying Big Data technology, including KG research, to government-scale problems, ethics and privacy are important issues to consider. Note that in some cases, industry and government interests can intersect in the Big Data research. Pan et al. (2017) is a useful example of how linked data and KGs can be exploited in large organizations.

Significant attention was given in this chapter to the Google Knowledge Graph. At this time, the blog post introducing the Google Knowledge Graph is still available online and can be accessed by consulting Singhal (2012). Since that time, many other papers have been written that have either described or improved on the Google Knowledge Graph in some aspects. Many modern papers on KGs directly cite the Google Knowledge Graph and its development as a motivating factor, sometimes for domain-specific cases. A partial list of works includes Hoffart et al. (2014), Ehrlinger and Wöß (2016), Steiner and Mirea

(2012), Steiner et al. (2012), Rotmensch et al. (2017), Vang (2013), Speer et al. (2017), and Paulheim (2017). Many patents have also been filed, a particularly important consideration when discussing innovation in industry. Two examples stemming from early work right after (or around the time of) the Google Knowledge Graph's blog announcement include Eder (2012) and Ryu et al. (2013).

The chapter also described the KV by Dong et al. (2014), which is believed to be contributing valuable research to the Google Knowledge Graph. The KV itself draws on a long line of research in IE and graph priors, with some important works noted in earlier chapters on IE. Other papers by Carlson et al. (2010), Lao et al. (2011), Li and Grishman (2013), Nakashole et al. (2011), Niu et al. (2012b), and Wick et al. (2013) must also be noted in having influenced the KV. OpenCeres, which does Open IE on semistructured web data, can be understood to be a more modern and updated version of KV; it was described by Lockard et al. (2019).

Social media has intersected significantly with KGs in recent years. We described the OGP as one contributing technology; good references for OGP include Haugen (2010) and Open Graph Protocol (2016). Beyond OGP, KGs have been used to inform a number of important social media applications. Pan et al. (2018) describe how to detect fake news in a content-based manner using KGs; similarly, Shiralkar et al. (2017) have used it to support fact-checking. Several other researchers have used KGs and social media for personalized recommendation and ranking; see Karidi et al. (2018) and Zhang et al. (2016), among others. Another related work is Choudhury et al. (2017), on the construction and querying of dynamic KGs, especially the kind that are constructed over social media. In chapter 7 on nontraditional IE, we covered a broader spectrum of work on extracting information from tweets and constructing a KG thereof.

Schema.org has rapidly expanded its presence on the web as a dominant form of structured data that can be processed and used by search engines. Good references include Guha et al. (2016) and Ronallo (2012), the latter of which also covers HTML5 microdata. An analysis of Schema.org is provided by Patel-Schneider (2014), and Meusel et al. (2015) does a web-scale study on its adoption and evolution over time. Mika (2015) provides an argument for why Schema.org is important for the web, and Nam and Kejriwal (2018) provide case studies on how organizations publish Schema.org markup. Hepp (2015) describes Schema.org for researchers and practitioners, especially with a view toward e-commerce. It is quite likely that we will continue to see increasing research on Schema.org during this decade as well.

OGD became a well-researched topic over the previous decade, owing not only to the rise of the Big Data movement, but also to governments releasing a lot of their data on web portals, often in a structured form. An excellent introduction to the OGD movement is Ubaldi (2013). In other relevant works, Ding et al. (2011) describes a portal for linked OGD ecosystems, while Vetrò et al. (2016) describes a framework for open data quality measurement (with an application toward OGD). Janssen et al. (2012) discusses the benefits and barriers of open data and open government, while Jetzek et al. (2014) more optimistically discusses innovations that could become possible through OGD. Another similar work along these lines is Chan (2013). Other good references, especially on specific initiatives or directives, include Janssen (2011) and Attard et al. (2015), the latter of which is a systematic review.

In the US, Data.gov has been the most prominent example of OGD. References for Data.gov (or on using it) include Ding et al. (2010a,b), Hendler et al. (2012), and Lakhani et al. (2002), among many others. More recent works include Wang et al. (2019) and Mahmud et al. (2020). In the UK, Shadbolt et al. (2012) discuss lessons derived from Data.gov.uk. For more details on the BBC, SW, and Linked Data, we recommend Raimond et al. (2014), which describes the BBC World Service radio archive, although several earlier papers on the BBC's use of semantic technology also can be consulted.

OSM is another valuable resource described briefly in this chapter, and that has also received interest from the SW and Linked Data communities. Haklay and Weber (2008) and Bennett (2010) are good references for learning about the OSM project, while Anelli et al. (2016) and Auer et al. (2009) describe how SW and Linked Data can be brought into the picture. Other related work, especially pertaining to data quality and other issues (such as crowdsourcing) that are important for these kinds of databases, includes Haklay (2010) and Budhathoki and Haythornthwaite (2013).

We concluded this chapter with the OKN, which is too recent to have gotten much research coverage thus far. Some references that mention it, however, are Sheth et al. (2019), Dietz et al. (2018), Xiaogang (2019), Kejriwal (2019), and Alarabiat et al. (2018). White papers and more information can also be downloaded from an NITRD website dedicated to the topic (which can be accessed at https://www.nitrd.gov/nitrdgroups/index.php?title= Open_Knowledge_Network). We note that the National Science Foundation has also allocated resources toward funding promising OKN initiatives.

15.8   Exercises

1. Try to look up a (subjectively determined) well-known, not as well-known, and completely unknown (e.g., your neighbor) entity on Google from the concept set {Person, Organization, Restaurant, Tourist Location}. For these $4 \times 3 = 12$ entities that you picked, how many were found to have a knowledge panel? Do all of your well-known entities have a knowledge panel, and do all of the completely unknown ones not have one? If there are unexpected cases, list a hypothetical explanation for the case. What would be one way for you to validate your hypothesis to determine if you're right?

2. Now let's consider the entities that are not as well known, but are also not completely unknown, however you might have interpreted that description. For such entities, if you found any that do not have a knowledge panel, what would be one way (short of

having direct edit access to the Google Knowledge Graph) to increase the chances of finding a knowledge panel on that entity a short time (say a week, or even a month) from today? *Hint: In reading our description of the Google Knowledge Graph, as well as other resources you can find about it online, what can you determine about the raw sources of information that ultimately get processed and eventually become entities, relations, and attributes in the Google Knowledge Graph?*

3. Suppose that you are opening a new restaurant and trying to set up a website for it. Other than the aesthetics of having a nice-looking website with no downtime, you are looking to leverage a Schema.org-based search engine optimization (SEO) strategy for appearing high in Google search rankings, and which may help attract more patrons. Describe what such a strategy would look like. What kinds of Schema.org snippets would you look into integrating into your website, and how often would you change them? Is timeliness very important? Why or why not?

4. By drawing on the examples and information listed in the OGP resource (http-s://ogp. me/), how might you integrate your restaurant's profile and information into a social graph (i.e., try to describe, being as specific as possible and using snippets of code, how you would turn your restaurant's webpage into a graph object using OGP).

5. List some commercial domains where you believe there is no use for Schema.org and/or where it is overkill to try and include it in a website. If you have found such a domain, could you generalize and state what properties of the domain (criteria) make it amenable or not amenable to the kinds of Schema.org SEO strategies that you considered for the restaurant domain in the previous exercise? Try to provide a list of five diverse domains that you believe would *not* be amenable to a Schema.org-based SEO strategy, and state the expected reasons (using your criteria).

6. Recall the OGD principles listed in table 15.2. Could you think of data sets that have the first four properties (i.e., they are complete, primary, timely, and accessible), but not the last four?

7. A think tank that studies the intersection of government and geospatial data hires you as a consultant expressing a desire to develop an app that their employees and social scientists can use to (i) visualize major cities and regions of the world using maps; and (ii) display demographic, economic, and other relevant socioeconomic and political indicators at appropriate granularities (e.g., county-level income data). You have been hired because of your expertise in KGs and the think tank's belief that a properly designed KG can help them develop a scalable and sustainable answer to their needs. You will be working with a user experience designer and developers, and your main task is to help them build such a KG. Making appropriate assumptions where needed, draft an architecture document for constructing, completing, and accessing the KG to serve the needs of the think tank as described. In particular, drawing on the material in both this chapter and chapter 14, be precise about the raw and auxiliary data sources

that you will use or need to realize this vision. Try to limit yourself to open data sets as much as possible.

8. You have been successful in the endeavor from exercise 7, and the think tank has received new funding due to the impressive capabilities of the KG. It now wants to develop a powerful new version of the app that is able to integrate news data on a daily basis. Specifically, they have hired a machine learning expert who will develop algorithms to derive real-valued signals (e.g., indicators of local violence, political unrest, strikes, and other significant events) from news data and send it to your KG. You may further assume that you have access to a service (e.g., LexisNexis: https://www.lexisnexis.com/en-us/gateway.page) that delivers a daily dump of news articles to the think tank's server, and you have a full suite of tools at your disposal, including Named Entity Recognition (NER), KG embeddings (KGEs), and others. How might you extend the architecture you drafted earlier? Would changes be needed at the level of the KG's ontology to accommodate these indicator signals? What additional open data sources could you bring to bear to help the machine learning expert achieve better accuracy?

16 Knowledge Graphs and Ontologies in Science

Overview. Scientific knowledge is one of the most important repositories of knowledge available to humanity. As scientific domains have proliferated and broadened in scope, particularly in rapidly advancing fields like biology and medicine, it has become all the more important to organize and represent that knowledge in a coherent manner. Ontologies and knowledge graphs (KGs) have emerged as fundamental technologies for accomplishing that goal. In this chapter, we provide an overview of KGs in selected scientific communities where KGs have had quite an impact in recent years (and thus provide important best-practice lessons), such as the life science, chemistry, and geoscience communities.

16.1 Introduction

Scientific knowledge is arguably one of the most important and trusted bodies of knowledge available to humanity, and it has been painstakingly developed and tested over many centuries of theorizing and hypothesis formulation, experimental design and execution, and refinement. Just like ordinary social communities, each scientific community has its own norms and views, but common among them all is the scientific method and a focus on experimental validation of hypotheses. In each community, the scientific method has led to vast repositories of *scientific facts*, many of which have been replicated in multiple experiments or otherwise have some provenance or citation (usually, but not always, through a peer-reviewed scientific publication or experiment of record) that can be used to determine the verity of the claim. Because the scientific method is inductive, a given hypothesis can be overturned in the face of new knowledge. Facts can also lose their status as facts if new experiments are unable to replicate the finding or if unintentional (and in some unfortunate cases, intentional) biases or mistakes are discovered to lie behind the data.

We provide this background to illustrate two critical aspects of a scientific domain: first, despite all the differences between individual fields of study, the scientific method, as well as a focus on high-quality, experimentally validated, and peer-reviewed knowledge, provides a strong guarantee of the quality of modern scientific knowledge generated; and second, science is both a *dynamic* and a *social* endeavor. Science is dynamic because the generation of new knowledge often leads to overturning of old hypotheses or proposals of new hypotheses (and sometimes the creation of entirely new areas of research), but it is also social because scientists rarely work in isolation—they must almost always draw on the findings of others in proposing their contributions. In other words, scientific knowledge is meant to be *shared*, and facts within an area of study have structure to them, as scientists within the field tend to use similar terminology and obey similar norms (notwithstanding the complexities that arise due to factions between communities and geopolitical differences). Intuitively, it is not hard to make the argument that scientific subfields have their own ontology, though it may not always be easy to encode an ontology (to satisfy everyone in the field) in a formal language like Web Ontology Language (OWL).

Going one step beyond ontologies, we argue that KGs are equally well suited to encoding, publishing, and sharing scientific knowledge for several reasons. The main reason is the structure of the data itself, because scientific knowledge as a high-quality repository is predominantly factual, though many facts can be superseded or refined in the face of new experiments and findings. On an auxiliary note, uncertainty and provenance are clearly important aspects that must be systematically accounted for, and although knowledge provenance is beyond the scope of this book (we provide guidance for the interested reader in the section entitled "Bibliographic Notes," at the end of this chapter), ontologies for codifying and capturing provenance currently exist in the Semantic Web (SW) community. Next, because of the increasingly social nature of science, as evidenced by the success of large consortia and ambitious scientific projects like the discovery of gravitational waves or experiments in the Large Hadron Collider (which required the participation of numerous scientists and disciplines), properly represented and published KGs can be immensely useful to all the different stakeholders for sharing and querying a body of scientific knowledge. Finally, because of the domain-specific nature of scientific knowledge (a different way to say this is that an ontology in biology is very different from an ontology in materials science), KGs are apt, as they are well suited for capturing domain knowledge. In fact, as we've seen in the vast majority of this text, the structure and schema of most KGs (the one exception being KGs constructed using Open IE techniques) is defined using a domain ontology.

One point of confusion that can arise in natural disciplines like biology or chemistry is between a KG and an ontology. Because such disciplines tend to make claims about concepts (e.g., water molecule) rather than a particular instance of the concept (a particular water molecule in the Pacific Ocean), it is common to define the knowledge in an ontology. This leads to an enormous ontology, with no corresponding KG. This makes the scientific domain very unique, in that ontologies, not KGs, are the first-class citizens; in fact, KGs rarely exist in a structured format. However, because of its size and complexity, the ontology serves the same purpose as a KG does in more common applications like e-commerce or search. With this in mind, in the rest of this chapter, we treat such ontologies just as we would the KGs that we have encountered thus far.

16.2 Biology

As biological information has accumulated, it has become increasingly important to describe and classify biological objects in meaningful ways. Many species- and domain-specific databases have strategies to organize and integrate such data, allowing users to sift through expanding volumes of information. However, biologists want to be able to use the information stored in disparate databases to ask interesting and relevant, field-specific questions. For example, a biologist might want to ask which genes or gene products contribute to the formation and development of an epithelial sheet. Researchers may not want to stop there, and they may want to be able to expand such queries to find gene products in different organisms that share characteristics. To support this kind of research, an ordinary database is not enough (i.e., searching for such information in the context of complex scientific tasks like examining microarray expression data or sequencing genotypes in a population is simply impossible without an ecosystem of computational tools, querying systems, and even annotation schemes).

Although the biological field has many good resources to draw upon, the dominant resource that is pertinent to KGs as we have presented them in this book is the *Gene Ontology* (GO). Despite what its name suggests, the Gene Ontology has emerged as something far more than an ontology (as would be understood in everyday practice), and it is now an ecosystem in itself, having inspired a range of downstream systems and applications. In the rest of this section, we describe the various aspects of the Gene Ontology in detail.

16.2.1 Gene Ontology

The need for a flexible, extensible resource in the life sciences was recognized well before the era of Big Data had begun in other areas, especially considering the many disparate data sources, varying information needs, and the dynamic, expanding nature of biological knowledge in irregular, often unpredictable, ways, given that some subfields can expand at faster rates than others. In response to this need, the Gene Ontology Consortium[1] was formed to "develop a comprehensive, computational model of biological systems, ranging from the molecular to the organism level, across the multiplicity of species in the tree of life." The original intent of the group was to construct a set of vocabularies that comprise terms that could be shared with a common understanding of the meaning of any term used and that could support cross-database queries. In this sense, this purpose was no different

---

[1] http://geneontology.org/. This website is also the source of the quote.

Table 16.1: Specific goals of the GO Consortium.

Goals of the GO Consortium
Compiling a comprehensive structured vocabulary of terms describing various elements of molecular biology shared among life forms. Furthermore, terms are defined, may have synonyms, and may be refined further into broader and narrower organizations. Also, separate vocabularies will be used to define the different dimensions of biology.
Describing the biological objects (in the model organism database of each contributing member) using the terms compiled in the first point.
Providing querying tools and mechanisms for manipulating the vocabularies, including (1) adding new vocabularies for additional aspects of biology, (2) permitting researchers to locate terms and biological objects via the web (or even more complex ways), and (3) allowing the setup of satellite databases where necessary.
Providing the tools to enable curators to assign GO terms to biological objects (including sequence-based methods, editorial annotations, protein binding experiments and microarrays).

from that of any group looking to define a class ontology for formalizing the terminology and semantics of their domain.

However, even very early on, novel extensions to the intent started to emerge. For example, it became clear that the combined set of annotations from the model organism groups would provide a useful resource for the community. This is a good example of a use-case that emerges organically. As a result of these annotations, in addition to developing the shared structured vocabularies, the GO project intended to develop an extensible database resource providing access not just to vocabularies, but also to annotation and query applications. The consortium also intended to release specialized data sets resulting from the use of the vocabularies in the annotation of genes and gene products. The goals of the GO Consortium are listed in table 16.1.

It should be noted that the consortium is also clear about what its goals are *not*. For example, the consortium has said clearly that the ontology is not a way to unify biological data sets, even though (at least in practice) the sharing of nomenclature has had that added welcome effect. The ontology is also not a dictated standard, in the sense of mandating nomenclature across databases. Rather, the goal is for groups to come together and arrive at a mutually acceptable consensus. Finally, the GO does not define homologies between gene products from different organisms. While usage of the ontology has resulted in shared annotations for gene products from different organisms, the annotation is not (in itself) sufficient for determining an evolutionary relationship.

16.2.1.1 Structure of the Ontology   To fulfill its goals, the GO Consortium developed three ontologies: *molecular function, biological process,* and *cellular component,* to describe attributes of gene products or gene product groups. The three ontologies are each represented by a separate root ontology term. All terms in a domain can trace their parentage to a root term, although there may be numerous paths via varying numbers of intermediary terms to an ontology root. The three root nodes are unrelated and do not have a common parent node; for this reason, it is more appropriate to think of the GO as a project rather than as a single ontology. One complication that can arise due to the presence of three ontologies is the use of graph-based (or other) software that can work with only one ontology at a time (i.e., requires a single root node). A workaround suggested by the GO itself for dealing with this issue is to introduce a fake term that serves as a single root and is the parent of the three existing root nodes.

While a molecular function describes what a gene product does at the biochemical level, a biological process describes a broad biological objective and a cellular component describes the location of a gene product (e.g., within a cellular structure). The three ontologies are directed acyclic graphs, and predominantly include both *"is a"* and *"part of"* relationship types. Each term in the ontology is an accessible object in the GO resource and has a unique identifier that can be used as a database cross-reference. Elements of GO terms, as per the latest edition, are described in table 16.2

Molecular Function. Within the molecular function ontology are terms describing molecular-level activities performed by gene products—specifically, activities that occur at the molecular level (e.g., catalysis or transport). In GO, molecular function terms represent activities rather than the entities (molecules or complexes) that perform these actions, and they do not specify where, when, or in what context the actions take place. Molecular functions generally correspond to activities that can be performed by individual gene products (a protein or ribonucleic acid), but some activities are performed by molecular complexes composed of multiple gene products. Examples of broad functional terms in the molecular function ontology include "enzyme," "transporter," and "ligand," while an example of a more specific functional term is "adenylate cyclase." Note that there is the potential for semantic confusion between a gene product and its molecular function because very often, a gene product, with enzymes being a particularly notorious example, is named by at least by one of its molecular functions (or a single function, if there is only one).

Biological Process. These terms describe the larger processes or biological programs that are accomplished by several molecular activities. Examples of broad biological process terms that occur in the biological process ontology include "cell growth and maintenance," with more specific examples being "pyrimidine metabolism" and "cAMP biosynthesis." However, a biological process in this context is not considered equivalent to a pathway, and the consortium has not (thus far) attempted to represent any of the dynamics or dependencies required for describing a pathway.

Table 16.2: Essential and optional elements (the latter indicated by *) in GO terms.

Term	Description
Unique identifier and term name	Every term has a human-readable term name (e.g., mitochondrion) and a GO ID, which is a unique seven-digit identifier prefixed by *GO*.
Aspect	Denotes which of the three subontologies (cellular component, biological process, or molecular function) the term belongs to.
Definition	A textual description of what the term represents, plus references to the source of the information.
Relationships to other terms	How the term relates to other terms in the ontology. All terms (other than the root terms representing each aspect) have an "is a" subclass relationship to another term.
Secondary IDs (also known as alternate IDs)*	Secondary IDs come about when two or more terms are identical in meaning and merged into a single term. All term IDs are preserved so that no information (e.g., annotations to the merged IDs) is lost.
Database cross-references (dbxrefs)*	Database cross-references refer to identical or very similar objects in other databases.
Synonyms*	Alternative words or phrases closely related in meaning to the term name, with indication of the relationship between the name and synonym given by the synonym scope (*exact, broad, narrow*, and *related*). Custom synonym types are also used in the ontology. For example, a number of synonyms are designated as systematic synonyms; synonyms of this type are exact synonyms of the term name.
Comment*	Any extra information about the term and its usage.
Subset*	Indicates that the term belongs to a designated subset of terms, e.g., one of the GO subsets.
Obsolete tag*	Indicates that the term has been deprecated and should not be used. A GO term is obsoleted when it is out of scope, misleadingly named or defined, or describes a concept that would be better represented in another way and needs to be removed from the published ontology. In these cases, the term and ID persist in the ontology, but the term is tagged as obsolete and all relationships to other terms are removed. A comment is added to the term which details the reason for the obsoletion and replacement terms are suggested, if possible.

Cellular Component. Terms in the cellular component ontology describe locations relative to cellular structures, in which a gene product performs a function, either cellular compartments (e.g., mitochondrion), or stable macromolecular complexes of which they are parts, such as ribosome. Examples of terms in the cellular component ontology include complexes where multiple gene products can be found, such as ribosome and proteasome, in addition to location terms like nuclear membrane, used to indicate places in a cell where a gene product is active. Unlike the other aspects of GO, cellular component classes refer not to processes, but a cellular anatomy.

We note that each term in these three ontologies is defined, with a citation to the source from which the definition was obtained. Query and implementation tools were also developed to exploit the detailed relationships captured in the ontologies. Each term in the ontology has a relationship with at least one other term, but the consortium made a conscious decision not to incorporate these relationships in the term identifiers themselves due to the expected dynamic nature of the ontology (i.e., it was expected that over time, the location of the term within an ontology—namely, its parents and children—would likely change, sometimes in completely unexpected ways).

16.2.1.2 Features and Improvements. Since the early 2000s, the GO has come a long way, and because of its uptake, has continued to be enhanced in its tools, resources, and policies, particularly with a view to improving annotation consistency and ensuring that annotations reflect the state of current biological knowledge. A specific concern addressed by the consortium was the use of inconsistent data representations through these enhancements. Recent improvements to the original GO are described next.

Ontology Development. The total number of GO terms has been steadily increasing, with over a 100 percent increase in just a decade (from around 18,000 to more than 40,000 between 2004 and 2014). Compared to the number of GO terms added to describe molecular functions and cellular components, the number of terms describing biological processes has increased at a higher rate, averaging 4,000 new ones every two years since 2011. There has also been a consistent increase in the number of manual annotations made by curators (e.g., the number of manually annotated gene products has grown to more than 400,000).

Development hasn't been equally divided among the various ontology classes, with the cellular component branch seeing more robust enhancements than others and facilitating the needs of multiple communities. For example, the Subcellular Anatomy Ontology was merged into the GO cellular component representation, leading to a single, unified ontology designed to serve the needs of both the neuroscience community and the wider biomedical research community already being served by the GO. In a similar vein, ontology editors have carried out an effort to update and refine other areas of the ontology (e.g., making enhancements in the OWL version of GO to better support quality control and classification as integral parts of the overall ontology development cycle). For other details on ontology development and enhancement, we refer the interested reader to the

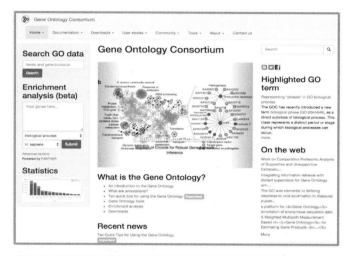

Figure 16.1: A snapshot of changes to the GO resource webpage from five years ago (top) to April 2019 (bottom).

"Bibliographic Notes" section. The GO webpage itself has also undergone design changes and improvements; figure 16.1 illustrates how the homepage has changed in the last five years.

Annotation. Annotation is an important part of a shared, growing resource like the GO. Over the last several years, the GO Consortium has introduced metadata to better describe annotation contexts, including relationships such as localization dependencies and transcription factors. Metadata to better describe the spatiotemporal aspects of processes such as cell type or developmental stages has also been introduced. The information expressed by these extensions refines functional annotations by representing relationships between a basic annotation and contextual information from within the GO (or even external ontologies). Extended annotations can enable complex queries and reasoning, which is an important goal in building such ontologies to begin with. The consortium has also encouraged experts to provide input in various biological areas. For example, a collaboration with the Transcription Factor Checkpoint database expanded annotations to human, mouse, and rat transcription factors, and the Developmental Functional Annotation at Tufts (DFLAT[2]) project improved the annotation quality of the genes involved in fetal development. A joint collaboration between Gramene and Ensembl Plants yielded initial GO annotations for tens of sequenced plant genomes with new releases. Ultimately, such annotations have significantly expanded the scope, quality, and use-cases made possible by the GO resource.

Public Access and Browsing. We earlier illustrated how the GO website has changed to a simpler, more streamlined look compared to just five years ago. New tools for browsing GO annotations were also released. The GO Consortium also provides platforms of interaction and welcomes participation from the community, both to address general inquiries and to address specific requests for the ontology. There are plug-ins for social media and GitHub on the webpage. These social and public-facing aspects of the GO are clearly considered to be important assets by the consortium, and are expected to be continued to be maintained and enhanced over time.

16.3 Chemistry

Chemistry is another important natural science discipline in which knowledge representation has found important use-cases and applications. We describe two important efforts, ChEBI and PubChem, in this domain. Note that the GO itself is liberally used in chemistry as well.

16.3.1 Chemical Entities of Biological Interest

Chemical Entities of Biological Interest (ChEBI) is a freely available dictionary of molecular entities focused on small chemical compounds (i.e., genome-encoded macromolecules, such as nucleic acids, proteins, and peptides derived from proteins by cleavage, are not generally included in ChEBI). The molecular entities in question are either natural or synthetic products that are used to intervene in the processes of living organisms; in essence, they encompass any constitutionally or isotopically distinct atom, molecule, ion, ion pair, or radical (among others) that is identifiable as a separately distinguishable entity.

In addition to molecular entities, ChEBI contains groups (parts of molecular entities) and classes of entities. It includes an ontological classification, whereby the relationships

---

[2] http://dflat.cs.tufts.edu/.

between molecular entities or classes of entities and their parents, children, or both are specified.

All the data in ChEBI is nonproprietary or derived from a nonproprietary source, and is available under the Creative Commons License. Furthermore, ChEBI data items have detailed provenance, in that they are traceable and explicitly referenced to the original source. A visualization of the ChEBI entity-centric dashboard for the molecular entity ecogonine benzoate is shown in figure 16.2. In addition to the visual structure of the molecule, the database contains an identifier for the entity (CHEBI:41001); a definition; a star-based annotation scheme that (in this case) confirms that the entity has been manually annotated by the ChEBI team; secondary IDs; supplier information; and chemical properties like Formula, Net Charge, and Average Mass. In this case, there is also a Wikipedia link. Although not shown here, other details that can be obtained by scrolling down the page include the IUPAC Name, roles classifications, registry numbers, and synonyms.

The reason that we illustrate the search dashboard here is to highlight a critical point that was first alluded to in the introduction when studying scientific knowledge repositories like ChEBI (namely, that such repositories meet the definition of a KG owing to their focus on entities, relationships, and connections between entities, despite the fact that they are not designated as KGs). Furthermore, in scientific databases such as these, it can be hard to distinguish where the ontology leaves off and the KG begins (if one even exists—some would argue that the ontology is all there is in a scientific repository). In practice, such a distinction is neither necessary nor wise, which makes these data sets different from traditional KGs constructed by natural-language systems over news or open-domain corpora. Unlike ordinary domains, where the ontology tends to be compact and the actual KG is much bigger, scientific KGs can be equivalently characterized as large ontologies.

Although ChEBI is reasonably compact (compared to other KGs), containing just over 18,000 entities in the early 2000s (and expanding to over 46,000 entries by 2016), it is differentiated by a strong focus on quality, with exceptional efforts afforded to International Union of Pure and Applied Chemistry (IUPAC) nomenclature rules, classification within the ontology, and best IUPAC practices when drawing chemical structures. The employed nomenclature and terminology in ChEBI is also recommended by the Nomenclature Committee of the International Union of Biochemistry and Molecular Biology (NC-IUBMB).

In recent years, programmatic access to ChEBI has significantly improved, as detailed in the section entitled "Software and Resources," at the end of this chapter. The documented use-cases of ChEBI include (1) being used as a source of stable unique identifiers for chemicals in annotations in a wide range of bioinformatics databases, including UniProt and systems biology models; (2) being used in text- and data-mining programs; (3) being linked to the GO, as well as several other ontologies, as the chemistry component; and (4) being used for SW applications [e.g., as the recent representation of PubChem content as the Resource Description Framework (RDF) in order to provide *rdf:type* tags for PubChem

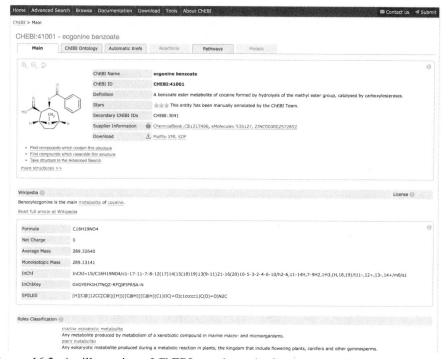

Figure 16.2: An illustration of ChEBI search results for the molecular entity "ecogonine benzoate."

chemicals, as discussed next]. In the decade since its introduction, ChEBI has gained widespread adoption and become an essential repository for chemistry and bioinformatics, supporting a robust set of applications and user types in multiple scientific contexts.

16.3.2 PubChem

PubChem is a public repository on chemical substances and their biological activities, and it was launched in 2004 as a component of the Molecular Libraries Roadmap Initiatives of the US National Institutes of Health (NIH). PubChem rapidly grew into a key chemical information resource for serving scientific communities in areas such as cheminformatics, chemical biology, and drug discovery. It contains one of the largest corpora of publicly available chemical information, with more than 157 million depositor-provided chemical substance descriptions, 60 million unique chemical structures, and 1 million biological assay descriptions, covering about 10,000 unique protein target sequences. This large repository of data is organized into three interlinked databases: *Substance, Compound*, and *BioAssay. Substance* stores depositor-contributed information, while the unique chemical structures extracted from the *Substance* database are stored in the *Compound* database. In contrast, the *BioAssay* database stores descriptions of biological assays on chemical substances.

PubChem has a strong community presence, with data provided by more than 350 contributors, including university labs, government agencies, pharmaceutical companies, and chemical vendors. Data provided by these contributors involves not just small molecules, but chemically modified macromolecules, lipids, and peptides, among other substances.

Originally, PubChem was not a KG; however, PubChemRDF changed this by encoding PubChem's data using RDF and harnessing ontological frameworks to facilitate PubChem data sharing, analysis, and integration with resources external to the National Center for Biotechnology Information (NCBI) and across scientific domains. Chemical and drug ontologies such as NDF-RT, NCI Thesaurus,[3] and ChEBI are used to annotate PubChem compounds and substances, while the GO and the Protein Ontology are used to annotate bioassay molecular targets. Furthermore, PubChemRDF exposes a number of semantic relationships among compounds, substances, bioassays, genes, and other elements.

Ultimately, PubChemRDF allows researchers to work with PubChem data locally using SW tools and systems. The selected data files in any subdomain can be downloaded from the PubChem File Transfer Protocol (FTP) site and imported into an RDF triple/quad-store (such as Apache Jena) that provides a SPARQL interface. The data can also be loaded into graph databases like Neo4j, and graph traversal and processing algorithms could be used to query the KG in advanced ways. Additionally, PubChemRDF provides programmatic data

---

[3] https://ncithesaurus.nci.nih.gov/ncitbrowser/.

access through a representational state transfer (REST)-ful interface and simple SPARQL-like query capabilities for grouping and filtering relevant results.

16.4   Earth, Environment, and Geosciences

Geoscience studies produce data from various observations, experiments, and simulations a very high rate. With the proliferation of applications and data formats, the geoscience research community faces many challenges in effectively managing and sharing resources, as well as efficiently integrating and analyzing the data.

16.4.1   Semantic Web for Earth and Environmental Terminology

Ontologies within the Semantic Web for Earth and Environmental Terminology (SWEET) together constitute an upper-level ontology for Earth system science. The SWEET ontologies include several thousand terms, spanning a broad extent of Earth system science and related concepts (such as data characteristics) using OWL.

SWEET consists of two types of ontologies: *faceted* and *integrative*. Figure 16.3, derived from the SWEET guide, shows their interrelationships. Tables 16.3 and 16.4 further describe these ontologies. As a set, the ontologies should be thought of as constituting a *concept space* for Earth system science. SWEET enables the same concept to be represented using various phrases to satisfy the needs of multiple users. Rather than define a compound concept such as air temperature, the SWEET ontologists decided to separate the physical property (e.g., temperature) from the element that the property applies to (e.g., air). This provides a more scalable solution to a growing knowledge base (KB). In this case, *compositional* knowledge of the independent concepts of the substance "air" and the property temperature provides a complete understanding of "air temperature," without a need to create an explicit definition of the compound concept. While such a decomposition does not preclude term recompositions, the compound terms are designated as synonymous with their integral parts. In other instances, the compound concepts contain more meaning than their component parts (e.g., static pressure) and are explicitly included in the ontology.

16.4.2   The GEON Portal and OpenTopography

One other solution that was proposed in the mid-2000s was the GEON (the GEOscience Network) Portal, which was focused on the same problem as the GO—namely, that information sources often fail to share a common terminology, have a variety of data representation formats and management architectures, and exhibit complex relationships between data and tools used to analyze the data. Creating an infrastructure to integrate, analyze, and model geoscience data poses many challenges due to the extreme heterogeneity of geoscience data formats, storage and computing systems and, most important, the ubiquity of differing conventions, terminologies, and ontological frameworks across disciplines. Dealing with this heterogeneity is important to facilitate interdisciplinary research, especially

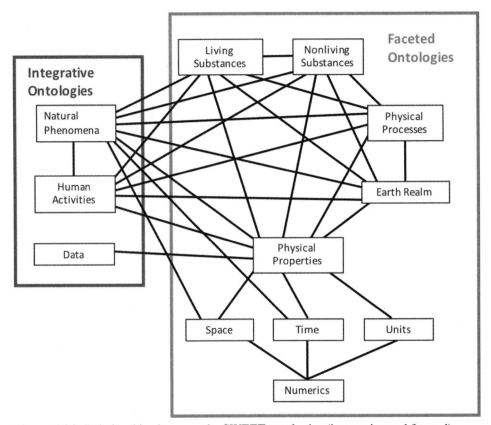

Figure 16.3: Relationships between the SWEET ontologies (integrative and faceted).

Table 16.3: Brief descriptions of faceted ontologies in SWEET.

Ontology	Description
Earth Realm	The spheres (e.g., atmosphere, ocean, and solid earth) of the Earth constitute the EarthRealm ontology, based upon the physical properties of the planet, including subrealms such as the ocean floor and atmospheric boundary layer. This ontology can be considered a state of the planet that is extendable to past or future time periods (as well as to other planets).
Nonliving Substances	The nonliving building blocks of nature include particles, electromagnetic radiation, and chemical compounds. These substances constitute an ontology of physics and chemistry.
Living Substances	The living substances include plant and animal species. This ontology was imported from the "biosphere" taxonomy of the Global Change Master Directory.
Physical Processes	Physical processes include processes that affect living and nonliving substances, such as diffusion and evaporation.
Physical Properties	A separate ontology was developed for physical properties, including those observable or associated with other components. Examples of physical properties include *temperature*, *pressure*, and *height*, and could apply to Nonliving Substances, Living Substances, and Physical Processes, among others. These properties typically are measured physical quantities (or qualities) with units.
Units	Units are defined using Unidata's UDUnits, a package that contains an extensive unit database and is available at *www.unidata.ucar.edu/software/udunits/*. The resulting ontology includes conversion factors among various units. Prefixed units such as *km* are defined as a special case of *m* with an appropriate conversion factor.
Time	Time is essentially a numerical scale with terminology specific to the temporal domain. In the Time Ontology, the temporal extents and relations are special cases of numeric extents and relations, respectively. Temporal extents include *duration*, *season*, *century*, and *1996*, while examples of temporal relations include *after* and *before*.
Space	Similar to Time, Space is a multidimensional numerical scale with terminology specific to the spatial domain. A Space Ontology was developed, in which the spatial extents and relations are special cases of numeric extents and relations, respectively. Spatial extent examples include *country*, *Antarctica*, and *equator*, and spatial relations include *above* and *northOf*.
Numerics	Numerical extents include *interval, point, 0*, and $\mathbb{R}^2$. Numerical relations include *greaterThan* and *max*. Multidimensional concepts were defined because they are not native to OWL and XML.

Table 16.4: Brief descriptions of integrative ontologies in SWEET.

Ontology	Description
Physical Phenomena	A Phenomena Ontology is used to define transient events. A phenomenon crosses bounds of other ontology elements. Examples include *hurricane, earthquake,* and *El Niño,* and each has associated Time, Space, Earth Realms, Nonliving Elements, and Living Elements. Specific instances of phenomena, spanning approximately 50 events over the past two decades, are also included.
Human Activities	This ontology is included for representing activities that humans engage in, such as commerce and fisheries. It is included because scientific processes and phenomena have human impacts, and there is a need for representing such activities.
Data	The Data Ontology provides support for data set concepts, including representation, storage, modeling, format, resources, services, and distribution.

in the face of pressing crises like climate change. Studying climate change using holistic and unbiased scientific principles require an integrated understanding of stratigraphy, sea-level changes, fossil record, isotopes, and tectonics. The proverbial scientist working on climate change must have access to data from a number of scientific processes. However, the expenses involved in collecting necessary information for a single scientist, or even a single group of scientists, can prove to be a formidable barrier impeding new and exciting directions of research.

The goal of GEON (which was funded by the US National Science Foundation) was to respond to the pressing need in the geosciences to interlink and share multidisciplinary data sets to understand the complex dynamics of Earth systems. The portal was already becoming popular in the mid-2000s, well before the current popularity of KGs. For instance, Nambiar et al. (2006) claimed that the publicly accessible portal contained more than 400 registered data sources, 600 services, more than 750 registered users, and 20 ontologies. Today, GEON has been largely superseded by a larger project called Open-Topography, for which it originally served as a proof-of-concept cyberinfrastructure. The term "cyberinfrastructure" was coined by the National Science Foundation in 2003 to describe the computer networks and application-specific software, tools, and data repositories that support research in a given discipline. OpenTopography facilitates community access to high-resolution, earth science–oriented, topography data, and related tools and resources through cyberinfrastructure developed at the San Diego Supercomputer Center at University of California, San Diego. Its goals include to democratize online access to high-resolution (meter to submeter scale), earth science–oriented topography data acquired with lidar and other technologies; harness cutting-edge cyberinfrastructure to provide web service–based data access, processing, and analysis capabilities that are scalable, extensible, and innovative; and foster interaction and knowledge exchange in the earth science lidar user community.

OpenTopography data access levels include the following:

1. **Google Earth.** Provides an excellent platform to deliver lidar-derived visualizations for research and outreach. These files display full-resolution images derived from lidar in the Google Earth virtual globe. The virtual globe environment provides a freely available and easily navigated viewer and enables quick integration of the lidar visualizations with imagery, geographic layers, and other relevant data available in Keyhole Markup Language (KML) format.

2. **Raster.** Precomputed raster data include digital elevation model layers computed from aerial lidar surveys and raster data from the Satellite Radar Topography Mission global data set. The digital elevation models from aerial lidar surveys are available as bare earth (ground), highest hit, or intensity (strength of laser pulse) tiles. Some data sets also have orthophotographs available. The digital elevation models are in common Geospatial Information Systems (GIS) formats and are compressed to reduce their size.

3. **Lidar point cloud data and on-demand processing.** Users are allowed to define an area of interest, as well as a subset of the data (e.g., "ground returns only"), and then to download the results of this query in ASCII or LAS binary point cloud formats. Also available is the option to generate custom derivative products such as digital elevation models produced with user-defined resolution and algorithm parameters and down-loaded in a number of different file formats. The system will also generate geomorphic metrics (e.g., slope maps) and dynamically generate data product visualizations for display in the web browser or Google Earth.

OpenTopography cyberinfrastructure is based on a multitiered service-oriented architecture for efficient web browser–based access to data and processing. It includes an infrastructure tier, an application tier, and a services tier. The infrastructure tier contains dedicated storage and compute resources, the application tier is where most users access data and processing, and the services tier includes algorithms (e.g., for visualization) and other domain-specific services such as orthoimagery, raster processing, and gridding.

16.4.3 Environment Ontology

The Environment Ontology (ENVO) is a community-led, open project that seeks to provide an ontology for specifying a wide range of environments relevant to multiple life science disciplines and, through an open participation model, to accommodate the terminological requirements of all those needing to annotate data using ontology classes. In short, it is a succinct, controlled description of environments. A broad definition of an environment includes the natural or anthropogenic systems that can surround an entity (living or non-living). ENVO is motivated by the finding that, like so many of the sciences, while all biologists have an intuitive understanding of what is meant by "environment," a rigorous definition of this class is nontrivial. For example, confusion often arises when attempting to distinguish an environment from a habitat or niche: as some studies have shown, the environment that an organism was observed in or isolated from may have little to do with its habitat or its niche.

ENVO is comprised of classes (terms) referring to key environment types that may be used to facilitate the retrieval and integration of a broad range of biological data. The ENVO Consortium did not develop ENVO in a vacuum; rather, it took into account the many existing resources addressing, among other entities, environment types. Like other domain scientists and scientific consortia, they were motivated by the value of unifying pre-existing resources in a foundational (or building-block) ontology developed within a *federated* framework (thereby facilitating sharing) and exclusively concerned with the specification of environment types (the selected domain of interest), independent of any particular application (facilitating reuse).

ENVO's most developed branches (which are of primary interest to annotators) are the *biome, environmental feature*, and *environmental material* hierarchies. The biome hierarchy recognizes two important subclasses: terrestrial biome and aquatic biome. Most subclasses in the terrestrial biome have been adapted from major (terrestrial) habitat types defined by the World Wide Fund for Nature (WWF). The aquatic biome class has two subclasses: the marine biome and freshwater biome classes. The former hierarchy has been enriched with detailed input from marine scientists and includes classes representing depth-dependent layers of the oceans and seas, along with biomes associated with geographic entities, while the latter is in a considerably less developed state and includes subclasses adapted from the WWF's freshwater ecosystem classification.

The environmental feature hierarchy comprises subbranches addressing a number of spatial scales (e.g., the geographic feature subclass contains subclasses adapted from geographic surveys like those of the US Geographic Survey), as well as features that are of smaller spatial scale (e.g., carcasses and fomites that are included as subclasses of mesoscopic physical object) and finally, subclasses of marine feature and organic feature that are presently used to temporarily accommodate user requests.

The environmental material hierarchy is less deep compared to the biome and environmental feature hierarchies. Broad subclasses such as soil, water, and sediment are subdivided either by using well-known schemes (e.g., the UN Food and Agriculture Organization soil classification), or by referring to commonly used terms in the relevant domain by engaging with experts.

Since its introduction, and just like the other examples described here, ENVO has been adopted by or used in several projects, and its initial scope has significantly expanded. The *-omics* community was an early adopter of ENVO, which is a recommended ontology in the core component of the Minimal Information about any (x) Sequence (MIxS) specification.

Outside the *-omics* community, StrainInfo, a service which indexes and allows searching over numerous microbial culture collections, has used ENVO in its semantic representation of isolation environment. Recent interaction with the Environments-EOL initiative, which is utilizing text-mining approaches to annotate Encyclopedia of Life pages with ENVO classes, is providing valuable guidance in ENVO's development. The developers of ENVO are also working with the eco-informatics community to map the environmental descriptors in ENVO to the SPIRE vocabulary. This allows ecological interaction data mapped to SPIRE to be remapped to ENVO. Finally, as ENVO annotations become more widely available, databases and data retrieval tools (such as the Genomic Metadata for Infectious Agents Database) are supporting queries over ENVO classes.

More recently, much of ENVO's existing content has been revised for improved semantic representation, with the ontology now containing representations for habitats, environmental processes, anthropogenic environments, and entities relevant to environmental health initiatives and the global Sustainable Development Agenda for 2030. Several branches of ENVO have been used to incubate and seed new ontologies in previously unrepresented domains such as food and agronomy. Through this expansion, ENVO has subsequently been shaped into a multidomain ontology that bridges domains such as biomedicine, natural and anthropogenic ecology, -omics, and even socioeconomic development.

16.5   Concluding Notes

In this chapter, we covered the use of KG technology within scientific domains such as life sciences, geosciences, and chemistry. While these are arguably the most influential applications of KGs in science, especially considering the conservative tendency of these communities with respect to quality, storage, protection, and use of data, there are several others that were not covered in this chapter. For example, within the social sciences (and especially the side of the community that intersects with network sciences), there has been a proliferation of rich, attributed graphs that look a lot less like traditional social networks and more like KGs. Within the computer sciences, there has always been a willingness to experiment with more cutting-edge technology, and KGs and ontologies exist for a wide variety of purposes, including for recording experimental computational results. We believe that the cases we have covered in this chapter have offered a good representation of the tendencies and use-cases of scientific communities in adopting KG technology. An important caveat that must be borne in mind when dealing with scientific KGs is that the distinction between an ontology and KG becomes blurred (purely as a pragmatic matter).

16.6   Software and Resources

Many of the resources covered in this chapter are publicly available; we provide links to the important ones. In the event that a link does not resolve, we recommend using a search engine to get an updated link.

Specifically, the primary landing page for the GO is geneontology.org/. From this page, the interested user can access many of the facilities discussed in the chapter, including the ontology itself (http://geneontology.org/docs/ontology-documentation/), the annotation (http://geneontology.org/docs/go-annotations/), and importantly, the causal activity model (http://geneontology.org/docs/gocam-overview/). There are also many tools available to browse, search, visualize, and curate the GO, available at http://geneontology.org/docs/tools-overview/. The Noctua Curation Platform for curators to create GO annotations is accessible at http://noctua.geneontology.org/. The GO wiki (http://wiki.geneontology.org/index.php/Main_Page) is also a great resource for potential users to learn more about the ecosystem and resources. It also contains a collected list of publications, talks and posters, by year and time periods.

Programmatic access to ChEBI has significantly improved lately by introducing a library, libChEBI, in Java, Python, and Matlab. The GiHub page for this resource is accessible at https://github.com/libChEBI. The addition of new tools, such as an analysis tool, BiNChE, and a query tool for the ontology, OntoQuery, have also significantly aided in making ChEBI accessible and useful for sophisticated analyses in the chemical sciences. These resources are accessible at https://www.ebi.ac.uk/chebi/tools/binche/ and https://www.ncbi.nlm.nih.gov/pubmed/24008420, respectively. For instance, BiNChE is a web-based enrichment analysis tool (although it is also available as a software library), and offers plain or weighted analysis options against the ChEBI role, structure or combined ontology. It was inspired by similar tools in the GO ecosystem. In contrast, OntoQuery was designed with a larger audience (including Semantic Web) in mind, since it allows for the easy formulation and execution of complex logical queries against the ontology. The formulation is easy because Description Logic (DL) queries can be posed in the relatively easy Manchester syntax and can be executed against the preloaded (and prereasoned) ontology. Additionally, OntoQuery offers syntax suggestions and corrections as a query is being typed, and supports composite queries using logical connectives like "and" and "or" of classes or relationships in the ontology. For example, OntoQuery would be able to retrieve results over ChEBI given a query such as "steriod and has_role some (human_metabolite or nematode_metabolite)."

PubChem data are available for bulk download on an FTP site (ftp://ftp.ncbi.nlm.nih.gov/pubchem). The PubChem Structure Download service, accessible at https://pubchem.ncbi.nlm.nih.gov/pc_fetch/pc_fetch.cgi, can also be used to download a subset of substance or compound records in PubChem, rather than all PubChem records. The records can be exported in several formats, including plain text, Extensible Markup Language (XML), and various other convenient modalities. Optionally, the files can be compressed in standard gzip or bzip2 formats. For more details, we recommend that the reader peruse the primary PubChem documentation at https://pubchemdocs.ncbi.nlm.nih.gov/downloads.

Concerning the geosciences resources, the OBO Foundry resources can be accessed at the following GitHub page: https://github.com/OBOFoun-dry/OBOFoundry.github.io/ blob/master/resources.md. ENVO is one example of an OBO Foundry ontology that we detailed in this chapter. The GitHub page linked here is useful because it contains many resources for getting started with ontologies (particularly scientific ontologies), and also contains links to tools and browsers. ENVO is published under a CC-BY license and is accessed at http://www.obofoundry.org/ontology/envo.html. The SWEET ontologies were previously downloadable from http://sweet.jpl.nasa.gov/sweet, but lately they have been inaccessible. Another link from where the main ontology is directly downloadable is http://iridl.ldeo.columbia.edu/ontologies/SWEET.owl. The main page for accessing Open-Topography resources is https://opentopography.org/.

16.7 Bibliographic Notes

Unlike many of the other chapters, for which we could draw on multiple surveys (and even books and metasurveys) as a bedrock of foundational material and recent advances, there is no one work (to our knowledge) that comprehensively describes KGs (or KBs) in even just the major natural sciences such as biology and chemistry. In this chapter, we took a per-field approach by describing developments as they have unfolded in individual areas of scientific knowledge. While there has been some work on curating multiple scientific KBs or even in producing metadata, a comprehensive description of the KBs themselves has been lacking in one single work.

Much effort was spent in the early part of this chapter on the GO, which remains, to our knowledge, the best-known and most widely deployed effort of applying KG technology in a scientific area. There are many good references for the GO, and we drew on a few of those in describing it in this chapter. A set of articles from the GO Consortium constitute excellent first reads; we recommend Gene Ontology Consortium (2004, 2008, 2012, 2015, 2017) and Gene Ontology Consortium et al. (2001). We also recommend foundational work by Ashburner et al. (2000) for interested readers. There has also been much secondary work to make sense of the GO itself. For example, Supek et al. (2011) propose a method to summarize and visualize GO terms to make a list of such terms easier of interpret. Other such studies include Boyle et al. (2004) and Martin et al. (2004).

Beyond the GO, ChEBI and PubChem are important resources for the chemistry domain. Good references include de Matos et al. (2010), Degtyarenko et al. (2007), Hastings et al. (2016), Kim et al. (2016), Wang et al. (2014), and Bolton et al. (2008). The paper describing PubChemRDF by Fu et al. (2015) is especially instructive because it directly involves

KG technology and has a close connection to SW tools, models, and languages such as RDF and SPARQL.

For the other resources mentioned here, good references describing SWEET include Raskin and Pan (2003), Raskin et al. (2004), and Raskin and Pan (2005). Good references for GEON and OpenTopography include Nambiar et al. (2006), Gahegan et al. (2009), Lin and Ludäscher (2004), Krishnan et al. (2011), and Crosby et al. (2013). Several good references exist for ENVO; we encourage the interested reader to consider Buttigieg et al. (2013, 2016). Note that there are other good resources for the geosciences beyond what was covered in this chapter; the abstract by Zaslavsky et al. (2016) provides pointers to a few of them.

16.8   Exercises

1. In the chapter introduction, we wrote that the scientific community tends to mostly publish knowledge as statements in an ontology, as opposed to a KG. Looking at the list here, can you determine what should be a concept in an ontology as opposed to an instance in a KG? If you choose the latter, explain why you would not put it in the ontology.

   (a) An element in the periodic table

   (b) A fungal specimen that was collected from a specific rainforest

   (c) The parameters in a differential equation describing a physical phenomena

   (d) The scientist who invented a cure for tuberculosis

   (e) The structure of the COVID-19 virus

2. We listed several optional elements for GO terms in table 16.2, such as Subset, Comment, and Obsolete tag. We would like to do a small sampling-based study to determine how many GO terms actually use these optional terms. To begin the study, pick 10 GO terms. You could do this by searching online or by browsing the GO website. Try to be as random as you can. What are these terms? Draw a table and list their unique identifiers and term names.

3. Considering only the six optional elements listed in table 16.2, how many GO terms in your sample have at least one value for each of these elements? Provide an individual percentage for each of these elements (e.g., you could state that 6 of the 10 terms in your sample have a value for Subset, while 8 have an associated comment).

4. When describing chemical entities and KGs for chemical entities, we considered both ChEBI and PubChem. We also used "ecogonine benzoate" to illustrate ChEBI. What is the identifier for this entity on PubChem? In comparing the entities for ChEBI and PubChem, what differences do you observe? Is there an equal amount of information about the entity on both portals?

5. List three differences between PubChem and ChEBI.

6. Consider the SWEET ontologies in figure 16.3. What distinguishes faceted from integrative ontologies? What do the edges mean?

7. Try to look up the details of the Data integrative ontology online. List some classes and properties in this ontology. What is a good use-case where use of this ontology is essential? Considering the ubiquity of data, why is it not linked to every single integrative and faceted ontology in figure 16.3?

17 Knowledge Graphs for Domain-Specific Social Impact

Overview. Constructing knowledge graphs (KGs) over arbitrary domains is a difficult problem that has recently emerged as both important and feasible. In previous chapters, we have already seen some use-cases, such as for understanding events and their dynamics. In some sense, every real-world KG exists in society and has social impact. However, many such KGs, including DBpedia and Wikidata, are designed more as jack-of-all-trades entities that can support a broad set of applications. In contrast, research on domain-specific KGs for social impact have tried to have a major influence on one major field or application. Particularly influential examples include building KGs for fighting human trafficking (HT), forecasting geopolitical events (and hence, better preparing for them), and effectively mobilizing resources after natural disasters. Despite their potential impact, such application domains (in the computational and KG communities) have not been as well covered historically, and are quite challenging to work with in practical settings. Fortunately, as we discuss in this chapter, there has been a recent surge of exciting research in this area, with demonstrable success.

17.1 Introduction

We are used to thinking of the web as a one-size-fits-all ecosystem. Everyone seems to use the same (or similar variants of) web technologies such as email clients, social media, news and Really Simple Syndication (RSS) feeds, Google, YouTube, and even knowledge sources like Wikipedia. We could even argue that this is why the web has been so successful because it is largely predicated on a set of uniform standards and protocols like HTTP.

It is easy to forget that the web also has a significant long tail, and there is much evidence, both empirical and anecdotal, showing the importance and ubiquity of the long tail. Think of all the restaurants that do not have a Wikipedia page, or websites that you visit for myriad purposes but that are not household names like Amazon. Moving beyond the long tail, it does not take much imagination to see that there are entire subsets of the web that are *domain-specific*. Every academic in computer science, for example, is familiar with bibliographic portals like Google Scholar, DBLP, PubMed, and several others. Artists, photographs, and numerous other domain experts have their own catalogs of go-to pages.

Sometimes there is a real need for us to limit our search and attention to pages belonging to a specific domain, not just the entire web.

A real-world example of such a domain expert in the securities fraud domain is an employee from the Securities and Exchange Commission (SEC) who is attempting to identify actionable cases of penny stock fraud. Penny stock offerings in over-the-counter (OTC) markets are frequently suspected of being fraudulent, but without specific evidence, usually in the form of a false factual claim (that is admissible as evidence), their trading cannot be halted. With thousands of penny stock offerings, investigators do not have the resources or time to Google and investigate all of them.

A technical workflow that addresses this problem would be to crawl a corpus of relevant pages from the web describing the domain, a process that was described in detail in chapter 3, using methods like focused crawling or the (much more recent) domain discovery tool (DDT). Once such a corpus is obtained, an expert in information extraction (IE) and machine learning would elicit opinions from the users on what fields (e.g., location, company, or stock ticker symbol) are important to the user for answering domain-specific questions, along with example extractions per field. This sequence of KG construction (KGC) steps results in the familiar KG, which is now amenable to aggregations and to both keyword and structured querying, using many of the querying and analytics techniques studied in part IV of this book. With a good interface, for example, the domain expert can identify all persons and organizations (usually shell companies) associated with a stock ticker symbol, aggregate prices, or suspicious activity by searching for hyped-up phrases that indicate fraud. Furthermore, even if the initial KGC procedures do not yield ideal quality, we demonstrated in part III some mechanisms (including representation learning, entity resolution, and data cleaning) that could be used to complete or identify the (initially constructed) noisy KG.

As described here, the full workflow of acquiring the data, constructing and completing the KG, and then querying it seems to be a straightforward series of steps. In practice, these procedures are expensive and technically difficult (as evidenced by the fact that they have taken up a large chunk of this very book). Certainly, the domain expert from the SEC does not have the time or inclination to build such an integrated system by herself, and she would likely not have the resources to construct a team of engineers and data scientists to do it for her. In summary, there are two problems, both difficult. First, how can we combine the sets of technologies described here, and in the rest of this book, into an integrated, end-to-end system? What should such a system look like? Second, how can we make the system accessible to domain experts who do not necessarily have the technical ability to write complex scripts, or who do not even have a background in machine learning?

To answer these questions and facilitate research into domain-specific search, the Memex program was established by the US Defense Advanced Research Projects Agency (DARPA) in the mid-2010s. The goal of Memex was to develop software that advanced online search

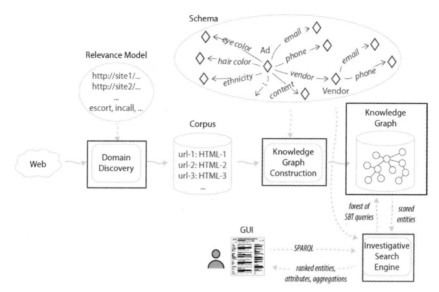

Figure 17.1: A typical workflow showing the working of the DIG system.

by allowing nontechnical users to create their own domain-specific search engines for discovering relevant content and organizing it in ways that were more useful to their specific problems. Next, we describe the Domain-Specific Insight Graphs (DIG) architecture that was a direct output of Memex and was developed by a multiorganizational team. However, we note that this system (or the Memex program) is not the only approach for using KGs to address social problems. We cover at least one other application, crisis informatics and disaster response, which also draws on KG research, but in an alternative way.

17.2 Domain-Specific Insight Graphs

Funded under the DARPA Memex program, the DIG architecture was designed to allow domain experts and users the ability to construct and search KGs without any programming. The domain-specific aspect of the system arises from its ability to permit the setup, tuning, and integration of KGC for a fixed but arbitrary domain. This is in complete contrast to Google, as described later in this chapter. The insights that can be derived from the system arise from its search facilities and graphical user interface (GUI), which offers a range of customizable options.

A typical workflow in DIG is conveyed in figure 17.1. First, in the *domain setup* phase, the system ingests the output of domain discovery (chapter 3); that is, a raw corpus of webpages by presenting an intuitive, multistep KGC to the user, who usually requires an hour or less of example-based training to learn how to navigate the steps and refine the outputs iteratively. Second, in the *domain exploration* phase, the system offers a search interface that can be used to navigate the KGs using a combination of search techniques, some of which were described in depth in part IV. Next, we briefly describe the main components of both phases, followed by a description of the applications with which it has been deployed.

17.2.1   Domain Setup

The first phase, *domain setup*, involves setting up the domain with the goal of answering a certain set of (possibly open-ended) questions that a user is interested in further exploring. This phase does not comprise a strictly linear set of steps but rather involves several inter-leaved steps (figure 17.2). At a high level, the user loads a sample of the corpus to explore, followed by defining wrappers using the Inferlink tool (briefly described subsequently), customizing domain-specific fields, and adding field-specific glossaries (if desired). Many of these extraction techniques were earlier covered in part II. Periodically, the user can *crystallize* a sequence of steps by running extractions to construct the KG and uploading the KG to an index. Once the upload is complete, users can demo their efforts by clicking on the Sample DigApp button in the upper-left corner of the screen shown in figure 17.2 to explore the KG using a search interface. The process is iterative: the user can always return to the dashboard to define or refine more fields, define more wrappers with Inferlink (a wrapper induction system offering a GUI), or input more glossaries.

Specifically, the different steps in setting up a domain are described next.

Loading Sample Pages. The original DIG system ingested webpages that have been crawled and placed in a distributed file system using the Common Data Repository (CDR) format with an ingestion schema that was collectively decided upon by the Memex program and its participants. The schema records not just the HTML content of pages, but also metadata, such as when the page was crawled and which crawler was used. Images are separately processed and stored. CDR was defined to be a special instance of the Javascript Object Notation (JSON) format, and more recent versions of DIG can directly process JSON. At this time, direct ingestion of formats other than CDR or JSON are being actively explored, including PDFs.

Defining Fields. DIG allows users to define their own fields and to customize the fields in several ways that directly influence their use during the domain exploration phase. To define a field, users click on the Fields tab (step 2 in figure 17.2), which provides them with an overview of fields that are already defined (including predefined fields like *location*), and also allows them to add and update fields. In addition to customizing the appearance of a field by assigning it a color and icon, users can set the importance of the field for search (on a scale of 1–10), declare the field to represent an entity by selecting the entity rather than the text option in Show as Links (thereby supporting entity-centric search, described in the section entitled "Domain Exploration," later in this chapter), and assign it a predefined extractor like a glossary.

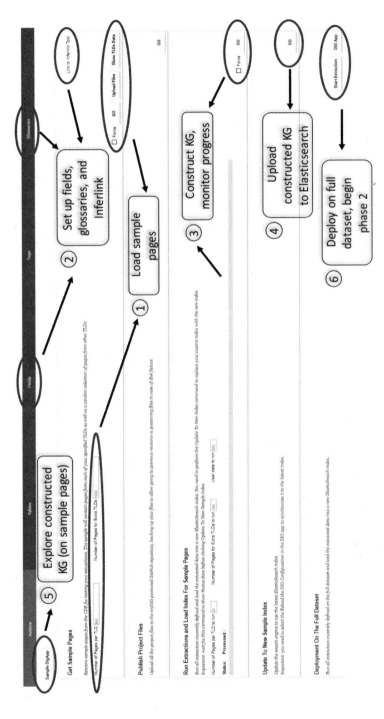

Figure 17.2: An illustration of the DIG application, involving several interleaved steps that a nontechnical subject matter (or domain) expert could take to set up their own domain-specific KG and search engine. The precise details and text on the dashboard are less important than the steps shown here and described in the text (and are being updated periodically).

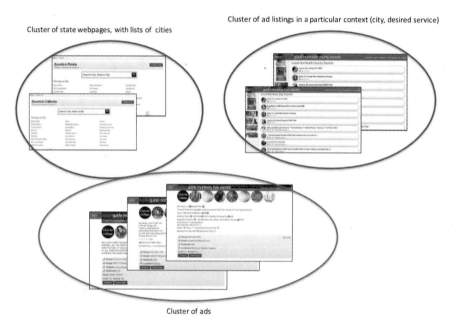

Figure 17.3: Examples of three clusters, each containing structurally and contextually similar webpages.

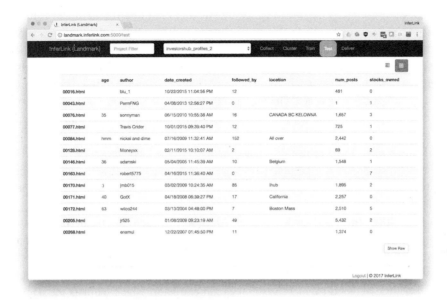

Figure 17.4: An illustration (from the *Securities Fraud* domain) of the semantic typing facility in Inferlink. To create this screen, semantic typing, in terms of the defined set of fields, has already been done. For example, the second column has been typed with "age" semantics and other elements.

Defining Wrappers Using the Inferlink Tool. Earlier, in chapter 5, we described wrappers as a means of extracting structured elements from webpages. The Inferlink tool, developed by a private company of the same name, offers an intuitive, graphical way of doing this. For convenient formalism, let us define a top-level domain (TLD) (such as backpage.com) T as a set $\{w_1, \ldots, w_n\}$ of webpages (e.g., backpage.com/chicago/1234). As a first step, Inferlink uses an *unsupervised template clustering algorithm* to partition T into clusters, such that webpages in each cluster are structurally and contextually similar to each other. Figure 17.3 provides some real-world intuition for the TLD backpage.com (e.g., Cluster 1 contains city-specific webpages containing categories of advertisements such as appliances and roommates; and Cluster 2 contains webpages describing city-specific appliance listings). The examples in figure 17.3 show that both structure and context are important. For example, while Clusters 2 and 3 are structurally similar, they are contextually different and thereby get separated into two clusters (rather than one).

Extraction setup proceeds as follows. Once they have chosen a relevant cluster, users see an illustration like the one in figure 17.4, wherein Inferlink extracts common structural elements from the webpages in the cluster and presents it to the users in a column layout, with one row per webpage and one column per structured element that is common to the webpages. Users can open a webpage by clicking on a link (the leftmost column in the screen shown in figure 17.4), delete a column, or assign it to a field that has already been defined. This is precisely the semantic typing step that was also discussed earlier in this book (chapter 4) in the context of Named Entity Recognition (NER); that is, it is not enough to extract just "Obama" in the sentence "Obama championed the Affordable Care Act"; a good NER must extract "Obama" as "Politician" or "Person," depending on what kinds of concepts have been defined in the underlying ontology). Users must separately type columns for each TLD cluster because different TLDs (and more generally, different clusters in the same TLDs) share different structures in the webpages they contain. However, users are guaranteed high precision in their results, and after some initial training, they do not have to know anything about wrappers or how they work in order to operate the Inferlink tool.

Defining Other Information Extraction Methods. In addition to the Inferlink tool, DIG offers implementations of methods suitable for IE from blocks of text or other content that are not delimited as structured HTML elements (i.e., delimited using HTML tags). To ease user effort, some generic extractors are pretrained and cannot be customized, but they can be disabled. A good example is the location extractor, which extracts the names of cities, states, and countries using a machine learning model that was trained offline. DIG also offers users the option to input a glossary (with incumbent options, such as whether the glossary terms should be interpreted case-sensitively) for a given field. This option was popular with domain experts who evaluated the system. The Glossaries tab is accessed in a similar way as Fields. The latest version of DIG also offers users an intuitive rule editor for expressing and testing simple natural-language rules or templates with extraction placeholders. For example, a name extractor can be set up with a pattern recognition rule like "Hi, my name is [NAME]."

Indexing the Constructed Knowledge Graph. In step 3 in figure 17.2, the user executes the defined IEs, including glossaries, Inferlink, and predefined extractors that have not been disabled, in order to construct a KG over a subset of TLDs and a sample of webpages from each TLD. While users are allowed to specify the sample size, the smaller the sample, the less representative the constructed KG, but the faster its execution. Hence, there is a trade-off. A status bar shows the user the progress of KGC. The constructed KG is indexed and stored in a NoSQL document store like Elasticsearch. In the domain exploration phase, this stored and indexed KG can be navigated in a variety of ways.

17.2.2   Domain Exploration

The domain exploration phase is the in-use phase, when the system is actually being used to satisfy information retrieval (IR) needs. Once the user has iterated enough times to be satisfied with the results on the sampled pages, she would initiate domain exploration by executing the KGC pipeline on the full corpus of webpages. The time until completion depends on the size of the corpus, as well as the computing power available.

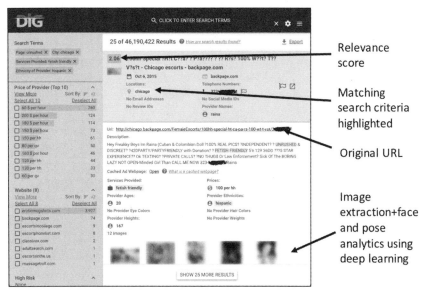

Relevance score

Matching search criteria highlighted

Original URL

Image extraction+face and pose analytics using deep learning

Figure 17.5: An illustration of the search capabilities offered by the DIG system, with HT investigations as the use-case. Critical details have been blurred or obfuscated due to the illicit nature of some of the material.

DIG offers users a range of search capabilities, including basic keyword search, structured search, and a novel search capability called *dossier generation*. We enumerate some of the options here, using the screenshot in figure 17.5 for illustration.

1. *Search using structure:* The user begins the search by filling out values in a form containing fields that she has declared (during domain setup) as being searchable (figure 17.6). The search engine in DIG, which is based on Elasticsearch in the back end, uses many of the techniques covered earlier, in part IV, to ensure that user intent is captured in a robust manner with good performance on the recall metric. In fields that have text semantics, like Description, keywords can be entered; these fields are like the search bar in engines like Google. While keyword search is designed to be primarily exploratory, structured search allows a user to quickly hone in on pages containing certain key details that the user has specified in the form. DIG uses ranking and relevance scoring techniques first developed in the IR community—namely, satisfying more criteria on a form will lead to a page having a higher ranking than another page that satisfies fewer criteria. Users can also make a search criterion strict by clicking on the star next to the field. This implies that the search is now a constraint: for a KG node, if the value is not found for that field, the node will be assigned a zero score and will never get retrieved or ranked in the interface.

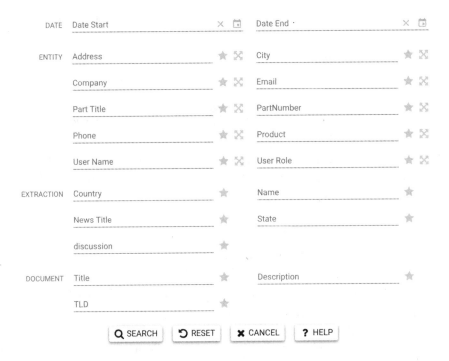

Figure 17.6: A structured search form in the DIG system. This form can be used for an ordinary *product* domain, but in this case, it was built for a prototype used to investigate the *counterfeit electronics* domain.

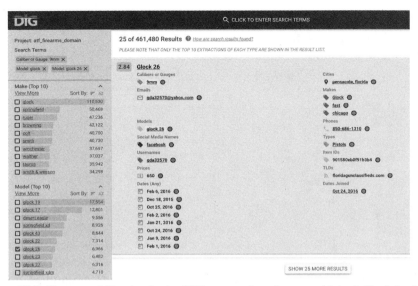

Figure 17.7: Facets and filtering in the DIG system (see the gray sidebar). By "checking" off certain boxes or adding more search terms (top of the sidebar), a user can try to make the search more precise.

2. *Facets and filtering:* As shown in figure 17.7, DIG supports faceted search and filtering on select fields (e.g., Model) that the user can specify during domain setup. In all of the investigate case studies in which DIG was evaluated, users made fairly intuitive choices: except for free-form fields like text, descriptions, or comments, they favored faceting over nonfaceting. In addition to allowing more informed search and filtering, facets help the user to see an overview of the search results. For example, in the screen, one can deduce that (among the *Model* extractions) *glock 19* and *glock 17* occurs far more often in the data than other models when searching for weapon models.

3. *Dossier generation (entity-centric search):* Dossier generation and summarization are important distinctions separating the domain exploration facilities of KG-centric systems like DIG from more generic Google search. An example is illustrated in figure 17.8 for the entity *glock 26*, which is presumably a model that an investigator in the Illegal Weapons Sales domain is interested in investigating further for suspicious activity. The entity dashboard summarizes the information about this particular entity by providing a (1) timeline of occurrences, (2) locations extracted from webpages from which the entity was extracted, (3) other entities cooccurring with the entity (along with *non-cooccurrence* information to enable intuitive significance comparisons), and (4) relevant pages related to that entity.

Figure 17.8: Entity-centric search (also called *dossier generation*) in the DIG system from the *illegal firearms sales* domain. In this case, an investigator could look up all information extracted for the entity "glock 26."

4. *Provenance:* DIG supports provenance both at the coarse-grained level of webpages and the fine-grained level of extractions. Concerning the latter, provenance information is obtained by clicking on the square next to an extraction, which brings up the specific extraction method, such as Inferlink, SpaCy, or glossary (figure 17.9), and in the case of context-based extractors that use natural-language techniques, the text surrounding the extraction. Multiple provenances are illustrated if applicable, as shown in the figure (e.g., glossary extractions from text that originated in different structures in a webpage). We also support webpage-level provenance by allowing the user to open the cached webpage in a new tab. It is important to show the cached, rather than the live, webpage (which can also be shown by clicking on the predefined URL extraction that exists for every webpage in the corpus) because the webpage may have changed, or even been removed, since domain discovery. Cached pages in the HT version of the system were recently admitted as evidence in court (see the section entitled "Bibliographic Notes," at the end of the chapter).

17.3   Alternative System: DeepDive

DeepDive is an alternative system for domain-specific KGC that was first presented in the early 2010s and has since expanded. The original DeepDive system was based on the classic entity-relationship model and employed techniques like distant supervision and Statistical Relational Learning (SRL) to combine various signals. In this sense, it was

Extraction Data Provenance

DOCUMENT ID	9E7837E816A928E93E551BC0A2CCBD8058701C758B47.
TEXT	brand - new game from **square enix** . - games from
METHOD	extract_using_dictionary from content_strict
TEXT	brand - new game from **square enix** . - games from
METHOD	extract_using_dictionary from content_relaxed
TEXT	brand - new game from **square enix** . - games from the
METHOD	extract_using_dictionary from html

Figure 17.9: Provenance in the DIG system for an extracted entity "square enix," which is a game. In addition to the document ID, the provenance shows that a single extraction algorithm, based on dictionaries (or glossaries), was used. For the third method, the source (on which the algorithm was executed) is the raw HTML, while for the other two, it is the scraped text. Here, *content_relaxed* means that the text was extracted in a recall-friendly way from the HTML (meaning that some irrelevant elements, such as ad and code snippets embedded in the HTML, were extracted in addition to the relevant content), while *content_strict* implies a more precision-friendly approach.

similar to other KGC architectures like YAGO and EntityCube. However, DeepDive went further in also offering deep Natural Language Processing (NLP) techniques to extract linguistic features, including dependency paths, from large quantities (up to terabytes) of text, as well as to perform web-scale statistical learning and inference. DeepDive operates by first converting diverse input data, such as ontologies and raw corpora, to relational features using both standard NLP tools and custom code. Next, these features are used to train statistical models capturing the relationships between linguistic patterns and target relations. By combining these models with domain knowledge (using statistical relational models like Markov Logic, as covered in chapter 9), DeepDive yields a domain-specific KG as its final output.

In terms of implementation, DeepDive used a declarative language that was similar to SQL, while inheriting Markov Logic Networks' (MLNs) formal semantics. We covered MLNs in the context of SRL (chapter 9). As with the Knowledge Vault that was covered in chapter 15, DeepDive produces marginal probabilities that are calibrated—that is, if we examined all facts output with a probability of 0.8 by DeepDive, it means that (in expectation) 80 percent of these facts would be correct. For more details on DeepDive, we point interested readers to references in the "Bibliographic Notes" section.

In comparing DIG and DeepDive, we note that while DeepDive also offers an impressive and unified array of KGC tools, it was not designed for the nonprogrammer, or for facilitating complex, entity-centric search of the kind that DIG has made possible, in both theory and practice. Furthermore, DeepDive is much more computationally intensive than DIG due to its heavy reliance on MLNs. According to Niu et al. (2012a), inference and learning in DeepDive can take hours, even on 1 TB RAM/48-core machines. While memory and computation requirements of both systems clearly depend on the size of the data, DIG does offer some simple facilities that can make it amenable to relatively low-power or low-memory settings (such as a laptop or desktop machine). Whether DIG or Deep-Dive is right for an application depends on the user, her technical prowess, and the desired methodology[1] for getting to the final KG.

17.4 Applications and Use-Cases

To draw the connection between KG capabilities and applications with social impact, we detail two broad application domains (namely, investigative domains, which include complex subdomains that are fields of study and application in their own right, including HT and securities fraud, and crisis informatics). Each of these illustrates, in its own specific way, the challenges involved in working with complex, real-world domains with nontechnical stakeholders and unusual desiderata compared to relatively normal (and significant) domains like e-commerce, as well as the creative ways in which KGs can help address these challenges.

17.4.1 Investigative Domains

KGC over investigative domains is part of a broader movement that popularly goes by the phrase "AI for social good." As artificial intelligence (AI) systems have proliferated in recent years, there has been increasing concern over several social and technological issues. Entire conferences and journals are now dedicated to this important issue. In part, the problem is social, because many of the most sophisticated AI tools either are developed in academic labs and not transitioned at all (beyond the lab) due to lack of software maturity or testing, or they are developed in industry and are largely proprietary. On the other hand, many of the agencies that can benefit most from AI do not have the resources to do research on this area, or to acquire the technology via licenses or other expensive means. Most do not have the resources to even facilitate transition (e.g., by retraining their employees or dedicating infrastructure to hosting the systems). Thus, it is all the more important to develop tools that nontechnical users can apply to their use-cases, so that the barrier for entry is not so high.

---

[1] One such aspect of this methodology would be the specific mechanism used for eliciting domain knowledge. DIG allows simpler means like glossaries and rules, while DeepDive offers SRL. Some kinds of domain knowledge are more apt for the latter, while others are better suited for the former.

We now describe a sample of investigative domains that have been investigated, at least in a prototypical state, using the DIG system, as well as other technologies that have emerged over the course of the Memex program, at institutions and companies across the United States, including the Jet Propulsion Laboratory at the National Aeronautics and Space Administration (NASA) and New York University[2]). Of these, the domain on which DIG was evaluated most extensively is HT. Thus, we pay special attention to this domain, which we cover last in this discussion.

17.4.1.1 Securities Fraud   Securities fraud, particularly penny stock fraud is a complex domain that falls under the direct authority of the SEC in the United States. Penny stock fraud is unusual because much of the activity that accompanies fraudulent behavior, including hype and promotional activity, is legally permitted. Many of the actual actors involved may not be physically present in the US, but for regulatory reasons, shell companies fronting such activity for promotional and legal purposes have to be registered in the US to trade stocks legitimately in OTC exchanges. In addition to the longer-term goal of investigating and gathering information on such shell companies and the people involved in them, investigators are interested in taking preventive activity. This can happen when a penny stock company is caught actively engaging in factually fraudulent hype (e.g., a false claim that a contract was just signed with a well-known customer firm), in which case trading can be halted, or even shut down. This is also why the step is *preventive*; trading is shut down before unwary investors buy in and subsequently end up losing their savings. The DIG system supports these goals by allowing users to aggregate information (in the crawled corpus, which contains many web domains) about suspicious penny stocks using the entity-centric search facilities, and to zero in on burgeoning promotional activity.

17.4.1.2 Illegal Firearms Sales   In the US, firearms sales are regulated in the sense that transactions cannot be conducted with arbitrary persons, or over arbitrary channels like the Internet. Investigators in the illegal firearms sales domain are interested in pinpointing activity that, either directly or indirectly, provides evidence for illicit sales that leave some digital trace. The domain is similar to the securities fraud domain (and dissimilar to the counterfeit electronics domain, described next), for the important reason that investigators limit their focus to domestic activities.

17.4.1.3 Counterfeit Electronics   Despite what the name suggests, investigators in the counterfeit electronics domain are interested, not in consumer electronics, but in microchips and Field-Programmable Gate Arrays (FPGAs), which form the computational backbones of more complex application devices. The latter may resemble FPGAs from

---

[2] In chapter 3, we described the DDT that was developed by a group at New York University, primarily in response to the Memex goals and challenges, although the scope of the system has since been extended.

genuine contractors, but they are fakes and may have malicious modifications at the hardware level. Certain countries, companies, and devices are more relevant to this kind of activity than others. We note that there is an obvious national security component to these investigations, and just as with the other domains described here, domain expertise plays a crucial role both in setting up the domain and in the knowledge discovery itself.

17.4.1.4 Human Trafficking   Data from various authoritative sources, including the National Human Trafficking Resource Center, show that HT is not only on the rise in the United States, but is a problem of international proportions. The advent of the web has made the problem worse. HT victims are advertised both on the open and the Dark Web, with estimates of the number of (not necessarily unique) published advertisements numbering in the tens, if not hundreds, of millions. In recent years, various agencies in the US have turned to technology to assist them in combating this problem through the suggestion of leads, evidence, and HT indicators. Entities are typically sex advertisers, such as *escorts*, but could also be latent entities such as *vendors* (sex rings, sometimes posing under the guise of spas and massage parlors), who organize the activity.

DIG, along with another search system called Tellfinder, has been in active use by law enforcement agencies to track potential HT activity. It was a direct output of the Memex program and was eventually transitioned to the office of the District Attorney for New York, along with other offices. At this time, it has contributed to the convictions of at least three traffickers, including a 97-years-to-life sentence for a trafficker in the San Francisco area. Tellfinder has had similar success. These cases indicate that the use of KGs and entity-centric technology can have real and lasting benefits for society, especially in terms of fighting difficult problems like HT.

17.4.1.5 Why Not Google?   As an aside, an important question that can, and does arise, when demonstrating such KG systems to nontechnical investigative users is "Why not just use Google for satisfying user intent?" In other words, why are investigative domains difficult for search engines like Google to handle? This is an important question because some of the challenges that emerge are, by no means, unique to investigative domains. We list some of these challenges next with the caveat that not every challenge applies to every investigative domain, and there are many noninvestigative domains to which these challenges also apply. We use the HT domain to illustrate the challenges more effectively, as all of these challenges have been observed in the HT domain. On occasion, we also invoke one of the other investigative domains, or even noninvestigative ones, where appropriate, as examples.

Nontraditional Domain. HT, and several domains like it, are largely characterized by illicit, organized activity, and they have not been as extensively researched as traditional domains (e.g., enterprise) are. Directly adapting existing techniques from these domains is problematic, along with using external knowledge bases (KBs) like Wikipedia, because the entities of interest (escorts and HT victims) are not described in such KBs. For example, we could not directly use tools like stemmers and tokenizers from standard NLP packages like Natural Language Toolkit (NLTK) because the corpus contains many nondictionary words and employs advanced obfuscation techniques. The problem is made much worse by the long-tail nature of both the HT domain and other domains, as one cannot tune an algorithm for webpages from a small number of root Uniform Resource Locators (URLs) such as backpage.com.

Scale and Irrelevance. The scale of the task (millions of webpages) and the size of the corpus preclude many KG systems from using serial algorithms that have a high memory imprint and long running times. Many of the most expensive tasks have to be run on scalable infrastructures like Apache Spark to be viable; furthermore, because an annotated ground-truth is often not available, and the corpora crawled by domain discovery tools tend to have many irrelevant webpages, core algorithms often have to be executed several times. Scale and irrelevance both proved to be key engineering challenges to be overcome when building scalable KG-powered systems that offer domain-specific benefits beyond Google.

Missing Values and Noise. In many cases, each page is typically missing information (e.g., hair color) that investigators would like to extract and use in their queries. However, it is typically unknown a priori which pages and web domains were missing values for which attributes. In many of these systems, it was often the case that extractors would get confused and extract noisy values for attributes that were either missing or well obfuscated. These observations strongly motivated the design of both extraction and query execution technology specifically for investigative search engines. Some of these techniques, including query reformulation, were covered earlier in this book in part IV; we also provide other pointers in the "Bibliographic Notes" section.

Information Obfuscation. A recurring challenge in domains like HT is *information obfuscation*, which includes obscure language models, excessive use of punctuation marks and special characters, presence of extraneous, hard-to-filter data (e.g., advertisements) in web pages, irrelevant pages, lack of representative examples for supervised extractors, data skew, and heterogeneity. Many pages exhibit more than one problem; for instance, a sampling of some pages in the Memex corpus used to evaluate systems on HT queries revealed that obfuscation was the norm rather than the exception. A concrete obfuscation example is an individual stating that her phone number[3] (+1-111-453-0004) was "1**1-1**4-5-3*-**-*oh-oh-oh***4." A successful system would not only recover the original number from this text, but also infer (based on other information on the page) that it is a number from the United States (+1). While some limited work has been done in dealing with obfuscation, the techniques that are required to address human-centric *semantic* obfuscation of the kind

---

[3] We have taken the liberty of modifying some of the digits in this example so that it is not a real phone number.

that predominates in HT are domain-specific, and they keep evolving as traffickers adjust their methods. Generic search engines are not optimized for such domain-specific shifts.

Complex Query Types. In the HT domain, investigators are interested in several kinds of queries. The simplest queries, in principle, are factoid queries (called *point fact* queries) that can be handled by key-value data stores like Elasticsearch assuming robust extractions, indexing, and similarity computations. More complex aggregation and cluster queries (e.g., "find and list all escorts by age and ethnicity in Seattle on Christmas Eve") over noisy data are far less straightforward. Even point fact queries turn out to be difficult when considering both the noise and the variability in the KGC.

Preclusion of Live Web Search. Despite all these problems, we could still very well question if there is not *some* way to pose the question as a Google query, at least to solve the initial problem of locating relevant web pages, followed by online (i.e., real time) execution of extraction technology. There are two problems with such a thesis, even assuming the efficiency of online extractions. First, investigators are often interested, not just in what escort ads are *presently* on the web, but also in escort ads published in the past (and which may have been taken down subsequently). Many ads are published only for a few days. Building cases against trafficking requires establishing a pattern of behavior over time, so it is important to retain pages that may not be available at the moment of search.

In summary, such searches are especially vital for the purposes of evidence gathering, which is directly relevant to the motivation of using the system for evidence-based social good. The second problem is that it is not obvious how keyword-based search engines can solve complex query types such as clustering and aggregation in a purely online fashion, using only a keyword index. Finally, traditional web search principles, which rely on hyperlinks for the robust functioning of ranking algorithms like PageRank, do not hold in the HT domain, where relevant hyperlinks in the HTML of an escort ad tend to be sparse. Most links are inserted by publishers to promote other content and cause traditional search crawlers to behave undesirably.

17.4.2   Crisis Informatics

The UN Office for the Coordination of Human Affairs (OCHA) reported that in 2016, more than a 100 million people were affected by natural disasters alone, while over 60 million people were forcibly displaced by violence and conflict. Since that time, the numbers have only gotten worse. Certain programs, again funded by agencies like DARPA, have attempted to use technology to address these problems where their impact is most calamitous (e.g., developing or remote regions of the planet). For example, the DARPA LORELEI (Low-Resource Languages for Emergent Incidents) program was established with the explicit agenda of providing situational awareness for emergent incidents, under the assumption that the emergent incident occurs in a region of the world where the predominant language is *computationally* low resource, by which we mean languages for which few automated or NLP tools actually exist. An example is Uyghur, a Turkic language spoken by about 10–25 million people in western China, but which has far fewer open-source NLP capabilities or research tools available in the public domain compared to major Western languages like English. The technologies resulting from LORELEI research, some of which have been demonstrated and are already undergoing transitioning, will be capable of supporting situational awareness based on low-resource foreign language sources within an extremely short time frame (about 24 hours after a new language requirement emerges).

What kinds of situational awareness would apply? The very basics, especially for text data, would be NLP tasks like machine translation (if the language is not in English), as well as inference and KGC on the translated text, including tasks such as NER and sentiment analysis. Additionally, once the KG is constructed, viable solutions to problems such as entity resolution and provenance reasoning are required to support detailed analytics that are ultimately visualized on a GUI. A major differentiator between crisis informatics systems and some of the other tools discussed earlier in this chapter is that the former must often work with sparse or otherwise context-poor data, of which short text social media (e.g., Twitter) is a good example. This entails the adoption of different kinds of IE (recall the different kinds of IE discussed in part II, including chapter 7, an entire chapter on social media and Open IE). A more advanced kind of situational awareness would rely on clustering and other kinds of semantic aggregation on a collection of (possibly streaming) messages, as many people will be discussing the same situation (e.g., an urgent need that has arisen on a particular street affected by a flood). Even the simply stated problems of binary classification and inference in the crisis informatics domain can get complicated. For example, one kind of inference that is useful to first responders is the level of *urgency* at both the message and the situation (cluster) levels. How to design good urgency detection algorithms for arbitrary disasters, or with only a few labels available, continues to be a dilemma for standard machine learning, which requires a reasonable number (or in the case of deep learning, a large number) of labels before the algorithms deliver a reasonable performance on test data.

A KG-centric system that is capable of providing some of the situational awareness mentioned above is THOR, whose name stands for "Text-enabled Humanitarian Operations in Real-time," which was developed under the aforementioned LORELEI program. The architecture of THOR is illustrated in figure 17.10, and a dashboard showing what it looks like in practice when executed in a real scenario or for a real data set shown in figure 17.11. The input to THOR is a streaming corpus of raw documents and a set of NLP modules collectively denoted as the Language Technology Development Environment (LTDE), which includes state-of-the-art implementations for NLP services such as machine translation and NER. The LTDE outputs are used to structure each raw document in the stream into a situation frame, serialized as a semistructured JSON document that contains a combination of

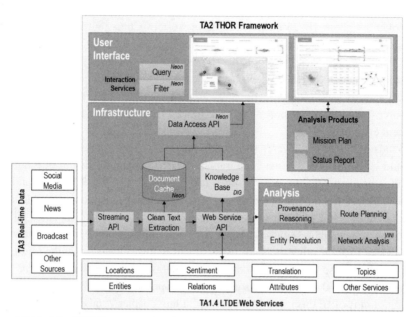

Figure 17.10: The THOR system developed for providing situational awareness to responders in the aftermath of natural disasters and other crises.

unstructured and structured data and metadata. These JSON documents are then visualized in an interactive GUI to support both search and analytics.

Although THOR is very different from KG construction systems like DIG and Deep-Dive, there are some similarities. Just like the other systems described earlier, for example, THOR is highly modular, allowing plug-and-play architecture that allows it to be customized for arbitrary user bases and disasters, as well as a combination of algorithmic and visualization utilities. For example, while the current version of THOR does not support route mapping or hotspot detection, these could potentially be added as layers on top of the default implementation if so desired by the organization using THOR. Even the visualization facilities in THOR are modular and tile-based. Among the analytics that are rendered in the GUI, the most important tile is on situation frames, which classify each JSON document as expressing one or more needs in preset categories such as food or water. By using methods like spatiotemporal rendering, these situations are ultimately designed to help field analysts decide where, when, and how to allocate resources to meet current situational needs.

17.4.3   COVID-19 and Medical Informatics

KGs and, more broadly, AI and informatics have been playing a prominent technological role in addressing the ongoing COVID-19 pandemic. A wide variety of data sets and

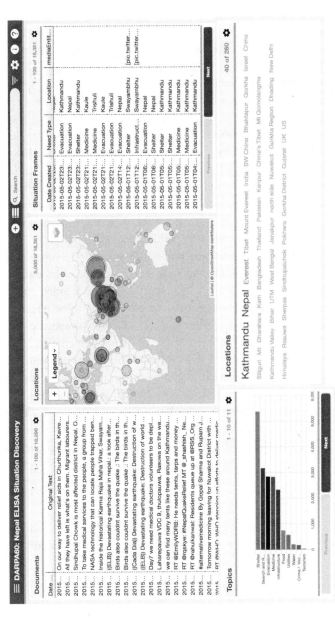

Figure 17.11: The THOR dashboard over a real data set collected from Twitter in the aftermath of a Nepal earthquake, which devastated the region in 2015. In general, THOR is capable of working over myriad kinds of data and disasters, especially in those regions of the world where the native language is not English.

resources that have been made available, often for free, in response to the crisis have facili-
tated the rapid application of these advanced technologies. A particularly valuable resource
has been the so-called CORD-19 corpus, which is a research data set comprising of over
57,000 scholarly articles (including over 45,000 with full text) about COVID-19 and other
related coronaviruses. It was prepared and released by the White House and a coalition
of leading research groups. Already some researchers have been applying (and releasing
the output of) IE and other KG construction techniques on this data set. For example,
Wang et al. (2020) created the CORD-NER data set, which is the output of comprehensive
NER application on the CORD-19 corpus (using distant or weak supervision). Their data
set covers 75 fine-grained entity types, including common biomedical entity types such
as genes and chemicals. It also covers new types related to COVID-19 studies, including
viral proteins, substrates, and immune response. The quality of NER was found to surpass
SciSpaCy (a version of SpaCy that is optimized for scientific text) based on a sample set of
documents. The authors have stated that they will continue to update CORD-NER based
on incremental updates and improvements to the underlying system. Although the outputs
of NER do not (by themselves) constitute a KG as we understand it, it is possible to express
the outputs as a set of triples and apply other techniques such as instance matching (IM)
and Probabilistic Soft Logic (PSL) to them. Several groups are already undertaking these
refined efforts to complete the KG (as discussed in part III), including our own.

Recently, Neo4j (chapter 12) built and released a proper KG on COVID-19 that integrates
publications, case statistics, genes, functions, molecular data, and other relevant information. According to the website,[4] the project is a "voluntary initiative of graph enthusiasts
and companies" and is therefore truly representative of a community effort. The website
also includes details on the schema used to represent the KG and the specific data sets
and infrastructure used. We also provide more guidance in the section entitled "Software
and Resources," at the end of this chapter. The fact that a collaboratively built KG, and
KG-supporting resources such as CORD-NER, could be set up mere weeks after public
data sets and resources were released is a testament to the maturity of the field of KGs,
the applicability of research that has been the sum total of decades-long contribution of
many practitioners and scientists, and the social recognition by many current scientists and
companies that KGs could indeed be used as a technology to help in the fight against the
disease.

17.5   Concluding Notes

In this chapter, we described some selected use-cases and architectures for constructing
domain-specific KGs (and KG-powered systems such as domain-specific search engines

---

[4] http://www.odbms.org/2020/03/we-build-a-knowledge-graph-on-covid-19/.

and intelligence tools for informatics and situational awareness), especially in areas of social impact such as HT and other crises. However, crises and illicit domains are by no means the only social domains that KG research can influence, and research on the application of KGs for social good continues to be very active. For example, very recently, there have been attempts to use KGs for doing better geopolitical forecasting. This is a difficult problem that, especially in today's political climate, can yield insights into, and benefits for, a range of stakeholders, including policy think tanks and intelligence agencies like Intelligence Advanced Research Projects Activity (IARPA), if performed with reasonable success. Successful geopolitical forecasting requires one to navigate a landscape of complex variables and to expend considerable time and resources on doing research. In recent work, the DIG system was used to process various important data sources, such as the Armed Conflict Location and Event Data (ACLED) project, the Political Instability Task Force (PITF), and the Famine Early Warning Systems Network (FEWS NET), in order to equip geopolitical forecasters with sophisticated facilities like structured search, maps, and dossier generation. While the jury is still out on whether providing such aids can yield a consistent improvement in overall forecasting accuracy, there is no question that KG-powered systems are providing more sophisticated decision aids that are bringing more tools to domain experts than was thought possible or feasible before. In domains like HT and other crisis informatics, the evidence (in favor of better response or more social impact) for providing such aids is fairly conclusive. We are confident that more such cases will crystallize and be publicized over time.

17.6 Software and Resources

The Inferlink tool, which played an important role in DIG and can be used in other systems as well, is described in detail at http://www.inferlink.com/our-work#research-capabilities-section. ETK, which provides the extraction capabilities in DIG but can similarly be extended or even used in a stand-alone fashion, is available at https://github.com/usc-isi-i2/etk. Details on DIG are available at http://usc-isi-i2.github.io/dig/. An alternative system, DeepDive, that can also be used to do relation extraction (RE) and build KGs using a relatively customized framework, may be accessed at http://deepdive.stanford.edu/relation_extraction. In chapter 3, we also mentioned the DDT, which provides an advanced interface for domain discovery and has also been used extensively in the Memex program, which funded much of the HT work discussed in this chapter. The DDT maintains a GitHub repository at https://domain-discovery-tool.readthedocs.io/en/latest/. Other useful resources available under Memex may be found at https://www.darpa.mil/opencatalog?ocSearch=m-emex&sort=program&ocFilter=all.

The THOR system, as a complete package, is not a fully open source package, although many individual modules are downloadable in some modality (e.g., as a Docker container or as source code). The ELISA system was one of the LTDEs (including machine translation and IE) implemented for THOR. IE modules used in ELISA expose some download links and modalities at https://blender.cs.illinois.edu/software/. Other research packages include tools for situational clustering of tweets (e.g., https://hub.docker.com/r/akarshdang/streaming-clustersv4), visualization of crisis-relevant classifications on social media data (e.g., https://github.com/ppplin-day/Situati-on-Awareness-Visualization), and urgency detection (e.g., https://hub.docker.com/r/ppplinday/emergence-detection). Sentiment analysis also plays a role in such systems, and many useful sentiment analysis tools are available, including free, relatively simple, but widely used (and arguably robust) packages, such as the lexicon- and rule-based tool VADER (https://github.com/cjhutto/vaderSentiment), as well as paid tools, especially for social media marketing. Deep learning has also been applied to sentiment analysis in recent years; see Zhang et al. (2018) for a survey and pointers.

There are several other projects that are using AI and knowledge management tools for crisis informatics. Good resources and pointers can be found on the pages for Project EPIC (https://epic.cs.colorado.edu/our_work/) and more recently, Co-Inform (http://people.kmi. open.ac.uk/harith/). Another valuable resource, especially for data sets and lexicons, is CrisisLex (https://crisislex.org/), which also contains tools that helps users and researchers create these collections and lexicons. In the "Bibliographic Notes" section, we also provide citations to other important works, many of which maintain project pages as well.

The Linguistic Data Consortium (LDC) has done much resource curation and annotation to support the larger goals of the LORELEI program under which THOR was funded. The LDC webpage describing current and recent projects may be accessed at https://www.ldc. upenn.edu/collabor-ations/current-projects. Note that a subscription is typically required to access and download many of these resources.

Toward the end of the chapter, we mentioned COVID-19, which is an ongoing crisis at this time, and has already had severe social, economic, and medical impacts. A silver lining has been the rallying of scientific and other communities of people, globally, for the purpose of finding ways of tackling the crisis together. On the technology front, there has been ample provision of software, data, and resources for fighting the crisis. We can only list a few here, although we also include websites that are attempting to list known resources on a single page:

1. The CORD-19 corpus is available on Kaggle: www.kaggle.com/allen-insti-tute-for-ai/CORD-19-research-challenge.

2. The Neo4j KG on COVID-19 is described at http://www.odbms.org/2020/03/we-build-a-knowledge-graph-on-covid-19/. Public access credentials are also available on that page.

3. Another example of a COVID-19 KG project released by a commercial effort (Yahoo) is described at https://yahoodevelopers.tumblr.com/post/616566-076523839488/yahoo-knowledge-graph-announces-covid-19-dataset.

4. CORD-NER is available at https://xuanwang91.github.io/2020-03-20-cord19-ner/.

5. In general, a detailed summary of the literature review, tools, data sets, and other contributions from the Kaggle community's COVID-19 work is maintained at https://www.kaggle.com/covid-19-contributions.

These sites present only one example of an aggregation of COVID-19 data sets and resources. A web search reveals many more, some of which are more official than others. Examples of aggregation pages include https://dataverse.harvard.edu/dataverse/2019ncov, https://browse.welch.jhmi.edu/covid-19/databases and https://guides.ucsf.edu/COVID19/data. Note that usually there is significant overlap, but on occasion, a good resource may be found or linked on selective aggregation websites. Furthermore, because the crisis continues to evolve very fast, we always recommend that the interested reader do a fresh web search, both to obtain new resources and to find the latest addresses of these resources.

17.7 Bibliographic Notes

As KGs are a relatively novel research area, using them for domain-specific social impact has only recently started becoming a serious topic of research, although the use-cases covered by this chapter (such as HT, but also natural disaster response) are important enough that they encompass individual domains of research in which KGs have played some role. By now, multiple papers have been published covering both direct and indirect applications of KG and KG-enabled search technology to HT, many of which cover research that was funded or conducted under the Memex program. There are also general studies about using technology to fight HT, as well as on better understanding the extent of this tragic crime. We cite a broad range of work here, including Szekely et al. (2015), Hultgren et al. (2016), Alvari et al. (2016), Kejriwal and Kapoor (2019), QC et al. (2016), Chen (2011), Harrendorf et al. (2010), Greiman and Bain (2013), Savona and Stefanizzi (2007), and Kejriwal and Szekely (2017a,c), for the interested reader to get started on this difficult subject. Work specifically related to DIG includes Szekely et al. (2015), Kejriwal et al. (2017a,b), Kejriwal and Szekely (2017c), and Kapoor et al. (2017). In the other direction, there has also been work on how the Internet, as well as technologies like mobile, have contributed to trafficking; we cite Musto and Boyd (2014), Dixon (2013), Sarkar (2015), Latonero et al. (2012), and Latonero (2012) as examples of research investigating this phenomenon.

A good reference for the DeepDive system, which has also been used for constructing KBs in difficult domains, is Niu et al. (2012a). Yang et al. (2016), though not specific to either HT or KGs, is also a worthwhile read for some of the conceptual underpinnings of the work cited earlier, as well as continuing work in this space.

Other related work, which is broader and more conceptual but critical to gaining a deeper understanding of these other domain-specific systems, includes Hogan et al. (2007), Lin et al. (2012), Saleiro et al. (2016), Tonon et al. (2012), Dalvi et al. (2009), Freitas et al.

(2012), Marchionini (2006), Jain et al. (2007), Anantharangachar et al. (2013), Nikolov et al. (2013), and Gupta et al. (2012). They cover a diverse set of topics, such as entity-centric search, ad-hoc object retrieval, exploratory search, structured querying over web ads and natural-language text, efficient combination of structured and full-text queries, ontology-guided IE, and scalable web search and query systems, all of which played some role in the construction and design of a system like DIG that was transitioned to law enforcement for fighting HT. Some of these topics (such as the combination of structured and full-text queries) fall into areas that have received a fuller treatment in part IV of this book.

Concerning natural disaster response, we note that the broader field of *crisis informatics* has become important, especially given the effects of climate change, record-setting summers and droughts, and the prevalence of more extreme weather events. For a background on crisis informatics, we highly recommend Hagar (2015), Reuter et al. (2018), Anderson and Schram (2011), Palen et al. (2007), and Palen and Anderson (2016) (with the last of these being a particularly instructive introduction); for a sense of how technology (especially social media) can have an impact in this area, we recommend Ukkusuri et al. (2014), Palen (2008), Heverin and Zach (2010), and Anderson et al. (2013). It is also instructive to consider the impact of funded projects in this space (e.g., Project EPIC is an important effort that was launched in September 2009 and supported by a \$2.8 million grant from the National Science Foundation). It takes a multilingual, multidisciplinary perspective and has led to a large number of publications, with the last few publications coming in 2015. The most recent examples include Kogan et al. (2015), Aydin and Anderson (2015), and Barrenechea et al. (2015).

KGs play a niche role in this space, though the LORELEI program has introduced advanced-language technologies to address the problem in parts of the world where English is not the dominant language; see Christianson et al. (2018) for an excellent overview. Throughout this book (but especially in part II), we have made note of the difficulties posed for IE (and, by extension, KGC and KG-enabled) systems in the cross-lingual and multilingual setting. When dealing with urgent crisis situations, especially in developing nations, addressing these difficulties while still managing inevitable performance degradation (compared to English-only systems and baselines) can make all the difference between a timely intervention and great loss of life. LORELEI provided the basis for an impressive research agenda that brought together natural-language and KG researchers; a good set of program-level references include Tong et al. (2018), Papadopoulos et al. (2017), Strassel et al. (2017), and Strassel and Tracey (2016), of which at least one of the outputs was THOR. Good references, as well as a demonstration article on THOR that inspired much of the material covered herein, include Kejriwal et al. (2018a,b), Malandrakis et al. (2018), Gu and Kejriwal (2018), Zhang et al. (2018), Kejriwal and Zhou (2019), Martinez et al. (2019), and Kejriwal and Gu (2019).

Note that, because LORELEI and Memex ended recently, the jury is still out on the full impact (and sustainability) of this research on society. Some of the systems that have been transitioned to real-world users or are still being transitioned may or may not survive, but we believe that there is enough momentum behind the broader agenda of AI for social good (of which KGs for social good is a part) that more such systems designed to have direct social impact will continue to emerge.

Of course, beyond the two mentioned here, there are other social domains where KGs are starting to gain traction, although the literature is piecemeal and not easy to track or collect into a comprehensive list of references. An important domain is healthcare; see Shi et al. (2017), Gatta et al. (2017), and Huang et al. (2017) for some direct applications of KGs in healthcare-related domains. Recently, there have also been patents [specifically, we note one by Sahu et al. (2018)] from industry, showing that this is not just an academic pursuit. Another important domain is government, on which we provided more details on how KGs can play an important role in chapter 15.

17.8 Exercises

1. Imagine that you are a doctor trying to find either a cure or vaccine for COVID-19. We described some KG efforts in the subsection entitled "COVID19 and Medical Informatics" that were under way as early as March 2020. For the KG to help you, as a doctor, in your job, what kinds of features should it support? Looking back at some of the other chapters in this section, could you think of essential data sets that should be incorporated into, or linked to, a COVID-19 KG?

2. Obfuscation of text is an important challenge for KGC systems when dealing with illicit domains like HT. Imagine an ordinary piece of text such as "Let us meet in the park. Call me at the number 123-456-7890 when you get here." Suppose that you were trying to obfuscate this message so that it is clear to a (reasonable, but arbitrary) human being what you are trying to express, but you want to deliberately make it harder for search engines and machine learning to extract critical information such as phone number. Think of three such ways to obfuscate the message and write your obfuscated messages.

3. Thinking back to the KGC systems in part II, what kinds of approaches could you use to extract a useful KG from millions of messages like these?

4. Considering the crisis informatics problem described earlier, list five open data sets that you could use to deliver more value to stakeholders in this space. Why would you advocate for those data sources, and what are some key things to be aware of when using or integrating these KGs?

5. How might a resource such as the Gene Ontology be of help in fighting COVID-19? Try to draw out a very specific scenario, and articulate your assumptions as clearly as possible.

6. Could you think of illicit domains that have significant presence on the web, but where KG technology, as described in this book, might not necessarily be applicable? Why or why not?

7. Suppose an illicit portal on the Dark Web wants to build a chatbot for its highest-paying customers to ensure that they do not have to wade through lots of obfuscation or irrelevant results, but they can find what they're looking for as efficiently as they can. Why would the portal not run into the same problem as you when trying to build such a chatbot? Does obfuscation really matter for the portal? Why or why not? *Hint: Think carefully about the raw data that your KGC systems have to work with when dealing with a domain from the outside, as well as the data that the portal would have access to. How does the portal ensure that obfuscation does not matter to, or get in the way of the chatbot, even if third-party providers are involved in listing on the portal?*

Bibliography

Abdelaziz, Ibrahim, Razen Harbi, Zuhair Khayyat, and Panos Kalnis. 2017. A survey and experimental comparison of distributed SPARQL engines for very large RDF data. In *Proceedings of the VLDB endowment* 10 (13): 2049–2060.

Abramova, Veronika, and Jorge Bernardino. 2013. NoSQL databases: MongoDB vs. Cassandra.. In *Proceedings of the international C* conference on computer science and software engineering*, 14–22. ACM.

Adelberg, Brad. 1998. NoDoSE—a tool for semi-automatically extracting structured and semistructured data from text documents. In *Proceedings of the 1998 ACM SIGMOD international conference on management of data*, 283–294.

Adomavicius, Gediminas, and Alexander Tuzhilin. 2005. Toward the next generation of recommender systems: A survey of the state-of-the-art and possible extensions. *IEEE transactions on knowledge and data engineering* 17 (6): 734–749.

Aggarwal, Nitish, Tamara Polajnar, and Paul Buitelaar. 2013. Cross-lingual natural language querying over the web of data. In *International conference on application of natural language to information systems*, 152–163. Springer.

Agichtein, Eugene, David Carmel, Dan Pelleg, Yuval Pinter, and Donna Harman. 2015. Overview of the TREC 2015 LiveQA track. In *Proceedings of the 2015 TREC conference on text retrieval*.

Aguilar, Jacqueline, Charley Beller, Paul McNamee, Benjamin Van Durme, Stephanie Strassel, Zhiyi Song, and Joe Ellis. 2014. A comparison of the events and relations across ACE, ERE, TAC-KBP, and FrameNet annotation standards. In *Proceedings of the second workshop on events: Definition, detection, coreference, and representation*, 45–53.

Ahn, David. 2006. The stages of event extraction. In *Proceedings of the workshop on annotating and reasoning about time and events*, 1–8.

Akbik, Alan, and Alexander Löser. 2012. Kraken: N-ary facts in open information extraction. In *Proceedings of the joint workshop on automatic knowledge base construction and web-scale knowledge extraction*, 52–56. Association for Computational Linguistics.

Akerkar, Rajendra. 2009. *Foundations of the Semantic Web: XML, RDF and ontology*. Alpha Science International, Ltd.

Alarabiat, Ayman, Delfina Soares, Luis Ferreira, and Filipe de Sá-Soares. 2018. Analyzing e-governance assessment initiatives: An exploratory study. In *Proceedings of the 19th annual international conference on digital government research: Governance in the data age*, 1–10.

Alfonseca, Enrique, and Suresh Manandhar. 2002. An unsupervised method for general named entity recognition and automated concept discovery. In *Proceedings of the 1st international conference on general WordNet, Mysore, India*, 34–43.

Allemang, Dean, and James Hendler. 2011. *Semantic Web for the working ontologist: Effective modeling in RDFS and OWL*. Elsevier.

Alvari, Hamidreza, Paulo Shakarian, and J. E. Kelly Snyder. 2016. A non-parametric learning approach to identify online human trafficking. In *Intelligence and security informatics (ISI), 2016 IEEE conference on*, 133–138. IEEE.

Amitay, Einat. 1998. Using common hypertext links to identify the best phrasal description of target web documents. In *Proceedings of the 1998 SIGIR post-conference workshop on hypertext information retrieval for the web*, Vol. 98.

An, Yoo Jung, James Geller, Yi-Ta Wu, and Soon Ae Chun. 2007. Semantic Deep Web: Automatic attribute extraction from the Deep Web data sources. In *Proceedings of the 2007 ACM symposium on applied computing*, 1667–1672.

Anantharangachar, Raghu, Srinivasan Ramani, and S. Rajagopalan. 2013. Ontology guided information extraction from unstructured text. *arXiv preprint arXiv:1302.1335*.

Anderson, Kenneth M., and Aaron Schram. 2011. Design and implementation of a data analytics infrastructure in support of crisis informatics research (Nier track). In *Proceedings of the 33rd international conference on software engineering*, 844–847.

Anderson, Kenneth Mark, Aaron Schram, Ali Alzabarah, and Leysia Palen. 2013. Architectural implications of social media analytics in support of crisis informatics research. *IEEE data engineering bulletin*, 36 (3): 13–20.

Anelli, Vito Walter, Andrea Calì, Tommaso Di Noia, Matteo Palmonari, and Azzurra Ragone. 2016. Exposing open street map in the linked data cloud. In *International conference on industrial, engineering, and other applications of applied intelligent systems*, 344–355. Springer.

Angeli, Gabor, Melvin Jose Johnson Premkumar, and Christopher D. Manning. 2015. Leveraging linguistic structure for open domain information extraction. In *Proceedings of the 53rd annual meeting of the Association for Computational Linguistics and the 7th international joint conference on natural language processing (Volume 1: Long papers)*, 344–354.

Angles, Renzo, Marcelo Arenas, Pablo Barceló, Peter Boncz, George Fletcher, Claudio Gutierrez, Tobias Lindaaker, Marcus Paradies, Stefan Plantikow, Juan Sequeda, et al. 2018. G-core: A core for future graph query languages. In *Proceedings of the 2018 international conference on management of data*, 1421–1432. ACM.

Angles, Renzo, Marcelo Arenas, Pablo Barceló, Aidan Hogan, Juan L Reutter, and Domagoj Vrgoc. 2016. Foundations of modern graph query languages. *CoRR, abs/1610.06264*.

Angles, Renzo, Marcelo Arenas, Pablo Barceló, Aidan Hogan, Juan Reutter, and Domagoj Vrgoč. 2017. Foundations of modern query languages for graph databases. *ACM computing surveys (CSUR)* 50 (5): 1–40.

Angles, Renzo, and Claudio Gutierrez. 2008. Survey of graph database models. *ACM computing surveys (CSUR)* 40 (1): 1–39.

Antoniou, Grigoris, and Frank Van Harmelen. 2004a. *A Semantic Web primer*. MIT Press.

Antoniou, Grigoris, and Frank Van Harmelen. 2004b. Web ontology language: OWL. In *Handbook on ontologies*, 67–92. Springer.

Appelt, Douglas E. 1999. Introduction to information extraction. *AI communications* 12 (3): 161–172.

Arasu, Arvind, and Hector Garcia-Molina. 2003. Extracting structured data from web pages. In *Proceedings of the 2003 ACM sigmod international conference on management of data*, 337–348.

Araujo, Samur, Duc Tran, Arjen DeVries, Jan Hidders, and Daniel Schwabe. 2012. Serimi: Class-based disambiguation for effective instance matching over heterogeneous web data. In *Webdb*, 25–30.

Archenaa, J., and E. A. Mary Anita. 2015. A survey of Big Data analytics in healthcare and government. *Procedia computer science* 50: 408–413.

Armstrong, Robert, Dayne Freitag, Thorsten Joachims, Tom Mitchell, et al. 1995. Webwatcher: A learning apprentice for the World Wide Web. In *AAAI spring symposium on information gathering from heterogeneous, distributed environments*, Vol. 93, 107. Stanford.

Arocena, G, and A Mendelzon. 1998. WebOQL: Restructuring documents, databases, and webs. In *Proceedings of the 1998 international conference on data engineering, Orlando*.

Asghar, Nabiha. 2016. Automatic extraction of causal relations from natural language texts: A comprehensive survey. *arXiv preprint arXiv:1605.07895*.

Ashburner, Michael, Catherine A. Ball, Judith A. Blake, David Botstein, Heather Butler, J. Michael Cherry, Allan P. Davis, Kara Dolinski, Selina S. Dwight, Janan T. Eppig, et al. 2000. Gene ontology: Tool for the unification of biology. *Nature genetics* 25 (1): 25–29.

Atefeh, Farzindar, and Wael Khreich. 2015. A survey of techniques for event detection in Twitter. *Computational intelligence* 31 (1): 132–164.

Attard, Judie, Fabrizio Orlandi, Simon Scerri, and Sören Auer. 2015. A systematic review of open government data initiatives. *Government information quarterly* 32 (4): 399–418.

Auer, Sören, Christian Bizer, Georgi Kobilarov, Jens Lehmann, Richard Cyganiak, and Zachary Ives. 2007. Dbpedia: A nucleus for a web of open data. In *The Semantic Web*, 722–735. Springer.

Auer, Sören, Jens Lehmann, and Sebastian Hellmann. 2009. LinkedGeoData: Adding a spatial dimension to the web of data. In *International Semantic Web conference*, 731–746. Springer.

Aydin, Ahmet Arif, and Kenneth M. Anderson. 2015. Incremental sorting for large dynamic data sets. In *2015 IEEE first international conference on Big Data computing service and applications*, 170–175. IEEE.

Bača, Radim, Michal Krátký, Irena Holubová, Martin Nečaský, Tomáš Skopal, Martin Svoboda, and Sherif Sakr. 2017. Structural XML query processing. *ACM computing surveys (CSUR)* 50 (5): 64.

Bach, Nguyen, and Sameer Badaskar. 2007. A review of relation extraction. *Literature review for Language and Statistics II* 2: 1–15.

Bach, Stephen H, Matthias Broecheler, Bert Huang, and Lise Getoor. 2017. Hinge-loss Karkov random fields and probabilistic soft logic. *Journal of machine learning research* 18 (1): 3846–3912.

Balikas, Georgios, Aris Kosmopoulos, Anastasia Krithara, Georgios Paliouras, and Ioannis Kakadiaris. 2015. Results of the BioASQ tasks of the question answering lab at CLEF 2015. In *Proceedings of the CEUR workshop*, Vol. 1391.

Banker, Kyle. 2011. *MongoDB in action*. Manning Publications.

Barabási, Albert-László. 2016. *Network science*. Cambridge University Press.

Barbehenn, Michael. 1998. A note on the complexity of Dijkstra's algorithm for graphs with weighted vertices. *IEEE transactions on computers* 47 (2): 263.

Barbieri, Davide Francesco, Daniele Braga, Stefano Ceri, Emanuele Della Valle, and Michael Grossniklaus. 2009. C-SPARQL: SPARQL for continuous querying. In *The 18th international conference on World Wide Web-WWW'09*, 1061–1062.

Barrenechea, Mario, Kenneth M. Anderson, Ahmet Arif Aydin, Mazin Hakeem, and Sahar Jambi. 2015. Getting the query right: User interface design of analysis platforms for crisis research. In *International conference on web engineering*, 547–564. Springer.

Batsakis, Sotiris, Euripides G. M. Petrakis, and Evangelos Milios. 2009. Improving the performance of focused web crawlers. *Data & knowledge engineering* 68 (10): 1001–1013.

Batzios, Alexandros, Christos Dimou, Andreas L. Symeonidis, and Pericles A. Mitkas. 2008. Biocrawler: An intelligent crawler for the Semantic Web. *Expert systems with applications* 35 (1–2): 524–530.

Bellogín, Alejandro, Pablo Castells, and Iván Cantador. 2017. Statistical biases in information retrieval metrics for recommender systems. *Information retrieval journal* 20 (6): 606–634.

Ben Abacha, Asma, and Pierre Zweigenbaum. 2012. Medical question answering: Translating medical questions into SPARQL queries. In *Proceedings of the 2nd ACM SIGHIT international health informatics symposium*, 41–50.

Bénel, Aurélien, Chao Zhou, and Jean-Pierre Cahier. 2010. Beyond Web 2.0 and beyond the Semantic Web. In *From CSCW to Web 2.0: European developments in collaborative design*, 155–171. Springer.

Benjelloun, Omar, Hector Garcia-Molina, David Menestrina, Qi Su, Steven Euijong Whang, and Jennifer Widom. 2009. Swoosh: A generic approach to entity resolution. *VLDB journal* 18 (1): 255–276.

Bennett, Jonathan. 2010. *OpenStreetMap*. Packt Publishing.

Berger, Seth I., and Ravi Iyengar. 2009. Network analyses in systems pharmacology. *Bioinformatics* 25 (19): 2466–2472.

Berners-Lee, Tim. 2011. Linked data-design issues. http://www.w3.org/DesignIssues/LinkedData.

Berners-Lee, Tim, et al. 1998. *Semantic Web road map*. http://www.w3.org/DesignIssues/Semantic.

Berners-Lee, Tim, Dan Connolly, and Ralph R. Swick. 1999. Web architecture: Describing and exchanging data. *W3C Nota* 7.

Berners-Lee, Tim, James Hendler, Ora Lassila, et al. 2001. The Semantic Web. *Scientific American* 284 (5): 28–37.

Bertot, John Carlo, Ursula Gorham, Paul T. Jaeger, Lindsay C. Sarin, and Heeyoon Choi. 2014. Big Data, open government and e-government: Issues, policies and recommendations. *Information polity* 19 (1, 2): 5–16.

Bhattacharya, Indrajit, and Lise Getoor. 2007. Collective entity resolution in relational data. *ACM Transactions on knowledge discovery from data (TKDD)* 1 (1): 5-es.

Biemann, Chris, Siegfried Handschuh, André Freitas, Farid Meziane, and Elisabeth Métais. 2015. *Proceedings of natural language processing and information systems: 20th international conference on applications of natural language to information systems, NLDB 2015, Passau, Germany, June 17–19, 2015*, Vol. 9103. Springer.

Bikel, Daniel M., Scott Miller, Richard Schwartz, and Ralph Weischedel. 1998. Nymble: A high-performance learning name-finder. *arXiv preprint cmp-lg/9803003*.

Bilal, Muhammad, Lukumon O. Oyedele, Junaid Qadir, Kamran Munir, Saheed O. Ajayi, Olugbenga O. Akinade, Hakeem A. Owolabi, Hafiz A. Alaka, and Maruf Pasha. 2016. Big Data in the construction industry: A review of present status, opportunities, and future trends. *Advanced engineering informatics* 30 (3): 500–521.

Bilenko, Mikhail, Beena Kamath, and Raymond J. Mooney. 2006. Adaptive blocking: Learning to scale up record linkage. In *Sixth international conference on data mining (ICDM'06)*, 87–96. IEEE.

Bilenko, Mikhail, and Raymond J. Mooney. 2003. Adaptive duplicate detection using learnable string similarity measures. In *Proceedings of the ninth ACM SIGKDD international conference on knowledge discovery and data mining*, 39–48. ACM.

Bizer, Christian. 2009. The emerging web of linked data. *IEEE intelligent systems* 24 (5): 87–92.

Bizer, Chris, Richard Cyganiak, Tom Heath, et al. 2007. How to publish linked data on the web. http://www4.wiwiss.fu-berlin.de/bizer/pub/LinkedDataTutorial.

Bizer, Christian, Tom Heath, and Tim Berners-Lee. 2011. Linked data: The story so far. In *Semantic services, interoperability, and web applications: Emerging concepts*, 205–227. IGI Global.

Bizer, Christian, Tom Heath, Kingsley Idehen, and Tim Berners-Lee. 2008. Linked data on the web (LDOW2008). In *Proceedings of the 17th international conference on World Wide Web*, 1265–1266. ACM.

Bizer, C., A. Jentzsch, and R. Cyganiak. 2011. State of the linked open data (lod) cloud, Technical report, April 5, 2011 (March 2011). http://www4.wiwiss.fu-berlin.

Bizer, Christian, Jens Lehmann, Georgi Kobilarov, Sören Auer, Christian Becker, Richard Cyganiak, and Sebastian Hellmann. 2009a. Dbpedia—A crystallization point for the web of data. *Journal of web semantics* 7 (3): 154–165.

Bizer, Christian, and Andreas Schultz. 2009. The Berlin SPARQL benchmark. *International journal on Semantic Web and information systems (IJSWIS)* 5 (2): 1–24.

Bizer, Christian, Julius Volz, Georgi Kobilarov, and Martin Gaedke. 2009b. Silk—A link discovery framework for the web of data. In *18th international World Wide Web conference*, Vol. 122.

Bobadilla, Jesús, Fernando Ortega, Antonio Hernando, and Abraham Gutiérrez. 2013. Recommender systems survey. *Knowledge-based systems* Vol. 46, 109–132.

Boicea, Alexandru, Florin Radulescu, and Laura Ioana Agapin. 2012. MongoDB vs. Oracle–Database comparison. In *2012 third international conference on emerging intelligent data and web technologies*, 330–335. IEEE.

Bolton, Evan E., Yanli Wang, Paul A. Thiessen, and Stephen H. Bryant. 2008. PubChem: Integrated platform of small molecules and biological activities. In *Annual reports in computational chemistry*, Vol. 4, 217–241. Elsevier.

Bondy, John Adrian, and Uppaluri Siva Ramachandra Murty. 1976. *Graph theory with applications*, Vol. 290. Macmillan.

Bontcheva, Kalina, Leon Derczynski, Adam Funk, Mark A. Greenwood, Diana Maynard, and Niraj Aswani. 2013. Twitie: An open-source information extraction pipeline for microblog text. In *Proceedings of the international conference recent advances in natural language processing (RANLP) 2013*, 83–90.

Bordes, Antoine, Y.-Lan Boureau, and Jason Weston. 2016. Learning end-to-end goal-oriented dialog. *arXiv preprint arXiv:1605.07683*.

Bordes, Antoine, Nicolas Usunier, Alberto Garcia-Duran, Jason Weston, and Oksana Yakhnenko. 2013. Translating embeddings for modeling multi-relational data. In *Advances in neural information processing systems*, 2787–2795.

Bordes, Antoine, Jason Weston, Ronan Collobert, and Yoshua Bengio. 2011. Learning structured embeddings of knowledge bases. In *Twenty-fifth AAAI conference on artificial intelligence*, 301–306.

Borgatti, Stephen P., Ajay Mehra, Daniel J. Brass, and Giuseppe Labianca. 2009. Network analysis in the social sciences. *Science* 323 (5916): 892–895.

Bosselut, Antoine, and Yejin Choi. 2019. Dynamic knowledge graph construction for zero-shot commonsense question answering. *arXiv preprint arXiv:1911.03876*.

Boston, Christopher, Sandra Carberry, and Hui Fang. 2012. Wikimantic: Disambiguation for short queries. In *International conference on application of natural language to information systems*, 140–151. Springer.

Bouraoui, Zied, Jose Camacho-Collados, and Steven Schockaert. 2019. Inducing relational knowledge from BERT. *arXiv preprint arXiv:1911.12753*.

Boyle, Elizabeth I., Shuai Weng, Jeremy Gollub, Heng Jin, David Botstein, J. Michael Cherry, and Gavin Sherlock. 2004. Go:: Termfinder—Open-source software for accessing gene ontology information and finding significantly enriched gene ontology terms associated with a list of genes. *Bioinformatics* 20 (18): 3710–3715.

Brachman, R. J., R. E. Fikes, and H. J. Levesque. 1983. Krypton: A functional approach to knowledge representation. *Computer*, Vol. 10, 67–73.

Brachman, R. J., and H. J. Levesque. 1985. *Readings in knowledge representation.* https://dl.acm.org/citation.cfm?id=577033. ACM.

Brin, Sergey, and Lawrence Page. 1998. The anatomy of a large-scale hypertextual web search engine. *Computer networks and ISDN systems*, Vol. 30, 1–7.

Brown, Susan Windisch, Claire Bonial, Leo Obrst, and Martha Palmer. 2017. The rich event ontology. In *Proceedings of the events and stories in the news workshop*, 87–97.

Budhathoki, Nama R., and Caroline Haythornthwaite. 2013. Motivation for open collaboration: Crowd and community models and the case of OpenStreetMap. *American behavioral scientist* 57 (5): 548–575.

Buitelaar, Paul, Philipp Cimiano, Peter Haase, and Michael Sintek. 2009. Towards linguistically grounded ontologies. In *European Semantic Web conference*, 111–125. Springer.

Burke, Robin. 2002. Hybrid recommender systems: Survey and experiments. *User modeling and user-adapted interaction* 12 (4): 331–370.

Buron, Maxime, François Goasdoué, Ioana Manolescu, and Marie-Laure Mugnier. 2019. Reformulation-based query answering for RDF graphs with RDFS ontologies. In *European Semantic Web conference*, 19–35. Springer.

Buttigieg, Pier Luigi, Norman Morrison, Barry Smith, Christopher J. Mungall, Suzanna E. Lewis, Envo Consortium, et al. 2013. The environment ontology: Contextualising biological and biomedical entities. *Journal of biomedical semantics* 4 (1): 43.

Buttigieg, Pier Luigi, Evangelos Pafilis, Suzanna E. Lewis, Mark P. Schildhauer, Ramona L. Walls, and Christopher J. Mungall. 2016. The environment ontology in 2016: Bridging domains with increased scope, semantic density, and interoperation. *Journal of biomedical semantics* 7 (1): 57.

Cafarella, Michael J., Alon Y. Halevy, Yang Zhang, Daisy Zhe Wang, and Eugene Wu. 2008. Uncovering the relational web. In *WebDB*.

Cafarella, Michael J., Jayant Madhavan, and Alon Halevy. 2009. Web-scale extraction of structured data. *ACM SIGMOD record* 37 (4): 55–61.

Cahoon, Brendon, and Kathryn S. McKinley. 1996. Performance evaluation of a distributed architecture for information retrieval. In *Proceedings of the 19th annual international ACM SIGIR conference on research and development in information retrieval*, 110–118.

Callan, Jamie. 2002. Distributed information retrieval. In *Advances in information retrieval*, 127–150. Springer.

Calvanese, Diego, Giuseppe De Giacomo, Domenico Lembo, Maurizio Lenzerini, and Riccardo Rosati. 2004. What to ask to a peer: Ontolgoy-based query reformulation. In *Proceedings of the ninth international conference on the principles of knowledge representation and reasoning*, 469–478.

Calvanese, Diego, Maurizio Lenzerini, and Daniele Nardi. 1998. Description logics for conceptual data modeling. In *Logics for databases and information systems*, 229–263. Springer.

Campos, David, Sérgio Matos, and José Luís Oliveira. 2012. Biomedical Named Entity Recognition: A survey of machine-learning tools. http://dx.doi.org/10.5772/51066.

Cao, Yunbo, Zhiyuan Chen, Jiamin Zhu, Pei Yue, Chin-Yew Lin, and Yong Yu. 2011. Leveraging unlabeled data to scale blocking for record linkage. In *Twenty-second international joint conference on artificial intelligence*, 2211–2217.

Cao, Zhe, Tao Qin, Tie-Yan Liu, Ming-Feng Tsai, and Hang Li. 2007. Learning to rank: From pairwise approach to listwise approach. In *Proceedings of the 24th international conference on machine learning*, 129–136.

Carlson, Andrew, Justin Betteridge, Bryan Kisiel, Burr Settles, Estevam R. Hruschka, and Tom M. Mitchell. 2010. Toward an architecture for never-ending language learning. In *Twenty-fourth AAAI conference on artificial intelligence*.

Carvalho, Danilo S., Cagatay Calli, André Freitas, and Edward Curry. 2014. Easyesa: A low-effort infrastructure for explicit semantic analysis. In *International Semantic Web conference (posters & demos)*, 177–180.

Cassandra, Apache. 2014. Apache Cassandra. Website. http://planetcassandra.org/what-is-apache-cassandra.

Cattell, Rick. 2011. Scalable SQL and NoSQL data stores. *ACM SIGMOD record* 39 (4): 12–27.

Cetto, Matthias, Christina Niklaus, André Freitas, and Siegfried Handschuh. 2018. Graphene: Semantically-linked propositions in open information extraction. *arXiv preprint arXiv:1807.11276.*

Chakrabarti, Soumen, Martin Van den Berg, and Byron Dom. 1999. Focused crawling: A new approach to topic-specific web resource discovery. *Computer networks* 31 (11–16): 1623–1640.

Chakraborty, Nilesh, Denis Lukovnikov, Gaurav Maheshwari, Priyansh Trivedi, Jens Lehmann, and Asja Fischer. 2019. Introduction to neural network–based approaches for question answering over knowledge graphs. *arXiv preprint arXiv:1907.09361.*

Chan, Calvin M. L.. 2013. From open data to open innovation strategies: Creating e-services using open government data. In *2013 46th Hawaii international conference on system sciences*, 1890–1899. IEEE.

Chang, Chia-Hui, Mohammed Kayed, Moheb R. Girgis, and Khaled F. Shaalan. 2006. A survey of web information extraction systems. *IEEE transactions on knowledge and data engineering* 18 (10): 1411–1428.

Chang, Chia-Hui, and Shih-Chien Kuo. 2004. OLERA: Semisupervised web-data extraction with visual support. *IEEE intelligent systems* 19 (6): 56–64.

Chang, Chia-Hui, and Shao-Chen Lui. 2001. IEPAD: Information extraction based on pattern discovery. In *Proceedings of the 10th international conference on World Wide Web*, 681–688.

Chapelle, Olivier, and Yi Chang. 2011. Yahoo! Learning to Rank Challenge overview. In *Proceedings of the Learning to Rank Challenge*, 1–24.

Chau, Michael, and Hsinchun Chen. 2003. Personalized and focused web spiders. In *Web intelligence*, 197–217. Springer.

Chen, Hsinchun. 2011. *Dark Web: Exploring and data mining the dark side of the Web*, Vol. 30. Springer.

Chen, Hsinchun, Roger H. L. Chiang, and Veda C Storey. 2012. Business intelligence and analytics: From Big Data to big impact. *MIS quarterly*, 1165–1188.

Chen, Jiaoyan, and Alexander Zipf. 2017. DeepVGI: Deep learning with volunteered geographic information. In *Proceedings of the 26th international conference on World Wide Web companion*, 771–772.

Chen, P., and Sidney Redner. 2010. Community structure of the physical review citation network. *Journal of informetrics* 4 (3): 278–290.

Cheong, Fah-Chun. 1996. *Internet agents: Spiders, wanderers, brokers, and bots*. New Riders Publishing.

Chinchor, Nancy A., and Beth Sundheim. 1995. Message Understanding Conference (MUC) tests of discourse processing. In *Proceedings of AAAI spring symposium on empirical methods in discourse interpretation and generation*, 21–26.

Cho, Junghoo, Hector Garcia-Molina, and Lawrence Page. 1998. Efficient crawling through URL ordering. *Computer networks and ISDN systems* 30 (1–7), 161–172.

Chodorow, Kristina. 2013. *MongoDB: The definitive guide: Powerful and scalable data storage*. O'Reilly Media.

Choi, Namyoun, Il-Yeol Song, and Hyoil Han. 2006. A survey on ontology mapping. *ACM SIGMOD record* 35 (3): 34–41.

Choudhury, Sutanay, Khushbu Agarwal, Sumit Purohit, Baichuan Zhang, Meg Pirrung, Will Smith, and Mathew Thomas. 2017. NOUS: Construction and querying of dynamic knowledge graphs. In *2017 IEEE 33rd international conference on data engineering (ICDE)*, 1563–1565. IEEE.

Christen, Peter. 2008. Febrl: A freely available record linkage system with a graphical user interface. In *Proceedings of the second Australasian workshop on health data and knowledge management*, Vol. 80, 17–25. Australian Computer Society.

Christen, Peter. 2011. A survey of indexing techniques for scalable record linkage and deduplication. *IEEE transactions on knowledge and data engineering* 24 (9): 1537–1555.

Christen, Peter. 2012. *Data matching: Concepts and techniques for record linkage, entity resolution, and duplicate detection*. Springer.

Christensen, Janara, Stephen Soderland, Oren Etzioni, et al. 2010. Semantic role labeling for open information extraction. In *Proceedings of the NAACL HLT 2010 first international workshop on formalisms and methodology for learning by reading*, 52–60. Association for Computational Linguistics.

Christianson, Caitlin, Jason Duncan, and Boyan Onyshkevych. 2018. Overview of the DARPA LORELEI program. *Machine translation* 32 (1–2): 3–9.

Christophides, Vassilis, Vasilis Efthymiou, and Kostas Stefanidis. 2015. Entity resolution in the web of data. *Synthesis lectures on the Semantic Web* 5 (3): 1–122.

Chu, Xu, Ihab F. Ilyas, Sanjay Krishnan, and Jiannan Wang. 2016. Data cleaning: Overview and emerging challenges. In *Proceedings of the 2016 international conference on management of data*, 2201–2206. ACM.

Cimiano, Philipp. 2009. Flexible semantic composition with DUDES. In *Proceedings of the eighth international conference on computational semantics*, 272–276. Association for Computational Linguistics.

Cimiano, Philipp, and Johanna Völker. 2005. Towards large-scale, open-domain and ontology-based named entity classification. In *Proceedings of the international conference on recent advances in natural language processing (RANLP)*, 166–172.

Cohen, Aaron M., and William R. Hersh. 2005. A survey of current work in biomedical text mining. *Briefings in bioinformatics* 6 (1): 57–71.

Cojan, Julien, Elena Cabrio, and Fabien Gandon. 2013. Filling the gaps among DBpedia multilingual chapters for question answering. In *Proceedings of the 5th annual ACM web science conference*, 33–42.

Collins, Michael, and Yoram Singer. 1999. Unsupervised models for named entity classification. In *1999 joint SIGDAT conference on empirical methods in natural language processing and very large corpora*, 100–110.

Connolly, Dan, Rohit Khare, and Adam Rifkin. 1997. The evolution of web documents: The ascent of XML. *World Wide Web journal* 2 (4): 119–128.

Costa, Vítor Santos, Ashwin Srinivasan, Rui Camacho, Hendrik Blockeel, Bart Demoen, Gerda Janssens, Jan Struyf, Henk Vandecasteele, and Wim Van Laer. 2003. Query transformations for improving the efficiency of ilp systems. *Journal of machine learning research* 4 (Aug.): 465–491.

Cox, Brad J. 1986. *Object-oriented programming: An evolutionary approach*. Addison-Wesley.

Crauser, Andreas, Kurt Mehlhorn, Ulrich Meyer, and Peter Sanders. 1998. A parallelization of Dijkstra's shortest-path algorithm. In *International symposium on mathematical foundations of computer science*, 722–731. Springer.

Crescenzi, Valter, and Giansalvatore Mecca. 1998. Grammars have exceptions. *Information systems* 23 (8): 539–565.

Crescenzi, Valter, Giansalvatore Mecca, Paolo Merialdo, et al. 2001. Roadrunner: Towards automatic data extraction from large web sites. In *VLDB*, Vol. 1, 109–118.

Crestan, Eric, and Patrick Pantel. 2011. Web-scale table census and classification. In *Proceedings of the fourth ACM international conference on web search and data mining*, 545–554.

Croft, W. Bruce, Donald Metzler, and Trevor Strohman. 2010. *Search engines: Information retrieval in practice*, Vol. 520. Addison-Wesley.

Crosby, Christopher, Viswanath Nandigam, Chaitan Baru, and J. Ramon Arrowsmith. 2013. Open-to-po-graphy: Enabling online access to high-resolution lidar topography data and processing tools. In *EGU general assembly conference abstracts*, Vol. 15, 13326.

Csuka, K., D. Gaastra, and Y. de Bruijn. 2018. Breaking captchas on the Dark Web. https://delaat.net/rp/2017-2018/p62/report.pdf

Cucchiarelli, Alessandro, and Paola Velardi. 2001. Unsupervised named entity recognition using syntactic and semantic contextual evidence. *Computational linguistics* 27 (1): 123–131.

Cumby, Chad M., and Dan Roth. 2003. On kernel methods for relational learning. In *Proceedings of the 20th international conference on machine learning (ICML-03)*, 107–114.

Cussens, James, and Stephen Pulman. 1999. Experiments in inductive chart parsing. In *International conference on learning language in logic*, 143–156. Springer.

Cyganiak, Richard. 2005. A relational algebra for SPARQL. Digital Media Systems Laboratory HP Laboratories Bristol. *HPL-2005-170* 35: 9.

Da Costa, Paulo Cesar G., Kathryn B. Laskey, and Kenneth J. Laskey. 2006. PR-OWL: A bayesian ontology language for the Semantic Web. In *Uncertainty reasoning for the Semantic Web*, Vol. 1, 88–107. Springer.

Dalvi, Nilesh, Ravi Kumar, Bo Pang, Raghu Ramakrishnan, Andrew Tomkins, Philip Bohannon, Sathiya Keerthi, and Srujana Merugu. 2009. A web of concepts. In *Proceedings of the twenty-eighth acm SIGMOD-SIGACT-SIGART symposium on principles of database systems*, 1–12. ACM.

Damova, Mariana, Atanas Kiryakov, Kiril Simov, and Svetoslav Petrov. 2010. Mapping the central LOD ontologies to proton upper-level ontology. *Ontology Matching*, 61.

Dang, Hoa Trang, Diane Kelly, and Jimmy J. Lin. 2007. Overview of the TREC 2007 question answering track. In *TREC*, Vol. 7, 63.

Dauphin, Yann N., Angela Fan, Michael Auli, and David Grangier. 2017. Language modeling with gated convolutional networks. In *Proceedings of the 34th international conference on machine learning*, Vol. 70, 933–941. *JMLR.org*.

Davis, R., H. Shrobe, and P. Szolovits. 1993. What is a knowledge representation? *AI magazine* 14 (1): 17.

Davoudian, Ali, Liu Chen, and Mengchi Liu. 2018. A survey on NoSQL stores. *ACM computing surveys (CSUR)* 51 (2): 40.

de Abreu, Sandra Collovini, Tiago Luis Bonamigo, and Renata Vieira. 2013. A review on relation extraction with an eye on Portuguese. *Journal of the Brazilian Computer Society* 19 (4): 553.

Decker, Stefan, Dan Brickley, Janne Saarela, and Jürgen Angele. 1998. A query and inference service for RDF. In *Ql98—the query languages workshop*, Vol. 96. World Wide Web Consortium (W3C).

Degtyarenko, Kirill, Paula de Matos, Marcus Ennis, Janna Hastings, Martin Zbinden, Alan Mc-Naught, Rafael Alcántara, Michael Darsow, Mickaël Guedj, and Michael Ashburner. 2007. ChEBI: A database and ontology for chemical entities of biological interest. *Nucleic acids research* 36 (Suppl_1): 344–350.

Dehaspe, Luc. 1997. Maximum entropy modeling with clausal constraints. In *International conference on inductive logic programming*, 109–124. Springer.

Deines, Irina, and Dirk Krechel. 2012. A German natural language interface for semantic search. In *Joint international semantic technology conference*, 278–289. Springer.

Del Corro, Luciano, and Rainer Gemulla. 2013. Clausie: Clause-based open information extraction. In *Proceedings of the 22nd international conference on World Wide Web*, 355–366. ACM.

Delmonte, Rodolfo. 2008. *Computational linguistic text processing—lexicon, grammar, parsing and anaphora resolution*. Nova Science Publishers.

de Matos, Paula, Adriano Dekker, Marcus Ennis, Janna Hastings, Kenneth Haug, Steve Turner, and Christoph Steinbeck. 2010. ChEBI: A chemistry ontology and database. *Journal of cheminformatics* 2 (S1): 6.

Devlin, Jacob, Ming-Wei Chang, Kenton Lee, and Kristina Toutanova. 2018. BERT: Pre-training of deep bidirectional transformers for language understanding. *arXiv preprint arXiv:1810.04805*.

Dietz, Laura, Chenyan Xiong, Jeff Dalton, and Edgar Meij. 2018. The second workshop on knowledge graphs and semantics for text retrieval, analysis, and understanding (KG4IR). In *The 41st international ACM SIGIR conference on research and development in information retrieval*, 1423–1426.

Dijkstra, Edsger W. 1959. A note on two problems in connexion with graphs. *Numerische mathematik* 1 (1): 269–271.

Diligenti, Michelangelo, Frans Coetzee, Steve Lawrence, C. Lee Giles, Marco Gori, et al. 2000. Focused crawling using context graphs. In *VLDB*, 527–534.

Dima, Corina. 2013. Intui2: A prototype system for question answering over linked data. In *Clef (working notes)*.

Ding, Li, Dominic DiFranzo, Alvaro Graves, James R. Michaelis, Xian Li, Deborah L. McGuinness, and Jim Hendler. 2010a. Data-gov wiki: Towards linking government data. In *AAAI spring symposium: Linked data meets artificial intelligence*, vol. 10, pp. 1–1.

Ding, Li, Dominic DiFranzo, Alvaro Graves, James R. Michaelis, Xian Li, Deborah L. McGuinness, and James A. Hendler. 2010b. TWC data-gov corpus: Incrementally generating linked government data from data. gov. In *Proceedings of the 19th international conference on World Wide Web*, 1383–1386. ACM.

Ding, Li, Tim Finin, Anupam Joshi, Rong Pan, R. Scott Cost, Yun Peng, Pavan Reddivari, V. C. Doshi, and Joel Sachs. 2004. Swoogle: A Semantic Web search and metadata engine. In *Proceedings of the 13th ACM conference on information and knowledge management*, Vol. 304, 652–659. Citeseer.

Ding, Li, Timothy Lebo, John S. Erickson, Dominic Difranzo, Gregory Todd Williams, Xian Li, James Michaelis, Alvaro Graves, Jin Guang Zheng, Zhenning Shangguan, et al. 2011. TWC LOGD: A portal for Linked Open Government Data ecosystems. *Journal of web semantics* 9 (3): 325–333.

Dixon Jr., Herbert B. 2013. Human trafficking and the internet (and other technologies, too). *Judges Journal* 52: 36.

Doan, AnHai, and Alon Y. Halevy. 2005. Semantic integration research in the database community: A brief survey. *AI magazine* 26 (1): 83.

Doan, AnHai, Alon Halevy, and Zachary Ives. 2012. *Principles of data integration.* Elsevier.

Doddington, George R., Alexis Mitchell, Mark A. Przybocki, Lance A. Ramshaw, Stephanie M. Strassel, and Ralph M. Weischedel. 2004. The automatic content extraction (ACE) program—tasks, data, and evaluation. In *Language Resources Evaluation conference (LREC)*, 2 (1): 837–840. Lisbon.

Domingos, Pedro, and Daniel Lowd. 2009. Markov Logic: An interface layer for artificial intelligence. *Synthesis lectures on artificial intelligence and machine learning* 3 (1): 1–155.

Dong, Xin, Evgeniy Gabrilovich, Geremy Heitz, Wilko Horn, Ni Lao, Kevin Murphy, Thomas Strohmann, Shaohua Sun, and Wei Zhang. 2014. Knowledge Vault: A web-scale approach to probabilistic knowledge fusion. In *Proceedings of the 20th ACM SIGKDD international conference on knowledge discovery and data mining*, 601–610. ACM.

Easley, David, and Jon Kleinberg. 2010. *Networks, crowds, and markets.* Cambridge University Press.

Ebraheem, Muhammad, Saravanan Thirumuruganathan, Shafiq Joty, Mourad Ouzzani, and Nan Tang. 2017. Deeper–deep entity resolution. *arXiv preprint arXiv:1710.00597.*

Eder, Jeffrey Scott. 2012. Knowledge graph–based search system Google Patents. US Patent App. 13/404,109.

Egele, Manuel, Leyla Bilge, Engin Kirda, and Christopher Kruegel. 2010. Captcha smuggling: Hijacking web browsing sessions to create captcha farms. In *Proceedings of the 2010 ACM symposium on applied computing*, 1865–1870.

Ehrig, Marc, and Alexander Maedche. 2003. Ontology-focused crawling of web documents. In *Proceedings of the 2003 ACM symposium on applied computing*, 1174–1178.

Ehrlinger, Lisa, and Wolfram Wöß. 2016. Towards a definition of knowledge graphs. *SEMANTiCS (Posters, Demos, SuCCESS)*, Vol. 48, 1–4.

Elango, Pradheep. 2005. Coreference resolution: A survey. University of Wisconsin, Madison, WI.

Ellenberg, Jordan. 2008. The Netflix challenge—a usd million prize for building a better recommendation engine is luring the biggest math brains around. meet the psychologist who just might outsmart them all. *Wired* 16 (3): 114.

Elmagarmid, Ahmed K., Panagiotis G. Ipeirotis, and Vassilios S. Verykios. 2006. Duplicate record detection: A survey. *IEEE transactions on knowledge and data engineering* 19 (1): 1–16.

Erxleben, Fredo, Michael Günther, Markus Krötzsch, Julian Mendez, and Denny Vrandečić. 2014. Introducing wikidata to the Linked Data web. In *International Semantic Web conference*, 50–65. Springer.

Esposito, Floriana, Stefano Ferilli, Teresa Basile, and Nicola Di Mauro. 2012. Social networks and statistical relational learning: A survey. *International journal of social network mining* 1 (2): 185–208.

Esteban, Cristóbal, Volker Tresp, Yinchong Yang, Stephan Baier, and Denis Krompaß. 2016. Predicting the co-evolution of event and knowledge graphs. In *2016 19th international conference on information fusion (fusion)*, 98–105. IEEE.

Ester, Martin, Matthias Groß, and Hans-Peter Kriegel. 2001. Focused web crawling: A generic framework for specifying the user interest and for adaptive crawling strategies. In *Proceedings of 27th international conference on very large data bases*, 321–329.

Etzioni, Oren, Michele Banko, Stephen Soderland, and Daniel S. Weld. 2008. Open information extraction from the web. *Communications of the ACM* 51 (12): 68–74.

Etzioni, Oren, Michael Cafarella, Doug Downey, Stanley Kok, Ana-Maria Popescu, Tal Shaked, Stephen Soderland, Daniel S. Weld, and Alexander Yates. 2004. Web-scale information extraction in KnowItAll: (preliminary results). In *Proceedings of the 13th international conference on World Wide Web*, 100–110.

Etzioni, Oren, Michael Cafarella, Doug Downey, Ana-Maria Popescu, Tal Shaked, Stephen Soderland, Daniel S. Weld, and Alexander Yates. 2005. Unsupervised named-entity extraction from the web: An experimental study. *Artificial intelligence* 165 (1): 91–134.

Euler, L. 1741. Solutio problematis ad geometriam situs pertinentis. *Commentarii academiae scientiarum Petropolitanae* 128–140.

Euzenat, Jérôme, Pavel Shvaiko, et al. 2007. *Ontology matching*, Vol. 18. Springer.

Evans, Richard, and Stafford Street. 2003. A framework for named entity recognition in the open domain. *Recent advances in natural language processing III: Selected papers from RANLP* 260 (267–274): 110.

Even, Shimon. 2011. *Graph algorithms*. Cambridge University Press.

Fader, Anthony, Stephen Soderland, and Oren Etzioni. 2011. Identifying relations for open information extraction. In *Proceedings of the conference on empirical methods in natural language processing*, 1535–1545. Association for Computational Linguistics.

Fakhraei, Shobeir, Bert Huang, Louiqa Raschid, and Lise Getoor. 2014. Network-based drug-target interaction prediction with probabilistic soft logic. *IEEE/ACM transactions on computational biology and bioinformatics* 11 (5): 775–787.

Fan, Miao, Qiang Zhou, Emily Chang, and Fang Zheng. 2014. Transition-based knowledge graph embedding with relational mapping properties. In *Proceedings of the 28th Pacific Asia conference on language, information and computing*, 328–337.

Färber, Michael, Basil Ell, Carsten Menne, and Achim Rettinger. 2015. A comparative survey of DBpedia, Freebase, OpenCyc, Wikidata, and YAGO. *Semantic Web journal* 1 (1): 1–5.

Felix, Cristian. 2019. *Designing mixed-initiative visual analytics systems for exploratory labeling of textual data*. PhD diss. New York University Tandon School of Engineering.

Fellegi, Ivan P., and Alan B. Sunter. 1969. A theory for record linkage. *Journal of the American Statistical Association* 64 (328): 1183–1210.

Feng, Jun, Minlie Huang, Mingdong Wang, Mantong Zhou, Yu Hao, and Xiaoyan Zhu. 2016. Knowledge graph embedding by flexible translation. In *Fifteenth international conference on the principles of knowledge representation and reasoning*, 557–560.

Fensel, Dieter, Umutcan Şimşek, Kevin Angele, Elwin Huaman, Elias Kärle, Oleksandra Panasiuk, Ioan Toma, Jürgen Umbrich, and Alexander Wahler. 2020. *Knowledge graphs: Methodology, tools and selected use cases*. Springer.

Ferrara, Alfio, Andriy Nikolov, and François Scharffe. 2011. Data linking for the Semantic Web. *International journal on Semantic Web and information systems (IJSWIS)* 7 (3): 46–76.

Feuerverger, Andrey, Yu He, and Shashi Khatri. 2012. Statistical significance of the Netflix challenge. *Statistical Science* (2012): 202–231.

Finkel, Jenny Rose, Trond Grenager, and Christopher Manning. 2005. Incorporating non-local information into information extraction systems by Gibbs sampling. In *Proceedings of the 43rd annual meeting on Association for Computational Linguistics*, 363–370. Association for Computational Linguistics.

Fox, Steve, Kuldeep Karnawat, Mark Mydland, Susan Dumais, and Thomas White. 2005. Evaluating implicit measures to improve web search. *ACM transactions on information systems (TOIS)* 23 (2): 147–168.

Frakes, William B. 1992. *Information retrieval: Data structures and algorithms*. Pearson Education India.

Francis, Nadime, Alastair Green, Paolo Guagliardo, Leonid Libkin, Tobias Lindaaker, Victor Marsault, Stefan Plantikow, Mats Rydberg, Petra Selmer, and Andrés Taylor. 2018. Cypher: An evolving query language for property graphs. In *Proceedings of the 2018 international conference on management of data*, 1433–1445. ACM.

Freitag, Dayne. 1998. Information extraction from HTML: Application of a general machine learning approach. In *AAAI/IAAI*, 517–523.

Freitas, André, Edward Curry, João Gabriel Oliveira, and Sean O'Riain. 2012. Querying heterogeneous datasets on the linked data web: Challenges, approaches, and trends. *IEEE internet computing* 16 (1): 24–33.

Freitas, André, Joao Gabriel Oliveira, Edward Curry, Seán O'Riain, and João Carlos Pereira da Silva. 2011. TREO: Combining entity-search, spreading activation and semantic relatedness for querying linked data. In *1st workshop on question answering over Linked Data (QALD-1)*, 24.

Freitas, André, João Gabriel Oliveira, Seán O'Riain, Edward Curry, and João Carlos Pereira Da Silva. 2011. Querying linked data using semantic relatedness: A vocabulary independent approach. In *International conference on application of natural language to information systems*, 40–51. Springer.

Friedman, Nir, Lise Getoor, Daphne Koller, and Avi Pfeffer. 1999. Learning probabilistic relational models. In *IJCAI*, Vol. 99, 1300–1309.

Fu, Gang, Colin Batchelor, Michel Dumontier, Janna Hastings, Egon Willighagen, and Evan Bolton. 2015. PubChemRDF: Towards the semantic annotation of PubChem compound and substance databases. *Journal of cheminformatics* 7 (1): 34.

Furche, Tim, Georg Gottlob, Giovanni Grasso, Christian Schallhart, and Andrew Sellers. 2013. Oxpath: A language for scalable data extraction, automation, and crawling on the deep web. *VLDB journal* 22 (1): 47–72.

Gahegan, Mark, Junyan Luo, Stephen D. Weaver, William Pike, and Tawan Banchuen. 2009. Connecting Geon: Making sense of the myriad resources, researchers and concepts that comprise a geoscience cyberinfrastructure. *Computers & geosciences* 35 (4): 836–854.

Garcia-Molina, Hector, Jeffrey D. Ullman, and Jennifer Widom. 2000. *Database system implementation*. Prentice Hall.

Gashteovski, Kiril, Rainer Gemulla, and Luciano del Corro. 2017. Minie: Minimizing facts in open information extraction. Association for Computational Linguistics.

Gatta, Roberto, Mauro Vallati, Jacopo Lenkowicz, Eric Rojas, Andrea Damiani, Lucia Sacchi, Berardino De Bari, Arianna Dagliati, Carlos Fernandez-Llatas, Matteo Montesi, et al. 2017. Generating and comparing knowledge graphs of medical processes using pMineR. In *Proceedings of the knowledge capture conference*, 1–4.

Gatterbauer, Wolfgang, Paul Bohunsky, Marcus Herzog, Bernhard Krüpl, and Bernhard Pollak. 2007. Towards domain-independent information extraction from web tables. In *Proceedings of the 16th international conference on World Wide Web*, 71–80.

Gavin, Anne-Claude, Markus Bösche, Roland Krause, Paola Grandi, Martina Marzioch, Andreas Bauer, Jörg Schultz, Jens M. Rick, Anne-Marie Michon, Cristina-Maria Cruciat, et al. 2002. Functional organization of the yeast proteome by systematic analysis of protein complexes. *Nature* 415 (6868): 141–147.

Gene Ontology Consortium. 2004. The Gene Ontology (GO) database and informatics resource. *Nucleic acids research* 32 (Suppl_1): 258–261.

Gene Ontology Consortium. 2008. The Gene Ontology project in 2008. *Nucleic acids research* 36 (Suppl_1): 440–444.

Gene Ontology Consortium. 2012. Gene Ontology annotations and resources. *Nucleic acids research* 41 (D1): 530–535.

Gene Ontology Consortium. 2015. Gene Ontology Consortium: Going forward. *Nucleic acids research* 43 (D1): 1049–1056.

Gene Ontology Consortium. 2017. Expansion of the Gene Ontology knowledge base and resources. *Nucleic acids research* 45 (D1): 331–338.

Gene Ontology Consortium, et al. 2001. Creating the Gene Ontology resource: Design and implementation. *Genome research* 11 (8): 1425–1433.

George, Lars. 2011. *HBase: The definitive guide: Random access to your planet-size data*. O'Reilly Media.

Gerner, Deborah J, Philip A Schrodt, Omür Yilmaz, and Rajaa Abu-Jabr. 2002a. Conflict and mediation event observations (CAMEO): A new event data framework for the analysis of foreign policy interactions. International Studies Association, New Orleans.

Gerner, Deborah J., Philip A. Schrodt, Omur Yilmaz, and Rajaa Abu-Jabr. 2002b. The creation of CAMEO (conflict and mediation event observations): An event data framework for a post cold war world. In *Annual meeting of the American Political Science Association*, Vol. 29.

Gero, John S. Design prototypes: A knowledge representation schema for design. *AI magazine* 11, no. 4 (1990): 26–26.

Gerry QC, Felicity, Julia Muraszkiewicz, and Niovi Vavoula. 2016. The role of technology in the fight against human trafficking: Reflections on privacy and data protection concerns. *Computer law and security review* 32 (2): 205–217.

Getoor, Lise, and Christopher P. Diehl. 2005. Link mining: A survey. *ACM SIGKDD explorations newsletter* 7 (2): 3–12.

Getoor, Lise, and Ashwin Machanavajjhala. 2012. Entity resolution: Theory, practice and open challenges. *Proceedings of the VLDB endowment* 5 (12): 2018–2019.

Getoor, Lise, and Ashwin Machanavajjhala. 2013. Entity resolution for Big Data. In *Proceedings of the 19th ACM SIGKDD international conference on knowledge discovery and data mining*, 1527. ACM.

Getoor, Lise, and Lilyana Mihalkova. 2011. Learning statistical models from relational data. In *Proceedings of the 2011 ACM SIGMOD international conference on management of data*, 1195–1198.

Getoor, Lise, and Ben Taskar. 2007. Statistical relational learning. MIT Press.

Giannone, Cristina, Valentina Bellomaria, and Roberto Basili. 2013. A HMM-based approach to question answering against linked data. In *CLEF (working notes)*. Citeseer.

Gliozzo, Alfio Massimiliano, and Aditya Kalyanpur. 2012. Predicting lexical answer types in open domain QA. *International journal on Semantic Web and information systems (IJSWIS)* 8 (3): 74–88.

Glushko, Robert J. 2013. The discipline of organizing. *Bulletin of the American society for information science and technology* 40 (1): 21–27.

Gong, Dihong, Daisy Zhe Wang, and Yang Peng. 2017. Multimodal learning for web information extraction. In *Proceedings of the 25th ACM international conference on multimedia*, 288–296.

Gormley, Clinton, and Zachary Tong. 2015. *Elasticsearch: The definitive guide: A distributed real-time search and analytics engine*. O'Reilly Media.

Gossweiler, Rich, Maryam Kamvar, and Shumeet Baluja. 2009. What's up captcha? A captcha based on image orientation. In *Proceedings of the 18th international conference on World Wide Web*, 841–850.

Goyal, Palash, and Emilio Ferrara. 2018. Graph embedding techniques, applications, and performance: A survey. *Knowledge-based systems*, Vol. 151, 78–94.

Greenberg, Steven A. 2009. How citation distortions create unfounded authority: Analysis of a citation network. *BMJ*, Vol. 339, 2680.

Greiman, Virginia, and Christina Bain. 2013. The emergence of cyber activity as a gateway to human trafficking. In *Proceedings of the 8th international conference on information warfare and security: ICIW 2013*, Vol. 90. Academic Conferences.

Grishman, Ralph, and Beth Sundheim. 1996. Message understanding conference—6: A brief history. In *Proceedings of the 16th international conference on computational linguistics—Volume 1*, pp. 466–471.

Gross, Jonathan L., and Jay Yellen. 2004. *Handbook of graph theory*. CRC Press.

Grover, Aditya, and Jure Leskovec. 2016. Node2vec: Scalable feature learning for networks. In *Proceedings of the 22nd ACM SIGKDD international conference on knowledge discovery and data mining*, 855–864.

Gu, Yao, and Mayank Kejriwal. 2018. Unsupervised hashtag retrieval and visualization for crisis informatics. *arXiv preprint arXiv:1801.05906.*

Guha, Ramanathan V., Dan Brickley, and Steve Macbeth. 2016. Schema.org: Evolution of structured data on the web. *Communications of the ACM* 59 (2): 44–51.

Guo, Shu, Quan Wang, Bin Wang, Lihong Wang, and Li Guo. 2015. Semantically smooth knowledge graph embedding. In *Proceedings of the 53rd annual meeting of the Association for Computational Linguistics and the 7th international joint conference on natural language processing (volume 1: Long papers)*, 84–94.

Guo, Shu, Quan Wang, Lihong Wang, Bin Wang, and Li Guo. 2016. Jointly embedding knowledge graphs and logical rules. In *Proceedings of the 2016 conference on empirical methods in natural language processing*, 192–202.

Gupta, Shubham, Pedro Szekely, Craig A Knoblock, Aman Goel, Mohsen Taheriyan, and Maria Muslea. 2012. Karma: A system for mapping structured sources into the Semantic Web. In *Extended Semantic Web conference*, 430–434. Springer.

Győrödi, Cornelia, Robert Győrödi, George Pecherle, and Andrada Olah. 2015. A comparative study: MongoDB vs. mySQL. In *2015 13th international conference on engineering of modern electric systems (EMES)*, 1–6. IEEE.

Hagar, Christine. 2015. Crisis informatics. In *Encyclopedia of information science and technology, third edition*, 1350–1358. IGI Global.

Haklay, Mordechai. 2010. How good is volunteered geographical information? A comparative study of OpenStreetMap and ordnance survey datasets. *Environment and planning B: Planning and design* 37 (4): 682–703.

Haklay, Mordechai, and Patrick Weber. 2008. OpenStreetMap: User-generated street maps. *IEEE pervasive computing* 7 (4): 12–18.

Hammer, Joachim, Jason McHugh, and Hector Garcia-Molina. 1997. Semistructured data: The TSIMMIS experience. In *Proceedings of the first East-European symposium on advances in databases and information systems*, Vol. 1, 1–13.

Han, Jing, E. Haihong, Guan Le, and Jian Du. 2011. Survey on NoSQL database. In *2011 6th international conference on pervasive computing and applications*, 363–366. IEEE.

Harrendorf, Stefan, Markku Heiskanen, and Steven Malby. 2010. *International statistics on crime and justice.* European Institute for Crime Prevention and Control, affiliated with the United Nations (HEUNI).

Hart, Glen, and Catherine Dolbear. 2016. *Linked data: A geographic perspective.* CRC Press.

Harth, Andreas, Jürgen Umbrich, and Stefan Decker. 2006. Multicrawler: A pipelined architecture for crawling and indexing Semantic Web data. In *International Semantic Web conference*, 258–271. Springer.

Hastings, Janna, Gareth Owen, Adriano Dekker, Marcus Ennis, Namrata Kale, Venkatesh Muthukrishnan, Steve Turner, Neil Swainston, Pedro Mendes, and Christoph Steinbeck. 2016. ChEBI in 2016: Improved services and an expanding collection of metabolites. *Nucleic acids research* 44 (D1): 1214–1219.

Haugen, Austin. 2010. The Open Graph Protocol design decisions. In *International Semantic Web conference*, 338. Springer.

Hearst, Marti A. 1992. Automatic acquisition of hyponyms from large text corpora. In *Proceedings of the 14th conference on computational linguistics*, Vol. 2, 539–545. Association for Computational Linguistics.

Heath, Tom, and Christian Bizer. 2011. Linked data: Evolving the web into a global data space. *Synthesis lectures on the Semantic Web: Theory and technology* 1 (1): 1–136.

Hecht, Robin, and Stefan Jablonski. 2011. NoSQL evaluation: A use case oriented survey. In *2011 international conference on cloud and service computing*, 336–341. IEEE.

Heidari, Safiollah, Yogesh Simmhan, Rodrigo N. Calheiros, and Rajkumar Buyya. 2018. Scalable graph processing frameworks: A taxonomy and open challenges. *ACM computing surveys (CSUR)* 51 (3): 1–53.

Hendler, James. 2001. Agents and the Semantic Web. *IEEE intelligent systems* 16 (2): 30–37.

Hendler, James A. 2009. Tonight's dessert: Semantic Web layer cakes. In *European Semantic Web conference*, 1. Springer.

Hendler, James, Jeanne Holm, Chris Musialek, and George Thomas. 2012. US government Linked Open Data: Semantic.data.gov. *IEEE intelligent systems*, Vol. 3, 25–31.

Hepp, Martin. 2015. The web of data for e-commerce: Schema.org and good relations for researchers and practitioners. In *International conference on web engineering*, 723–727. Springer.

Hernández, Daniel, Aidan Hogan, and Markus Krötzsch. 2015. Reifying RDF: What works well with Wikidata? *SSWS@ ISWC*, Vol. 1457, 32–47.

Hernández, Mauricio A., and Salvatore J. Stolfo. 1995. The merge/purge problem for large databases. In *ACM SIGMOD record*, Vol. 24, 127–138. ACM.

Herzig, Daniel M., Peter Mika, Roi Blanco, and Thanh Tran. 2013. Federated entity search using on-the-fly consolidation. In *International Semantic Web conference*, 167–183. Springer.

Heverin, Thomas, and Lisl Zach. 2010. *Microblogging for crisis communication: Examination of Twitter use in response to a 2009 violent crisis in the Seattle-Tacoma, Washington, area.* ISCRAM.

Hewitt, Eben. 2010. *Cassandra: The definitive guide.* O'Reilly Media.

Hirschman, Lynette, Alexander Yeh, Christian Blaschke, and Alfonso Valencia. 2005. Overview of BioCreAtIvE: Critical assessment of information extraction for biology. *BMC Bioinformatics* 6, S1.

Hitzler, Pascal, Markus Krötzsch, Bijan Parsia, Peter F. Patel-Schneider, Sebastian Rudolph, et al. 2009. OWL 2 web ontology language primer. *W3C recommendation* 27 (1): 1–122.

Hixon, Ben, Peter Clark, and Hannaneh Hajishirzi. 2015. Learning knowledge graphs for question answering through conversational dialog. In *Proceedings of the 2015 conference of the North American chapter of the Association for Computational Linguistics: Human language technologies*, 851–861.

Hoffart, Johannes, Dragan Milchevski, and Gerhard Weikum. 2014. STICS: Searching with strings, things, and cats. In *Proceedings of the 37th international ACM SIGIR conference on research and development in information retrieval*, 1247–1248.

Hoffmann, Raphael, Congle Zhang, Xiao Ling, Luke Zettlemoyer, and Daniel S. Weld. 2011. Knowledge-based weak supervision for information extraction of overlapping relations. In *Proceedings of the 49th annual meeting of the Association for Computational Linguistics: Human language technologies*, Vol. 1, 541–550. Association for Computational Linguistics.

Höffner, Konrad, and Jens Lehmann. 2014. Towards question answering on statistical linked data. In *Proceedings of the 10th international conference on semantic systems*, 61–64.

Höffner, Konrad, Sebastian Walter, Edgard Marx, Ricardo Usbeck, Jens Lehmann, and Axel-Cyrille Ngonga Ngomo. 2017. Survey on challenges of question answering in the Semantic Web. *Semantic Web* 8 (6): 895–920.

Hogan, Aidan, Eva Blomqvist, Michael Cochez, Claudia d'Amato, Gerard de Melo, Claudio Gutierrez, Jos Emilio Labra Gayo, Sabrina Kirrane, Sebastian Neumaier, Axel Polleres, Roberto Navigli, Axel-Cyrille Ngonga Ngomo, Sabbir M. Rashid, Anisa Rula, Lukas Schmelzeisen, Juan Sequeda, Steffen Staab, and Antoine Zimmermann. 2020. Knowledge Graphs. *arXiv preprint arXiv:2003.02320.*

Hogan, Aidan, Andreas Harth, Jürgen Umrich, and Stefan Decker. 2007. Towards a scalable search and query engine for the web. In *Proceedings of the 16th international conference on World Wide Web*, 1301–1302. ACM.

Hogan, Aidan, Andreas Harth, Jürgen Umbrich, Sheila Kinsella, Axel Polleres, and Stefan Decker. 2011. Searching and browsing linked data with SWSE: The Semantic Web search engine. *Journal of web semantics* 9 (4): 365–401.

Hogue, Andrew, and David Karger. 2005. Thresher: Automating the unwrapping of semantic content from the World Wide Web. In *Proceedings of the 14th international conference on World Wide Web*, 86–95.

Hong, Jer Lang. 2010. Deep Web data extraction. In *2010 IEEE international conference on systems, man and cybernetics*, 3420–3427. IEEE.

Hopkins, Brian, and Robin J. Wilson. 2004. The truth about Königsberg. *College mathematics journal* 35 (3): 198–207.

Horrocks, Ian, Peter F. Patel-Schneider, Harold Boley, Said Tabet, Benjamin Grosof, Mike Dean, et al. 2004. SWRL: A Semantic Web rule language combining OWL and RuleML. *W3C member submission* 21 (79): 1–31.

Hripcsak, George, and Adam S. Rothschild. 2005. Agreement, the F-measure, and reliability in information retrieval. *Journal of the American Medical Informatics Association* 12 (3): 296–298.

Hsu, Chun-Nan, and Ming-Tzung Dung. 1998. Generating finite-state transducers for semi-structured data extraction from the web. *Information systems* 23 (8): 521–538.

Hua, Wen, Dat T. Huynh, Saeid Hosseini, Jiaheng Lu, and Xiaofang Zhou. 2012. Information extraction from microblogs: A survey. *International journal of software and informatics* 6 (4): 495–522.

Huang, Jeff, and Efthimis N. Efthimiadis. 2009. Analyzing and evaluating query reformulation strategies in web search logs. In *Proceedings of the 18th ACM conference on information and knowledge management*, 77–86.

Huang, Jiewen, Daniel J. Abadi, and Kun Ren. 2011. Scalable SPARQL querying of large RDF graphs. *Proceedings of the VLDB endowment* 4 (11): 1123–1134.

Huang, Zhisheng, Jie Yang, Frank van Harmelen, and Qing Hu. 2017. Constructing knowledge graphs of depression. In *International conference on health information science*, 149–161. Springer.

Huffman, S. 1996. Learning information extraction patterns from examples. In *International Joint Conference on Artificial Intelligence*, 246–260. Springer.

Hultgren, Marisa, Murray E. Jennex, John Persano, and Cezar Ornatowski. 2016. Using knowledge management to assist in identifying human sex trafficking. In *2016 49th Hawaii international conference on system sciences*, 4344–4353. IEEE.

Hummon, Norman P., and Patrick Dereian. 1989. Connectivity in a citation network: The development of DNA theory. *Social networks* 11 (1): 39–63.

Humphreys, Kevin, Robert Gaizauskas, and Saliha Azzam. 1997. Event coreference for information extraction. In *Proceedings of a workshop on operational factors in practical, robust anaphora resolution for unrestricted texts*, 75–81.

Huttunen, Silja, Roman Yangarber, and Ralph Grishman. 2002. Diversity of scenarios in information extraction. In *Language Resources and Evaluation Conference (LREC)*, 1443–1450.

Inferlink R&D Capabilities. http://www.inferlink.com/our-work#research-capabilities-section. Accessed: 2020-03-10.

ISI extraction toolkit repository. https://github.com/usc-isi-i2/etk. Accessed: 2020-03-10.

Jain, Alpa, AnHai Doan, and Luis Gravano. 2007. SQL queries over unstructured text databases. In *2007 IEEE 23rd international conference on data engineering*, 1255–1257. IEEE.

Jain, Prateek, Pascal Hitzler, Peter Z. Yeh, Kunal Verma, and Amit P. Sheth. 2010. Linked data is merely more data. In *2010 AAAI spring symposium series*.

Janssen, Katleen. 2011. The influence of the PSI directive on open government data: An overview of recent developments. *Government information quarterly* 28 (4): 446–456.

Janssen, Marijn, Yannis Charalabidis, and Anneke Zuiderwijk. 2012. Benefits, adoption barriers and myths of open data and open government. *Information systems management* 29 (4): 258–268.

Janssen, Marijn, and Jeroen van den Hoven. 2015. *Big and Open Linked Data (BOLD) in government: A challenge to transparency and privacy?* Elsevier.

Jetschni, Jonas, and Vera G. Meister. 2017. Schema engineering for enterprise knowledge graphs: A reflecting survey and case study. In *2017 eighth international conference on intelligent computing and information systems (ICICIS)*, 271–277. IEEE.

Jetzek, Thorhildur, Michel Avital, and Niels Bjorn-Andersen. 2014. Data-driven innovation through open government data. *Journal of theoretical and applied electronic commerce research* 9 (2): 100–120.

Ji, Guoliang, Shizhu He, Liheng Xu, Kang Liu, and Jun Zhao. 2015. Knowledge graph embedding via dynamic mapping matrix. In *Proceedings of the 53rd annual meeting of the Association for Computational Linguistics and the 7th international joint conference on natural language processing (volume 1: Long papers)*, 687–696.

Ji, Guoliang, Kang Liu, Shizhu He, and Jun Zhao. 2016. Knowledge graph completion with adaptive sparse transfer matrix. In *Thirtieth AAAI conference on artificial intelligence*, vol. 16, 985–991.

Ji, Heng, and Ralph Grishman. 2006. Data selection in semi-supervised learning for name tagging. In *Proceedings of the workshop on information extraction beyond the document*, 48–55. Association for Computational Linguistics.

Ji, Heng, and Ralph Grishman. 2008. Refining event extraction through cross-document inference. In *Proceedings of ACL-08: HLT*, 254–262.

Jiang, Jing. 2012. Information extraction from text. In *Mining text data*, 11–41. Springer.

Jiang, Xiaotian, Quan Wang, Peng Li, and Bin Wang. 2016. Relation extraction with multi-instance multi-label convolutional neural networks. In *Proceedings of COLING 2016, the 26th international conference on computational linguistics: Technical papers*, 1471–1480.

Jones, Rosie, Rayid Ghani, Tom Mitchell, and Ellen Riloff. 2003. Active learning for information extraction with multiple view feature sets. *Proceedings of adaptive text extraction and mining, EMCL/PKDD-03, Cavtat-Dubrovnik, Croatia* (2003): 26–34.

Joshi, Amit Krishna, Prateek Jain, Pascal Hitzler, Peter Z. Yeh, Kunal Verma, Amit P. Sheth, and Mariana Damova. 2012. Alignment-based querying of Linked Open Data. In *OTM confederated international conferences on the move to meaningful internet systems*, 807–824. Springer.

Jung, Hanmin, Sung-Pil Choi, Seungwoo Lee, and Sa-Kwang Song. 2012. Survey on kernel-based relation extraction. In *Theory and Applications for Advanced Text Mining*. IntechOpen.

Junghanns, Martin, André Petermann, Martin Neumann, and Erhard Rahm. 2017. Management and analysis of big graph data: Current systems and open challenges. In *Handbook of Big Data technologies*, 457–505. Springer.

Kaiser, Katharina, and Silvia Miksch. 2005. Information extraction. A survey. Vienna University of Technology. *Asgaard-TR-2005-6*. http://publik.tuwien.ac.at/files/pub-inf_2999.pdf.

Kapoor, Rahul, Mayank Kejriwal, and Pedro Szekely. 2017. Using contexts and constraints for improved geotagging of human trafficking webpages. *arXiv preprint arXiv:1704.05569*.

Karidi, Danae Pla, Yannis Stavrakas, and Yannis Vassiliou. 2018. Tweet and followee personalized recommendations based on knowledge graphs. *Journal of ambient intelligence and humanized computing* 9 (6): 2035–2049.

Kejriwal, Mayank. 2014. Populating entity name systems for Big Data integration. In *International Semantic Web conference*, 521–528. Springer.

Kejriwal, Mayank. 2016. *Populating a linked data entity name system: A Big Data solution to unsupervised instance matching*, Vol. 27. IOS Press.

Kejriwal, Mayank. 2019. *Domain-specific knowledge graph construction*. Springer.

Kejriwal, Mayank, Jiayuan Ding, Runqi Shao, Anoop Kumar, and Pedro Szekely. 2017b. Flagit: A system for minimally supervised human trafficking indicator mining. *arXiv preprint arXiv:1712.03086*.

Kejriwal, Mayank, Daniel Gilley, Pedro Szekely, and Jill Crisman. 2018b. Thor: Text-enabled analytics for humanitarian operations. In *Companion proceedings of the the web conference 2018*, 147–150.

Kejriwal, Mayank, and Yao Gu. 2019. A pipeline for rapid post-crisis Twitter data acquisition, filtering and visualization. *Technologies* 7 (2): 33.

Kejriwal, Mayank, and Rahul Kapoor. 2019. Network-theoretic information extraction quality assessment in the human trafficking domain. *Applied network science* 4 (1): 44.

Kejriwal, Mayank, and Daniel P Miranker. 2013. An unsupervised algorithm for learning blocking schemes. In *2013 IEEE 13th international conference on data mining*, 340–349. IEEE.

Kejriwal, Mayank, and Daniel P. Miranker. 2015a. Semi-supervised instance matching using boosted classifiers. In *European Semantic Web conference*, 388–402. Springer.

Kejriwal, Mayank, and Daniel P. Miranker. 2015b. An unsupervised instance matcher for schema-free RDF data. *Web semantics: Science, services and agents on the World Wide Web* 35: 102–123.

Kejriwal, Mayank, Jing Peng, Haotian Zhang, and Pedro Szekely. 2018a. Structured event entity resolution in humanitarian domains. In *International Semantic Web conference*, 233–249. Springer.

Kejriwal, Mayank, Thomas Schellenberg, and Pedro Szekely. 2017a. A semantic search engine for investigating human trafficking. In *International Semantic Web conference (posters, demos and industry tracks)*, Vol. 1963, CEUR-WS.

Kejriwal, Mayank, and Pedro Szekely. 2017a. Information extraction in illicit web domains. In *Proceedings of the 26th international conference on World Wide Web*, 997–1006. International World Wide Web Conferences Steering Committee.

Kejriwal, Mayank, and Pedro Szekely. 2017b. An investigative search engine for the human trafficking domain. In *International Semantic Web conference*, 247–262. Springer.

Kejriwal, Mayank, and Pedro Szekely. 2017c. Knowledge graphs for social good: An entity-centric search engine for the human trafficking domain. *IEEE transactions on Big Data*, no. 99.

Kejriwal, Mayank, and Peilin Zhou. 2019. Saviz: Interactive exploration and visualization of situation labeling classifiers over crisis social media data. In *Proceedings of the 2019 IEEE/ACM international conference on advances in social networks analysis and mining*, 705–708.

Kendall, Elisa F., and Deborah L. McGuinness. 2019. Ontology engineering. *Synthesis lectures on the Semantic Web: Theory and technology* 9 (1): i–102.

Kersting, Kristian, and Luc De Raedt. 2001. Adaptive bayesian logic programs. In *International conference on inductive logic programming*, 104–117. Springer.

Khan, Maqbool, Xiaotong Wu, Xiaolong Xu, and Wanchun Dou. 2017. Big Data challenges and opportunities in the hype of industry 4.0. In *2017 IEEE international conference on communications (ICC)*, 1–6. IEEE.

Khetrapal, Ankur, and Vinay Ganesh. 2006. Hbase and hypertable for large-scale distributed storage systems. *Department of Computer Science, Purdue University* 10 (1376616.1376726).

Khosravi, Hassan, and Bahareh Bina. 2010. A survey on statistical relational learning. In *Canadian conference on artificial intelligence*, 256–268. Springer.

Kim, Gang-Hoon, Silvana Trimi, and Ji-Hyong Chung. 2014. Big-Data applications in the government sector. *Communications of the ACM* 57 (3): 78–85.

Kim, Jun-Tae, and Dan I. Moldovan. 1995. Acquisition of linguistic patterns for knowledge-based information extraction. *IEEE transactions on knowledge and data engineering* 7 (5): 713–724.

Kim, Sunghwan, Paul A. Thiessen, Evan E. Bolton, Jie Chen, Gang Fu, Asta Gindulyte, Lianyi Han, Jane He, Siqian He, Benjamin A. Shoemaker, et al. 2016. PubChem substance and compound databases. *Nucleic acids research* 44 (D1): 1202–1213.

Kimmig, Angelika, Stephen Bach, Matthias Broecheler, Bert Huang, and Lise Getoor. 2012. A short introduction to probabilistic soft logic. In *Proceedings of the NIPS workshop on probabilistic programming: Foundations and applications*, 1–4.

Kimmig, Angelika, Lilyana Mihalkova, and Lise Getoor. 2015. Lifted graphical models: A survey. *Machine learning* 99 (1): 1–45.

Kleinberg, Jon M. 1999. Authoritative sources in a hyperlinked environment. *Journal of the ACM (JACM)* 46 (5): 604–632.

Kleinberg, Jon M. 2007. Challenges in mining social network data: Processes, privacy, and paradoxes. In *Proceedings of the 13th ACM SIGKDD international conference on knowledge discovery and data mining*, 4–5. ACM.

Klímek, Jakub, Petr Škoda, and Martin Nečaskỳ. 2019. Survey of tools for linked data consumption. *Semantic Web* 10 (4): 665–720.

Klinov, Pavel. 2008. Pronto: A non-monotonic probabilistic description logic reasoner. In *European Semantic Web conference*, 822–826. Springer.

Knoblock, Craig A., and Pedro Szekely. 2015. Exploiting semantics for Big Data integration. *AI magazine* 36, no. 1 (2015): 25–38.

Knoblock, Craig A., Pedro Szekely, José Luis Ambite, Aman Goel, Shubham Gupta, Kristina Lerman, Maria Muslea, Mohsen Taheriyan, and Parag Mallick. 2012. Semi-automatically mapping structured sources into the Semantic Web. In *Extended Semantic Web conference*, 375–390. Springer.

Knoke, David, and Song Yang. 2008. *Social network analysis*, Vol. 154. SAGE.

Kobilarov, Georgi, Tom Scott, Yves Raimond, Silver Oliver, Chris Sizemore, Michael Smethurst, Christian Bizer, and Robert Lee. 2009. Media meets Semantic Web—How the BBC uses DBpedia and linked data to make connections. In *European Semantic Web conference*, 723–737. Springer.

Kogan, Marina, Leysia Palen, and Kenneth M. Anderson. 2015. Think local, retweet global: Retweeting by the geographically-vulnerable during Hurricane Sandy. In *Proceedings of the 18th ACM conference on computer-supported cooperative work and social computing*, 981–993.

Kok, Stanley, and Pedro Domingos. 2005. Learning the structure of Markov Logic Networks. In *Proceedings of the 22nd international conference on machine learning*, 441–448.

Kok, Stanley, and Pedro Domingos. 2009. Learning Markov Logic Network structure via hypergraph lifting. In *Proceedings of the 26th annual international conference on machine learning*, 505–512.

Koller, Daphne, and Nir Friedman. 2009. *Probabilistic graphical models: Principles and techniques.* MIT Press.

Kooli, Nihel, Robin Allesiardo, and Erwan Pigneul. 2018. Deep learning–based approach for entity resolution in databases. In *Asian conference on intelligent information and database systems*, 3–12. Springer.

Köpcke, Hanna, Andreas Thor, and Erhard Rahm. 2010. Evaluation of entity resolution approaches on real–world match problems. *Proceedings of the VLDB endowment* 3 (1–2): 484–493.

Kouki, Pigi, Shobeir Fakhraei, James Foulds, Magdalini Eirinaki, and Lise Getoor. 2015. Hyper: A flexible and extensible probabilistic framework for hybrid recommender systems. In *Proceedings of the 9th ACM conference on recommender systems*, 99–106.

Krishnamurthy, Yamuna, Kien Pham, Aécio Santos, and Juliana Freire. 2016. Interactive exploration for domain discovery on the web. In *ACM KDD workshop on interactive data exploration and analytics (IDEA)*, 64–71.

Krishnan, Sriram, Christopher Crosby, Viswanath Nandigam, Minh Phan, Charles Cowart, Chaitanya Baru, and Ramon Arrowsmith. 2011. Opentopography: A services-oriented architecture for community access to lidar topography. In *Proceedings of the 2nd international conference on computing for geospatial research and applications*, 1–8.

Krotov, Vlad, and Leiser Silva. 2018. Legality and ethics of web scraping. In *24th Americas conference on information systems (AMCIS), New Orleans*, pp. 1–5.

Krötzsch, Markus, Frantisek Simancik, and Ian Horrocks. 2012. A description logic primer. *arXiv preprint arXiv:1201.4089.*

Krupka, George R. 1995. Sra: Description of the SRA system as used for MUC-6. In *Proceedings of the 6th conference on message understanding*, 221–235. Association for Computational Linguistics.

Kuc, Rafal, and Marek Rogozinski. 2013. *Elasticsearch server.* Packt Publishing Ltd.

Kuhlins, S., and R. Tredwell. 2002. Toolkits for generating wrappers. In *Net. ObjectDays: International conference on object-oriented and internet-based technologies, concepts, and applications for a networked world*, 184–198. Springer.

Kumar, Shantanu. 2017. A survey of deep learning methods for relation extraction. *arXiv preprint arXiv:1705.03645.*

Kushmerick, Nicholas, and Bernd Thomas. 2003. Adaptive information extraction: Core technologies for information agents. In *Intelligent information agents*, 79–103. Springer.

Kushmerick, Nicholas, Daniel S. Weld, and Robert Doorenbos. 1997. *Wrapper induction for information extraction.* University of Washington.

Labrinidis, Alexandros, and Hosagrahar V. Jagadish. 2012. Challenges and opportunities with big data. *Proceedings of the VLDB Endowment* 5 (12): 2032–2033.

Laender, Alberto H. F., Berthier Ribeiro-Neto, and Altigran S. Da Silva. 2002. Debye—data extraction by example. *Data & knowledge engineering* 40 (2): 121–154.

Laender, Alberto H. F., Berthier A. Ribeiro-Neto, Altigran S. Da Silva, and Juliana S Teixeira. 2002. A brief survey of web data extraction tools. *ACM SIGMOD record* 31 (2): 84–93.

Lakhani, Karim R., Robert D. Austin, and Yumi Yi. 2002. *Data.gov.* Harvard Business School.

Lakshman, Avinash, and Prashant Malik. 2010. Cassandra: A decentralized structured storage system. *ACM SIGOPS Operating Systems Review* 44 (2): 35–40.

Lao, Ni, Tom Mitchell, and William W Cohen. 2011. Random walk inference and learning in a large-scale knowledge base. In *Proceedings of the conference on empirical methods in natural language processing*, 529–539. Association for Computational Linguistics.

Lassila, Ora. 1998. Web metadata: A matter of semantics. *IEEE internet computing* 2 (4): 30–37.

Lassila, Ora, Ralph R. Swick, et al. 1998. Resource description framework (RDF) model and syntax specification. http://citeseerx.ist.psu.edu/viewdoc/summary?doi=10.1.1.44.6030.

Latonero, Mark. 2012. Technology and human trafficking: The rise of mobile and the diffusion of technology-facilitated trafficking. Available at *SSRN 2177556.* https://technologyandtrafficking.usc.edu/files/2012/11/USC-Annenberg-Technology-and-Human-Trafficking-2012.pdf.

Latonero, Mark, Jennifer Musto, Zhaleh Boyd, Ev Boyle, Amber Bissel, Kari Gibson, and Joanne Kim. 2012. *The rise of mobile and the diffusion of technology-facilitated trafficking.* University of Southern California, Center on Communication Leadership.

Leaman, Robert, and Graciela Gonzalez. 2008. BANNER: An executable survey of advances in biomedical named entity recognition. In *Pacific symposium on biocomputing 2008*, 652–663.

Leavitt, Neal. 2010. Will NoSQL databases live up to their promise? *Computer* 43 (2): 12–14.

Lee, Jay, Hung-An Kao, Shanhu Yang, et al. 2014. Service innovation and smart analytics for industry 4.0 and Big Data environment. *Procedia CIRP* 16 (1): 3–8.

Lehmann, Jens, Tim Furche, Giovanni Grasso, Axel-Cyrille Ngonga Ngomo, Christian Schallhart, Andrew Sellers, Christina Unger, Lorenz Bühmann, Daniel Gerber, Konrad Höffner, et al. 2012. DEQA: Deep Web extraction for question answering. In *International Semantic Web conference*, 131–147. Springer.

Leskovec, Jure, Daniel Huttenlocher, and Jon Kleinberg. 2010. Predicting positive and negative links in online social networks. In *Proceedings of the 19th international conference on World Wide Web*, 641–650. ACM.

Levesque, H. J. 1986. Knowledge representation and reasoning. *Annual review of computer science* 1 (1): 255–287. doi:10.1146/annurev.cs.01.060186.001351.

Lewis, Patrick, Ludovic Denoyer, and Sebastian Riedel. 2019. Unsupervised question answering by cloze translation. *arXiv preprint arXiv:1906.04980*.

Li, Chenliang, Aixin Sun, and Anwitaman Datta. 2012. Twevent: Segment-based event detection from tweets. In *Proceedings of the 21st ACM international conference on information and knowledge management*, 155–164.

Li, Hang, and Zhengdong Lu. 2016. Deep learning for information retrieval. In *Proceedings of the 39th international ACM SIGIR conference on research and development in information retrieval*, 1203–1206.

Li, Qi, Heng Ji, and Liang Huang. 2013. Joint event extraction via structured prediction with global features. In *Proceedings of the 51st annual meeting of the Association for Computational Linguistics (volume 1: Long papers)*, 73–82.

Li, Xiang, and Ralph Grishman. 2013. Confidence estimation for knowledge base population. In *Proceedings of the international conference: Recent advances in natural language processing (RANLP) 2013*, 396–401.

Li, Xin, Hsinchun Chen, Zan Huang, and Mihail C Roco. 2007. Patent citation network in nanotechnology (1976–2004). *Journal of nanoparticle research* 9 (3): 337–352.

Liao, Shasha, and Ralph Grishman. 2010. Using document-level cross-event inference to improve event extraction. In *Proceedings of the 48th annual meeting of the Association for Computational Linguistics*, 789–797. Association for Computational Linguistics.

Lin, Dekang. 1998. Automatic retrieval and clustering of similar words. In *COLING 1998 volume 2: The 17th international conference on computational linguistics*.

Lin, Kai, and Bertram Ludäscher. 2004. Geon: Ontology-enabled map integration. In *2004 ESRI international user conference: Redlands, California, ESRI professional papers*, http://gis.esri.com/library/userconf/proc04/abstracts/a1796.html, 1–10.

Lin, Thomas, Patrick Pantel, Michael Gamon, Anitha Kannan, and Ariel Fuxman. 2012. Active objects: Actions for entity-centric search. In *Proceedings of the 21st international conference on World Wide Web*, 589–598. ACM.

Lin, Yankai, Zhiyuan Liu, Maosong Sun, Yang Liu, and Xuan Zhu. 2015. Learning entity and relation embeddings for knowledge graph completion. In *Twenty-ninth AAAI conference on artificial intelligence*, 2181–2187.

Lin, Yankai, Shiqi Shen, Zhiyuan Liu, Huanbo Luan, and Maosong Sun. 2016. Neural relation extraction with selective attention over instances. In *Proceedings of the 54th annual meeting of the Association for Computational Linguistics (volume 1: Long papers)*, 2124–2133.

Liu, Bing, Robert Grossman, and Yanhong Zhai. 2003. Mining data records in web pages. In *Proceedings of the ninth ACM SIGKDD international conference on knowledge discovery and data mining*, 601–606.

Liu, Ling, Calton Pu, and Wei Han. 2000. XWRAP: An XML-enabled wrapper construction system for web information sources. In *Proceedings of 16th international conference on data engineering (cat. no. 00cb37073)*, 611–621. IEEE.

Liu, Tie-Yan, et al. 2009. Learning to rank for information retrieval. *Foundations and trends® in information retrieval* 3 (3): 225–331.

Liu, Wei, Xiaofeng Meng, and Weiyi Meng. 2009. Vide: A vision-based approach for Deep Web data extraction. *IEEE transactions on knowledge and data engineering* 22 (3): 447–460.

Liu, Yinhan, Myle Ott, Naman Goyal, Jingfei Du, Mandar Joshi, Danqi Chen, Omer Levy, Mike Lewis, Luke Zettlemoyer, and Veselin Stoyanov. 2019. RoBERTa: A robustly optimized BERT pre-training approach. *arXiv preprint arXiv:1907.11692*.

Lockard, Colin, Prashant Shiralkar, and Xin Luna Dong. 2019. Openceres: When open information extraction meets the semi-structured web. In *Proceedings of the 2019 conference of the North American chapter of the Association for Computational Linguistics: Human language technologies, volume 1 (long and short papers)*, 3047–3056.

Luke, Sean, Lee Spector, David Rager, and James Hendler. 1997. Ontology-based web agents. In *Proceedings of the first international conference on autonomous agents*, 59–66.

Lyman, Peter and Hal R. Varian. How much information? Internet [Online]. School of Information Management and Systems, University of California, Berkeley. http://www2.sims.berkeley.edu/research/projects/how-much-info-2003.

Madhyastha, Harsha V., N. Balakrishnan, and K. R. Ramakrishnan. 2003. Event information extraction using link grammar. In *Proceedings of the seventeenth workshop on parallel and distributed simulation*, 16–22. IEEE.

Maedche, Alexander, and Steffen Staab. 2001. Ontology learning for the Semantic Web. *IEEE Intelligent systems* 16 (2): 72–79.

Mahmud, S. M. Hasan, Md. Altab Hossin, Md. Rezwan Hasan, Hosney Jahan, Sheak Rashed Haider Noori, and Md. Razu Ahmed. 2020. Publishing CSV data as linked data on the web. In *Proceedings of ICETIT 2019*, 805–817. Springer.

Malandrakis, Nikolaos, Anil Ramakrishna, Victor Martinez, Tanner Sorensen, Dogan Can, and Shrikanth Narayanan. 2018. The ELISA situation frame extraction for low-resource languages pipeline for LoReHLT2016. *Machine translation* 32 (1–2): 127–142.

Manning, Christopher D., Prabhakar Raghavan, and Hinrich Schütze. 2008. *Introduction to information retrieval*. Cambridge University Press.

Manning, Christopher D., and Hinrich Schütze. 1999. *Foundations of statistical natural language processing*. MIT press.

Manning, Christopher D., Mihai Surdeanu, John Bauer, Jenny Finkel, Steven J. Bethard, and David McClosky. 2014. The Stanford CoreNLP natural language processing toolkit. In *Association for Computational Linguistics (ACL) system demonstrations*, 55–60. http://www.aclweb.org/anthology/P/P14/P14-5010.

Manola, Frank. 1998. Towards a richer web object model. *ACM SIGMOD Record* 27 (1): 76–80.

Manola, Frank. 1999. Technologies for a web object model. *IEEE internet computing* 3 (1): 38–47.

Marchionini, Gary. 2006. Exploratory search: From finding to understanding. *Communications of the ACM* 49 (4): 41–46.

Markman, A. B.. 2013. *Knowledge representation*. Psychology Press.

Martin, David, Christine Brun, Elisabeth Remy, Pierre Mouren, Denis Thieffry, and Bernard Jacq. 2004. GOToolBox: Functional analysis of gene datasets based on gene ontology. *Genome biology* 5 (12): R101.

Martinez, Victor R., Anil Ramakrishna, Ming-Chang Chiu, Karan Singla, and Shrikanth Narayanan. 2019. A system for the 2019 sentiment, emotion and cognitive state task of DARPA's LORELEI project. In *2019 8th international conference on affective computing and intelligent interaction (ACII)*, 1–6. IEEE.

Mausam, Mausam. 2016. Open information extraction systems and downstream applications. In *Proceedings of the twenty-fifth international joint conference on artificial intelligence*, 4074–4077.

Maynard, Diana, Kalina Bontcheva, and Isabelle Augenstein. 2016. Natural language processing for the Semantic Web. *Synthesis lectures on the Semantic Web: Theory and technology* 6 (2): 1–194.

McBride, Brian. 2004. The Resource Description Framework (RDF) and its vocabulary description language RDFS. In *Handbook on ontologies*, 51–65. Springer.

McCallum, Andrew, and Wei Li. 2003. Early results for named entity recognition with conditional random fields, feature induction and web-enhanced lexicons. In *Proceedings of the seventh conference on natural language learning at HLT-NAACL 2003*, Vol. 4, 188–191. Association for Computational Linguistics.

McCallum, Andrew, Kamal Nigam, and Lyle H. Ungar. 2000. Efficient clustering of high-dimensional data sets with application to reference matching. In *Proceedings of the sixth ACM SIGKDD international conference on knowledge discovery and data mining*, 169–178.

McClosky, David, Mihai Surdeanu, and Christopher D. Manning. 2011. Event extraction as dependency parsing. In *Proceedings of the 49th annual meeting of the Association for Computational Linguistics: Human language technologies*, Vol. 1, 1626–1635. Association for Computational Linguistics.

McGuinness, Deborah L., Frank Van Harmelen, et al. 2004. OWL Web Ontology Language overview. *W3C recommendation* 10 (10).

McIlraith, Sheila A., Tran Cao Son, and Honglei Zeng. 2001. Semantic Web services. *IEEE intelligent systems* 16 (2): 46–53.

Mei, Hongyuan, Sheng Zhang, Kevin Duh, and Benjamin Van Durme. 2018. Halo: Learning semantics-aware representations for cross-lingual information extraction. *arXiv preprint arXiv:1805.08271*.

Melo, Dora, Irene Pimenta Rodrigues, and Vitor Nogueira. 2011. Cooperative question answering for the Semantic Web. In *Actas das Jornadas de Informática da Universidade de Évora 2011*, 1–6. Escola de Ciências e Tecnologia, Universidade de Évora, November 16.

Mesquita, Filipe, Jordan Schmidek, and Denilson Barbosa. 2013. Effectiveness and efficiency of open relation extraction. In *Proceedings of the 2013 conference on empirical methods in natural language processing*, 447–457.

Meusel, Robert, Christian Bizer, and Heiko Paulheim. 2015. A web-scale study of the adoption and evolution of the Schema.org vocabulary over time. In *Proceedings of the 5th international conference on web intelligence, mining and semantics*, 1–11.

Michelson, Matthew, and Craig A Knoblock. 2006. Learning blocking schemes for record linkage. In *AAAI*, Vol. 6, 440–445.

Mika, Peter. 2015. On Schema.org and why it matters for the web. *IEEE internet computing* 19 (4): 52–55.

Mikheev, Andrei, Marc Moens, and Claire Grover. 1999. Named entity recognition without gazetteers. In *Ninth conference of the European chapter of the Association for Computational Linguistics*.

Mikolov, Tomas, Ilya Sutskever, Kai Chen, Greg S. Corrado, and Jeff Dean. 2013. Distributed representations of words and phrases and their compositionality. In *Advances in neural information processing systems*, 3111–3119.

Miller, George A. 1998. *WordNet: An electronic lexical database*. MIT Press.

Miller, Justin J. 2013. Graph database applications and concepts with Neo4j. In *Proceedings of the Southern Association for Information Systems conference*, Vol. 2324.

Miller, Robert C., and Krishna Bharat. 1998. Sphinx: A framework for creating personal, site-specific web crawlers. *Computer networks and ISDN systems* 30 (1–7): 119–130.

Mintz, Mike, Steven Bills, Rion Snow, and Dan Jurafsky. 2009. Distant supervision for relation extraction without labeled data. In *Proceedings of the joint conference of the 47th annual meeting of the ACL and the 4th international joint conference on natural language processing of the AFNLP*, Vol. 2, 1003–1011. Association for Computational Linguistics.

Möhring, Rolf H., Heiko Schilling, Birk Schütz, Dorothea Wagner, and Thomas Willhalm. 2007. Partitioning graphs to speed up Dijkstra's algorithm. *Journal of experimental algorithmics (JEA)*, Vol. 11, 2–8.

Mooney, R.. 1999. Relational learning of pattern-match rules for information extraction. In *Proceedings of the sixteenth national conference on artificial intelligence*, Vol. 334, 328–334.

Moraes, Felipe, Rodrygo L. T. Santos, and Nivio Ziviani. 2017. On effective dynamic search in specialized domains. In *Proceedings of the ACM SIGIR international conference on theory of information retrieval*, 177–184.

Moreno, Jakob L. 1946. Sociogram and sociomatrix. *Sociometry*, Vol. 9, 348–349.

Morgan, Mena Badieh Habib, and Maurice Van Keulen. 2014. Information extraction for social media. In *Proceedings of the third workshop on Semantic Web and information extraction*, 9–16.

Mouzannar, Hussein, Yara Rizk, and Mariette Awad. 2018. Damage identification in social media posts using multimodal deep learning. In *Proceedings of the 15th ISCRAM conference, Rochester, NY*.

Mudgal, Sidharth, Han Li, Theodoros Rekatsinas, AnHai Doan, Youngchoon Park, Ganesh Krishnan, Rohit Deep, Esteban Arcaute, and Vijay Raghavendra. 2018. Deep learning for entity matching: A design space exploration. In *Proceedings of the 2018 international conference on management of data*, 19–34. ACM.

Muggleton, Stephen, et al. 1996. Stochastic logic programs. *Advances in inductive logic programming*, Vol. 32, 254–264.

Muslea, Ion, Steve Minton, and Craig Knoblock. 1999. A hierarchical approach to wrapper induction. In *Proceedings of the third annual conference on autonomous agents*, 190–197.

Musto, Jennifer Lynne, and Danah Boyd. 2014. The trafficking-technology nexus. *Social politics* 21 (3): 461–483.

Nadeau, D., and S. Sekine. A survey of named entity recognition and classification. *Lingvisticae Investigationes* 30, no. 1 (2007): 3–26.

Nadeau, David, Peter D. Turney, and Stan Matwin. 2006. Unsupervised named-entity recognition: Generating gazetteers and resolving ambiguity. In *Conference of the Canadian Society for Computational Studies of Intelligence*, 266–277. Springer.

Nakashole, Ndapandula, Martin Theobald, and Gerhard Weikum. 2011. Scalable knowledge harvesting with high precision and high recall. In *Proceedings of the fourth ACM international conference on web search and data mining*, 227–236.

Nam, Daye, and Mayank Kejriwal. 2018. How do organizations publish semantic markup? Three case studies using public schema.org crawls. *Computer* 51 (6): 42–51.

Nambiar, Ullas, Bertram Ludaescher, Kai Lin, and Chaitan Baru. 2006. The Geon portal: Accelerating knowledge discovery in the geosciences. In *Proceedings of the 8th annual ACM international workshop on web information and data management*, 83–90.

Naumann, Felix, and Melanie Herschel. 2010. An introduction to duplicate detection. *Synthesis lectures on data management* 2 (1): 1–87.

Neapolitan, Richard E. 2012. *Probabilistic reasoning in expert systems: Theory and algorithms*. Create-Space Independent Publishing Platform.

Neelakantan, Arvind, Benjamin Roth, and Andrew McCallum. 2015. Compositional vector space models for knowledge base inference. *arXiv preprint arXiv:1504.06662*.

Nenkova, Ani, and Kathleen McKeown. 2012. A survey of text summarization techniques. In *Mining text data*, 43–76. Springer.

Nentwig, Markus, Michael Hartung, Axel-Cyrille Ngonga Ngomo, and Erhard Rahm. 2017. A survey of current link discovery frameworks. *Semantic Web* 8 (3): 419–436.

Neville, Jennifer, David Jensen, Lisa Friedland, and Michael Hay. 2003. Learning relational probability trees. In *Proceedings of the ninth ACM SIGKDD international conference on knowledge discovery and data mining*, 625–630.

Neville, Jennifer, Matthew Rattigan, and David Jensen. 2003. Statistical Relational Learning: Four claims and a survey. In *IJCAI 2003 workshop on learning statistical models from relational data*.

Ngo, Liem, and Peter Haddawy. 1997. Answering queries from context-sensitive probabilistic knowledge bases. *Theoretical computer science* 171 (1–2): 147–177.

Ngomo, Axel-Cyrille Ngonga. 2012. Link discovery with guaranteed reduction ratio in affine spaces with Minkowski measures. In *International Semantic Web conference*, 378–393. Springer.

Nguyen, Dat Quoc. 2017. An overview of embedding models of entities and relationships for knowledge base completion. *arXiv preprint arXiv:1703.08098*.

Nguyen, Thien Huu, and Ralph Grishman. 2015. Relation extraction: Perspective from convolutional neural networks. In *Proceedings of the 1st workshop on vector space modeling for natural language processing*, 39–48.

Nickel, Maximilian, Kevin Murphy, Volker Tresp, and Evgeniy Gabrilovich. 2015. A review of relational machine learning for knowledge graphs. *Proceedings of the IEEE* 104 (1): 11–33.

Nickel, Maximilian, Lorenzo Rosasco, and Tomaso Poggio. 2016. Holographic embeddings of knowledge graphs. In *Thirtieth AAAI conference on artificial intelligence*, 1955–1961.

Nickel, Maximilian, Volker Tresp, and Hans-Peter Kriegel. 2011. A three-way model for collective learning on multi-relational data. In *International Conference on Machine Learning (ICML)*, Vol. 11, 809–816.

Niklaus, Christina, Matthias Cetto, André Freitas, and Siegfried Handschuh. 2018. A survey on open information extraction. *arXiv preprint arXiv:1806.05599*.

Nikolov, Andriy, Mathieu d'Aquin, and Enrico Motta. 2012. Unsupervised learning of link discovery configuration. In *Extended Semantic Web conference*, 119–133. Springer.

Nikolov, Andriy, Andreas Schwarte, and Christian Hütter. 2013. FedSearch: Efficiently combining structured queries and full-text search in a SPARQL federation. In *International Semantic Web conference*, 427–443. Springer.

Niu, Feng, Ce Zhang, Christopher Ré, and Jude Shavlik. 2012a. DeepDive: Web-scale knowledge-base construction using statistical learning and inference. *VLDS* 12: 25–28.

Niu, Feng, Ce Zhang, Christopher Ré, and Jude Shavlik. 2012b. Elementary: Large-scale knowledge-base construction via machine learning and statistical inference. *International journal on Semantic Web and information systems (IJSWIS)* 8 (3): 42–73.

Novak, Blaž. 2004. A survey of focused web crawling algorithms. *Proceedings of the Special Interest Group on Knowledge Discovery and Data Mining (SIKDD)*, 55–58.

Open Graph Protocol. 2016. The Open Graph Protocol. https://ogp.me.

Palen, Leysia. 2008. Online social media in crisis events. *Educause quarterly* 31 (3): 76–78.

Palen, Leysia, and Kenneth M. Anderson. 2016. Crisis informatics-new data for extraordinary times. *Science* 353 (6296): 224–225.

Palen, Leysia, Sarah Vieweg, Jeannette Sutton, Sophia B. Liu, and Amanda Hughes. 2007. Crisis informatics: Studying crisis in a networked world. In *Proceedings of the third international conference on e-social science*, 7–9. Citeseer.

Palmer, David D., and David Day. 1997. A statistical profile of the named entity task. In *Fifth conference on applied natural language processing*, 190–193.

Pan, Jeff Z., Siyana Pavlova, Chenxi Li, Ningxi Li, Yangmei Li, and Jinshuo Liu. 2018. Content-based fake news detection using knowledge graphs. In *International Semantic Web conference*, 669–683. Springer.

Pan, Jeff Z., Guido Vetere, Jose Manuel Gomez-Perez, and Honghan Wu. 2017. *Exploiting linked data and knowledge graphs in large organisations*. Springer.

Pang, Liang, Yanyan Lan, Jiafeng Guo, Jun Xu, Jingfang Xu, and Xueqi Cheng. 2017. DeepRank: A new deep architecture for relevance ranking in information retrieval. In *Proceedings of the 2017 ACM conference on information and knowledge management*, 257–266.

Papadakis, George, Ekaterini Ioannou, Claudia Niederée, and Peter Fankhauser. 2011. Efficient entity resolution for large heterogeneous information spaces. In *Proceedings of the fourth ACM international conference on web search and data mining*, 535–544. ACM.

Papadopoulos, Pavlos, Ruchir Travadi, Colin Vaz, Nikolaos Malandrakis, Ulf Hermjakob, Nima Pourdamghani, Michael Pust, Boliang Zhang, Xiaoman Pan, Di Lu, et al. 2017. Team ELISA system for DARPA LORELEI speech evaluation 2016. In *Interspeech*, 2053–2057.

Parker, Zachary, Scott Poe, and Susan V. Vrbsky. 2013. Comparing NoSQL mongoDB to an SQL DB. In *Proceedings of the 51st ACM southeast conference*, 5. ACM.

Paro, Alberto. 2015. *Elasticsearch cookbook*. Packt Publishing Ltd.

Pasca, Marius, Dekang Lin, Jeffrey Bigham, Andrei Lifchits, and Alpa Jain. 2006. Organizing and searching the World Wide Web of facts—step one: The one-million fact extraction challenge. In *AAAI*, Vol. 6, 1400–1405.

Passin, Thomas B. 2004. *Explorer's guide to the Semantic Web*. Manning Greenwich.

Patel-Schneider, Peter F. 2014. Analyzing Schema.org. In *International Semantic Web conference*, 261–276. Springer.

Paulheim, Heiko. 2017. Knowledge graph refinement: A survey of approaches and evaluation methods. *Semantic Web* 8 (3): 489–508.

Pawar, Sachin, Girish K. Palshikar, and Pushpak Bhattacharyya. 2017. Relation extraction: A survey. *arXiv preprint arXiv:1712.05191*.

Pearl, Judea. 2014. *Probabilistic reasoning in intelligent systems: Networks of plausible inference*. Elsevier.

Pedersen, Ted, Siddharth Patwardhan, Jason Michelizzi, et al. 2004. WordNet:: Similarity-measuring the relatedness of concepts. In *AAAI*, Vol. 4, 25–29.

Peng, Fuchun, and Andrew McCallum. 2006. Information extraction from research papers using conditional random fields. *Information processing and management* 42 (4): 963–979.

Pérez, Jorge, Marcelo Arenas, and Claudio Gutierrez. 2006. Semantics and complexity of SPARQL. In *International Semantic Web conference*, 30–43. Springer.

Perozzi, Bryan, Rami Al-Rfou, and Steven Skiena. 2014. DeepWalk: Online learning of social representations. In *Proceedings of the 20th ACM SIGKDD international conference on knowledge discovery and data mining*, 701–710.

Peters, Matthew E., Mark Neumann, Mohit Iyyer, Matt Gardner, Christopher Clark, Kenton Lee, and Luke Zettlemoyer. 2018. Deep contextualized word representations. *arXiv preprint arXiv:1802.05365*.

Petroni, Fabio, Tim Rocktäschel, Patrick Lewis, Anton Bakhtin, Yuxiang Wu, Alexander H. Miller, and Sebastian Riedel. 2019. Language models as knowledge bases? *arXiv preprint arXiv:1909.01066*.

Phi, Van-Thuy, Joan Santoso, Van-Hien Tran, Hiroyuki Shindo, Masashi Shimbo, and Yuji Matsumoto. 2019. Distant supervision for relation extraction via piecewise attention and bag-level contextual inference. *IEEE access* 7: 103570–103582.

Phillips, William, and Ellen Riloff. 2002. Exploiting strong syntactic heuristics and co-training to learn semantic lexicons. In *Proceedings of the 2002 conference on empirical methods in natural language processing (EMNLP 2002)*, 125–132.

Pirolli, Peter, James Pitkow, and Ramana Rao. 1996. Silk from a sow's ear: Extracting usable structures from the web. In *Proceedings of the SIGCHI conference on human factors in computing systems*, 118–125.

Piskorski, Jakub, and Roman Yangarber. 2013. Information extraction: Past, present and future. In *Multi-source, multilingual information extraction and summarization*, 23–49. Springer.

Poibeau, Thierry, Horacio Saggion, Jakub Piskorski, and Roman Yangarber. 2012. *Multi-source, multilingual information extraction and summarization.* Springer.

Popescu, Ana-Maria, Marco Pennacchiotti, and Deepa Paranjpe. 2011. Extracting events and event descriptions from Twitter. In *Proceedings of the 20th international conference companion on World Wide Web*, 105–106.

Popescul, Alexandrin, and Lyle H. Ungar. 2003. Statistical Relational Learning for link prediction. In *IJCAI workshop on learning statistical models from relational data*, Vol. 2003. Citeseer.

Pujara, Jay, Hui Miao, Lise Getoor, and William Cohen. 2013. Knowledge graph identification. In *International Semantic Web conference*, 542–557. Springer.

Qi, Guilin, Huajun Chen, Kang Liu, Haofen Wang, Qiu Ji, and Tianxing Wu. 2020. *Knowledge graph.* Springer.

Qin, Tao, Tie-Yan Liu, Jun Xu, and Hang Li. 2010. LETOR: A benchmark collection for research on learning to rank for information retrieval. *Information retrieval* 13 (4): 346–374.

Quilitz, Bastian, and Ulf Leser. 2008. Querying distributed RDF data sources with SPARQL. In *European Semantic Web conference*, 524–538. Springer.

Rabiner, Lawrence, and B. Juang. 1986. An introduction to Hidden Markov Models. *IEEE ASP magazine* 3 (1): 4–16.

Radford, Alec, Karthik Narasimhan, Tim Salimans, and Ilya Sutskever. 2018. Improving language understanding by generative pre-training. https://s3-us-west-2.amazonaws.com/openai-assets/researchcovers/languageunsupervised/language understanding paper.pdf.

Radford, Alec, Jeffrey Wu, Rewon Child, David Luan, Dario Amodei, and Ilya Sutskever. 2019. Language models are unsupervised multitask learners. *OpenAI blog* 1 (8): 9.

Radlinski, Filip, and Nick Craswell. 2010. Comparing the sensitivity of information retrieval metrics. In *Proceedings of the 33rd international ACM SIGIR conference on research and development in information retrieval*, 667–674.

Raghavan, Sriram, and Hector Garcia-Molina. 2001. Crawling the hidden web. In *Proceedings of the 27th International Conference on Very Large Data Bases,* 129–138. Morgan Kaufmann.

Rahm, Erhard, and Philip A. Bernstein. 2001. A survey of approaches to automatic schema matching. *VLDB journal* 10 (4): 334–350.

Raimond, Yves, Tristan Ferne, Michael Smethurst, and Gareth Adams. 2014. The BBC World Service archive prototype. *Journal of web semantics*, Vol. 27, 2–9.

Rajpurkar, Pranav, Jian Zhang, Konstantin Lopyrev, and Percy Liang. 2016. SQuAD: 100,000+ questions for machine comprehension of text. *arXiv preprint arXiv:1606.05250.*

Ramadan, Banda, and Peter Christen. 2015. Unsupervised blocking key selection for real-time entity resolution. In *Pacific-Asia conference on knowledge discovery and data mining*, 574–585. Springer.

Rana, Ram Kumar, and Nidhi Tyagi. 2012. A novel architecture of ontology-based Semantic Web crawler. *International journal of computer applications* 44 (18): 31–36.

Raskin, Rob, and Michael Pan. 2003. Semantic Web for Earth and Environmental Terminology (SWEET). In *Proceedings of the workshop on Semantic Web technologies for searching and retrieving scientific data*, Vol. 25.

Raskin, Rob, Michael Pan, and Chris Mattmann. 2004. Enabling semantic interoperability for earth science data. In *4th NASA earth science technology conference*. Citeseer.

Raskin, Robert G., and Michael J. Pan. 2005. Knowledge representation in the Semantic Web for Earth and Environmental Terminology (SWEET). *Computers and geosciences* 31 (9): 1119–1125.

Ratner, Alexander, Stephen H Bach, Henry Ehrenberg, Jason Fries, Sen Wu, and Christopher Ré. 2020. Snorkel: Rapid training data creation with weak supervision. *VLDB journal* 29 (2): 709–730.

Reddy, Siva, Danqi Chen, and Christopher D. Manning. 2019. CoQA: A conversational question answering challenge. *Transactions of the Association for Computational Linguistics*, Vol. 7, 249–266.

Rennie, Jason, Andrew McCallum, et al. 1999. Using reinforcement learning to spider the web efficiently. *ICML*, Vol. 99, 335–343.

Rettinger, Achim, Matthias Nickles, and Volker Tresp. 2011. Statistical relational learning of trust. *Machine learning* 82 (2): 191–209.

Reuter, Christian, Amanda Lee Hughes, and Marc-André Kaufhold. 2018. Social media in crisis management: An evaluation and analysis of crisis informatics research. *International journal of human–computer interaction* 34 (4): 280–294.

Reutter, Juan L, Miguel Romero, and Moshe Y. Vardi. 2017. Regular queries on graph databases. *Theory of computing systems* 61 (1): 31–83.

Richardson, Matthew, and Pedro Domingos. 2006. Markov Logic Networks. *Machine learning* 62 (1–2): 107–136.

Riedel, Sebastian, Limin Yao, and Andrew McCallum. 2010. Modeling relations and their mentions without labeled text. In *Joint European conference on machine learning and knowledge discovery in databases*, 148–163. Springer.

Riloff, Ellen, et al. 1993. Automatically constructing a dictionary for information extraction tasks. In *AAAI*, Vol. 1, 811–816. Citeseer.

Riloff, Ellen, Rosie Jones, et al. 1999. Learning dictionaries for information extraction by multi-level bootstrapping. In *AAAI/IAAI*, 474–479.

Ritter, Alan, Sam Clark, Mausam, and Oren Etzioni. 2011. Named entity recognition in tweets: An experimental study. In *EMNLP*, 1524–1534.

Ritter, Alan, Oren Etzioni, and Sam Clark. 2012. Open domain event extraction from Twitter. In *Proceedings of the 18th ACM SIGKDD international conference on knowledge discovery and data mining*, 1104–1112.

Roberts, Adam, Colin Raffel, and Noam Shazeer. 2020. How much knowledge can you pack into the parameters of a language model? *arXiv preprint arXiv:2002.08910*.

Rogers, Anna, Olga Kovaleva, and Anna Rumshisky. 2020. A primer in BERTology: What we know about how BERT works. *arXiv preprint arXiv:2002.12327*.

Ronallo, Jason. 2012. HTML5 microdata and Schema.org. *Code4Lib Journal*. https://code4lib.org/conference/2012/ronallo/.

Rossi, Ryan A., Luke K. McDowell, David William Aha, and Jennifer Neville. 2012. Transforming graph data for statistical relational learning. *Journal of artificial intelligence research*, Vol. 45, 363–441.

Rotmensch, Maya, Yoni Halpern, Abdulhakim Tlimat, Steven Horng, and David Sontag. 2017. Learning a health knowledge graph from electronic medical records. *Scientific reports* 7 (1): 1–11.

Ryu, Pum Mo, Myung Gil Jang, Hyunki Kim, YiGyu Hwang, Soojong Lim, Jeong Heo, Chung Hee Lee, Hyo-Jung Oh, Changki Lee, Miran Choi, et al. 2013. Apparatus and method for knowledge graph stabilization. Google Patents. US Patent 8,407,253.

Sahoo, Satya S., Wolfgang Halb, Sebastian Hellmann, Kingsley Idehen, Ted Thibodeau Jr., Sören Auer, Juan Sequeda, and Ahmed Ezzat. 2009. A survey of current approaches for mapping of relational databases to RDF. *W3C RDB2RDF Incubator Group report*, Vol. 1, 113–130.

Sahu, Archana, Kaushik Baruah, Sumit Negi, and Om D. Deshmukh. 2018. Method and system for content processing to query multiple healthcare-related knowledge graphs. Google Patents. US Patent App. 15/355,085.

Sahuguet, Arnaud, and Fabien Azavant. 2001. Building intelligent web applications using lightweight wrappers. *Data and knowledge engineering* 36 (3): 283–316.

Sakai, Tetsuya. 2007. On the reliability of information retrieval metrics based on graded relevance. *Information processing and management* 43 (2): 531–548.

Sakai, Tetsuya, and Noriko Kando. 2008. On information retrieval metrics designed for evaluation with incomplete relevance assessments. *Information retrieval* 11 (5): 447–470.

Sakr, Sherif, and Ghazi Al-Naymat. 2010. Relational processing of RDF queries: A survey. *ACM SIGMOD record* 38 (4): 23–28.

Sakr, Sherif, Marcin Wylot, Raghava Mutharaju, Danh Le Phuoc, and Fundulaki Irini. 2019. *Linked data: Storing, querying, and reasoning*. Springer.

Saleiro, Pedro, Jorge Teixeira, Carlos Soares, and Eugénio Oliveira. 2016. TimeMachine: Entity-centric search and visualization of news archives. In *European conference on information retrieval*, 845–848. Springer.

Sang, Erik F., and Fien De Meulder. 2003. Introduction to the CoNLL-2003 shared task: Language-independent named entity recognition. *arXiv preprint cs/0306050*.

Sanh, Victor, Lysandre Debut, Julien Chaumond, and Thomas Wolf. 2019. DistilBERT, a distilled version of BERT: Smaller, faster, cheaper and lighter. *arXiv preprint arXiv:1910.01108*.

Sankaranarayanan, Jagan, Hanan Samet, Benjamin E. Teitler, Michael D. Lieberman, and Jon Sperling. 2009. Twitterstand: News in tweets. In *Proceedings of the 17th ACM SIGSPATIAL international conference on advances in geographic information systems*, 42–51.

Santos, Henrique, Victor Dantas, Vasco Furtado, Paulo Pinheiro, and Deborah L. McGuinness. 2017. From data to city indicators: A knowledge graph for supporting automatic generation of dashboards. In *European Semantic Web conference*, 94–108. Springer.

Sarawagi, Sunita. 2002. Automation in information extraction and integration. In *Tutorial of the 28th international conference on very large data bases (VLDB). http://www2.cs.uh.edu/ ce-ick/6340/Extraction.pdf*.

Sarawagi, Sunita, and William W. Cohen. 2005. Semi-Markov conditional random fields for information extraction. In *Advances in neural information processing systems*, 1185–1192.

Sarawagi, Sunita, et al. 2008. Information extraction. *Foundations and trends® in databases* 1 (3): 261–377.

Sarkar, Siddhartha. 2015. Use of technology in human trafficking networks and sexual exploitation: A cross-sectional multi-country study. *Transnational social review* 5 (1): 55–68.

Sato, Taisuke, and Yoshitaka Kameya. 1997. PRISM: a language for symbolic-statistical modeling. In *IJCAI*, Vol. 97, 1330–1339.

Savona, Ernesto U., and Sonia Stefanizzi. 2007. *Measuring human trafficking*. Springer.

Schätzle, Alexander, Martin Przyjaciel-Zablocki, Simon Skilevic, and Georg Lausen. 2016. S2RDF: Rdf querying with SPARQL on Spark. *Proceedings of the VLDB endowment* 9 (10): 804–815.

Schmachtenberg, Max, Christian Bizer, and Heiko Paulheim. 2014. Adoption of the linked data best practices in different topical domains. In *International Semantic Web conference*, 245–260. Springer.

Schmidek, Jordan, and Denilson Barbosa. 2014. Improving open relation extraction via sentence re-structuring. In *Proceedings of the Ninth International Conference on Language Resources and Evaluation*, 3720–3723.

Schmidt, Michael, Thomas Hornung, Georg Lausen, and Christoph Pinkel. 2009. SP2Bench: A SPARQL performance benchmark. In *2009 IEEE 25th international conference on data engineering*, 222–233. IEEE.

Schreiber, Falk, and Henning Schwöbbermeyer. 2005. MAVisto: A tool for the exploration of network motifs. *Bioinformatics* 21 (17): 3572–3574.

Schulz, Klaus U., and Stoyan Mihov. 2002. Fast string correction with Levenshtein automata. *International journal on document analysis and recognition* 5 (1): 67–85.

Schum, David A. 2001. *The evidential foundations of probabilistic reasoning*. Northwestern University Press.

Sclaroff, Stan. 1995. *World Wide Web image search engines*. Technical report, Boston University Computer Science Department.

Sekine, Satoshi, and Chikashi Nobata. 2004. Definition, dictionaries and tagger for extended named entity hierarchy. In *Proceedings of the Ninth International Conference on Language Resources and Evaluation*.

Sequeda, Juan F., Syed Hamid Tirmizi, Oscar Corcho, and Daniel P. Miranker. 2011. Survey of directly mapping SQL databases to the Semantic Web. *The knowledge engineering review* 26 (4): 445–486.

Severyn, Aliaksei, and Alessandro Moschitti. 2015. Learning to rank short text pairs with convolutional deep neural networks. In *Proceedings of the 38th international ACM SIGIR conference on research and development in information retrieval*, 373–382.

Shaalan, Khaled. 2014. A survey of Arabic named entity recognition and classification. *Computational linguistics* 40 (2): 469–510.

Shadbolt, Nigel, Tim Berners-Lee, and Wendy Hall. 2006. The Semantic Web revisited. *IEEE intelligent systems* 21 (3): 96–101.

Shadbolt, Nigel, Kieron O'Hara, Tim Berners-Lee, Nicholas Gibbins, Hugh Glaser, Wendy Hall, et al. 2012. Linked open government data: Lessons from data.gov.uk. *IEEE intelligent systems* 27 (3): 16–24.

Shaffer, Clifford A. 1997. *A practical introduction to data structures and algorithm analysis*. Prentice Hall.

Shang-Hua Teng, Qi Lu, M. Eichstaedt, D. Ford, and T. Lehman. 1999. Collaborative web crawling: Information gathering/processing over internet. In *Proceedings of the 32nd annual Hawaii international conference on systems sciences. 1999. HICSS-32*. Abstracts and CD-ROM of full papers, Vol. Track 5, 12. doi:10.1109/HICSS.1999.772945.

Shao, Jingyu, and Qing Wang. 2018. Active blocking scheme learning for entity resolution. In *Pacific-Asia conference on knowledge discovery and data mining*, 350–362. Springer.

Sharma, Vijay Kumar, and Namita Mittal. 2016. Cross-lingual information retrieval (CLIR): Review of tools, challenges and translation approaches. In *Information systems design and intelligent applications*, 699–708. Springer.

Shekarpour, Saeedeh, Axel-Cyrille Ngonga Ngomo, and Sören Auer. 2012. Query segmentation and resource disambiguation leveraging background knowledge. In *Wole@ISWC*, 82–93.

Shekarpour, Saeedeh, Axel-Cyrille Ngonga Ngomo, and Sören Auer. 2013. Question answering on interlinked data. In *Proceedings of the 22nd international conference on World Wide Web*, 1145–1156.

Sheth, Amit, Swati Padhee, and Amelie Gyrard. 2019. Knowledge graphs and knowledge networks: The story in brief. *IEEE internet computing* 23 (4): 67–75.

Shi, Longxiang, Shijian Li, Xiaoran Yang, Jiaheng Qi, Gang Pan, and Binbin Zhou. 2017. Semantic health knowledge graph: Semantic integration of heterogeneous medical knowledge and services. *BioMed research international* 2017: 2858423. doi: 10.1155/2017/2858423.

Shinyama, Yusuke, and Satoshi Sekine. 2004. Named entity discovery using comparable news articles. In *Proceedings of the 20th international conference on computational linguistics*, 848. Association for Computational Linguistics.

Shiralkar, Prashant, Alessandro Flammini, Filippo Menczer, and Giovanni Luca Ciampaglia. 2017. Finding streams in knowledge graphs to support fact checking. In *2017 IEEE international conference on data mining (ICDM)*, 859–864. IEEE.

Shizhu, He, Zhang Yuanzhe, Liu Kang, and Zhao Jun 2014. Casia@v2: A MLN-based question answering system over linked data. *http://ceur-ws.org/Vol-1180/CLEF2014wn-QA-ShizhuEt2014.pdf*.

Singh, Ved Prakash, and Preet Pal. 2014. Survey of different types of captcha. *International journal of computer science and information technologies* 5 (2): 2242–2245.

Singhal, Amit. 2012. Introducing the knowledge graph: Things, not strings. *Official Google blog*. Available: *https://www.blog.google/products/search/introducing-knowledge-graph-things-not/*.

Singla, Parag, and Pedro Domingos. 2005. Discriminative training of Markov Logic Networks. In *AAAI*, Vol. 5, 868–873.

Singla, Parag, and Pedro Domingos. 2006. Entity resolution with Markov Logic. In *Sixth international conference on data mining (ICDM'06)*, 572–582. IEEE.

Sirin, Evren, and Bijan Parsia. 2007. SPARQL-DL: SPARQL query for OWL-DL. In *OWLED*, Vol. 258. Citeseer.

Smeaton, Alan F., Gary Keogh, Cathal Gurrin, Kieran McDonald, and Tom Sødring. 2002. Analysis of papers from twenty-five years of SIGIR conferences: What have we been doing for the last quarter of a century? In *ACM SIGIR forum*, Vol. 36, 39–43. ACM.

Smirnova, Alisa, and Philippe Cudré-Mauroux. 2018. Relation extraction using distant supervision: A survey. *ACM computing surveys (CSUR)* 51 (5): 1–35.

Socher, Richard, Danqi Chen, Christopher D. Manning, and Andrew Ng. 2013. Reasoning with neural tensor networks for knowledge base completion. In *Advances in neural information processing systems*, 926–934.

Soderland, Stephen. 1999. Learning information extraction rules for semi-structured and free text. *Machine learning* 34 (1–3): 233–272.

Soderland, Stephen, David Fisher, Jonathan Aseltine, and Wendy Lehnert. 1995. Crystal: Inducing a conceptual dictionary. *arXiv preprint cmp-lg/9505020*.

Song, Zhiyi, Ann Bies, Stephanie Strassel, Tom Riese, Justin Mott, Joe Ellis, Jonathan Wright, Seth Kulick, Neville Ryant, and Xiaoyi Ma. 2015. From light to rich ERE: Annotation of entities, relations, and events. In *Proceedings of the the 3rd workshop on events: Definition, detection, coreference, and representation*, 89–98.

Sowa, J. F. 2000. *Knowledge representation: Logical, philosophical, and computational foundations*. Brooks/Cole.

Sowa, J. F. 2014. *Principles of semantic networks: Explorations in the representation of knowledge*. Morgan Kaufmann.

Spector, Lee. 1997. Ontology-based web agents. In *Proceedings of first international conference on autonomous agents*, 59–66. Citeseer.

Speer, Robyn, Joshua Chin, and Catherine Havasi. 2017. ConceptNet 5.5: An open multilingual graph of general knowledge. In *Thirty-first AAAI conference on artificial intelligence*, 4444–4451.

Spertus, Ellen. 1997. Parasite: Mining structural information on the web. *Computer networks and ISDN systems* 29 (8–13): 1205–1215.

Stanovsky, Gabriel, Jessica Ficler, Ido Dagan, and Yoav Goldberg. 2016. Getting more out of syntax with props. *arXiv preprint arXiv:1603.01648*.

Stanovsky, Gabriel, Julian Michael, Luke Zettlemoyer, and Ido Dagan. 2018. Supervised open information extraction. In *North American Chapter of the Association for Computational Linguistics (NAACL-HLT)*, 885–895.

Steiner, Thomas, and Stefan Mirea. 2012. Seki@home, or crowdsourcing an open knowledge graph. In *Proceedings of the first international workshop on knowledge extraction and consolidation from social media (KECSM 2012)*, Vol. 7.

Steiner, Thomas, Ruben Verborgh, Raphaël Troncy, Joaquim Gabarro, and Rik Van de Walle. 2012. Adding realtime coverage to the Google Knowledge Graph. In *11th international Semantic Web conference, Posters and Demonstrations Track (ISWC-PD 2012)*, 65–68. Citeseer.

Straccia, Umberto, and Raphaël Troncy. 2006. Towards distributed information retrieval in the Semantic Web: Query reformulation using the OMAP framework. In *European Semantic Web conference*, 378–392. Springer.

Strassel, Stephanie, and Jennifer Tracey. 2016. LORELEI language packs: Data, tools, and resources for technology development in low-resource languages. In *Proceedings of the tenth international conference on language resources and evaluation (LREC'16)*, 3273–3280.

Strassel, Stephanie M., Ann Bies, and Jennifer Tracey. 2017. Situational awareness for low-resource languages: The LORELEI situation frame annotation task. In *SMERP@ECIR*, 32–41.

Strauch, Christof, and Walter Kriha. 2011. NoSQL databases. Lecture Notes, Selected topics on software-technology ultra-large scale sites, Stuttgart Media University 20. *https://www.christof-strauch.de/nosqldbs.pdf*.

Sun, Jianling, and Qiang Jin. 2010. Scalable RDF store based on HBase and MapReduce. In *2010 3rd international conference on advanced computer theory and engineering (ICACTE)*, Vol. 1, V1-633. IEEE.

Sun, Wen, Achille Fokoue, Kavitha Srinivas, Anastasios Kementsietsidis, Gang Hu, and Guotong Xie. 2015. SQLGraph: An efficient relational-based property graph store. In *Proceedings of the 2015 ACM SIGMOD international conference on management of data*, 1887–1901. ACM.

Sun, Yang, Isaac G. Councill, and C. Lee Giles. 2010. The ethicality of web crawlers. In *2010 IEEE/WIC/ACM international conference on web intelligence and intelligent agent technology*, Vol. 1, 668–675. IEEE.

Supek, Fran, Matko Bošnjak, Nives Škunca, and Tomislav Šmuc. 2011. Revigo summarizes and visualizes long lists of gene ontology terms. *PloS one* 6 (7).

Surdeanu, Mihai, Julie Tibshirani, Ramesh Nallapati, and Christopher D. Manning. 2012. Multi-instance multi-label learning for relation extraction. In *Proceedings of the 2012 joint conference on empirical methods in natural language processing and computational natural language learning*, 455–465. Association for Computational Linguistics.

Sutton, Charles, Andrew McCallum, et al. 2012. An introduction to conditional random fields. *Foundations and trends® in machine learning* 4 (4): 267–373.

Szekely, Pedro, Craig A. Knoblock, Shubham Gupta, Mohsen Taheriyan, and Bo Wu. 2011. Exploiting semantics of web services for geospatial data fusion. In *Proceedings of the 1st ACM SIGSPATIAL international workshop on spatial semantics and ontologies*, 32–39.

Szekely, Pedro, Craig A. Knoblock, Jason Slepicka, Andrew Philpot, Amandeep Singh, Chengye Yin, Dipsy Kapoor, Prem Natarajan, Daniel Marcu, Kevin Knight, et al. 2015. Building and using a knowledge graph to combat human trafficking. In *International Semantic Web conference*, 205–221. Springer.

Szekely, Pedro, Craig A. Knoblock, Fengyu Yang, Xuming Zhu, Eleanor E. Fink, Rachel Allen, and Georgina Goodlander. 2013. Connecting the Smithsonian American Art Museum to the linked data cloud. In *Extended Semantic Web conference*, 593–607. Springer.

Tang, Duyu, Bing Qin, and Ting Liu. 2015a. Document modeling with gated recurrent neural network for sentiment classification. In *Proceedings of the 2015 conference on empirical methods in natural language processing*, 1422–1432.

Tang, Jian, Meng Qu, Mingzhe Wang, Ming Zhang, Jun Yan, and Qiaozhu Mei. 2015b. Line: Large-scale information network embedding. In *Proceedings of the 24th international conference on World Wide Web*, 1067–1077.

Tang, Jie, Tiancheng Lou, and Jon Kleinberg. 2012. Inferring social ties across heterogenous networks. In *Proceedings of the fifth ACM international conference on web search and data mining*, 743–752. ACM.

Tarjan, Robert. 1972. Depth-first search and linear graph algorithms. *SIAM journal on computing* 1 (2): 146–160.

Taskar, Ben, Vassil Chatalbashev, and Daphne Koller. 2004. Learning associative Markov networks. In *Proceedings of the twenty-first international conference on machine learning*, 102.

Thelwall, Mike, and David Stuart. 2006. Web crawling ethics revisited: Cost, privacy, and denial of service. *Journal of the American Society for Information Science and Technology* 57 (13): 1771–1779.

Tiwary, U. S., and Tanveer Siddiqui. 2008. *Natural language processing and information retrieval.* Oxford University Press.

Tong, Audrey, Lukas Diduch, Jonathan Fiscus, Yasaman Haghpanah, Shudong Huang, David Joy, Kay Peterson, and Ian Soboroff. 2018. Overview of the NIST 2016 LOREHLT evaluation. *Machine translation* 32 (1–2): 11–30.

Tonon, Alberto, Gianluca Demartini, and Philippe Cudré-Mauroux. 2012. Combining inverted indices and structured search for ad-hoc object retrieval. In *Proceedings of the 35th international ACM SIGIR conference on research and development in information retrieval*, 125–134. ACM.

Trivedi, Rakshit, Hanjun Dai, Yichen Wang, and Le Song. 2017. Know-evolve: Deep temporal reasoning for dynamic knowledge graphs. In *Proceedings of the 34th international conference on machine learning*, Vol. 70, 3462–3471. JMLR.org.

Tsatsaronis, George, Georgios Balikas, Prodromos Malakasiotis, Ioannis Partalas, Matthias Zschunke, Michael R. Alvers, Dirk Weissenborn, Anastasia Krithara, Sergios Petridis, Dimitris Polychronopoulos, et al. 2015. An overview of the bioasq large-scale biomedical semantic indexing and question answering competition. *BMC bioinformatics* 16 (1): 138.

Tsatsaronis, George, Michael Schroeder, Georgios Paliouras, Yannis Almirantis, Ion Androutsopoulos, Eric Gaussier, Patrick Gallinari, Thierry Artieres, Michael R. Alvers, Matthias Zschunke, et al. 2012. BioASQ: A challenge on large-scale biomedical semantic indexing and question answering. In *2012 AAAI fall symposium series*.

Ubaldi, Barbara. 2013. Open government data: Towards empirical analysis of Open Government Data initiatives. *OECD working papers on public governance* 22 (2013). doi: 10.1787/19934351.

Ukkusuri, Satish V., Xianyuan Zhan, Arif Mohaimin Sadri, and Qing Ye. 2014. Use of social media data to explore crisis informatics: Study of 2013 Oklahoma tornado. *Transportation research record* 2459 (1): 110–118.

Unger, Christina, Lorenz Bühmann, Jens Lehmann, Axel-Cyrille Ngonga Ngomo, Daniel Gerber, and Philipp Cimiano. 2012. Template-based question answering over RDF data. In *Proceedings of the 21st international conference on World Wide Web*, 639–648.

Unger, Christina, and Philipp Cimiano. 2011a. Pythia: Compositional meaning construction for ontology-based question answering on the Semantic Web. In *International conference on application of natural language to information systems*, 153–160. Springer.

Unger, Christina, and Philipp Cimiano. 2011b. Representing and resolving ambiguities in ontology-based question answering. In *Proceedings of the TextInfer 2011 workshop on textual entailment*, 40–49. Association for Computational Linguistics.

Usbeck, Ricardo, Axel-Cyrille Ngonga Ngomo, Lorenz Bühmann, and Christina Unger. 2015. Hawk—hybrid question answering using linked data. In *European Semantic Web conference*, 353–368. Springer.

Van Hooland, Seth, and Ruben Verborgh. 2014. *Linked data for libraries, archives and museums: How to clean, link and publish your metadata.* Facet Publishing.

Vang, Katrine Juel. 2013. Ethics of Google's Knowledge Graph: Some considerations. *Journal of information, communication and ethics in society* 11, no. 4: 245–260.

Vetrò, Antonio, Lorenzo Canova, Marco Torchiano, Camilo Orozco Minotas, Raimondo Iemma, and Federico Morando. 2016. Open data quality measurement framework: Definition and application to open government data. *Government information quarterly* 33 (2): 325–337.

Viswanathan, Amar, James R. Michaelis, Taylor Cassidy, Geeth de Mel, and James Hendler. 2017. In-context query reformulation for failing SPARQL queries. In *Ground/air multisensor interoperability, integration, and networking for persistent ISR VIII*, vol. 10190, 101900M. International Society for Optics and Photonics.

Von Ahn, Luis, Manuel Blum, Nicholas J. Hopper, and John Langford. 2003. Captcha: Using hard AI problems for security. In *International conference on the theory and applications of cryptographic techniques*, 294–311. Springer.

Vora, Mehul Nalin. 2011. Hadoop-HBase for large-scale data. In *Proceedings of 2011 international conference on computer science and network technology*, Vol. 1, 601–605. IEEE.

Vrandečić, Denny, and Markus Krötzsch. 2014. Wikidata: A free collaborative knowledge base. *Communications of the ACM* 57, no. 10: 78–85.

Wang, Alex, and Kyunghyun Cho. 2019. BERT has a mouth, and it must speak: BERT as a Markov Random Field language model. *arXiv preprint arXiv:1902.04094*.

Wang, Haoyu, Ming Tan, Mo Yu, Shiyu Chang, Dakuo Wang, Kun Xu, Xiaoxiao Guo, and Saloni Potdar. 2019. Extracting multiple-relations in one-pass with pre-trained transformers. *arXiv preprint arXiv:1902.01030*.

Wang, Jiannan, Tim Kraska, Michael J. Franklin, and Jianhua Feng. 2012. Crowder: Crowdsourcing entity resolution. *Proceedings of the VLDB endowment* 5 (11): 1483–1494.

Wang, Jiying, and Fred H. Lochovsky. 2002. Wrapper induction based on nested pattern discovery. *World Wide Web internet and web information systems*.

Wang, Jue, and Pedro M. Domingos. 2008. Hybrid Markov Logic Networks. In *AAAI*, Vol. 8, 1106–1111.

Wang, Quan, Zhendong Mao, Bin Wang, and Li Guo. 2017. Knowledge graph embedding: A survey of approaches and applications. *IEEE transactions on knowledge and data engineering* 29 (12): 2724–2743.

Wang, Xuan, Xiangchen Song, Yingjun Guan, Bangzheng Li, and Jiawei Han. 2020. Comprehensive named entity recognition on CORD-19 with distant or weak supervision. *arXiv preprint arXiv:2003.12218*.

Wang, Yanli, Tugba Suzek, Jian Zhang, Jiyao Wang, Siqian He, Tiejun Cheng, Benjamin A. Shoemaker, Asta Gindulyte, and Stephen H. Bryant. 2014. PubChem bioassay: 2014 update. *Nucleic acids research* 42 (D1): 1075–1082.

Wang, Yongyi, Hui Zhang, Dan Wu, and Jiangping Chen. 2019. Health data on data.gov: A research on status quo of open health data. *iConference 2019 Proceedings*. *http://hdl.handle.net/2142/103362*.

Wang, Zhen, Jianwen Zhang, Jianlin Feng, and Zheng Chen. 2014a. Knowledge graph embedding by translating on hyperplanes. In *Proceedings of the twenty-eighth AAAI conference on artificial intelligence*, 1112–1119.

Wang, Zhen, Jianwen Zhang, Jianlin Feng, and Zheng Chen. 2014b. Knowledge graph and text jointly embedding. In *Proceedings of the 2014 conference on empirical methods in natural language processing (EMNLP)*, 1591–1601.

Wang, Zhigang, Juanzi Li, Zhiyuan Liu, and Jie Tang. 2016. Text-enhanced representation learning for knowledge graph. In *Proceedings of the twenty-fifth IJCAI conference on artificial intelligence*, 1293–1299.

Wasserman, Stanley, and Katherine Faust. 1994. *Social network analysis: Methods and applications.* Cambridge University Press.

Wei, Zhuoyu, Jun Zhao, Kang Liu, Zhenyu Qi, Zhengya Sun, and Guanhua Tian. 2015. Large-scale knowledge base completion: Inferring via grounding network sampling over selected instances. In *Proceedings of the 24th ACM international on conference on information and knowledge management*, 1331–1340.

Weiss, Ron, Bienvenido Vélez, and Mark A. Sheldon. 1996. HyPursuit: A hierarchical network search engine that exploits content-link hypertext clustering. In *Proceedings of the the seventh ACM conference on hypertext*, 180–193.

Wellman, Michael P., John S. Breese, and Robert P. Goldman. 1992. From knowledge bases to decision models. *Knowledge engineering review* 7 (1): 35–53.

Wen, Tsung-Hsien, Yishu Miao, Phil Blunsom, and Steve Young. 2017. Latent intention dialogue models. In *Proceedings of the 34th international conference on machine learning*, vol. 70, 3732–3741. *JMLR.org.*

Wernicke, Sebastian, and Florian Rasche. 2006. FANMOD: A tool for fast network motif detection. *Bioinformatics* 22 (9): 1152–1153.

West, Douglas Brent. 1996. *Introduction to graph theory*, Vol. 2. Prentice Hall.

Weston, Jason E. 2016. Dialog-based language learning. In *Proceedings of the thirtieth international conference on neural information processing systems*, 829–837.

Weston, Jason, Antoine Bordes, Oksana Yakhnenko, and Nicolas Usunier. 2013. Connecting language and knowledge bases with embedding models for relation extraction. *arXiv preprint arXiv:1307.7973.*

Whang, Steven Euijong, David Menestrina, Georgia Koutrika, Martin Theobald, and Hector Garcia-Molina. 2009. Entity resolution with iterative blocking. In *Proceedings of the 2009 ACM SIGMOD international conference on management of data*, 219–232. ACM.

White, Aaron Steven, Drew Reisinger, Keisuke Sakaguchi, Tim Vieira, Sheng Zhang, Rachel Rudinger, Kyle Rawlins, and Benjamin Van Durme. 2016. Universal decompositional semantics on universal dependencies. In *Proceedings of the 2016 conference on empirical methods in natural language processing*, 1713–1723.

Wick, Michael, Sameer Singh, Ari Kobren, and Andrew McCallum. 2013. Assessing confidence of knowledge base content with an experimental study in entity resolution. In *Proceedings of the 2013 workshop on automated knowledge base construction*, 13–18.

Witten, Ian H., Eibe Frank, Mark A. Hall, and Christopher J. Pal. 2016. *Data mining: Practical machine learning tools and techniques.* Morgan Kaufmann.

Wolf, Thomas, Lysandre Debut, Victor Sanh, Julien Chaumond, Clement Delangue, Anthony Moi, Pierric Cistac, Tim Rault, Rémi Louf, Morgan Funtowicz, et al. 2019. Transformers: State-of-the-art natural language processing. *arXiv preprint arXiv:1910.03771.*

Wood, David, Marsha Zaidman, Luke Ruth, and Michael Hausenblas. 2014. *Linked data.* Manning Publications.

Wu, Fei, and Daniel S. Weld. 2010. Open information extraction using Wikipedia. In *Proceedings of the 48th annual meeting of the Association for Computational Linguistics*, 118–127. Association for Computational Linguistics.

Xiao, Han, Minlie Huang, Yu Hao, and Xiaoyan Zhu. 2015. TransA: An adaptive approach for knowledge graph embedding. *arXiv preprint arXiv:1509.05490*.

Xiao, Han, Minlie Huang, and Xiaoyan Zhu. 2016. TransG: A generative model for knowledge graph embedding. In *Proceedings of the 54th annual meeting of the Association for Computational Linguistics (volume 1: Long papers)*, 2316–2325.

Xiaogang, M. A. 2019. Geo-data science: Leveraging geoscience research with geoinformatics, semantics and open data. *Acta geologica sinica (English edition)* 93: 44–47.

Xie, Ruobing, Zhiyuan Liu, Jia Jia, Huanbo Luan, and Maosong Sun. 2016. Representation learning of knowledge graphs with entity descriptions. In *Thirtieth AAAI conference on artificial intelligence*, 2659–2665.

Xie, Ruobing, Zhiyuan Liu, and Maosong Sun. 2016. Representation learning of knowledge graphs with hierarchical types. In *International Joint Conference on Artificial Intelligence (IJCAI)*, 2965–2971.

Xu, Kai, Zhanfan Zhou, Tianyong Hao, and Wenyin Liu. 2017. A bidirectional LSTM and conditional random fields approach to medical named entity recognition. In *International conference on advanced intelligent systems and informatics*, 355–365. Springer.

Xu, Kun, Sheng Zhang, Yansong Feng, and Dongyan Zhao. 2014. Answering natural language questions via phrasal semantic parsing. In *Natural language processing and Chinese computing*, 333–344. Springer.

Xu, Li Da, and Lian Duan. 2019. Big Data for cyber physical systems in industry 4.0: A survey. *Enterprise information systems* 13 (2): 148–169.

Yadav, Vikas, and Steven Bethard. 2019. A survey on recent advances in Named Entity Recognition from deep learning models. *http://arxiv.org/abs/1910.11470*.

Yahya, Mohamed, Klaus Berberich, Shady Elbassuoni, Maya Ramanath, Volker Tresp, and Gerhard Weikum. 2012. Deep answers for naturally asked questions on the web of data. In *Proceedings of the 21st international conference on World Wide Web*, 445–449.

Yahya, Mohamed, Steven Whang, Rahul Gupta, and Alon Halevy. 2014. Renoun: Fact extraction for nominal attributes. In *Proceedings of the 2014 conference on empirical methods in natural language processing (EMNLP)*, 325–335.

Yan, Jihong, Chengyu Wang, Wenliang Cheng, Ming Gao, and Aoying Zhou. 2018. A retrospective of knowledge graphs. *Frontiers of computer science* 12 (1): 55–74.

Yang, Grace Hui, Marc Sloan, and Jun Wang. 2016. Dynamic information retrieval modeling. *Synthesis lectures on information concepts, retrieval, and services* 8 (3): 1–144.

Yang, Wei, Yuqing Xie, Aileen Lin, Xingyu Li, Luchen Tan, Kun Xiong, Ming Li, and Jimmy Lin. 2019a. End-to-end open-domain question answering with BERTserini. *arXiv preprint arXiv:1902.01718*.

Yang, Xiwang, Yang Guo, Yong Liu, and Harald Steck. 2014. A survey of collaborative filtering–based social recommender systems. *Computer communications* 41: 1–10.

Yang, Zhilin, Zihang Dai, Yiming Yang, Jaime Carbonell, Russ R. Salakhutdinov, and Quoc V. Le. 2019b. XLnet: Generalized autoregressive pretraining for language understanding. In *Advances in neural information processing systems*, 5754–5764.

Yangarber, Roman, Winston Lin, and Ralph Grishman. 2002. Unsupervised learning of generalized names. In *Proceedings of the 19th international conference on computational linguistics*, Vol. 1, 1–7. Association for Computational Linguistics.

Ye, Guixin, Zhanyong Tang, Dingyi Fang, Zhanxing Zhu, Yansong Feng, Pengfei Xu, Xiaojiang Chen, and Zheng Wang. 2018. Yet another text captcha solver: A generative adversarial network-based approach. In *Proceedings of the 2018 ACM SIGSAC conference on computer and communications security*, 332–348.

Ye, Hai, Wenhan Chao, Zhunchen Luo, and Zhoujun Li. 2016. Jointly extracting relations with class ties via effective deep ranking. *arXiv preprint arXiv:1612.07602*.

Yin, Shen, and Okyay Kaynak. 2015. Big Data for modern industry: Challenges and trends [point of view]. *Proceedings of the IEEE* 103 (2): 143–146.

Yin, Wenpeng, Katharina Kann, Mo Yu, and Hinrich Schütze. 2017. Comparative study of CNN and RNN for natural language processing. *arXiv preprint arXiv:1702.01923*.

Younis, Eman M. G., Christopher B. Jones, Vlad Tanasescu, and Alia I. Abdelmoty. 2012. Hybrid geo-spatial query methods on the Semantic Web with a spatially-enhanced index of DBpedia. In *International conference on geographic information science*, 340–353. Springer.

Yubo, Chen, Xu Liheng, Liu Kang, Zeng Daojian, Zhao Jun, et al. 2015. Event extraction via dynamic multi-pooling convolutional neural networks. In *Proceedings of the 53rd annual meeting of the Association for Computational Linguistics and the 7th international joint conference on natural language processing (Volume 1: Long Papers)*, 167–176.

Yuvarani, Meiyappan, A. Kannan, et al. 2006. LSCrawler: A framework for an enhanced focused web crawler based on link semantics. In *2006 IEEE/WIC/ACM international conference on web intelligence (WI 2006 main conference proceedings)(WI'06)*, 794–800. IEEE.

Zadeh, Lofti A. 1996. Knowledge Representation in Fuzzy Logic, In *Fuzzy Sets, Fuzzy Logic, and Fuzzy Systems: Selected Papers by Lotfi A. Zadeh*, 764–774.

Zaslavsky, Ilya, Stephen M. Richard, Amarnath Gupta, David Valentine, Thomas Whitenack, Ibrahim Burak Ozyurt, Jeffrey S. Grethe, and Adam Schachne. 2016. Integrating semantic information in metadata descriptions for a geoscience-wide resource inventory. In *AGU fall meeting abstracts 2016*: IN21D–03.

Zaveri, Amrapali, Anisa Rula, Andrea Maurino, Ricardo Pietrobon, Jens Lehmann, and Sören Auer. 2016. Quality assessment for linked data: A survey. *Semantic Web* 7 (1): 63–93.

Zeng, Daojian, Kang Liu, Siwei Lai, Guangyou Zhou, Jun Zhao, et al. 2014. Relation classification via convolutional deep neural network. In *Proceedings of COLING 2014, the 25th international conference on computational linguistics: Technical papers*, 2335–2344.

Zeng, Daojian, Kang Liu, Yubo Chen, and Jun Zhao. 2015. Distant supervision for relation extraction via piecewise convolutional neural networks. In *Proceedings of the 2015 conference on empirical methods in natural language processing*, 1753–1762.

Zhang, Baichuan, Sutanay Choudhury, Mohammad Al Hasan, Xia Ning, Khushbu Agarwal, Sumit Purohit, and Paola Pesntez Cabrera. 2016. Trust from the past: Bayesian personalized ranking based link prediction in knowledge graphs. *arXiv preprint arXiv:1601.03778*.

Zhang, Dongxu, Subhabrata Mukherjee, Colin Lockard, Xin Luna Dong, and Andrew McCallum. 2019. OpenKI: Integrating open information extraction and knowledge bases with relation inference. *arXiv preprint arXiv:1904.12606.*

Zhang, Lei, Shuai Wang, and Bing Liu. 2018. Deep learning for sentiment analysis: A survey. *Wiley interdisciplinary reviews: Data mining and knowledge discovery* 8 (4): e1253.

Zhang, N., J. C. Creput, W. Hongjian, C. Meurie, and Y. Ruichek. 2013. Query answering using user feedback and context gathering for web of data. In *3rd international conference on advanced communications and computation (INFOCOMP)*, 33–38.

Zhang, Sheng, Kevin Duh, and Benjamin Van Durme. 2017. Selective decoding for cross-lingual open information extraction. In *Proceedings of the eighth international joint conference on natural language processing (volume 1: Long papers)*, 832–842.

Zhang, Tongtao, Ananya Subburathinam, Ge Shi, Lifu Huang, Di Lu, Xiaoman Pan, Manling Li, Boliang Zhang, Qingyun Wang, Spencer Whitehead, et al. 2018. GAIA-a multi-media multi-lingual knowledge extraction and hypothesis generation system. In *Text analysis conference (TAC) knowledge base population workshop*. https://tac.nist.gov/publications/2018/participant.papers/TAC2018.GAIA.proceedings.pdf.

Zhang, Tongtao, Spencer Whitehead, Hanwang Zhang, Hongzhi Li, Joseph Ellis, Lifu Huang, Wei Liu, Heng Ji, and Shih-Fu Chang. 2017. Improving event extraction via multimodal integration. In *Proceedings of the 25th ACM international conference on multimedia*, 270–278.

Zhang, Weinan, Tianming Du, and Jun Wang. 2016. Deep learning over multi-field categorical data. In *European conference on information retrieval*, 45–57. Springer.

Zhong, Huaping, Jianwen Zhang, Zhen Wang, Hai Wan, and Zheng Chen. 2015. Aligning knowledge and text embeddings by entity descriptions. In *Proceedings of the 2015 conference on empirical methods in natural language processing*, 267–272.

Zhou, Deyu, Liangyu Chen, and Yulan He. 2015. An unsupervised framework of exploring events on Twitter: Filtering, extraction and categorization. In *Twenty-ninth AAAI conference on artificial intelligence*, 2468–2474.

Zhou, Deyu, Dayou Zhong, and Yulan He. 2014. Biomedical relation extraction: From binary to complex. *Computational and mathematical methods in medicine, 2014*, 298473, doi: 10.1155/2014/298473.

Zou, Lei, Ruizhe Huang, Haixun Wang, Jeffrey Xu Yu, Wenqiang He, and Dongyan Zhao. 2014. Natural language question answering over RDF: A graph data-driven approach. In *Proceedings of the 2014 ACM SIGMOD international conference on management of data*, 313–324.

Index